Greek and Roman Lives

DOVER · **GIANT THRIFT** · EDITIONS

Greek and Roman Lives

PLUTARCH

Translated by John Dryden
Revised and Edited by Arthur Hugh Clough

DOVER PUBLICATIONS, INC.
Mineola, New York

DOVER GIANT THRIFT EDITIONS

GENERAL EDITOR: MARY CAROLYN WALDREP
EDITOR OF THIS VOLUME: T. N. R. ROGERS

Bibliographical Note

This Dover edition, first published in 2005, is a new selection, comprising ten lives plus most of Arthur Hugh Clough's Introduction, from *Plutarch's Lives: The Translation Called Dryden's*, published by Little, Brown and Co., Boston, in 1864. (With regard to the translation's attribution to Dryden, see the Introduction.) We have Americanized the spelling and punctuation of the translation, but not those of Clough's Introduction. The lives are unabridged; we have removed from the Introduction the first three paragraphs (about half a page), which were irrelevant to the present edition. Notes in brackets have been added by the editor of this Dover volume.

Library of Congress Cataloging-in-Publication Data

Plutarch.
    [Lives. English. Selections]
    Greek and Roman lives / Plutarch ; translated by John Dryden ; revised and edited by Arthur Hugh Clough.
        p. cm. — (Dover giant thrift editions)
    "This Dover edition, first published in 2005, is a new selection, comprising ten lives plus most of Arthur Hugh Clough's Introduction, from Plutarch's Lives: the translation called Dryden's, published by Little, Brown and Co., Boston, in 1864. The lives are unabridged."
    ISBN 0-486-44576-3 (pbk.)
    1. Greece—Biography—Early works to 1800. 2. Rome—Biography—Early works to 1800. I. Dryden, John, 1631–1700. II. Clough, Arthur Hugh, 1819–1861. III. Title. IV. Series.

DE7.P513 2005
920.038—dc22

2005049661

Manufactured in the United States of America
Dover Publications, Inc., 31 East 2nd Street, Mineola, N.Y. 11501

Contents

INTRODUCTION

by Arthur Hugh Clough

THE PLAIN FACTS of Plutarch's own life may be given in a very short compass. He was born, probably, in the reign of Claudius, about A.D. 45 or 50. His native place was Chæronea, in Bœotia, where his family had long been settled and was of good standing and local reputation. He studied at Athens under a philosopher named Ammonius. He visited Egypt. Later in life, some time before A.D. 90, he was at Rome "on public business," a deputation, perhaps, from Chæronea. He continued there long enough to give lectures which attracted attention. Whether he visited Italy once only, or more often, is uncertain.

He was intimate with Sosius Senecio, to all appearances the same who was four times consul. The acquaintance may have sprung up at Rome, where Sosius, a much younger man than himself,[1] may have first seen him as a lecturer; or they may have previously known each other in Greece.

To Greece and to Chæronea he returned, and appears to have spent in the little town, which he was loth "to make less by the withdrawal of even one inhabitant," the remainder of his life. He took part in the public business of the place and the neighbourhood. He was archon in the town, and officiated many years as a priest of Apollo, apparently at Delphi.

He was married, and was the father of at least five children, of whom two sons, at any rate, survived to manhood. His greatest work, his Biographies, and several of his smaller writings, belong to this later period of his life, under the reign of Trajan. Whether he survived to the time of Hadrian is doubtful. If A.D. 45 be taken by way of conjecture for the date of his birth, A.D. 120, Hadrian's fourth year, may be assumed, in like manner, as pretty nearly that of his death. All that is certain is that he lived to be old; that in one of his fictitious dialogues he describes himself as a young man conversing on philosophy with Ammonius in the time of Nero's visit to Greece, A.D. 66–67; and that he was certainly alive and

---

[1] Unless the expression "my sons your companions" ought to be taken as a piece of pleasantry.

still writing in A.D. 106, the winter which Trajan, after building his bridge over the Danube, passed in Dacia. "We are told," he says, in his Inquiry into the Principle of Cold, "by those who are now wintering with the Emperor on the Danube, that the freezing of water will crush boats to pieces."

To this bare outline of certainties, several names and circumstances may be added from his writings; on which indeed alone we can safely rely for the very outline itself. There are a few allusions and anecdotes in the Lives, and from his miscellaneous compositions, his Essays, Lectures, Dialogues, Table-Talk, etc., the imagination may furnish itself with a great variety of curious and interesting suggestions.

The name of his great-grandfather, Nicarchus, is incidentally recorded in the life of Antony. "My great-grandfather used," he says, "to tell, how in Antony's last war the whole of the citizens of Chæronea were put in requisition to bring down corn to the coast of the gulf of Corinth, each man carrying a certain load, and soldiers standing by to urge them on with the lash." One such journey was made, and they had measured out their burdens for the second, when news arrived of the defeat at Actium.[2] Lamprias, his grandfather, is also mentioned in the same life. Philotas, the physician, had told him an anecdote illustrating the luxuriousness of Antony's life in Egypt. His father is more than once spoken of in the minor works, but never mentioned by his name.

The name of Ammonius, his teacher and preceptor at Athens, occurs repeatedly in the minor works, and is once specially mentioned in the Lives; a descendant of Themistocles had studied with Plutarch under Ammonius. We find it mentioned that he three times held the office, once so momentous in the world's history, of *strategus* at Athens.[3] This, like that of the Bœotarchs in Bœotia, continued under the Empire to be intrusted to native citizens, and judging from what is said in the little treatise of Political Precepts, was one of the more important places under the Roman provincial governor.

"Once," Plutarch tells us, "our teacher, Ammonius, observing at his afternoon lecture that some of his auditors had been indulging too freely at breakfast, gave directions, in our presence, for chastisement to be administered to his own son, *because,* he said, *the young man has declined to*

---

[2] There appears, however, to be no sure reason for saying that Plutarch himself remembered seeing his great-grandfather, and hearing him tell the story.

[3] This may throw some doubt on the statement (with which, however, it is perhaps not absolutely incompatible) made by the Byzantine historian Eunapius that "Ammonius, the teacher of the divine Plutarch, was an Egyptian."

Plutarch was certainly skilled in all the wisdom of the Græco-Egyptians; see his treatise addressed to the learned lady Clea, on Isis and Osiris; but he may, for anything we know, have stayed long and studied much at Alexandria.

take his breakfast unless he has sour wine with it, fixing his eyes at the same time on the offending members of the class."

The following anecdote appears to belong to some period a little later than that of his studies at Athens. "I remember, when I myself was still a young man, I was sent in company with another on a deputation to the proconsul; my colleague, it so happened, was unable to proceed, and I saw the proconsul and performed the commission alone. Upon my return when I was about to lay down my office, and to give an account of its discharge, my father got up in the assembly and bade me privately to take care not to say *I* went, but *we* went, nor *I* said, but *we* said, and in the whole narration to give my companion his share."

Of his stay in Italy, his visit to or residence in Rome, we know little beyond the statement which he gives us in the life of Demosthenes, that public business and visitors who came to see him on subjects of philosophy, took up so much of his time that he learned, at that time, but little of the Latin language. He must have travelled about, for he saw the bust or statue of Marius at Ravenna, as he informs us in the beginning of Marius's life. He undertook, he tells us in his essay on Brotherly Affection, the office, whilst he was in Rome, of arbitrating between two brothers, one of whom was considered to be a lover of philosophy. "But he had," he says, "in reality, no legitimate title to the name either of brother or of philosopher. When I told him I should expect from him the behaviour of a philosopher towards one, who was, first of all, an ordinary person making no such profession, and, in the second place, a brother, *as for the first point,* replied he, *it may be well enough, but I don't attach any great importance to the fact of two people having come from the same pair of bodies;"* an impious piece of freethinking which met, of course, with Plutarch's indignant rebuke and reprobation.

A more remarkable anecdote is related in his discourse on Inquisitiveness. Among other precepts for avoiding or curing the fault, "We should habituate ourselves," he says, "when letters are brought to us, not to open them instantly and in a hurry, not to bite the strings in two, as many people will, if they do not succeed at once with their fingers; when a messenger comes, not to run to meet him; not to jump up, when a friend says he has something new to tell us; rather, if he has some good or useful advice to give us. Once when I was lecturing at Rome, Rusticus, whom Domitian afterwards, out of jealousy of his reputation, put to death, was one of my hearers; and while I was going on, a soldier came in and brought him a letter from the Emperor. And when every one was silent, and I stopped in order to let him read the letter, he declined to do so, and put it aside until I had finished and the audience withdrew; an example of serious and dignified behaviour which excited much admiration."

L. Junius Arulenus Rusticus, the friend of Pliny and Tacitus, glorified among the Stoic martyrs whose names are written in the life of Agricola, was in youth the ardent disciple of Thrasea Pætus; and when Pætus was destined by Nero for death, and the Senate was prepared to pass the decree for his condemnation, Rusticus, in the fervour of his feelings, was eager to interpose the veto still attaching in form to the office, which he happened then to hold, of tribune, and was scarcely withheld by his master from a demonstration which would but have added him, before his time, to the catalogue of victims. After performing, in the civil wars ensuing on the death of Nero, the duties of prætor, he published in Domitian's time a life of Thrasea, as did Senecio one of Helvidius, and Tacitus, probably himself, that of Agricola: the bold language of which insured his death. Among the teachers who afterwards gave instruction to the youthful Marcus Aurelius, we read the name of an Arulenus Rusticus, probably his grandson, united with that of Sextus of Chæronea, Plutarch's nephew, "who taught me," says the virtuous Emperor, "by his own example, the just and wise habits he recommended," and to whose door, in late life, he was still seen to go, still desirous, as he said, to be a learner.

It does not, of course, follow from the terms in which the story is related, that the incident occurred in Domitian's time, and that it was to Domitian's letter that Plutarch's discourse was preferred. But that Plutarch was at Rome in or after Domitian's reign, seems to be fairly inferred from the language in which he speaks of the absurd magnificence of Domitian's palaces and other imperial buildings.

His two brothers, Timon and Lamprias, are frequently mentioned in his Essays and Dialogues. They, also, appear to have been pupils of Ammonius. In the treatise on Affection between Brothers, after various examples of the strength of this feeling, occurs the following passage: "And for myself," he says, "that among the many favours for which I have to thank the kindness of fortune, my brother Timon's affection to me is one, past and present, that may be put in the balance against all the rest, is what every one that has so much as met with us must be aware of, and our friends, of course, know well."

His wife was Timoxena, the daughter of Alexion. The circumstances of his domestic life receive their best illustration from his letter addressed to this wife, on the loss of their one daughter, born to them, it would appear, late in life, long after her brothers. "Plutarch to his wife, greeting. The messengers you sent to announce our child's death, apparently missed the road to Athens. I was told about my daughter on reaching Tanagra. Everything relating to the funeral I suppose to have been already performed; my desire is that all these arrangements may have been so made, as will now and in the future be most consoling to yourself. If there is anything which you have wished to do and have omitted, awaiting my opinion, and think would be a relief to you, it shall be attended to, apart from all excess and superstition, which no one would like less than yourself. Only, my wife, let me hope, that you will maintain both me and yourself within the reasonable limits of grief. What our loss really amounts to, I know and estimate for myself. But should I find your distress excessive, my trouble on your account will be greater than on that of our loss. I am not a 'stock or stone,' as you, my partner in the care of our numerous children, every one of whom we have ourselves brought up at home, can testify. And this child, a daughter, born to your wishes after four sons, and affording me the opportunity of recording your name, I am well aware was a special object of affection."

The sweet temper and the pretty ways of the child, he proceeds to say, make the privation peculiarly painful. "Yet why," he says, "should we forget the reasonings we have often addressed to others, and regard our present pain as obliterating and effacing our former joys?" Those who had been present had spoken to him in terms of admiration of the calmness and simplicity of her behaviour. The funeral had been devoid of any useless and idle sumptuosity, and her own house of all display of extravagant lamentation. This was indeed no wonder to him, who knew how much her plain and unluxurious living had surprised his philosophical friends and visitors, and who well remembered her composure under the previous loss of the eldest of her children, and again, "when our beautiful Charon left us." "I recollect," he says, "that some acquaintance from abroad were coming up with me from the sea when the tidings of the child's decease were brought, and they followed with our other friends to the house; but the perfect order and tranquillity they found there made them believe, as I afterwards was informed they had related, that nothing had happened, and that the previous intelligence had been a mistake."

The Consolation (so the letter is named) closes with expressions of belief in the immortality of each human soul; in which the parents are sustained and fortified by the tradition of their ancestors, and the revelations to which they had both been admitted, conveyed in the mystic Dionysian ceremonies.

There is a phrase in the letter which might be taken to imply that, at the time of his domestic misfortune, Plutarch and Timoxena were already grandparents. The marriage of their son Autobulus is the occasion of one of the dinner parties recorded in the Symposiac Questions; and in one of the dialogues there is a distinct allusion to Autobulus's son. Plutarch inscribes the little treatise in explanation of the Timæus to his two sons, Autobulus and Plutarch. They must certainly have been grown-up men, to have anything to do with so difficult a subject. In his Inquiry as to the Way in which the Young should read the Poets, "It is not easy," he says, addressing Marcus Sedatus, "to restrain altogether from such reading young people of the age of my Soclarus and your Cleander." But whether Soclarus was a son, or a grandson, or some more distant relative, or, which is possible, a pupil, does not appear. Eurydice, to whom and to Pollianus, her newly espoused husband, he addresses his Marriage Precepts, seems to be spoken of as a recent inmate of his house; but it cannot he inferred that she was a daughter, nor does it seem likely that the little Timoxena's place was ever filled up.[4]

The office of Archon, which Plutarch held in his native municipality, was probably only an annual one; but very likely he served it more than once. He seems to have busied himself about all the little matters of the town, and to have made it a point to undertake the humblest duties. After relating the story of Epaminondas giving dignity to the office of Chief Scavenger, "And I, too, for that matter," he says, "am often a jest to my neighbours, when they see me, as they frequently do, in public, occupied on very similar duties; but the story told about Antisthenes comes to my assistance. When some one expressed surprise at his carrying home some picked fish from market in his own hands, *It is*, he answered, *for myself*. Conversely, when I am reproached with standing by and watching while tiles are measured out, and stone and mortar brought up, *This service*, I say, *is not for myself*, it is for my country."

In the little essay on the question, Whether an Old Man should continue in Public Life, written in the form of an exhortation of Euphanes, an ancient and distinguished member of the Areopagus at Athens, and of the Amphictyonic council, not to relinquish his duties, "Let there be no severance," he says, "in our long companionship, and let neither the one nor the other of us forsake the life that was our choice." And, alluding to his own functions as priest of Apollo at Delphi, "You know," he adds in another place, "that I have served the Pythian God for many *pythiads*[5] past, yet you would not now tell me, *you have taken part enough in the sacrifices, processions, and dances, and it is high time, Plutarch, now you are an old man, to lay aside your garland, and retire as superannuated from the oracle*."

Even in these, the comparatively few, more positive and matter-of-fact passages of allusion and anecdote, there is enough to bring up something of a picture of a happy domestic life, half academic, half municipal, passed among affectionate relatives and well-known friends, inclining most to literary and moral studies, yet not cut off from the duties and avocations of the citizen. We cannot, of course, to go yet further, accept the scenery

---

[4] That he had more than two sons who grew up, at any rate, to youth, appears from a passage where he speaks of his younger sons having stayed too long at the theatre, and being, in consequence, too late at supper.

[5] Periods of four years elapsing between the celebrations of the Pythian games, like the Olympiads for the Olympic games.

of the fictitious Dialogues as historical; yet there is much of it which may be taken as, so to say, pictorially just; and there is, probably, a good deal here and there that is literally true to the fact. The Symposiac, or After-Dinner Questions, collected in nine books, and dedicated to Sosius Senecio, were discussed, we are told, many of them, in the company of Sosius himself, both at Rome and in Greece, as, for example, when he was with them at the marriage festivities of Autobulus. Lamprias and Timon, the author's brothers, are frequent speakers, each with a distinctly traced character, in these conversations; the father, and the elder Lamprias, the grandfather, both take an occasional, and the latter a lively part; there is one whole book in which Ammonius predominates; the scene is now at Delphi, and now at Athens, sometimes perhaps, but rarely, at Rome, sometimes at the celebrations of the Games. Plutarch, in his priestly capacity, gives an entertainment in honour of a poetic victor at the Pythia, there is an Isthmian dinner at Corinth, and an Olympian party at Elis. As an adopted Athenian citizen of the Leontid tribe, he attends the celebration of the success of his friend, the philosophic poet Serapion. The *dramatis personæ* of the various little pieces form a company, when put together, of more than eighty names, philosophers, rhetoricians, and grammarians, several physicians, Euthydemus his colleague in the priesthood, Alexion his father-in-law, and four or five other connections by marriage, Favorinus the philosopher of Arles in Provence, afterwards favoured by Hadrian, to whom he dedicates one of his treatises, and who in return wrote an essay called Plutarchus, on the Academic Philosophy. Serapion entertains them in a garden on the banks of the Cephisus. They dine with a friendly physician on the heights of Hyampolis, and meet in a party at the baths of Ædepsus. The questions are of the most miscellaneous description, grave sometimes, and moral, grammatical and antiquarian, and often festive and humorous. *In what sense does Plato say that God uses geometry? Why do we hear better by night than by day? Why are dreams least true in autumn? Which existed first, the hen or the egg? Which of Venus's hands did Diomed wound?* Lamprias, the grandfather, finds fault with his son, Plutarch's father, for *inviting too many guests* to the parties given "when we came home from Alexandria." Ammonius, in office as general at Athens, gives a dinner to the young men who had distinguished themselves at a trial of skill in grammar, rhetoric, geometry, and poetry; and anecdotes are told on the occasion *of verses aptly or inaptly quoted.*

Of the other minor works, some look a good deal like lectures delivered at Rome, and afterwards published with little dedications prefixed. We have a disquisition on the Advantages we can derive from our Enemies addressed to Cornelius Pulcher, a discourse On Fate, to Piso, and On Brotherly Affection, to Nigrinus and Quintus. Many, however, are dialogues and conversations, with a good deal of the same varied scenery and exuberant detail which embellish the Table-Talk.

In a conversation which he had been present at, "long ago, when Nero was staying in Greece," between Ammonius and some other friends, the meaning of the strange inscription at Delphi, the two letters EI, is debated. A visitor is conducted by some of Plutarch's friends over the sacred buildings at Delphi, and in the intervals between the somewhat tedious speeches of the professional guides, who showed the sights, a discussion takes place on the Nature of the Oracles. "It happened a little before the Pythian games in the time of Callistratus, there met us at Delphi two travellers, from the extremities of the world, Demetrius, the grammarian, on his way home to Tarsus from Britain, and Cleombrotus the Lacedæmonian, just returned from a journey he had made for his pleasure and instruction in Upper Egypt, and far out into the Erythræan Sea." The question somehow or other occurs, and the dialogue, Of the Cessation of Oracles, ensues; one passage of which is the famous story of the voice that proclaimed the death of the great Pan. Autobulus is talking with Soclarus, the companion of his son, about an encomium which they had heard on hunting; the best praise they can give it is, that it diverts into a less objectionable course the passion which finds one vent in seeing the contests of gladiators. Up come presently a large party of young men, lovers of hunting and fishing, and the question of the Superior Sagacity of Land or of Water Animals is formally pleaded by two selected orators. Stories are told of elephants; and Aristotimus, the advocate of the land animals, relates a sight (of the dog imitating in a play the effects of poison) which he himself, he says, saw in Rome, and which was so perfectly acted as to cause emotion in the spectators, the Emperor included; the aged Vespasian himself being present, in the theatre of Marcellus. It reads very much as if Plutarch, and not Aristotimus, had been the eye-witness.[6]

Autobulus occurs again in the Dialogue on Love. At the request of his friend Flavianus, he repeats a long conversation, attended with curious incidents, in which his father had taken part on Mount Helicon, "once long ago, before we were born, when he brought our mother, after the

---

[6]Something also of a personal remembrance of Vespasian's unrelentingly severe temper may be thought to appear in the story, related in the Dialogue on Love, of the Gaulish rebel Sabinus, and his wife Eponina, mentioned by Tacitus in his Histories, who, after living in an underground concealment several years, were discovered and put to death. Two sons were born to them in their hiding-place, "one of whom," says Plutarch, "was here with us in Delphi only a little while ago," and he is disposed, he adds, "to attribute the subsequent extinction of the race of Vespasian to divine displeasure at this cruel and unfeeling act."

dispute and variance which had arisen between their parents, that she might offer a sacrifice to Love at the feast held at Thespiæ."

The variance alluded to must clearly have been a fact. And, in general, though these playful fictions or semi-fictions, which form the machinery of the dialogues, are not indeed to be accepted in a literal way, they possess an authenticity which we cannot venture to attribute to the professedly historical statements about their author, given in later writers. Suidas, the lexicographer, repeats a mere romance when he tells us that Trajan gave him the dignity of consul, and issued orders that none of the magistrates in Illyria should do anything without consulting him. Syncellus, the Byzantine historian, under the record of one of the first years of Hadrian's reign, is equally or even more extravagant, relating that Plutarch, the philosopher of Chæronea, was in his old age appointed by the emperor to the office of governor of Greece. Though the period of Trajan and the Antonines was the golden age of philosophers, whose brief persecution under Domitian seems to have won them for a while a sort of spiritual supremacy, similar to that which, after Diocletian, was wrested from them by the ministers of the new religion, still these assertions are on the face of them entirely incredible.

There is a letter, indeed, given among Plutarch's printed works, in which a collection of Sayings of Kings and Commanders is dedicated to Trajan; and though much doubt is entertained, it is not at all improbable that it is Plutarch's own writing. There is nothing remarkable in its contents, and it is most noticeable for the contrast in tone which it presents to another letter, undoubtedly spurious, first published in Latin by John of Salisbury, which is a very preceptorial lecture to Trajan, his pupil, by Plutarch, his supposed former teacher.

A list of Plutarch's works, including many of which nothing remains, is also given by Suidas, as made by Lamprias, Plutarch's son; and a little prefatory letter to a friend, whom he had known in Asia, and who had written to ask for the information, is prefixed to the catalogue. The catalogue itself may be correct enough, but the name of Lamprias occurs nowhere in all Plutarch's extant works as that of one of his sons; and it cannot but be suspected that this family name was adopted, and this letter to the nameless friend in Asia composed, by some grammarian long after, who desired to give interest to an ordinary list of the author's extant writings.

In reading Plutarch, the following points should be remembered. He is a moralist rather than an historian. His interest is less for politics and the changes of empires, and much more for personal character and individual actions and motives to action; duty performed and rewarded; arro-

gance chastised, hasty anger corrected; humanity, fair dealing, and generosity triumphing in the visible, or relying on the invisible world. His
mind in his biographic memoirs is continually running on the
Aristotelian Ethics and the high Platonic theories, which formed the religion of the educated population of his time.

The time itself is a second point; that of Nerva, Trajan, and Hadrian;
the commencement of the best and happiest age of the great Roman imperial period. The social system, spreading over all the coasts of the
Mediterranean Sea, of which Greece and Italy were the centres, and to
which the East and the furthest known West were brought into relation,
had then reached its highest mark of advance and consummation. The
laws of Rome and the philosophy of Greece were powerful from the
Tigris to the British islands. It was the last great era of Greek and Roman
literature. Epictetus was teaching in Greek the virtues which Marcus
Aurelius was to illustrate as emperor. Dio Chrysostom and Arrian were
recalling the memory of the most famous Attic rhetoricians and historians, and while Plutarch wrote in Chæronea, Tacitus, Pliny the Younger,
Martial, and Juvenal were writing at Rome. It may be said too, perhaps,
not untruly, that the Latin, the metropolitan writers, less faithfully represent the general spirit and character of the time than what came from the
pen of a simple Bœotian provincial, writing in a more universal language,
and unwarped by the strong local reminiscences of the old home of the
Senate and the Republic. Tacitus and Juvenal have more, perhaps, of the
"antique Roman" than of the citizen of the great Mediterranean Empire.
The evils of the imperial government, as felt in the capital city, are depicted in the Roman prose and verse more vividly and more vehemently
than suits a general representation of the state of the imperial world, even
under the rule of Domitian himself.

It is, at any rate, the serener aspect and the better era that the life and
writings of Plutarch reflect. His language is that of a man happy in himself and in what is around him. His natural cheerfulness is undiminished,
his easy and joyous simplicity is unimpaired, his satisfactions are not sad-
dened or imbittered by any overpowering recollections of years passed
under the immediate present terrors of imperial wickedness. Though he
also could remember Nero, and had been a man when Domitian was an
emperor, the utmost we can say is, that he shows, perhaps, the instructed
happiness of one who had lived into good times out of evil, and that the
very vigour of his content proves that its roots were fixed amongst circumstances not too indulgent or favourable.

Much has been said of Plutarch's inaccuracy; and it cannot be denied
that he is careless about numbers, and occasionally contradicts his own
statements. A greater fault, perhaps, is his passion for anecdote; he cannot
forbear from repeating stories, the improbability of which he is the first

to recognise; which, nevertheless, by mere repetition, leave unjust impressions. He is unfair in this way to Demosthenes and to Pericles, against the latter of whom, however, he doubtless inherited the prejudices which Plato handed down to the philosophers.

It is true, also, that his unhistorical treatment of the subjects of his biography makes him often unsatisfactory and imperfect in the portraits he draws. Much, of course, in the public lives of statesmen can find its only explanation in their political position; and of this Plutarch often knows and thinks little. So far as the researches of modern historians have succeeded in really recovering a knowledge of relations of this sort, so far, undoubtedly, these biographies stand in need of their correction. Yet in the uncertainty which must attend all modern restorations, it is agreeable, and surely, also, profitable, to recur to portraits drawn ere new thoughts and views had occupied the civilised world, without reference to such disputable grounds of judgment, simply upon the broad principles of the ancient moral code of right and wrong.

Making some little deductions in cases such as those that have been mentioned, allowing for a little over-love of story, and for some considerable quasi-religious hostility to the democratic leaders who excited the scorn of Plato, if we bear in mind, also, that in narratives like that of Theseus, he himself confesses his inability to disengage fact from fable, it may be said that in Plutarch's Lives the readers of all ages will find instructive and faithful biographies of the great men of Greece and Rome. Or, at any rate, if in Plutarch's time it was too late to think of really faithful biographies, we have here the faithful record of the historical tradition of his age. This is what, in the second century of our era, Greeks and Romans loved to believe about their warriors and statesmen of the past. As a picture, at least, of the best Greek and Roman moral views and moral judgments, as a presentation of the results of Greek and Roman moral thought, delivered not under the pressure of calamity, but as they existed in ordinary times, and actuated plain-living people in country places in their daily life, Plutarch's writings are of indisputable value; and it may be said, also, that Plutarch's character, as depicted in them, possesses a natural charm of pleasantness and amiability which it is not easy to match among all extant classical authors.

The present translation is a revision of that published at the end of the seventeenth century, with a life of Plutarch written by Dryden, whose name, it was presumed, would throw some reflected lustre on the humbler workmen who performed, better or worse, the more serious labour. There is, of course, a great inequality in their work. But the translation by Langhorne, for which, in the middle of the last century, the older volumes were discarded, is so inferior in liveliness, and is in fact so dull and heavy a book that, in default of an entirely new translation, some advantage, it is hoped, may be gained by the revival here attempted. It would not have been needed, had Mr. Long not limited the series which he published, with very useful notes, in Mr. Knight's Shilling Library, to the lives connected with the Civil Wars of Rome.

Dryden's Life of Plutarch is, like many of Dryden's writings, hasty yet well written, inaccurate but agreeable to read; that by Dacier, printed in the last volume of his French translations, is, in many respects, very good. The materials for both were collected, and the references accumulated, by Rualdus, in his laborious Life appended to the old Paris folios of 1624. But everything that is of any value is given in the articles in Fabricius's *Bibliotheca Græca,* and, with the most recent additions, in Pauly's *German Cyclopædia.* Much that is useful is found, as might be expected, in Clinton's *Fasti Romani,* from which the following table is taken:—

DATE	OCCURRENCES	AUTHORS
A.D.		

41. Accession of Claudius.

54. Accession of Nero.

66. Nero comes into Greece; alluded to in Plutarch's Dialogue, On the EI at Delphi.

67. Nero celebrates the Isthmian Games; alluded to in Plutarch's Life of Flamininus.

> Seneca.
> Lucan.
> Persius.

68. Galba is Emperor. Civil wars.

69. Vitellius, Otho, Vespasian.

70. Taking of Jerusalem.

74. The Philosophers are expelled from Rome.

79. Death of Sabinus, the Gaul.
Death of Vespasian, and accession of Titus.
Eruption of Vesuvius; alluded to by Plutarch, as a recent occurrence, in his Enquiry why the Pythian Oracles are no longer delivered in verse.

> Death of Pliny the Elder.

81. Accession of Domitian.

90. The Philosophers are again expelled from Rome, after the death of Rusticus.

> Quintilian.
> Statius.
> Silius Italicus.
> Martial.

96. Accession of Nerva.

98. Accession of Trajan.

100. Pliny's Panegyric.

103. Epictetus is teaching at Nicopolis, Arrian attending him.

104. Pliny in Bithynia.

106. Trajan winters on the Danube; alluded to by Plutarch, On the Principle of Cold.

113. Erection of Trajan's Column.

114. Trajan's Parthian Victories. Plutarch had written his life of Antony before these.

117. Accession of Hadrian.
In Hadrian's third year, Plutarch, according to Eusebius, was still alive.

> *Dio Chrysostom.*
> Tacitus, born about A.D. 60.
> *Plutarch.*
> *Epictetus.*
> *Arrian.*
> Pliny the Younger, born A.D. 61.
> Juvenal, born A.D. 59.
> *Favorinus.*
> Suetonius, born about A.D. 70.

138. Accession of Antoninus.

161. Accession of Marcus Aurelius.

181. Accession of Commodus.

> *Ptolemy.*
> *Appian.*
> *Pausanias.*
> *Galen.*
> *Lucian.*
> *Athenæus.*
> *Dion Cassius.*

NOTE.—*The authors whose names are printed in italics are Greek writers.*

The fault which runs through all the earlier biographies, from that of Rualdus downward, is the assumption, wholly untenable, that Plutarch passed many years, as many, perhaps, as forty, at Rome. The entire character of his life is of course altered by such an impression. It is, therefore, not worth while reprinting here the life originally prefixed by Dryden to the translations which, with more or less of alteration, follow in the present volumes. One or two characteristic extracts may be sufficient. The first may throw some light on a subject which to modern readers is a little obscure. Dryden is wrong in one or two less important points, but his general view of the *dæmonic* belief which pervades Plutarch's writings is tolerably to the purpose.

"We can only trace the rest of his opinions from his philosophy, which we have said in the general to be Platonic, though it cannot also be denied that there was a tincture in it of the Electic[7] sect, which was begun by Potamon under the empire of Augustus, and which selected from all the other sects what seemed most probable in their opinions, not adhering singularly to any of them, nor rejecting everything. I will only touch his belief of spirits. In his two Treatises of Oracles, the one concerning the Reason of their Cessation, the other inquiring Why they were not given in Verse as in former times, he seems to assert the Pythagorean doctrine of Transmigration of Souls. We have formerly shown that he owned the unity of a Godhead; whom, according to his attributes, he calls by several names, as Jupiter from his almighty power, Apollo from his wisdom, and so of the rest; but under him he places those beings whom he styles *Genii* or *Dæmons,* of a middle nature, between divine and human; for he thinks it absurd that there should be no mean between the two extremes of an immortal and a mortal being; that there cannot be in nature so vast a flaw, without some intermedial kind of life, partaking of them both. As, therefore, we find the intercourse between the soul and body to be made by the animal spirits, so between divinity and humanity there is this species of dæmons. Who,[8] having first been men, and followed the strict rules of virtue, have purged off the grossness and feculency of their earthly being, are exalted into these genii; and are from thence either raised higher into an ethereal life, if they still continue virtuous, or tumbled down again into mortal bodies, and sinking into flesh after they have lost that purity which constituted their glorious being. And this sort of Genii are those who, as our author imagines, presided over oracles; spirits which have so much of their terrestrial principles remaining in them as to be subject to passions and inclinations; usually

---

[7] He means the Eclectic as it is more usually called.
[8] He means, I believe, *Those who;* apparently the word *and* should be omitted in line 24, before *sinking into flesh.*

beneficent, sometimes malevolent to mankind, according as they refine themselves, or gather dross, and are declining into mortal bodies. The cessation, or rather the decrease of oracles (for some of them were still remaining in Plutarch's time), he attributes either to the death of those dæmons, as appears by the story of the Egyptian Thamus, who was commanded to declare that the great god Pan was dead, or to their forsaking of those places where they formerly gave out their oracles, from whence they were driven by stronger Genii into banishment for a certain revolution of ages. Of this last nature were the war of the giants against the gods, the dispossession of Saturn by Jupiter, the banishment of Apollo from heaven, the fall of Vulcan, and many others; all which, according to our author, were the battles of these Genii or Dæmons amongst themselves. But supposing, as Plutarch evidently does, that these spirits administered, under the Supreme Being, the affairs of men, taking care of the virtuous, punishing the bad, and sometimes communicating with the best, as, particularly, the Genius of Socrates always warned him of approaching dangers, and taught him to avoid them, I cannot but wonder that every one who has hitherto written Plutarch's Life, and particularly Rualdus, the most knowing of them all, should so confidently affirm that these oracles were given by bad spirits, according to Plutarch. As Christians, indeed, we may think them so; but that Plutarch so thought is a most apparent falsehood. 'Tis enough to convince a reasonable man, that our author in his old age (and that then he doted not, we may see by the treatise he has written, That old men ought to have the management of public affairs), I say that then he initiated himself in the sacred rites of Delphos, and died, for ought we know, Apollo's priest. Now it is not to be imagined that he thought the God he served a *Cacodæmon,* or, as we call him, a devil. Nothing could be further from the opinion and practice of this holy philosopher than so gross an impiety. The story of the Pythias, or priestess of Apollo, which he relates immediately before the ending of that treatise, concerning the Cessation of Oracles, confirms my assertion rather than shakes it; for 'tis there delivered, 'That going with great reluctation into the sacred place to be inspired, she came out foaming at the mouth, her eyes goggling, her breast heaving, her voice undistinguishable and shrill, as if she had an earthquake within her, labouring for vent; and, in short, that thus tormented with the god, whom she was not able to support, she died distracted in a few days after. For he had said before that the divineress ought to have no perturbations of mind or impure passions at the time when she was to consult the oracle, and if she had, she was no more fit to be inspired than an instrument untuned to render an harmonious sound.' And he gives us to suspect, by what he says at the close of this relation, 'That this Pythias had not lived chastely for some time before it; so that her death appears more like a

punishment inflicted for loose living, by some holy Power, than the mere
malignancy of a Spirit delighted naturally in mischief.' There is another
observation which indeed comes nearer to their purpose, which I will
digress so far as to relate, because it somewhat appertains to our own
country. 'There are many islands,' says he, 'which lie scattering about
Britain, after the manner of our Sporades; they are unpeopled, and some
of them are called the Islands of the Heroes, or the Genii.' One
Demetrius was sent by the emperor (who by computation of the time
must either be Caligula or Claudius[9]) to discover those parts, and arriving at one of the islands next adjoining to the before mentioned, which
was inhabited by some few Britons (but those held sacred and inviolable
by all their countrymen), immediately after his arrival, the air grew black
and troubled, strange apparitions were seen, the winds raised a tempest,
and fiery spouts or whirlwinds appeared dancing towards the earth.
When these prodigies were ceased, the islanders informed him that some
one of the aerial beings, superior to our nature, then ceased to live. For
as a taper, while yet burning, affords a pleasant, harmless light, but is noi-
some and offensive when extinguished, so those heroes shine benignly
on us and do us good, but at their death turn all things topsy-turvy, raise
up tempests, and infect the air with pestilential vapours. By those holy
and inviolable men, there is no question but he means our Druids, who
were nearest to the Pythagoreans of any sect; and this opinion of the
Genii might probably be one of theirs. Yet it proves not that all dæmons
were thus malicious, only those who were to be condemned hereafter
into human bodies, for their misdemeanours in their aerial being. But 'tis
time to leave a subject so very fanciful, and so little reasonable as this. I
am apt to imagine the natural vapours, arising in the cave where the temple afterwards was built, might work upon the spirits of those who entered the holy place, as they did on the shepherd Coretas, who first found
it out by accident, and incline them to enthusiasm and prophetic madness; that as the strength of those vapours diminished (which were generally in caverns, as that of Mopsus, of Trophonius, and this of Delphos),
so the inspiration decreased by the same measures; that they happened to
be stronger when they killed the Pythias, who being conscious of this,
was so unwilling to enter; that the oracles ceased to be given in verse
when poets ceased to be the priests, and that the Genius of Socrates
(whom he confessed never to have seen, but only to have heard inwardly,
and unperceived by others) was no more than the strength of his imagination; or, to speak in the language of a Christian Platonist, his guardian
angel."

The concluding passage of the life may serve as a conclusion to this

---

[9] Undoubtedly much later.

prefatory essay. It is as follows: "And now, with the usual vanity of Dutch prefacers, I could load our author with the praises and commemorations of writers; for both ancient and modern have made honourable mention of him. But to cumber pages with this kind of stuff were to raise a distrust in common readers that Plutarch wants them. Rualdus, indeed, has collected ample testimonies of them; but I will only recite the names of some, and refer you to him for the particular quotations. He reckons Gellius, Eusebius, Himerius the Sophister, Eunapius, Cyrillus of Alexandria, Theodoret, Agathias, Photius and Xiphilin, patriarchs of Constantinople, Johannes Sarisberiensis, the famous Petrarch, Petrus Victorius, and Justus Lipsius.

"But Theodorus Gaza, a man learned in the Latin tongue, and a great restorer of the Greek, who lived above two hundred years ago, deserves to have his suffrage set down in words at length; for the rest have only commended Plutarch more than any single author, but he has extolled him above all together.

"'Tis said that, having this extravagant question put to him by a friend, that if learning must suffer a general shipwreck, and he had only his choice left him of preserving one author, who should be the man he would preserve, he answered, Plutarch; and probably might give this reason, that in saving him, he should secure the best collection of them all.

"The epigram of Agathias deserves also to be remembered. This author flourished about the year five hundred, in the reign of the Emperor Justinian. The verses are extant in the Anthologia, and with the translation of them I will conclude the praises of our author; having first admonished you, that they are supposed to be written on a statue erected by the Romans to his memory.

"'Chæronean Plutarch, to thy deathless praise
Does martial Rome this grateful statue raise,
Because both Greece and she thy fame have shared,
(Their heroes written, and their lives compared).
But thou thyself couldst never write thy own;
Their lives have parallels, but thine has none.'"

THE GREEKS

SOLON

DIDYMUS, the grammarian, in his answer to Asclepiades concerning Solon's Tables of Law, mentions a passage of one Philocles, who states that Solon's father's name was Euphorion, contrary to the opinion of all others who have written concerning him; for they generally agree that he was the son of Execestides, a man of moderate wealth and power in the city, but of a most noble stock, being descended from Codrus; his mother, as Heraclides Ponticus affirms, was cousin to Pisistratus's mother, and the two at first were great friends, partly because they were akin, and partly because of Pisistratus's noble qualities and beauty. And they say Solon loved him; and that is the reason, I suppose, that when afterwards they differed about the government, their enmity never produced any hot and violent passion, they remembered their old kindnesses, and retained—

"Still in its embers living the strong fire"

of their love and dear affection. For that Solon was not proof against beauty, nor of courage to stand up to passion and meet it—

"Hand to hand as in the ring,"

we may conjecture by his poems, and one of his laws, in which there are practices forbidden to slaves, which he would appear, therefore, to recommend to freemen. Pisistratus, it is stated, was similarly attached to one Charmus; he it was who dedicated the figure of Love in the Academy, where the runners in the sacred torch race light their torches. Solon, as Hermippus writes, when his father had ruined his estate in doing benefits and kindnesses to other men, though he had friends enough that were willing to contribute to his relief, yet was ashamed to be beholden to others, since he was descended from a family who were accustomed to do kindnesses rather than receive them; and therefore applied himself to merchandise in his youth; though others assure us that he traveled rather to get learning and experience than to make money. It is certain that he was a lover of knowledge, for when he was old he would say, that he—

"Each day grew older, and learnt something new;"

and yet no admirer of riches, esteeming as equally wealthy the man—

> "Who hath both gold and silver in his hand,
> Horses and mules, and acres of wheat-land,
> And him whose all is decent food to eat,
> Clothes to his back and shoes upon his feet,
> And a young wife and child, since so 'twill be,
> And no more years than will with that agree;"

and in another place—

> "Wealth I would have, but wealth by wrong procure
> I would not; justice, e'en if slow, is sure."

And it is perfectly possible for a good man and a statesman, without being solicitous for superfluities, to show some concern for competent necessaries. In his time, as Hesiod says,—"Work was a shame to none," nor was distinction made with respect to trade, but merchandise was a noble calling, which brought home the good things which the barbarous nations enjoyed, was the occasion of friendship with their kings, and a great source of experience. Some merchants have built great cities, as Protis, the founder of Massilia, to whom the Gauls, near the Rhone, were much attached. Some report also, that Thales and Hippocrates the mathematician traded; and that Plato defrayed the charges of his travels by selling oil in Egypt. Solon's softness and profuseness, his popular rather than philosophical tone about pleasure in his poems, have been ascribed to his trading life; for, having suffered a thousand dangers, it was natural they should be recompensed with some gratifications and enjoyments; but that he accounted himself rather poor than rich is evident from the lines—

> "Some wicked men are rich, some good are poor,
> We will not change our virtue for their store:
> Virtue's a thing that none can take away;
> But money changes owners all the day."

At first he used his poetry only in trifles, not for any serious purpose, but simply to pass away his idle hours; but afterwards he introduced moral sentences and state matters, which he did, not to record them merely as an historian, but to justify his own actions, and sometimes to correct, chastise, and stir up the Athenians to noble performances. Some report that he designed to put his laws into heroic verse, and that they began thus:—

"We humbly beg a blessing on our laws
From mighty Jove, and honor, and applause."

In philosophy, as most of the wise men then, he chiefly esteemed the political part of morals; in physics, he was very plain and antiquated, as appears by this:—

"It is the clouds that make the snow and hail,
And thunder comes from lightning without fail;
The sea is stormy when the winds have blown,
But it deals fairly when 'tis left alone."

And, indeed, it is probable that at that time Thales alone had raised philosophy above mere practice into speculation; and the rest of the wise men were so called from prudence in political concerns. It is said, that they had an interview at Delphi, and another at Corinth, by the procurement of Periander, who made a meeting for them, and a supper. But their reputation was chiefly raised by sending the tripod to them all, by their modest refusal, and complaisant yielding to one another. For, as the story goes, some of the Coans fishing with a net, some strangers, Milesians, bought the draught at a venture; the net brought up a golden tripod, which, they say, Helen, at her return from Troy, upon the remembrance of an old prophecy, threw in there. Now, the strangers at first contesting with the fishers about the tripod, and the cities espousing the quarrel so far as to engage themselves in a war, Apollo decided the controversy by commanding to present it to the wisest man; and first it was sent to Miletus to Thales, the Coans freely presenting him with that for which they fought against the whole body of the Milesians; but Thales declaring Bias the wiser person, it was sent to him; from him to another; and so, going round them all, it came to Thales a second time; and, at last, being carried from Miletus to Thebes, was there dedicated to Apollo Ismenius. Theophrastus writes that it was first presented to Bias at Priene; and next to Thales at Miletus, and so through all it returned to Bias, and was afterwards sent to Delphi. This is the general report, only some, instead of a tripod, say this present was a cup sent by Crœsus; others, a piece of plate that one Bathycles had left. It is stated, that Anacharsis and Solon, and Solon and Thales, were familiarly acquainted and some have delivered parts of their discourse; for, they say, Anacharsis, coming to Athens, knocked at Solon's door, and told him, that he, being a stranger, was come to be his guest, and contract a friendship with him; and Solon replying, "It is better to make friends at home," Anacharsis replied, "Then you that are at home make friendship with me." Solon, somewhat surprised at the readiness of the repartee, received him kindly, and kept him some time with him, being already engaged in public business and the compilation of his laws; which when Anacharsis understood, he laughed at him for imagining the dishonesty and covetousness of his countrymen could be restrained by written laws, which were like spiders' webs, and would catch, it is true, the weak and poor, but easily be broken by the mighty and rich. To this Solon rejoined that men keep their promises when neither side can get anything by the breaking of them; and he would so fit his laws to the citizens, that all should understand it was more eligible to be just than to break the laws. But the event rather agreed with the conjecture of Anacharsis than Solon's hope. Anacharsis, being once at the Assembly, expressed his wonder at the fact that in Greece wise men spoke and fools decided.

Solon went, they say, to Thales, at Miletus, and wondered that Thales took no care to get him a wife and children. To this, Thales made no answer for the present; but a few days after procured a stranger to pretend that he had left Athens ten days ago; and Solon inquiring what news there, the man, according to his instructions, replied, "None but a young man's funeral, which the whole city attended; for he was the son, they said, of an honorable man, the most virtuous of the citizens, who was not then at home, but had been traveling a long time." Solon replied, "What a miserable man is he! But what was his name?" "I have heard it," says the man, "but have now forgotten it, only there was a great talk of his wisdom and his justice." Thus Solon was drawn on by every answer, and his fears heightened, till at last, being extremely concerned, he mentioned his own name, and asked the stranger if that young man was called Solon's son; and the stranger assenting, he began to beat his head, and to do and say all that is usual with men in transports of grief. But Thales took his hand, and, with a smile, said, "These things, Solon, keep me from marriage and rearing children, which are too great for even your constancy to support; however, be not concerned at the report, for it is a fiction." This Hermippus relates, from Patæcus, who boasted that he had Æsop's soul.

However, it is irrational and poor-spirited not to seek conveniences for fear of losing them, for upon the same account we should not allow ourselves to like wealth, glory, or wisdom, since we may fear to be deprived of all these; nay, even virtue itself, than which there is no greater nor more desirable possession, is often suspended by sickness or drugs. Now Thales, though unmarried, could not be free from solicitude unless he likewise felt no care for his friends, his kinsmen, or his country; yet we are told he adopted Cybisthus, his sister's son. For the soul, having a principle of kindness in itself, and being born to love, as well as perceive, think, or remember, inclines and fixes upon some stranger, when a man has none of his own to embrace. And alien or illegitimate objects insinuate themselves into his affections, as into some estate that lacks lawful heirs; and with affection come anxiety and care; insomuch that you may see men that use the strongest language against the marriage-bed and the fruit of it, when some servant's or concubine's child is sick or dies, almost killed with grief, and abjectly lamenting. Some have given way to shameful and desperate sorrow at the loss of a dog or horse; others have borne the deaths of virtuous children without any extravagant or unbecoming grief, have passed the rest of their lives like men, and according to the principles of reason. It is not affection, it is weakness, that brings men, unarmed against fortune by reason, into these endless pains and terrors; and they indeed have not even the present enjoyment of what they dote upon, the possibility of the future loss causing them continual pangs, tremors, and distresses. We must not provide against the loss of wealth by poverty, or of friends by refusing all acquaintance, or of children by having none, but by morality and reason. But of this too much.

Now, when the Athenians were tired with a tedious and difficult war that they conducted against the Megarians for the island Salamis, and made a law that it should be death for any man, by writing or speaking, to assert that the city ought to endeavor to recover it, Solon, vexed at the disgrace, and perceiving thousands of the youth wished for somebody to begin, but did not dare to stir first for fear of the law, counterfeited a distraction, and by his own family it was spread about the city that he was mad. He then secretly composed some elegiac verses, and getting them by heart, that it might seem extempore, ran out into the marketplace with a cap upon his head, and, the people gathering about him, got upon the herald's stand, and sang that elegy which begins thus:—

> "I am a herald come from Salamis the fair,
> My news from thence my verses shall declare."

The poem is called Salamis; it contains a hundred verses very elegantly written; when it had been sung, his friends commended it, and especially Pisistratus exhorted the citizens to obey his directions; insomuch that they recalled the law, and renewed the war under Solon's conduct. The popular tale is, that with Pisistratus he sailed to Colias, and, finding the women, according to the custom of the country there, sacrificing to Ceres, he sent a trusty friend to Salamis, who should pretend himself a renegade, and advise them, if they desired to seize the chief Athenian women, to come with him at once to Colias; the Megarians presently sent off men in the vessel with him; and Solon, seeing it put off from the island, commanded the women to be gone, and some beardless youths, dressed in their clothes, their shoes and caps, and privately armed with daggers, to dance and play near the shore till the enemies had landed and the vessel was in their power. Things being thus ordered, the Megarians were lured with the appearance, and, coming to the shore, jumped out, eager who should first seize a prize, so that not one of them escaped; and the Athenians set sail for the island and took it.

Others say that it was not taken this way, but that he first received this oracle from Delphi:—

> "Those heroes that in fair Asopia rest,
> All buried with their faces to the west,
> Go and appease with offerings of the best;"

and that Solon, sailing by night to the island, sacrificed to the heroes Periphemus and Cychreus, and then taking five hundred Athenian volunteers (a law having passed that those that took the island should be highest in the government), with a number of fisher-boats and one thirty-oared ship, anchored in a bay of Salamis that looks towards Nisæa; and the Megarians that were then in the island, hearing only an uncertain report, hurried to their arms, and sent a ship to reconnoiter the enemies. This ship Solon took, and, securing the Megarians, manned it with Athenians, and gave them orders to sail to the island with as much privacy as possible; meantime he, with the other soldiers, marched against the Megarians by land, and whilst they were fighting, those from the ship took the city. And this narrative is confirmed by the following solemnity, that was afterwards observed: An Athenian ship used to sail silently at first to the island, then, with noise and a great shout, one leapt out armed, and with a loud cry ran to the promontory Sciradium to meet those that approached upon the land. And just by there stands a temple which Solon dedicated to Mars. For he beat the Megarians, and as many as were not killed in the battle he sent away upon conditions.

The Megarians, however, still contending, and both sides having received considerable losses, they chose the Spartans for arbitrators. Now, many affirm that Homer's authority did Solon a considerable kindness, and that, introducing a line into the Catalog of Ships, when the matter was to be determined, he read the passage as follows:—

> "Twelve ships from Salamis stout Ajax brought,
> And ranked his men where the Athenians fought."

The Athenians, however, call this but an idle story, and report that Solon made it appear to the judges, that Philæus and Eurysaces, the sons of Ajax, being made citizens of Athens, gave them the island, and that one of them dwelt at Brauron in Attica, the other at Melite; and they have a township of Philaidæ, to which Pisistratus belonged, deriving its name from this Philæus. Solon took a farther argument against the Megarians from the dead bodies, which, he said, were not buried after their fashion, but according to the Athenian; for the Megarians turn the corpse to the east, the Athenians to the west. But Hereas the Megarian denies this, and affirms that they likewise turn the body to the west, and also that the Athenians have a separate tomb for everybody, but the Megarians put two or three into one. However, some of Apollo's oracles, where he calls Salamis Ionian, made much for Solon. This matter was determined by five Spartans, Critolaidas, Amompharetus, Hypsechidas, Anaxilas, and Cleomenes.

For this, Solon grew famed and powerful; but his advice in favor of defending the oracle at Delphi, to give aid, and not to suffer the Cirrhæans to profane it, but to maintain the honor of the god, got him most repute among the Greeks; for upon his persuasion the Amphictyons undertook the war, as, amongst others, Aristotle affirms, in his enumeration of the victors at the Pythian games, where he makes Solon the author of this counsel. Solon, however, was not general in that expedition, as Hermippus states, out of Evanthes the Samian; for Æschines the orator says no such thing, and, in the Delphian register, Alcmæon, not Solon, is named as commander of the Athenians.

Now the Cylonian pollution had a long while disturbed the commonwealth, ever since the time when Megacles the archon persuaded the conspirators with Cylon that took sanctuary in Minerva's temple to come down and stand to a fair trial. And they, tying a thread to the image, and holding one end of it, went down to the tribunal; but when they came to the temple of the Furies, the thread broke of its own accord, upon which, as if the goddess had refused them protection, they were seized by Megacles and the other magistrates; as many as were without the temples were stoned, those that fled for sanctuary were butchered at the altar, and only those escaped who made supplication to the wives of the magistrates. But they from that time were considered under pollution, and regarded with hatred. The remainder of the faction of Cylon grew strong again, and had continual quarrels with the family of Megacles; and now the quarrel being at its height, and the people divided, Solon, being in reputation, interposed with the chiefest of the Athenians, and by entreaty and admonition persuaded the polluted to submit to a trial and the decision of three hundred noble citizens. And Myron of Phlya being their accuser, they were found guilty, and as many as were then alive were banished, and the bodies of the dead were dug up, and scattered beyond the confines of the country. In the midst of these distractions, the Megarians falling upon them, they lost Nisæa and Salamis again; besides, the city was disturbed with superstitious fears and strange appearances, and the priests declared that the sacrifices intimated some villainies and pollutions that were to be expiated. Upon this, they sent for Epimenides the Phæstian from Crete, who is counted the seventh wise man by those that will not admit Periander into the number. He seems to have been thought a favorite of heaven, possessed of knowl-

edge in all the supernatural and ritual parts of religion; and, therefore, the
men of his age called him a new Curies, and son of a nymph named
Balte. When he came to Athens, and grew acquainted with Solon, he
served him in many instances, and prepared the way for his legislation.
He made them moderate in their forms of worship, and abated their
mourning by ordering some sacrifices presently after the funeral, and taking off those severe and barbarous ceremonies which the women usually
practiced; but the greatest benefit was his purifying and sanctifying the
city, by certain propitiatory and expiatory lustrations, and foundation of
sacred buildings; by that means making them more submissive to justice,
and more inclined to harmony. It is reported that, looking upon
Munychia, and considering a long while, he said to those that stood by,
"How blind is man in future things! for did the Athenians foresee what
mischief this would do their city, they would even eat it with their own
teeth to be rid of it." A similar anticipation is ascribed to Thales; they say
he commanded his friends to bury him in an obscure and contemned
quarter of the territory of Miletus, saying that it should some day be the
marketplace of the Milesians. Epimenides, being much honored, and receiving from the city rich offers of large gifts and privileges, requested
but one branch of the sacred olive, and, on that being granted, returned.

The Athenians, now the Cylonian sedition was over and the polluted
gone into banishment, fell into their old quarrels about the government,
there being as many different parties as there were diversities in the country. The Hill quarter favored democracy, the Plain, oligarchy, and those
that lived by the Seaside stood for a mixed sort of government, and so
hindered either of the other parties from prevailing. And the disparity of
fortune between the rich and the poor, at that time, also reached its
height; so that the city seemed to be in a truly dangerous condition, and
no other means for freeing it from disturbances and settling it to be possible but a despotic power. All the people were indebted to the rich; and
either they tilled their land for their creditors, paying them a sixth part
of the increase, and were, therefore, called Hectemorii and Thetes, or else
they engaged their body for the debt, and might be seized, and either sent
into slavery at home, or sold to strangers; some (for no law forbade it)
were forced to sell their children, or fly their country to avoid the cruelty of their creditors; but the most part and the bravest of them began
to combine together and encourage one another to stand to it, to choose
a leader, to liberate the condemned debtors, divide the land, and change
the government.

Then the wisest of the Athenians, perceiving Solon was of all men the
only one not implicated in the troubles, that he had not joined in the ex-
actions of the rich, and was not involved in the necessities of the poor,
pressed him to succor the commonwealth and compose the differences.

Though Phanias the Lesbian affirms, that Solon, to save his country, put a trick upon both parties, and privately promised the poor a division of the lands, and the rich, security for their debts. Solon, however, himself says that it was reluctantly at first that he engaged in state affairs, being afraid of the pride of one party and the greediness of the other; he was chosen archon, however, after Philombrotus, and empowered to be an arbitrator and lawgiver; the rich consenting because he was wealthy, the poor because he was honest. There was a saying of his current before the election, that when things are *even* there never can be war, and this pleased both parties, the wealthy and the poor; the one conceiving him to mean, when all have their fair proportion; the others, when all are absolutely equal. Thus, there being great hopes on both sides, the chief men pressed Solon to take the government into his own hands, and, when he was once settled, manage the business freely and according to his pleasure; and many of the commons, perceiving it would be a difficult change to be effected by law and reason, were willing to have one wise and just man set over the affairs; and some say that Solon had this oracle from Apollo—

"Take the mid-seat, and be the vessel's guide;
    Many in Athens are upon your side."

But chiefly his familiar friends chid him for disaffecting monarchy only because of the name, as if the virtue of the ruler could not make it a lawful form; Euboea had made this experiment when it chose Tynnondas, and Mitylene, which had made Pittacus its prince; yet this could not shake Solon's resolution; but, as they say, he replied to his friends, that it was true a tyranny was a very fair spot, but it had no way down from it; and in a copy of verses to Phocus he writes—

"that I spared my land,
    And withheld from usurpation and from violence my hand,
    And forbore to fix a stain and a disgrace on my good name,
    I regret not; I believe that it will be my chiefest fame."

From which it is manifest that he was a man of great reputation before he gave his laws. The several mocks that were put upon him for refusing the power, he records in these words:—

"Solon surely was a dreamer, and a man of simple mind;
    When the gods would give him fortune, he of his own will declined;
    When the net was full of fishes, over-heavy thinking it,
    He declined to haul it up, through want of heart and want of wit.
    Had but I that chance of riches and of kingship, for one day,
    I would give my skin for flaying, and my house to die away."

Thus he makes the many and the low people speak of him. Yet, though he refused the government, he was not too mild in the affair; he did not show himself mean and submissive to the powerful, nor make his laws to pleasure those that chose him. For where it was well before, he applied no remedy, nor altered anything, for fear lest—

> "Overthrowing altogether and disordering the state,"

he should be too weak to new-model and recompose it to a tolerable condition; but what he thought he could effect by persuasion upon the pliable, and by force upon the stubborn, this he did, as he himself says—

> "With force and justice working both in one."

And, therefore, when he was afterwards asked if he had left the Athenians the best laws that could be given, he replied, "The best they could receive." The way which, the moderns say, the Athenians have of softening the badness of a thing, by ingeniously giving it some pretty and innocent appellation, calling harlots, for example, mistresses, tributes customs, a garrison a guard, and the jail the chamber, seems originally to have been Solon's contrivance, who called canceling debts Seisacthea, a relief, or disencumbrance. For the first thing which he settled was, that what debts remained should be forgiven, and no man, for the future, should engage the body of his debtor for security. Though some, as Androtion, affirm that the debts were not canceled, but the interest only lessened, which sufficiently pleased the people; so that they named this benefit the Seisacthea, together with the enlarging their measures, and raising the value of their money; for he made a pound, which before passed for seventy-three drachmas, go for a hundred; so that, though the number of pieces in the payment was equal, the value was less; which proved a considerable benefit to those that were to discharge great debts, and no loss to the creditors. But most agree that it was the taking off the debts that was called Seisacthea, which is confirmed by some places in his poem, where he takes honor to himself, that—

> "The mortgage-stones that covered her, by me
>   Removed,—the land that was a slave is free";

that some who had been seized for their debts he had brought back from other countries, where—

> "—so far their lot to roam,
> They had forgot the language of their home";

and some he had set at liberty—

> "Who here in shameful servitude were held."

While he was designing this, a most vexatious thing happened; for when he had resolved to take off the debts, and was considering the proper form and fit beginning for it, he told some of his friends, Conon, Clinias, and Hipponicus, in whom he had a great deal of confidence, that he would not meddle with the lands, but only free the people from their debts; upon which they, using their advantage, made haste and borrowed some considerable sums of money, and purchased some large farms; and when the law was enacted, they kept the possessions, and would not return the money; which brought Solon into great suspicion and dislike, as if he himself had not been abused, but was concerned in the contrivance. But he presently stopped this suspicion, by releasing his debtors of five talents (for he had lent so much), according to the law; others, as Polyzelus the Rhodian, say fifteen; his friends, however, were ever afterward called Chreocopidæ, repudiators.

In this he pleased neither party, for the rich were angry for their money, and the poor that the land was not divided, and, as Lycurgus ordered in his commonwealth, all men reduced to equality. He, it is true, being the eleventh from Hercules, and having reigned many years in Lacedæmon, had got a great reputation and friends and power, which he could use in modeling his state; and, applying force more than persuasion, insomuch that he lost his eye in the scuffle, was able to employ the most effectual means for the safety and harmony of a state, by not permitting any to be poor or rich in his commonwealth. Solon could not rise to that in his polity, being but a citizen of the middle classes; yet he acted fully up to the height of his power, having nothing but the good-will and good opinion of his citizens to rely on; and that he offended the most part, who looked for another result, he declares in the words—

"Formerly they boasted of me vainly; with averted eyes
    Now they look askance upon me; friends no more, but enemies."

And yet had any other man, he says, received the same power—

"He would not have forborne, nor let alone,
        But made the fattest of the milk his own."

Soon, however, becoming sensible of the good that was done, they laid by their grudges, made a public sacrifice, calling it Seisacthea, and chose Solon to new-model and make laws for the commonwealth, giving him the entire power over everything, their magistracies, their assemblies, courts, and councils; that he should appoint the number, times of meeting, and what estate they must have that could be capable of these, and dissolve or continue any of the present constitutions, according to his pleasure.

First, then, he repealed all Draco's laws, except those concerning homicide, because they were too severe, and the punishment too great; for death was appointed for almost all offenses, insomuch that those that were convicted of idleness were to die, and those that stole a cabbage or an apple to suffer even as villains that committed sacrilege or murder. So that Demades, in after time, was thought to have said very happily, that Draco's laws were written not with ink but blood; and he himself, being once asked why he made death the punishment of most offenses, replied, "Small ones deserve that, and I have no higher for the greater crimes."

Next, Solon, being willing to continue the magistracies in the hands of the rich men, and yet receive the people into the other part of the government, took an account of the citizens' estates, and those that were worth five hundred measures of fruit, dry and liquid, he placed in the first rank, calling them Pentacosiomedimni; those that could keep an horse, or were worth three hundred measures, were named Hippada Teluntes, and made the second class; the Zeugitæ, that had two hundred measures, were in the third; and all the others were called Thetes, who were not admitted to any office, but could come to the assembly, and act as jurors; which at first seemed nothing, but afterwards was found an enormous privilege, as almost every matter of dispute came before them in this latter capacity. Even in the cases which he assigned to the archons' cognizance, he allowed an appeal to the courts. Besides, it is said that he was obscure and ambiguous in the wording of his laws, on purpose to increase the honor of his courts; for since their differences could not be adjusted by the letter, they would have to bring all their causes to the judges, who thus were in a manner masters of the laws. Of this equalization he himself makes mention in this manner:—

> "Such power I gave the people as might do,
> Abridged not what they had, now lavished new.
> Those that were great in wealth and high in place,
> My counsel likewise kept from all disgrace.
> Before them both I held my shield of might,
> And let not either touch the other's right."

And for the greater security of the weak commons, he gave general liberty of indicting for an act of injury; if any one was beaten, maimed, or suffered any violence, any man that would and was able, might prosecute the wrongdoer; intending by this to accustom the citizens, like members of the same body, to resent and be sensible of one another's injuries. And there is a saying of his agreeable to this law, for, being asked what city was best modeled, "That," said he, "where those that are not injured try and punish the unjust as much as those that are."

When he had constituted the Areopagus of those who had been yearly archons, of which he himself was a member therefore, observing that the people, now free from their debts, were unsettled and imperious, he formed another council of four hundred, a hundred out of each of the four tribes, which was to inspect all matters before they were propounded to the people, and to take care that nothing but what had been first examined should be brought before the general assembly. The upper council, or Areopagus, he made inspectors and keepers of the laws, conceiving that the commonwealth, held by these two councils, like anchors, would be less liable to be tossed by tumults, and the people be more quiet. Such is the general statement, that Solon instituted the Areopagus; which seems to be confirmed, because Draco makes no mention of the Areopagites, but in all causes of blood refers to the Ephetæ; yet Solon's thirteenth table contains the eighth law set down in these very words: "Whoever before Solon's archonship were disfranchised, let them be restored, except those that, being condemned by the Areopagus, Ephetæ, or in the Prytaneum by the kings, for homicide, murder, or designs against the government, were in banishment when this law was made"; and these words seem to show that the Areopagus existed before Solon's laws, for who could be condemned by that council before his time, if he was the first that instituted the court? unless, which is probable, there is some ellipsis, or want of precision, in the language, and it should run thus:—"Those that are convicted of such offenses as belong to the cognizance of the Areopagites, Ephetæ, or the Prytanes, when this law was made," shall remain still in disgrace, whilst others are restored; of this the reader must judge.

Amongst his other laws, one is very peculiar and surprising, which disfranchises all who stand neuter in a sedition; for it seems he would not have any one remain insensible and regardless of the public good, and securing his private affairs, glory that he has no feeling of the distempers of his country; but at once join with the good party and those that have the right upon their side, assist and venture with them, rather than keep out of harm's way and watch who would get the better. It seems an absurd and foolish law which permits an heiress, if her lawful husband fail her, to take his nearest kinsman; yet some say this law was well contrived against those who, conscious of their own unfitness, yet, for the sake of the portion, would match with heiresses, and make use of law to put a violence upon nature; for now, since she can quit him for whom she pleases, they would either abstain from such marriages, or continue them with disgrace, and suffer for their covetousness and designed affront; it is well done, moreover, to confine her to her husband's nearest kinsman, that the children may be of the same family. Agreeable to this is the law that the bride and bridegroom shall be shut into a chamber, and eat a quince together; and that the husband of an heiress shall consort with her thrice a month; for though there be no children, yet it is an honor and due affection which an husband ought to pay to a virtuous, chaste wife; it takes off all petty differences, and will not permit their little quarrels to proceed to a rupture.

In all other marriages he forbade dowries to be given; the wife was to have three suits of clothes, a little inconsiderable household stuff, and that was all; for he would not have marriages contracted for gain or an estate, but for pure love, kind affection, and birth of children. When the mother of Dionysius desired him to marry her to one of his citizens, "Indeed," said he, "by my tyranny I have broken my country's laws, but cannot put a violence upon those of nature by an unseasonable marriage." Such disorder is never to be suffered in a commonwealth, nor such unseasonable and unloving and unperforming marriages, which attain no due end or fruit; any provident governor or lawgiver might say to an old man that takes a young wife what is said to Philoctetes in the tragedy—

"Truly, in a fit state thou to marry!"

and if he find a young man, with a rich and elderly wife, growing fat in his place, like the partridges, remove him to a young woman of proper age. And of this enough.

Another commendable law of Solon's is that which forbids men to speak evil of the dead; for it is pious to think the deceased sacred, and just, not to meddle with those that are gone, and politic, to prevent the perpetuity of discord. He likewise forbade them to speak evil of the living in the temples, the courts of justice, the public offices, or at the games, or else to pay three drachmas to the person, and two to the public. For never to be able to control passion shows a weak nature and ill-breeding; and always to moderate it is very hard, and to some impossible. And laws must look to possibilities, if the maker designs to punish few in order to their amendment, and not many to no purpose.

He is likewise much commended for his law concerning wills; for before him none could be made, but all the wealth and estate of the deceased belonged to his family; but he, by permitting them, if they had no children, to bestow it on whom they pleased, showed that he esteemed friendship a stronger tie than kindred, and affection than necessity; and made every man's estate truly his own. Yet he allowed not all sorts of legacies, but those only which were not extorted by the frenzy of a disease, charms, imprisonment, force, or the persuasions of a wife; with good reason thinking that being seduced into wrong was as bad as being forced, and that between deceit and necessity, flattery and compulsion, there was little difference, since both may equally suspend the exercise of reason.

He regulated the walks, feasts, and mourning of the women, and took away everything that was either unbecoming or immodest; when they walked abroad, no more than three articles of dress were allowed them;

an obol's worth of meat and drink; and no basket above a cubit high; and at night they were not to go about unless in a chariot with a torch before them. Mourners tearing themselves to raise pity, and set wailings, and at one man's funeral to lament for another, he forbade. To offer an ox at the grave was not permitted, nor to bury above three pieces of dress with the body, or visit the tombs of any besides their own family, unless at the very funeral; most of which are likewise forbidden by our laws, but this is further added in ours, that those that are convicted of extravagance in their mournings are to be punished as soft and effeminate by the censors of women.

Observing the city to be filled with persons that flocked from all parts into Attica for security of living, and that most of the country was barren and unfruitful, and that traders at sea import nothing to those that could give them nothing in exchange, he turned his citizens to trade, and made a law that no son should be obliged to relieve a father who had not bred him up to any calling. It is true, Lycurgus, having a city free from all strangers, and land, according to Euripides—

"Large for large hosts, for twice their number much,"

and, above all, an abundance of laborers about Sparta, who should not be left idle, but be kept down with continual toil and work, did well to take off his citizens from laborious and mechanical occupations, and keep them to their arms, and teach them only the art of war. But Solon, fitting his laws to the state of things, and not making things to suit his laws, and finding the ground scarce rich enough to maintain the husbandmen, and altogether incapable of feeding an unoccupied and leisured multitude, brought trades into credit, and ordered the Areopagites to examine how every man got his living, and chastise the idle. But that law was yet more rigid which, as Heraclides Ponticus delivers, declared the sons of unmarried mothers not obliged to relieve their fathers; for he that avoids the honorable form of union shows that he does not take a woman for children, but for pleasure, and thus gets his just reward, and has taken away from himself every title to upbraid his children, to whom he has made their very birth a scandal and reproach.

Solon's laws in general about women are his strangest; for he permitted any one to kill an adulterer that found him in the act; but if any one forced a free woman, a hundred drachmas was the fine; if he enticed her, twenty; except those that sell themselves openly, that is, harlots, who go openly to those that hire them. He made it unlawful to sell a daughter or a sister, unless, being yet unmarried, she was found wanton. Now it is irrational to punish the same crime sometimes very severely and without remorse, and sometimes very lightly, and as it were in sport, with a trivial fine; unless there being little money then in Athens, scarcity made those mulcts the more grievous punishment. In the valuation for sacrifices, a sheep and a bushel were both estimated at a drachma; the victor in the Isthmian games was to have for reward a hundred drachmas; the conqueror in the Olympian, five hundred; he that brought a wolf, five drachmas; for a whelp, one; the former sum, as Demetrius the Phalerian asserts, was the value of an ox, the latter, of a sheep. The prices which Solon, in his sixteenth table, sets on choice victims, were naturally far greater; yet they, too, are very low in comparison of the present. The Athenians were, from the beginning, great enemies to wolves, their fields being better for pasture than corn. Some affirm their tribes did not take their names from the sons of Ion, but from the different sorts of occupation that they followed; the soldiers were called Hoplitæ, the craftsmen Ergades, and, of the remaining two, the farmers Gedeontes, and the shepherds and graziers Ægicores.

Since the country has but few rivers, lakes, or large springs, and many used wells which they had dug, there was a law made, that, where there was a public well within a *hippicon,* that is, four furlongs, all should draw at that; but when it was farther off, they should try and procure a well of their own; and, if they had dug ten fathoms deep and could find no water, they had liberty to fetch a pitcherful of four gallons and a half in a day from their neighbors'; for he thought it prudent to make provision against want, but not to supply laziness. He showed skill in his orders about planting, for any one that would plant another tree was not to set it within five feet of his neighbor's field; but if a fig or an olive not within nine; for their roots spread farther, nor can they be planted near all sorts of trees without damage, for they draw away the nourishment, and in some cases are noxious by their effluvia. He that would dig a pit or a ditch was to dig it at the distance of its own depth from his neighbor's ground; and he that would raise stocks of bees was not to place them within three hundred feet of those which another had already raised.

He permitted only oil to be exported, and those that exported any other fruit, the archon was solemnly to curse, or else pay an hundred drachmas himself; and this law was written in his first table, and, therefore, let none think it incredible, as some affirm, that the exportation of figs was once unlawful, and the informer against the delinquents called a sycophant. He made a law, also, concerning hurts and injuries from beasts, in which he commands the master of any dog that bit a man to deliver him up with a log about his neck, four and a half feet long; a happy device for men's security. The law concerning naturalizing strangers is of doubtful character; he permitted only those to be made free of Athens who were in perpetual exile from their own country, or came with their whole family to trade there; this he did, not to discourage strangers, but rather to invite them to a permanent participation in the privileges of the government; and, besides, he thought those would prove the more faithful citizens who had been forced from their own country, or voluntarily forsook it. The law of public entertainment (*parasitein* is his name for it) is also peculiarly Solon's; for if any man came often, or if he that was invited refused, they were punished, for he concluded that one was greedy, the other a contemner of the state.

All his laws he established for an hundred years, and wrote them on wooden tables or rollers, named axones, which might be turned round in oblong cases; some of their relics were in my time still to be seen in the Prytaneum, or common hall, at Athens. These, as Aristotle states, were called cyrbes, and there is a passage of Cratinus the comedian—

> "By Solon, and by Draco, if you please,
> Whose Cyrbes make the fires that parch our peas."

But some say those are properly cyrbes, which contain laws concerning sacrifices and the rites of religion, and all the others axones. The council all jointly swore to confirm the laws, and every one of the Thesmothetæ vowed for himself at the stone in the marketplace, that if he broke any of the statutes, he would dedicate a golden statue, as big as himself, at Delphi.

Observing the irregularity of the months, and that the moon does not always rise and set with the sun, but often in the same day overtakes and gets before him, he ordered the day should be named the Old and New, attributing that part of it which was before the conjunction to the old moon, and the rest to the new, he being the first, it seems, that understood that verse of Homer—

> "The end and the beginning of the month,"—

and the following day he called the new moon. After the twentieth he did not count by addition, but, like the moon itself in its wane, by subtraction; thus up to the thirtieth.

Now when these laws were enacted, and some came to Solon every day, to commend or dispraise them, and to advise, if possible, to leave out or put in something, and many criticized and desired him to explain, and tell the meaning of such and such a passage, he, knowing that to do it was useless, and not to do it would get him ill-will, and desirous to bring himself out of all straits, and to escape all displeasure and exceptions, it being a hard thing, as he himself says—

> "In great affairs to satisfy all sides,"

as an excuse for traveling, bought a trading vessel, and, having obtained leave for ten years' absence, departed, hoping that by that time his laws would have become familiar.

His first voyage was for Egypt, and he lived, as he himself says—

"Near Nilus' mouth, by fair Canopus' shore,"

and spent some time in study with Psenophis of Heliopolis, and Sonchis the Saite, the most learned of all the priests; from whom, as Plato says, getting knowledge of the Atlantic story, he put it into a poem, and proposed to bring it to the knowledge of the Greeks. From thence he sailed to Cyprus, where he was made much of by Philocyprus, one of the kings there, who had a small city built by Demophon, Theseus's son, near the river Clarius, in a strong situation, but incommodious and uneasy of access. Solon persuaded him, since there lay a fair plain below, to remove, and build there a pleasanter and more spacious city. And he stayed himself, and assisted in gathering inhabitants, and in fitting it both for defense and convenience of living; insomuch that many flocked to Philocyprus, and the other kings imitated the design; and, therefore, to honor Solon, he called the city Soli, which was formerly named Æpea. And Solon himself, in his Elegies, addressing Philocyprus, mentions this foundation in these words:—

> "Long may you live, and fill the Solian throne,
> Succeeded still by children of your own;
> And from your happy island while I sail,
> Let Cyprus send for me a favoring gale;
> May she advance, and bless your new command,
> Prosper your town, and send me safe to land."

That Solon should discourse with Crœsus, some think not agreeable with chronology; but I cannot reject so famous and well-attested a narrative, and, what is more, so agreeable to Solon's temper, and so worthy his wisdom and greatness of mind, because, forsooth, it does not agree with some chronological canons, which thousands have endeavored to regulate, and yet, to this day, could never bring their differing opinions to any agreement. They say, therefore, that Solon, coming to Crœsus at his request, was in the same condition as an inland man when first he goes to see the sea; for as he fancies every river he meets with to be the ocean, so Solon, as he passed through the court, and saw a great many nobles richly dressed, and proudly attended with a multitude of guards and foot-boys, thought every one had been the king, till he was brought to Crœsus, who was decked with every possible rarity and curiosity, in ornaments of jewels, purple, and gold, that could make a grand and gorgeous spectacle of him. Now when Solon came before him, and seemed not at all surprised, nor gave Crœsus those compliments he expected, but showed himself to all discerning eyes to be a man that despised the gaudiness and petty ostentation of it, he commanded them to open all his treasure houses, and carry him to see his sumptuous furniture and luxuries, though he did not wish it; Solon could judge of him well enough by the first sight of him; and, when he returned from viewing all, Crœsus asked him if ever he had known a happier man than he. And when Solon answered that he had known one Tellus, a fellow-citizen of his own, and told him that this Tellus had been an honest man, had had good children, a competent estate, and died bravely in battle for his country, Crœsus took him for an ill-bred fellow and a fool, for not measuring happiness by the abundance of gold and silver, and preferring the life and death of a private and mean man before so much power and empire. He asked him, however, again, if, besides Tellus, he knew any other man more happy. And Solon replying, Yes, Cleobis and Biton, who were loving brothers, and extremely dutiful sons to their mother, and, when the oxen delayed her, harnessed themselves to the wagon, and drew her to Juno's temple, her neighbors all calling her happy, and she herself rejoicing; then, after sacrificing and feasting, they went to rest, and never rose again, but died in the midst of their honor a painless and tranquil death, "What," said Crœsus, angrily, "and dost not thou reckon us amongst the happy men at all?" Solon, unwilling either to flatter or exasperate him more, replied, "The gods, O king, have given the Greeks all other gifts in moderate degree; and so our wisdom, too, is a cheerful and a homely, not a noble and kingly wisdom; and this, observing the numerous misfortunes that attend all conditions, forbids us to grow insolent upon our present enjoyments, or to admire any man's happiness that may yet, in course of time, suffer change. For the uncertain future has yet to come, with every possible variety of fortune; and him only to whom the divinity has continued happiness unto the end, we call happy; to salute as happy one that is still in the midst of life and hazard, we think as little safe and conclusive as to crown and proclaim as victorious the wrestler that is yet in the ring." After this, he was dismissed, having given Crœsus some pain, but no instruction.

Æsop, who wrote the fables, being then at Sardis upon Crœsus's invitation, and very much esteemed, was concerned that Solon was so ill-received, and gave him this advice: "Solon, let your converse with kings be either short or seasonable." "Nay, rather," replied Solon, "either short or reasonable." So at this time Crœsus despised Solon; but when he was overcome by Cyrus, had lost his city, was taken alive, condemned to be burnt, and laid bound upon the pile before all the Persians and Cyrus himself, he cried out as loud as possibly he could three times, "O Solon!" and Cyrus being surprised, and sending some to inquire what man or god this Solon was, whom alone he invoked in this extremity, Crœsus told him the whole story, saying, "He was one of the wise men of Greece, whom I sent for, not to be instructed, or to learn any thing that I wanted, but that he should see and be a witness of my happiness; the loss of which was, it seems, to be a greater evil than the enjoyment was a good; for when I had them they were goods only in opinion, but now the loss of them has brought upon me intolerable and real evils. And he, conjecturing from what then was, this that now is, bade me look to the end of my life, and not rely and grow proud upon uncertainties." When this was told Cyrus, who was a wiser man than Crœsus, and saw in the present example Solon's maxim confirmed, he not only freed Crœsus from punishment, but honored him as long as he lived; and Solon had the glory, by the same saying, to save one king and instruct another.

When Solon was gone, the citizens began to quarrel; Lycurgus headed the Plain; Megacles, the son of Alcmæon, those to the Seaside; and Pisistratus the Hill party, in which were the poorest people, the Thetes, and greatest enemies to the rich; insomuch that, though the city still used the new laws, yet all looked for and desired a change of government, hoping severally that the change would be better for them, and put them above the contrary faction. Affairs standing thus, Solon returned, and was reverenced by all, and honored; but his old age would not permit him to be as active, and to speak in public, as formerly; yet, by privately conferring with the heads of the factions, he endeavored to compose the differences, Pisistratus appearing the most tractable; for he was extremely smooth and engaging in his language, a great friend to the poor, and moderate in his resentments; and what nature had not given him, he had the skill to imitate; so that he was trusted more than the others, being accounted a prudent and orderly man, one that loved equality, and would be an enemy to any that moved against the present settlement. Thus he deceived the majority of people; but Solon quickly discovered his character, and found out his design before any one else; yet did not hate him upon this, but endeavored to humble him, and bring him off from his ambition, and often told him and others, that if any one could banish the passion for pre-eminence from his mind, and cure him of his desire of absolute power, none would make a more virtuous man or a more excellent citizen. Thespis, at this time, beginning to act tragedies, and the thing, because it was new, taking very much with the multitude, though it was not yet made a matter of competition, Solon, being by nature fond of hearing and learning something new, and now, in his old age, living idly, and enjoying himself, indeed, with music and with wine, went to see Thespis himself, as the ancient custom was, act; and after the play was done, he addressed him, and asked him if he was not ashamed to tell so many lies before such a number of people; and Thespis replying that it was no harm to say or do so in play, Solon vehemently struck his staff against the ground: "Ay," said he, "if we honor and commend such play as this, we shall find it some day in our business."

Now when Pisistratus, having wounded himself, was brought into the marketplace in a chariot, and stirred up the people, as if he had been thus treated by his opponents because of his political conduct, and a great many were enraged and cried out, Solon, coming close to him, said, "This, O son of Hippocrates, is a bad copy of Homer's Ulysses; you do, to trick your countrymen, what he did to deceive his enemies." After this, the people were eager to protect Pisistratus, and met in an assembly, where one Ariston making a motion that they should allow Pisistratus fifty clubmen for a guard to his person, Solon opposed it, and said, much to the same purport as what he has left us in his poems—

> "You dote upon his words and taking phrase;"

and again—

> "True, you are singly each a crafty soul,
> But all together make one empty fool."

But observing the poor men bent to gratify Pisistratus, and tumultuous, and the rich fearful and getting out of harm's way, he departed, saying he was wiser than some and stouter than others; wiser than those that did not understand the design, stouter than those that, though they understood it, were afraid to oppose the tyranny. Now, the people, having passed the law, were not nice with Pisistratus about the number of his clubmen, but took no notice of it, though he enlisted and kept as many as he would, until he seized the Acropolis. When that was done, and the city in an uproar, Megacles, with all his family, at once fled; but Solon, though he was now very old, and had none to back him, yet came into the marketplace and made a speech to the citizens, partly blaming their inadvertency and meanness of spirit, and in part urging and exhorting them not thus tamely to lose their liberty; and likewise then spoke that memorable saying, that, before, it was an easier task to stop the rising tyranny, but now the greater and more glorious action to destroy it, when it was begun already, and had gathered strength. But all being afraid to side with him, he returned home, and, taking his arms, he brought them out and laid them in the porch before his door, with these words: "I have done my part to maintain my country and my laws," and then he busied himself no more. His friends advising him to fly, he refused; but wrote poems, and thus reproached the Athenians in them:—

> "If now you suffer, do not blame the Powers,
> For they are good, and all the fault was ours.
> All the strongholds you put into his hands,
> And now his slaves must do what he commands."

And many telling him that the tyrant would take his life for this, and asking what he trusted to, that he ventured to speak so boldly, he replied, "To my old age." But Pisistratus, having got the command, so extremely courted Solon, so honored him, obliged him, and sent to see him, that Solon gave him his advice, and approved many of his actions; for he retained most of Solon's laws, observed them himself, and compelled his friends to obey. And he himself, though already absolute ruler, being accused of murder before the Areopagus, came quietly to clear himself; but his accuser did not appear. And he added other laws, one of which is that the maimed in the wars should be maintained at the public charge; this Heraclides Ponticus records, and that Pisistratus followed Solon's example in this, who had decreed it in the case of one Thersippus, that was maimed; and Theophrastus asserts that it was Pisistratus, not Solon, that made that law against laziness, which was the reason that the country was more productive, and the city tranquiller.

Now Solon, having begun the great work in verse, the history or fable of the Atlantic Island, which he had learned from the wise men in Sais, and thought convenient for the Athenians to know, abandoned it; not, as Plato says, by reason of want of time, but because of his age, and being discouraged at the greatness of the task; for that he had leisure enough, such verses testify, as—

"Each day grow older, and learn something new";

and again—

"But now the Powers of Beauty, Song, and Wine,
Which are most men's delights, are also mine."

Plato, willing to improve the story of the Atlantic Island, as if it were a fair estate that wanted an heir and came with some title to him, formed, indeed, stately entrances, noble enclosures, large courts, such as never yet introduced any story, fable, or poetic fiction; but, beginning it late, ended his life before his work; and the reader's regret for the unfinished part is the greater, as the satisfaction he takes in that which is complete is extraordinary. For as the city of Athens left only the temple of Jupiter Olympius unfinished, so Plato, amongst all his excellent works, left this only piece about the Atlantic Island imperfect. Solon lived after Pisistratus seized the government, as Heraclides Ponticus asserts, a long time; but Phanias the Eresian says not two full years; for Pisistratus began his tyranny when Comias was archon, and Phanias says Solon died under Hegestratus, who succeeded Comias. The story that his ashes were scattered about the island Salamis is too strange to be easily believed, or be thought anything but a mere fable; and yet it is given, amongst other good authors, by Aristotle, the philosopher.

THEMISTOCLES

THE BIRTH of Themistocles was somewhat too obscure to do him honor. His father, Neocles, was not of the distinguished people of Athens, but of the township of Phrearrhi, and of the tribe Leontis; and by his mother's side, as it is reported, he was base-born—

> "I am not of the noble Grecian race,
> I'm poor Abrotonon, and born in Thrace;
> Let the Greek women scorn me, if they please,
> I was the mother of Themistocles."

Yet Phanias writes that the mother of Themistocles was not of Thrace, but of Caria, and that her name was not Abrotonon, but Euterpe; and Neanthes adds farther that she was of Halicarnassus in Caria. And, as illegitimate children, including those that were of half-blood or had but one parent an Athenian, had to attend at the Cynosarges (a wrestling-place outside the gates, dedicated to Hercules, who was also of half-blood amongst the gods, having had a mortal woman for his mother), Themistocles persuaded several of the young men of high birth to accompany him to anoint and exercise themselves together at Cynosarges; an ingenious device for destroying the distinction between the noble and the base-born, and between those of the whole and those of the half-blood of Athens. However, it is certain that he was related to the house of the Lycomedæ; for Simonides records, that he rebuilt the chapel of Phlya, belonging to that family, and beautified it with pictures and other ornaments, after it had been burnt by the Persians.

It is confessed by all that from his youth he was of a vehement and impetuous nature, of a quick apprehension, and a strong and aspiring bent for action and great affairs. The holidays and intervals in his studies he did not spend in play or idleness, as other children, but would be always inventing or arranging some oration or declamation to himself, the subject of which was generally the excusing or accusing his companions, so that his master would often say to him, "You, my boy, will be nothing small, but great one way or other, for good or else for bad." He received reluctantly and carelessly instructions given him to improve his manners and behavior, or to teach him any pleasing or graceful accomplishment, but whatever was said to improve him in sagacity, or in management of affairs, he would give attention to, beyond one of his years, from confidence in his natural capacities for such things. And thus afterwards, when in company where people engaged themselves in what are commonly thought the liberal and elegant amusements, he was obliged to defend himself against the observations of those who considered themselves highly accomplished, by the somewhat arrogant retort, that he certainly could not make use of any stringed instrument, could only, were a small and obscure city put into his hands, make it great and glorious. Notwithstanding this, Stesimbrotus says that Themistocles was a hearer of Anaxagoras, and that he studied natural philosophy under Melissus, contrary to chronology; for Melissus commanded the Samians in their siege by Pericles, who was much Themistocles's junior; and with Pericles, also, Anaxagoras was intimate. They, therefore, might rather be credited, who report, that Themistocles was an admirer of Mnesiphilus the Phrearrhian, who was neither rhetorician nor natural philosopher, but a professor of that which was then called wisdom, consisting in a sort of political shrewdness and practical sagacity, which had begun and continued, almost like a sect of philosophy, from Solon; but those who came afterwards, and mixed it with pleadings and legal artifices, and transformed the practical part of it into a mere art of speaking and an exercise of words, were generally called sophists. Themistocles resorted to Mnesiphilus when he had already embarked in politics.

In the first essays of his youth he was not regular nor happily balanced; he allowed himself to follow mere natural character, which, without the control of reason and instruction, is apt to hurry, upon either side, into sudden and violent courses, and very often to break away and determine upon the worst; as he afterwards owned himself, saying, that the wildest colts make the best horses, if they only get properly trained and broken in. But those who upon this fasten stories of their own invention, as of his being disowned by his father, and that his mother died for grief of her son's ill fame, certainly calumniate him; and there are others who relate, on the contrary, how that to deter him from public business, and to let him see how the vulgar behave themselves towards their leaders when they have at last no farther use of them, his father showed him the old galleys as they lay forsaken and cast about upon the seashore.

Yet it is evident that his mind was early imbued with the keenest interest in public affairs, and the most passionate ambition for distinction. Eager from the first to obtain the highest place, he unhesitatingly accepted the hatred of the most powerful and influential leaders in the city, but more especially of Aristides, the son of Lysimachus, who always opposed him. And yet all this great enmity between them arose, it appears, from a very boyish occasion, both being attached to the beautiful Stesilaus of Ceos, as Ariston the philosopher tells us; ever after which they took opposite sides, and were rivals in politics. Not but that the incompatibility of their lives and manners may seem to have increased the difference, for Aristides was of a mild nature, and of a nobler sort of character, and, in public matters, acting always with a view, not to glory or popularity, but to the best interest of the state consistently with safety and honesty, he was often forced to oppose Themistocles, and interfere against the increase of his influence, seeing him stirring up the people to all kinds of enterprises, and introducing various innovations. For it is said that Themistocles was so transported with the thoughts of glory and so inflamed with the passion for great actions, that, though he was still young when the battle of Marathon was fought against the Persians, upon the skillful conduct of the general, Miltiades, being everywhere talked about, he was observed to be thoughtful and reserved, alone by himself; he passed the nights without sleep, and avoided all his usual places of recreation, and to those who wondered at the change, and inquired the reason of it, he gave the answer, that "the trophy of Miltiades would not let him sleep." And when others were of opinion that the battle of Marathon would be an end to the war, Themistocles thought that it was but the beginning of far greater conflicts, and for these, to the benefit of all Greece, he kept himself in continual readiness, and his city also in proper training, foreseeing from far before what would happen.

And, first of all, the Athenians being accustomed to divide amongst themselves the revenue proceeding from the silver mines at Laurium, he was the only man that durst propose to the people that this distribution should cease, and that with the money ships should be built to make war against the Æginetans, who were the most flourishing people in all Greece, and by the number of their ships held the sovereignty of the sea; and Themistocles thus was more easily able to persuade them, avoiding all mention of danger from Darius or the Persians, who were at a great distance, and their coming very uncertain, and at that time not much to be feared; but, by a seasonable employment of the emulation and anger felt by the Athenians against the Æginetans, he induced them to preparation. So that with this money a hundred ships were built, with which they afterwards fought against Xerxes. And henceforward, little by little, turning and drawing the city down towards the sea, in the belief that, whereas by land they were not a fit match for their next neighbors, with their ships they might be able to repel the Persians and command Greece, thus, as Plato says, from steady soldiers he turned them into mariners and seamen tossed about the sea, and gave occasion for the reproach against him, that he took away from the Athenians the spear and the shield, and bound them to the bench and the oar. These measures he carried in the assembly, against the opposition, as Stesimbrotus relates, of Miltiades; and whether or no he hereby injured the purity and true balance of government may be a question for philosophers, but that the deliverance of Greece came at that time from the sea, and that these galleys restored Athens again after it was destroyed, were others wanting, Xerxes himself would be sufficient evidence, who, though his land-forces were still entire, after his defeat at sea, fled away, and thought himself no longer able to encounter the Greeks; and, as it seems to me, left Mardonius behind him, not out of any hopes he could have to bring them into subjection, but to hinder them from pursuing him.

Themistocles is said to have been eager in the acquisition of riches, according to some, that he might be the more liberal; for loving to sacrifice often, and to be splendid in his entertainment of strangers, he required a plentiful revenue; yet he is accused by others of having been parsimonious and sordid to that degree that he would sell provisions which were sent to him as a present. He desired Diphilides, who was a breeder of horses, to give him a colt, and when he refused it, threatened that in a short time he would turn his house into a wooden horse, intimating that he would stir up dispute and litigation between him and some of his relations.

He went beyond all men in the passion for distinction. When he was still young and unknown in the world, he entreated Episcles of Hermione, who had a good hand at the lute and was much sought after by the Athenians, to come and practice at home with him, being ambitious of having people inquire after his house and frequent his company. When he came to the Olympic games, and was so splendid in his equipage and entertainments, in his rich tents and furniture, that he strove to outdo Cimon, he displeased the Greeks, who thought that such magnificence might be allowed in one who was a young man and of a great family, but was a great piece of insolence in one as yet undistinguished, and without title or means for making any such display. In a dramatic contest, the play he paid for won the prize, which was then a matter that excited much emulation; he put up a tablet in record of it, with the inscription: "Themistocles of Phrearrhi was at the charge of it; Phrynichus made it; Adimantus was archon." He was well liked by the common people, would salute every particular citizen by his own name, and always show himself a just judge in questions of business between private men; he said to Simonides, the poet of Ceos, who desired something of him, when he was commander of the army, that was not reasonable, "Simonides, you would be no good poet if you wrote false measure, nor should I be a good magistrate if for favor I made false law." And at another time, laughing at Simonides, he said that he was a man of little judgment to speak against the Corinthians, who were inhabitants of a great city, and to have his own picture drawn so often, having so ill-looking a face.

Gradually growing to be great, and winning the favor of the people, he at last gained the day with his faction over that of Aristides, and procured his banishment by ostracism. When the king of Persia was now advancing against Greece, and the Athenians were in consultation who should be general, and many withdrew themselves of their own accord, being terrified with the greatness of the danger, there was one Epicydes, a popular speaker, son to Euphemides, a man of an eloquent tongue, but of a faint heart, and a slave to riches, who was desirous of the command, and was looked upon to be in a fair way to carry it by the number of votes; but Themistocles, fearing that, if the command should fall into such hands, all would be lost, bought off Epicydes and his pretensions, it is said, for a sum of money.

When the king of Persia sent messengers into Greece, with an interpreter, to demand earth and water, as an acknowledgment of subjection, Themistocles, by the consent of the people, seized upon the interpreter, and put him to death, for presuming to publish the barbarian orders and decrees in the Greek language; this is one of the actions he is commended for, as also for what he did to Arthmius of Zelea, who brought gold from the king of Persia to corrupt the Greeks, and was, by an order from Themistocles, degraded and disfranchised, he and his children and his posterity; but that which most of all redounded to his credit was, that he put an end to all the civil wars of Greece, composed their differences, and persuaded them to lay aside all enmity during the war with the Persians; and in this great work, Chileus the Arcadian was, it is said, of great assistance to him.

Having taken upon himself the command of the Athenian forces, he immediately endeavored to persuade the citizens to leave the city, and to embark upon their galleys, and meet with the Persians at a great distance from Greece; but many being against this, he led a large force, together with the Lacedæmonians, into Tempe, that in this pass they might maintain the safety of Thessaly, which had not as yet declared for the king; but when they returned without performing anything; and it was known that not only the Thessalians, but all as far as Bœotia, was going over to Xerxes, then the Athenians more willingly hearkened to the advice of Themistocles to fight by sea, and sent him with a fleet to guard the straits of Artemisium.

When the contingents met here, the Greeks would have the Lacedæmonians to command, and Eurybiades to be their admiral; but the Athenians, who surpassed all the rest together in number of vessels, would not submit to come after any other, till Themistocles, perceiving the danger of the contest, yielded his own command to Eurybiades, and got the Athenians to submit, extenuating the loss by persuading them, that if in this war they behaved themselves like men, he would answer for it after that, that the Greeks, of their own will, would submit to their command. And by this moderation of his, it is evident that he was the chief means of the deliverance of Greece, and gained the Athenians the glory of alike surpassing their enemies in valor, and their confederates in wisdom.

As soon as the Persian armada arrived at Aphetæ, Eurybiades was astonished to see such a vast number of vessels before him, and, being informed that two hundred more were sailing around behind the island of Sciathus, he immediately determined to retire farther into Greece, and to sail back into some part of Peloponnesus, where their land army and their fleet might join, for he looked upon the Persian forces to be altogether unassailable by sea. But the Eubœans, fearing that the Greeks would forsake them and leave them to the mercy of the enemy, sent Pelagon to confer privately with Themistocles, taking with him a good sum of money, which, as Herodotus reports, he accepted and gave to Eurybiades. In this affair none of his own countrymen opposed him so much as Architeles, captain of the sacred galley, who, having no money to supply his seamen, was eager to go home; but Themistocles so incensed the Athenians against him, that they set upon him and left him not so much as his supper, at which Architeles was much surprised, and took it very ill; but Themistocles immediately sent him in a chest a service of provisions, and at the bottom of it a talent of silver, desiring him to sup tonight, and tomorrow provide for his seamen; if not, he would report it among the Athenians that he had received money from the enemy. So Phanias the Lesbian tells the story.

Though the fights between the Greeks and Persians in the straits of Eubœa were not so important as to make any final decision of the war, yet the experience which the Greeks obtained in them was of great advantage, for thus, by actual trial and in real danger, they found out that neither number of ships, nor riches and ornaments, nor boasting shouts, nor barbarous songs of victory, were any way terrible to men that knew how to fight, and were resolved to come hand to hand with their enemies; these things they were to despise, and to come up close and grapple with their foes. This Pindar appears to have seen, and says justly enough of the fight at Artemisium, that—

> "There the sons of Athens set
> The stone that freedom stands on yet."

For the first step towards victory undoubtedly is to gain courage. Artemisium is in Eubœa, beyond the city of Histiæa, a sea beach open to the north; most nearly opposite to it stands Olizon, in the country which formerly was under Philoctetes; there is a small temple there, dedicated to Diana, surnamed of the Dawn, and trees about it, around which again stand pillars of white marble; and if you rub them with your hand, they send forth both the smell and color of saffron. On one of the pillars these verses are engraved:—

> "With numerous tribes from Asia's regions brought
> The sons of Athens on these waters fought;
> Erecting, after they had quelled the Mede,
> To Artemis this record of the deed."

There is a place still to be seen upon this shore, where, in the middle of a great heap of sand, they take out from the bottom a dark powder like ashes, or something that has passed the fire; and here, it is supposed, the shipwrecks and bodies of the dead were burnt.

But when news came from Thermopylæ to Artemisium informing them that king Leonidas was slain, and that Xerxes had made himself master of all the passages by land, they returned back to the interior of Greece, the Athenians having the command of the rear, the place of honor and danger, and much elated by what had been done.

As Themistocles sailed along the coast, he took notice of the harbors and fit places for the enemies' ships to come to land at, and engraved large letters in such stones as he found there by chance, as also in others which he set up on purpose near to the landing-places, or where they were to water; in which inscriptions he called upon the Ionians to forsake the Medes, if it were possible, and come over to the Greeks, who were their proper founders and fathers, and were now hazarding all for their liberties; but, if this could not be done, at any rate to impede and disturb the Persians in all engagements. He hoped that these writings would prevail with the Ionians to revolt, or raise some trouble by making their fidelity doubtful to the Persians.

Now, though Xerxes had already passed through Doris and invaded the country of Phocis, and was burning and destroying the cities of the Phocians, yet the Greeks sent them no relief; and, though the Athenians earnestly desired them to meet the Persians in Bœotia, before they could come into Attica, as they themselves had come forward by sea at Artemisium, they gave no ear to their request, being wholly intent upon Peloponnesus, and resolved to gather all their forces together within the Isthmus, and to build a wall from sea to sea in that narrow neck of land; so that the Athenians were enraged to see themselves betrayed, and at the same time afflicted and dejected at their own destitution. For to fight alone against such a numerous army was to no purpose, and the only expedient now left them was to leave their city and cling to their ships; which the people were very unwilling to submit to, imagining that it would signify little now to gain a victory, and not understanding how there could be deliverance any longer after they had once forsaken the temples of their gods and exposed the tombs and monuments of their ancestors to the fury of their enemies.

Themistocles, being at a loss and not able to draw the people over to his opinion by any human reason, set his machines to work, as in a theater, and employed prodigies and oracles. The serpent of Minerva, kept in the inner part of her temple, disappeared; the priest gave it out to the people that the offerings which were set for it were found untouched, and declared, by the suggestion of Themistocles, that the goddess had left the city, and taken her flight before them towards the sea. And he often urged them with the oracle which bade them trust to walls of wood, showing them that walls of wood could signify nothing else but ships; and that the island of Salamis was termed in it, not miserable or unhappy, but had the epithet of divine, for that it should one day be associated with a great good fortune of the Greeks. At length his opinion prevailed, and he obtained a decree that the city should be committed to the protection of Minerva, "Queen of Athens"; that they who were of age to bear arms should embark, and that each should see to sending away his children, women, and slaves where he could. This decree being confirmed, most of the Athenians removed their parents, wives, and children to Trœzen, where they were received with eager goodwill by the Trœzenians, who passed a vote that they should be maintained at the public charge, by a daily payment of two obols to everyone, and leave be given to the children to gather fruit where they pleased, and schoolmasters paid to instruct them. This vote was proposed by Nicagoras.

There was no public treasure at that time in Athens; but the council of Areopagus, as Aristotle says, distributed to everyone that served eight drachmas, which was a great help to the manning of the fleet; but Clidemus ascribes this also to the art of Themistocles. When the Athenians were on their way down to the haven of Piræus, the shield with the head of Medusa was missing; and he, under the pretext of searching for it, ransacked all places, and found among their goods considerable sums of money concealed, which he applied to the public use; and with this the soldiers and seamen were well provided for their voyage.

When the whole city of Athens were going on board, it afforded a spectacle worthy alike of pity and admiration, to see them thus send away their fathers and children before them, and, unmoved with their cries and tears, pass over into the island. But that which stirred compassion most of all was, that many old men, by reason of their great age, were left behind; and even the tame domestic animals could not be seen without some pity, running about the town and howling, as desirous to be carried along with their masters that had kept them; among which it is reported that Xanthippus, the father of Pericles, had a dog that would not endure to stay behind, but leaped into the sea, and swam along by the galley's side till he came to the island of Salamis, where he fainted away and died, and that spot in the island, which is still called the Dog's Grave, is said to be his.

Among the great actions of Themistocles at this crisis, the recall of Aristides was not the least, for, before the war, he had been ostracized by the party which Themistocles headed, and was in banishment; but now, perceiving that the people regretted his absence, and were fearful that he might go over to the Persians to revenge himself, and thereby ruin the affairs of Greece, Themistocles proposed a decree that those who were banished for a time might return again, to give assistance by word and deed to the cause of Greece with the rest of their fellow-citizens.

Eurybiades, by reason of the greatness of Sparta, was admiral of the Greek fleet, but yet was faint-hearted in time of danger, and willing to weigh anchor and set sail for the isthmus of Corinth, near which the land army lay encamped; which Themistocles resisted; and this was the occasion of the well-known words, when Eurybiades, to check his impatience, told him that at the Olympic games they that start up before the rest are lashed; "And they," replied Themistocles, "that are left behind are not crowned." Again, Eurybiades lifting up his staff as if he were going to strike, Themistocles said, "Strike if you will, but hear"; Eurybiades, wondering much at his moderation, desired him to speak, and Themistocles now brought him to a better understanding. And when one who stood by him told him that it did not become those who had neither city nor house to lose, to persuade others to relinquish their habitations and forsake their countries, Themistocles gave this reply: "We have indeed left our houses and our walls, base fellow, not thinking it fit to become slaves for the sake of things that have no life nor soul; and yet our city is the greatest of all Greece, consisting of two hundred galleys, which are here to defend you, if you please; but if you run away and betray us, as you did once before, the Greeks shall soon hear news of the Athenians possessing as fair a country, and as large and free a city, as that they have lost." These expressions of Themistocles made Eurybiades suspect that if he retreated the Athenians would fall off from him. When one of Eretria began to oppose him, he said, "Have you anything to say of war, that are like an inkfish? you have a sword, but no heart." Some say that while Themistocles was thus speaking upon the deck, an owl was seen flying to the right hand of the fleet, which came and sat upon the top of the mast; and this happy omen so far disposed the Greeks to follow his advice, that they presently prepared to fight. Yet, when the enemy's fleet was arrived at the haven of Phalerum, upon the coast of Attica, and with the number of

their ships concealed all the shore, and when they saw the king himself
in person come down with his land army to the seaside, with all his forces
united, then the good counsel of Themistocles was soon forgotten, and
the Peloponnesians cast their eyes again towards the isthmus, and took it
very ill if any one spoke against their returning home; and, resolving to
depart that night, the pilots had orders what course to steer.

Themistocles, in great distress that the Greeks should retire, and lose
the advantage of the narrow seas and strait passage, and slip home every
one to his own city, considered with himself, and contrived that stratagem that was carried out by Sicinnus. This Sicinnus was a Persian captive, but a great lover of Themistocles, and the attendant of his children.
Upon this occasion, he sent him privately to Xerxes, commanding him
to tell the king that Themistocles, the admiral of the Athenians, having
espoused his interest, wished to be the first to inform him that the Greeks
were ready to make their escape, and that he counseled him to hinder
their flight, to set upon them while they were in this confusion and at a
distance from their land army, and hereby destroy all their forces by sea.
Xerxes was very joyful at this message, and received it as from one who
wished him all that was good, and immediately issued instructions to the
commanders of his ships, that they should instantly set out with two hundred galleys to encompass all the islands, and enclose all the straits and
passages, that none of the Greeks might escape, and that they should afterwards follow with the rest of their fleet at leisure. This being done,
Aristides, the son of Lysimachus, was the first man that perceived it, and
went to the tent of Themistocles, not out of any friendship, for he had
been formerly banished by his means, as has been related, but to inform
him how they were encompassed by their enemies. Themistocles, knowing the generosity of Aristides, and much struck by his visit at that time,
imparted to him all that he had transacted by Sicinnus, and entreated him
that, as he would be more readily believed among the Greeks, he would
make use of his credit to help to induce them to stay and fight their enemies in the narrow seas. Aristides applauded Themistocles, and went to
the other commanders and captains of the galleys, and encouraged them
to engage; yet they did not perfectly assent to him, till a galley of Tenos,
which deserted from the Persians, of which Panætius was commander,
came in, while they were still doubting, and confirmed the news that all
the straits and passages were beset; and then their rage and fury, as well as
their necessity, provoked them all to fight.

As soon as it was day, Xerxes placed himself high up, to view his fleet,
and how it was set in order. Phanodemus says, he sat upon a promontory
above the temple of Hercules, where the coast of Attica is separated from
the island by a narrow channel; but Acestodorus writes, that it was in the
confines of Megara, upon those hills which are called the Horns, where

he sat in a chair of gold, with many secretaries about him to write down all that was done in the fight.

When Themistocles was about to sacrifice, close to the admiral's galley, there were three prisoners brought to him, fine-looking men, and richly dressed in ornamented clothing and gold, said to be the children of Artayctes and Sandauce, sister to Xerxes. As soon as the prophet Euphrantides saw them, and observed that at the same time the fire blazed out from the offerings with a more than ordinary flame, and that a man sneezed on the right, which was an intimation of a fortunate event, he took Themistocles by the hand, and bade him consecrate the three young men for sacrifice, and offer them up with prayers for victory to Bacchus the Devourer; so should the Greeks not only save themselves, but also obtain victory. Themistocles was much disturbed at this strange and terrible prophecy, but the common people, who in any difficult crisis and great exigency ever look for relief rather to strange and extravagant than to reasonable means, calling upon Bacchus with one voice, led the captives to the altar, and compelled the execution of the sacrifice as the prophet had commanded. This is reported by Phanias the Lesbian, a philosopher well read in history.

The number of the enemy's ships the poet Æschylus gives in his tragedy called the Persians, as on his certain knowledge, in the following words:—

> "Xerxes, I know, did into battle lead
>   One thousand ships; of more than usual speed
>   Seven and two hundred. So is it agreed."

The Athenians had a hundred and eighty; in every ship eighteen men fought upon the deck, four of whom were archers and the rest men-at-arms.

As Themistocles had fixed upon the most advantageous place, so, with no less sagacity, he chose the best time of fighting; for he would not run the prows of his galleys against the Persians, nor begin the fight till the time of day was come, when there regularly blows in a fresh breeze from the open sea, and brings in with it a strong swell into the channel; which was no inconvenience to the Greek ships, which were low-built, and little above the water, but did much hurt to the Persians, which had high sterns and lofty decks, and were heavy and cumbrous in their movements, as it presented them broadside to the quick charges of the Greeks, who kept their eyes upon the motions of Themistocles, as their best example, and more particularly because, opposed to his ship, Ariamenes, admiral to Xerxes, a brave man and by far the best and worthiest of the king's brothers, was seen throwing darts and shooting arrows from his huge galley, as from the walls of a castle. Aminias the Decelean and

Sosicles the Pedian, who sailed in the same vessel, upon the ships meet- ing stem to stem, and transfixing each the other with their brazen prows, so that they were fastened together, when Ariamenes attempted to board theirs, ran at him with their pikes, and thrust him into the sea; his body, as it floated amongst other shipwrecks, was known to Artemisia, and car- ried to Xerxes.

It is reported that, in the middle of the fight, a great flame rose into the air above the city of Eleusis, and that sounds and voices were heard through all the Thriasian plain, as far as the sea, sounding like a number of men accompanying and escorting the mystic Iacchus, and that a mist seemed to form and rise from the place from whence the sounds came, and, passing forward, fell upon the galleys. Others believed that they saw apparitions, in the shape of armed men, reaching out their hands from the island of Ægina before the Grecian galleys; and supposed they were the Æacidæ, whom they had invoked to their aid before the battle. The first man that took a ship was Lycomedes the Athenian, captain of a gal- ley, who cut down its ensign, and dedicated it to Apollo the Laurel- crowned. And as the Persians fought in a narrow arm of the sea, and could bring but part of their fleet to fight, and fell foul of one another, the Greeks thus equaled them in strength, and fought with them till the evening forced them back, and obtained, as says Simonides, that noble and famous victory, than which neither amongst the Greeks nor barbar- ians was ever known more glorious exploit on the seas; by the joint valor, indeed, and zeal of all who fought, but by the wisdom and sagacity of Themistocles.

After this sea fight, Xerxes, enraged at his ill fortune, attempted, by casting great heaps of earth and stones into the sea, to stop up the chan- nel and to make a dam, upon which he might lead his land forces over into the island of Salamis.

Themistocles, being desirous to try the opinion of Aristides, told him that he proposed to set sail for the Hellespont, to break the bridge of ships, so as to shut up, he said, Asia a prisoner within Europe; but Aristides, disliking the design, said: "We have hitherto fought with an enemy who has regarded little else but his pleasure and luxury; but if we shut him up within Greece, and drive him to necessity, he that is master of such great forces will no longer sit quietly with an umbrella of gold over his head, looking upon the fight for his pleasure; but in such a strait will attempt all things; he will be resolute, and appear himself in person upon all occasions, he will soon correct his errors, and supply what he has formerly omitted through remissness, and will be better advised in all things. Therefore, it is noways our interest, Themistocles," he said, "to take away the bridge that is already made, but rather to build another, if it were possible, that he might make his retreat with the more expedition."

To which Themistocles answered, "If this be requisite, we must immediately use all diligence, art, and industry, to rid ourselves of him as soon as may be;" and to this purpose he found out among the captives one of the king of Persia's eunuchs, named Arnaces, whom he sent to the king, to inform him that the Greeks, being now victorious by sea, had decreed to sail to the Hellespont, where the boats were fastened together, and destroy the bridge; but that Themistocles, being concerned for the king, revealed this to him, that he might hasten towards the Asiatic seas, and pass over into his own dominions; and in the mean time would cause delays and hinder the confederates from pursuing him. Xerxes no sooner heard this, but, being very much terrified, he proceeded to retreat out of Greece with all speed. The prudence of Themistocles and Aristides in this was afterwards more fully understood at the battle of Platæa, where Mardonius, with a very small fraction of the forces of Xerxes, put the Greeks in danger of losing all.

Herodotus writes that of all the cities of Greece, Ægina was held to have performed the best service in the war; while all single men yielded to Themistocles, though, out of envy, unwillingly; and when they returned to the entrance of Peloponnesus, where the several commanders delivered their suffrages at the altar, to determine who was most worthy, every one gave the first vote for himself and the second for Themistocles. The Lacedæmonians carried him with them to Sparta, where, giving the rewards of valor to Eurybiades, and of wisdom and conduct to Themistocles, they crowned him with olive, presented him with the best chariot in the city, and sent three hundred young men to accompany him to the confines of their country. And at the next Olympic games, when Themistocles entered the course, the spectators took no farther notice of those who were contesting the prizes, but spent the whole day in looking upon him, showing him to the strangers, admiring him, and applauding him by clapping their hands, and other expressions of joy, so that he himself, much gratified, confessed to his friends that he then reaped the fruit of all his labors for the Greeks.

He was, indeed, by nature, a great lover of honor, as is evident from the anecdotes recorded of him. When chosen admiral by the Athenians, he would not quite conclude any single matter of business, either public or private, but deferred all till the day they were to set sail, that, by dispatching a great quantity of business all at once, and having to meet a great variety of people, he might make an appearance of greatness and power. Viewing the dead bodies cast up by the sea, he perceived bracelets and necklaces of gold about them, yet passed on, only showing them to a friend that followed him, saying, "Take you these things, for you are not Themistocles." He said to Antiphates, a handsome young man, who had formerly avoided, but now in his glory courted him, "Time, young man,

has taught us both a lesson." He said that the Athenians did not honor
him or admire him, but made, as it were, a sort of plane tree of him; sheltered themselves under him in bad weather, and as soon as it was fine,
plucked his leaves and cut his branches. When the Seriphian told him that
he had not obtained this honor by himself, but by the greatness of the
city, he replied, "You speak truth; I should never have been famous if I
had been of Seriphus; nor you, had you been of Athens." When another
of the generals, who thought he had performed considerable service for
the Athenians, boastingly compared his actions with those of
Themistocles, he told him that once upon a time the Day after the
Festival found fault with the Festival: "On you there is nothing but hurry
and trouble and preparation, but, when I come, everybody sits down quietly and enjoys himself"; which the Festival admitted was true, but "if I
had not come first, you would not have come at all." "Even so," he said,
"if Themistocles had not come before, where had you been now?"
Laughing at his own son, who got his mother, and, by his mother's
means, his father also, to indulge him, he told him that he had the most
power of any one in Greece: "For the Athenians command the rest of
Greece, I command the Athenians, your mother commands me, and you
command your mother." Loving to be singular in all things, when he had
land to sell, he ordered the crier to give notice that there were good
neighbors near it. Of two who made love to his daughter, he preferred
the man of worth to the one who was rich, saying he desired a man
without riches, rather than riches without a man. Such was the character of his sayings.

After these things, he began to rebuild and fortify the city of Athens,
bribing, as Theopompus reports, the Lacedæmonian ephors not to be
against it, but, as most relate it, overreaching and deceiving them. For,
under pretext of an embassy, he went to Sparta, where, upon the
Lacedæmonians charging him with rebuilding the walls, and Poliarchus
coming on purpose from Ægina to denounce it, he denied the fact, bidding them to send people to Athens to see whether it were so or no; by
which delay he got time for the building of the wall, and also placed
these ambassadors in the hands of his countrymen as hostages for him;
and so, when the Lacedæmonians knew the truth, they did him no hurt,
but, suppressing all display of their anger for the present, sent him away.

Next he proceeded to establish the harbor of Piræus, observing the
great natural advantages of the locality and desirous to unite the whole
city with the sea, and to reverse, in a manner, the policy of ancient
Athenian kings, who, endeavoring to withdraw their subjects from the
sea, and to accustom them to live, not by sailing about, but by planting
and tilling the earth, spread the story of the dispute between Minerva and
Neptune for the sovereignty of Athens, in which Minerva, by producing

to the judges an olive tree, was declared to have won; whereas Themistocles did not only knead up, as Aristophanes says, the port and the city into one, but made the city absolutely the dependent and the adjunct of the port, and the land of the sea, which increased the power and confidence of the people against the nobility; the authority coming into the hands of sailors and boatswains and pilots. Thus it was one of the orders of the thirty tyrants, that the hustings in the assembly, which had faced towards the sea, should be turned round towards the land; implying their opinion that the empire by sea had been the origin of the democracy, and that the farming population were not so much opposed to oligarchy.

Themistocles, however, formed yet higher designs with a view to naval supremacy. For, after the departure of Xerxes, when the Grecian fleet was arrived at Pagasæ, where they wintered, Themistocles, in a public oration to the people of Athens, told them that he had a design to perform something that would tend greatly to their interests and safety, but was of such a nature that it could not be made generally public. The Athenians ordered him to impart it to Aristides only; and, if he approved of it, to put it in practice. And when Themistocles had discovered to him that his design was to burn the Grecian fleet in the haven of Pagasæ, Aristides, coming out to the people, gave this report of the stratagem contrived by Themistocles, that no proposal could be more politic, or more dishonorable; on which the Athenians commanded Themistocles to think no farther of it.

When the Lacedæmonians proposed, at the general council of the Amphictyonians, that the representatives of those cities which were not in the league, nor had fought against the Persians, should be excluded, Themistocles, fearing that the Thessalians, with those of Thebes, Argos, and others, being thrown out of the council, the Lacedæmonians would become wholly masters of the votes, and do what they pleased, supported the deputies of the cities, and prevailed with the members then sitting to alter their opinion on this point, showing them that there were but one-and-thirty cities which had partaken in the war, and that most of these, also, were very small; how intolerable would it be, if the rest of Greece should be excluded, and the general council should come to be ruled by two or three great cities. By this, chiefly, he incurred the displeasure of the Lacedæmonians, whose honors and favors were now shown to Cimon, with a view to making him the opponent of the state policy of Themistocles.

He was also burdensome to the confederates, sailing about the islands and collecting money from them. Herodotus says, that, requiring money of those of the island of Andros, he told them that he had brought with him two goddesses, Persuasion and Force; and they answered him that they had also two great goddesses, which prohibited them from giving him any money, Poverty and Impossibility. Timocreon, the Rhodian poet, reprehends him somewhat bitterly for being wrought upon by money to let some who were banished return, while abandoning himself, who was his guest and friend. The verses are these:—

"Pausanias you may praise, and Xanthippus he be for,
 For Leutychidas, a third; Aristides, I proclaim,
 From the sacred Athens came,
 The one true man of all; for Themistocles Latona doth abhor,
 The liar, traitor, cheat, who, to gain his filthy pay,
 Timocreon, his friend, neglected to restore
 To his native Rhodian shore;
 Three silver talents took, and departed (curses with him) on his way,
 Restoring people here, expelling there, and killing here,
 Filling evermore his purse: and at the Isthmus gave a treat,
 To be laughed at, of cold meat,
 Which they ate, and prayed the gods some one else might give the
   feast another year."

But after the sentence and banishment of Themistocles, Timocreon reviles him yet more immoderately and wildly in a poem which begins thus:—

> "Unto all the Greeks repair
> O Muse, and tell these verses there,
> As is fitting and is fair."

The story is, that it was put to the question whether Timocreon should be banished for siding with the Persians, and Themistocles gave his vote against him. So when Themistocles was accused of intriguing with the Medes, Timocreon made these lines upon him:—

"So now Timocreon, indeed, is not the sole friend of the Mede,
 There are some knaves besides; nor is it only mine that fails,
 But other foxes have lost tails.—"

When the citizens of Athens began to listen willingly to those who traduced and reproached him, he was forced, with somewhat obnoxious frequency, to put them in mind of the great services he had performed, and ask those who were offended with him whether they were weary with receiving benefits often from the same person, so rendering himself more odious. And he yet more provoked the people by building a temple to Diana with the epithet of Aristobule, or Diana of Best Counsel; intimating thereby, that he had given the best counsel, not only to the

Athenians, but to all Greece. He built this temple near his own house, in the district called Melite, where now the public officers carry out the bodies of such as are executed, and throw the halters and clothes of those that are strangled or otherwise put to death. There is to this day a small figure of Themistocles in the temple of Diana of Best Counsel, which represents him to be a person not only of a noble mind, but also of a most heroic aspect. At length the Athenians banished him, making use of the ostracism to humble his eminence and authority, as they ordinarily did with all whom they thought too powerful, or, by their greatness, disproportionable to the equality thought requisite in a popular government. For the ostracism was instituted, not so much to punish the offender, as to mitigate and pacify the violence of the envious, who delighted to humble eminent men, and who, by fixing this disgrace upon them, might vent some part of their rancor.

Themistocles being banished from Athens, while he stayed at Argos the detection of Pausanias happened, which gave such advantage to his enemies, that Leobotes of Agraule, son of Alcmæon, indicted him of treason, the Spartans supporting him in the accusation.

When Pausanias went about this treasonable design, he concealed it at first from Themistocles, though he were his intimate friend; but when he saw him expelled out of the commonwealth, and how impatiently he took his banishment, he ventured to communicate it to him, and desired his assistance, showing him the king of Persia's letters, and exasperating him against the Greeks, as a villainous, ungrateful people. However, Themistocles immediately rejected the proposals of Pausanias, and wholly refused to be a party in the enterprise, though he never revealed his communications, nor disclosed the conspiracy to any man, either hoping that Pausanias would desist from his intentions, or expecting that so inconsiderate an attempt after such chimerical objects would be discovered by other means.

After that Pausanias was put to death, letters and writings being found concerning this matter, which rendered Themistocles suspected, the Lacedæmonians were clamorous against him, and his enemies among the Athenians accused him; when, being absent from Athens, he made his defense by letters, especially against the points that had been previously alleged against him. In answer to the malicious detractions of his enemies, he merely wrote to the citizens, urging that he who was always ambitious to govern, and not of a character or a disposition to serve, would never sell himself and his country into slavery to a barbarous and hostile nation.

Notwithstanding this, the people, being persuaded by his accusers, sent officers to take him and bring him away to be tried before a council of the Greeks, but, having timely notice of it, he passed over into the island of Corcyra, where the state was under obligations to him; for, being chosen as arbitrator in a difference between them and the Corinthians, he decided the controversy by ordering the Corinthians to pay down twenty talents, and declaring the town and island of Leucas a joint colony from both cities. From thence he fled into Epirus, and, the Athenians and Lacedæmonians still pursuing him, he threw himself upon chances of safety that seemed all but desperate. For he fled for refuge to Admetus, king of the Molossians, who had formerly made some request to the Athenians, when Themistocles was in the height of his authority, and had been disdainfully used and insulted by him, and had let it appear plain enough that, could he lay hold of him, he would take his revenge. Yet in this misfortune, Themistocles, fearing the recent hatred of his neighbors and fellow citizens more than the old displeasure of the king, put himself at his mercy and became a humble suppliant to Admetus, after a peculiar manner different from the custom of other countries. For taking the king's son, who was then a child, in his arms, he laid himself down at his hearth, this being the most sacred and only manner of supplication among the Molossians, which was not to be refused. And some say that his wife, Phthia, intimated to Themistocles this way of petitioning, and placed her young son with him before the hearth; others, that king Admetus, that he might be under a religious obligation not to deliver him up to his pursuers, prepared and enacted with him a sort of stage-play to this effect. At this time, Epicrates of Acharnæ privately conveyed his wife and children out of Athens, and sent them hither, for which afterwards Cimon condemned him and put him to death, as Stesimbrotus reports, and yet somehow, either forgetting this himself, or making Themistocles to be little mindful of it, says presently that he sailed into Sicily, and desired in marriage the daughter of Hiero, tyrant of Syracuse, promising to bring the Greeks under his power; and, on Hiero refusing him, departed thence into Asia; but this is not probable.

For Theophrastus writes, in his work on Monarchy, that when Hiero sent racehorses to the Olympian games, and erected a pavilion sumptuously furnished, Themistocles made an oration to the Greeks, inciting them to pull down the tyrant's tent, and not to suffer his horses to run. Thucydides says, that, passing overland to the Ægaean Sea, he took ship at Pydna in the bay of Therme, not being known to any one in the ship, till, being terrified to see the vessel driven by the winds near to Naxos, which was then besieged by the Athenians, he made himself known to the master and pilot, and, partly entreating them, partly threatening that if they went on shore he would accuse them, and make the Athenians to believe that they did not take him in out of ignorance, but that he had corrupted them with money from the beginning, he compelled them to bear off and stand out to sea, and sail forward towards the coast of Asia.

A great part of his estate was privately conveyed away by his friends, and sent after him by sea into Asia; besides which there was discovered and confiscated to the value of fourscore talents, as Theophrastus writes; Theopompus says a hundred; though Themistocles was never worth three talents before he was concerned in public affairs.

When he arrived at Cyme, and understood that all along the coast there were many laid wait for him, and particularly Ergoteles and Pythodorus (for the game was worth the hunting for such as were thankful to make money by any means, the king of Persia having offered by public proclamation two hundred talents to him that should take him), he fled to Ægae, a small city of the Æolians, where no one knew him but only his host Nicogenes, who was the richest man in Æolia, and well known to the great men of Inner Asia. While Themistocles lay hid for some days in his house, one night, after a sacrifice and supper ensuing, Olbius, the attendant upon Nicogenes's children, fell into a sort of frenzy and fit of inspiration, and cried out in verse—

> "Night shall speak, and night instruct thee,
> By the voice of night conduct thee."

After this, Themistocles, going to bed, dreamed that he saw a snake coil itself up upon his belly, and so creep to his neck; then, as soon as it touched his face, it turned into an eagle, which spread its wings over him, and took him up and flew away with him a great distance; then there appeared a herald's golden wand, and upon this at last it set him down securely, after infinite terror and disturbance.

His departure was effected by Nicogenes by the following artifice: The barbarous nations, and amongst them the Persians especially, are extremely jealous, severe, and suspicious about their women, not only their wives, but also their bought slaves and concubines, whom they keep so strictly that no one ever sees them abroad; they spend their lives shut up within doors, and, when they take a journey, are carried in close tents, curtained in on all sides, and set upon a wagon. Such a traveling carriage being prepared for Themistocles, they hid him in it and carried him on his journey, and told those whom they met or spoke with upon the road that they were conveying a young Greek woman out of Ionia to a nobleman at court.

Thucydides and Charon of Lampsacus say that Xerxes was dead, and that Themistocles had an interview with his son; but Ephorus, Dinon, Clitarchus, Heraclides, and many others, write that he came to Xerxes. The chronological tables better agree with the account of Thucydides, and yet neither can their statements be said to be quite set at rest.

When Themistocles was come to the critical point, he applied himself first to Artabanus, commander of a thousand men, telling him that he was a Greek, and desired to speak with the king about important affairs concerning which the king was extremely solicitous. Artabanus answered him: "O stranger, the laws of men are different, and one thing is honorable to one man, and to others another; but it is honorable for all to honor and observe their own laws. It is the habit of the Greeks, we are told, to honor, above all things, liberty and equality; but amongst our many excellent laws, we account this the most excellent, to honor the king, and to worship him, as the image of the great preserver of the universe; if, then, you shall consent to our laws, and fall down before the king and worship him, you may both see him and speak to him; but if your mind be otherwise, you must make use of others to intercede for you, for it is not the national custom here for the king to give audience to anyone that doth not fall down before him." Themistocles, hearing this, replied, "Artabanus, I that come hither to increase the power and glory of the king, will not only submit myself to his laws, since so it hath pleased the god who exalteth the Persian empire to this greatness, but will also cause many more to be worshippers and adorers of the king. Let not this, therefore, be an impediment why I should not communicate to the king what I have to impart." Artabanus asking him, "Who must we tell him that you are? for your words signify you to be no ordinary person," Themistocles answered, "No man, O Artabanus, must be informed of this before the king himself." Thus Phanias relates; to which Eratosthenes, in his treatise on Riches, adds, that it was by the means of a woman of Eretria, who was kept by Artabanus, that he obtained this audience and interview with him.

When he was introduced to the king, and had paid his reverence to him, he stood silent, till the king commanding the interpreter to ask him who he was, he replied, "O king, I am Themistocles the Athenian, driven into banishment by the Greeks. The evils that I have done to the Persians are numerous; but my benefits to them yet greater, in withholding the Greeks from pursuit, so soon as the deliverance of my own country allowed me to show kindness also to you. I come with a mind suited to my present calamities; prepared alike for favors and for anger; to welcome your gracious reconciliation, and to deprecate your wrath. Take my own countrymen for witnesses of the services I have done for Persia, and make use of this occasion to show the world your virtue, rather than to satisfy your indignation. If you save me, you will save your suppliant; if otherwise, will destroy an enemy of the Greeks." He talked also of divine admonitions, such as the vision which he saw at Nicogenes's house, and the direction given him by the oracle of Dodona, where Jupiter commanded him to go to him that had a name like his, by which he understood that he was sent from Jupiter to him, seeing that they both were great, and had the name of kings.

The king heard him attentively, and, though he admired his temper and courage, gave him no answer at that time; but, when he was with his intimate friends, rejoiced in his great good fortune, and esteemed himself very happy in this, and prayed to his god Arimanius, that all his enemies might be ever of the same mind with the Greeks, to abuse and expel the bravest men amongst them. Then he sacrificed to the gods, and presently fell to drinking, and was so well pleased, that in the night, in the middle of his sleep, he cried out for joy three times, "I have Themistocles the Athenian."

In the morning, calling together the chief of his court, he had Themistocles brought before him, who expected no good of it, when he saw, for example, the guards fiercely set against him as soon as they learnt his name, and giving him ill language. As he came forward towards the king, who was seated, the rest keeping silence, passing by Roxanes, a commander of a thousand men, he heard him, with a slight groan, say, without stirring out of his place, "You subtle Greek serpent, the king's good genius hath brought thee hither." Yet, when he came into the presence, and again fell down, the king saluted him, and spoke to him kindly, telling him he was now indebted to him two hundred talents; for it was just and reasonable that he should receive the reward which was proposed to whosoever should bring Themistocles; and promising much more, and encouraging him, he commanded him to speak freely what he would concerning the affairs of Greece. Themistocles replied, that a man's discourse was like to a rich Persian carpet, the beautiful figures and patterns of which can only be shown by spreading and extending it out; when it is contracted and folded up, they are obscured and lost; and, therefore, he desired time. The king being pleased with the comparison, and bidding him take what time he would, he desired a year; in which time, having learnt the Persian language sufficiently, he spoke with the king by himself without the help of an interpreter, it being supposed that he discoursed only about the affairs of Greece; but there happening, at the same time, great alterations at court, and removals of the king's favorites, he drew upon himself the envy of the great people, who imagined that he had taken the boldness to speak concerning them. For the favors shown to other strangers were nothing in comparison with the honors conferred on him; the king invited him to partake of his own pastimes and recreations both at home and abroad, carrying him with him a-hunting, and made him his intimate so far that he permitted him to see the queen-mother, and converse frequently with her. By the king's command, he also was made acquainted with the Magian learning.

When Demaratus the Lacedæmonian, being ordered by the king to ask whatsoever he pleased, that it should immediately be granted him, desired that he might make his public entrance, and be carried in state through the city of Sardis, with the tiara set in the royal manner upon his head, Mithropaustes, cousin to the king, touched him on the head, and told him that he had no brains for the royal tiara to cover, and if Jupiter should give him his lightning and thunder, he would not any the more be Jupiter for that; the king also repulsed him with anger, resolving never to be reconciled to him, but to be inexorable to all supplications on his behalf. Yet Themistocles pacified him, and prevailed with him to forgive him. And it is reported that the succeeding kings, in whose reigns there was a greater communication between the Greeks and Persians, when they invited any considerable Greek into their service, to encourage him, would write, and promise him that he should be as great with them as Themistocles had been. They relate, also, how Themistocles, when he was in great prosperity, and courted by many, seeing himself splendidly served at his table, turned to his children and said, "Children, we had been undone if we had not been undone." Most writers say that he had three cities given him, Magnesia, Myus, and Lampsacus, to maintain him in bread, meat, and wine. Neanthes of Cyzicus, and Phanias, add two more, the city of Palæscepsis, to provide him with clothes, and Percote, with bedding and furniture for his house.

As he was going down towards the sea-coast to take measures against Greece, a Persian whose name was Epixyes, governor of the upper Phrygia, laid wait to kill him, having for that purpose provided a long time before a number of Pisidians, who were to set upon him when he should stop to rest at a city that is called Lion's-head. But Themistocles, sleeping in the middle of the day, saw the Mother of the gods appear to him in a dream and say unto him, "Themistocles, keep back from the Lion's-head, for fear you fall into the lion's jaws; for this advice I expect that your daughter Mnesiptolema should be my servant." Themistocles was much astonished, and, when he had made his vows to the goddess, left the broad road, and making a circuit, went another way, changing his intended station to avoid that place, and at night took up his rest in the fields. But one of the sumpter horses, which carried the furniture for his tent, having fallen that day into the river, his servants spread out the tapestry, which was wet, and hung it up to dry; in the meantime the Pisidians made towards them with their swords drawn, and, not discerning exactly by the moon what it was that was stretched out, thought it to be the tent of Themistocles, and that they should find him resting himself within it; but when they came near, and lifted up the hangings, those who watched there fell upon them and took them. Themistocles, having escaped this great danger, in admiration of the goodness of the goddess that appeared to him, built, in memory of it, a temple in the city of Magnesia, which he dedicated to Dindymene, Mother of the gods, in which he consecrated and devoted his daughter Mnesiptolema to her service.

When he came to Sardis, he visited the temples of the gods, and observing, at his leisure, their buildings, ornaments, and the number of their offerings, he saw in the temple of the Mother of the gods the statue of a virgin in brass, two cubits high, called the water bringer. Themistocles had caused this to be made and set up when he was surveyor of the waters at Athens, out of the fines of those whom he detected in drawing off and diverting the public water by pipes for their private use; and whether he had some regret to see this image in captivity, or was desirous to let the Athenians see in what great credit and authority he was with the king, he entered into a treaty with the governor of Lydia to persuade him to send this statue back to Athens, which so enraged the Persian officer, that he told him he would write the king word of it. Themistocles, being affrighted hereat, got access to his wives and concubines, by presents of money to whom he appeased the fury of the governor; and afterwards behaved with more reserve and circumspection, fearing the envy of the Persians, and did not, as Theopompus writes, continue to travel about Asia, but lived quietly in his own house in Magnesia, where for a long time he passed his days in great security, being courted by all, and enjoying rich presents, and honored equally with the greatest persons in the Persian empire; the king, at that time, not minding his concerns with Greece, being taken up with the affairs of inner Asia.

But when Egypt revolted, being assisted by the Athenians, and the Greek galleys roved about as far as Cyprus and Cilicia, and Cimon had made himself master of the seas, the king turned his thoughts thither, and, bending his mind chiefly to resist the Greeks, and to check the growth of their power against him, began to raise forces, and send out commanders, and to dispatch messengers to Themistocles at Magnesia, to put him in mind of his promise, and to summon him to act against the Greeks. Yet this did not increase his hatred nor exasperate him against the Athenians, neither was he in any way elevated with the thoughts of the honor and powerful command he was to have in this war; but judging, perhaps, that the object would not be attained, the Greeks having at that time, beside other great commanders, Cimon, in particular, who was gaining wonderful military successes; but chiefly being ashamed to sully the glory of his former great actions, and of his many victories and trophies, he determined to put a conclusion to his life, agreeable to its previous course. He sacrificed to the gods, and invited his friends; and, having entertained them and shaken hands with them, drank bull's blood, as is the usual story; as others state, a poison producing instant death; and ended his days in the city of Magnesia, having lived sixty-five years, most of which he had spent in politics and in the wars, in government and command. The king, being informed of the cause and manner of his death, admired him more than ever, and continued to show kindness to his friends and relations.

Themistocles left three sons by Archippe, daughter to Lysander of Alopece,—Archeptolis, Polyeuctus, and Cleophantus. Plato, the philosopher, mentions the last as a most excellent horseman, but otherwise insignificant person; of two sons yet older than these, Neocles and Diocles, Neocles died when he was young by the bite of a horse, and Diocles was adopted by his grandfather, Lysander. He had many daughters, of whom Mnesiptolema, whom he had by a second marriage, was wife to Archeptolis, her brother by another mother; Italia was married to Panthoides, of the island of Chios; Sybaris to Nicomedes the Athenian. After the death of Themistocles, his nephew, Phrasicles, went to Magnesia, and married, with her brothers' consent, another daughter, Nicomache, and took charge of her sister Asia, the youngest of all the children.

The Magnesians possess a splendid sepulchre of Themistocles, placed in the middle of their marketplace. It is not worth while taking notice of what Andocides states in his Address to his Friends concerning his remains, how the Athenians robbed his tomb, and threw his ashes into the air; for he feigns this, to exasperate the oligarchical faction against the people; and there is no man living but knows that Phylarchus simply invents in his history, where he all but uses an actual stage machine, and brings in Neocles and Demopolis as the sons of Themistocles, to incite or move compassion, as if he were writing a tragedy. Diodorus the cosmographer says, in his work on Tombs, but by conjecture rather than of certain knowledge, that near to the haven of Piræus, where the land runs out like an elbow from the promontory of Alcimus, when you have doubled the cape and passed inward where the sea is always calm, there is a large piece of masonry, and upon this the tomb of Themistocles, in the shape of an altar; and Plato the comedian confirms this, he believes, in these verses:—

> "Thy tomb is fairly placed upon the strand,
> Where merchants still shall greet it with the land;
> Still in and out 'twill see them come and go,
> And watch the galleys as they race below."

Various honors also and privileges were granted to the kindred of Themistocles at Magnesia, which were observed down to our times, and were enjoyed by another Themistocles of Athens, with whom I had an intimate acquaintance and friendship in the house of Ammonius the philosopher.

PERICLES

CÆSAR once, seeing some wealthy strangers at Rome, carrying up and down with them in their arms and bosoms young puppy-dogs and monkeys, embracing and making much of them, took occasion not unnaturally to ask whether the women in their country were not used to bear children; by that prince-like reprimand gravely reflecting upon persons who spend and lavish upon brute beasts that affection and kindness which nature has implanted in us to be bestowed on those of our own kind. With like reason may we blame those who misuse that love of inquiry and observation which nature has implanted in our souls, by expending it on objects unworthy of the attention either of their eyes or their ears, while they disregard such as are excellent in themselves, and would do them good.

The mere outward sense, being passive in responding to the impression of the objects that come in its way and strike upon it, perhaps cannot help entertaining and taking notice of everything that addresses it, be it what it will, useful or unuseful; but, in the exercise of his mental perception every man, if he chooses, has a natural power to turn himself upon all occasions, and to change and shift with the greatest ease to what he shall himself judge desirable. So that it becomes a man's duty to pursue and make after the best and choicest of everything, that he may not only employ his contemplation, but may also be improved by it. For as that color is more suitable to the eye whose freshness and pleasantness stimulates and strengthens the sight, so a man ought to apply his intellectual perception to such objects as, with the sense of delight, are apt to call it forth, and allure it to its own proper good and advantage.

Such objects we find in the acts of virtue, which also produce in the minds of mere readers about them an emulation and eagerness that may lead them on to imitation. In other things there does not immediately follow upon the admiration and liking of the thing done any strong desire of doing the like. Nay, many times, on the very contrary, when we are pleased with the work, we slight and set little by the workman or artist himself, as, for instance, in perfumes and purple dyes, we are taken with the things themselves well enough, but do not think dyers and perfumers otherwise than low and sordid people. It was not said amiss by Antisthenes, when people told him that one Ismenias was an excellent piper, "It may be so," said he, "but he is but a wretched human being, otherwise he would not have been an excellent piper." And King Philip, to the same purpose, told his son Alexander, who once at a merry-meeting played a piece of music charmingly and skillfully, "Are you not ashamed, son, to play so well?" For it is enough for a king or prince to find leisure sometimes to hear others sing, and he does the muses quite honor enough when he pleases to be but present, while others engage in such exercises and trials of skill.

He who busies himself in mean occupations produces, in the very pains he takes about things of little or no use, an evidence against himself of his negligence and indisposition to what is really good. Nor did any generous and ingenuous young man, at the sight of the statue of Jupiter at Pisa, ever desire to be a Phidias, or on seeing that of Juno at Argos, long to be a Polycletus, or feel induced by his pleasure in their poems to wish to be an Anacreon or Philetas or Archilochus. For it does not necessarily follow that, if a piece of work please for its gracefulness, therefore he that wrought it deserves our admiration. Whence it is that neither do such things really profit or advantage the beholders, upon the sight of which no zeal arises for the imitation of them, nor any impulse or inclination, which may prompt any desire or endeavor of doing the like. But virtue, by the bare statement of its actions, can so affect men's minds as to create at once both admiration of the things done and desire to imitate the doers of them. The goods of fortune we would possess and would enjoy; those of virtue we long to practice and exercise; we are content to receive the former from others, the latter we wish others to experience from us. Moral good is a practical stimulus; it is no sooner seen, than it inspires an impulse to practice, and influences the mind and character not by a mere imitation which we look at, but by the statement of the fact creates a moral purpose which we form.

And so we have thought fit to spend our time and pains in writing of the lives of famous persons; and have composed this tenth book upon that subject, containing the life of Pericles, and that of Fabius Maximus, who carried on the war against Hannibal, men alike, as in their other virtues and good parts, so especially in their mild and upright temper and demeanor, and in that capacity to bear the cross-grained humors of their fellow-citizens and colleagues in office which made them both most useful and serviceable to the interests of their countries. Whether we take a right aim at our intended purpose, it is left to the reader to judge by what he shall here find.

Pericles was of the tribe Acamantis, and the township Cholargus, of the noblest birth both on his father's and mother's side. Xanthippus, his father, who defeated the king of Persia's generals in the battle of Mycale, took to wife Agariste, the grandchild of Clisthenes, who drove out the sons of Pisistratus, and nobly put an end to their tyrannical usurpation, and, moreover, made a body of laws, and settled a model of government admirably tempered and suited for the harmony and safety of the people.

His mother, being near her time, fancied in a dream that she was brought to bed of a lion, and a few days after was delivered of Pericles, in other respects perfectly formed, only his head was somewhat longish and out of proportion. For which reason almost all the images and statues that were made of him have the head covered with a helmet, the workmen apparently being willing not to expose him. The poets of Athens called him *Schinocephalos,* or squill-head, from *schinos,* a squill, or sea-onion. One of the comic poets, Cratinus, in the Chirons, tells us that—

> "Old Chronos once took queen Sedition to wife;
> Which two brought to life
> That tyrant far-famed,
> Whom the gods the supreme skull-compeller have named";

and, in the Nemesis, addresses him—

> "Come, Jove, thou *head* of gods."

And a second, Teleclides, says, that now, in embarrassment with political difficulties, he sits in the city—

> "Fainting underneath the load
> Of his own head; and now abroad,
> From his huge gallery of a pate,
> Sends forth trouble to the state."

And a third, Eupolis, in the comedy called the Demi, in a series of questions about each of the demagogues, whom he makes in the play to come up from hell, upon Pericles being named last, exclaims—

> "And here by way of summary, now we've done,
> Behold, in brief, the heads of all in one."

The master that taught him music, most authors are agreed, was Damon (whose name, they say, ought to be pronounced with the first syllable short). Though Aristotle tells us that he was thoroughly practiced in all accomplishments of this kind by Pythoclides. Damon, it is not unlikely, being a sophist, out of policy sheltered himself under the profession of music to conceal from people in general his skill in other things, and under this pretense attended Pericles, the young athlete of politics, so to say, as his training-master in these exercises. Damon's lyre, however, did not prove altogether a successful blind; he was banished the country by ostracism for ten years, as a dangerous intermeddler and a favorer of arbitrary power, and, by this means, gave the stage occasion to play upon him. As, for instance, Plato, the comic poet, introduces a character who questions him—

> "Tell me, if you please,
> Since you're the Chiron who taught Pericles."

Pericles, also, was a hearer of Zeno, the Eleatic, who treated of natural philosophy in the same manner as Parmenides did, but had also perfected himself in an art of his own for refuting and silencing opponents in argument; as Timon of Phlius describes it—

> "Also the two-edged tongue of mighty Zeno, who,
> Say what one would, could argue it untrue."

But he that saw most of Pericles, and furnished him most especially with a weight and grandeur of sense, superior to all arts of popularity, and in general gave him his elevation and sublimity of purpose and of character, was Anaxagoras of Clazomenæ; whom the men of those times called by the name of Nous, that is, mind, or intelligence, whether in admiration of the great and extraordinary gift he had displayed for the science of nature, or because that he was the first of the philosophers who did not refer the first ordering of the world to fortune or chance, nor to necessity or compulsion, but to a pure, unadulterated intelligence, which in all other existing mixed and compound things acts as a principle of discrimination, and of combination of like with like.

For this man, Pericles entertained an extraordinary esteem and admiration, and filling himself with this lofty, and, as they call it, up-in-the-air sort of thought, derived hence not merely, as was natural, elevation of purpose and dignity of language, raised far above the base and dishonest buffooneries of mob eloquence, but, besides this, a composure of countenance, and a serenity and calmness in all his movements, which no occurrence whilst he was speaking could disturb, a sustained and even tone of voice, and various other advantages of a similar kind, which produced the greatest effect on his hearers. Once, after being reviled and ill-spoken of all day long in his own hearing by some vile and abandoned fellow in the open marketplace, where he was engaged in the dispatch of some urgent affair, he continued his business in perfect silence, and in the evening returned home composedly, the man still dogging him at the heels, and pelting him all the way with abuse and foul language; and stepping into his house, it being by this time dark, he ordered one of his servants to take a light, and to go along with the man and see him safe home. Ion, it is true, the dramatic poet, says that Pericles's manner in company was somewhat over-assuming and pompous; and that into his high-bearing there entered a good deal of slightingness and scorn of others; he reserves his commendation for Cimon's ease and pliancy and natural grace in society. Ion, however, who must needs make virtue, like a show of tragedies, include some comic scenes, we shall not altogether rely upon; Zeno used to bid those who called Pericles's gravity the affectation of a charlatan, to go and affect the like themselves; inasmuch as this mere counterfeiting might in time insensibly instill into them a real love and knowledge of those noble qualities.

Nor were these the only advantages which Pericles derived from Anaxagoras's acquaintance; he seems also to have become, by his instructions, superior to that superstition with which an ignorant wonder at appearances, for example, in the heavens, possesses the minds of people unacquainted with their causes, eager for the supernatural, and excitable through an inexperience which the knowledge of natural causes removes, replacing wild and timid superstition by the good hope and assurance of an intelligent piety.

There is a story that once Pericles had brought to him from a country farm of his a ram's head with one horn, and that Lampon, the diviner, upon seeing the horn grow strong and solid out of the midst of the forehead, gave it as his judgment, that, there being at that time two potent factions, parties, or interests in the city, the one of Thucydides and the other of Pericles, the government would come about to that one of them in whose ground or estate this token or indication of fate had shown itself. But that Anaxagoras, cleaving the skull in sunder, showed to the bystanders that the brain had not filled up its natural place, but being oblong, like an egg, had collected from all parts of the vessel which contained it in a point to that place from whence the root of the horn took its rise. And that, for that time, Anaxagoras was much admired for his explanation by those that were present; and Lampon no less a little while after, when Thucydides was overpowered, and the whole affairs of the state and government came into the hands of Pericles.

And yet, in my opinion, it is no absurdity to say that they were both in the right, both natural philosopher and diviner, one justly detecting the cause of this event, by which it was produced, the other the end for which it was designed. For it was the business of the one to find out and give an account of what it was made, and in what manner and by what means it grew as it did; and of the other to foretell to what end and purpose it was so made, and what it might mean or portend. Those who say that to find out the cause of a prodigy is in effect to destroy its supposed signification as such, do not take notice that, at the same time, together with divine prodigies, they also do away with signs and signals of human art and concert, as, for instance, the clashings of quoits, fire beacons, and the shadows on sundials, every one of which has its cause, and by that cause and contrivance is a sign of something else. But these are subjects, perhaps, that would better befit another place.

Pericles, while yet but a young man, stood in considerable apprehension of the people, as he was thought in face and figure to be very like the tyrant Pisistratus, and those of great age remarked upon the sweetness of his voice, and his volubility and rapidity in speaking, and were struck with amazement at the resemblance. Reflecting, too, that he had a considerable estate, and was descended of a noble family, and had friends of great influence, he was fearful all this might bring him to be banished as a dangerous person; and for this reason meddled not at all with state affairs, but in military service showed himself of a brave and intrepid nature. But when Aristides was now dead, and Themistocles driven out, and Cimon was for the most part kept abroad by the expeditions he made in parts out of Greece, Pericles, seeing things in this posture, now advanced and took his side, not with the rich and few, but with the many and poor, contrary to his natural bent, which was far from democratical; but, most likely fearing he might fall under suspicion of aiming at arbitrary power, and seeing Cimon on the side of the aristocracy, and much beloved by the better and more distinguished people, he joined the party of the people, with a view at once both to secure himself and procure means against Cimon.

He immediately entered, also, on quite a new course of life and management of his time. For he was never seen to walk in any street but that which led to the marketplace and council hall, and he avoided invitations of friends to supper, and all friendly visiting and intercourse whatever; in all the time he had to do with the public, which was not a little, he was never known to have gone to any of his friends to a supper, except that once when his near kinsman Euryptolemus married, he remained present till the ceremony of the drink offering, and then immediately rose from table and went his way. For these friendly meetings are very quick to defeat any assumed superiority, and in intimate familiarity an exterior of gravity is hard to maintain. Real excellence, indeed, is most recognized when most openly looked into; and in really good men, nothing which meets the eyes of external observers so truly deserves their admiration, as their daily common life does that of their nearer friends. Pericles, however, to avoid any feeling of commonness, or any satiety on the part of the people, presented himself at intervals only, not speaking to every business, nor at all times coming into the assembly, but, as Critolaus says, reserving himself, like the Salaminian galley, for great occasions, while matters of lesser importance were dispatched by friends or other speakers under his direction. And of this number we are told Ephialtes made one, who broke the power of the council of Areopagus, giving the people, according to Plato's expression, so copious and so strong a draught of liberty, that growing wild and unruly, like an unmanageable horse, it, as the comic poets say—

> "—got beyond all keeping in,
> Champing at Eubœa, and among the islands leaping in."

The style of speaking most consonant to his form of life and the dignity of his views he found, so to say, in the tones of that instrument with which Anaxagoras had furnished him; of his teaching he continually availed himself, and deepened the colors of rhetoric with the dye of natural science. For having, in addition to his great natural genius, attained, by the study of nature, to use the words of the divine Plato, this height of intelligence, and this universal consummating power, and drawing hence whatever might be of advantage to him in the art of speaking, he showed himself far superior to all others. Upon which account, they say, he had his nickname given him, though some are of opinion he was named the Olympian from the public buildings with which he adorned the city; and others again, from his great power in public affairs, whether of war or peace. Nor is it unlikely that the confluence of many attributes may have conferred it on him. However, the comedies represented at the time, which, both in good earnest and in merriment, let fly many hard words at him, plainly show that he got that appellation especially from his speaking; they speak of his "thundering and lightning" when he harangued the people, and of his wielding a dreadful thunderbolt in his tongue.

A saying also of Thucydides, the son of Melesias, stands on record, spoken by him by way of pleasantry upon Pericles's dexterity. Thucydides was one of the noble and distinguished citizens, and had been his greatest opponent; and, when Archidamus, the king of the Lacedæmonians, asked him whether he or Pericles were the better wrestler, he made this answer: "When I," said he, "have thrown him and given him a fair fall, by persisting that he had no fall, he gets the better of me, and makes the bystanders, in spite of their own eyes, believe him." The truth, however, is, that Pericles himself was very careful what and how he was to speak, insomuch that, whenever he went up to the hustings, he prayed the gods that no one word might unawares slip from him unsuitable to the matter and the occasion.

He has left nothing in writing behind him, except some decrees; and there are but very few of his sayings recorded; one, for example, is, that he said Ægina must, like a gathering in a man's eye, be removed from Piræus; and another, that he said he saw already war moving on its way towards them out of Peloponnesus. Again, when on a time Sophocles, who was his fellow-commissioner in the generalship, was going on board with him, and praised the beauty of a youth they met with in the way to the ship, "Sophocles," said he, "a general ought not only to have clean hands but also clean eyes." And Stesimbrotus tells us that, in his encomium on those who fell in battle at Samos, he said they were become immortal, as the gods were. "For," said he, "we do not see them themselves, but only by the honors we pay them, and by the benefits they do us, attribute to them immortality; and the like attributes belong also to those that die in the service of their country."

Since Thucydides describes the rule of Pericles as an aristocratical government, that went by the name of a democracy, but was, indeed, the supremacy of a single great man, while many others say, on the contrary, that by him the common people were first encouraged and led on to such evils as appropriations of subject territory; allowances for attending theaters, payments for performing public duties, and by these bad habits were, under the influence of his public measures, changed from a sober, thrifty people, that maintained themselves by their own labors, to lovers of expense, intemperance, and license, let us examine the cause of this change by the actual matters of fact.

At the first, as has been said, when he set himself against Cimon's great authority, he did caress the people. Finding himself come short of his competitor in wealth and money, by which advantages the other was enabled to take care of the poor, inviting every day some one or other of the citizens that was in want to supper, and bestowing clothes on the aged people, and breaking down the hedges and enclosures of his grounds, that all that would might freely gather what fruit they pleased, Pericles, thus outdone in popular arts, by the advice of one Damonides of Œa, as Aristotle states, turned to the distribution of the public moneys; and in a short time having bought the people over, what with moneys allowed for shows and for service on juries, and what with other forms of pay and largess, he made use of them against the council of Areopagus, of which he himself was no member, as having never been appointed by lot either chief archon, or lawgiver, or king, or captain. For from of old these offices were conferred on persons by lot, and they who had acquitted themselves duly in the discharge of them were advanced to the court of Areopagus. And so Pericles, having secured his power in interest with the populace, directed the exertions of his party against this council with such success, that most of those causes and matters which had been used to be tried there were, by the agency of Ephialtes, removed from its cognizance; Cimon, also, was banished by ostracism as a favorer of the Lacedæmonians and a hater of the people, though in wealth and noble birth he was among the first, and had won several most glorious victories over the barbarians, and had filled the city with money and spoils of war; as is recorded in the history of his life. So vast an authority had Pericles obtained among the people.

The ostracism was limited by law to ten years; but the Lacedæmonians, in the meantime, entering with a great army into the territory of Tanagra, and the Athenians going out against them, Cimon, coming from his banishment before his time was out, put himself in arms and array with those of his fellow-citizens that were of his own tribe, and desired by his deeds to wipe off the suspicion of his favoring the Lacedæmonians, by venturing his own person along with his countrymen. But Pericles's friends, gathering in a body, forced him to retire as a banished man. For which cause also Pericles seems to have exerted himself more in that than in any battle, and to have been conspicuous above all for his exposure of himself to danger. All Cimon's friends, also, to a man, fell together side by side, whom Pericles had accused with him of taking part with the Lacedæmonians. Defeated in this battle on their own frontiers, and expecting a new and perilous attack with return of spring, the Athenians now felt regret and sorrow for the loss of Cimon, and repentance for their expulsion of him. Pericles, being sensible of their feelings, did not hesitate or delay to gratify it, and himself made the motion for recalling him home. He, upon his return, concluded a peace betwixt the two cities; for the Lacedæmonians entertained as kindly feelings towards him as they did the reverse towards Pericles and the other popular leaders.

Yet some there are who say that Pericles did not propose the order for Cimon's return till some private articles of agreement had been made between them, and this by means of Elpinice, Cimon's sister; that Cimon, namely, should go out to sea with a fleet of two hundred ships, and be commander-in-chief abroad, with a design to reduce the king of Persia's territories, and that Pericles should have the power at home.

This Elpinice, it was thought, had before this time procured some favor for her brother Cimon at Pericles's hands, and induced him to be more remiss and gentle in urging the charge when Cimon was tried for his life; for Pericles was one of the committee appointed by the commons to plead against him. And when Elpinice came and besought him in her brother's behalf, he answered, with a smile, "O Elpinice, you are too old a woman to undertake such business as this." But, when he appeared to impeach him, he stood up but once to speak, merely to acquit himself of his commission, and went out of court, having done Cimon the least prejudice of any of his accusers.

How, then, can one believe Idomeneus, who charges Pericles as if he had by treachery procured the murder of Ephialtes, the popular statesman, one who was his friend, and of his own party in all his political course, out of jealousy, forsooth, and envy of his great reputation? This historian, it seems, having raked up these stories, I know not whence, has befouled with them a man who, perchance, was not altogether free from fault or blame, but yet had a noble spirit, and a soul that was bent on honor; and where such qualities are, there can no such cruel and brutal passion find harbor or gain admittance. As to Ephialtes, the truth of the story, as Aristotle has told it, is this: that having made himself formidable to the oligarchical party, by being an uncompromising asserter of the people's rights in calling to account and prosecuting those who any way wronged them, his enemies, lying in wait for him, by the means of Aristodicus the Tanagræan, privately dispatched him.

Cimon, while he was admiral, ended his days in the Isle of Cyprus. And the aristocratical party, seeing that Pericles was already before this grown to be the greatest and foremost man of all the city, but nevertheless wishing there should be somebody set up against him, to blunt and turn the edge of his power, that it might not altogether prove a monarchy, put forward Thucydides of Alopece, a discreet person, and a near kinsman of Cimon's, to conduct the opposition against him; who, indeed, though less skilled in warlike affairs than Cimon was, yet was better versed in speaking and political business, and keeping close guard in the city, and engaging with Pericles on the hustings, in a short time brought the government to an equality of parties. For he would not suffer those who were called the honest and good (persons of worth and distinction) to be scattered up and down and mix themselves and be lost among the populace, as formerly, diminishing and obscuring their superiority amongst the masses; but taking them apart by themselves and uniting them in one body, by their combined weight he was able, as it were upon the balance, to make a counterpoise to the other party.

For, indeed, there was from the beginning a sort of concealed split, or seam, as it might be in a piece of iron, marking the different popular and aristocratical tendencies; but the open rivalry and contention of these two opponents made the gash deep, and severed the city into the two parties of the people and the few. And so Pericles, at that time more than at any other, let loose the reins to the people, and made his policy subservient to their pleasure, contriving continually to have some great public show or solemnity, some banquet, or some procession or other in the town to please them, coaxing his countrymen like children with such delights and pleasures as were not, however, unedifying. Besides that every year he sent out threescore galleys, on board of which there went numbers of the citizens, who were in pay eight months, learning at the same time and practicing the art of seamanship.

He sent, moreover, a thousand of them into the Chersonese as planters, to share the land among them by lot, and five hundred more into the isle of Naxos, and half that number to Andros, a thousand into

Thrace to dwell among the Bisaltæ, and others into Italy, when the city Sybaris, which now was called Thurii, was to be repeopled. And this he did to ease and discharge the city of an idle, and, by reason of their idleness, a busy, meddling crowd of people; and at the same time to meet the necessities and restore the fortunes of the poor townsmen, and to intimidate, also, and check their allies from attempting any change, by posting such garrisons, as it were, in the midst of them.

That which gave most pleasure and ornament to the city of Athens, and the greatest admiration and even astonishment to all strangers, and that which now is Greece's only evidence that the power she boasts of and her ancient wealth are no romance or idle story, was his construction of the public and sacred buildings. Yet this was that of all his actions in the government which his enemies most looked askance upon and caviled at in the popular assemblies, crying out how that the commonwealth of Athens had lost its reputation and was ill spoken of abroad for removing the common treasure of the Greeks from the isle of Delos into their own custody; and how that their fairest excuse for so doing, namely, that they took it away for fear the barbarians should seize it, and on purpose to secure it in a safe place, this Pericles had made unavailable, and how that "Greece cannot but resent it as an insufferable affront, and consider herself to be tyrannized over openly, when she sees the treasure, which was contributed by her upon a necessity for the war, wantonly lavished out by us upon our city, to gild her all over, and to adorn and set her forth, as it were some vain woman, hung round with precious stones and figures and temples, which cost a world of money."

Pericles, on the other hand, informed the people, that they were in no way obliged to give any account of those moneys to their allies, so long as they maintained their defense, and kept off the barbarians from attacking them; while in the meantime they did not so much as supply one horse or man or ship, but only found money for the service; "which money," said he, "is not theirs that give it, but theirs that receive it, if so be they perform the conditions upon which they receive it." And that it was good reason, that, now the city was sufficiently provided and stored with all things necessary for the war, they should convert the overplus of its wealth to such undertakings, as would hereafter, when completed, give them eternal honor, and, for the present, while in process, freely supply all the inhabitants with plenty. With their variety of workmanship and of occasions for service, which summon all arts and trades and require all hands to be employed about them, they do actually put the whole city, in a manner, into state pay; while at the same time she is both beautified and maintained by herself. For as those who are of age and strength for war are provided for and maintained in the armaments abroad by their pay out of the public stock, so, it being his desire and design that the undisciplined mechanic multitude that stayed at home should not go without their share of public salaries, and yet should not have them given them for sitting still and doing nothing, to that end he thought fit to bring in among them, with the approbation of the people, these vast projects of buildings and designs of works, that would be of some continuance before they were finished, and would give employment to numerous arts, so that the part of the people that stayed at home might, no less than those that were at sea or in garrisons or on expeditions, have a fair and just occasion of receiving the benefit and having their share of the public moneys.

The materials were stone, brass, ivory, gold, ebony cypress wood; and the arts or trades that wrought and fashioned them were smiths and carpenters, molders, founders and braziers, stonecutters, dyers, goldsmiths, ivory workers, painters, embroiderers, turners; those again that conveyed them to the town for use, merchants and mariners and ship masters by sea, and by land cartwrights, cattle breeders, wagoners, rope makers, flax workers, shoemakers and leather-dressers, roadmakers, miners. And every trade in the same nature, as a captain in an army has his particular company of soldiers under him, had its own hired company of journeymen and laborers belonging to it banded together as in array, to be as it were the instrument and body for the performance of the service. Thus, to say all in a word, the occasions and services of these public works distributed plenty through every age and condition.

As then grew the works up, no less stately in size than exquisite in form, the workmen striving to outvie the material and the design with the beauty of their workmanship, yet the most wonderful thing of all was the rapidity of their execution.

Undertakings, any one of which singly might have required, they thought, for their completion, several successions and ages of men, were every one of them accomplished in the height and prime of one man's political service. Although they say, too, that Zeuxis once, having heard Agatharchus the painter boast of dispatching his work with speed and ease, replied, "I take a long time." For ease and speed in doing a thing do not give the work lasting solidity or exactness of beauty; the expenditure of time allowed to a man's pains beforehand for the production of a thing is repaid by way of interest with a vital force for its preservation when once produced. For which reason Pericles's works are especially admired, as having been made quickly, to last long. For every particular piece of his work was immediately, even at that time, for its beauty and elegance, antique; and yet in its vigor and freshness looks to this day as if it were just executed. There is a sort of bloom of newness upon those works of his, preserving them from the touch of time, as if they had some perennial spirit and undying vitality mingled in the composition of them.

Phidias had the oversight of all the works, and was surveyor-general, though upon the various portions other great masters and workmen were employed. For Callicrates and Ictinus built the Parthenon; the chapel at Eleusis, where the mysteries were celebrated, was begun by Corœbus, who erected the pillars that stand upon the floor or pavement, and joined them to the architraves; and after his death Metagenes of Xypete added the frieze and the upper line of columns; Xenocles of Cholargus roofed or arched the lantern on top of the temple of Castor and Pollux; and the long wall, which Socrates says he himself heard Pericles propose to the people, was undertaken by Callicrates. This work Cratinus ridicules, as long in finishing—

> "'Tis long since Pericles, if words would do it,
>   Talked up the wall; yet adds not one mite to it."

The Odeum, or music room, which in its interior was full of seats and ranges of pillars, and outside had its roof made to slope and descend from one single point at the top, was constructed, we are told, in imitation of the King of Persia's Pavilion; this likewise by Pericles's order; which Cratinus again, in his comedy called The Thracian Women, made an occasion of raillery—

> "So, we see here,
>   Jupiter Long-pate Pericles appear,
>   Since ostracism time, he's laid aside his head,
>   And wears the new Odeum in its stead."

Pericles also, eager for distinction, then first obtained the decree for a contest in musical skill to be held yearly at the Panathenæa, and he himself, being chosen judge, arranged the order and method in which the competitors should sing and play on the flute and on the harp. And both at that time, and at other times also, they sat in this music room to see and hear all such trials of skill.

The propylæa, or entrances to the Acropolis, were finished in five years' time, Mnesicles being the principal architect. A strange accident happened in the course of building, which showed that the goddess was not averse to the work, but was aiding and cooperating to bring it to perfection. One of the artificers, the quickest and the handiest workman among them all, with a slip of his foot fell down from a great height, and lay in a miserable condition, the physicians having no hope of his recovery. When Pericles was in distress about this, Minerva appeared to him at night in a dream, and ordered a course of treatment, which he applied, and in a short time and with great ease cured the man. And upon this occasion it was that he set up a brass statue of Minerva, surnamed Health, in the citadel near the altar, which they say was there before. But it was

Phidias who wrought the goddess's image in gold, and he has his name inscribed on the pedestal as the workman of it; and indeed the whole work in a manner was under his charge, and he had, as we have said already, the oversight over all the artists and workmen, through Pericles's friendship for him; and this, indeed, made him much envied, and his patron shamefully slandered with stories, as if Phidias were in the habit of receiving, for Pericles's use, freeborn women that came to see the works. The comic writers of the town, when they had got hold of this story, made much of it, and bespattered him with all the ribaldry they could invent, charging him falsely with the wife of Menippus, one who was his friend and served as lieutenant under him in the wars; and with the birds kept by Pyrilampes, an acquaintance of Pericles, who, they pretended, used to give presents of peacocks to Pericles's female friends. And how can one wonder at any number of strange assertions from men whose whole lives were devoted to mockery, and who were ready at any time to sacrifice the reputation of their superiors to vulgar envy and spite, as to some evil genius, when even Stesimbrotus the Thasian has dared to lay to the charge of Pericles a monstrous and fabulous piece of criminality with his son's wife? So very difficult a matter is it to trace and find out the truth of anything by history, when, on the one hand, those who afterwards write it find long periods of time intercepting their view, and, on the other hand, the contemporary records of any actions and lives, partly through envy and ill-will, partly through favor and flattery, pervert and distort truth.

When the orators, who sided with Thucydides and his party, were at one time crying out, as their custom was, against Pericles, as one who squandered away the public money, and made havoc of the state revenues, he rose in the open assembly and put the question to the people, whether they thought that he had laid out much; and they saying, "Too much, a great deal." "Then," said he, "since it is so, let the cost not go to your account, but to mine; and let the inscription upon the buildings stand in my name." When they heard him say thus, whether it were out of a surprise to see the greatness of his spirit or out of emulation of the glory of the works, they cried aloud, bidding him to spend on, and lay out what he thought fit from the public purse, and to spare no cost, till all were finished.

At length, coming to a final contest with Thucydides which of the two should ostracize the other out of the country, and having gone through this peril, he threw his antagonist out, and broke up the confederacy that had been organized against him. So that now all schism and division being at an end, and the city brought to evenness and unity, he got all Athens and all affairs that pertained to the Athenians into his own hands, their tributes, their armies, and their galleys, the islands, the sea, and their

wide-extended power, partly over other Greeks and partly over barbarians, and all that empire, which they possessed, founded and fortified
upon subject nations and royal friendships and alliances.

After this he was no longer the same man he had been before, nor as
tame and gentle and familiar as formerly with the populace, so as readily
to yield to their pleasures and to comply with the desires of the multitude, as a steersman shifts with the winds. Quitting that loose, remiss, and,
in some cases, licentious court of the popular will, he turned those soft
and flowery modulations to the austerity of aristocratical and regal rule;
and employing this uprightly and undeviatingly for the country's best interests, he was able generally to lead the people along, with their own
wills and consents, by persuading and showing them what was to be
done; and sometimes, too, urging and pressing them forward extremely
against their will, he made them, whether they would or no, yield submission to what was for their advantage. In which, to say the truth, he
did but like a skillful physician, who, in a complicated and chronic disease, as he sees occasion, at one while allows his patient the moderate use
of such things as please him, at another while gives him keen pains and
drugs to work the cure. For there arising and growing up, as was natural,
all manner of distempered feelings among a people which had so vast a
command and dominion, he alone, as a great master, knowing how to
handle and deal fitly with each one of them, and, in an especial manner,
making that use of hopes and fears, as his two chief rudders, with the one
to check the career of their confidence at any time, with the other to
raise them up and cheer them when under any discouragement, plainly
showed by this, that rhetoric, or the art of speaking, is, in Plato's language,
the government of the souls of men, and that her chief business is to address the affections and passions, which are as it were the strings and keys
to the soul, and require a skillful and careful touch to be played on as they
should be. The source of this predominance was not barely his power of
language, but, as Thucydides assures us, the reputation of his life, and the
confidence felt in his character; his manifest freedom from every kind of
corruption, and superiority to all considerations of money. Notwithstanding he had made the city Athens, which was great of itself, as great
and rich as can be imagined, and though he were himself in power and
interest more than equal to many kings and absolute rulers, who some of
them also bequeathed by will their power to their children, he, for his
part, did not make the patrimony his father left him greater than it was
by one drachma.

Thucydides, indeed, gives a plain statement of the greatness of his
power; and the comic poets, in their spiteful manner, more than hint at
it, styling his companions and friends the new Pisistratidæ, and calling on
him to abjure any intention of usurpation, as one whose eminence was

too great to be any longer proportionable to and compatible with a
democracy or popular government. And Teleclides says the Athenians had
surrendered up to him—

"The tribute of the cities, and with them, the cities too, to do with them
    as he pleases, and undo;
To build up, if he likes, stone walls around a town; and again, if so he likes,
    to pull them down;
Their treaties and alliances, power, empire, peace, and war, their wealth
    and their success forevermore."

Nor was all this the luck of some happy occasion; nor was it the mere
bloom and grace of a policy that flourished for a season; but having for
forty years together maintained the first place among statesmen such as
Ephialtes and Leocrates and Myronides and Cimon and Tolmides and
Thucydides were, after the defeat and banishment of Thucydides, for no
less than fifteen years longer, in the exercise of one continuous unintermitted command in the office, to which he was annually re-elected, of
General, he preserved his integrity unspotted; though otherwise he was
not altogether idle or careless in looking after his pecuniary advantage;
his paternal estate, which of right belonged to him, he so ordered that it
might neither through negligence be wasted or lessened, nor yet, being
so full of business as he was, cost him any great trouble or time with taking care of it; and put it into such a way of management as he thought
to be the most easy for himself, and the most exact. All his yearly products and profits he sold together in a lump, and supplied his household
needs afterwards by buying everything that he or his family wanted out
of the market. Upon which account, his children, when they grew to age,
were not well pleased with his management, and the women that lived
with him were treated with little cost, and complained of this way of
housekeeping, where everything was ordered and set down from day to
day, and reduced to the greatest exactness; since there was not there, as is
usual in a great family and a plentiful estate, anything to spare, or over
and above; but all that went out or came in, all disbursements and all receipts, proceeded as it were by number and measure. His manager in all
this was a single servant, Evangelus by name, a man either naturally gifted
or instructed by Pericles so as to excel every one in this art of domestic
economy.

All this, in truth, was very little in harmony with Anaxagoras's wisdom;
if, indeed, it be true that he, by a kind of divine impulse and greatness of
spirit, voluntarily quitted his house, and left his land to lie fallow and to
be grazed by sheep like a common. But the life of a contemplative
philosopher and that of an active statesman are, I presume, not the same
thing; for the one merely employs, upon great and good objects of

thought, an intelligence that requires no aid of instruments nor supply of any external materials; whereas the other, who tempers and applies his virtue to human uses, may have occasion for affluence, not as a matter of necessity, but as a noble thing; which was Pericles's case, who relieved numerous poor citizens.

However, there is a story that Anaxagoras himself, while Pericles was taken up with public affairs, lay neglected, and that, now being grown old, he wrapped himself up with a resolution to die for want of food; which being by chance brought to Pericles's ear, he was horror-struck, and instantly ran thither, and used all the arguments and entreaties he could to him, lamenting not so much Anaxagoras's condition as his own, should he lose such a counselor as he had found him to be; and that, upon this, Anaxagoras unfolded his robe, and showing himself, made answer: "Pericles," said he, "even those who have occasion for a lamp supply it with oil."

The Lacedæmonians beginning to show themselves troubled at the growth of the Athenian power, Pericles, on the other hand, to elevate the people's spirit yet more, and to raise them to the thought of great actions, proposed a decree, to summon all the Greeks in what part soever, whether of Europe or Asia, every city, little as well as great, to send their deputies to Athens to a general assembly, or convention, there to consult and advise concerning the Greek temples which the barbarians had burnt down, and the sacrifices which were due from them upon vows they had made to their gods for the safety of Greece when they fought against the barbarians; and also concerning the navigation of the sea, that they might henceforward all of them pass to and fro and trade securely, and be at peace among themselves.

Upon this errand, there were twenty men, of such as were above fifty years of age, sent by commission; five to summon the Ionians and Dorians in Asia, and the islanders as far as Lesbos and Rhodes; five to visit all the places in the Hellespont and Thrace, up to Byzantium; and other five besides these to go to Bœotia and Phocis and Peloponnesus, and from hence to pass through the Locrians over to the neighboring continent as far as Acarnania and Ambracia; and the rest to take their course through Eubœa to the Œtaeans and the Malian Gulf, and to the Achæans of Phthiotis and the Thessalians; all of them to treat with the people as they passed, and to persuade them to come and take their part in the debates for settling the peace and jointly regulating the affairs of Greece.

Nothing was effected, nor did the cities meet by their deputies, as was desired; the Lacedæmonians, as it is said, crossing the design underhand, and the attempt being disappointed and baffled first in Peloponnesus. I thought fit, however, to introduce the mention of it, to show the spirit of the man and the greatness of his thoughts.

In his military conduct, he gained a great reputation for wariness; he would not by his goodwill engage in any fight which had much uncertainty or hazard; he did not envy the glory of generals whose rash adventures fortune favored with brilliant success, however they were admired by others; nor did he think them worthy his imitation, but always used to say to his citizens that, so far as lay in his power, they should continue immortal, and live forever. Seeing Tolmides, the son of Tolmæus, upon the confidence of his former successes, and flushed with the honor his military actions had procured him, making preparations to attack the Bœotians in their own country, when there was no likely opportunity, and that he had prevailed with the bravest and most enterprising of the youth to enlist themselves as volunteers in the service, who besides his other force made up a thousand, he endeavored to withhold him and to advise him from it in the public assembly, telling him in a memorable saying of his, which still goes about, that, if he would not take Pericles's advice, yet he would not do amiss to wait and be ruled by time, the wisest counselor of all. This saying, at that time, was but slightly commended; but within a few days after, when news was brought that Tolmides himself had been defeated and slain in battle near Coronea, and that many brave citizens had fallen with him, it gained him great repute as well as good-will among the people, for wisdom and for love of his countrymen.

But of all his expeditions, that to the Chersonese gave most satisfaction and pleasure, having proved the safety of the Greeks who inhabited there. For not only by carrying along with him a thousand fresh citizens of Athens he gave new strength and vigor to the cities, but also by belting the neck of land, which joins the peninsula to the continent, with bulwarks and forts from sea to sea, he put a stop to the inroads of the Thracians, who lay all about the Chersonese, and closed the door against a continual and grievous war, with which that country had been long harassed, lying exposed to the encroachments and influx of barbarous neighbors, and groaning under the evils of a predatory population both upon and within its borders.

Nor was he less admired and talked of abroad for his sailing round the Peloponnesus, having set out from Pegæ, or The Fountains, the port of Megara, with a hundred galleys. For he not only laid waste the seacoast, as Tolmides had done before, but also, advancing far up into the mainland with the soldiers he had on board, by the terror of his appearance drove many within their walls; and at Nemea, with main force, routed and raised a trophy over the Sicyonians, who stood their ground and joined battle with him. And having taken on board a supply of soldiers into the galleys out of Achaia, then in league with Athens, he crossed with the fleet to the opposite continent, and, sailing along by the mouth of the river Achelous, overran Acarnania, and shut up the Œniadæ within their city walls, and having ravaged and wasted their country, weighed anchor for home with the double advantage of having shown himself formidable to his enemies, and at the same time safe and energetic to his fellow citizens; for there was not so much as any chance miscarriage that happened, the whole voyage through, to those who were under his charge.

Entering also the Euxine Sea with a large and finely equipped fleet, he obtained for the Greek cities any new arrangements they wanted, and entered into friendly relations with them; and to the barbarous nations, and kings and chiefs round about them, displayed the greatness of the power of the Athenians, their perfect ability and confidence to sail wherever they had a mind, and to bring the whole sea under their control. He left the Sinopians thirteen ships of war, with soldiers under the command of Lamachus, to assist them against Timesileus the tyrant; and when he and his accomplices had been thrown out, obtained a decree that six hundred of the Athenians that were willing should sail to Sinope and plant themselves there with the Sinopians, sharing among them the houses and land which the tyrant and his party had previously held.

But in other things he did not comply with the giddy impulses of the citizens, nor quit his own resolutions to follow their fancies, when, carried away with the thought of their strength and great success, they were eager to interfere again in Egypt, and to disturb the king of Persia's maritime dominions. Nay, there were a good many who were, even then, possessed with that unblessed and inauspicious passion for Sicily, which afterward the orators of Alcibiades's party blew up into a flame. There were some also who dreamt of Tuscany and of Carthage, and not without plausible reason in their present large dominion and the prosperous course of their affairs.

But Pericles curbed this passion for foreign conquest, and unsparingly pruned and cut down their ever busy fancies for a multitude of undertakings; and directed their power for the most part to securing and consolidating what they had already got, supposing it would be quite enough for them to do, if they could keep the Lacedæmonians in check; to whom he entertained all along a sense of opposition; which, as upon many other occasions, so he particularly showed by what he did in the time of the holy war. The Lacedæmonians, having gone with an army to Delphi, restored Apollo's temple, which the Phocians had got into their possession, to the Delphians; immediately after their departure, Pericles, with another army, came and restored the Phocians. And the Lacedæmonians, having engraven the record of their privilege of consulting the oracle before others, which the Delphians gave them, upon the forehead of the brazen wolf which stands there, he, also, having received from the Phocians the like privilege for the Athenians, had it cut upon the same wolf of brass on his right side.

That he did well and wisely in thus restraining the exertions of the Athenians within the compass of Greece, the events themselves that happened afterward bore sufficient witness. For, in the first place, the Eubœans revolted, against whom he passed over with forces; and then, immediately after, news came that the Megarians were turned their enemies, and a hostile army was upon the borders of Attica, under the conduct of Plistoanax, king of the Lacedæmonians. Wherefore Pericles came with his army back again in all haste out of Eubœa, to meet the war which threatened at home; and did not venture to engage a numerous and brave army eager for battle; but perceiving that Plistoanax was a very young man, and governed himself mostly by the counsel and advice of Cleandrides, whom the ephors had sent with him, by reason of his youth, to be a kind of guardian and assistant to him, he privately made trial of this man's integrity, and, in a short time, having corrupted him with money, prevailed with him to withdraw the Peloponnesians out of Attica. When the army had retired and dispersed into their several states, the Lacedæmonians in anger fined their king in so large a sum of money, that, unable to pay it, he quitted Lacedæmon; while Cleandrides fled, and had sentence of death passed upon him in his absence. This was the father of Gylippus, who overpowered the Athenians in Sicily. And it seems that this covetousness was an hereditary disease transmitted from father to son; for Gylippus also afterwards was caught in foul practices, and expelled from Sparta for it. But this we have told at large in the account of Lysander.

When Pericles, in giving up his accounts of this expedition, stated a disbursement of ten talents, as laid out upon fit occasion, the people, without any question, nor troubling themselves to investigate the mystery, freely allowed of it. And some historians, in which number is Theophrastus the philosopher, have given it as a truth that Pericles every year used to send privately the sum of ten talents to Sparta, with which he complimented those in office, to keep off the war; not to purchase peace neither, but time, that he might prepare at leisure, and be the better able to carry on war hereafter.

Immediately after this, turning his forces against the revolters, and passing over into the island of Eubœa with fifty sail of ships and five thousand men in arms, he reduced their cities, and drove out the citizens of the Chalcidians, called Hippobotæ, horse-feeders, the chief persons for wealth and reputation among them; and removing all the Histiæans out of the country, brought in a plantation of Athenians in their room; making them his one example of severity, because they had captured an Attic ship and killed all on board.

After this, having made a truce between the Athenians and Lace-.

dæmonians for thirty years, he ordered, by public decree, the expedition against the Isle of Samos, on the ground, that, when they were bid to leave off their war with the Milesians they had not complied. And as these measures against the Samians are thought to have been taken to please Aspasia, this may be a fit point for inquiry about the woman, what art or charming faculty she had that enabled her to captivate, as she did, the greatest statesmen, and to give the philosophers occasion to speak so much about her, and that, too, not to her disparagement. That she was a Milesian by birth, the daughter of Axiochus, is a thing acknowledged. And they say it was in emulation of Thargelia, a courtesan of the old Ionian times, that she made her addresses to men of great power. Thargelia was a great beauty, extremely charming, and at the same time sagacious; she had numerous suitors among the Greeks, and brought all who had to do with her over to the Persian interest, and by their means, being men of the greatest power and station, sowed the seeds of the Median faction up and down in several cities. Aspasia, some say, was courted and caressed by Pericles upon account of her knowledge and skill in politics. Socrates himself would sometimes go to visit her, and some of his acquaintance with him; and those who frequented her company would carry their wives with them to listen to her. Her occupation was anything but creditable, her house being a home for young courtesans. Æschines tells us, also, that Lysicles, a sheep dealer, a man of low birth and character, by keeping Aspasia company after Pericles's death, came to be a chief man in Athens. And in Plato's Menexenus, though we do not take the introduction as quite serious, still thus much seems to be historical, that she had the repute of being resorted to by many of the Athenians for instruction in the art of speaking. Pericles's inclination for her seems, however, to have rather proceeded from the passion of love. He had a wife that was near of kin to him, who had been married first to Hipponicus, by whom she had Callias, surnamed the Rich; and also she brought Pericles, while she lived with him, two sons, Xanthippus and Paralus. Afterwards, when they did not well agree, nor like to live together, he parted with her, with her own consent, to another man, and himself took Aspasia, and loved her with wonderful affection; every day, both as he went out and as he came in from the marketplace, he saluted and kissed her.

In the comedies she goes by the nicknames of the new Omphale and Deianira, and again is styled Juno. Cratinus, in downright terms, calls her a harlot.

> "To find him a Juno the goddess of lust
>   Bore that harlot past shame,
>   Aspasia by name."

It should seem also that he had a son by her; Eupolis, in his Demi, introduced Pericles asking after his safety, and Myronides replying,

> "My son?" "He lives: a man he had been long,
> But that the harlot-mother did him wrong."

Aspasia, they say, became so celebrated and renowned, that Cyrus also,
who made war against Artaxerxes for the Persian monarchy, gave her
whom he loved the best of all his concubines the name of Aspasia, who
before that was called Milto. She was a Phocæan by birth, the daughter
of one Hermotimus, and, when Cyrus fell in battle, was carried to the
king, and had great influence at court. These things coming into my
memory as I am writing this story, it would be unnatural for me to omit
them.

Pericles, however, was particularly charged with having proposed to
the assembly the war against the Samians, from favor to the Milesians,
upon the entreaty of Aspasia. For the two states were at war for the possession of Priene; and the Samians, getting the better, refused to lay down
their arms and to have the controversy betwixt them decided by arbitra-
tion before the Athenians. Pericles, therefore, fitting out a fleet, went and
broke up the oligarchical government at Samos, and taking fifty of the
principal men of the town as hostages, and as many of their children, sent
them to the isle of Lemnos, there to be kept, though he had offers, as
some relate, of a talent apiece for himself from each one of the hostages,
and of many other presents from those who were anxious not to have a
democracy. Moreover, Pisuthnes the Persian, one of the king's lieutenants, bearing some goodwill to the Samians, sent him ten thousand
pieces of gold to excuse the city. Pericles, however, would receive none
of all this; but after he had taken that course with the Samians which he
thought fit, and set up a democracy among them, sailed back to Athens.

But they, however, immediately revolted, Pisuthnes having privily got
away their hostages for them, and provided them with means for the war.
Whereupon Pericles came out with a fleet a second time against them,
and found them not idle nor slinking away, but manfully resolved to try
for the dominion of the sea. The issue was that, after a sharp sea fight
about the island called Tragia, Pericles obtained a decisive victory, having
with forty-four ships routed seventy of the enemy's, twenty of which
were carrying soldiers.

Together with his victory and pursuit, having made himself master of
the port, he laid siege to the Samians, and blocked them up, who yet, one
way or another, still ventured to make sallies, and fight under the city
walls. But after that another greater fleet from Athens was arrived, and
that the Samians were now shut up with a close leaguer on every side,
Pericles, taking with him sixty galleys, sailed out into the main sea, with

the intention, as most authors give the account, to meet a squadron of Phœnician ships that were coming for the Samians' relief, and to fight them at as great distance as could be from the island; but, as Stesimbrotus says, with a design of putting over to Cyprus, which does not seem to be probable. But whichever of the two was his intention, it seems to have been a miscalculation. For on his departure, Melissus, the son of Ithagenes, a philosopher, being at that time the general in Samos, despising either the small number of the ships that were left or the inexperience of the commanders, prevailed with the citizens to attack the Athenians. And the Samians having won the battle, and taken several of the men prisoners, and disabled several of the ships, were masters of the sea, and brought into port all necessaries they wanted for the war, which they had not before. Aristotle says, too, that Pericles himself had been once before this worsted by this Melissus in a sea fight.

The Samians, that they might requite an affront which had before been put upon them, branded the Athenians, whom they took prisoners, in their foreheads, with the figure of an owl. For so the Athenians had marked them before with a Samæna, which is a sort of ship, low and flat in the prow, so as to look snub-nosed, but wide and large and well-spread in the hold, by which it both carries a large cargo and sails well. And it was so called, because the first of that kind was seen at Samos, having been built by order of Polycrates the tyrant. These brands upon the Samians' foreheads, they say, are the allusion in the passage of Aristophanes, where he says—

"For, oh, the Samians are a lettered people."

Pericles, as soon as news was brought him of the disaster that had befallen his army, made all the haste he could to come in to their relief, and having defeated Melissus, who bore up against him, and put the enemy to flight, he immediately proceeded to hem them in with a wall, resolving to master them and take the town, rather with some cost and time than with the wounds and hazards of his citizens. But as it was a hard matter to keep back the Athenians, who were vexed at the delay, and were eagerly bent to fight, he divided the whole multitude into eight parts, and arranged by lot that that part which had the white bean should have leave to feast and take their ease, while the other seven were fighting. And this is the reason, they say, that people, when at any time they have been merry, and enjoyed themselves, call it white day, in allusion to this white bean.

Ephorus the historian tells us besides, that Pericles made use of engines of battery in this siege, being much taken with the curiousness of the invention, with the aid and presence of Artemon himself, the engineer, who, being lame, used to be carried about in a litter, where the works required his attendance, and for that reason was called Periphoretus.[1] But Heraclides Ponticus disproves this out of Anacreon's poems, where mention is made of this Artemon Periphoretus several ages before the Samian war, or any of these occurrences. And he says that Artemon, being a man who loved his ease, and had a great apprehension of danger, for the most part kept close within doors, having two of his servants to hold a brazen shield over his head, that nothing might fall upon him from above; and if he were at any time forced upon necessity to go abroad, that he was carried about in a little hanging bed, close to the very ground, and that for this reason he was called Periphoretus.

In the ninth month, the Samians surrendering themselves and delivering up the town, Pericles pulled down their walls, and seized their shipping, and set a fine of a large sum of money upon them, part of which they paid down at once, and they agreed to bring in the rest by a certain time, and gave hostages for security. Duris the Samian makes a tragical drama out of these events, charging the Athenians and Pericles with a great deal of cruelty, which neither Thucydides, nor Ephorus, nor Aristotle have given any relation of, and probably with little regard to truth; how, for example, he brought the captains and soldiers of the galleys into the marketplace at Miletus, and there having bound them fast to boards for ten days, then, when they were already all but half dead, gave order to have them killed by beating out their brains with clubs, and their dead bodies to be flung out into the open streets and fields, unburied. Duris, however, who, even where he has no private feeling concerned, is not wont to keep his narrative within the limits of truth, is the more likely upon this occasion to have exaggerated the calamities which befell his country, to create odium against the Athenians. Pericles, however, after the reduction of Samos, returning back to Athens, took care that those who died in the war should be honorably buried, and made a funeral harangue, as the custom is, in their commendation at their graves, for which he gained great admiration. As he came down from the stage on which he spoke, the rest of the women came and complimented him, taking him by the hand, and crowning him with garlands and ribbons, like a victorious athlete in the games; but Elpinice, coming near to him, said, "These are brave deeds, Pericles, that you have done, and such as deserve our chaplets; who have lost us many a worthy citizen, not in a war with Phœnicians or Medes, like my brother Cimon, but for the overthrow of an allied and kindred city." As Elpinice spoke these words, he, smiling quietly, as it is said, returned her answer with this verse:—

"Old women should not seek to be perfumed."

---

[1] ["Carried around."]

Ion says of him that, upon this exploit of his, conquering the Samians, he indulged very high and proud thoughts of himself: whereas Agamemnon was ten years taking a barbarous city, he had in nine months' time vanquished and taken the greatest and most powerful of the Ionians. And indeed it was not without reason that he assumed this glory to himself, for, in real truth, there was much uncertainty and great hazard in this great war, if so be, as Thucydides tells us, the Samian state were within a very little of wresting the whole power and dominion of the sea out of the Athenians' hands.

After this was over, the Peloponnesian war beginning to break out in full tide, he advised the people to send help to the Corcyrsæans, who were attacked by the Corinthians, and to secure to themselves an island possessed of great naval resources, since the Peloponnesians were already all but in actual hostilities against them. The people readily consenting to the motion, and voting an aid and succor for them, he dispatched Lacedæmonius, Cimon's son, having only ten ships with him, as it were out of a design to affront him; for there was a great kindness and friendship betwixt Cimon's family and the Lacedæmonians; so, in order that Lacedæmonius might lie the more open to a charge, or suspicion at least, of favoring the Lacedæmonians and playing false, if he performed no considerable exploit in this service, he allowed him a small number of ships, and sent him out against his will; and indeed he made it somewhat his business to hinder Cimon's sons from rising in the state, professing that by their very names they were not to be looked upon as native and true Athenians, but foreigners and strangers, one being called Lacedæmonius, another Thessalus, and the third Eleus; and they were all three of them, it was thought, born of an Arcadian woman. Being, however, ill spoken of on account of these ten galleys, as having afforded but a small supply to the people that were in need, and yet given a great advantage to those who might complain of the act of intervention, Pericles sent out a larger force afterwards to Corcyra, which arrived after the fight was over. And when now the Corinthians, angry and indignant with the Athenians, accused them publicly at Lacedæmon, the Megarians joined with them, complaining that they were, contrary to common right and the articles of peace sworn to among the Greeks, kept out and driven away from every market and from all ports under the control of the Athenians. The Æginetans, also, professing to be ill-used and treated with violence, made supplications in private to the Lacedæmonians for redress, though not daring openly to call the Athenians in question. In the meantime, also, the city Potidæa, under the dominion of the Athenians, but a colony formerly of the Corinthians, had revolted, and was beset with a formal siege, and was a further occasion of precipitating the war.

Yet notwithstanding all this, there being embassies sent to Athens, and

Archidamus, the king of the Lacedæmonians, endeavoring to bring the greater part of the complaints and matters in dispute to a fair determination, and to pacify and allay the hearts of the allies, it is very likely that the war would not upon any other grounds of quarrel have fallen upon the Athenians, could they have been prevailed with to repeal the ordinance against the Megarians, and to be reconciled to them. Upon which account, since Pericles was the man who mainly opposed it, and stirred up the people's passions to persist in their contention with the Megarians, he was regarded as the sole cause of the war.

They say, moreover, that ambassadors went, by order, from Lacedæmon to Athens about this very business, and that when Pericles was urging a certain law which made it illegal to take down or withdraw the tablet of the decree, one of the ambassadors, Polyalces by name, said, "Well, do not take it down then, but *turn* it; there is no law, I suppose, which forbids that;" which, though prettily said, did not move Pericles from his resolution. There may have been, in all likelihood, something of a secret grudge and private animosity which he had against the Megarians. Yet, upon a public and open charge against them, that they had appropriated part of the sacred land on the frontier, he proposed a decree that a herald should be sent to them, and the same also to the Lacedæmonians, with an accusation of the Megarians; an order which certainly shows equitable and friendly proceeding enough. And after that the herald who was sent, by name Anthemocritus, died, and it was believed that the Megarians had contrived his death, then Charinus proposed a decree against them, that there should be an irreconcilable and implacable enmity thenceforward betwixt the two commonwealths; and that if any one of the Megarians should but set his foot in Attica, he should be put to death; and that the commanders, when they take the usual oath, should, over and above that, swear that they will twice every year make an inroad into the Megarian country; and that Anthemocritus should be buried near the Thracian Gates, which are now called the Dipylon, or Double Gate.

On the other hand, the Megarians, utterly denying and disowning the murder of Anthemocritus, throw the whole matter upon Aspasia and Pericles, availing themselves of the famous verses in the Acharnians—

> "To Megara some of our madcaps ran,
> And stole Simætha thence, their courtesan.
> Which exploit the Megarians to outdo,
> Came to Aspasia's house, and took off two."

The true occasion of the quarrel is not so easy to find out. But of inducing the refusal to annul the decree, all alike charge Pericles. Some say he met the request with a positive refusal, out of high spirit and a view of the state's best interest, accounting that the demand made in those embassies was designed for a trial of their compliance, and that a concession would be taken for a confession of weakness, as if they durst not do otherwise; while other some there are who say that it was rather out of arrogance and a willful spirit of contention, to show his own strength, that he took occasion to slight the Lacedæmonians. The worst motive of all, which is confirmed by most witnesses, is to the following effect: Phidias the Molder had, as has before been said, undertaken to make the statue of Minerva. Now he, being admitted to friendship with Pericles, and a great favorite of his, had many enemies upon this account, who envied and maligned him; who also, to make trial in a case of his, what kind of judges the commons would prove, should there be occasion to bring Pericles himself before them, having tampered with Menon, one who had been a workman with Phidias, stationed him in the marketplace, with a petition desiring public security upon his discovery and impeachment of Phidias. The people admitting the man to tell his story, and the prosecution proceeding in the assembly, there was nothing of theft or cheat proved against him; for Phidias, from the very first beginning, by the advice of Pericles, had so wrought and wrapt the gold that was used in the work about the statue, that they might take it all off and make out the just weight of it, which Pericles at that time bade the accusers do. But the reputation of his works was what brought envy upon Phidias, especially that where he represents the fight of the Amazons upon the goddess's shield, he had introduced a likeness of himself as a bald old man holding up a great stone with both hands, and had put in a very fine representation of Pericles fighting with an Amazon. And the position of the hand, which holds out the spear in front of the face, was ingeniously contrived to conceal in some degree the likeness, which, meantime, showed itself on either side.

Phidias then was carried away to prison, and there died of a disease; but, as some say, of poison, administered by the enemies of Pericles, to raise a slander, or a suspicion at least, as though he had procured it. The informer Menon, upon Glycon's proposal, the people made free from payment of taxes and customs, and ordered the generals to take care that nobody should do him any hurt. About the same time, Aspasia was indicted of impiety, upon the complaint of Hermippus the comedian, who also laid further to her charge that she received into her house freeborn women for the uses of Pericles. And Diopithes proposed a decree, that public accusation should be laid against persons who neglected religion, or taught new doctrines about things above, directing suspicion, by means of Anaxagoras, against Pericles himself. The people receiving and admitting these accusations and complaints, at length, by this means, they came to enact a decree, at the motion of Dracontides, that Pericles should bring in the accounts of the moneys he had expended, and lodge them with the Prytanes; and that the judges, carrying their suffrage from the altar in the Acropolis, should examine and determine the business in the city. This last clause Hagnon took out of the decree, and moved that the causes should be tried before fifteen hundred jurors, whether they should be styled prosecutions for robbery, or bribery, or any kind of malversation. Aspasia, Pericles begged off, shedding, as Æschines says, many tears at the trial, and personally entreating the jurors. But fearing how it might go with Anaxagoras, he sent him out of the city. And finding that in Phidias's case he had miscarried with the people, being afraid of impeachment, he kindled the war, which hitherto had lingered and smothered, and blew it up into a flame; hoping, by that means, to disperse and scatter these complaints and charges, and to allay their jealousy; the city usually throwing herself upon him alone, and trusting to his sole conduct, upon the urgency of great affairs and public dangers, by reason of his authority and the sway he bore.

These are given out to have been the reasons which induced Pericles not to suffer the people of Athens to yield to the proposals of the Lacedæmonians; but their truth is uncertain.

The Lacedæmonians, for their part, feeling sure that if they could once remove him, they might be at what terms they pleased with the Athenians, sent them word that they should expel the "Pollution" with which Pericles on the mother's side was tainted, as Thucydides tells us. But the issue proved quite contrary to what those who sent the message expected; instead of bringing Pericles under suspicion and reproach, they raised him into yet greater credit and esteem with the citizens, as a man whom their enemies most hated and feared. In the same way, also, before Archidamus, who was at the head of the Peloponnesians, made his invasion into Attica, he told the Athenians beforehand, that if Archidamus, while he laid waste the rest of the country, should forbear and spare his estate, either on the ground of friendship or right of hospitality that was betwixt them, or on purpose to give his enemies an occasion of traducing him; that then he did freely bestow upon the state all his land and the buildings upon it for the public use. The Lacedæmonians, therefore, and their allies, with a great army, invaded the Athenian territories, under the conduct of King Archidamus, and laying waste the country, marched on as far as Acharnæ, and there pitched their camp, presuming that the Athenians would never endure that, but would come out and fight them for their country's and their honor's sake. But Pericles looked upon it as dangerous to engage in battle, to the risk of the city itself, against sixty thousand men-at-arms of Peloponnesians and Bœotians; for so many they were in number that made the inroad at first; and he endeavored to appease those who were desirous to fight, and were grieved and discontented to see how things went, and gave them good words, saying, that "trees, when they are lopped and cut, grow up again in a short time, but men, being once lost, cannot easily be recovered." He did not convene the people into an assembly, for fear lest they should force him to act against his judgment; but, like a skillful steersman or pilot of a ship, who, when a sudden squall comes on, out at sea, makes all his arrangements, sees that all is tight and fast, and then follows the dictates of his skill, and minds the business of the ship, taking no notice of the tears and entreaties of the seasick and fearful passengers, so he, having shut up the city gates, and placed guards at all posts for security, followed his own reason and judgment, little regarding those that cried out against him and were angry at his management, although there were a great many of his friends that urged him with requests, and many of his enemies threatened and accused him for doing as he did, and many made songs and lampoons upon him, which were sung about the town to his disgrace, reproaching him with the cowardly exercise of his office of general, and the tame abandonment of everything to the enemy's hands.

Cleon, also, already was among his assailants, making use of the feeling against him as a step to the leadership of the people, as appears in the anapaestic verses of Hermippus—

> "Satyr-king, instead of swords,
>   Will you always handle words?
>   Very brave indeed we find them,
>   But a Teles lurks behind them.

> "Yet to gnash your teeth you're seen,
>   When the little dagger keen,
>   Whetted every day anew,
>   Of sharp Cleon touches you."

Pericles, however, was not at all moved by any attacks, but took all patiently, and submitted in silence to the disgrace they threw upon him and the ill-will they bore him; and, sending out a fleet of a hundred galleys to Peloponnesus, he did not go along with it in person, but stayed behind, that he might watch at home and keep the city under his own control, till the Peloponnesians broke up their camp and were gone. Yet to soothe the common people, jaded and distressed with the war, he relieved them with distributions of public moneys, and ordained new divisions of subject land. For having turned out all the people of Ægina, he parted the island among the Athenians, according to lot. Some comfort, also, and ease in their miseries, they might receive from what their enemies endured. For the fleet, sailing round the Peloponnese, ravaged a great deal of the country, and pillaged and plundered the towns and smaller cities; and by land he himself entered with an army the Megarian country, and made havoc of it all. Whence it is clear that the Peloponnesians, though they did the Athenians much mischief by land, yet suffering as much themselves from them by sea, would not have protracted the war to such a length, but would quickly have given it over, as Pericles at first foretold they would, had not some divine power crossed human purposes.

In the first place, the pestilential disease, or plague, seized upon the city, and ate up all the flower and prime of their youth and strength. Upon occasion of which, the people, distempered and afflicted in their souls, as well as in their bodies, were utterly enraged like madmen against Pericles, and, like patients grown delirious, sought to lay violent hands on their physician, or, as it were, their father. They had been possessed, by his enemies, with the belief that the occasion of the plague was the crowding of the country people together into the town, forced as they were now, in the heat of the summer-weather, to dwell many of them together even as they could, in small tenements and stifling hovels, and to be tied to a lazy course of life within doors, whereas before they lived in a pure, open, and free air. The cause and author of all this, said they, is he who on account of the war has poured a multitude of people from the country in upon us within the walls, and uses all these men that he has here upon no employ or service, but keeps them pent up like cattle, to be overrun with infection from one another, affording them neither shift of quarters nor any refreshment.

With the design to remedy these evils, and do the enemy some inconvenience, Pericles got a hundred and fifty galleys ready, and having embarked many tried soldiers, both foot and horse, was about to sail out, giving great hope to his citizens, and no less alarm to his enemies, upon the sight of so great a force. And now the vessels having their complement of men, and Pericles being gone aboard his own galley, it happened that the sun was eclipsed, and it grew dark on a sudden, to the affright of all, for this was looked upon as extremely ominous. Pericles, therefore, perceiving the steersman seized with fear and at a loss what to do, took his cloak and held it up before the man's face, and, screening him with it so that he could not see, asked him whether he imagined there was any great hurt, or the sign of any great hurt in this, and he answering No, "Why," said he, "and what does that differ from this, only that what has caused that darkness there, is something greater than a cloak?" This is a story which philosophers tell their scholars. Pericles, however, after putting out to sea, seems not to have done any other exploit befitting such preparations, and when he had laid siege to the holy city Epidaurus, which gave him some hope of surrender, miscarried in his design by reason of the sickness. For it not only seized upon the Athenians, but upon all others, too, that held any sort of communication with the army. Finding after this the Athenians ill-affected and highly displeased with

him, he tried and endeavored what he could to appease and reencourage
them. But he could not pacify or allay their anger, nor persuade or prevail with them any way, till they freely passed their votes upon him, resumed their power, took away his command from him, and fined him in
a sum of money; which, by their account that say least, was fifteen talents, while they who reckon most name fifty. The name prefixed to the
accusation was Cleon, as Idomeneus tells us; Simmias, according to
Theophrastus; and Heraclides Ponticus gives it as Lacratidas.

After this, public troubles were soon to leave him unmolested; the people, so to say, discharged their passion in their stroke, and lost their stings
in the wound. But his domestic concerns were in an unhappy condition,
many of his friends and acquaintance having died in the plague time, and
those of his family having long since been in disorder and in a kind of
mutiny against him. For the eldest of his lawfully begotten sons,
Xanthippus by name, being naturally prodigal, and marrying a young and
expensive wife, the daughter of Tisander, son of Epilycus, was highly offended at his father's economy in making him but a scanty allowance, by
little and little at a time. He sent, therefore, to a friend one day and borrowed some money of him in his father Pericles's name, pretending it was
by his order. The man coming afterward to demand the debt, Pericles was
so far from yielding to pay it, that he entered an action against him. Upon
which the young man, Xanthippus, thought himself so ill used and disobliged that he openly reviled his father; telling first, by way of ridicule,
stories about his conversations at home, and the discourses he had with
the sophists and scholars that came to his house. As for instance, how one
who was a practicer of the five games of skill, having with a dart or
javelin unawares against his will struck and killed Epitimus the
Pharsalian, his father spent a whole day with Protagoras in a serious dispute, whether the javelin, or the man that threw it, or the masters of the
games who appointed these sports, were, according to the strictest and
best reason, to be accounted the cause of this mischance. Besides this,
Stesimbrotus tells us that it was Xanthippus who spread abroad among
the people the infamous story concerning his own wife; and in general
that this difference of the young man's with his father, and the breach betwixt them, continued never to be healed or made up till his death. For
Xanthippus died in the plague time of the sickness. At which time
Pericles also lost his sister, and the greatest part of his relations and
friends, and those who had been most useful and serviceable to him in
managing the affairs of state. However, he did not shrink or give in upon
these occasions, nor betray or lower his high spirit and the greatness of
his mind under all his misfortunes; he was not even so much as seen to
weep or to mourn, or even attend the burial of any of his friends or relations, till at last he lost his only remaining legitimate son. Subdued by

this blow, and yet striving still, as far as he could, to maintain his principle, and to preserve and keep up the greatness of his soul, when he came, however, to perform the ceremony of putting a garland of flowers upon the head of the corpse, he was vanquished by his passion at the sight, so that he burst into exclamations, and shed copious tears, having never done any such thing in all his life before.

The city having made trial of other generals for the conduct of war, and orators for business of state, when they found there was no one who was of weight enough for such a charge, or of authority sufficient to be trusted with so great a command, regretted the loss of him, and invited him again to address and advise them, and to reassume the office of general. He, however, lay at home in dejection and mourning; but was persuaded by Alcibiades and others of his friends to come abroad and show himself to the people; who having, upon his appearance, made their acknowledgments, and apologized for their untowardly treatment of him, he undertook the public affairs once more; and, being chosen general, requested that the statute concerning base-born children, which he himself had formerly caused to be made, might be suspended; that so the name and race of his family might not, for absolute want of a lawful heir to succeed, be wholly lost and extinguished. The case of the statute was thus: Pericles, when long ago at the height of his power in the state, having then, as has been said, children lawfully begotten, proposed a law that those only should be reputed true citizens of Athens who were born of such parents as were both Athenians. After this, the king of Egypt having sent to the people, by way of present, forty thousand bushels of wheat, which were to be shared out among the citizens, a great many actions and suits about legitimacy occurred, by virtue of that edict; cases which, till that time, had not been known nor taken notice of; and several persons suffered by false accusations. There were little less than five thousand who were convicted and sold for slaves; those who, enduring the test, remained in the government and passed muster for true Athenians were found upon the poll to be fourteen thousand and forty persons in number.

It looked strange that a law, which had been carried so far against so many people, should be canceled again by the same man that made it; yet the present calamity and distress which Pericles labored under in his family broke through all objections, and prevailed with the Athenians to pity him, as one whose losses and misfortunes had sufficiently punished his former arrogance and haughtiness. His sufferings deserved, they thought, their pity, and even indignation, and his request was such as became a man to ask and men to grant; they gave him permission to enroll his son in the register of his fraternity, giving him his own name. This son afterward, after having defeated the Peloponnesians at Arginusæ, was, with his fellow-generals, put to death by the people.

About the time when his son was enrolled, it should seem, the plague seized Pericles, not with sharp and violent fits, as it did others that had it, but with a dull and lingering distemper, attended with various changes and alterations, leisurely, by little and little, wasting the strength of his body, and undermining the noble faculties of his soul. So that Theophrastus, in his Morals, when discussing whether men's characters change with their circumstances, and their moral habits, disturbed by the ailings of their bodies, start aside from the rules of virtue, has left it upon record, that Pericles, when he was sick, showed one of his friends that came to visit him an amulet or charm that the women had hung about his neck; as much as to say, that he was very sick indeed when he would admit of such a foolery as that was.

When he was now near his end, the best of the citizens and those of his friends who were left alive, sitting about him, were speaking of the greatness of his merit, and his power, and reckoning up his famous actions and the number of his victories; for there were no less than nine trophies, which, as their chief commander and conqueror of their enemies, he had set up for the honor of the city. They talked thus together among themselves, as though he were unable to understand or mind what they said, but had now lost his consciousness. He had listened, however, all the while, and attended to all, and, speaking out among them, said that he wondered they should commend and take notice of things which were as much owing to fortune as to anything else, and had happened to many other commanders, and, at the same time, should not speak or make mention of that which was the most excellent and greatest thing of all. "For," said he, "no Athenian, through my means, ever wore mourning."

He was indeed a character deserving our high admiration, not only for his equitable and mild temper, which all along in the many affairs of his life, and the great animosities which he incurred, he constantly maintained; but also for the high spirit and feeling which made him regard it the noblest of all his honors that, in the exercise of such immense power, he never had gratified his envy or his passion, nor ever had treated any enemy as irreconcilably opposed to him. And to me it appears that this one thing gives that otherwise childish and arrogant title a fitting and becoming significance; so dispassionate a temper, a life so pure and unblemished, in the height of power and place, might well be called Olympian, in accordance with our conceptions of the divine beings, to whom, as the natural authors of all good and of nothing evil, we ascribe the rule and government of the world. Not as the poets represent, who, while confounding us with their ignorant fancies, are themselves confuted by their own poems and fictions, and call the place, indeed, where they say the gods make their abode, a secure and quiet seat, free from all hazards and commotions, untroubled with winds or with clouds, and equally through all time illumined with a soft serenity and a pure light as though such were a home most agreeable for a blessed and immortal nature; and yet, in the meanwhile, affirm that the gods themselves are full of trouble and enmity and anger and other passions, which no way become or belong to even men that have any understanding. But this will, perhaps, seem a subject fitter for some other consideration, and that ought to be treated of in some other place.

The course of public affairs after his death produced a quick and speedy sense of the loss of Pericles. Those who, while he lived, resented his great authority, as that which eclipsed themselves, presently after his quitting the stage, making trial of other orators and demagogues, readily acknowledged that there never had been in nature such a disposition as his was, more moderate and reasonable in the height of that state he took upon him, or more grave and impressive in the mildness which he used. And that invidious arbitrary power, to which formerly they gave the name of monarchy and tyranny, did then appear to have been the chief bulwark of public safety; so great a corruption and such a flood of mischief and vice followed, which he, by keeping weak and low, had withheld from notice, and had prevented from attaining incurable height through a licentious impunity.

ALCIBIADES

ALCIBIADES, as it is supposed, was anciently descended from Eurysaces, the son of Ajax, by his father's side; and by his mother's side from Alcmæon. Dinomache, his mother, was the daughter of Megacles. His father, Clinias, having fitted out a galley at his own expense, gained great honor in the sea fight at Artemisium, and was afterwards slain in the battle of Coronea, fighting against the Bœotians. Pericles and Ariphron, the sons of Xanthippus, nearly related to him, became the guardians of Alcibiades. It has been said not untruly that the friendship which Socrates felt for him has much contributed to his fame; and certain it is, that, though we have no account from any writer concerning the mother of Nicias or Demosthenes, of Lamachus or Phormion, of Thrasybulus or Theramenes, notwithstanding these were all illustrious men of the same period, yet we know even the nurse of Alcibiades, that her country was Lacedæmon, and her name Amycla; and that Zopyrus was his teacher and attendant; the one being recorded by Antisthenes, and the other by Plato.

It is not, perhaps, material to say anything of the beauty of Alcibiades, only that it bloomed with him in all the ages of his life, in his infancy, in his youth, and in his manhood; and, in the peculiar character becoming to each of these periods, gave him, in every one of them, a grace and a charm. What Euripides says, that—

"Of all fair things the autumn, too, is fair,"

is by no means universally true. But it happened so with Alcibiades, amongst few others, by reason of his happy constitution and natural vigor of body. It is said that his lisping, when he spoke, became him well, and gave a grace and persuasiveness to his rapid speech. Aristophanes takes notice of it in the verses in which he jests at Theorus; "How like a *colax* he is," says Alcibiades, meaning a *corax*; on which it is remarked,

"How very happily he lisped the truth."

Archippus also alludes to it in a passage where he ridicules the son of Alcibiades:—

> "That people may believe him like his father,
> He walks like one dissolved in luxury,
> Lets his robe trail behind him on the ground,
> Carelessly leans his head, and in his talk
> Affects to lisp."

His conduct displayed many great inconsistencies and variations, not unnaturally, in accordance with the many and wonderful vicissitudes of his fortunes; but among the many strong passions of his real character, the one most prevailing of all was his ambition and desire of superiority, which appears in several anecdotes told of his sayings whilst he was a child. Once being hard pressed in wrestling, and fearing to be thrown, he got the hand of his antagonist to his mouth, and bit it with all his force; and when the other loosed his hold presently, and said, "You bite, Alcibiades, like a woman." "No," replied he, "like a lion." Another time as he played at dice in the street, being then but a child, a loaded cart came that way, when it was his turn to throw; at first he called to the driver to stop, because he was to throw in the way over which the cart was to pass; but the man giving him no attention and driving on, when the rest of the boys divided and gave way, Alcibiades threw himself on his face before the cart, and, stretching himself out, bade the carter pass on now if he would; which so startled the man, that he put back his horses, while all that saw it were terrified, and, crying out, ran to assist Alcibiades. When he began to study, he obeyed all his other masters fairly well, but refused to learn upon the flute, as a sordid thing, and not becoming a free citizen; saying that to play on the lute or the harp does not in any way disfigure a man's body or face, but one is hardly to be known by the most intimate friends when playing on the flute. Besides, one who plays on the harp may speak or sing at the same time; but the use of the flute stops the mouth, intercepts the voice, and prevents all articulation. "Therefore," said he, "let the Theban youths pipe, who do not know how to speak, but we Athenians, as our ancestors have told us, have Minerva for our patroness, and Apollo for our protector, one of whom threw away the flute, and the other stripped the Flute-player of his skin." Thus, between raillery and good earnest, Alcibiades kept not only himself but others from learning, as it presently became the talk of the young boys, how Alcibiades despised playing on the flute, and ridiculed those who studied it. In consequence of which, it ceased to be reckoned amongst the liberal accomplishments, and became generally neglected.

It is stated in the invective which Antiphon wrote against Alcibiades, that once, when he was a boy, he ran away to the house of Democrates, one of those who made a favorite of him, and that Ariphon had determined to cause proclamation to be made for him, had not Pericles diverted him from it, by saying, that if he were dead, the proclaiming of him could only cause it to be discovered one day sooner, and if he were safe, it would be a reproach to him as long as he lived. Antiphon also says, that he killed one of his own servants with the blow of a staff in Sibyrtius's wrestling ground. But it is unreasonable to give credit to all that is objected by an enemy, who makes open profession of his design to defame him.

It was manifest that the many well-born persons who were continually seeking his company, and making their court to him, were attracted and captivated by his brilliant and extraordinary beauty only. But the affection which Socrates entertained for him is a great evidence of the natural noble qualities and good disposition of the boy, which Socrates, indeed, detected both in and under his personal beauty; and, fearing that his wealth and station, and the great number both of strangers and Athenians who flattered and caressed him, might at last corrupt him, resolved, if possible, to interpose, and preserve so hopeful a plant from perishing in the flower, before its fruit came to perfection. For never did fortune surround and enclose a man with so many of those things which we vulgarly call goods, or so protect him from every weapon of philosophy, and fence him from every access of free and searching words, as she did Alcibiades; who, from the beginning, was exposed to the flatteries of those who sought merely his gratification, such as might well unnerve him, and indispose him to listen to any real adviser or instructor. Yet such was the happiness of his genius, that he discerned Socrates from the rest, and admitted him, whilst he drove away the wealthy and the noble who made court to him. And, in a little time, they grew intimate, and Alcibiades, listening now to language entirely free from every thought of unmanly fondness and silly displays of affection, finding himself with one who sought to lay open to him the deficiencies of his mind, and repress his vain and foolish arrogance—

"Dropped like the craven cock his conquered wing."

He esteemed these endeavors of Socrates as most truly a means which the gods made use of for the care and preservation of youth, and began to think meanly of himself and to admire him; to be pleased with his kindness, and to stand in awe of his virtue; and, unawares to himself, there became formed in his mind that reflex image and reciprocation of Love, or Anteros, that Plato talks of. It was a matter of general wonder, when people saw him joining Socrates in his meals and his exercises, living with him in the same tent, whilst he was reserved and rough to all others who made their addresses to him, and acted, indeed, with great insolence to some of them. As in particular to Anytus, the son of Anthemion, one who was very fond of him, and invited him to an entertainment which he had prepared for some strangers. Alcibiades refused the invitation; but, having drunk to excess at his own house with some of his companions, went thither with them to play some frolic; and, standing at the door of the room where the guests were enjoying themselves, and seeing the tables covered with gold and silver cups, he commanded his servants to take away the one-half of them, and carry them to his own house; and then, disdaining so much as to enter into the room himself, as soon as he had done this, went away. The company was indignant, and exclaimed at his rude and insulting conduct; Anytus, however, said, on the contrary, he had shown great consideration and tenderness in taking only a part when he might have taken all.

He behaved in the same manner to all others who courted him except only one stranger, who, as the story is told, having but a small estate, sold it all for about a hundred staters, which he presented to Alcibiades, and besought him to accept. Alcibiades, smiling and well pleased at the thing, invited him to supper, and, after a very kind entertainment, gave him his gold again, requiring him, moreover, not to fail to be present the next day, when the public revenue was offered to farm, and to outbid all others. The man would have excused himself, because the contract was so large, and would cost many talents; but Alcibiades, who had at that time a private pique against the existing farmers of the revenue, threatened to have him beaten if he refused. The next morning, the stranger, coming to the marketplace, offered a talent more than the existing rate; upon which the farmers, enraged and consulting together, called upon him to name his sureties, concluding that he could find none. The poor man, being startled at the proposal, began to retire; but Alcibiades, standing at a distance, cried out to the magistrates, "Set my name down, he is a friend of mine; I will be security for him." When the other bidders heard this, they perceived that all their contrivance was defeated; for their way was, with the profits of the second year to pay the rent for the year preceding; so that, not seeing any other way to extricate themselves out of the difficulty, they began to entreat the stranger, and offered him a sum of money. Alcibiades would not suffer him to accept of less than a talent; but when that was paid down, he commanded him to relinquish the bargain, having by this device relieved his necessity.

Though Socrates had many and powerful rivals, yet the natural good qualities of Alcibiades gave his affection the mastery. His words overcame him so much, as to draw tears from his eyes, and to disturb his very soul. Yet sometimes he would abandon himself to flatterers, when they proposed to him varieties of pleasure, and would desert Socrates; who, then, would pursue him, as if he had been a fugitive slave. He despised everyone else, and had no reverence or awe for any but him. Cleanthes the philosopher, speaking of one to whom he was attached, says his only hold

on him was by his ears, while his rivals had all the others offered them;
and there is no question that Alcibiades was very easily caught by pleasures; and the expression used by Thucydides about the excesses of his
habitual course of living gives occasion to believe so. But those who endeavored to corrupt Alcibiades took advantage chiefly of his vanity and
ambition, and thrust him on unseasonably to undertake great enterprises,
persuading him, that as soon as he began to concern himself in public affairs, he would not only obscure the rest of the generals and statesmen,
but outdo the authority and the reputation which Pericles himself had
gained in Greece. But in the same manner as iron which is softened by
the fire grows hard with the cold, and all its parts are closed again; so, as
often as Socrates observed Alcibiades to be misled by luxury or pride, he
reduced and corrected him by his addresses, and made him humble and
modest, by showing him in how many things he was deficient, and how
very far from perfection in virtue.

When he was past his childhood, he went once to a grammar-school,
and asked the master for one of Homer's books; and he making answer
that he had nothing of Homer's, Alcibiades gave him a blow with his fist,
and went away. Another schoolmaster telling him that he had Homer
corrected by himself; "How," said Alcibiades, "and do you employ your
time in teaching children to read? You, who are able to amend Homer,
may well undertake to instruct men." Being once desirous to speak with
Pericles, he went to his house and was told there that he was not at
leisure, but busied in considering how to give up his accounts to the
Athenians; Alcibiades, as he went away, said, it "were better for him to
consider how he might avoid giving up his accounts at all."

Whilst he was very young, he was a soldier in the expedition against
Potidæa, where Socrates lodged in the same tent with him, and stood
next to him in battle. Once there happened a sharp skirmish, in which
they both behaved with signal bravery; but Alcibiades receiving a wound,
Socrates threw himself before him to defend him, and beyond any question saved him and his arms from the enemy, and so in all justice might
have challenged the prize of valor. But the generals appearing eager to
adjudge the honor to Alcibiades, because of his rank, Socrates, who desired to increase his thirst after glory of a noble kind, was the first to give
evidence for him, and pressed them to crown him, and to decree to him
the complete suit of armor. Afterwards, in the battle of Delium, when the
Athenians were routed, and Socrates with a few others was retreating on
foot, Alcibiades, who was on horseback, observing it, would not pass on,
but stayed to shelter him from the danger, and brought him safe off,
though the enemy pressed hard upon them, and cut off many. But this
happened some time after.

He gave a box on the ear to Hipponicus, the father of Callias, whose birth and wealth made him a person of great influence and repute. And this he did unprovoked by any passion or quarrel between them, but only because, in a frolic, he had agreed with his companions to do it. People were justly offended at this insolence when it became known through the city; but early the next morning, Alcibiades went to his house and knocked at the door, and, being admitted to him, took off his outer garment, and, presenting his naked body, desired him to scourge and chastise him as he pleased. Upon this Hipponicus forgot all his resentment, and not only pardoned him, but soon after gave him his daughter Hipparete in marriage. Some say that it was not Hipponicus, but his son Callias, who gave Hipparete to Alcibiades, together with a portion of ten talents, and that after, when she had a child, Alcibiades forced him to give ten talents more, upon pretense that such was the agreement if she brought him any children. Afterwards, Callias, for fear of coming to his death by his means, declared, in a full assembly of the people, that if he should happen to die without children, the state should inherit his house and all his goods. Hipparete was a virtuous and dutiful wife, but, at last, growing impatient of the outrages done to her by her husband's continual entertaining of courtesans, as well strangers as Athenians, she departed from him and retired to her brother's house. Alcibiades seemed not at all concerned at this, and lived on still in the same luxury; but the law requiring that she should deliver to the archon in person, and not by proxy, the instrument by which she claimed a divorce, when, in obedience to the law, she presented herself before him to perform this, Alcibiades came in, caught her up, and carried her home through the marketplace, no one daring to oppose him nor to take her from him. She continued with him till her death, which happened not long after, when Alcibiades had gone to Ephesus. Nor is this violence to be thought so very enormous or unmanly. For the law, in making her who desires to be divorced appear in public, seems to design to give her husband an opportunity of treating with her, and of endeavoring to retain her.

Alcibiades had a dog which cost him seventy minas, and was a very large one, and very handsome. His tail, which was his principal ornament, he caused to be cut off, and his acquaintances exclaiming at him for it, and telling him that all Athens was sorry for the dog, and cried out upon him for this action, he laughed, and said, "Just what I wanted has happened, then. I wished the Athenians to talk about this, that they might not say something worse of me."

It is said that the first time he came into the assembly was upon occasion of a largess of money which he made to the people. This was not done by design, but as he passed along he heard a shout, and inquiring the cause, and having learned that there was a donative making to the people, he went in amongst them and gave money also. The multitude thereupon applauding him, and shouting, he was so transported at it, that he forgot a quail which he had under his robe, and the bird, being frighted with the noise, flew off; upon which the people made louder acclamations than before, and many of them started up to pursue the bird; and one Antiochus, a pilot, caught it and restored it to him, for which he was ever after a favorite with Alcibiades.

He had great advantages for entering public life; his noble birth, his riches, the personal courage he had shown in divers battles, and the multitude of his friends and dependents, threw open, so to say, folding doors for his admittance. But he did not consent to let his power with the people rest on anything, rather than on his own gift of eloquence. That he was a master in the art of speaking, the comic poets bear him witness; and the most eloquent of public speakers, in his oration against Midias, allows that Alcibiades, among other perfections, was a most accomplished orator. If, however, we give credit to Theophrastus, who of all philosophers was the most curious inquirer, and the greatest lover of history, we are to understand that Alcibiades had the highest capacity for inventing, for discerning what was the right thing to be said for any purpose, and on any occasion; but, aiming not only at saying what was required, but also at saying it well, in respect, that is, of words and phrases, when these did not readily occur, he would often pause in the middle of his discourse for want of the apt word, and would be silent and stop till he could recollect himself, and had considered what to say.

His expenses in horses kept for the public games, and in the number of his chariots, were matter of great observation; never did anyone but he, either private person or king, send seven chariots to the Olympic games. And to have carried away at once the first, the second, and the fourth prize, as Thucydides says, or the third, as Euripides relates it, outdoes far away every distinction that ever was known or thought of in that kind. Euripides celebrates his success in this manner:—

> "—But my song to you,
> Son of Clinias, is due.
> Victory is noble; how much more
> To do as never Greek before;
> To obtain in the great chariot race
> The first, the second, and third place;
> With easy step advanced to fame,
> To bid the herald three times claim
> The olive for one victor's name."

The emulation displayed by the deputations of various states in the presents which they made to him, rendered this success yet more illustrious. The Ephesians erected a tent for him, adorned magnificently; the city of

Chios furnished him with provender for his horses and with great numbers of beasts for sacrifice; and the Lesbians sent him wine and other provisions for the many great entertainments which he made. Yet in the midst of all this he escaped not without censure, occasioned either by the ill-nature of his enemies or by his own misconduct. For it is said, that one Diomedes, an Athenian, a worthy man and a friend to Alcibiades, passionately desiring to obtain the victory at the Olympic games, and having heard much of a chariot which belonged to the state at Argos, where he knew that Alcibiades had great power and many friends, prevailed with him to undertake to buy the chariot. Alcibiades did indeed buy it, but then claimed it for his own, leaving Diomedes to rage at him, and to call upon the gods and men to bear witness to the injustice. It would seem there was a suit at law commenced upon this occasion, and there is yet extant an oration concerning the chariot, written by Isocrates in defense of the son of Alcibiades. But the plaintiff in this action is named Tisias, and not Diomedes.

As soon as he began to intermeddle in the government, which was when he was very young, he quickly lessened the credit of all who aspired to the confidence of the people except Phæax, the son of Erasistratus, and Nicias, the son of Niceratus, who alone could contest it with him. Nicias was arrived at a mature age, and was esteemed their first general. Phæax was but a rising statesman like Alcibiades; he was descended from noble ancestors, but was his inferior, as in many other things, so, principally, in eloquence. He possessed rather the art of persuading in private conversation than of debate before the people, and was, as Eupolis said of him—

"The best of talkers, and of speakers worst."

There is extant an oration written by Phæax against Alcibiades, in which, amongst other things, it is said, that Alcibiades made daily use at his table of many gold and silver vessels, which belonged to the commonwealth, as if they had been his own.

There was a certain Hyperbolus, of the township of Perithœdæ, whom Thucydides also speaks of as a man of bad character, a general butt for the mockery of all the comic writers of the time, but quite unconcerned at the worst things they could say, and, being careless of glory, also insensible of shame; a temper which some people call boldness and courage, whereas it is indeed impudence and recklessness. He was liked by nobody, yet the people made frequent use of him, when they had a mind to disgrace or calumniate any persons in authority. At this time, the people, by his persuasions, were ready to proceed to pronounce the sentence of ten years' banishment, called ostracism. This they made use of to humiliate and drive out of the city such citizens as outdid the rest in credit and power, indulging not so much perhaps their apprehensions as their jealousies in this way. And when, at this time, there was no doubt but that the ostracism would fall upon one of those three, Alcibiades contrived to form a coalition of parties, and, communicating his project to Nicias, turned the sentence upon Hyperbolus himself. Others say, that it was not with Nicias, but Phæax, that he consulted, and by help of his party procured the banishment of Hyperbolus, when he suspected nothing less. For, before that time, no mean or obscure person had ever fallen under that punishment, so that Plato, the comic poet, speaking of Hyperbolus, might well say—

> "The man deserved the fate; deny't who can?
> Yes, but the fate did not deserve the man;
> Not for the like of him and his slave-brands
> Did Athens put the sherd into our hands."

But we have given elsewhere a fuller statement of what is known to us of the matter.

Alcibiades was not less disturbed at the distinctions which Nicias gained amongst the enemies of Athens than at the honors which the Athenians themselves paid to him. For though Alcibiades was the proper appointed person to receive all Lacedæmonians when they came to Athens, and had taken particular care of those that were made prisoners at Pylos, yet, after they had obtained the peace and restitution of the captives, by the procurement chiefly of Nicias, they paid him very special attentions. And it was commonly said in Greece, that the war was begun by Pericles, and that Nicias made an end of it, and the peace was generally called the peace of Nicias. Alcibiades was extremely annoyed at this, and, being full of envy, set himself to break the league. First, therefore, observing that the Argives, as well out of fear as hatred to the Lacedæmonians, sought for protection against them, he gave them a secret assurance of alliance with Athens. And communicating, as well in person as by letters, with the chief advisers of the people there, he encouraged them not to fear the Lacedæmonians, nor make concessions to them, but to wait a little, and keep their eyes on the Athenians, who, already, were all but sorry they had made peace, and would soon give it up. And, afterwards, when the Lacedæmonians had made a league with the Bœotians, and had not delivered up Panactum entire, as they ought to have done by the treaty, but only after first destroying it, which gave great offense to the people of Athens, Alcibiades laid hold of that opportunity to exasperate them more highly. He exclaimed fiercely against Nicias, and accused him of many things, which seemed probable enough: as that, when he was general, he made no attempt himself to capture their enemies that were shut up in the isle of Sphacteria, but, when they were afterwards made prisoners by others, he procured their release and sent them back to the Lacedæmonians, only to get favor with them; that he would not make use of his credit with them to prevent their entering into this confederacy with the Bœotians and Corinthians, and yet, on the other side, that he sought to stand in the way of those Greeks who were inclined to make an alliance and friendship with Athens, if the Lacedæmonians did not like it.

It happened, at the very time when Nicias was by these arts brought into disgrace with the people, that ambassadors arrived from Lacedæmon, who, at their first coming, said what seemed very satisfactory, declaring that they had full powers to arrange all matters in dispute upon fair and equal terms. The council received their propositions, and the people were to assemble on the morrow to give them audience. Alcibiades grew very apprehensive of this, and contrived to gain a secret conference with the ambassadors. When they were met, he said: "What is it you intend, you men of Sparta? Can you be ignorant that the council always act with moderation and respect towards ambassadors, but that the people are full of ambition and great designs? So that, if you let them know what full powers your commission gives you, they will urge and press you to unreasonable conditions. Quit, therefore, this indiscreet simplicity, if you expect to obtain equal terms from the Athenians, and would not have things extorted from you contrary to your inclinations, and begin to treat with the people upon some reasonable articles, not avowing yourselves plenipotentiaries; and I will be ready to assist you, out of good-will to the Lacedæmonians." When he had said thus, he gave them his oath for the performance of what he promised, and by this way drew them from Nicias to rely entirely upon himself, and left them full of admiration of the discernment and sagacity they had seen in him. The next day, when the people were assembled and the ambassadors introduced, Alcibiades, with great apparent courtesy, demanded of them, With what powers they were come? They made answer that they were not come as plenipotentiaries.

Instantly upon that, Alcibiades, with a loud voice, as though he had received and not done the wrong, began to call them dishonest prevaricators, and to urge that such men could not possibly come with a purpose to say or do anything that was sincere. The council was incensed, the people were in a rage, and Nicias, who knew nothing of the deceit and the imposture, was in the greatest confusion, equally surprised and ashamed at such a change in the men. So thus the Lacedæmonian ambassadors were utterly rejected, and Alcibiades was declared general, who presently united the Argives, the Eleans, and the people of Mantinea, into a confederacy with the Athenians.

No man commended the method by which Alcibiades effected all this, yet it was a great political feat thus to divide and shake almost all Peloponnesus, and to combine so many men in arms against the Lacedæmonians in one day before Mantinea; and, moreover, to remove the war and the danger so far from the frontier of the Athenians, that even success would profit the enemy but little, should they be conquerors, whereas, if they were defeated, Sparta itself was hardly safe.

After this battle at Mantinea, the select thousand of the army of the Argives attempted to overthrow the government of the people in Argos, and make themselves masters of the city; and the Lacedæmonians came to their aid and abolished the democracy. But the people took arms again, and gained the advantage, and Alcibiades came in to their aid and completed the victory, and persuaded them to build long walls, and by that means to join their city to the sea, and so to bring it wholly within the reach of the Athenian power. To this purpose, he procured them builders and masons from Athens, and displayed the greatest zeal for their service, and gained no less honor and power to himself than to the commonwealth of Athens. He also persuaded the people of Patræ to join their city to the sea, by building long walls; and when some one told them, by way of warning, that the Athenians would swallow them up at last, Alcibiades made answer, "Possibly it may be so, but it will be by little and little, and beginning at the feet, whereas the Lacedæmonians will begin at the head and devour you all at once." Nor did he neglect either to advise the Athenians to look to their interests by land, and often put the young men in mind of the oath which they had made at Agraulos, to the effect that they would account wheat and barley, and vines and olives, to be the limits of Attica; by which they were taught to claim a title to all land that was cultivated and productive.

But with all these words and deeds, and with all this sagacity and eloquence, he intermingled exorbitant luxury and wantonness, in his eating and drinking and dissolute living; wore long purple robes like a woman, which dragged after him as he went through the marketplace; caused the planks of his galley to be cut away, that so he might lie the softer, his bed not being placed on the boards, but hanging upon girths. His shield, again, which was richly gilded, had not the usual ensigns of the Athenians, but a Cupid, holding a thunderbolt in his hand, was painted upon it. The sight of all this made the people of good repute in the city feel disgust and abhorrence, and apprehension also, at his free living and his contempt of law, as things monstrous in themselves and indicating designs of usurpation. Aristophanes has well expressed the people's feeling towards him—

"They love, and hate, and cannot do without him."

And still more strongly, under a figurative expression,—

"Best rear no lion in your state, 'tis true;
But treat him like a lion if you do."

The truth is, his liberalities, his public shows, and other munificence to the people, which were such as nothing could exceed, the glory of his ancestors, the force of his eloquence, the grace of his person, his strength of body, joined with his great courage and knowledge in military affairs, prevailed upon the Athenians to endure patiently his excesses, to indulge many things to him, and, according to their habit, to give the softest names to his faults, attributing them to youth and good nature. As, for example, he kept Agatharcus, the painter, a prisoner till he had painted his whole house, but then dismissed him with a reward. He publicly struck Taureas, who exhibited certain shows in opposition to him and contended with him for the prize. He selected for himself one of the captive Melian women, and had a son by her, whom he took care to educate. This the Athenians styled great humanity; and yet he was the principal cause of the slaughter of all the inhabitants of the isle of Melos who were of age to bear arms, having spoken in favor of that decree. When Aristophon, the painter, had drawn Nemea sitting and holding Alcibiades in her arms, the multitude seemed pleased with the piece, and thronged to see it, but older people disliked and disrelished it, and looked on these things as enormities, and movements towards tyranny. So that it was not said amiss by Archestratus, that Greece could not support a second Alcibiades. Once, when Alcibiades succeeded well in an oration which he made, and the whole assembly attended upon him to do him honor, Timon the misanthrope did not pass slightly by him, nor avoid him, as he did others, but purposely met him, and, taking him by the hand, said, "Go on boldly, my son, and increase in credit with the people, for thou wilt one day bring them calamities enough." Some that were present laughed at the saying, and some reviled Timon; but there were others upon whom it made a deep impression; so various was the judgment which was made of him, and so irregular his own character.

The Athenians, even in the lifetime of Pericles, had already cast a longing eye upon Sicily; but did not attempt anything till after his death. Then, under pretense of aiding their confederates, they sent succors upon all occasions to those who were oppressed by the Syracusans, preparing the way for sending over a greater force. But Alcibiades was the person who inflamed this desire of theirs to the height, and prevailed with them no longer to proceed secretly, and by little and little, in their design, but to sail out with a great fleet, and undertake at once to make themselves masters of the island. He possessed the people with great hopes, and he himself entertained yet greater; and the conquest of Sicily, which was the utmost bound of their ambition, was but the mere outset of his expectation. Nicias endeavored to divert the people from the expedition, by representing to them that the taking of Syracuse would be a work of great difficulty; but Alcibiades dreamed of nothing less than the conquest of Carthage and Libya, and by the accession of these conceiving himself at once made master of Italy and of Peloponnesus, seemed to look upon Sicily as little more than a magazine for the war. The young men were soon elevated with these hopes, and listened gladly to those of riper years, who talked wonders of the countries they were going to; so that you might see great numbers sitting in the wrestling grounds and public places, drawing on the ground the figure of the island and the situation of Libya and Carthage. Socrates the philosopher and Meton the astrologer are said, however, never to have hoped for any good to the commonwealth from this war; the one, it is to be supposed, presaging what would ensue, by the intervention of his attendant Genius; and the other, either upon rational consideration of the project or by use of the art of divination, conceived fears for its issue, and, feigning madness, caught up a burning torch, and seemed as if he would have set his own house on fire. Others report, that he did not take upon him to act the madman, but secretly in the night set his house on fire, and the next morning besought the people, that for his comfort, after such a calamity, they would spare his son from the expedition. By which artifice, he deceived his fellow-citizens, and obtained of them what he desired.

Together with Alcibiades, Nicias, much against his will, was appointed general: and he endeavored to avoid the command, not the less on account of his colleague. But the Athenians thought the war would proceed more prosperously, if they did not send Alcibiades free from all restraint, but tempered his heat with the caution of Nicias. This they chose the rather to do, because Lamachus, the third general, though he was of mature years, yet in several battles had appeared no less hot and rash than Alcibiades himself. When they began to deliberate of the number of forces, and of the manner of making the necessary provisions, Nicias made another attempt to oppose the design, and to prevent the war; but Alcibiades contradicted him, and carried his point with the people. And one Demostratus, an orator, proposing to give the generals absolute power over the preparations and the whole management of the war, it was presently decreed so. When all things were fitted for the voyage, many unlucky omens appeared. At that very time the feast of Adonis happened, in which the women were used to expose, in all parts of the city, images resembling dead men carried out to their burial, and to represent funeral solemnities by lamentations and mournful songs. The mutilation, however, of the images of Mercury, most of which, in one night, had their faces all disfigured, terrified many persons who were wont to despise most things of that nature. It was given out that it was done by the

Corinthians, for the sake of the Syracusans, who were their colony, in hopes that the Athenians, by such prodigies, might be induced to delay or abandon the war. But the report gained no credit with the people, nor yet the opinion of those who would not believe that there was anything ominous in the matter, but that it was only an extravagant action, committed, in that sort of sport which runs into license, by wild young men coming from a debauch. Alike enraged and terrified at the thing, looking upon it to proceed from a conspiracy of persons who designed some commotions in the state, the council, as well as the assembly of the people, which was held frequently in a few days' space, examined diligently everything that might administer ground for suspicion. During this examination, Androcles, one of the demagogues, produced certain slaves and strangers before them who accused Alcibiades and some of his friends of defacing other images in the same manner, and of having profanely acted the sacred mysteries at a drunken meeting, where one Theodorus represented the herald, Polytion the torch-bearer, and Alcibiades the chief priest, while the rest of the party appeared as candidates for initiation, and received the title of Initiates. These were the matters contained in the articles of information, which Thessalus, the son of Cimon, exhibited against Alcibiades, for his impious mockery of the goddesses Ceres and Proserpine. The people were highly exasperated and incensed against Alcibiades upon this accusation, which, being aggravated by Androcles, the most malicious of all his enemies, at first disturbed his friends exceedingly. But when they perceived that all the seamen designed for Sicily were for him, and the soldiers also, and when the Argive and Mantinean auxiliaries, a thousand men at arms, openly declared that they had undertaken this distant maritime expedition for the sake of Alcibiades, and that if he was ill-used they would all go home, they recovered their courage, and became eager to make use of the present opportunity for justifying him. At this his enemies were again discouraged, fearing lest the people should be more gentle to him in their sentence, because of the occasion they had for his service. Therefore, to obviate this, they contrived that some other orators, who did not appear to be enemies to Alcibiades, but really hated him no less than those who avowed it, should stand up in the assembly and say that it was a very absurd thing that one who was created general of such an army with absolute power, after his troops were assembled, and the confederates were come, should lose the opportunity, whilst the people were choosing his judges by lot, and appointing times for the hearing of the cause. And, therefore, let him set sail at once, good fortune attend him; and when the war should be at an end, he might then in person make his defense according to the laws.

Alcibiades perceived the malice of this postponement, and, appearing in the assembly, represented that it was monstrous for him to be sent with the command of so large an army, when he lay under such accusations and calumnies; that he deserved to die, if he could not clear himself of the crimes objected to him; but when he had so done, and had proved his innocence, he should then cheerfully apply himself to the war, as standing no longer in fear of false accusers. But he could not prevail with the people, who commanded him to sail immediately. So he departed, together with the other generals, having with them near 140 galleys, 5,100 men at arms, and about 1,300 archers, slingers, and light-armed men, and all the other provisions corresponding.

Arriving on the coast of Italy, he landed at Rhegium, and there stated his views of the manner in which they ought to conduct the war. He was opposed by Nicias; but Lamachus being of his opinion, they sailed for Sicily forthwith, and took Catana. This was all that was done while he was there, for he was soon after recalled by the Athenians to abide his trial. At first, as we before said, there were only some slight suspicions advanced against Alcibiades, and accusations by certain slaves and strangers. But afterwards, in his absence, his enemies attacked him more violently, and confounded together the breaking the images with the profanation of the mysteries, as though both had been committed in pursuance of the same conspiracy for changing the government. The people proceeded to imprison all that were accused, without distinction, and without hearing them, and repented now, considering the importance of the charge, that they had not immediately brought Alcibiades to his trial and given judgment against him. Any of his friends or acquaintance who fell into the people's hands, whilst they were in this fury, did not fail to meet with very severe usage. Thucydides has omitted to name the informers, but others mention Dioclides and Teucer. Amongst whom is Phrynichus, the comic poet, in whom we find the following:—

> "O dearest Hermes! only do take care,
>   And mind you do not miss your footing there;
>   Should you get hurt, occasion may arise
>   For a new Dioclides to tell lies."

To which he makes Mercury return this answer:—

> "will so, for I feel no inclination
>   To reward Teucer for more information."

The truth is, his accusers alleged nothing that was certain or solid against him. One of them, being asked how he knew the men who defaced the images, replying, that he saw them by the light of the moon, made a palpable misstatement, for it was just new moon when the fact was committed. This made all men of understanding cry out upon the thing; but the people were as eager as ever to receive further accusations, nor was their first heat at all abated, but they instantly seized and imprisoned every one that was accused. Amongst those who were detained in prison for their trials was Andocides the orator, whose descent the historian Hellanicus deduces from Ulysses. He was always supposed to hate popular government, and to support oligarchy. The chief ground of his being suspected of defacing the images was because the great Mercury, which stood near his house, and was an ancient monument of the tribe Ægeïs, was almost the only statue of all the remarkable ones which remained entire. For this cause, it is now called the Mercury of Andocides, all men giving it that name, though the inscription is evidence to the contrary. It happened that Andocides, amongst the rest who were prisoners upon the same account, contracted particular acquaintance and intimacy with one Timæus, a person inferior to him in repute, but of remarkable dexterity and boldness. He persuaded Andocides to accuse himself and some few others of this crime, urging to him that, upon his confession, he would be, by the decree of the people, secure of his pardon, whereas the event of judgment is uncertain to all men, but to great persons, such as he was, most formidable. So that it was better for him, if he regarded himself, to save his life by a falsity, than to suffer an infamous death, as really guilty of the crime. And if he had regard to the public good, it was commendable to sacrifice a few suspected men, by that means to rescue many excellent persons from the fury of the people. Andocides was prevailed upon, and accused himself and some others, and, by the terms of the decree, obtained his pardon, while all the persons named by him, except some few who had saved themselves by flight, suffered death. To gain the greater credit to his information, he accused his own servants amongst others. But notwithstanding this, the people's anger was not wholly appeased; and being now no longer diverted by the mutilators, they were at leisure to pour out their whole rage upon Alcibiades. And, in conclusion, they sent the galley named the Salaminian to recall him. But they expressly commanded those that were sent to use no violence, nor seize upon his person, but address themselves to him in the mildest terms, requiring him to follow them to Athens in order to abide his trial, and clear himself before the people. For they feared mutiny and sedition in the army in an enemy's country, which indeed it would have been easy for Alcibiades to effect, if he had wished it. For the soldiers were dispirited upon his departure, expecting for the future tedious delays, and that the war would be drawn out into a lazy length by Nicias, when Alcibiades, who was the spur to action, was taken away. For though Lamachus was a soldier, and a man of courage, poverty deprived him of authority and respect in the army. Alcibiades, just upon his departure, prevented Messena from falling into the hands of the Athenians. There were some in that city who were upon the point of delivering it up, but he, knowing the persons, gave information to some friends of the Syracusans, and so defeated the whole contrivance. When he arrived at Thurii, he went on shore, and, concealing himself there, escaped those who searched after him. But to one who knew him, and asked him if he durst not trust his own native country, he made answer, "In everything else, yes; but in a matter that touches my life, I would not even my own mother, lest she might by mistake throw in the black ball instead of the white." When, afterwards, he was told that the assembly had pronounced judgment of death against him, all he said was, "I will make them feel that I am alive."

The information against him was conceived in this form:—

"Thessalus, the son of Cimon, of the township of Lacia, lays information that Alcibiades, the son of Clinias, of the township of the Scambonidæ, has committed a crime against the goddesses Ceres and Proserpine, by representing in derision the holy mysteries, and showing them to his companions in his own house. Where, being habited in such robes as are used by the chief priest when he shows the holy things, he named himself the chief priest, Polytion the torch-bearer, and Theodorus, of the township of Phegæa, the herald; and saluted the rest of his company as Initiates and Novices, all which was done contrary to the laws and institutions of the Eumolpidæ, and the heralds and priests of the temple at Eleusis."

He was condemned as contumacious upon his not appearing, his property confiscated, and it was decreed that all the priests and priestesses should solemnly curse him. But one of them, Theano, the daughter of Menon, of the township of Agraule, is said to have opposed that part of the decree, saying that her holy office obliged her to make prayers, but not execrations.

Alcibiades, lying under these heavy decrees and sentences, when first he fled from Thurii, passed over into Peloponnesus and remained some time at Argos. But being there in fear of his enemies, and seeing himself utterly hopeless of return to his native country, he sent to Sparta, desiring safe conduct, and assuring them that he would make them amends by his future services for all the mischief he had done them while he was their enemy. The Spartans giving him the security he desired, he went eagerly, was well received, and, at his very first coming, succeeded in inducing them, without any further caution or delay, to send aid to the Syracusans; and so roused and excited them, that they forthwith dispatched Gylippus into Sicily to crush the forces which the Athenians had in Sicily. A second point was to renew the war upon the Athenians at home. But the third thing, and the most important of all, was to make them fortify Decelea, which above everything reduced and wasted the resources of the Athenians.

The renown which he earned by these public services was equaled by the admiration he attracted to his private life; he captivated and won over everybody by his conformity to Spartan habits. People who saw him wearing his hair close cut, bathing in cold water, eating coarse meal, and dining on black broth, doubted, or rather could not believe, that he ever had a cook in his house, or had ever seen a perfumer, or had worn a mantle of Milesian purple. For he had, as it was observed, this peculiar talent and artifice for gaining men's affections, that he could at once comply with and really embrace and enter into their habits and ways of life, and change faster than the chameleon. One color, indeed, they say the chameleon cannot assume: it cannot make itself appear white; but Alcibiades, whether with good men or with bad, could adapt himself to his company, and equally wear the appearance of virtue or vice. At Sparta, he was devoted to athletic exercises, was frugal and reserved; in Ionia, luxurious, gay, and indolent; in Thrace, always drinking; in Thessaly, ever on horseback; and when he lived with Tisaphernes, the Persian satrap, he exceeded the Persians themselves in magnificence and pomp. Not that his natural disposition changed so easily, nor that his real character was so very variable, but, whenever he was sensible that by pursuing his own inclinations he might give offense to those with whom he had occasion to converse, he transformed himself into any shape, and adopted any fashion, that he observed to be most agreeable to them. So that to have seen him at Lacedæmon, a man, judging by the outward appearance, would have said, "'Tis not Achilles's son, but he himself, the very man" that Lycurgus designed to form; while his real feelings and acts would have rather provoked the exclamation, "'Tis the same woman still." For while king Agis was absent, and abroad with the army, he corrupted his wife Timæa, and had a child born by her. Nor did she even deny it, but when she was brought to bed of a son, called him in public Leotychides, but, amongst her confidants and attendants, would whisper that his name was Alcibiades. To such a degree was she transported by her passion for him. He, on the other side, would say, in his vain way, he had not done this thing out of mere wantonness of insult, nor to gratify a passion, but that his race might one day be kings over the Lacedæmonians.

There were many who told Agis that this was so, but time itself gave the greatest confirmation to the story. For Agis, alarmed by an earthquake, had quitted his wife, and for ten months after was never with her; Leotychides, therefore, being born after those ten months, he would not acknowledge him for his son; which was the reason that afterwards he was not admitted to the succession.

After the defeat which the Athenians received in Sicily, ambassadors were dispatched to Sparta at once from Chios and Lesbos and Cyzicus, to signify their purpose of revolting from the Athenians. The Bœotians interposed in favor of the Lesbians, and Pharnabazus of the Cyzicenes, but the Lacedæmonians, at the persuasion of Alcibiades, chose to assist Chios before all others. He himself, also, went instantly to sea, procured the immediate revolt of almost all Ionia, and, cooperating with the Lacedæmonian generals, did great mischief to the Athenians. But Agis was his enemy, hating him for having dishonored his wife, and also impatient of his glory, as almost every enterprise and every success was ascribed to Alcibiades. Others, also, of the most powerful and ambitious amongst the Spartans, were possessed with jealousy of him, and at last prevailed with the magistrates in the city to send orders into Ionia that he should be killed. Alcibiades, however, had secret intelligence of this, and in apprehension of the result, while he communicated all affairs to the Lacedæmonians, yet took care not to put himself into their power. At last he retired to Tisaphernes, the king of Persia's satrap, for his security, and immediately became the first and most influential person about him. For this barbarian, not being himself sincere, but a lover of guile and wickedness, admired his address and wonderful subtlety. And, indeed, the charm of daily intercourse with him was more than any character could resist or any disposition escape. Even those who feared and envied him could not but take delight, and have a sort of kindness for him, when they saw him and were in his company. So that Tisaphernes, otherwise a cruel character, and, above all other Persians, a hater of the Greeks, was yet so won by the flatteries of Alcibiades, that he set himself even to exceed him in responding to them. The most beautiful of his parks, containing salubrious streams and meadows, where he had built pavilions, and places of retirement royally and exquisitely adorned, received by his direction the name of Alcibiades, and was always so called and so spoken of.

Thus Alcibiades, quitting the interests of the Spartans, whom he could no longer trust, because he stood in fear of Agis, endeavored to do them ill offices, and render them odious to Tisaphernes, who, by his means, was hindered from assisting them vigorously, and from finally ruining the Athenians. For his advice was to furnish them but sparingly with money, and so wear them out, and consume them insensibly; when they had wasted their strength upon one another, they would both become ready to submit to the king. Tisaphernes readily pursued his counsel, and so openly expressed the liking and admiration which he had for him, that Alcibiades was looked up to by the Greeks of both parties, and the Athenians, now in their misfortunes, repented them of their severe sentence against him. And he, on the other side, began to be troubled for them, and to fear lest, if that commonwealth were utterly destroyed, he should fall into the hands of the Lacedæmonians, his enemies.

At that time the whole strength of the Athenians was in Samos. Their fleet maintained itself here, and issued from these headquarters to reduce such as had revolted, and protect the rest of their territories; in one way or other still contriving to be a match for their enemies at sea. What they stood in fear of was Tisaphernes and the Phœnician fleet of one hundred and fifty galleys, which was said to be already under sail; if those came, there remained then no hopes for the commonwealth of Athens. Understanding this, Alcibiades sent secretly to the chief men of the Athenians, who were then at Samos, giving them hopes that he would make Tisaphernes their friend; he was willing, he implied, to do some favor, not to the people, nor in reliance upon them, but to the better citizens, if only, like brave men, they would make the attempt to put down the insolence of the people, and, by taking upon them the government, would endeavor to save the city from ruin. All of them gave a ready ear to the proposal made by Alcibiades, except only Phrynichus of the township of Dirades, one of the generals, who suspected, as the truth was, that Alcibiades concerned not himself whether the government were in the people or the better citizens, but only sought by any means to make way for his return into his native country, and to that end inveighed against the people, thereby to gain the others, and to insinuate himself into their good opinion. But when Phrynichus found his counsel to be rejected, and that he was himself become a declared enemy of Alcibiades, he gave secret intelligence to Astyochus, the enemy's admiral, cautioning him to beware of Alcibiades, and to seize him as a double dealer, unaware that one traitor was making discoveries to another. For Astyochus, who was eager to gain the favor of Tisaphernes, observing the credit Alcibiades had with him, revealed to Alcibiades all that Phrynichus had said against him. Alcibiades at once dispatched messengers to Samos, to accuse Phrynichus of the treachery. Upon this, all the commanders were enraged with Phrynichus, and set themselves against him, and he, seeing no other way to extricate himself from the present danger, attempted to remedy one evil by a greater. He sent to Astyochus to reproach him for betraying him, and to make an offer to him at the same time to deliver into his hands both the army and the navy of the Athenians. This occasioned no damage to the Athenians, because Astyochus repeated his treachery and revealed also this proposal to Alcibiades. But this again was foreseen by Phrynichus, who, expecting a second accusation from Alcibiades, to anticipate him advertised the Athenians beforehand that the enemy was ready to sail in order to surprise them, and therefore advised them to fortify their camp, and to be in a readiness to go aboard their ships. While the Athenians were intent upon doing these things, they received other letters from Alcibiades, admonishing them to beware of Phrynichus as one who designed to betray their fleet to the enemy, to which they then gave no credit at all, conceiving that Alcibiades, who

knew perfectly the counsels and preparations of the enemy, was merely
making use of that knowledge in order to impose upon them in this false
accusation of Phrynichus. Yet, afterwards, when Phrynichus was stabbed
with a dagger in the marketplace by Hermon, one of the guards, the
Athenians, entering into an examination of the cause, solemnly condemned Phrynichus of treason, and decreed crowns to Hermon and his
associates. And now the friends of Alcibiades, carrying all before them at
Samos, dispatched Pisander to Athens, to attempt a change of government, and to encourage the aristocratical citizens to take upon themselves the government, and overthrow the democracy, representing to
them that, upon these terms, Alcibiades would procure them the friendship and alliance of Tisaphernes.

This was the color and pretense made use of by those who desired to
change the government of Athens to an oligarchy. But as soon as they
prevailed, and had got the administration of affairs into their hands, under
the name of the Five Thousand (whereas, indeed, they were but four
hundred), they slighted Alcibiades altogether, and prosecuted the war
with less vigor; partly because they durst not yet trust the citizens, who
secretly detested this change, and partly because they thought the
Lacedæmonians, who always befriended the government of the few,
would be inclined to give them favorable terms.

The people in the city were terrified into submission, many of those
who had dared openly to oppose the four hundred having been put to
death. But those who were at Samos, indignant when they heard this
news, were eager to set sail instantly for the Piræus; and, sending for
Alcibiades, they declared him general, requiring him to lead them on to
put down the tyrants. He, however, in that juncture, did not, as it might
have been thought a man would, on being suddenly exalted by the favor
of a multitude, think himself under an obligation to gratify and submit
to all the wishes of those who, from a fugitive and an exile, had created
him general of so great an army, and given him the command of such a
fleet. But, as became a great captain, he opposed himself to the precipi-
tate resolutions which their rage led them to, and, by restraining them
from the great error they were about to commit, unequivocally saved the
commonwealth. For if they then had sailed to Athens, all Ionia and the
islands and the Hellespont would have fallen into the enemies' hands
without opposition, while the Athenians, involved in civil war, would
have been fighting with one another within the circuit of their own
walls. It was Alcibiades alone, or at least principally, who prevented all this
mischief; for he not only used persuasion to the whole army, and showed
them the danger, but applied himself to them, one by one, entreating
some, and constraining others. He was much assisted, however, by
Thrasybulus of Stiria, who, having the loudest voice, as we are told, of all

the Athenians, went along with him, and cried out to those who were ready to be gone. A second great service which Alcibiades did for them was, his undertaking that the Phœnician fleet, which the Lacedæmonians expected to be sent to them by the king of Persia, should either come in aid of the Athenians or otherwise should not come at all. He sailed off with all expedition in order to perform this, and the ships, which had already been seen as near as Aspendus, were not brought any further by Tisaphernes, who thus deceived the Lacedæmonians; and it was by both sides believed that they had been diverted by the procurement of Alcibiades. The Lacedæmonians, in particular, accused him, that he had advised the Barbarian to stand still, and suffer the Greeks to waste and destroy one another, as it was evident that the accession of so great a force to either party would enable them to take away the entire dominion of the sea from the other side.

Soon after this, the four hundred usurpers were driven out, the friends of Alcibiades vigorously assisting those who were for the popular government. And now the people in the city not only desired, but commanded Alcibiades to return home from his exile. He, however, desired not to owe his return to the mere grace and commiseration of the people, and resolved to come back, not with empty hands, but with glory, and after some service done. To this end, he sailed from Samos with a few ships, and cruised on the sea of Cnidos, and about the isle of Cos; but receiving intelligence there that Mindarus, the Spartan admiral, had sailed with his whole army into the Hellespont, and that the Athenians had followed him, he hurried back to succor the Athenian commanders, and, by good fortune, arrived with eighteen galleys at a critical time. For both the fleets having engaged near Abydos, the fight between them had lasted till night, the one side having the advantage on one quarter, and the other on another. Upon his first appearance, both sides formed a false impression; the enemy was encouraged, and the Athenians terrified. But Alcibiades suddenly raised the Athenian ensign in the admiral ship, and fell upon those galleys of the Peloponnesians which had the advantage and were in pursuit. He soon put these to flight, and followed them so close that he forced them on shore, and broke the ships in pieces, the sailors abandoning them and swimming away, in spite of all the efforts of Pharnabazus, who had come down to their assistance by land and did what he could to protect them from the shore. In fine, the Athenians, having taken thirty of the enemy's ships, and recovered all their own, erected a trophy. After the gaining of so glorious a victory, his vanity made him eager to show himself to Tisaphernes, and, having furnished himself with gifts and presents, and an equipage suitable to his dignity, he set out to visit him. But the thing did not succeed as he had imagined, for Tisaphernes had been long suspected by the Lacedæmonians, and was afraid to fall into disgrace with his king upon that account, and therefore thought that Alcibiades arrived very opportunely, and immediately caused him to be seized, and sent away prisoner to Sardis; fancying, by this act of injustice, to clear himself from all former imputations.

But about thirty days after, Alcibiades escaped from his keepers, and, having got a horse, fled to Clazomenæ, where he procured Tisaphernes' additional disgrace by professing he was a party to his escape. From there he sailed to the Athenian camp, and, being informed there that Mindarus and Pharnabazus were together at Cyzicus, he made a speech to the soldiers, telling them that sea fighting, land fighting, and, by the gods, fighting against fortified cities too, must be all one for them, as, unless they conquered everywhere, there was no money for them. As soon as ever he got them on shipboard, he hasted to Proconnesus, and gave command to seize all the small vessels they met, and guard them safely in the interior of the fleet, that the enemy might have no notice of his coming; and a great storm of rain, accompanied with thunder and darkness, which happened at the same time, contributed much to the concealment of his enterprise. Indeed, it was not only undiscovered by the enemy, but the Athenians themselves were ignorant of it, for he commanded them suddenly on board, and set sail when they had abandoned all intention of it. As the darkness presently passed away, the Peloponnesian fleet were seen riding out at sea in front of the harbor of Cyzicus. Fearing, if they discovered the number of his ships, they might endeavor to save themselves by land, he commanded the rest of the captains to slacken, and follow him slowly, whilst he, advancing with forty ships, showed himself to the enemy, and provoked them to fight. The enemy, being deceived as to their numbers, despised them, and, supposing they were to contend with those only, made themselves ready and began the fight. But as soon as they were engaged, they perceived the other part of the fleet coming down upon them, at which they were so terrified that they fled immediately. Upon that, Alcibiades, breaking through the midst of them with twenty of his best ships, hastened to the shore, disembarked, and pursued those who abandoned their ships and fled to land, and made a great slaughter of them. Mindarus and Pharnabazus, coming to their succor, were utterly defeated. Mindarus was slain upon the place, fighting valiantly; Pharnabazus saved himself by flight. The Athenians slew great numbers of their enemies, won much spoil, and took all their ships. They also made themselves masters of Cyzicus, which was deserted by Pharnabazus, and destroyed its Peloponnesian garrison, and thereby not only secured to themselves the Hellespont, but by force drove the Lacedæmonians from out of all the rest of the sea. They intercepted some letters written to the ephors, which gave an account of this fatal overthrow, after their short laconic manner. "Our hopes are at an end. Mindarus is slain. The men starve. We know not what to do."

The soldiers who followed Alcibiades in this last fight were so exalted with their success, and felt that degree of pride, that, looking on themselves as invincible, they disdained to mix with the other soldiers, who had been often overcome. For it happened not long before, Thrasyllus had received a defeat near Ephesus, and, upon that occasion, the Ephesians erected their brazen trophy to the disgrace of the Athenians. The soldiers of Alcibiades reproached those who were under the command of Thrasyllus with this misfortune, at the same time magnifying themselves and their own commander, and it went so far that they would not exercise with them, nor lodge in the same quarters. But soon after, Pharnabazus, with a great force of horse and foot, falling upon the soldiers of Thrasyllus, as they were laying waste the territory of Abydos, Alcibiades came to their aid, routed Pharnabazus, and, together with Thrasyllus, pursued him till it was night; and in this action the troops united, and returned together to the camp, rejoicing and congratulating one another. The next day he erected a trophy, and then proceeded to lay waste with fire and sword the whole province which was under Pharnabazus, where none ventured to resist; and he took divers priests and priestesses, but released them without ransom. He prepared next to attack the Chalcedonians, who had revolted from the Athenians, and had received a Lacedæmonian governor and garrison. But having intelligence that they had removed their corn and cattle out of the fields, and were conveying it all to the Bithynians, who were their friends, he drew down his army to the frontier of the Bithynians, and then sent a herald to charge them with this proceeding. The Bithynians, terrified at his approach, delivered up to him the booty, and entered into alliance with him.

Afterwards he proceeded to the siege of Chalcedon, and enclosed it with a wall from sea to sea. Pharnabazus advanced with his forces to raise the siege, and Hippocrates, the governor of the town, at the same time, gathering together all the strength he had, made a sally upon the Athenians. Alcibiades divided his army so as to engage them both at once, and not only forced Pharnabazus to a dishonorable flight, but defeated Hippocrates, and killed him and a number of the soldiers with him. After this he sailed into the Hellespont, in order to raise supplies of money, and took the city of Selymbria, in which action, through his precipitation, he exposed himself to great danger. For some within the town had undertaken to betray it into his hands, and, by agreement, were to give him a signal by a lighted torch about midnight. But one of the conspirators beginning to repent himself of the design, the rest, for fear of being discovered, were driven to give the signal before the appointed hour. Alcibiades, as soon as he saw the torch lifted up in the air, though his army was not in readiness to march, ran instantly towards the walls, taking with him about thirty men only, and commanding the rest of the army to follow him with all possible speed. When he came thither, he found the gate opened for him and entered with his thirty men, and about twenty more light-armed men who were come up to them. They were no sooner in the city, but he perceived the Selymbrians all armed, coming down upon him; so that there was no hope of escaping if he stayed to receive them; and, on the other hand, having been always successful till that day, wherever he commanded, he could not endure to be defeated and fly. So, requiring silence by sound of a trumpet, he commanded one of his men to make proclamation that the Selymbrians should not take arms against the Athenians. This cooled such of the inhabitants as were fiercest for the fight, for they supposed that all their enemies were within the walls, and it raised the hopes of others who were disposed to an accommodation. Whilst they were parleying, and propositions making on one side and the other, Alcibiades's whole army came up to the town. And now, conjecturing rightly that the Selymbrians were well inclined to peace, and fearing lest the city might be sacked by the Thracians, who came in great numbers to his army to serve as volunteers, out of kindness for him, he commanded them all to retreat without the walls. And upon the submission of the Selymbrians, he saved them from being pillaged, only taking of them a sum of money, and, after placing an Athenian garrison in the town, departed.

During this action, the Athenian captains who besieged Chalcedon concluded a treaty with Pharnabazus upon these articles: that he should give them a sum of money; that the Chalcedonians should return to the subjection of Athens; and that the Athenians should make no inroad into the province whereof Pharnabazus was governor; and Pharnabazus was also to provide safe conducts for the Athenian ambassadors to the king of Persia. Afterwards, when Alcibiades returned thither, Pharnabazus required that he also should be sworn to the treaty; but he refused it, unless Pharnabazus would swear at the same time. When the treaty was sworn to on both sides, Alcibiades went against the Byzantines, who had revolted from the Athenians, and drew a line of circumvallation about the city. But Anaxilaus and Lycurgus, together with some others, having undertaken to betray the city to him upon his engagement to preserve the lives and property of the inhabitants, he caused a report to be spread abroad, as if, by reason of some unexpected movement in Ionia, he should be obliged to raise the siege. And, accordingly, that day he made a show to depart with his whole fleet; but returned the same night, and went ashore with all his men at arms, and, silently and undiscovered, marched up to the walls. At the same time, his ships rowed into the harbor with all possible violence, coming on with much fury, and with great shouts and outcries. The Byzantines, thus surprised and astonished, while they all hurried to the defense of their port and shipping, gave opportunity to those who favored the Athenians securely to receive Alcibiades into the city. Yet the enterprise was not accomplished without fighting, for the Peloponnesians, Bœotians, and Megarians not only repulsed those who came out of the ships, and forced them on board again, but, hearing that the Athenians were entered on the other side, drew up in order and went to meet them. Alcibiades, however, gained the victory after some sharp fighting, in which he himself had the command of the right wing, and Theramenes of the left, and took about three hundred, who survived of the enemy, prisoners of war. After the battle, not one of the Byzantines was slain, or driven out of the city, according to the terms upon which the city was put into his hands, that they should receive no prejudice in life or property. And thus Anaxilaus, being afterwards accused at Lacedæmon for this treason, neither disowned nor professed to be ashamed of the action; for he urged that he was not a Lacedæmonian, but a Byzantine, and saw not Sparta, but Byzantium, in extreme danger; the city so blockaded that it was not possible to bring in any new provisions, and the Peloponnesians and Bœotians, who were in garrison, devouring the old stores, whilst the Byzantines, with their wives and children, were starving; that he had not, therefore, betrayed his country to enemies, but had delivered it from the calamities of war, and had but followed the example of the most worthy Lacedæmonians, who esteemed nothing to be honorable and just, but what was profitable for their country. The Lacedæmonians, upon hearing his defense, respected it, and discharged all that were accused.

And now Alcibiades began to desire to see his native country again, or rather to show his fellow-citizens a person who had gained so many victories for them. He set sail for Athens, the ships that accompanied him being adorned with great numbers of shields and other spoils, and towing after them many galleys taken from the enemy, and the ensigns and ornaments of many others which he had sunk and destroyed; all of them together amounting to two hundred. Little credit, perhaps, can be given to what Duris the Samian, who professed to be descended from Alcibiades, adds, that Chrysogonus, who had gained a victory at the Pythian games, played upon his flute for the galleys, whilst the oars kept time with the music; and that Callippides, the tragedian, attired in his buskins, his purple robes, and other ornaments used in the theater, gave the word to the rowers, and that the admiral galley entered into the port with a purple sail. Neither Theopompus, nor Ephorus, nor Xenophon, mention them. Nor, indeed, is it credible, that one who returned from so long an exile, and such variety of misfortunes, should

come home to his countrymen in the style of revelers breaking up
from a drinking-party. On the contrary, he entered the harbor full of
fear, nor would he venture to go on shore, till, standing on the deck,
he saw Euryptolemus, his cousin, and others of his friends and acquaintance, who were ready to receive him, and invited him to land.
As soon as he was landed, the multitude who came out to meet him
scarcely seemed so much as to see any of the other captains, but came
in throngs about Alcibiades, and saluted him with loud acclamations,
and still followed him; those who could press near him crowned him
with garlands, and they who could not come up so close yet stayed to
behold him afar off, and the old men pointed him out, and showed
him to the young ones. Nevertheless, this public joy was mixed with
some tears, and the present happiness was allayed by the remembrance
of the miseries they had endured. They made reflections, that they
could not have so unfortunately miscarried in Sicily, or been defeated
in any of their other expectations, if they had left the management of
their affairs formerly, and the command of their forces, to Alcibiades,
since, upon his undertaking the administration, when they were in a
manner driven from the sea, and could scarce defend the suburbs of
their city by land, and, at the same time, were miserably distracted with
intestine factions, he had raised them up from this low and deplorable
condition, and had not only restored them to their ancient dominion
of the sea, but had also made them everywhere victorious over their
enemies on land.

There had been a decree for recalling him from his banishment already
passed by the people, at the instance of Critias, the son of Callæschrus, as
appears by his elegies, in which he puts Alcibiades in mind of this service:—

> "From my proposal did that edict come,
>   Which from your tedious exile brought you home.
>   The public vote at first was moved by me,
>   And my voice put the seal to the decree."

The people being summoned to an assembly, Alcibiades came in amongst
them, and first bewailed and lamented his own sufferings, and, in gentle
terms complaining of the usage he had received, imputed all to his hard
fortune, and some ill genius that attended him: then he spoke at large of
their prospects, and exhorted them to courage and good hope. The people crowned him with crowns of gold, and created him general, both at
land and sea, with absolute power. They also made a decree that his estate should be restored to him, and that the Eumolpidae and the holy
heralds should absolve him from the curses which they had solemnly
pronounced against him by sentence of the people. Which when all the

rest obeyed, Theodorus, the high-priest, excused himself, "For," said he, "if he is innocent, I never cursed him."

But notwithstanding the affairs of Alcibiades went so prosperously, and so much to his glory, yet many were still somewhat disturbed, and looked upon the time of his arrival to be ominous. For on the day that he came into the port, the feast of the goddess Minerva, which they call the Plynteria, was kept. It is the twenty-fifth day of Thargelion, when the Praxiergidæ solemnize their secret rites, taking all the ornaments from off her image, and keeping the part of the temple where it stands close covered. Hence the Athenians esteem this day most inauspicious, and never undertake any thing of importance upon it; and, therefore, they imagined that the goddess did not receive Alcibiades graciously and propitiously, thus hiding her face and rejecting him. Yet, notwithstanding, everything succeeded according to his wish. When the one hundred galleys, that were to return with him, were fitted out and ready to sail, an honorable zeal detained him till the celebration of the mysteries was over. For ever since Decelea had been occupied, as the enemy commanded the roads leading from Athens to Eleusis, the procession, being conducted by sea, had not been performed with any proper solemnity; they were forced to omit the sacrifices and dances and other holy ceremonies, which had usually been performed in the way, when they led forth Iacchus. Alcibiades, therefore, judged it would be a glorious action, which would do honor to the gods and gain him esteem with men, if he restored the ancient splendor to these rites, escorting the procession again by land, and protecting it with his army in the face of the enemy. For either, if Agis stood still and did not oppose, it would very much diminish and obscure his reputation, or, in the other alternative, Alcibiades would engage in a holy war, in the cause of the gods, and in defense of the most sacred and solemn ceremonies; and this in the sight of his country, where he should have all his fellow-citizens witnesses of his valor. As soon as he had resolved upon this design, and had communicated it to the Eumolpidae and heralds, he placed sentinels on the tops of the hills, and at the break of day sent forth his scouts. And then taking with him the priests and Initiates and the Initiators, and encompassing them with his soldiers, he conducted them with great order and profound silence; an august and venerable procession, wherein all who did not envy him said he performed at once the office of a high priest and of a general. The enemy did not dare to attempt anything against them, and thus he brought them back in safety to the city. Upon which, as he was exalted in his own thought, so the opinion which the people had of his conduct was raised to that degree, that they looked upon their armies as irresistible and invincible while he commanded them; and he so won, indeed, upon the lower and meaner sort of people, that they passionately desired to have him "tyrant" over them, and some of them did not scruple to tell him so, and to advise him to put himself out of the reach of envy, by abolishing the laws and ordinances of the people, and suppressing the idle talkers that were ruining the state, that so he might act and take upon him the management of affairs, without standing in fear of being called to an account.

How far his own inclinations led him to usurp sovereign power is uncertain, but the most considerable persons in the city were so much afraid of it, that they hastened him on shipboard as speedily as they could, appointing the colleagues whom he chose, and allowing him all other things as he desired. Thereupon he set sail with a fleet of one hundred ships, and, arriving at Andros, he there fought with and defeated as well the inhabitants as the Lacedæmonians who assisted them. He did not, however, take the city; which gave the first occasion to his enemies for all their accusations against him. Certainly, if ever man was ruined by his own glory, it was Alcibiades. For his continual success had produced such an idea of his courage and conduct that, if he failed in anything he undertook, it was imputed to his neglect, and no one would believe it was through want of power. For they thought nothing was too hard for him, if he went about it in good earnest. They fancied, every day, that they should hear news of the reduction of Chios, and of the rest of Ionia, and grew impatient that things were not effected as fast and as rapidly as they could wish for them. They never considered how extremely money was wanting, and that, having to carry on war with an enemy who had supplies of all things from a great king, he was often forced to quit his armament in order to procure money and provisions for the subsistence of his soldiers. This it was which gave occasion for the last accusation which was made against him. For Lysander, being sent from Lacedæmon with a commission to be admiral of their fleet, and being furnished by Cyrus with a great sum of money, gave every sailor four obols a day, whereas before they had but three. Alcibiades could hardly allow his men three obols, and therefore was constrained to go into Caria to furnish himself with money. He left the care of the fleet, in his absence, to Antiochus, an experienced seaman, but rash and inconsiderate, who had express orders from Alcibiades not to engage, though the enemy provoked him. But he slighted and disregarded these directions to that degree, that, having made ready his own galley and another, he stood for Ephesus, where the enemy lay, and, as he sailed before the heads of their galleys, used every provocation possible, both in words and deeds. Lysander at first manned out a few ships, and pursued him. But all the Athenian ships coming in to his assistance, Lysander, also, brought up his whole fleet, which gained an entire victory. He slew Antiochus himself, took many men and ships, and erected a trophy.

As soon as Alcibiades heard this news, he returned to Samos, and loosing from thence with his whole fleet, came and offered battle to Lysander. But Lysander, content with the victory he had gained, would not stir. Amongst others in the army who hated Alcibiades, Thrasybulus, the son of Thrason, was his particular enemy, and went purposely to Athens to accuse him, and to exasperate his enemies in the city against him. Addressing the people, he represented that Alcibiades had ruined their affairs and lost their ships by mere self-conceited neglect of his duties, committing the government of the army, in his absence, to men who gained his favor by drinking and scurrilous talking, whilst he wandered up and down at pleasure to raise money, giving himself up to every sort of luxury and excess amongst the courtesans of Abydos and Ionia, at a time when the enemy's navy were on the watch close at hand. It was also objected to him, that he had fortified a castle near Bisanthe in Thrace, for a safe retreat for himself, as one that either could not, or would not, live in his own country. The Athenians gave credit to these informations, and showed the resentment and displeasure which they had conceived against him by choosing other generals.

As soon as Alcibiades heard of this, he immediately forsook the army, afraid of what might follow; and, collecting a body of mercenary soldiers, made war upon his own account against those Thracians who called themselves free, and acknowledged no king. By this means he amassed to himself a considerable treasure, and, at the same time, secured the bordering Greeks from the incursions of the barbarians.

Tydeus, Menander, and Adimantus, the new-made generals, were at that time posted at Ægospotami, with all the ships which the Athenians had left. From whence they were used to go out to sea every morning, and offer battle to Lysander, who lay near Lampsacus; and when they had done so, returning back again, lay, all the rest of the day, carelessly and without order, in contempt of the enemy. Alcibiades, who was not far off, did not think so slightly of their danger, nor neglect to let them know it, but, mounting his horse, came to the generals, and represented to them that they had chosen a very inconvenient station, where there was no safe harbor, and where they were distant from any town; so that they were constrained to send for their necessary provisions as far as Sestos. He also pointed out to them their carelessness in suffering the soldiers, when they went ashore, to disperse and wander up and down at their pleasure, while the enemy's fleet, under the command of one general, and strictly obedient to discipline, lay so very near them. He advised them to remove the fleet to Sestos. But the admirals not only disregarded what he said, but Tydeus, with insulting expressions, commanded him to be gone, saying, that now not he, but others, had the command of the forces. Alcibiades, suspecting something of treachery in them, departed, and told his friends, who accompanied him out of the camp, that if the generals had not used him with such insupportable contempt, he would within a few days have forced the Lacedæmonians, however unwilling, either to have fought the Athenians at sea, or to have deserted their ships. Some looked upon this as a piece of ostentation only; others said, the thing was probable, for that he might have brought down by land great numbers of the Thracian cavalry and archers, to assault and disorder them in their camp. The event, however, soon made it evident how rightly he had judged of the errors which the Athenians committed. For Lysander fell upon them on a sudden, when they least suspected it, with such fury that Conon alone, with eight galleys, escaped him; all the rest, which were about two hundred, he took and carried away, together with three thousand prisoners, whom he put to death. And within a short time after, he took Athens itself, burnt all the ships which he found there, and demolished their long walls.

After this, Alcibiades, standing in dread of the Lacedæmonians, who were now masters both at sea and land, retired into Bithynia. He sent thither great treasure before him, took much with him, but left much more in the castle where he had before resided. But he lost great part of his wealth in Bithynia, being robbed by some Thracians who lived in those parts, and thereupon determined to go to the court of Artaxerxes, not doubting but that the king, if he would make trial of his abilities, would find him not inferior to Themistocles, besides that he was recommended by a more honorable cause. For he went not, as Themistocles did, to offer his service against his fellow citizens, but against their enemies, and to implore the king's aid for the defense of his country. He concluded that Pharnabazus would most readily procure him a safe conduct, and therefore went into Phrygia to him, and continued to dwell there some time, paying him great respect, and being honorably treated by him. The Athenians, in the meantime, were miserably afflicted at their loss of empire; but when they were deprived of liberty also, and Lysander set up thirty despotic rulers in the city, in their ruin now they began to turn to those thoughts which, while safety was yet possible, they would not entertain; they acknowledged and bewailed their former errors and follies, and judged this second ill usage of Alcibiades to be of all the most inexcusable. For he was rejected without any fault committed by himself; and only because they were incensed against his subordinate for having shamefully lost a few ships, they much more shamefully deprived the commonwealth of its most valiant and accomplished general. Yet in this sad state of affairs, they had still some faint hopes left them, nor would they utterly despair of the Athenian commonwealth, while Alcibiades was safe. For they persuaded themselves that if before, when he was an exile, he could not content himself to live idly and at ease, much less now,

if he could find any favorable opportunity, would he endure the insolence of the Lacedæmonians, and the outrages of the Thirty. Nor was it
an absurd thing in the people to entertain such imaginations, when the
Thirty themselves were so very solicitous to be informed and to get intelligence of all his actions and designs. In fine, Critias represented to
Lysander that the Lacedæmonians could never securely enjoy the dominion of Greece till the Athenian democracy was absolutely destroyed;
and, though now the people of Athens seemed quietly and patiently to
submit to so small a number of governors, yet so long as Alcibiades lived,
the knowledge of this fact would never suffer them to acquiesce in their
present circumstances.

Yet Lysander would not be prevailed upon by these representations, till
at last he received secret orders from the magistrates of Lacedaemon, expressly requiring him to get Alcibiades dispatched: whether it was that
they feared his energy and boldness in enterprising what was hazardous,
or that it was done to gratify King Agis. Upon receipt of this order,
Lysander sent away a messenger to Pharnabazus, desiring him to put it in
execution. Pharnabazus committed the affair to Magæus, his brother, and
to his uncle Susamithres. Alcibiades resided at that time in a small village
in Phrygia, together with Timandra, a mistress of his. As he slept, he had
this dream: he thought himself attired in his mistress's habit, and that she,
holding him in her arms, dressed his head and painted his face as if he
had been a woman; others say, he dreamed that he saw Magæus cut off
his head and burn his body; at any rate, it was but a little while before his
death that he had these visions. Those who were sent to assassinate him
had not courage enough to enter the house, but surrounded it first, and
set it on fire. Alcibiades, as soon as he perceived it, getting together great
quantities of clothes and furniture, threw them upon the fire to choke it,
and, having wrapped his cloak about his left arm, and holding his naked
sword in his right, he cast himself into the middle of the fire, and escaped
securely through it before his clothes were burnt. The barbarians, as soon
as they saw him, retreated, and none of them durst stay to wait for him,
or to engage with him, but, standing at a distance, they slew him with
their darts and arrows. When he was dead the barbarians departed, and
Timandra took up his dead body, and, covering and wrapping it up in
her own robes, she buried it as decently and as honorably as her circumstances would allow. It is said, that the famous Lais, who was called the
Corinthian, though she was a native of Hyccara, a small town in Sicily,
from whence she was brought a captive, was the daughter of this
Timandra. There are some who agree with this account of Alcibiades's
death in all points, except that they impute the cause of it neither to
Pharnabazus, nor Lysander, nor the Lacedæmonians; but, they say, he was
keeping with him a young lady of a noble house, whom he had de-

bauched, and that her brothers, not being able to endure the indignity, set fire by night to the house where he was living, and, as he endeavored to save himself from the flames, slew him with their darts, in the manner just related.

ALEXANDER

IT BEING my purpose to write the lives of Alexander the king, and of Cæsar, by whom Pompey was destroyed, the multitude of their great actions affords so large a field that I were to blame if I should not by way of apology forewarn my reader that I have chosen rather to epitomize the most celebrated parts of their story, than to insist at large on every particular circumstance of it. It must be borne in mind that my design is not to write histories, but lives. And the most glorious exploits do not always furnish us with the clearest discoveries of virtue or vice in men; sometimes a matter of less moment, an expression or a jest, informs us better of their characters and inclinations, than the most famous sieges, the greatest armaments, or the bloodiest battles whatsoever. Therefore as portrait painters are more exact in the lines and features of the face, in which the character is seen, than in the other parts of the body, so I must be allowed to give my more particular attention to the marks and indications of the souls of men, and while I endeavor by these to portray their lives, may be free to leave more weighty matters and great battles to be treated of by others.

It is agreed on by all hands, that on the father's side, Alexander descended from Hercules by Caranus, and from Æacus by Neoptolemus on the mother's side. His father Philip, being in Samothrace, when he was quite young, fell in love there with Olympias, in company with whom he was initiated in the religious ceremonies of the country, and her father and mother being both dead, soon after, with the consent of her brother, Arymbas, he married her. The night before the consummation of their marriage, she dreamed that a thunderbolt fell upon her body, which kindled a great fire, whose divided flames dispersed themselves all about, and then were extinguished. And Philip, some time after he was married, dreamt that he sealed up his wife's body with a seal, whose impression, as he fancied, was the figure of a lion. Some of the diviners interpreted this as a warning to Philip to look narrowly to his wife; but Aristander of Telmessus, considering how unusual it was to seal up anything that was empty, assured him the meaning of his dream was that the queen was with child of a boy, who would one day prove as stout and courageous as a lion. Once, moreover, a serpent was found lying by Olympias as she slept, which more than anything else, it is said, abated Philip's passion for her; and whether he feared her as an enchantress, or thought she had commerce with some god, and so looked on himself as excluded, he was ever after less fond of her conversation. Others say that the women of this country, having always been extremely addicted to the enthusiastic Orphic rites and the wild worship of Bacchus (upon which account they were called Clodones, and Mimallones), imitated in many things the practices of the Edonian and Thracian women about Mount Hæmus, from whom the word *threskeuein* seems to have been derived, as a special term for superfluous and over-curious forms of adoration; and that Olympias, zealously affecting these fanatical and enthusiastic inspirations, to perform them with more barbaric dread, was wont in the dances proper to these ceremonies to have great tame serpents about her, which sometimes creeping out of the ivy and the mystic fans, sometimes winding themselves about the sacred spears, and the women's chaplets, made a spectacle which the men could not look upon without terror.

Philip, after this vision, sent Chæron of Megalopolis to consult the oracle of Apollo at Delphi, by which he was commanded to perform sacrifice, and henceforth pay particular honor, above all other gods, to Ammon; and was told he should one day lose that eye with which he presumed to peep through the chink of the door, when he saw the god, under the form of a serpent, in the company of his wife. Eratosthenes says that Olympias, when she attended Alexander on his way to the army in his first expedition, told him the secret of his birth, and bade him behave himself with courage suitable to his divine extraction. Others again affirm that she wholly disclaimed any pretensions of the kind, and was wont to say, "When will Alexander leave off slandering me to Juno?" Alexander was born the sixth of Hecatombæon, which month the Macedonians call Lous, the same day that the temple of Diana at Ephesus was burnt; which Hegesias of Magnesia makes the occasion of a conceit, frigid enough to have stopped the conflagration. The temple, he says, took fire and was burnt while its mistress was absent, assisting at the birth of Alexander. And all the Eastern soothsayers who happened to be then at Ephesus, looking upon the ruin of this temple to be the forerunner of some other calamity, ran about the town, beating their faces, and crying that this day had brought forth something that would prove fatal and destructive to all Asia.

Just after Philip had taken Potidæa, he received these three messages at one time, that Parmenio had overthrown the Illyrians in a great battle, that his racehorse had won the course at the Olympic games, and that his wife had given birth to Alexander; with which being naturally well pleased, as an addition to his satisfaction, he was assured by the diviners that a son whose birth was accompanied with three such successes could not fail of being invincible.

The statues that gave the best representation of Alexander's person were those of Lysippus, (by whom alone he would suffer his image to be made), those peculiarities which many of his successors afterwards and his friends used to affect to imitate, the inclination of his head a little on one side towards his left shoulder, and his melting eye, having been expressed by this artist with great exactness. But Apelles, who drew him with thunderbolts in his hand, made his complexion browner and darker than it was naturally; for he was fair and of a light color, passing into ruddiness in his face and upon his breast. Aristoxenus in his Memoirs tells us that a most agreeable odor exhaled from his skin, and that his breath and body all over was so fragrant as to perfume the clothes which he wore next him; the cause of which might probably be the hot and adust temperament of his body. For sweet smells, Theophrastus conceives, are produced by the concoction of moist humors by heat, which is the reason that those parts of the world which are driest and most burnt up afford spices of the best kind, and in the greatest quantity; for the heat of the sun exhausts all the superfluous moisture which lies in the surface of bodies, ready to generate putrefaction. And this hot constitution, it may be, rendered Alexander so addicted to drinking, and so choleric. His temperance, as to the pleasures of the body, was apparent in him in his very childhood, as he was with much difficulty incited to them, and always used them with great moderation; though in other things he was extremely eager and vehement, and in his love of glory, and the pursuit of it, he showed a solidity of high spirit and magnanimity far above his age. For he neither sought nor valued it upon every occasion, as his father Philip did (who affected to show his eloquence almost to a degree of pedantry, and took care to have the victories of his racing chariots at the Olympic games engraved on his coin), but when he was asked by some about him, whether he would run a race in the Olympic games, as he was very swift-footed, he answered, he would, if he might have kings to run with him. Indeed, he seems in general to have looked with indifference, if not with dislike, upon the professed athletes. He often appointed prizes, for which not only tragedians and musicians, pipers and harpers, but rhapsodists also, strove to outvie one another; and delighted in all manner of hunting and cudgel-playing, but never gave any encouragement to contests either of boxing or of the pancratium.

While he was yet very young, he entertained the ambassadors from the king of Persia, in the absence of his father, and entering much into conversation with them, gained so much upon them by his affability, and the questions he asked them, which were far from being childish or trifling, (for he inquired of them the length of the ways, the nature of the road into inner Asia, the character of their king, how he carried himself to his enemies, and what forces he was able to bring into the field), that they were struck with admiration of him, and looked upon the ability so much famed of Philip to be nothing in comparison with the forwardness and high purpose that appeared thus early in his son. Whenever he heard Philip had taken any town of importance, or won any signal victory, instead of rejoicing at it altogether, he would tell his companions that his father would anticipate everything, and leave him and them no opportunities of performing great and illustrious actions. For being more bent upon action and glory than either upon pleasure or riches, he esteemed all that he should receive from his father as a diminution and prevention of his own future achievements; and would have chosen rather to succeed to a kingdom involved in troubles and wars, which would have afforded him frequent exercise of his courage, and a large field of honor, than to one already flourishing and settled, where his inheritance would be an inactive life and the mere enjoyment of wealth and luxury.

The care of his education, as it might be presumed, was committed to a great many attendants, preceptors, and teachers, over the whole of whom Leonidas, a near kinsman of Olympias, a man of an austere temper, presided, who did not indeed himself decline the name of what in reality is a noble and honorable office, but in general his dignity, and his near relationship, obtained him from other people the title of Alexander's foster father and governor. But he who took upon him the actual place and style of his pedagogue was Lysimachus the Acarnanian, who, though he had nothing specially to recommend him, but his lucky fancy of calling himself Phoenix, Alexander Achilles, and Philip Peleus, was therefore well enough esteemed, and ranked in the next degree after Leonidas.

Philonicus the Thessalian brought the horse Bucephalus to Philip, offering to sell him for thirteen talents; but when they went into the field to try him, they found him so very vicious and unmanageable, that he reared up when they endeavored to mount him, and would not so much as endure the voice of any of Philip's attendants. Upon which, as they were leading him away as wholly useless and untractable, Alexander, who stood by, said, "What an excellent horse do they lose, for want of address and boldness to manage him!" Philip at first took no notice of what he said; but when he heard him repeat the same thing several times, and saw he was much vexed to see the horse sent away, "Do you reproach," said he to him, "those who are older than yourself, as if you knew more, and were better able to manage him than they?" "I could manage this horse," replied he, "better than others do." "And if you do not," said Philip, "what will you forfeit for your rashness?" "I will pay," answered Alexander, "the whole price of the horse." At this the whole company fell a-laughing; and as soon as the wager was settled amongst them, he immediately ran to the horse, and taking hold of the bridle, turned him directly towards the sun, having, it seems, observed that he was disturbed at and afraid of the motion of his own shadow; then letting him go forward a little, still keeping the reins in his hand, and stroking him gently when he found him begin to grow eager and fiery, he let fall his upper garment softly, and with one nimble leap securely mounted him, and when he was seated, by little and little drew in the bridle, and curbed him without either striking or spurring him. Presently, when he found him free from all rebelliousness, and only impatient for the course, he let him go at full speed, inciting him now with a commanding voice, and urging him also with his heel. Philip and his friends looked on at first in silence and anxiety for the result, till seeing him turn at the end of his career, and come back rejoicing and triumphing for what he had performed, they all burst out into acclamations of applause; and his father, shedding tears, it is said, for joy, kissed him as he came down from his horse, and in his transport said, "O my son, look thee out a kingdom equal to and worthy of thyself, for Macedonia is too little for thee."

After this, considering him to be of a temper easy to be led to his duty by reason, but by no means to be compelled, he always endeavored to persuade rather than to command or force him to anything; and now looking upon the instruction and tuition of his youth to be of greater difficulty and importance than to be wholly trusted to the ordinary masters in music and poetry, and the common school subjects, and to require, as Sophocles says—

"The bridle and the rudder too,"

he sent for Aristotle, the most learned and most celebrated philosopher of his time, and rewarded him with a munificence proportionable to and becoming the care he took to instruct his son. For he repeopled his native city Stagira, which he had caused to be demolished a little before, and restored all the citizens who were in exile or slavery to their habitations. As a place for the pursuit of their studies and exercises, he assigned the temple of the Nymphs, near Mieza, where, to this very day, they show you Aristotle's stone seats and the shady walks which he was wont to frequent. It would appear that Alexander received from him not only his doctrines of Morals and of Politics, but also something of those more abstruse and profound theories which these philosophers, by the very names they gave them, professed to reserve for oral communication to the initiated, and did not allow many to become acquainted with. For when he was in Asia, and heard Aristotle had published some treatises of that kind, he wrote to him, using very plain language to him in behalf of philosophy, the following letter. "Alexander to Aristotle, greeting. You have not done well to publish your books of oral doctrine; for what is there now that we excel others in, if those things which we have been particularly instructed in be laid open to all? For my part, I assure you, I had rather excel others in the knowledge of what is excellent, than in the extent of my power and dominion. Farewell." And Aristotle, soothing this passion for preeminence, speaks, in his excuse for himself, of these doctrines as in fact both published and not published: as indeed, to say the truth, his books on metaphysics are written in a style which makes them useless for ordinary teaching, and instructive only, in the way of memoranda, for those who have been already conversant in that sort of learning.

Doubtless also it was to Aristotle that he owed the inclination he had, not to the theory only, but likewise to the practice of the art of medicine. For when any of his friends were sick, he would often prescribe them their course of diet, and medicines proper to their disease, as we may find in his epistles. He was naturally a great lover of all kinds of learning and reading; and Onesicritus informs us that he constantly laid Homer's Iliads, according to the copy corrected by Aristotle, called the casket copy, with his dagger under his pillow, declaring that he esteemed it a perfect portable treasure of all military virtue and knowledge. When he was in the upper Asia, being destitute of other books, he ordered Harpalus to send him some; who furnished him with Philistus's History, a great many of the plays of Euripides, Sophocles, and Æschylus, and some dithyrambic odes, composed by Telestes and Philoxenus. For a while he loved and cherished Aristotle no less, as he was wont to say himself, than if he had been his father, giving this reason for it, that as he had received life from the one, so the other had taught him to live well. But afterwards, upon some mistrust of him, yet not so great as to make him do him any hurt, his familiarity and friendly kindness to him abated so much of its former force and affectionateness, as to make it evident he was alienated from him. However, his violent thirst after and passion for learning, which were once implanted, still grew up with him, and never decayed; as appears by his veneration of Anaxarchus, by the present of fifty talents which he sent to Xenocrates, and his particular care and esteem of Dandamis and Calanus.

While Philip went on his expedition against the Byzantines, he left Alexander, then sixteen years old, his lieutenant in Macedonia, committing the charge of his seal to him; who, not to sit idle, reduced the rebellious Mædi, and having taken their chief town by storm, drove out the barbarous inhabitants, and planting a colony of several nations in their room, called the place after his own name, Alexandropolis. At the battle of Chæronea, which his father fought against the Grecians, he is said to have been the first man that charged the Thebans' sacred band. And even in my remembrance, there stood an old oak near the river Cephisus, which people called Alexander's oak, because his tent was pitched under it. And not far off are to be seen the graves of the Macedonians who fell in that battle. This early bravery made Philip so fond of him, that nothing pleased him more than to hear his subjects call himself their general and Alexander their king.

But the disorders of his family, chiefly caused by his new marriages and attachments (the troubles that began in the women's chambers spreading, so to say, to the whole kingdom), raised various complaints and differences between them, which the violence of Olympias, a woman of a jealous and implacable temper, made wider, by exasperating Alexander against his father. Among the rest, this accident contributed most to their falling out. At the wedding of Cleopatra, whom Philip fell in love with and married, she being much too young for him, her uncle Attalus in his drink desired the Macedonians would implore the gods to give them a lawful successor to the kingdom by his niece. This so irritated Alexander, that throwing one of the cups at his head, "You villain," said he, "what, am I then a bastard?" Then Philip, taking Attalus's part, rose up and would have run his son through; but by good fortune for them both, either his over-hasty rage, or the wine he had drunk, made his foot slip, so that he fell down on the floor. At which Alexander reproachfully insulted over him: "See there," said he, "the man who makes preparations to pass out of Europe into Asia, overturned in passing from one seat to another." After this debauch, he and his mother Olympias withdrew from Philip's company, and when he had placed her in Epirus, he himself retired into Illyria.

About this time, Demaratus the Corinthian, an old friend of the family, who had the freedom to say anything among them without offense, coming to visit Philip, after the first compliments and embraces were over, Philip asked him whether the Grecians were at amity with one another. "It ill becomes you," replied Demaratus, "to be so solicitous about Greece, when you have involved your own house in so many dissensions and calamities." He was so convinced by this seasonable reproach, that he immediately sent for his son home, and by Demaratus's mediation prevailed with him to return. But this reconciliation lasted not long; for when Pixodorus, viceroy of Caria, sent Aristocritus to treat for a match between his eldest daughter and Philip's son Arrhidæus, hoping by this alliance to secure his assistance upon occasion, Alexander's mother, and some who pretended to be his friends, presently filled his head with tales and calumnies, as if Philip, by a splendid marriage and important alliance, were preparing the way for settling the kingdom upon Arrhidæus. In alarm at this, he dispatched Thessalus, the tragic actor, into Caria, to dispose Pixodorus to slight Arrhidæus, both as illegitimate and a fool, and rather to accept of himself for his son-in-law. This proposition was much more agreeable to Pixodorus than the former. But Philip, as soon as he was made acquainted with this transaction, went to his son's apartment, taking with him Philotas, the son of Parmenio, one of Alexander's intimate friends and companions, and there reproved him severely, and reproached him bitterly, that he should be so degenerate, and unworthy of the power he was to leave him, as to desire the alliance of a mean Carian, who was at best but the slave of a barbarous prince. Nor did this satisfy his resentment, for he wrote to the Corinthians to send Thessalus to him in chains, and banished Harpalus, Nearchus, Erigyius, and Ptolemy, his son's friends and favorites, whom Alexander afterwards recalled and raised to great honor and preferment.

Not long after this, Pausanias, having had an outrage done to him at the instance of Attalus and Cleopatra, when he found he could get no reparation for his disgrace at Philip's hands, watched his opportunity and murdered him. The guilt of which fact was laid for the most part upon Olympias, who was said to have encouraged and exasperated the enraged youth to revenge; and some sort of suspicion attached even to Alexander himself, who, it was said, when Pausanias came and complained to him of the injury he had received, repeated the verse out of Euripides's Medea—

"On husband, and on father, and on bride."

However, he took care to find out and punish the accomplices of the conspiracy severely, and was very angry with Olympias for treating Cleopatra inhumanly in his absence.

Alexander was but twenty years old when his father was murdered, and succeeded to a kingdom beset on all sides with great dangers and rancorous enemies. For not only the barbarous nations that bordered on Macedonia were impatient of being governed by any but their own native princes; but Philip likewise, though he had been victorious over the Grecians, yet, as the time had not been sufficient for him to complete his conquest and accustom them to his sway, had simply left all things in a general disorder and confusion. It seemed to the Macedonians a very critical time; and some would have persuaded Alexander to give up all thought of retaining the Grecians in subjection by force of arms, and rather to apply himself to win back by gentle means the allegiance of the tribes who were designing revolt, and try the effect of indulgence in arresting the first motions towards revolution. But he rejected this counsel as weak and timorous, and looked upon it to be more prudence to secure himself by resolution and magnanimity, than, by seeming to truckle to any, to encourage all to trample on him. In pursuit of this opinion, he reduced the barbarians to tranquility, and put an end to all fear of war from them, by a rapid expedition into their country as far as the river

Danube, where he gave Syrmus, king of the Triballians, an entire over-throw. And hearing the Thebans were in revolt, and the Athenians in correspondence with them, he immediately marched through the pass of Thermopylæ, saying that to Demosthenes, who had called him a child while he was in Illyria and in the country of the Triballians, and a youth when he was in Thessaly, he would appear a man before the walls of Athens.

When he came to Thebes, to show how willing he was to accept of their repentance for what was past, he only demanded of them Phœnix and Prothytes, the authors of the rebellion, and proclaimed a general pardon to those who would come over to him. But when the Thebans merely retorted by demanding Philotas and Antipater to be delivered into their hands, and by a proclamation on their part invited all who would assert the liberty of Greece to come over to them, he presently applied himself to make them feel the last extremities of war. The Thebans indeed defended themselves with a zeal and courage beyond their strength, being much outnumbered by their enemies. But when the Macedonian garrison sallied out upon them from the citadel, they were so hemmed in on all sides that the greater part of them fell in the battle; the city itself, being taken by storm, was sacked and razed, Alexander's hope being that so severe an example might terrify the rest of Greece into obedience, and also in order to gratify the hostility of his confederates, the Phocians and Platæans. So that, except the priests, and some few who had heretofore been the friends and connections of the Macedonians, the family of the poet Pindar, and those who were known to have opposed the public vote for the war, all the rest, to the number of thirty thousand, were publicly sold for slaves; and it is computed that upwards of six thousand were put to the sword.

Among the other calamities that befell the city, it happened that some Thracian soldiers, having broken into the house of a matron of high character and repute, named Timoclea, their captain, after he had used violence with her, to satisfy his avarice as well as lust, asked her, if she knew of any money concealed; to which she readily answered she did, and bade him follow her into a garden, where she showed him a well, into which, she told him, upon the taking of the city she had thrown what she had of most value. The greedy Thracian presently stooping down to view the place where he thought the treasure lay, she came behind him and pushed him into the well, and then flung great stones in upon him, till she had killed him. After which, when the soldiers led her away bound to Alexander, her very mien and gait showed her to be a woman of dignity, and of a mind no less elevated, not betraying the least sign of fear or astonishment. And when the king asked her who she was, "I am," said she, "the sister of Theagenes, who fought the battle of Chæronea with your father Philip, and fell there in command for the liberty of Greece." Alexander was so surprised, both at what she had done and what she said, that he could not choose but give her and her children their freedom to go whither they pleased. After this he received the Athenians into favor, although they had shown themselves so much concerned at the calamity of Thebes that out of sorrow they omitted the celebration of the Mysteries, and entertained those who escaped with all possible humanity. Whether it were, like the lion, that his passion was now satisfied, or that, after an example of extreme cruelty, he had a mind to appear merciful, it happened well for the Athenians; for he not only forgave them all past offenses, but bade them to look to their affairs with vigilance, remembering that if he should miscarry, they were likely to be the arbiters of Greece. Certain it is, too, that in after time he often repented of his severity to the Thebans, and his remorse had such influence on his temper as to make him ever after less rigorous to all others. He imputed also the murder of Clitus, which he committed in his wine, and the unwillingness of the Macedonians to follow him against the Indians, by which his enterprise and glory was left imperfect, to the wrath and vengeance of Bacchus, the protector of Thebes. And it was observed that whatsoever any Theban, who had the good fortune to survive this victory, asked of him, he was sure to grant without the least difficulty.

Soon after, the Grecians, being assembled at the Isthmus, declared their resolution of joining with Alexander in the war against the Persians, and proclaimed him their general. While he stayed here, many public ministers and philosophers came from all parts to visit him and congratulated him on his election, but contrary to his expectation, Diogenes of Sinope, who then was living at Corinth, thought so little of him, that instead of coming to compliment him, he never so much as stirred out of the suburb called the Cranium, where Alexander found him lying along in the sun. When he saw so much company near him, he raised himself a little, and vouchsafed to look upon Alexander; and when he kindly asked him whether he wanted anything, "Yes," said he, "I would have you stand from between me and the sun." Alexander was so struck at this answer, and surprised at the greatness of the man, who had taken so little notice of him, that as he went away, he told his followers, who were laughing at the moroseness of the philosopher, that if he were not Alexander, he would choose to be Diogenes.

Then he went to Delphi, to consult Apollo concerning the success of the war he had undertaken, and happening to come on one of the forbidden days, when it was esteemed improper to give any answers from the oracle, he sent messengers to desire the priestess to do her office; and when she refused, on the plea of a law to the contrary, he went up himself, and began to draw her by force into the temple, until tired and overcome with his importunity, "My son," said she, "thou art invincible." Alexander taking hold of what she spoke, declared he had received such an answer as he wished for, and that it was needless to consult the god any further. Among other prodigies that attended the departure of his army, the image of Orpheus at Libethra, made of cypress wood, was seen to sweat in great abundance, to the discouragement of many. But Aristander told him that, far from presaging any ill to him, it signified he should perform acts so important and glorious as would make the poets and musicians of future ages labor and sweat to describe and celebrate them.

His army, by their computation who make the smallest amount, consisted of thirty thousand foot and four thousand horse; and those who make the most of it, speak but of forty-three thousand foot and three thousand horse. Aristobulus says, he had not a fund of above seventy talents for their pay, nor had he more than thirty days' provision, if we may believe Duris; Onesicritus tells us he was two hundred talents in debt. However narrow and disproportionable the beginnings of so vast an undertaking might seem to be, yet he would not embark his army until he had informed himself particularly what means his friends had to enable them to follow him, and supplied what they wanted, by giving good farms to some, a village to one, and the revenue of some hamlet or harbor town to another. So that at last he had portioned out or engaged almost all the royal property; which giving Perdiccas an occasion to ask him what he would leave himself, he replied, his hopes. "Your soldiers," replied Perdiccas, "will be your partners in those," and refused to accept of the estate he had assigned him. Some others of his friends did the like, but to those who willingly received or desired assistance of him, he liberally granted it, as far as his patrimony in Macedonia would reach, the most part of which was spent in these donations.

With such vigorous resolutions, and his mind thus disposed, he passed the Hellespont, and at Troy sacrificed to Minerva, and honored the memory of the heroes who were buried there, with solemn libations; especially Achilles, whose gravestone he anointed, and with his friends, as the ancient custom is, ran naked about his sepulchre, and crowned it with garlands, declaring how happy he esteemed him, in having while he lived so faithful a friend, and when he was dead, so famous a poet to proclaim his actions. While he was viewing the rest of the antiquities and curiosities of the place, being told he might see Paris's harp, if he pleased, he said he thought it not worth looking on, but he should be glad to see that of Achilles, to which he used to sing the glories and great actions of brave men.

In the meantime Darius's captains, having collected large forces, were encamped on the further bank of the river Granicus, and it was necessary to fight, as it were, in the gate of Asia for an entrance into it. The depth of the river, with the unevenness and difficult ascent of the opposite bank, which was to be gained by main force, was apprehended by most, and some pronounced it an improper time to engage, because it was unusual for the kings of Macedonia to march with their forces in the month called Dæsius. But Alexander broke through these scruples, telling them they should call it a second Artemisius. And when Parmenio advised him not to attempt anything that day, because it was late, he told him that he should disgrace the Hellespont should he fear the Granicus. And so, without more saying, he immediately took the river with thirteen troops of horse, and advanced against whole showers of darts thrown from the steep opposite side, which was covered with armed multitudes of the enemy's horse and foot, notwithstanding the disadvantage of the ground and the rapidity of the stream; so that the action seemed to have more of frenzy and desperation in it, than of prudent conduct. However, he persisted obstinately to gain the passage, and at last with much ado making his way up the banks, which were extremely muddy and slippery, he had instantly to join in a mere confused hand-to-hand combat with the enemy, before he could draw up his men, who were still passing over, into any order. For the enemy pressed upon him with loud and warlike outcries; and charging horse against horse, with their lances, after they had broken and spent these, they fell to it with their swords. And Alexander, being easily known by his buckler, and a large plume of white feathers on each side of his helmet, was attacked on all sides, yet escaped wounding, though his cuirass was pierced by a javelin in one of the joinings. And Rhœsaces and Spithridates, two Persian commanders, falling upon him at once, he avoided one of them, and struck at Rhœsaces, who had a good cuirass on, with such force that, his spear breaking in his hand, he was glad to betake himself to his dagger. While they were thus engaged, Spithridates came up on one side of him, and raising himself upon his horse, gave him such a blow with his battle-axe on the helmet that he cut off the crest of it with one of his plumes, and the helmet was only just so far strong enough to save him, that the edge of the weapon touched the hair of his head. But as he was about to repeat his stroke, Clitus, called the black Clitus, prevented him, by running him through the body with his spear. At the same time Alexander dispatched Rhœsaces with his sword. While the horse were thus dangerously engaged, the Macedonian phalanx passed the river, and the foot on each side advanced to fight. But the enemy, hardly sustaining the first onset, soon gave ground and fled, all but the mercenary Greeks, who, making a stand upon a rising ground, desired quarter, which Alexander, guided rather by passion than judgment, refused to grant, and charging them himself first, had his horse (not Bucephalus, but another) killed under him. And this obstinacy of his to cut off these experienced desperate men cost him the lives of more of his own soldiers than all the battle before, besides those who were wounded. The Persians lost in this battle twenty thousand foot and two thousand five hundred horse. On Alexander's side, Aristobulus says there were not wanting above four and thirty, of whom nine were foot soldiers; and in memory of them he caused so many statues of brass, of Lysippus's making, to be erected. And that the Grecians might participate in the honor of his victory, he sent a portion of the spoils home to them, particularly to the Athenians three hundred bucklers, and upon all the rest he ordered this inscription to be set: "Alexander the son of Philip, and the Grecians, except the Lacedæmonians, won these from the barbarians who inhabit Asia." All the plate and purple garments, and other things of the same kind that he took from the Persians, except a very small quantity which he reserved for himself, he sent as a present to his mother.

This battle presently made a great change of affairs to Alexander's advantage. For Sardis itself, the chief seat of the barbarian's power in the maritime provinces, and many other considerable places were surrendered to him; only Halicarnassus and Miletus stood out, which he took by force, together with the territory about them. After which he was a little unsettled in his opinion how to proceed. Sometimes he thought it best to find out Darius as soon as he could, and put all to the hazard of a battle; another while he looked upon it as a more prudent course to make an entire reduction of the seacoast, and not to seek the enemy till he had first exercised his power here and made himself secure of the resources of these provinces. While he was thus deliberating what to do, it happened that a spring of water near the city of Xanthus in Lycia, of its own accord swelled over its banks, and threw up a copper plate upon the margin, in which was engraven in ancient characters, that the time would come, when the Persian empire should be destroyed by the Grecians. Encouraged by this accident, he proceeded to reduce the maritime parts of Cilicia and Phœnicia, and passed his army along the seacoasts of Pamphylia with such expedition that many historians have described and extolled it with that height of admiration, as if it were no less than a miracle, and an extraordinary effect of divine favor, that the waves which usually come rolling in violently from the main, and hardly ever leave so much as a narrow beach under the steep, broken cliffs at any time uncovered, should on a sudden retire to afford him passage. Menander, in one of his comedies, alludes to this marvel when he says—

> "Was Alexander ever favored more?
> Each man I wish for meets me at my door,

And should I ask for passage through the sea,
The sea I doubt not would retire for me."

But Alexander himself in his epistles mentions nothing unusual in this at all, but says he went from Phaselis, and passed through what they call the Ladders. At Phaselis he stayed some time, and finding the statue of Theodectes, who was a native of this town and was now dead, erected in the marketplace, after he had supped, having drunk pretty plentifully, he went and danced about it, and crowned it with garlands, honoring not ungracefully in his sport, the memory of a philosopher whose conversation he had formerly enjoyed when he was Aristotle's scholar.

Then he subdued the Pisidians who made head against him, and conquered the Phrygians, at whose chief city, Gordium, which is said to be the seat of the ancient Midas, he saw the famous chariot fastened with cords made of the rind of the corner-tree, which whosoever should untie, the inhabitants had a tradition, that for him was reserved the empire of the world. Most authors tell the story that Alexander, finding himself unable to untie the knot, the ends of which were secretly twisted round and folded up within it, cut it asunder with his sword. But Aristobulus tells us it was easy for him to undo it, by only pulling the pin out of the pole, to which the yoke was tied, and afterwards drawing off the yoke itself from below. From hence he advanced into Paphlagonia and Cappadocia, both which countries he soon reduced to obedience, and then hearing of the death of Memnon, the best commander Darius had upon the seacoasts, who, if he had lived, might, it was supposed, have put many impediments and difficulties in the way of the progress of his arms, he was the rather encouraged to carry the war into the upper provinces of Asia.

Darius was by this time upon his march from Susa, very confident, not only in the number of his men, which amounted to six hundred thousand, but likewise in a dream, which the Persian soothsayers interpreted rather in flattery to him than according to the natural probability. He dreamed that he saw the Macedonian phalanx all on fire, and Alexander waiting on him, clad in the same dress which he himself had been used to wear when he was courier to the late king; after which, going into the temple of Belus, he vanished out of his sight. The dream would appear to have supernaturally signified to him the illustrious actions the Macedonians were to perform, and that as he, from a courier's place, had risen to the throne, so Alexander should come to be master of Asia, and not long surviving his conquests, conclude his life with glory. Darius's confidence increased the more, because Alexander spent so much time in Cilicia, which he imputed to his cowardice. But it was sickness that detained him there, which some say he contracted from his fatigues, others from bathing in the river Cydnus, whose waters were exceedingly cold. However it happened, none of his physicians would venture to give him any remedies, they thought his case so desperate, and were so afraid of the suspicions and ill will of the Macedonians if they should fail in the cure; till Philip, the Acarnanian, seeing how critical his case was, but relying on his own well-known friendship for him, resolved to try the last efforts of his art, and rather hazard his own credit and life than suffer him to perish for want of physic, which he confidently administered to him, encouraging him to take it boldly, if he desired a speedy recovery, in order to prosecute the war. At this very time, Parmenio wrote to Alexander from the camp, bidding him have a care of Philip, as one who was bribed by Darius to kill him, with great sums of money, and a promise of his daughter in marriage. When he had perused the letter, he put it under his pillow, without showing it so much as to any of his most intimate friends, and when Philip came in with the potion, he took it with great cheerfulness and assurance, giving him meantime the letter to read. This was a spectacle well worth being present at, to see Alexander take the draught and Philip read the letter at the same time, and then turn and look upon one another, but with different sentiments; for Alexander's looks were cheerful and open, to show his kindness to and confidence in his physician, while the other was full of surprise and alarm at the accusation, appealing to the gods to witness his innocence, sometimes lifting up his hands to heaven, and then throwing himself down by the bedside, and beseeching Alexander to lay aside all fear, and follow his directions without apprehension. For the medicine at first worked so strongly as to drive, so to say, the vital forces into the interior; he lost his speech, and falling into a swoon, had scarce any sense or pulse left. However, in no long time, by Philip's means, his health and strength returned, and he showed himself in public to the Macedonians, who were in continual fear and dejection until they saw him abroad again.

There was at this time in Darius's army a Macedonian refugee, named Amyntas, one who was pretty well acquainted with Alexander's character. This man, when he saw Darius intended to fall upon the enemy in the passes and defiles, advised him earnestly to keep where he was, in the open and extensive plains, it being the advantage of a numerous army to have field room enough when it engages with a lesser force. Darius, instead of taking his counsel, told him he was afraid the enemy would endeavor to run away, and so Alexander would escape out of his hands. "That fear," replied Amyntas, "is needless, for assure yourself that far from avoiding you, he will make all the speed he can to meet you, and is now most likely on his march towards you." But Amyntas's counsel was to no purpose, for Darius immediately decamping, marched into Cilicia at the same time that Alexander advanced into Syria to meet him; and missing

one another in the night, they both turned back again. Alexander, greatly
pleased with the event, made all the haste he could to fight in the defiles,
and Darius to recover his former ground, and draw his army out of so
disadvantageous a place. For now he began to perceive his error in engaging himself too far in a country in which the sea, the mountains, and
the river Pinarus running through the midst of it, would necessitate him
to divide his forces, render his horse almost unserviceable, and only cover
and support the weakness of the enemy. Fortune was not kinder to
Alexander in the choice of the ground, than he was careful to improve it
to his advantage. For being much inferior in numbers, so far from allowing himself to be outflanked, he stretched his right wing much further
out than the left wing of his enemies, and fighting there himself in the
very foremost ranks, put the barbarians to flight. In this battle he was
wounded in the thigh, Chares says by Darius, with whom he fought hand
to hand. But in the account which he gave Antipater of the battle, though
indeed he owns he was wounded in the thigh with a sword, though not
dangerously, yet he takes no notice who it was that wounded him.

Nothing was wanting to complete this victory, in which he overthrew
above a hundred and ten thousand of his enemies, but the taking the person of Darius, who escaped very narrowly by flight. However, having
taken his chariot and his bow, he returned from pursuing him, and found
his own men busy in pillaging the barbarians' camp, which (though to
disburden themselves they had left most of their baggage at Damascus)
was exceedingly rich. But Darius's tent, which was full of splendid furniture and quantities of gold and silver, they reserved for Alexander himself, who, after he had put off his arms, went to bathe himself, saying, "Let
us now cleanse ourselves from the toils of war in the bath of Darius."
"Not so," replied one of his followers, "but in Alexander's rather; for the
property of the conquered is and should be called the conqueror's." Here,
when he beheld the bathing vessels, the water pots, the pans, and the
ointment boxes, all of gold curiously wrought, and smelt the fragrant
odors with which the whole place was exquisitely perfumed, and from
thence passed into a pavilion of great size and height, where the couches
and tables and preparations for an entertainment were perfectly magnificent, he turned to those about him and said, "This, it seems, is royalty."

But as he was going to supper, word was brought him that Darius's
mother and wife and two unmarried daughters, being taken among the
rest of the prisoners, upon the sight of his chariot and bow were all in
mourning and sorrow, imagining him to be dead. After a little pause,
more livelily affected with their affliction than with his own success, he
sent Leonnatus to them to let them know Darius was not dead, and that
they need not fear any harm from Alexander, who made war upon him
only for dominion; they should themselves be provided with everything

they had been used to receive from Darius. This kind message could not but be very welcome to the captive ladies, especially being made good by actions no less humane and generous. For he gave them leave to bury whom they pleased of the Persians, and to make use for this purpose of what garments and furniture they thought fit out of the booty. He diminished nothing of their equipage, or of the attentions and respect formerly paid them, and allowed larger pensions for their maintenance than they had before. But the noblest and most royal part of their usage was, that he treated these illustrious prisoners according to their virtue and character, not suffering them to hear, or receive, or so much as to apprehend anything that was unbecoming. So that they seemed rather lodged in some temple, or some holy virgin chambers, where they enjoyed their privacy sacred and uninterrupted, than in the camp of an enemy. Nevertheless Darius's wife was accounted the most beautiful princess then living, as her husband the tallest and handsomest man of his time, and the daughters were not unworthy of their parents. But Alexander, esteeming it more kingly to govern himself than to conquer his enemies, sought no intimacy with any one of them, nor indeed with any other woman before marriage, except Barsine, Memnon's widow, who was taken prisoner at Damascus. She had been instructed in the Grecian learning, was of a gentle temper, and, by her father, Artabazus, royally descended, which good qualities, added to the solicitations and encouragement of Parmenio, as Aristobulus tells us, made him the more willing to attach himself to so agreeable and illustrious a woman. Of the rest of the female captives, though remarkably handsome and well proportioned, he took no further notice than to say jestingly that Persian women were terrible eyesores. And he himself, retaliating, as it were, by the display of the beauty of his own temperance and self-control, bade them be removed, as he would have done so many lifeless images. When Philoxenus, his lieutenant on the seacoast, wrote to him to know if he would buy two young boys of great beauty, whom one Theodorus, a Tarentine, had to sell, he was so offended that he often expostulated with his friends what baseness Philoxenus had ever observed in him that he should presume to make him such a reproachful offer. And he immediately wrote him a very sharp letter, telling him Theodorus and his merchandise might go with his goodwill to destruction. Nor was he less severe to Hagnon, who sent him word he would buy a Corinthian youth named Crobylus, as a present for him. And hearing that Damon and Timotheus, two of Parmenio's Macedonian soldiers, had abused the wives of some strangers who were in his pay, he wrote to Parmenio, charging him strictly, if he found them guilty, to put them to death, as wild beasts that were only made for the mischief of mankind. In the same letter he added, that he had not so much as seen or desired to see the wife of Darius, no, nor suffered anybody to speak of her beauty before him. He was wont to say that sleep and the act of generation chiefly made him sensible that he was mortal; as much as to say, that weariness and pleasure proceed both from the same frailty and imbecility of human nature.

In his diet, also, he was most temperate, as appears, omitting many other circumstances, by what he said to Ada, whom he adopted, with the title of mother, and afterwards created queen of Caria. For when she, out of kindness, sent him every day many curious dishes and sweetmeats, and would have furnished him with some cooks and pastry men, who were thought to have great skill, he told her he wanted none of them, his preceptor, Leonidas, having already given him the best, which were a night march to prepare for breakfast, and a moderate breakfast to create an appetite for supper. Leonidas also, he added, used to open and search the furniture of his chamber, and his wardrobe, to see if his mother had left him anything that was delicate or superfluous. He was much less addicted to wine than was generally believed; that which gave people occasion to think so of him was, that when he had nothing else to do, he loved to sit long and talk, rather than drink, and over every cup hold a long conversation. For when his affairs called upon him, he would not be detained, as other generals often were, either by wine, or sleep, nuptial solemnities, spectacles, or any other diversion whatsoever; a convincing argument of which is, that in the short time he lived, he accomplished so many and so great actions. When he was free from employment, after he was up, and had sacrificed to the gods, he used to sit down to breakfast, and then spend the rest of the day in hunting, or writing memoirs, giving decisions on some military questions, or reading. In marches that required no great haste, he would practice shooting as he went along, or to mount a chariot and alight from it in full speed. Sometimes, for sport's sake, as his journals tell us, he would hunt foxes and go fowling. When he came in for the evening, after he had bathed and was anointed, he would call for his bakers and chief cooks, to know if they had his dinner ready. He never cared to dine till it was pretty late and beginning to be dark, and was wonderfully circumspect at meals that everyone who sat with him should be served alike and with proper attention; and his love of talking, as was said before, made him delight to sit long at his wine. And then, though otherwise no prince's conversation was ever so agreeable, he would fall into a temper of ostentation and soldierly boasting, which gave his flatterers a great advantage to ride him, and made his better friends very uneasy. For though they thought it too base to strive who should flatter him most, yet they found it hazardous not to do it; so that between the shame and the danger, they were in a great strait how to behave themselves. After such an entertainment, he was wont to bathe, and then perhaps he would sleep till noon, and sometimes all day long. He was so very temperate in his eating, that when any rare fish or fruits were sent him, he would distribute them among his friends, and often reserve nothing for himself. His table, however, was always magnificent, the expense of it still increasing with his good fortune, till it amounted to ten thousand drachmas a day, to which sum he limited it, and beyond this he would suffer none to lay out in any entertainment where he himself was the guest.

After the battle of Issus, he sent to Damascus to seize upon the money and baggage, the wives and children, of the Persians, of which spoil the Thessalian horsemen had the greatest share; for he had taken particular notice of their gallantry in the fight, and sent them thither on purpose to make their reward suitable to their courage. Not but that the rest of the army had so considerable a part of the booty as was sufficient to enrich them all. This first gave the Macedonians such a taste of the Persian wealth and women and barbaric splendor of living, that they were ready to pursue and follow upon it with all the eagerness of hounds upon a scent. But Alexander, before he proceeded any further, thought it necessary to assure himself of the seacoast. Those who governed in Cyprus put that island into his possession, and Phoenicia, Tyre only excepted, was surrendered to him. During the siege of this city, which with mounds of earth cast up, and battering engines, and two hundred galleys by sea, was carried on for seven months together, he dreamt that he saw Hercules upon the walls, reaching out his hands, and calling to him. And many of the Tyrians in their sleep fancied that Apollo told them he was displeased with their actions, and was about to leave them and go over to Alexander. Upon which, as if the god had been a deserting soldier, they seized him, so to say, in the act, tied down the statue with ropes, and nailed it to the pedestal, reproaching him that he was a favorer of Alexander. Another time Alexander dreamed he saw a satyr mocking him at a distance, and when he endeavored to catch him, he still escaped from him, till at last with much perseverance, and running about after him, he got him into his power. The soothsayers, making two words of *Satyrus,* assured him that Tyre should be his own. The inhabitants at this time show a spring of water, near which they say Alexander slept when he fancied the satyr appeared to him.

While the body of the army lay before Tyre, he made an excursion against the Arabians who inhabit the Mount Antilibanus, in which he hazarded his life extremely to bring off his master Lysimachus, who would needs go along with him, declaring he was neither older nor inferior in courage to Phœnix, Achilles's guardian. For when, quitting their horses, they began to march up the hills on foot, the rest of the soldiers outwent them a great deal, so that night drawing on, and the enemy near, Alexander was fain to stay behind so long, to encourage and help up the lagging and tired old man, that before he was aware, he was left behind, a great way from his soldiers, with a slender attendance, and forced to pass an extremely cold night in the dark, and in a very inconvenient place; till seeing a great many scattered fires of the enemy at some distance, and trusting to his agility of body, and as he was always wont by undergoing toils and labors himself to cheer and support the Macedonians in any distress, he ran straight to one of the nearest fires, and with his dagger dispatching two of the barbarians that sat by it, snatched up a lighted brand, and returned with it to his own men. They immediately made a great fire, which so alarmed the enemy that most of them fled, and those that assaulted them were soon routed, and thus they rested securely the remainder of the night. Thus Chares writes.

But to return to the siege, it had this issue. Alexander, that he might refresh his army, harassed with many former encounters, had led only a small party towards the walls, rather to keep the enemy busy than with any prospect of much advantage. It happened at this time that Aristander, the soothsayer, after he had sacrificed, upon view of the entrails, affirmed confidently to those who stood by that the city should be certainly taken that very month, upon which there was a laugh and some mockery among the soldiers, as this was the last day of it. The king seeing him in perplexity, and always anxious to support the credit of the predictions, gave order that they should not count it as the thirtieth, but as the twenty-third of the month, and ordering the trumpets to sound, attacked the walls more seriously than he at first intended. The sharpness of the assault so inflamed the rest of his forces who were left in the camp, that they could not hold from advancing to second it, which they performed with so much vigor that the Tyrians retired, and the town was carried that very day. The next place he sat down before was Gaza, one of the largest cities of Syria, where this accident befell him. A large bird flying over him let a clod of earth fall upon his shoulder, and then, settling upon one of the battering engines, was suddenly entangled and caught in the nets, composed of sinews, which protected the ropes with which the machine was managed. This fell out exactly according to Aristander's prediction, which was, that Alexander should be wounded and the city reduced.

From hence he sent great part of the spoils to Olympias, Cleopatra, and the rest of his friends, not omitting his preceptor Leonidas, on whom he bestowed five hundred talents' weight of frankincense, and a hundred of myrrh, in remembrance of the hopes he had once expressed of him when he was but a child. For Leonidas, it seems, standing by him one day while he was sacrificing, and seeing him take both his hands full of incense to throw into the fire, told him it became him to be more sparing in his offerings, and not be so profuse till he was master of the countries which those sweet gums and spices came from. So Alexander now wrote to him, saying, "We have sent you abundance of myrrh and frankincense, that for the future you may not be stingy to the gods." Among the treasures and other booty that was taken from Darius, there was a very precious casket, which being brought to Alexander for a great rarity, he asked those about him what they thought fittest to be laid up in it; and when they had delivered their various opinions, he told them he should keep Homer's Iliad in it. This is attested by many credible authors, and if what those of Alexandria tell us, relying upon the authority of Heraclides, be true, Homer was neither an idle nor an unprofitable companion to him in his expedition. For when he was master of Egypt, designing to settle a colony of Grecians there, he resolved to build a large and populous city, and give it his own name. In order to which, after he had measured and staked out the ground with the advice of the best architects, he chanced one night in his sleep to see a wonderful vision; a grey-headed old man, of a venerable aspect, appeared to stand by him, and pronounce these verses:—

"An island lies, where loud the billows roar,
    Pharos they call it, on the Egyptian shore."

Alexander upon this immediately rose up and went to Pharos, which, at that time, was an island lying a little above the Canobic mouth of the river Nile, though it has now been joined to the mainland by a mole. As soon as he saw the commodious situation of the place, it being a long neck of land, stretching like an isthmus between large lagoons and shallow waters on one side and the sea on the other, the latter at the end of it making a spacious harbor, he said, Homer, besides his other excellences, was a very good architect, and ordered the plan of a city to be drawn out answerable to the place. To do which, for want of chalk, the soil being black, they laid out their lines with flour, taking in a pretty large compass of ground in a semicircular figure, and drawing into the inside of the circumference equal straight lines from each end, thus giving it something of the form of a cloak or cape; while he was pleasing himself with his design, on a sudden an infinite number of great birds of several kinds, rising like a black cloud out of the river and the lake, devoured every morsel of the flour that had been used in setting out the lines; at which omen even Alexander himself was troubled, till the augurs restored his confidence again by telling him it was a sign the city he was about to build would not only abound in all things within itself, but also be the nurse and feeder of many nations. He commanded the workmen to proceed, while he went to visit the temple of Ammon.

This was a long and painful, and, in two respects, a dangerous journey; first, if they should lose their provision of water, as for several days none could be obtained; and, secondly, if a violent south wind should rise upon them, while they were traveling through the wide extent of deep sands, as it is said to have done when Cambyses led his army that way, blowing the sand together in heaps, and raising, as it were, the whole desert like a sea upon them, till fifty thousand were swallowed up and destroyed by it. All these difficulties were weighed and represented to him; but Alexander was not easily to be diverted from anything he was bent upon. For fortune having hitherto seconded him in his designs, made him resolute and firm in his opinions, and the boldness of his temper raised a sort of passion in him for surmounting difficulties; as if it were not enough to be always victorious in the field, unless places and seasons and nature herself submitted to him. In this journey, the relief and assistance the gods afforded him in his distresses were more remarkable, and obtained greater belief than the oracles he received afterwards, which, however, were valued and credited the more on account of those occurrences. For first, plentiful rains that fell preserved them from any fear of perishing by drought, and, allaying the extreme dryness of the sand, which now became moist and firm to travel on, cleared and purified the air. Besides this, when they were out of their way, and were wandering up and down, because the marks which were wont to direct the guides were disordered and lost, they were set right again by some ravens, which flew before them when on their march, and waited for them when they lingered and fell behind; and the greatest miracle, as Callisthenes tells us, was that if any of the company went astray in the night, they never ceased croaking and making a noise till by that means they had brought them into the right way again. Having passed through the wilderness, they came to the place; where the high priest at the first salutation bade Alexander welcome from his father Ammon. And being asked by him whether any of his father's murderers had escaped punishment, he charged him to speak with more respect, since his was not a mortal father. Then Alexander, changing his expression, desired to know of him if any of those who murdered Philip were yet unpunished, and further concerning dominion, whether the empire of the world was reserved for him? This, the god answered, he should obtain, and that Philip's death was fully revenged, which gave him so much satisfaction that he made splendid offerings to Jupiter, and gave the priests very rich presents. This is what most authors write concerning the oracles. But Alexander, in a letter to his mother, tells her there were some secret answers, which at his return he would communicate to her only. Others say that the priest, desirous as a piece of courtesy to address him in Greek, "O Paidion," by a slip in pronunciation ended with the *s* instead of the *n,* and said, "O Paidios," which mistake Alexander was well enough pleased with, and it went for current that the oracle had called him so.[1]

---

[1] [The priest addressed him as "son of god" instead of "young man."]

Among the sayings of one Psammon, a philosopher, whom he heard in Egypt, he most approved of this, that all men are governed by God, because in everything, that which is chief and commands is divine. But what he pronounced himself upon this subject was even more like a philosopher, for he said, God was the common father of us all, but more particularly of the best of us. To the barbarians he carried himself very haughtily, as if he were fully persuaded of his divine birth and parentage; but to the Grecians more moderately, and with less affectation of divinity, except it were once in writing to the Athenians about Samos, when he tells them that he should not himself have bestowed upon them that free and glorious city; "You received it," he says, "from the bounty of him who at that time was called my lord and father," meaning Philip. However, afterwards being wounded with an arrow, and feeling much pain, he turned to those about him, and told them, "This, my friends, is real flowing blood, not ichor—

"Such as immortal gods are wont to shed."

And another time, when it thundered so much that everybody was afraid, and Anaxarchus, the sophist, asked him if he who was Jupiter's son could do anything like this, "Nay," said Alexander, laughing, "I have no desire to be formidable to my friends, as you would have me, who despised my table for being furnished with fish, and not with the heads of governors of provinces." For in fact it is related as true, that Anaxarchus, seeing a present of small fishes, which the king sent to Hephæstion, had used this expression, in a sort of irony, and disparagement of those who undergo vast labors and encounter great hazards in pursuit of magnificent objects, which after all bring them little more pleasure or enjoyment than what others have. From what I have said upon this subject, it is apparent that Alexander in himself was not foolishly affected, or had the vanity to think himself really a god, but merely used his claims to divinity as a means of maintaining among other people the sense of his superiority.

At his return out of Egypt into Phœnicia, he sacrificed and made solemn processions, to which were added shows of lyric dances and tragedies, remarkable not merely for the splendor of the equipage and decorations, but for the competition among those who exhibited them. For the kings of Cyprus were here the exhibitors, just in the same manner as at Athens those who are chosen by lot out of the tribes. And, indeed, they showed the greatest emulation to outvie each other; especially Nicocreon, king of Salamis, and Pasicrates of Soli, who furnished the chorus, and defrayed the expenses of the two most celebrated actors, Athenodorus and Thessalus, the former performing for Pasicrates, and the latter for Nicocreon. Thessalus was most favored by Alexander, though it did not appear till Athenodorus was declared victor by the plurality of votes. For then at his going away, he said the judges deserved to be commended for what they had done, but that he would willingly have lost part of his kingdom rather than to have seen Thessalus overcome. However, when he understood Athenodorus was fined by the Athenians for being absent at the festivals of Bacchus, though he refused his request that he would write a letter in his behalf, he gave him a sufficient sum to satisfy the penalty. Another time, when Lycon of Scarphia happened to act with great applause in the theater, and in a verse which he introduced into the comic part which he was acting, begged for a present of ten talents, he laughed and gave him the money.

Darius wrote him a letter, and sent friends to intercede with him, requesting him to accept as a ransom of his captives the sum of a thousand talents, and offering him in exchange for his amity and alliance all the countries on this side the river Euphrates, together with one of his daughters in marriage. These propositions he communicated to his friends, and when Parmenio told him that, for his part, if he were Alexander, he should readily embrace them, "So would I," said Alexander, "if I were Parmenio." Accordingly, his answer to Darius was, that if he would come and yield himself up into his power, he would treat him with all possible kindness; if not, he was resolved immediately to go himself and seek him. But the death of Darius's wife in childbirth made him soon after regret one part of this answer, and he showed evident marks of grief at being thus deprived of a further opportunity of exercising his clemency and good nature, which he manifested, however, as far as he could, by giving her a most sumptuous funeral.

Among the eunuchs who waited in the queen's chamber, and were taken prisoners with the women, there was one Tireus, who, getting out of the camp, fled away on horseback to Darius, to inform him of his wife's death. He, when he heard it, beating his head, and bursting into tears and lamentations, said, "Alas! how great is the calamity of the Persians! Was it not enough that their king's consort and sister was a prisoner in her lifetime, but she must, now she is dead, also be but meanly and obscurely buried?" "Oh king," replied the eunuch, "as to her funeral rites, or any respect or honor that should have been shown in them, you have not the least reason to accuse the ill fortune of your country; for to my knowledge neither your queen Statira when alive, nor your mother, nor children, wanted anything of their former happy condition, unless it were the light of your countenance, which I doubt not but the lord Oromasdes will yet restore to its former glory. And after her decease, I assure you, she had not only all due funeral ornaments, but was honored also with the tears of your very enemies; for Alexander is as gentle after victory as he is terrible in the field." At the hearing of these words, such was the grief and emotion of Darius's mind, that they carried him into extravagant suspicions; and taking Tireus aside into a more private part of his tent, "Unless thou likewise," said he to him, "hast deserted me, together with the good fortune of Persia, and art become a Macedonian in thy heart; if thou yet ownest me for thy master Darius, tell me, I charge thee, by the veneration thou payest the light of Mithras, and this right hand of thy king, do I not lament the least of Statira's misfortunes in her captivity and death? Have I not suffered something more injurious and deplorable in her lifetime? And had I not been miserable with less dishonor if I had met with a more severe and inhuman enemy? For how is it possible a young man as he is should treat the wife of his opponent with so much distinction, were it not from some motive that does me disgrace?" Whilst he was yet speaking, Tireus threw himself at his feet, and besought him neither to wrong Alexander so much, nor his dead wife and sister, as to give utterance to any such thoughts, which deprived him of the greatest consolation left him in his adversity, the belief that he was overcome by a man whose virtues raised him above human nature; that he ought to look upon Alexander with love and admiration, who had given no less proofs of his continence towards the Persian women, than of his valor among the men. The eunuch confirmed all he said with solemn and dreadful oaths, and was further enlarging upon Alexander's moderation and magnanimity on other occasions, when Darius, breaking away from him into the other division of the tent, where his friends and courtiers were, lifted up his hands to heaven, and uttered this prayer, "Ye gods," said he, "of my family, and of my kingdom, if it be possible, I beseech you to restore the declining affairs of Persia, that I may leave them in as flourishing a condition as I found them, and have it in my power to make a grateful return to Alexander for the kindness which in my adversity he has shown to those who are dearest to me. But if, indeed, the fatal time be come, which is to give a period to the Persian monarchy, if our ruin be a debt that must be paid to the divine jealousy and the vicissitude of things, then I beseech you grant that no other man but Alexander may sit upon the throne of Cyrus." Such is the narrative given by the greater number of the historians.

But to return to Alexander. After he had reduced all Asia on this side the Euphrates, he advanced towards Darius, who was coming down against him with a million of men. In his march, a very ridiculous passage happened. The servants who followed the camp for sport's sake divided themselves into two parties, and named the commander of one of them Alexander, and of the other Darius. At first they only pelted one another with clods of earth, but presently took to their fists, and at last, heated with the contention, they fought in good earnest with stones and clubs, so that they had much ado to part them; till Alexander, upon hearing of it, ordered the two captains to decide the quarrel by single combat, and armed him who bore his name himself, while Philotas did the same to him who represented Darius. The whole army were spectators of this encounter, willing from the event of it to derive an omen of their own future success. After they had fought stoutly a pretty long while, at last he who was called Alexander had the better, and for a reward of his prowess, had twelve villages given him, with leave to wear the Persian dress. So we are told by Eratosthenes.

But the great battle of all that was fought with Darius was not, as most writers tell us, at Arbela, but at Gaugamela, which, in their language, signifies the camel's house, forasmuch as one of their ancient kings having escaped the pursuit of his enemies on a swift camel, in gratitude to his beast, settled him at this place, with an allowance of certain villages and rents for his maintenance. It came to pass that in the month Boëdromion, about the beginning of the feast of Mysteries at Athens, there was an eclipse of the moon, the eleventh night after which, the two armies being now in view of one another, Darius kept his men in arms, and by torch-light took a general review of them. But Alexander, while his soldiers slept, spent the night before his tent with his diviner, Aristander, performing certain mysterious ceremonies, and sacrificing to the god Fear. In the meanwhile the oldest of his commanders, and chiefly Parmenio, when they beheld all the plain between Niphates and the Gordyæan mountains shining with the lights and fires which were made by the barbarians, and heard the uncertain and confused sound of voices out of their camp, like the distant roaring of a vast ocean, were so amazed at the thoughts of such a multitude, that after some conference among themselves, they concluded it an enterprise too difficult and hazardous for them to engage so numerous an enemy in the day, and therefore meeting the king as he came from sacrificing, besought him to attack Darius by night, that the darkness might conceal the danger of the ensuing battle. To this he gave them the celebrated answer, "I will not steal a victory," which though some at the time thought a boyish and inconsiderate speech, as if he played with danger, others, however, regarded as an evidence that he confided in his present condition, and acted on a true judgment of the future, not wishing to leave Darius, in case he were worsted, the pretext of trying his fortune again, which he might suppose himself to have, if he could impute his overthrow to the disadvantage of the night, as he did before to the mountains, the narrow passages, and the sea. For while he had such numerous forces and large dominions still remaining, it was not any want of men or arms that could induce him to give up the war, but only the loss of all courage and hope upon the conviction of an undeniable and manifest defeat.

After they were gone from him with this answer, he laid himself down in his tent and slept the rest of the night more soundly than was usual with him, to the astonishment of the commanders, who came to him early in the morning, and were fain themselves to give order that the soldiers should breakfast. But at last, time not giving them leave to wait any longer, Parmenio went to his bedside, and called him twice or thrice by his name, till he waked him, and then asked him how it was possible, when he was to fight the most important battle of all, he could sleep as soundly as if he were already victorious. "And are we not so, indeed," replied Alexander, smiling, "since we are at last relieved from the trouble of wandering in pursuit of Darius through a wide and wasted country, hoping in vain that he would fight us?" And not only before the battle, but in the height of the danger, he showed himself great, and manifested the self-possession of a just foresight and confidence. For the battle for some time fluctuated and was dubious. The left wing, where Parmenio commanded, was so impetuously charged by the Bactrian horse that it was disordered and forced to give ground, at the same time that Mazæus had sent a detachment round about to fall upon those who guarded the baggage, which so disturbed Parmenio that he sent messengers to acquaint Alexander that the camp and baggage would be all lost unless he immediately relieved the rear by a considerable reinforcement drawn out of the front. This message being brought him just as he was giving the signal to those about him for the onset, he bade them tell Parmenio that he must have surely lost the use of his reason, and had forgotten, in his alarm, that soldiers, if victorious, become masters of their enemies' baggage; and if defeated, instead of taking care of their wealth or their slaves, have nothing more to do but to fight gallantly and die with honor. When he had said this, he put on his helmet, having the rest of his arms on before he came out of his tent, which were coat of the Sicilian make, girt close about him, and over that a breastpiece of thickly quilted linen, which was taken among other booty at the battle of Issus. The helmet, which was made by Theophilus, though of iron, was so well wrought and polished that it was as bright as the most refined silver. To this was fitted a gorget of the same metal, set with precious stones. His sword, which was the weapon he most used in fight, was given him by the king of the Citieans, and was of an admirable temper and lightness. The belt which he also wore in all engagements was of much richer workmanship than the rest of his armor. It was a work of the ancient Helicon, and had been presented to him by the Rhodians, as mark of their respect to him. So long as he was engaged in drawing up his men, or riding about to give orders or directions, or to view them, he spared Bucephalus, who was now growing old, and made use of another horse; but when he was actually to fight, he sent for him again, and as soon as he was mounted, commenced the attack.

He made the longest address that day to the Thessalians and other

Greeks, who answered him with loud shouts, desiring him to lead them on against the barbarians, upon which he shifted his javelin into his left hand, and with his right lifted up towards heaven, besought the gods, as Callisthenes tells us, that if he was of a truth the son of Jupiter, they would be pleased to assist and strengthen the Grecians. At the same time the augur Aristander, who had a white mantle about him, and a crown of gold on his head, rode by and showed them an eagle that soared just over Alexander, and directed his flight towards the enemy; which so animated the beholders, that after mutual encouragements and exhortations, the horse charged at full speed, and were followed in a mass by the whole phalanx of the foot. But before they could well come to blows with the first ranks, the barbarians shrunk back, and were hotly pursued by Alexander, who drove those that fled before him into the middle of the battle, where Darius himself was in person, whom he saw from a distance over the foremost ranks, conspicuous in the midst of his life-guard, a tall and fine-looking man, drawn in a lofty chariot, defended by an abundance of the best horse, who stood close in order about it, ready to receive the enemy. But Alexander's approach was so terrible, forcing those who gave back upon those who yet maintained their ground, that he beat down and dispersed them almost all. Only a few of the bravest and valiantest opposed the pursuit, who were slain in their king's presence, falling in heaps upon one another, and in the very pangs of death striving to catch hold of the horses. Darius now seeing all was lost, that those who were placed in front to defend him were broken and beat back upon him, that he could not turn or disengage his chariot without great difficulty, the wheels being clogged and entangled among the dead bodies, which lay in such heaps as not only stopped, but almost covered the horses, and made them rear and grow so unruly that the frightened charioteer could govern them no longer, in this extremity was glad to quit his chariot and his arms, and mounting, it is said, upon a mare that had been taken from her foal, betook himself to flight. But he had not escaped so either, if Parmenio had not sent fresh messengers to Alexander, to desire him to return and assist him against a considerable body of the enemy which yet stood together, and would not give ground. For, indeed, Parmenio is on all hands accused of having been sluggish and unserviceable in this battle, whether age had impaired his courage, or that, as Callisthenes says, he secretly disliked and envied Alexander's growing greatness. Alexander, though he was not a little vexed to be so recalled and hindered from pursuing his victory, yet concealed the true reason from his men, and causing a retreat to be sounded, as if it were too late to continue the execution any longer, marched back towards the place of danger, and by the way met with the news of the enemy's total overthrow and flight.

This battle being thus over, seemed to put a period to the Persian empire; and Alexander, who was now proclaimed king of Asia, returned thanks to the gods in magnificent sacrifices, and rewarded his friends and followers with great sums of money, and places, and governments of provinces. And eager to gain honor with the Grecians, he wrote to them that he would have all tyrannies abolished, that they might live free according to their own laws, and specially to the Platæans, that their city should be rebuilt, because their ancestors had permitted their countrymen of old to make their territory the seat of the war when they fought with the barbarians for their common liberty. He sent also part of the spoils into Italy, to the Crotoniats, to honor the zeal and courage of their citizen Phayllus, the wrestler, who, in the Median war, when the other Grecian colonies in Italy disowned Greece, that he might have a share in the danger, joined the fleet at Salamis, with a vessel set forth at his own charge. So affectionate was Alexander to all kind of virtue, and so desirous to preserve the memory of laudable actions.

From hence he marched through the province of Babylon, which immediately submitted to him, and in Ecbatana was much surprised at the sight of the place where fire issues in a continuous stream, like a spring of water, out of a cleft in the earth, and the stream of naphtha, which, not far from this spot, flows out so abundantly as to form a sort of lake. This naphtha, in other respects resembling bitumen, is so subject to take fire, that before it touches the flame, it will kindle at the very light that surrounds it, and often inflame the intermediate air also. The barbarians, to show the power and nature of it, sprinkled the street that led to the king's lodgings with little drops of it, and when it was almost night, stood at the further end with torches, which being applied to the moistened places, the first at once taking fire, instantly, as quick as a man could think of it, it caught from one end to another, in such a manner that the whole street was one continued flame. Among those who used to wait on the king and find occasion to amuse him when he anointed and washed himself, there was one Athenophanes, an Athenian, who desired him to make an experiment of the naphtha upon Stephanus, who stood by in the bathing place, a youth with a ridiculously ugly face, whose talent was singing well, "For," said he, "if it take hold of him and is not put out, it must undeniably be allowed to be of the most invincible strength." The youth, as it happened, readily consented to undergo the trial, and as soon as he was anointed and rubbed with it, his whole body broke out into such a flame, and was so seized by the fire, that Alexander was in the greatest perplexity and alarm for him, and not without reason; for nothing could have prevented his being consumed by it, if by good chance there had not been people at hand with a great many vessels of water for the service of the bath, with all which they had much ado to extinguish the fire; and his body was so burned all over, that he was not cured of it for a good while after. And thus it is not without some plausibility that they endeavor to reconcile the fable to truth, who say this was the drug in the tragedies with which Medea anointed the crown and veil which she gave to Creon's daughter. For neither the things themselves, nor the fire, could kindle of its own accord, but being prepared for it by the naphtha, they imperceptibly attracted and caught a flame which happened to be brought near them. For the rays and emanations of fire at a distance have no other effect upon some bodies than bare light and heat, but in others, where they meet with airy dryness, and also sufficient rich moisture, they collect themselves and soon kindle and create a transformation. The manner, however, of the production of naphtha admits of a diversity of opinion on whether this liquid substance that feeds the flame does not rather proceed from a soil that is unctuous and productive of fire, as that of the province of Babylon is, where the ground is so very hot that oftentimes the grains of barley leap up and are thrown out, as if the violent inflammation had made the earth throb; and in the extreme heats the inhabitants are wont to sleep upon skins filled with water. Harpalus, who was left governor of this country, and was desirous to adorn the palace gardens and walks with Grecian plants, succeeded in raising all but ivy, which the earth would not bear, but constantly killed. For being a plant that loves a cold soil, the temper of this hot and fiery earth was improper for it. But such digressions as these the impatient reader will be more willing to pardon, if they are kept within a moderate compass.

At the taking of Susa, Alexander found in the palace forty thousand talents in money ready coined, besides an unspeakable quantity of other furniture and treasure; amongst which was five thousand talents' worth of Hermionian purple, that had been laid up there a hundred and ninety years, and yet kept its color as fresh and lively as at first. The reason of which, they say, is that in dyeing the purple they made use of honey, and of white oil in the white tincture, both which after the like space of time preserve the clearness and brightness of their luster. Dinon also relates that the Persian kings had water fetched from the Nile and the Danube, which they laid up in their treasuries as a sort of testimony of the greatness of their power and universal empire.

The entrance into Persia was through a most difficult country, and was guarded by the noblest of the Persians, Darius himself having escaped further. Alexander, however, chanced to find a guide in exact correspondence with what the Pythia had foretold when he was a child, that a lycus should conduct him into Persia. For by such an one, whose father was a Lycian, and his mother a Persian, and who spoke both languages, he was now led into the country, by a way something about, yet without fetching any considerable compass. Here a great many of the prisoners were put to the sword, of which himself gives this account, that he commanded them to be killed in the belief that it would be for his advantage. Nor was the money found here less, he says, than at Susa, besides other movables and treasure, as much as ten thousand pair of mules and five thousand camels could well carry away. Amongst other things he happened to observe a large statue of Xerxes thrown carelessly down to the ground in the confusion made by the multitude of soldiers pressing into the palace. He stood still, and accosting it as if it had been alive, "Shall we," said he, "neglectfully pass thee by, now thou art prostrate on the ground, because thou once invadedst Greece, or shall we erect thee again in consideration of the greatness of thy mind and thy other virtues?" But at last, after he had paused some time, and silently considered with himself, he went on without taking any further notice of it. In this place he took up his winter quarters, and stayed four months to refresh his soldiers. It is related that the first time he sat on the royal throne of Persia, under the canopy of gold, Demaratus, the Corinthian, who was much attached to him and had been one of his father's friends, wept, in an old man's manner, and deplored the misfortune of those Greeks whom death had deprived of the satisfaction of seeing Alexander seated on the throne of Darius.

From hence designing to march against Darius, before he set out he diverted himself with his officers at an entertainment of drinking and other pastimes, and indulged so far as to let every one's mistress sit by and drink with them. The most celebrated of them was Thais, an Athenian, mistress of Ptolemy, who was afterwards king of Egypt. She, partly as a sort of well-turned compliment to Alexander, partly out of sport, as the drinking went on, at last was carried so far as to utter a saying, not misbecoming her native country's character, though somewhat too lofty for her own condition. She said it was indeed some recompense for the toils she had undergone in following the camp all over Asia, that she was that day treated in, and could insult over, the stately palace of the Persian monarchs. But, she added, it would please her much better if, while the king looked on, she might in sport, with her own hands, set fire to the court of that Xerxes who reduced the city of Athens to ashes, that it might be recorded to posterity that the women who followed Alexander had taken a severer revenge on the Persians for the sufferings and affronts of Greece, than all the famed commanders had been able to do by sea or land. What she said was received with such universal liking and murmurs of applause, and so seconded by the encouragement and eagerness of the company, that the king himself, persuaded to be of the party, started from his seat, and with a chaplet of flowers on his head and a lighted torch in his hand, led them the way, while they went after him in a riotous manner, dancing and making loud cries about the place; which when the rest of the Macedonians perceived, they also in great delight ran thither with torches; for they hoped the burning and destruction of the royal palace was an argument that he looked homeward, and had no design to reside among the barbarians. Thus some writers give their account of this action, while others say it was done deliberately; however, all agree that he soon repented of it, and gave order to put out the fire.

Alexander was naturally most munificent, and grew more so as his fortune increased, accompanying what he gave with that courtesy and freedom which, to speak truth, is necessary to make a benefit really obliging. I will give a few instances of this kind. Ariston, the captain of the Paeonians, having killed an enemy, brought his head to show him, and told him that in his country such a present was recompensed with a cup of gold. "With an empty one," said Alexander, smiling, "but I drink to you in this, which I give you full of wine." Another time, as one of the common soldiers was driving a mule laden with some of the king's treasure, the beast grew tired, and the soldier took it upon his own back, and began to march with it, till Alexander, seeing the man so overcharged, asked what was the matter; and when he was informed, just as he was ready to lay down his burden for weariness, "Do not faint now," said he to him, "but finish the journey, and carry what you have there to your own tent for yourself." He was always more displeased with those who would not accept of what he gave than with those who begged of him. And therefore he wrote to Phocion, that he would not own him for his friend any longer if he refused his presents. He had never given anything to Serapion, one of the youths that played at ball with him, because he did not ask of him, till one day, it coming to Serapion's turn to play, he still threw the ball to others, and when the king asked him why he did not direct it to him, "Because you do not ask for it," said he; which answer pleased him so that he was very liberal to him afterwards. One Proteas, a pleasant, jesting, drinking fellow, having incurred his displeasure, got his friends to intercede for him, and begged his pardon himself with tears, which at last prevailed, and Alexander declared he was friends with him. "I cannot believe it," said Proteas, "unless you first give me some pledge of it." The king understood his meaning, and presently ordered five talents to be given him. How magnificent he was in enriching his friends, and those who attended on his person, appears by a letter which Olympias wrote to him, where she tells him he should reward and honor those about him in a more moderate way. "For now," said she, "you make them all equal to kings, you give them power and opportunity of making many friends of their own, and in the meantime you leave yourself destitute." She often wrote to him to this purpose, and he never communicated her letters to anybody, unless it were one which he opened when Hephæstion was by, whom he permitted, as his custom was, to read it along with him; but then as soon as he had done, he took off his ring, and set the seal upon Hephæstion's lips. Mazæus, who was the most considerable man in Darius's court, had a son who was already governor of a province. Alexander bestowed another upon him that was better; he, however, modestly refused, and told him, instead of one Darius, he went the way to make many Alexanders. To Parmenio he gave Bagoas's house, in which he found a wardrobe of apparel worth more than a thousand talents. He wrote to Antipater, commanding him to keep a life-guard about him for the security of his person against conspiracies. To his mother he sent many presents, but would never suffer her to meddle with matters of state or war, not indulging her busy temper, and when she fell out with him upon this account, he bore her ill humor very patiently. Nay more, when he read a long letter from Antipater, full of accusations against her, "Antipater," he said, "does not know that one tear of a mother effaces a thousand such letters as these."

But when he perceived his favorites grow so luxurious and extravagant in their way of living and expenses, that Hagnon, the Teian, wore silver nails in his shoes, that Leonnatus employed several camels only to bring him powder out of Egypt to use when he wrestled, and that Philotas had hunting nets a hundred furlongs in length, that more used precious ointment than plain oil when they went to bathe, and that they carried about servants everywhere with them to rub them and wait upon them in their chambers, he reproved them in gentle and reasonable terms, telling them he wondered that they who had been engaged in so many signal battles did not know by experience, that those who labor sleep more sweetly and soundly than those who are labored for, and could fail to see by comparing the Persians' manner of living with their own that it was the most abject and slavish condition to be voluptuous, but the most noble and royal to undergo pain and labor. He argued with them further, how it was possible for anyone who pretended to be a soldier, either to look well after his horse, or to keep his armor bright and in good order, who thought it much to let his hands be serviceable to what was nearest to him, his own body. "Are you still to learn," said he, "that the end and perfection of our victories is to avoid the vices and infirmities of those whom we subdue?" And to strengthen his precepts by example, he applied himself now more vigorously than ever to hunting and warlike expeditions, embracing all opportunities of hardship and danger, insomuch that a Lacedæmonian, who was there on an embassy to him, and chanced to be by when he encountered with and mastered a huge lion, told him he had fought gallantly with the beast, which of the two should be king. Craterus caused a representation to be made of this adventure, consisting of the lion and the dogs, of the king engaged with the lion, and himself coming in to his assistance, all expressed in figures of brass, some of which were by Lysippus, and the rest by Leochares; and had it dedicated in the temple of Apollo at Delphi. Alexander exposed his person to danger in this manner, with the object both of inuring himself and inciting others to the performance of brave and virtuous actions.

But his followers, who were grown rich, and consequently proud, longed to indulge themselves in pleasure and idleness, and were weary of marches and expeditions, and at last went on so far as to censure and speak ill of him. All which at first he bore very patiently, saying it became a king well to do good to others, and be evil spoken of. Meantime, on the smallest occasions that called for a show of kindness to his friends, there was every indication on his part of tenderness and respect. Hearing Peucestes was bitten by a bear, he wrote to him that he took it unkindly he should send others notice of it, and not make him acquainted with it; "But now," said he, "since it is so, let me know how you do, and whether any of your companions forsook you when you were in danger, that I may punish them." He sent Hephæstion, who was absent about some business, word how, while they were fighting for their diversion with an ichneumon, Craterus was by chance run through both thighs with Perdiccas's javelin. And upon Peucestes's recovery from a fit of sickness, he sent a letter of thanks to his physician Alexippus. When Craterus was ill, he saw a vision in his sleep, after which he offered sacrifices for his health, and bade him to do so likewise. He wrote also to Pausanias, the physician, who was about to purge Craterus with hellebore, partly out of an anxious concern for him, and partly to give him a caution how he used that medicine. He was so tender of his friends' reputation that he imprisoned Ephialtes and Cissus, who brought him the first news of Harpalus's flight and withdrawal from his service, as if they had falsely accused him. When he sent the old and infirm soldiers home, Eurylochus, a citizen of Ægæ, got his name enrolled among the sick, though he ailed nothing, which being discovered, he confessed he was in love with a young woman named Telesippa, and wanted to go along with her to the seaside. Alexander inquired to whom the woman belonged, and being told she was a free courtesan, "I will assist you," said he to Eurylochus, "in your amour, if your mistress be to be gained either by presents or persuasions; but we must use no other means, because she is free-born."

It is surprising to consider upon what slight occasions he would write letters to serve his friends. As when he wrote one in which he gave order to search for a youth that belonged to Seleucus, who was run away into Cilicia; and in another, thanked and commended Peucestes for apprehending Nicon, a servant of Craterus; and in one to Megabyzus, concerning a slave that had taken sanctuary in a temple, gave direction that he should not meddle with him while he was there, but if he could entice him out by fair means, then he gave him leave to seize him. It is reported of him that when he first sat in judgment upon capital causes, he would lay his hand upon one of his ears while the accuser spoke, to keep it free and unprejudiced in behalf of the party accused. But afterwards such a multitude of accusations were brought before him, and so many proved true, that he lost his tenderness of heart, and gave credit to those also that were false; and especially when anybody spoke ill of him, he would be transported out of his reason, and show himself cruel and inexorable, valuing his glory and reputation beyond his life or kingdom.

He now, as we said, set forth to seek Darius, expecting he should be put to the hazard of another battle, but heard he was taken and secured by Bessus, upon which news he sent home the Thessalians, and gave them a largess of two thousand talents over and above the pay that was due to them. This long and painful pursuit of Darius—for in eleven days he marched thirty-three hundred furlongs—harassed his soldiers so that most of them were ready to give it up, chiefly for want of water. While they were in this distress, it happened that some Macedonians, who had fetched water in skins upon their mules from a river they had found out, came about noon to the place where Alexander was, and seeing him almost choked with thirst, presently filled a helmet and offered it him. He asked them to whom they were carrying the water; they told him to their children, adding, that if his life were but saved, it was no matter for them, they should be able well enough to repair that loss, though they all perished. Then he took the helmet into his hands, and looking round about, when he saw all those who were near him stretching their heads out and looking earnestly after the drink, he returned it again with thanks without tasting a drop of it, "For," said he, "if I alone should drink, the rest will be out of heart." The soldiers no sooner took notice of his temperance and magnanimity upon this occasion, but they one and all cried out to him to lead them forward boldly, and began whipping on their horses. For whilst they had such a king, they said, they defied both weariness and thirst, and looked upon themselves to be little less than immortal. But though they were all equally cheerful and willing, yet not above three-score horse were able, it is said, to keep up and to fall in with Alexander upon the enemy's camp, where they rode over abundance of gold and silver that lay scattered about, and passing by a great many chariots full of women that wandered here and there for want of drivers, they endeavored to overtake the first of those that fled, in hopes to meet with Darius among them. And at last, after much trouble, they found him lying in a chariot, wounded all over with darts, just at the point of death. However, he desired they would give him some drink, and when he had drunk a little cold water, he told Polystratus, who gave it him, that it had become the last extremity of his ill fortune to receive benefits and not be able to return them. "But Alexander," said he, "whose kindness to my mother, my wife, and my children I hope the gods will recompense, will doubt-less thank you for your humanity to me. Tell him, therefore, in token of my acknowledgment, I give him this right hand," with which words he took hold of Polystratus's hand and died. When Alexander came up to them, he showed manifest tokens of sorrow, and taking off his own cloak, threw it upon the body to cover it. And some time afterwards, when Bessus was taken, he ordered him to be torn in pieces in this manner. They fastened him to a couple of trees which were bound down so as to meet, and then being let loose, with a great force returned to their places, each of them carrying that part of the body along with it that was tied to it. Darius's body was laid in state, and sent to his mother with pomp suitable to his quality. His brother Exathres, Alexander received into the number of his intimate friends.

And now with the flower of his army he marched into Hyrcania, where he saw a large bay of an open sea, apparently not much less than the Euxine, with water, however, sweeter than that of other seas, but could learn nothing of certainty concerning it, further than that in all probability it seemed to him to be an arm issuing from the lake of Mæotis. However, the naturalists were better informed of the truth, and had given an account of it many years before Alexander's expedition; that of four gulfs which out of the main sea enter into the continent, this, known indifferently as the Caspian and as the Hyrcanian Sea, is the most northern. Here the barbarians, unexpectedly meeting with those who led Bucephalus, took them prisoners, and carried the horse away with them, at which Alexander was so much vexed that he sent a herald to let them know he would put them all to the sword, men, women, and children, without mercy, if they did not restore him. But on their doing so, and at the same time surrendering their cities into his hands, he not only treated them kindly, but also paid a ransom for his horse to those who took him.

From hence he marched into Parthia, where not having much to do, he first put on the barbaric dress, perhaps with the view of making the work of civilizing them the easier, as nothing gains more upon men than a conformity to their fashions and customs. Or it may have been as a first trial, whether the Macedonians might be brought to *adore* as the Persians did their kings, by accustoming them by little and little to bear with the alteration of his rule and course of life in other things. However, he fol-lowed not the Median fashion, which was altogether foreign and un-couth, and adopted neither the trousers nor the sleeved vest, nor the tiara for the head, but taking a middle way between the Persian mode and the Macedonian, so contrived his habit that it was not so flaunting as the one, and yet more pompous and magnificent than the other. At first he wore this habit only when he conversed with the barbarians, or within doors, among his intimate friends and companions, but afterwards he appeared in it abroad, when he rode out, and at public audiences, a sight which the Macedonians beheld with grief; but they so respected his other virtues and good qualities that they felt it reasonable in some things to gratify his fancies and his passion of glory, in pursuit of which he hazarded himself so far, that, besides his other adventures, he had but lately been wounded in the leg by an arrow, which had so shattered the shank-bone that splinters were taken out. And on another occasion he received a violent blow with a stone upon the nape of the neck, which dimmed his sight for a good while afterwards. And yet all this could not hinder him from exposing himself freely to any dangers, insomuch that he passed the river Orexartes, which he took to be the Tanais, and putting the Scythians to flight, followed them above a hundred furlongs, though suffering all the time from a diarrhœa.

Here many affirm that the Amazon came to give him a visit. So Clitarchus, Polyclitus, Onesicritus, Antigenes, and Ister tell us. But Aristobulus and Chares, who held the office of reporter of requests, Ptolemy and Anticlides, Philon the Theban, Philip of Theangela, Hecatæus the Eretrian, Philip the Chalcidian, and Duris the Samian say it is wholly a fiction. And truly Alexander himself seems to confirm the latter statement, for in a letter in which he gives Antipater an account of all that happened, he tells him that the king of Scythia offered him his daughter in marriage, but makes no mention at all of the Amazon. And many years after, when Onesicritus read this story in his fourth book to Lysimachus, who then reigned, the king laughed quietly and asked, "Where could I have been at that time?"

But it signifies little to Alexander whether this be credited or no. Certain it is, that apprehending the Macedonians would be weary of pursuing the war, he left the greater part of them in their quarters; and having with him in Hyrcania the choice of his men only, amounting to twenty thousand foot and three thousand horse, he spoke to them to this effect: That hitherto the barbarians had seen them no otherwise than as it were in a dream, and if they should think of returning when they had only alarmed Asia, and not conquered it, their enemies would set upon them as upon so many women. However, he told them he would keep none of them with him against their will, they might go if they pleased; he should merely enter his protest, that when on his way to make the Macedonians the masters of the world, he was left alone with a few friends and volunteers. This is almost word for word, as he wrote in a letter to Antipater, where he adds, that when he had thus spoken to them, they all cried out, they would go along with him whithersoever it was his pleasure to lead them. After succeeding with these, it was no hard matter for him to bring over the multitude, which easily followed the example of their betters. Now, also, he more and more accommodated himself in his way of living to that of the natives, and tried to bring them, also, as near as he could to the Macedonian customs, wisely considering that whilst he was engaged in an expedition which would carry him far from thence, it would be wiser to depend upon the goodwill which might arise from intermixture and association as a means of maintaining tranquillity, than upon force and compulsion. In order to this, he chose out thirty thousand boys, whom he put under masters to teach them the Greek tongue, and to train them up to arms in the Macedonian discipline. As for his marriage with Roxana, whose youthfulness and beauty had charmed him at a drinking entertainment, where he first happened to see her taking part in a dance, it was, indeed, a love affair, yet it seemed at the same time to be conducive to the object he had in hand. For it gratified the conquered people to see him choose a wife from among themselves, and it made them feel the most lively affection for him, to find that in the only passion which he, the most temperate of men, was overcome by, he yet forbore till he could obtain her in a lawful and honorable way.

Noticing, also, that among his chief friends and favorites, Hephæstion most approved all that he did, and complied with and imitated him in his change of habits, while Craterus continued strict in the observation of the customs and fashions of his own country, he made it his practice to employ the first in all transactions with the Persians, and the latter when he had to do with the Greeks or Macedonians. And in general he showed more affection for Hephæstion, and more respect for Craterus; Hephæstion, as he used to say, being Alexander's, and Craterus the king's friend. And so these two friends always bore in secret a grudge to each other, and at times quarreled openly, so much so that once in India they drew upon one another, and were proceeding in good earnest, with their friends on each side to second them, when Alexander rode up and publicly reproved Hephæstion, calling him fool and madman, not to be sensible that without his favor he was nothing. He rebuked Craterus, also, in private, severely, and then causing them both to come into his presence, he reconciled them, at the same time swearing by Ammon and the rest of the gods, that he loved them two above all other men, but if ever he perceived them fall out again he would be sure to put both of them to death, or at least the aggressor. After which they neither ever did or said anything, so much as in jest, to offend one another.

There was scarcely anyone who had greater repute among the Macedonians than Philotas, the son of Parmenio. For besides that he was valiant and able to endure any fatigue of war, he was also next to Alexander himself the most munificent, and the greatest lover of his friends, one of whom asking him for some money, he commanded his steward to give it him; and when he told him he had not wherewith,

"Have you not any plate, then," said he, "or any clothes of mine to sell?" But he carried his arrogance and his pride of wealth and his habits of display and luxury to a degree of assumption unbecoming a private man; and affecting all the loftiness without succeeding in showing any of the grace or gentleness of true greatness, by this mistaken and spurious majesty he gained so much envy and ill-will, that Parmenio would sometimes tell him, "My son, to be not quite so great would be better." For he had long before been complained of, and accused to Alexander. Particularly when Darius was defeated in Cilicia, and an immense booty was taken at Damascus, among the rest of the prisoners who were brought into the camp, there was one Antigone of Pydna, a very handsome woman, who fell to Philotas's share. The young man one day in his cups, in the vaunting, outspoken, soldier's manner, declared to his mistress, that all the great actions were performed by him and his father, the glory and benefit of which, he said, together with the title of king, the boy Alexander reaped and enjoyed by their means. She could not hold, but discovered what he had said to one of her acquaintance, and he, as is usual in such cases, to another, till at last the story came to the ears of Craterus, who brought the woman secretly to the king. When Alexander had heard what she had to say, he commanded her to continue her intrigue with Philotas, and give him an account from time to time of all that should fall from him to this purpose. He, thus unwittingly caught in a snare, to gratify sometimes a fit of anger, sometimes a mere love of vainglory, let himself utter numerous foolish, indiscreet speeches against the king in Antigone's hearing, of which, though Alexander was informed and convinced by strong evidence, yet he would take no notice of it at present, whether it was that he confided in Parmenio's affection and loyalty, or that he apprehended their authority and interest in the army. But about this time, one Limnus, a Macedonian of Chalastra, conspired against Alexander's life, and communicated his design to a youth whom he was fond of, named Nicomachus, inviting him to be of the party. But he, not relishing the thing, revealed it to his brother Balinus, who immediately addressed himself to Philotas, requiring him to introduce them both to Alexander, to whom they had something of great moment to impart which very nearly concerned him. But he, for what reason is uncertain, went not with them, professing that the king was engaged with affairs of more importance. And when they had urged him a second time, and were still slighted by him, they applied themselves to another, by whose means being admitted into Alexander's presence, they first told about Limnus's conspiracy, and by the way let Philotas's negligence appear, who had twice disregarded their application to him. Alexander was greatly incensed, and on finding that Limnus had defended himself, and had been killed by the soldier who was sent to seize him, he was still more discomposed, thinking he had thus lost the means of detecting the plot. As soon as his displeasure against Philotas began to appear, presently all his old enemies showed themselves, and said openly, the king was too easily imposed on, to imagine that one so inconsiderable as Limnus, a Chalastrian, should of his own head undertake such an enterprise; that in all likelihood he was but subservient to the design, an instrument that was moved by some greater spring; that those ought to be more strictly examined about the matter whose interest it was so much to conceal it. When they had once gained the king's ear for insinuations of this sort, they went on to show a thousand grounds of suspicion against Philotas, till at last they prevailed to have him seized and put to the torture, which was done in the presence of the principal officers, Alexander himself being placed behind some tapestry to understand what passed. Where, when he heard in what a miserable tone, and with what abject submissions Philotas applied himself to Hephæstion, he broke out, it is said, in this manner: "Are you so mean-spirited and effeminate, Philotas, and yet can engage in so desperate a design?" After his death, he presently sent into Media, and put also Parmenio, his father, to death, who had done brave service under Philip, and was the only man, of his older friends and counselors, who had encouraged Alexander to invade Asia. Of three sons whom he had had in the army, he had already lost two, and now was himself put to death with the third. These actions rendered Alexander an object of terror to many of his friends, and chiefly to Antipater, who, to strengthen himself, sent messengers privately to treat for an alliance with the Ætolians, who stood in fear of Alexander, because they had destroyed the town of the Œniadæ; on being informed of which, Alexander had said the children of the Œniadæ need not revenge their fathers' quarrel, for he would himself take care to punish the Ætolians.

Not long after this happened, the deplorable end of Clitus, which to those who barely hear the matter, may seem more inhuman than that of Philotas; but if we consider the story with its circumstance of time, and weigh the cause, we shall find it to have occurred rather through a sort of mischance of the king's, whose anger and overdrinking offered an occasion to the evil genius of Clitus. The king had a present of Grecian fruit brought him from the seacoast, which was so fresh and beautiful that he was surprised at it, and called Clitus to him to see it, and to give him a share of it. Clitus was then sacrificing, but he immediately left off and came, followed by three sheep, on whom the drink offering had been already poured preparatory to sacrificing them. Alexander, being informed of this, told his diviners, Aristander and Cleomantis the Lacedæmonian, and asked them what it meant; on whose assuring him it was an ill omen, he commanded them in all haste to offer sacrifices for Clitus's safety, forasmuch as three days before he himself had seen a strange vision in his sleep, of Clitus all in mourning, sitting by Parmenio's sons who were dead. Clitus, however, stayed not to finish his devotions, but came straight to supper with the king, who had sacrificed to Castor and Pollux. And when they had drunk pretty hard, some of the company fell asinging the verses of one Pranichus, or as others say of Pierion, which were made upon those captains who had been lately worsted by the barbarians, on purpose to disgrace and turn them to ridicule. This gave offense to the older men who were there, and they upbraided both the author and the singer of the verses, though Alexander and the younger men about him were much amused to hear them, and encouraged them to go on, till at last Clitus, who had drunk too much, and was besides of a froward and willful temper, was so nettled that he could hold no longer, saying it was not well done to expose the Macedonians so before the barbarians and their enemies, since though it was their unhappiness to be overcome, yet they were much better men than those who laughed at them. And when Alexander remarked that Clitus was pleading his own cause, giving cowardice the name of misfortune, Clitus started up: "This cowardice, as you are pleased to term it," said he to him, "saved the life of a son of the gods, when in flight from Spithridates's sword; and it is by the expense of Macedonian blood, and by these wounds, that you are now raised to such a height as to be able to disown your father Philip, and call yourself the Son of Ammon." "Thou base fellow," said Alexander, who was now thoroughly exasperated, "dost thou think to utter these things everywhere of me, and stir up the Macedonians to sedition, and not be punished for it?" "We are sufficiently punished already," answered Clitus, "if this be the recompense of our toils, and we must esteem theirs a happy lot who have not lived to see their countrymen scourged with Median rods and forced to sue to the Persians to have access to their king." While he talked thus at random, and those near Alexander got up from their seats and began to revile him in turn, the elder men did what they could to compose the disorder. Alexander, in the meantime turning about to Xenodochus, the Pardian, and Artemius, the Colophonian, asked them if they were not of opinion that the Greeks, in comparison with the Macedonians, behaved themselves like so many demigods among wild beasts. But Clitus for all this would not give over, desiring Alexander to speak out if he had anything more to say, or else why did he invite men who were freeborn and accustomed to speak their minds openly without restraint to sup with him. He had better live and converse with barbarians and slaves who would not scruple to bow the knee to his Persian girdle and his white tunic. Which words so provoked Alexander that, not able to suppress his anger any longer, he threw one of the apples that lay upon the table at him, and hit him, and then looked about for his sword. But Aristophanes, one of his life-guard, had hid that out of the way, and others came about

him and besought him, but in vain; for breaking from them, he called out
aloud to his guards in the Macedonian language, which was a certain sign
of some great disturbance in him, and commanded a trumpeter to sound,
giving him a blow with his clenched fist for not instantly obeying him;
though afterwards the same man was commended for disobeying an
order which would have put the whole army into tumult and confusion.
Clitus, still refusing to yield, was with much trouble forced by his friends
out of the room. But he came in again immediately at another door, very
irreverently and confidently singing the verses out of Euripides's
Andromache—

"In Greece, alas! how ill things ordered are!"

Upon this, at last, Alexander, snatching a spear from one of the soldiers,
met Clitus as he was coming forward and was putting by the curtain that
hung before the door, and ran him through the body. He fell at once with
a cry and a groan. Upon which the king's anger immediately vanishing,
he came perfectly to himself, and when he saw his friends about him all
in a profound silence, he pulled the spear out of the dead body, and
would have thrust it into his own throat, if the guards had not held his
hands, and by main force carried him away into his chamber, where all
that night and the next day he wept bitterly, till being quite spent with
lamenting and exclaiming, he lay as it were speechless, only fetching deep
sighs. His friends apprehending some harm from his silence, broke into
the room, but he took no notice of what any of them said, till Aristander
putting him in mind of the vision he had seen concerning Clitus, and the
prodigy that followed, as if all had come to pass by an unavoidable fatal-
ity, he then seemed to moderate his grief. They now brought
Callisthenes, the philosopher, who was the near friend of Aristotle, and
Anaxarchus of Abdera, to him. Callisthenes used moral language, and
gentle and soothing means, hoping to find access for words of reason,
and get a hold upon the passion. But Anaxarchus, who had always taken
a course of his own in philosophy, and had a name for despising and
slighting his contemporaries, as soon as he came in, cried out aloud, "Is
this the Alexander whom the whole world looks to, lying here weeping
like a slave, for fear of the censure and reproach of men, to whom he
himself ought to be a law and measure of equity, if he would use the right
his conquests have given him as supreme lord and governor of all, and
not be the victim of a vain and idle opinion? Do not you know," said he,
"that Jupiter is represented to have Justice and Law on each hand of him,
to signify that all the actions of a conqueror are lawful and just?" With
these and the like speeches, Anaxarchus indeed allayed the king's grief,
but withal corrupted his character, rendering him more audacious and
lawless than he had been. Nor did he fail by these means to insinuate

himself into his favor, and to make Callisthenes's company, which at all times, because of his austerity, was not very acceptable, more uneasy and disagreeable to him.

It happened that, these two philosophers meeting at an entertainment where conversation turned on the subject of climate and the temperature of the air, Callisthenes joined with their opinion, who held that those countries were colder, and the winter sharper there than in Greece. Anaxarchus would by no means allow this, but argued against it with some heat. "Surely," said Callisthenes, "you cannot but admit this country to be colder than Greece, for there you used to have but one threadbare cloak to keep out the coldest winter, and here you have three good warm mantles one over another." This piece of raillery irritated Anaxarchus and the other pretenders to learning, and the crowd of flatterers in general could not endure to see Callisthenes so much admired and followed by the youth, and no less esteemed by the older men for his orderly life, and his gravity, and for being contented with his condition; all confirming what he had professed about the object he had in his journey to Alexander, that it was only to get his countrymen recalled from banishment, and to rebuild and repeople his native town. Besides the envy which his great reputation raised, he also, by his own deportment, gave those who wished him ill opportunity to do him mischief. For when he was invited to public entertainments, he would most times refuse to come, or if he were present at any, he put a constraint upon the company by his austerity and silence, which seemed to intimate his disapproval of what he saw. So that Alexander himself said in application to him,—

> "That vain pretense to wisdom I detest,
> Where a man's blind to his own interest."

Being with many more invited to sup with the king, he was called upon when the cup came to him, to make an oration extempore in praise of the Macedonians; and he did it with such a flow of eloquence, that all who heard it rose from their seats to clap and applaud him, and threw their garland upon him; only Alexander told him out of Euripides,

> "I wonder not that you have spoke so well,
> 'Tis easy on good subjects to excel."

"Therefore," said he, "if you will show the force of your eloquence, tell my Macedonians their faults, and dispraise them, that by hearing their errors they may learn to be better for the future." Callisthenes presently obeyed him, retracting all he had said before, and, inveighing against the Macedonians with great freedom, added, that Philip thrived and grew powerful, chiefly by the discord of the Grecians, applying this verse to him—

"In civil strife e'en villains rise to fame";

which so offended the Macedonians, that he was odious to them ever after. And Alexander said, that instead of his eloquence, he had only made his ill will appear in what he had spoken. Hermippus assures us that one Strœbus, a servant whom Callisthenes kept to read to him, gave this account of these passages afterwards to Aristotle; and that when he perceived the king grow more and more averse to him, two or three times, as he was going away, he repeated the verses—

"Death seiz'd at last on great Patroclus too,
Though he in virtue far exceeded you."

Not without reason, therefore, did Aristotle give this character of Callisthenes, that he was, indeed, a powerful speaker, but had no judgment. He acted certainly a true philosopher's part in positively refusing, as he did, to pay adoration; and by speaking out openly against that which the best and gravest of the Macedonians only repined at in secret, he delivered the Grecians and Alexander himself from a great disgrace, when the practice was given up. But he ruined himself by it, because he went too roughly to work, as if he would have forced the king to that which he should have effected by reason and persuasion. Chares of Mitylene writes, that at a banquet Alexander, after he had drunk, reached the cup to one of his friends, who, on receiving it, rose up towards the domestic altar, and when he had drunk, first adored and then kissed Alexander, and afterwards laid himself down at the table with the rest. Which they all did one after another, till it came to Callisthenes's turn, who took the cup and drank, while the king, who was engaged in conversation with Hephæstion, was not observing, and then came and offered to kiss him. But Demetrius, surnamed Phidon, interposed, saying, "Sir, by no means let him kiss you, for he only of us all has refused to adore you"; upon which the king declined it, and all the concern Callisthenes showed was, that he said aloud, "Then I go away with a kiss less than the rest." The displeasure he incurred by this action procured credit for Hephæstion's declaration that he had broken his word to him in not paying the king the same veneration that others did, as he had faithfully promised to do. And to finish his disgrace, a number of such men as Lysimachus and Hagnon now came in with their asseverations that the sophist went about everywhere boasting of his resistance to arbitrary power, and that the young men all ran after him, and honored him as the only man among so many thousands who had the courage to preserve his liberty. Therefore when Hermolaus's conspiracy came to be discovered, the charges which his enemies brought against him were the more easily believed, particularly that when the young man asked him what he should do to be the most illustrious person on earth, he told him the readiest way was to kill him who was already so; and that to incite him to commit the deed, he bade him not be awed by the golden couch, but remember Alexander was a man equally infirm and vulnerable as another. However, none of Hermolaus's accomplices, in the utmost extremity, made any mention of Callisthenes's being engaged in the design. Nay, Alexander himself, in the letters which he wrote soon after to Craterus, Attalus, and Alcetas, tells them that the young men who were put to the torture, declared they had entered into the conspiracy of themselves, without any others being privy to or guilty of it. But yet afterwards, in a letter to Antipater, he accuses Callisthenes. "The young men," he says, "were stoned to death by the Macedonians, but for the sophist" (meaning Callisthenes), "I will take care to punish him with them too who sent him to me, and who harbor those in their cities who conspire against my life," an unequivocal declaration against Aristotle, in whose house Callisthenes, for his relationship's sake, being his niece Hero's son, had been educated. His death is variously related. Some say he was hanged by Alexander's orders; others, that he died of sickness in prison; but Chares writes he was kept in chains seven months after he was apprehended, on purpose that he might be proceeded against in full council, when Aristotle should be present; and that growing very fat, and contracting a disease of vermin, he there died, about the time that Alexander was wounded in India, in the country of the Malli Oxydracæ, all which came to pass afterwards.

For to go on in order, Demaratus of Corinth, now quite an old man, had made a great effort, about this time, to pay Alexander a visit; and when he had seen him, said he pitied the misfortune of those Grecians, who were so unhappy as to die before they had beheld Alexander seated on the throne of Darius. But he did not long enjoy the benefit of the king's kindness for him, any otherwise than that soon after falling sick and dying, he had a magnificent funeral, and the army raised him a monument of earth, fourscore cubits high, and of a vast circumference. His ashes were conveyed in a very rich chariot, drawn by four horses, to the seaside.

Alexander, now intent upon his expedition into India, took notice that his soldiers were so charged with booty that it hindered their marching. Therefore, at break of day, as soon as the baggage wagons were laden, first he set fire to his own, and to those of his friends, and then commanded those to be burnt which belonged to the rest of the army. An act which in the deliberation of it had seemed more dangerous and difficult than it proved in the execution, with which few were dissatisfied; for most of the soldiers, as if they had been inspired, uttering loud outcries and warlike shoutings, supplied one another with what was absolutely necessary, and burnt and destroyed all that was superfluous, the sight of which redoubled Alexander's zeal and eagerness for his design. And, indeed, he was now grown very severe and inexorable in punishing those who committed any fault. For he put Menander, one of his friends, to death for deserting a fortress where he had placed him in garrison, and shot Orsodates, one of the barbarians who revolted from him, with his own hand.

At this time a sheep happened to yean a lamb, with the perfect shape and color of a tiara upon the head, and testicles on each side; which portent Alexander regarded with such dislike, that he immediately caused his Babylonian priests, whom he usually carried about with him for such purposes, to purify him, and told his friends he was not so much concerned for his own sake as for theirs, out of an apprehension that after his death the divine power might suffer his empire to fall into the hands of some degenerate, impotent person. But this fear was soon removed by a wonderful thing that happened not long after, and was thought to presage better. For Proxenus, a Macedonian, who was the chief of those who looked to the king's furniture, as he was breaking up the ground near the river Oxus, to set up the royal pavilion, discovered a spring of a fat, oily liquor, which, after the top was taken off, ran pure, clear oil, without any difference either of taste or smell, having exactly the same smoothness and brightness, and that, too, in a country where no olives grew. The water, indeed, of the river Oxus, is said to be the smoothest to the feeling of all waters, and to leave a gloss on the skins of those who bathe themselves in it. Whatever might be the cause, certain it is that Alexander was wonderfully pleased with it, as appears by his letters to Antipater, where he speaks of it as one of the most remarkable presages that God had ever favored him with. The diviners told him it signified his expedition would be glorious in the event, but very painful, and attended with many difficulties; for oil, they said, was bestowed on mankind by God as a refreshment of their labors.

Nor did they judge amiss, for he exposed himself to many hazards in the battles which he fought, and received very severe wounds, but the greatest loss in his army was occasioned through the unwholesomeness of the air and the want of necessary provisions. But he still applied himself to overcome fortune and whatever opposed him, by resolution and virtue, and thought nothing impossible to true intrepidity, and on the other hand nothing secure or strong for cowardice. It is told of him that when he besieged Sisimithres, who held an inaccessible, impregnable rock against him, and his soldiers began to despair of taking it, he asked Oxyartes whether Sisimithres was a man of courage, who assuring him he was the greatest coward alive, "Then you tell me," said he, "that the place may easily be taken, since what is in command of it is weak." And in a little time he so terrified Sisimithres that he took it without any difficulty. At an attack which he made upon such another precipitous place with some of his Macedonian soldiers, he called to one whose name was Alexander, and told him he at any rate must fight bravely, if it were but for his name's sake. The youth fought gallantly and was killed in the action, at which he was sensibly afflicted. Another time, seeing his men march slowly and unwillingly to the siege of the place called Nysa, because of a deep river between them and the town, he advanced before them, and standing upon the bank, "What a miserable man," said he, "am I, that I have not learned to swim!" and then was hardly dissuaded from endeavoring to pass it upon his shield. Here, after the assault was over, the ambassadors who from several towns which he had blocked up came to submit to him and make their peace, were surprised to find him still in his armor, without anyone in waiting or attendance upon him, and when at last some one brought him a cushion, he made the eldest of them, named Acuphis, take it and sit down upon it. The old man, marveling at his magnanimity and courtesy, asked him what his countrymen should do to merit his friendship. "I would have them," said Alexander, "choose you to govern them, and send one hundred of the most worthy men among them to remain with me as hostages." Acuphis laughed and answered, "I shall govern them with more ease, sir, if I send you so many of the worst, rather than the best of my subjects."

The extent of King Taxiles's dominions in India was thought to be as large as Egypt, abounding in good pastures, and producing beautiful fruits. The king himself had the reputation of a wise man, and at his first interview with Alexander, he spoke to him in these terms: "To what purpose," said he, "should we make war upon one another, if the design of your coming into these parts be not to rob us of our water or our necessary food, which are the only things that wise men are indispensably obliged to fight for? As for other riches and possessions, as they are accounted in the eye of the world, if I am better provided of them than you, I am ready to let you share with me; but if fortune has been more liberal to you than me, I have no objection to be obliged to you." This discourse pleased Alexander so much, that embracing him, "Do you think," said he to him, "your kind words and courteous behavior will bring you off in this interview without a contest? No, you shall not escape so. I shall contend and do battle with you so far, that how obliging soever you are, you shall not have the better of me." Then, receiving some presents from him, he returned him others of greater value, and to complete his bounty gave him in money ready coined one thousand talents; at which his old friends were much displeased, but it gained him the hearts of many of the barbarians. But the best soldiers of the Indians now entering into the pay of several of the cities, undertook to defend them, and did it so bravely, that they put Alexander to a great deal of trouble, till at last, after a capitulation, upon the surrender of the place, he fell upon them as they were marching away, and put them all to the sword. This one breach of his word remains as a blemish upon his achievements in war, which he otherwise had performed throughout with that justice and honor that became a king. Nor was he less incommoded by the Indian philosophers, who inveighed against those princes who joined his party, and solicited the free nations to oppose him. He took several of these also and caused them to be hanged.

Alexander, in his own letters, has given us an account of his war with Porus. He says the two armies were separated by the river Hydaspes, on whose opposite bank Porus continually kept his elephants in order of battle, with their heads towards their enemies, to guard the passage; that he, on the other hand, made every day a great noise and clamor in his camp, to dissipate the apprehensions of the barbarians; that one stormy dark night he passed the river, at a distance from the place where the enemy lay, into a little island, with part of his foot and the best of his horse. Here there fell a most violent storm of rain, accompanied with lightning and whirlwinds, and seeing some of his men burnt and dying with the lightning, he nevertheless quitted the island and made over to the other side. The Hydaspes, he says, now after the storm, was so swollen and grown so rapid as to have made a breach in the bank, and a part of the river was now pouring in here, so that when he came across it was with difficulty he got a footing on the land, which was slippery and un-steady, and exposed to the force of the currents on both sides. This is the occasion when he is related to have said, "O ye Athenians, will ye believe what dangers I incur to merit your praise?" This, however, is Onesicritus's story. Alexander says, here the men left their boats, and passed the breach in their armor, up to the breast in water, and that then he advanced with his horse about twenty furlongs before his foot, concluding that if the enemy charged him with their cavalry he should be too strong for them; if with their foot, his own would come up time enough to his assistance. Nor did he judge amiss; for being charged by a thousand horse and sixty armed chariots, which advanced before their main body, he took all the chariots, and killed four hundred horse upon the place. Porus, by this time guessing that Alexander himself had crossed over, came on with his whole army, except a party which he left behind, to hold the rest of the Macedonians in play, if they should attempt to pass the river. But he, ap-prehending the multitude of the enemy, and to avoid the shock of their elephants, dividing his forces, attacked their left wing himself, and com-manded Cœnus to fall upon the right, which was performed with good success. For by this means both wings being broken, the enemies fell back in their retreat upon the center, and crowded in upon their elephants. There rallying, they fought a hand-to-hand battle, and it was the eighth hour of the day before they were entirely defeated. This description the conqueror himself has left us in his own epistles.

Almost all the historians agree in relating that Porus was four cubits and a span high, and that when he was upon his elephant, which was of the largest size, his stature and bulk were so answerable, that he appeared to be proportionably mounted, as a horseman on his horse. This elephant, during the whole battle, gave many singular proofs of sagacity and of particular care of the king, whom as long as he was strong and in a condition to fight, he defended with great courage, repelling those who set upon him; and as soon as he perceived him overpowered with his numerous wounds and the multitude of darts that were thrown at him, to prevent his falling off, he softly knelt down and began to draw out the darts with his proboscis. When Porus was taken prisoner, and Alexander asked him how he expected to be used, he answered, "As a king." For that expression, he said, when the same question was put to him a second time, comprehended everything. And Alexander, accordingly, not only suffered him to govern his own kingdom as satrap under himself, but gave him also the additional territory of various independent tribes whom he subdued, a district which, it is said, contained fifteen several nations and five thousand considerable towns, besides abundance of villages. To another government, three times as large as this, he appointed Philip, one of his friends.

Some little time after the battle with Porus, Bucephalus died, as most of the authorities state, under cure of his wounds, or as Onesicritus says, of fatigue and age, being thirty years old. Alexander was no less concerned at his death than if he had lost an old companion or an intimate friend, and built a city, which he named Bucephalia, in memory of him, on the bank of the river Hydaspes. He also, we are told, built another city, and called it after the name of a favorite dog, Peritas, which he had brought up himself. So Sotion assures us he was informed by Potamon of Lesbos.

But this last combat with Porus took off the edge of the Macedonians' courage, and stayed their further progress into India. For having found it hard enough to defeat an enemy who brought but twenty thousand foot and two thousand horse into the field, they thought they had reason to oppose Alexander's design of leading them on to pass the Ganges, too, which they were told was thirty-two furlongs broad and a hundred fathoms deep, and the banks on the further side covered with multitudes of enemies. For they were told that the kings of the Gandaritans and Præsians expected them there with eighty thousand horse, two hundred thousand foot, eight thousand armed chariots, and six thousand fighting elephants. Nor was this a mere vain report, spread to discourage them. For Androcottus, who not long after reigned in those parts, made a present of five hundred elephants at once to Seleucus, and with an army of six hundred thousand men subdued all India. Alexander at first was so grieved and enraged at his men's reluctancy that he shut himself up in his tent and threw himself upon the ground, declaring, if they would not pass the Ganges, he owed them no thanks for anything they had hitherto done, and that to retreat now was plainly to confess himself vanquished. But at last the reasonable persuasions of his friends and the cries and lamentations of his soldiers, who in a suppliant manner crowded about the entrance of his tent, prevailed with him to think of returning. Yet he could not refrain from leaving behind him various deceptive memorials of his expedition, to impose upon aftertimes, and to exaggerate his glory with posterity, such as arms larger than were really worn, and mangers for horses, with bits of bridles above the usual size, which he set up, and distributed in several places. He erected altars, also, to the gods, which the kings of the Præsians even in our time do honor to when they pass the river, and offer sacrifice upon them after the Grecian manner. Androcottus, then a boy, saw Alexander there, and is said often afterwards to have been heard to say, that he missed but little of making himself master of those countries; their king, who then reigned, was so hated and despised for the viciousness of his life and the meanness of his extraction.

Alexander was now eager to see the ocean. To which purpose he caused a great many rowboats and rafts to be built, in which he fell gently down the rivers at his leisure, yet so that his navigation was neither unprofitable nor inactive. For by several descents upon the banks, he made himself master of the fortified towns, and consequently of the country on both sides. But at a siege of a town of the Mallians, who have the repute of being the bravest people of India, he ran in great danger of his life. For having beaten off the defendants with showers of arrows, he was the first man that mounted the wall by a scaling ladder, which, as soon as he was up, broke and left him almost alone, exposed to the darts which the barbarians threw at him in great numbers from below. In this distress, turning himself as well as he could, he leaped down in the midst of his enemies, and had the good fortune to light upon his feet. The brightness and clattering of his armor when he came to the ground made the barbarians think they saw rays of light, or some bright phantom playing before his body, which frightened them so at first that they ran away and dispersed. Till seeing him seconded but by two of his guards, they fell upon him hand to hand, and some, while he bravely defended himself, tried to wound him through his armor with their swords and spears. And one who stood further off drew a bow with such strength that the arrow, finding its way through his cuirass, stuck in his ribs under the breast. This stroke was so violent that it made him give back, and set one knee to the ground, upon which the man ran up with his drawn scimitar, thinking to dispatch him; and had done it, if Peucestes and Limnæus had not interposed, who were both wounded, Limnæus mortally; but Peucestes stood his ground, while Alexander killed the barbarian. But this did not free him from danger; for besides many other wounds, at last he received so weighty a stroke of a club upon his neck that he was forced to lean his body against the wall, still, however, facing the enemy. At this extremity, the Macedonians made their way in and gathered round him. They took him up, just as he was fainting away, having lost all sense of what was done near him, and conveyed him to his tent, upon which it was presently reported all over the camp that he was dead. But when they had with great difficulty and pains sawed off the shaft of the arrow, which was of wood, and so with much trouble got off his cuirass, they came to cut out the head of it, which was three fingers broad and four long, and stuck fast in the bone. During the operation he was taken with almost mortal swoonings, but when it was out he came to himself again. Yet though all danger was past, he continued very weak, and confined himself a great while to a regular diet and the method of his cure, till one day hearing the Macedonians clamoring outside in their eagerness to see him, he took his cloak and went out. And having sacrificed to the gods, without more delay he went on board again, and as he coasted along subdued a great deal of the country on both sides, and several considerable cities.

In this voyage, he took ten of the Indian philosophers prisoners, who had been most active in persuading Sabbas to revolt, and had caused the Macedonians a great deal of trouble. These men, called Gymnosophists, were reputed to be extremely ready and succinct in their answers, which he made trial of, by putting difficult questions to them, letting them know that those whose answers were not pertinent should be put to death, of which he made the eldest of them judge. The first, being asked which he thought the most numerous, the dead or the living, answered, "The living, because those who are dead are not at all." Of the second, he desired to know whether the earth or the sea produced the largest beasts; who told him, "The earth, for the sea is but a part of it." His question to the third was, "Which is the cunningest of beasts?" "That," said he, "which men have not yet found out." He bade the fourth tell him what argument he used to Sabbas to persuade him to revolt. "No other," said he, "than that he should either live or die nobly." Of the fifth he asked, Which was eldest, night or day? The philosopher replied, "Day was eldest, by one day at least." But perceiving Alexander not well satisfied with that account, he added, that he ought not to wonder if strange questions had as strange answers made to them. Then he went on and inquired of the next, what a man should do to be exceedingly beloved. "He must be very powerful," said he, "without making himself too much feared." The answer of the seventh to his question, how a man might become a god, was, "By doing that which was impossible for men to do." The eighth told him, "Life is stronger than death, because it supports so many miseries." And the last being asked, how long he thought it decent for a man to live, said, "Till death appeared more desirable than life." Then Alexander turned to him whom he had made judge, and commanded him to give sentence. "All that I can determine," said he, "is that they have every one answered worse than another." "Nay," said the king, "then you shall die first, for giving such a sentence." "Not so, O king," replied the gymnosophist, "unless you said falsely that he should die first who made the worst answer." In conclusion he gave them presents and dismissed them.

But to those who were in greatest reputation among them, and lived a private quiet life, he sent Onesicritus, one of Diogenes the Cynic's disciples, desiring them to come to him. Calanus, it is said, very arrogantly and roughly commanded him to strip himself, and hear what he said naked, otherwise he would not speak a word to him, though he came from Jupiter himself. But Dandamis received him with more civility, and hearing him discourse of Socrates, Pythagoras, and Diogenes, told him he thought them men of great parts, and to have erred in nothing so much as in having too great respect for the laws and customs of their country. Others say Dandamis only asked him the reason why Alexander undertook so long a journey to come into those parts. Taxiles, however, persuaded Calanus to wait upon Alexander. His proper name was Sphines, but because he was wont to say *Cale,* which in the Indian tongue is a form of salutation, to those he met with anywhere, the Greeks called him Calanus. He is said to have shown Alexander an instructive emblem of government, which was this. He threw a dry shriveled hide upon the ground, and trod upon the edges of it. The skin, when it was pressed in one place, still rose up in another, wheresoever he trod round about it, till he set his foot in the middle, which made all the parts lie even and quiet. The meaning of this similitude being that he ought to reside most in the middle of his empire, and not spend too much time on the borders of it.

His voyage down the rivers took up seven months' time, and when he came to the sea, he sailed to an island which he himself called Scillustis, others Psiltucis, where going ashore, he sacrificed, and made what observations he could as to the nature of the sea and the seacoast. Then having besought the gods that no other man might ever go beyond the bounds of this expedition, he ordered his fleet, of which he made Nearchus admiral, and Onesicritus pilot, to sail round about, keeping the

Indian shore on the right hand, and returned himself by land through the country of the Orites, where he was reduced to great straits for want of provisions, and lost a vast number of men, so that of an army of one hundred and twenty thousand foot and fifteen thousand horse, he scarcely brought back above a fourth part out of India, they were so diminished by diseases, ill diet, and the scorching heats, but most by famine. For their march was through an uncultivated country whose inhabitants fared hardly, possessing only a few sheep, and those of a wretched kind, whose flesh was rank and unsavory, by their continual feeding upon sea-fish.

After sixty days' march he came into Gedrosia, where he found great plenty of all things, which the neighboring kings and governors of provinces, hearing of his approach, had taken care to provide. When he had here refreshed his army, he continued his march through Carmania, feasting all the way for seven days together. He with his most intimate friends banqueted and reveled night and day upon a platform erected on a lofty, conspicuous scaffold, which was slowly drawn by eight horses. This was followed by a great many chariots, some covered with purple and embroidered canopies, and some with green boughs, which were continually supplied afresh, and in them the rest of his friends and commanders drinking, and crowned with garlands of flowers. Here was now no target or helmet or spear to be seen; instead of armor, the soldiers handled nothing but cups and goblets and Thericlean drinking vessels, which, along the whole way, they dipped into large bowls and jars, and drank healths to one another, some seating themselves to it, others as they went along. All places resounded with music of pipes and flutes, with harping and singing, and women dancing as in the rites of Bacchus. For this disorderly, wandering march, besides the drinking part of it, was accompanied with all the sportiveness and insolence of bacchanals, as much as if the god himself had been there to countenance and lead the procession. As soon as he came to the royal palace of Gedrosia, he again refreshed and feasted his army; and one day after he had drunk pretty hard, it is said, he went to see a prize of dancing contended for, in which his favorite Bagoas, having gained the victory, crossed the theater in his dancing habit, and sat down close by him, which so pleased the Macedonians that they made loud acclamations for him to kiss Bagoas, and never stopped clapping their hands and shouting till Alexander put his arms round him and kissed him.

Here his admiral, Nearchus, came to him, and delighted him so with the narrative of his voyage, that he resolved himself to sail out of the mouth of the Euphrates with a great fleet, with which he designed to go round by Arabia and Africa, and so by Hercules's Pillars into the Mediterranean; in order for which, he directed all sorts of vessels to be built at Thapsacus, and made great provisions everywhere of seamen and pilots. But the tidings of the difficulties he had gone through in his Indian expedition, the danger of his person among the Mallians, the reported loss of a considerable part of his forces, and a general doubt as to his own safety, had begun to give occasion for revolt among many of the conquered nations, and for acts of great injustice, avarice, and insolence on the part of the satraps and commanders in the provinces, so that there seemed to be an universal fluctuation and disposition to change. Even at home, Olympias and Cleopatra had raised a faction against Antipater, and divided his government between them, Olympias seizing upon Epirus, and Cleopatra upon Macedonia. When Alexander was told of it, he said his mother had made the best choice, for the Macedonians would never endure to be ruled by a woman. Upon this he dispatched Nearchus again to his fleet, to carry the war into the maritime provinces, and as he marched that way himself he punished those commanders who had behaved ill, particularly Oxyartes, one of the sons of Abuletes, whom he killed with his own hand, thrusting him through the body with his spear. And when Abuletes, instead of the necessary provisions which he ought to have furnished, brought him three thousand talents in coined money, he ordered it to be thrown to his horses, and when they would not touch it, "What good," he said, "will this provision do us?" and sent him away to prison.

When he came into Persia, he distributed money among the women, as their own kings had been wont to do, who as often as they came thither gave every one of them a piece of gold; on account of which custom, some of them, it is said, had come but seldom, and Ochus was so sordidly covetous that, to avoid this expense, he never visited his native country once in all his reign. Then finding Cyrus's sepulchre opened and rifled, he put Polymachus, who did it, to death, though he was a man of some distinction, a born Macedonian of Pella. And after he had read the inscription, he caused it to be cut again below the old one in Greek characters; the words being these: "O man, whosoever thou art, and from whencesoever thou comest (for I know thou wilt come), I am Cyrus, the founder of the Persian empire; do not grudge me this little earth which covers my body." The reading of this sensibly touched Alexander, filling him with the thought of the uncertainty and mutability of human affairs. At the same time Calanus, having been a little while troubled with a disease in the bowels, requested that he might have a funeral pile erected, to which he came on horseback, and after he had said some prayers and sprinkled himself and cut off some of his hair to throw into the fire, before he ascended it, he embraced and took leave of the Macedonians who stood by, desiring them to pass that day in mirth and good-fellowship with their king, whom in a little time, he said, he doubted not but to see again at Babylon. Having thus said, he lay down, and covering up his face, he stirred not when the fire came near him, but continued still in the same posture as at first, and so sacrificed himself, as it was the ancient custom of the philosophers in those countries to do. The same thing was done long after by another Indian, who came with Cæsar to Athens, where they still show you "the Indian's monument." At his return from the funeral pile, Alexander invited a great many of his friends and principal officers to supper, and proposed a drinking match, in which the victor should receive a crown. Promachus drank twelve quarts of wine, and won the prize, which was a talent from them all; but he survived his victory but three days, and was followed, as Chares says, by forty-one more, who died of the same debauch, some extremely cold weather having set in shortly after.

At Susa, he married Darius's daughter Statira, and celebrated also the nuptials of his friends, bestowing the noblest of the Persian ladies upon the worthiest of them, at the same time making it an entertainment in honor of the other Macedonians whose marriages had already taken place. At this magnificent festival, it is reported, there were no less than nine thousand guests, to each of whom he gave a golden cup for the libations. Not to mention other instances of his wonderful magnificence, he paid the debts of his army, which amounted to nine thousand eight hundred and seventy talents. But Antigenes, who had lost one of his eyes, though he owed nothing, got his name set down in the list of those who were in debt, and bringing one who pretended to be his creditor, and to have supplied him from the bank, received the money. But when the cheat was found out, the king was so incensed at it, that he banished him from court, and took away his command, though he was an excellent soldier, and a man of great courage. For when he was but a youth, and served under Philip at the siege of Perinthus, where he was wounded in the eye by an arrow shot out of an engine, he would neither let the arrow be taken out, nor be persuaded to quit the field, till he had bravely repulsed the enemy and forced them to retire into the town. Accordingly he was not able to support such a disgrace with any patience, and it was plain that grief and despair would have made him kill himself, but that the king, fearing it, not only pardoned him, but let him also enjoy the benefit of his deceit.

The thirty thousand boys whom he left behind him to be taught and disciplined were so improved at his return, both in strength and beauty, and performed their exercises with such dexterity and wonderful agility, that he was extremely pleased with them, which grieved the Macedonians, and made them fear he would have the less value for them. And when he proceeded to send down the infirm and maimed soldiers to the sea, they said they were unjustly and infamously dealt with, after they were worn out in his service upon all occasions, now to be turned away with disgrace and sent home into their country among their friends and relations in a worse condition than when they came out; therefore they desired him to dismiss them one and all, and to account his Macedonians useless, now he was so well furnished with a set of dancing boys, with whom, if he pleased, he might go on and conquer the world. These speeches so incensed Alexander that, after he had given them a great deal of reproachful language in his passion, he drove them away, and committed the watch to Persians, out of whom he chose his guards and attendants. When the Macedonians saw him escorted by these men, and themselves excluded and shamefully disgraced, their high spirits fell, and conferring with one another, they found that jealousy and rage had almost distracted them. But at last coming to themselves again, they went without their arms, with only their under garments on, crying and weeping, to offer themselves at his tent, and desired him to deal with them as their baseness and ingratitude deserved. However, this would not prevail; for though his anger was already something mollified, yet he would not admit them into his presence, nor would they stir from thence, but continued two days and nights before his tent, bewailing themselves, and imploring him as their lord to have compassion on them. But the third day he came out to them, and seeing them very humble and penitent, he wept himself a great while, and after a gentle reproof spoke kindly to them, and dismissed those who were unserviceable with magnificent rewards, and with this recommendation to Antipater, that when they came home, at all public shows and in the theaters, they should sit on the best and foremost seats, crowned with chaplets of flowers. He ordered, also, that the children of those who had lost their lives in his service should have their fathers' pay continued to them.

When he came to Ecbatana in Media, and had dispatched his most urgent affairs, he began to divert himself again with spectacles and public entertainments, to carry on which he had a supply of three thousand actors and artists, newly arrived out of Greece. But they were soon interrupted by Hephæstion's falling sick of a fever, in which, being a young man and a soldier too, he could not confine himself to so exact a diet as was necessary; for whilst his physician Glaucus was gone to the theater, he ate a fowl for his dinner, and drank a large draught of wine, upon which he became very ill, and shortly after died. At this misfortune, Alexander was so beyond all reason transported that, to express his sorrow, he immediately ordered the manes and tails of all his horses and mules to be cut, and threw down the battlements of the neighboring cities. The poor physician he crucified, and forbade playing on the flute or any other musical instrument in the camp a great while, till directions came from the oracle of Ammon, and enjoined him to honor Hephæstion, and sacrifice to him as to a hero. Then seeking to alleviate his grief in war, he set out, as it were, to a hunt and chase of men, for he fell upon the Cossæans, and put the whole nation to the sword. This was called a sacrifice to Hephæstion's ghost. In his sepulchre and monument and the adorning of them he intended to bestow ten thousand talents; and designing that the excellence of the workmanship and the singularity of the design might outdo the expense, his wishes turned, above all other artists, to Stasicrates, because he always promised something very bold, unusual, and magnificent in his projects. Once when they had met before, he had told him that, of all the mountains he knew, that of Athos in Thrace was the most capable of being adapted to represent the shape and lineaments of a man; that if he pleased to command him, he would make it the noblest and most durable statue in the world, which in its left hand should hold a city of ten thousand inhabitants, and out of its right should pour a copious river into the sea. Though Alexander declined this proposal, yet now he spent a great deal of time with workmen to invent and contrive others even more extravagant and sumptuous.

As he was upon his way to Babylon, Nearchus, who had sailed back out of the ocean up the mouth of the river Euphrates, came to tell him he had met with some Chaldæan diviners, who had warned him against Alexander's going thither. Alexander, however, took no thought of it, and went on, and when he came near the walls of the place, he saw a great many crows fighting with one another, some of whom fell down just by him. After this, being privately informed that Apollodorus, the governor of Babylon, had sacrificed, to know what would become of him, he sent for Pythagoras, the soothsayer, and on his admitting the thing, asked him in what condition he found the victim; and when he told him the liver was defective in its lobe, "A great presage indeed!" said Alexander. However, he offered Pythagoras no injury, but was sorry that he had neglected Nearchus's advice, and stayed for the most part outside the town, removing his tent from place to place, and sailing up and down the Euphrates. Besides this, he was disturbed by many other prodigies. A tame ass fell upon the biggest and handsomest lion that he kept, and killed him by a kick. And one day after he had undressed himself to be anointed, and was playing at ball, just as they were going to bring his clothes again, the young men who played with him perceived a man clad in the king's robes, with a diadem upon his head, sitting silently upon his throne. They asked him who he was, to which he gave no answer a good while, till at last, coming to himself, he told them his name was Dionysius, that he was of Messenia, that for some crime of which he was accused he was brought thither from the seaside, and had been kept long in prison, that Serapis appeared to him, had freed him from his chains, conducted him to that place, and commanded him to put on the king's robe and diadem, and to sit where they found him, and to say nothing.

Alexander, when he heard this, by the direction of his soothsayers, put the fellow to death, but he lost his spirits, and grew diffident of the protection and assistance of the gods, and suspicious of his friends. His greatest apprehension was of Antipater and his sons, one of whom, Iolaus, was his chief cupbearer; and Cassander, who had lately arrived, and had been bred up in Greek manners, the first time he saw some of the barbarians adore the king could not forbear laughing at it aloud, which so incensed Alexander that he took him by the hair with both hands and dashed his head against the wall. Another time, Cassander would have said something in defense of Antipater to those who accused him, but Alexander interrupting him said, "What is it you say? Do you think people, if they had received no injury, would come such a journey only to calumniate your father?" To which when Cassander replied, that their coming so far from the evidence was a great proof of the falseness of their charges, Alexander smiled, and said those were some of Aristotle's sophisms, which would serve equally on both sides; and added, that both he and his father should be severely punished, if they were found guilty of the least injustice towards those who complained. All which made such a deep impression of terror in Cassander's mind that, long after when he was king of Macedonia and master of Greece, as he was walking up and down at Delphi, and looking at the statues, at the sight of that of Alexander he was suddenly struck with alarm, and shook all over, his eyes rolled, his head grew dizzy, and it was long before he recovered himself.

When once Alexander had given way to fears of supernatural influence, his mind grew so disturbed and so easily alarmed that, if the least unusual or extraordinary thing happened, he thought it a prodigy or a presage, and his court was thronged with diviners and priests whose business was to sacrifice and purify and foretell the future. So miserable a thing is incredulity and contempt of divine power on the one hand, and so miserable, also, superstition on the other, which like water, where the level has been lowered, flowing in and never stopping, fills the mind with slavish fears and follies, as now in Alexander's case. But upon some answers which were brought him from the oracle concerning Hephæstion, he laid aside his sorrow, and fell again to sacrificing and drinking; and having given Nearchus a splendid entertainment, after he had bathed, as was his custom, just as he was going to bed, at Medius's request he went to supper with him. Here he drank all the next day, and was attacked with a fever, which seized him, not as some write, after he had drunk of the bowl of Hercules; nor was he taken with any sudden pain in his back, as if he had been struck with a lance, for these are the inventions of some authors who thought it their duty to make the last scene of so great an action as tragical and moving as they could. Aristobulus tells us, that in the rage of his fever and a violent thirst, he took a draught of wine, upon which he fell into delirium, and died on the thirtieth day of the month Dæsius.

But the journals give the following record. On the eighteenth day of the month, he slept in the bathing room on account of his fever. The next day he bathed and removed into his chamber, and spent his time in playing at dice with Medius. In the evening he bathed and sacrificed, and ate freely, and had the fever on him through the night. On the twentieth, after the usual sacrifices and bathing, he lay in the bathing room and heard Nearchus's narrative of his voyage, and the observations he had made in the great sea. The twenty-first he passed in the same manner, his fever still increasing, and suffered much during the night. The next day the fever was very violent, and he had himself removed and his bed set by the great bath, and discoursed with his principal officers about finding fit men to fill up the vacant places in the army. On the twenty-fourth he was much worse, and was carried out of his bed to assist at the sacrifices, and gave order that the general officers should wait within the court, whilst the inferior officers kept watch without doors. On the twenty-fifth he was removed to his palace on the other side the river, where he slept a little, but his fever did not abate, and when the generals came into his chamber, he was speechless and continued so the following day. The Macedonians, therefore, supposing he was dead, came with great clamors to the gates, and menaced his friends so that they were forced to admit them, and let them all pass through unarmed along by his bedside. The same day Python and Seleucus were dispatched to the temple of Serapis to inquire if they should bring Alexander thither, and were answered by the god that they should not remove him. On the twenty-eighth, in the evening, he died. This account is most of it word for word as it is written in the diary.

At the time, nobody had any suspicion of his being poisoned, but upon some information given six years after, they say Olympias put many to death, and scattered the ashes of Iolaus, then dead, as if he had given it him. But those who affirm that Aristotle counseled Antipater to do it, and that by his means the poison was brought, adduce one Hagnothemis as their authority, who, they say, heard King Antigonus speak of it, and tell us that the poison was water, deadly cold as ice, distilled from a rock in the district of Nonacris, which they gathered like a thin dew, and kept in an ass's hoof; for it was so very cold and penetrating that no other vessel would hold it. However, most are of opinion that all this is a mere made-up story, no slight evidence of which is, that during the dissensions among the commanders, which lasted several days, the body continued clear and fresh, without any sign of such taint or corruption, though it lay neglected in a close, sultry place.

Roxana, who was now with child, and upon that account much hon-

ored by the Macedonians, being jealous of Statira, sent for her by a counterfeit letter, as if Alexander had been still alive; and when she had her in
her power, killed her and her sister, and threw their bodies into a well,
which they filled up with earth, not without the privity and assistance of
Perdiccas, who in the time immediately following the king's death, under
cover of the name of Arrhidæus, whom he carried about him as a sort of
guard to his person, exercised the chief authority. Arrhidæus, who was
Philip's son by an obscure woman of the name of Philinna, was himself
of weak intellect, not that he had been originally deficient either in body
or mind; on the contrary, in his childhood, he had showed a happy and
promising character enough. But a diseased habit of body, caused by
drugs which Olympias gave him, had ruined, not only his health, but his
understanding.

THE ROMANS

CAIUS MARIUS

WE ARE altogether ignorant of any third name of Caius Marius; as also of Quintus Sertorius, that possessed himself of Spain; or of Lucius Mummius that destroyed Corinth, though this last was surnamed Achaicus from his conquests, as Scipio was called Africanus, and Metellus, Macedonicus. Hence Posidonius draws his chief argument to confute those that hold the third to be the Roman proper name, as Camillus, Marcellus, Cato; as in this case, those that had but two names would have no proper name at all. He did not, however, observe that by his own reasoning he must rob the women absolutely of their names; for none of them have the first, which Posidonius imagines the proper name with the Romans. Of the other two, one was common to the whole family, Pompeii, Manlii, Cornelii (as with us Greeks the Heraclidæ and Pelopidæ), the other titular and personal, taken either from their natures or actions or bodily characteristics, as Macrinus, Torquatus, Sylla; such as are Mnemon, Grypus, or Callinicus among the Greeks.[1] On the subject of names, however, the irregularity of custom, would we insist upon it, might furnish us with discourse enough.

There is a likeness of Marius in stone at Ravenna, in Gaul, which I myself saw, quite corresponding with that roughness and harshness of character that is ascribed to him. Being naturally valiant and warlike, and more acquainted also with the discipline of the camp than of the city, he could not moderate his passion when in authority. He is said never to have either studied Greek, or to have made use of that language in any matter of consequence; thinking it ridiculous to bestow time in that learning, the teachers of which were little better than slaves. So after his second triumph, when at the dedication of a temple he presented some

---

[1] [Macrinus evidently meant "skinny"; Torquatus, "neck chain." It is said that Sulla's (or Sylla's) name came from a word meaning "red"; according to Plutarch (see page 228 below), he got the name because of his blotchy red complexion. Mnemon meant "memory"; Grypus meant "hooked" or "crooked"; and Callinicus, "beautiful victory."]

shows after the Greek fashion, coming into the theater, he only sat down and immediately departed. And, accordingly, as Plato often used to say to Xenocrates the philosopher, who was thought to show more than ordinary harshness of disposition, "I pray you, good Xenocrates, sacrifice to the Graces"; so if any could have persuaded Marius to pay his devotions to the Greek Muses and Graces, he had never brought his incomparable actions, both in war and peace, to so unworthy a conclusion, or wrecked himself, so to say, upon an old age of cruelty and vindictiveness, through passion, ill-timed ambition, and insatiable cupidity. But this will further appear by and by from the facts.

He was born of parents altogether obscure and indigent, who supported themselves by their daily labor; his father of the same name with himself, his mother called Fulcinia. He had spent a considerable part of his life before he saw and tasted the pleasures of the city; having passed previously in Cirrhæaton, a village of the territory of Arpinum, a life, compared with city delicacies, rude and unrefined, yet temperate, and conformable to the ancient Roman severity. He first served as a soldier in the war against the Celtiberians, when Scipio Africanus besieged Numantia; where he signalized himself to his general by courage far above his comrades, and, particularly, by his cheerfully complying with Scipio's reformation of his army, before almost ruined by pleasures and luxury. It is stated, too, that he encountered and vanquished an enemy in single combat, in his general's sight. In consequence of all this he had several honors conferred upon him; and once when at an entertainment a question arose about commanders, and one of the company (whether really desirous to know, or only in complaisance) asked Scipio where the Romans, after him, should obtain such another general, Scipio, gently clapping Marius on the shoulder as he sat next him, replied, "Here, perhaps." So promising was his early youth of his future greatness, and so discerning was Scipio to detect the distant future in the present first beginnings. It was this speech of Scipio, we are told, which, like a divine admonition, chiefly emboldened Marius to aspire to a political career. He sought, and by the assistance of Cæcilius Metellus, of whose family he as well as his father were dependents, obtained the office of tribune of the people. In which place, when he brought forward a bill for the regulation of voting, which seemed likely to lessen the authority of the great men in the courts of justice, the consul Cotta opposed him, and persuaded the senate to declare against the law and call Marius to account for it. He, however, when this decree was prepared, coming into the senate, did not behave like a young man newly and undeservedly advanced to authority, but, assuming all the courage that his future actions would have warranted, threatened Cotta, unless he recalled the decree, to throw him into prison. And on his turning to Metellus, and asking his vote, and Metellus rising up to concur with the consul, Marius, calling for the officer outside, commanded him to take Metellus into custody. He appealed to the other tribunes, but not one of them assisted him; so that the senate, immediately complying, withdrew the decree. Marius came forth with glory to the people and confirmed his law, and was henceforth esteemed a man of undaunted courage and assurance, as well as a vigorous opposer of the senate in favor of the commons. But he immediately lost their opinion of him by a contrary action; for when a law for the distribution of corn was proposed, he vigorously and successfully resisted it, making himself equally honored by both parties, in gratifying neither, contrary to the public interest.

After his tribuneship, he was candidate for the office of chief ædile; there being two orders of them, one the curules, from the stool with crooked feet on which they sat when they performed their duty; the other and inferior, called ædiles of the people. As soon as they have chosen the former, they give their voices again for the latter. Marius, finding he was likely to be put by for the greater, immediately changed and stood for the less; but because he seemed too forward and hot, he was disappointed of that also. And yet though he was in one day twice frustrated of his desired preferment (which never happened to any before), yet he was not at all discouraged, but a little while after sought for the prætorship and was nearly suffering a repulse, and then, too, though he was returned last of all, was nevertheless accused of bribery.

Cassius Sabaco's servant, who was observed within the rails among those who voted, chiefly occasioned the suspicion, as Sabaco was an intimate friend of Marius; but on being called to appear before the judges, he alleged that, being thirsty by reason of the heat, he called for cold water, and that his servant brought him a cup, and as soon as he had drunk, departed; he was, however, excluded from the senate by the succeeding censors, and not undeservedly either, as was thought, whether it might be for his false evidence, or his want of temperance. Caius Herennius was also cited to appear as evidence, but pleaded that it was not customary for a patron (the Roman word for *protector*) to witness against his clients, and that the law excused them from that harsh duty; and both Marius and his parents had always been clients to the family of the Herennii. And when the judges would have accepted of this plea, Marius himself opposed it, and told Herennius, that when he was first created magistrate he ceased to be his client; which was not altogether true. For it is not every office that frees clients and their posterity from the observance due to their patrons, but only those to which the law has assigned a curule chair. Notwithstanding, though at the beginning of the suit it went somewhat hard with Marius, and he found the judges no way favorable to him, yet, at last, their voices being equal, contrary to all ex-pectation, he was acquitted.

In his prætorship he did not get much honor, yet after it he obtained the further Spain; which province he is said to have cleared of robbers, with which it was much infested, the old barbarous habits still prevailing, and the Spaniards, in those days, still regarding robbery as a piece of valor. In the city he had neither riches nor eloquence to trust to, with which the leading men of the time obtained power with the people, but his ve-hement disposition, his indefatigable labors, and his plain way of living, of themselves gained him esteem and influence; so that he made an hon-orable match with Julia, of the distinguished family of the Cæsars, to whom that Cæsar was nephew who was afterwards so great among the Romans, and, in some degree, from his relationship, made Marius his ex-ample, as in his life we have observed.

Marius is praised for both temperance and endurance, of which latter he gave a decided instance in an operation of surgery. For having, as it seems, both his legs full of great tumors, and disliking the deformity, he determined to put himself into the hands of an operator; when, without being tied, he stretched out one of his legs, and silently, without chang-ing countenance, endured most excessive torments in the cutting, never either flinching or complaining; but when the surgeon went to the other, he declined to have it done, saying, "I see the cure is not worth the pain."

The consul Cæcilius Metellus, being declared general in the war against Jugurtha in Africa, took with him Marius for lieutenant; where, eager himself to do great deeds and services that would get him distinction, he did not, like others, consult Metellus's glory and the serving his interest, and attributing his honor of lieutenancy not to Metellus, but to fortune, which had presented him with a proper opportunity and theater of great actions, he exerted his utmost courage. That war, too, affording several dif-ficulties, he neither declined the greatest, nor disdained undertaking the least of them; but surpassing his equals in counsel and conduct, and matching the very common soldiers in labor and abstemiousness, he gained great popularity with them; as indeed any voluntary partaking with people in their labor is felt as an easing of that labor, as it seems to take away the constraint and necessity of it. It is the most obliging sight in the world to the Roman soldier to see a commander eat the same bread as himself, or lie upon an ordinary bed, or assist the work in the drawing a trench and raising a bulwark. For they do not so much admire those that confer honors and riches upon them, as those that partake of the same labor and danger with themselves; but love them better that will vouch-safe to join in their work, than those that encourage their idleness.

Marius thus employed, and thus winning the affections of the soldiers, before long filled both Africa and Rome with his fame, and some, too, wrote home from the army that the war with Africa would never be brought to a conclusion unless they chose Caius Marius consul. All which was evidently unpleasing to Metellus; but what more especially grieved him was the calamity of Turpillius. This Turpillius had, from his ancestors, been a friend of Metellus, and kept up a constant hospitality with him; and was now serving in the war, in command of the smiths and carpenters of the army. Having the charge of a garrison in Vaga, a considerable city, and trusting too much to the inhabitants, because he treated them civilly and kindly, he unawares fell into the enemy's hands. They received Jugurtha into the city; yet, nevertheless, at their request, Turpillius was dismissed safe and without receiving any injury; whereupon he was accused of betraying it to the enemy. Marius, being one of the council of war, was not only violent against him himself, but also incensed most of the others, so that Metellus was forced, much against his will, to put him to death. Not long after the accusation proved false, and when others were comforting Metellus, who took heavily the loss of his friend, Marius, rather insulting and arrogating it to himself, boasted in all companies that he had involved Metellus in the guilt of putting his friend to death.

Henceforward they were at open variance; and it is reported that Metellus once, when Marius was present, said, insultingly, "You, sir, design to leave us to go home and stand for the consulship, and will not be content to wait and be consul with this boy of mine?" Metellus's son being a mere boy at the time. Yet for all this Marius being very importunate to be gone, after several delays, he was dismissed about twelve days before the election of consuls; and performed that long journey from the camp to the seaport of Utica in two days and a night, and there doing sacrifice before he went on shipboard, it is said the augur told him that heaven promised him some incredible good fortune, and such as was beyond all expectation. Marius, not a little elated with this good omen, began his voyage, and in four days, with a favorable wind, passed the sea; he was welcomed with great joy by the people, and being brought into the assembly by one of the tribunes, sued for the consulship, inveighing in all ways against Metellus, and promising either to slay Jugurtha or take him alive.

He was elected triumphantly, and at once proceeded to levy soldiers, contrary both to law and custom, enlisting slaves and poor people; whereas former commanders never accepted of such, but bestowed arms, like other favors, as a matter of distinction, on persons who had the proper qualification, a man's property being thus a sort of security for his good behavior. These were not the only occasions of ill-will against Marius; some haughty speeches, uttered with great arrogance and contempt, gave great offense to the nobility; as, for example, his saying that he had carried off the consulship as a spoil from the effeminacy of the wealthy and high-born citizens, and telling the people that he gloried in wounds he had himself received for them, as much as others did in the monuments of dead men, and images of their ancestors. Often speaking of the commanders that had been unfortunate in Africa, naming Bestia, for example, and Albinus, men of very good families, but unfit for war, and who had miscarried through want of experience, he asked the people about him if they did not think that the ancestors of these nobles had much rather have left a descendant like him, since they themselves grew famous not by nobility, but by their valor and great actions? This he did not say merely out of vanity and arrogance, or that he were willing, without any advantage, to offend the nobility; but the people always delighting in affronts and scurrilous contumelies against the senate, making boldness of speech their measure of greatness of spirit, continually encouraged him in it, and strengthened his inclination not to spare persons of repute, so he might gratify the multitude.

As soon as he arrived again in Africa, Metellus, no longer able to control his feelings of jealousy, and his indignation that now when he had really finished the war, and nothing was left but to secure the person of Jugurtha, Marius, grown great merely through his ingratitude to him, should come to bereave him both of his victory and triumph, could not bear to have any interview with him; but retired himself, whilst Rutilius, his lieutenant, surrendered up the army to Marius, whose conduct, however, in the end of the war, met with some sort of retribution, as Sylla deprived him of the glory of the action, as he had done Metellus. I shall state the circumstances briefly here as they are given at large in the life of Sylla. Bocchus was king of the more distant barbarians, and was father-in-law to Jugurtha, yet sent him little or no assistance in his war, professing fears of his unfaithfulness, and really jealous of his growing power; but after Jugurtha fled, and in his distress came to him as his last hope, he received him as a suppliant, rather because ashamed to do otherwise, than out of real kindness; and when he had him in his power, he openly entreated Marius on his behalf, and interceded for him with bold words, giving out that he would by no means deliver him. Yet privately designing to betray him, he sent for Lucius Sylla, quæstor to Marius, and who had on a previous occasion befriended Bocchus in the war. When Sylla, relying on his word, came to him, the African began to doubt and repent of his purpose, and for several days was unresolved with himself, whether he should deliver Jugurtha or retain Sylla; at length he fixed upon his former treachery, and put Jugurtha alive into Sylla's possession. Thus was the first occasion given of that fierce and implacable hostility which so nearly ruined the whole Roman empire. For many that envied Marius attributed the success wholly to Sylla; and Sylla himself got a seal made on which was engraved Bocchus betraying Jugurtha to him, and constantly used it, irritating the hot and jealous temper of Marius, who was naturally greedy of distinction, and quick to resent any claim to share in his glory, and whose enemies took care to promote the quarrel, ascribing the beginning and chief business of the war to Metellus, and its conclusion to Sylla; that so the people might give over admiring and esteeming Marius as the worthiest person.

But these envyings and calumnies were soon dispersed and cleared away from Marius by the danger that threatened Italy from the west; when the city, in great need of a good commander, sought about whom she might set at the helm to meet the tempest of so great a war, no one would have anything to say to any members of noble or potent families who offered themselves for the consulship, and Marius, though then absent, was elected.

Jugurtha's apprehension was only just known, when the news of the invasion of the Teutones and Cimbri began. The accounts at first exceeded all credit, as to the number and strength of the approaching army; but in the end, report proved much inferior to the truth, as they were three hundred thousand effective fighting men, besides a far greater number of women and children. They professed to be seeking new countries to sustain these great multitudes, and cities where they might settle and inhabit, in the same way as they had heard the Celti before them had driven out the Tyrrhenians, and possessed themselves of the best part of Italy. Having had no commerce with the southern nations, and traveling over a wide extent of country, no man knew what people they were, or whence they came, that thus like a cloud burst over Gaul and Italy; yet by their gray eyes and the largeness of their stature, they were conjectured to be some of the German races dwelling by the northern sea; besides that, the Germans call plunderers Cimbri.

There are some that say that the country of the Celti, in its vast size and extent, reaches from the furthest sea and the arctic regions to the lake Mæotis[2] eastward, and to that part of Scythia which is near Pontus, and that there the nations mingle together; that they did not swarm out of their country all at once, or on a sudden, but advancing by force of arms, in the summer season, every year, in the course of time they crossed the whole continent. And thus, though each party had several appellations, yet the whole army was called by the common name of Celto-Scythians. Others say that the Cimmerii, anciently known to the Greeks, were only a small part of the nation, who were driven out upon some quarrel among the Scythians, and passed all along from the lake Mæotis to Asia, under the conduct of one Lygdamis; and that the greater and more warlike part of them still inhabit the remotest regions lying upon the outer

---

[2][Now called the Sea of Azov—the shallow northern branch of the Black Sea between Russia and Ukraine.]

ocean. These, they say, live in a dark and woody country hardly penetrable by the sunbeams, the trees are so close and thick, extending into the interior as far as the Hercynian forest;[3] and their position on the earth is under that part of heaven where the pole is so elevated that, by the declination of the parallels, the zenith of the inhabitants seems to be but little distant from it; and that their days and nights being almost of an equal length, they divide their year into one of each. This was Homer's occasion for the story of Ulysses calling up the dead, and from this region the people, anciently called Cimmerii, and afterwards, by an easy change, Cimbri, came into Italy. All this, however, is rather conjecture than an authentic history.

Their numbers, most writers agree, were not less, but rather greater than was reported. They were of invincible strength and fierceness in their wars, and hurried into battle with the violence of a devouring flame; none could withstand them: all they assaulted became their prey. Several of the greatest Roman commanders with their whole armies, that advanced for the defense of Transalpine Gaul, were ingloriously overthrown, and, indeed, by their faint resistance, chiefly gave them the impulse of marching towards Rome. Having vanquished all they had met, and found abundance of plunder, they resolved to settle themselves nowhere till they should have razed the city and wasted all Italy. The Romans, being from all parts alarmed with this news, sent for Marius to undertake the war, and nominated him the second time consul, though the law did not permit any one that was absent, or that had not waited a certain time after his first consulship, to be again created. But the people rejected all opposers, for they considered this was not the first time that the law gave place to the common interest; nor the present occasion less urgent than that when, contrary to law, they made Scipio consul, not in fear for the destruction of their own city, but desiring the ruin of that of the Carthaginians.

Thus it was decided; and Marius, bringing over his legions out of Africa on the very first day of January, which the Romans count the beginning of the year, received the consulship, and then, also, entered in triumph, showing Jugurtha a prisoner to the people, a sight they had despaired of ever beholding, nor could any, so long as he lived, hope to reduce the enemy in Africa; so fertile in expedients was he to adapt himself to every turn of fortune, and so bold as well as subtle. When, however, he was led in triumph, it is said that he fell distracted, and when he was afterwards thrown into prison, where some tore off his clothes by force, and others, whilst they struggled for his golden earring, with it pulled off the tip of his ear, and when he was, after this, cast naked into the dungeon, in his

---

[3][A huge area including the Black Forest and its environs.]

amazement and confusion, with a ghastly laugh, he cried out, "O Hercules! how cold your bath is!" Here for six days struggling with hunger, and to the very last minute desirous of life, he was overtaken by the just reward of his villainies. In this triumph was brought, as is stated, of gold three thousand and seven pounds weight, of silver bullion five thousand seven hundred and seventy-five, of money in gold and silver coin two hundred and eighty-seven thousand drachmas. After the solemnity, Marius called together the senate in the capitol, and entered, whether through inadvertency or unbecoming exultation with his good fortune, in his triumphal habit; but presently observing the senate offended at it, went out, and returned in his ordinary purple-bordered robe.

On the expedition he carefully disciplined and trained his army whilst they were on their way, giving them practice in long marches, and running of every sort, and compelling every man to carry his own baggage and prepare his own victuals; insomuch that thenceforward laborious soldiers, who did their work silently without grumbling, had the name of "Marius's mules." Some, however, think the proverb had a different occasion; that when Scipio besieged Numantia, and was careful to inspect not only their horses and arms, but their mules and carriages too, and see how well equipped and in what readiness each one's was, Marius brought forth his horse which he had fed extremely well, and a mule in better case, stronger and gentler than those of others; that the general was very well pleased, and often afterwards mentioned Marius's beasts; and that hence the soldiers, when speaking jestingly in the praise of a drudging, laborious fellow, called him Marius's mule.

But to proceed; very great good fortune seemed to attend Marius, for by the enemy in a manner changing their course, and falling first upon Spain, he had time to exercise his soldiers, and confirm their courage, and, which was most important, to show them what he himself was. For that fierce manner of his in command, and inexorableness in punishing, when his men became used not to do amiss or disobey, was felt to be wholesome and advantageous, as well as just, and his violent spirit, stern voice, and harsh aspect, which in a little while grew familiar to them, they esteemed terrible not to themselves, but only to their enemies. But his uprightness in judging more especially pleased the soldiers, one remarkable instance of which is as follows. One Caius Lusius, his own nephew, had a command under him in the army, a man not in other respects of bad character, but shamefully licentious with young men. He had one young man under his command called Trebonius, with whom notwithstanding many solicitations he could never prevail. At length one night he sent a messenger for him, and Trebonius came, as it was not lawful for him to refuse when he was sent for, and being brought into his tent, when Lusius began to use violence with him, he drew his sword and

ran him through. This was done whilst Marius was absent. When he returned, he appointed Trebonius a time for his trial, where, whilst many
accused him, and not any one appeared in his defense, he himself boldly
related the whole matter, and brought witness of his previous conduct to
Lusius, who had frequently offered him considerable presents. Marius,
admiring his conduct and much pleased, commanded the garland, the
usual Roman reward of valor, to be brought, and himself crowned
Trebonius with it, as having performed an excellent action, at a time that
very much wanted such good examples.

This being told at Rome, proved no small help to Marius towards his
third consulship; to which also conduced the expectation of the barbarians at the summer season, the people being unwilling to trust their fortunes with any other general but him. However, their arrival was not so
early as was imagined, and the time of Marius's consulship was again expired. The election coming on, and his colleague being dead, he left the
command of the army to Manius Aquilius, and hastened to Rome,
where, several eminent persons being candidates for the consulship,
Lucius Saturninus, who more than any of the other tribunes swayed the
populace, and of whom Marius himself was very observant, exerted his
eloquence with the people, advising them to choose Marius consul. He
playing the modest part, and professing to decline the office, Saturninus
called him traitor to his country, if, in such apparent danger, he would
avoid command. And though it was not difficult to discover that he was
merely helping Marius in putting this pretense upon the people, yet, considering that the present juncture much required his skill, and his good
fortunes, too, they voted him the fourth time consul, and made Catulus
Lutatius his colleague, a man very much esteemed by the nobility and
not unagreeable to the commons.

Marius, having notice of the enemy's approach, with all expedition
passed the Alps, and pitching his camp by the river Rhone, took care first
for plentiful supplies of victuals; lest at any time he should be forced to
fight at a disadvantage for want of necessaries. The carriage of provision
for the army from the sea, which was formerly long and expensive, he
made speedy and easy. For the mouth of the Rhone, by the influx of the
sea, being barred and almost filled up with sand and mud mixed with
clay, the passage there became narrow, difficult, and dangerous for the
ships that brought their provisions. Hither, therefore, bringing his army,
then at leisure, he drew a great trench; and by turning the course of a
great part of the river, brought it to a convenient point on the shore
where the water was deep enough to receive ships of considerable burden, and where there was a calm and easy opening to the sea. And this
still retains the name it took from him.

The enemy dividing themselves into two parts, the Cimbri arranged to go against Catulus higher up through the country of the Norici, and to force that passage; the Teutones and Ambrones to march against Marius by the seaside through Liguria. The Cimbri were a considerable time in doing their part. But the Teutones and Ambrones with all expedition passing over the interjacent country, soon came in sight, in numbers beyond belief, of a terrible aspect, and uttering strange cries and shouts. Taking up a great part of the plain with their camp, they challenged Marius to battle; he seemed to take no notice of them, but kept his soldiers within their fortification, and sharply reprehended those that were too forward and eager to show their courage, and who, out of passion, would needs be fighting, calling them traitors to their country, and telling them they were not now to think of the glory of triumphs and trophies, but rather how they might repel such an impetuous tempest of war and save Italy.

Thus he discoursed privately with his officers and equals, but placed the soldiers by turns upon the bulwarks to survey the enemy, and so made them familiar with their shape and voice, which were indeed altogether extravagant and barbarous, and he caused them to observe their arms, and way of using them, so that in a little time what at first appeared terrible to their apprehensions, by often viewing became familiar. For he very rationally supposed that the strangeness of things often makes them seem formidable when they are not so; and that by our better acquaintance, even things which are really terrible lose much of their frightfulness. This daily converse not only diminished some of the soldiers' fears, but their indignation warmed and inflamed their courage when they heard the threats and insupportable insolence of their enemies; who not only plundered and depopulated all the country round, but would even contemptuously and confidently attack the ramparts.

Complaints of the soldiers now began to come to Marius's ears. "What effeminacy does Marius see in us, that he should thus like women lock us up from encountering our enemies? Come on, let us show ourselves men, and ask him if he expects others to fight for Italy; and means merely to employ us in servile offices, when he would dig trenches, cleanse places of mud and dirt, and turn the course of rivers? It was to do such works as these, it seems, that he gave us all our long training; he will return home, and boast of these great performances of his consulships to the people. Does the defeat of Carbo and Cæpio, who were vanquished by the enemy, affright him? Surely they were much inferior to Marius both in glory and valor, and commanded a much weaker army: at the worst, it is better to be in action, though we suffer for it like them, than to sit idle spectators of the destruction of our allies and companions." Marius, not a little pleased to hear this, gently appeased them, pretending that he did not distrust their valor, but that he took his measures as to the time and place of victory from some certain oracles.

And, in fact, he used solemnly to carry about in a litter a Syrian woman, called Martha, a supposed prophetess, and to do sacrifice by her directions. She had formerly been driven away by the senate, to whom she addressed herself, offering to inform them about these affairs, and to foretell future events; and after this betook herself to the women, and gave them proofs of her skill, especially Marius's wife, at whose feet she sat when she was viewing a contest of gladiators, and correctly foretold which of them should overcome. She was for this and the like predictings sent by her to Marius and the army, where she was very much looked up to, and, for the most part, carried about in a litter. When she went to sacrifice, she wore a purple robe lined and buckled up, and had in her hand a little spear trimmed with ribbons and garlands. This theatrical show made many question whether Marius really gave any credit to her himself, or only played the counterfeit, when he showed her publicly, to impose upon the soldiers.

What, however, Alexander the Myndian relates about the vultures does really deserve admiration; that always before Marius's victories there appeared two of them, and accompanied the army, which were known by their brazen collars (the soldiers having caught them and put these about their necks, and so let them go, from which time they in a manner knew and saluted the soldiers), and whenever these appeared in their marches, they used to rejoice at it, and thought themselves sure of some success. Of the many other prodigies that then were taken notice of, the greater part were but of the ordinary stamp; it was, however, reported that at Ameria and Tuder, two cities in Italy, there were seen at nights in the sky flaming darts and shields, now waved about, and then again clashing against one another, all in accordance with the postures and motions soldiers use in fighting; that at length one party retreating, and the other pursuing, they all disappeared westward. Much about the same time came Bataces, one of Cybele's priests, from Pessinus, and reported how the goddess had declared to him, out of her oracle, that the Romans should obtain the victory. The senate giving credit to him, and voting the goddess a temple to be built in hopes of the victory, Aulus Pompeius, a tribune, prevented Bataces, when he would have gone and told the people this same story, calling him impostor, and ignominiously pulling him off the hustings; which action in the end was the main thing that gained credit for the man's story, for Aulus had scarce dissolved the assembly, and returned home, when a violent fever seized him, and it was matter of universal remark, and in everybody's mouth, that he died within a week after.

Now the Teutones, whilst Marius lay quiet, ventured to attack his camp; from whence, however, being encountered with showers of darts, and losing several of their men, they determined to march forward, hoping to reach the other side of the Alps without opposition, and, packing

up their baggage, passed securely by the Roman camp, where the greatness of their number was especially made evident by the long time they
took in their march, for they were said to be six days continually going
on in passing Marius's fortifications; they marched pretty near, and revil-
ingly asked the Romans if they would send any commands by them to
their wives, for they would shortly be with them. As soon as they were
passed and had gone on a little distance ahead, Marius began to move,
and follow them at his leisure, always encamping at some small distance
from them; choosing also strong positions, and carefully fortifying them,
that he might quarter with safety. Thus they marched till they came to
the place called Sextilius's Waters, from whence it was but a short way before being amidst the Alps, and here Marius put himself in readiness for
the encounter.

He chose a place for his camp of considerable strength, but where
there was a scarcity of water; designing, it is said, by this means, also, to
put an edge on his soldiers' courage; and when several were not a little
distressed, and complained of thirst, pointing to a river that ran near the
enemy's camp: "There," said he, "you may have drink, if you will buy it
with your blood." "Why, then," replied they, "do you not lead us to them,
before our blood is dried up in us?" He answered, in a softer tone, "Let
us first fortify our camp," and the soldiers, though not without repining,
proceeded to obey. Now a great company of their boys and camp followers, having neither drink for themselves nor for their horses, went
down to that river; some taking axes and hatchets, and some, too, swords
and darts with their pitchers, resolving to have water though they fought
for it. These were first encountered by a small party of the enemies; for
most of them had just finished bathing, and were eating and drinking,
and several were still bathing, the country thereabouts abounding in hot
springs; so that the Romans partly fell upon them whilst they were enjoying themselves and occupied with the novel sights and pleasantness of
the place. Upon hearing the shouts, greater numbers still joining in the
fight, it was not a little difficult for Marius to contain his soldiers, who
were afraid of losing the camp servants; and the more warlike part of the
enemies, who had overthrown Manlius and Cæpio (they were called
Ambrones, and were in number, one with another, above thirty thousand), taking the alarm, leaped up and hurried to arms.

These, though they had just been gorging themselves with food, and
were excited and disordered with drink, nevertheless did not advance
with an unruly step, or in mere senseless fury, nor were their shouts mere
inarticulate cries; but clashing their arms in concert and keeping time as
they leapt and bounded onward, they continually repeated their own
name, "Ambrones!" either to encourage one another, or to strike the
greater terror into their enemies. Of all the Italians in Marius's army, the

Ligurians were the first that charged; and when they caught the word of the enemy's confused shout, they, too, returned the same, as it was an ancient name also in their country, the Ligurians always using it when speaking of their descent. This acclamation, bandied from one army to the other before they joined, served to rouse and heighten their fury, while the men on either side strove, with all possible vehemence, the one to overshout the other.

The river disordered the Ambrones; before they could draw up all their army on the other side of it, the Ligurians presently fell upon the van, and began to charge them hand to hand. The Romans, too, coming to their assistance, and from the higher ground pouring upon the enemy, forcibly repelled them, and the most of them (one thrusting another into the river) were there slain, and filled it with their blood and dead bodies. Those that got safe over, not daring to make head, were slain by the Romans, as they fled to their camp and wagons; where the women meeting them with swords and hatchets, and making a hideous outcry, set upon those that fled as well as those that pursued, the one as traitors, the other as enemies, and, mixing themselves with the combatants, with their bare arms pulling away the Romans' shields, and laying hold on their swords, endured the wounds and slashing of their bodies to the very last with undaunted resolution. Thus the battle seems to have happened at that river rather by accident than by the design of the general.

After the Romans were retired from the great slaughter of the Ambrones, night came on; but the army was not indulged, as was the usual custom, with songs of victory, drinking in their tents, and mutual entertainments and (what is most welcome to soldiers after successful fighting) quiet sleep, but they passed that night, above all others, in fears and alarm. For their camp was without either rampart or palisade, and there remained thousands upon thousands of their enemies yet unconquered; to whom were joined as many of the Ambrones as escaped. There were heard from these all through the night wild bewailings, nothing like the sighs and groans of men, but a sort of wild-beast-like howling and roaring, joined with threats and lamentations rising from the vast multitude, and echoed among the neighboring hills and hollow banks of the river. The whole plain was filled with hideous noise, insomuch that the Romans were not a little afraid, and Marius himself was apprehensive of a confused tumultuous night engagement. But the enemy did not stir either this night or the next day, but were employed in disposing and drawing themselves up to the greatest advantage.

Of this occasion Marius made good use; for there were beyond the enemies some wooded ascents and deep valleys thickly set with trees, whither he sent Claudius Marcellus, secretly, with three thousand regular soldiers, giving him orders to post them in ambush there, and show themselves at the rear of the enemies when the fight was begun. The others, refreshed with victuals and sleep, as soon as it was day he drew up before the camp, and commanded the horse to sally out into the plain, at the sight of which the Teutones could not contain themselves till the Romans should come down and fight them on equal terms, but hastily arming themselves, charged in their fury up the hillside. Marius, sending officers to all parts, commanded his men to stand still and keep their ground; when they came within reach, to throw their javelins, then use their swords, and, joining their shields, force them back; pointing out to them that the steepness of the ground would render the enemy's blows inefficient, nor could their shields be kept close together, the inequality of the ground hindering the stability of their footing.

This counsel he gave them, and was the first that followed it; for he was inferior to none in the use of his body, and far excelled all in resolution. The Romans accordingly stood for their approach, and, checking them in their advance upwards, forced them little by little to give way and yield down the hill, and here, on the level ground, no sooner had the Ambrones begun to restore their van into a posture of resistance, but they found their rear disordered. For Marcellus had not let slip the opportunity; but as soon as the shout was raised among the Romans on the hills, he, setting his men in motion, fell in upon the enemy behind, at full speed, and with loud cries, and routed those nearest him, and they, breaking the ranks of those that were before them, filled the whole army with confusion. They made no long resistance after they were thus broke in upon, but having lost all order, fled.

The Romans, pursuing them, slew and took prisoners above one hundred thousand, and possessing themselves of their spoil, tents, and carriages, voted all that was not purloined to Marius's share, which, though so magnificent a present, yet was generally thought less than his conduct deserved in so great a danger. Other authors give a different account, both about the division of the plunder and the number of the slain. They say, however, that the inhabitants of Massilia made fences round their vineyards with the bones, and that the ground, enriched by the moisture of the putrefied bodies (which soaked in with the rain of the following winter), yielded at the season a prodigious crop, and fully justified Archilochus, who said, that the fallows thus are fattened. It is an observation, also, that extraordinary rains pretty generally fall after great battles; whether it be that some divine power thus washes and cleanses the polluted earth with showers from above, or that moist and heavy evaporations, steaming forth from the blood and corruption, thicken the air, which naturally is subject to alteration from the smallest causes.

After the battle, Marius chose out from amongst the barbarians' spoils and arms those that were whole and handsome, and that would make the greatest show in his triumph; the rest he heaped upon a large pile, and offered a very splendid sacrifice. Whilst the army stood round about with their arms and garlands, himself attired (as the fashion is on such occasions) in the purple-bordered robe, taking a lighted torch, and with both hands lifting it up towards heaven, he was then going to put it to the pile, when some friends were espied with all haste coming towards him on horseback. Upon which every one remained in silence and expectation. They, upon their coming up, leapt off and saluted Marius, bringing him the news of his fifth consulship, and delivered him letters to that effect. This gave the addition of no small joy to the solemnity; and while the soldiers clashed their arms and shouted, the officers again crowned Marius with a laurel wreath, and he thus set fire to the pile, and finished his sacrifice.

But whatever it be which interferes to prevent the enjoyment of prosperity ever being pure and sincere, and still diversifies human affairs with the mixture of good and bad, whether fortune or divine displeasure, or the necessity of the nature of things, within a few days Marius received an account of his colleague, Catulus, which, as a cloud in serenity and calm, terrified Rome with the apprehension of another imminent storm. Catulus, who marched against the Cimbri, despairing of being able to defend the passes of the Alps, lest, being compelled to divide his forces into several parties, he should weaken himself, descended again into Italy, and posted his army behind the river Adige; where he occupied the passages with strong fortifications on both sides the river, and made a bridge, that so he might cross to the assistance of his men on the other side, if so be the enemy, having forced their way through the mountain passes, should storm the fortresses. The barbarians, however, came on with such insolence and contempt of their enemies, that to show their strength and courage, rather than out of any necessity, they went naked in the showers of snow, and through the ice and deep snow climbed up to the tops of the hills, and from thence, placing their broad shields under their bodies, let themselves slide from the precipices along their vast slippery descents.

When they had pitched their camp at a little distance from the river, and surveyed the passage, they began to pile it up, giant-like, tearing down the neighboring hills; and brought trees pulled up by the roots, and heaps of earth to the river, damming up its course; and with great heavy materials which they rolled down the stream and dashed against the bridge, they forced away the beams which supported it; in consequence of which the greatest part of the Roman soldiers, much affrighted, left the camp and fled. Here Catulus showed himself a generous and noble general, in preferring the glory of his people before his own; for when he could not prevail with his soldiers to stand to their colors, but saw how they all deserted them, he commanded his own standard to be taken up, and running to the foremost of those that fled, he led them forward, choosing rather that the disgrace should fall upon himself than upon his country, and that they should not seem to fly, but, following their captain, to make a retreat. The barbarians assaulted and took the fortress on the other side the Adige; where much admiring the few Romans there left, who had shown extreme courage, and had fought worthily of their country, they dismissed them upon terms, swearing them upon their brazen bull, which was afterwards taken in the battle, and carried, they say, to Catulus's house, as the chief trophy of victory.

Thus falling in upon the country destitute of defense, they wasted it on all sides. Marius was presently sent for to the city; where, when he arrived, every one supposing he would triumph, the senate, too, unanimously voting it, he himself did not think it convenient: whether that he were not willing to deprive his soldiers and officers of their share of the glory, or that, to encourage the people in this juncture, he would leave the honor due to his past victory on trust, as it were, in the hands of the city and its future fortune; deferring it now to receive it afterwards with the greater splendor. Having left such orders as the occasion required, he hastened to Catulus, whose drooping spirits he much raised, and sent for his own army from Gaul; and as soon as it came, passing the river Po, he endeavored to keep the barbarians out of that part of Italy which lies south of it.

They professed they were in expectation of the Teutones, and, saying they wondered they were so long in coming, deferred the battle; either that they were really ignorant of their defeat or were willing to seem so. For they certainly much maltreated those that brought them such news, and, sending to Marius, required some part of the country for themselves and their brethren, and cities fit for them to inhabit. When Marius inquired of the ambassadors who their brethren were, upon their saying the Teutones, all that were present began to laugh; and Marius scoffingly answered them; "Do not trouble yourselves for your brethren, for we have already provided lands for them, which they shall possess forever." The ambassadors, understanding the mockery, broke into insults, and threatened that the Cimbri would make him pay for this, and the Teutones, too, when they came. "They are not far off," replied Marius, "and it will be unkindly done of you to go away before greeting your brethren." Saying so, he commanded the kings of the Teutones to be brought out as they were, in chains; for they were taken by the Sequani among the Alps, before they could make their escape. This was no sooner made known to the Cimbri, but they with all expedition came against Marius, who then lay still and guarded his camp.

It is said that, against this battle, Marius first altered the construction of the Roman javelins. For before, at the place where the wood was joined to the iron, it was made fast with two iron pins; but now Marius let one of them alone as it was, and pulling out the other, put a weak wooden peg in its place, thus contriving that when it was driven into the enemy's shield, it should not stand right out, but the wooden peg breaking, the iron should bend, and so the javelin should hold fast by its crooked point and drag. Bœorix, king of the Cimbri, came with a small party of horse to the Roman camp, and challenged Marius to appoint the time and place where they might meet and fight for the country. Marius answered that the Romans never consulted their enemies when to fight; however, he would gratify the Cimbri so far; and so they fixed upon the third day after and for the place, the plain near Vercellæ, which was convenient enough for the Roman horse, and afforded room for the enemy to display their numbers.

They observed the time appointed, and drew out their forces against each other. Catulus commanded twenty thousand three hundred, and Marius thirty-two thousand, who were placed in the two wings, leaving Catulus the center. Sylla, who was present at the fight, gives this account; saying, also, that Marius drew up his army in this order, because he expected that the armies would meet on the wings, since it generally happens that in such extensive fronts the center falls back, and thus he would have the whole victory to himself and his soldiers, and Catulus would not be even engaged. They tell us, also, that Catulus himself alleged this in vindication of his honor, accusing, in various ways, the enviousness of Marius. The infantry of the Cimbri marched quietly out of their fortifications, having their flanks equal to their front; every side of the army taking up thirty furlongs. Their horse, that were in number fifteen thousand, made a very splendid appearance. They wore helmets, made to resemble the heads and jaws of wild beasts, and other strange shapes, and heightening these with plumes of feathers, they made themselves appear taller than they were. They had breastplates of iron, and white glittering shields; and for their offensive arms, every one had two darts, and when they came hand to hand, they used large and heavy swords.

The cavalry did not fall directly upon the front of the Romans, but, turning to the right, they endeavored to draw them on in that direction by little and little, so as to get them between themselves and their infantry, who were placed in the left wing. The Roman commanders soon perceived the design, but could not contain the soldiers; for one happening to shout out that the enemy fled, they all rushed to pursue them, while the whole barbarian foot came on, moving like a great ocean. Here Marius, having washed his hands, and lifting them up towards heaven, vowed an hecatomb to the gods; and Catulus, too, in the same posture, solemnly promised to consecrate a temple to the "Fortune of that day."

They say, too, that Marius, having the victim shown to him as he was sacrificing, cried out with a loud voice, "The victory is mine."

However, in the engagement, according to the accounts of Sylla and
his friends, Marius met with what might be called a mark of divine displeasure. For a great dust being raised, which (as it might very probably
happen) almost covered both the armies, he, leading on his forces to the
pursuit, missed the enemy, and having passed by their array, moved, for a
good space, up and down the field; meanwhile the enemy, by chance, engaged with Catulus, and the heat of the battle was chiefly with him and
his men, among whom Sylla says he was; adding, that the Romans had
great advantage of the heat and sun that shone in the faces of the Cimbri.
For they, well able to endure cold, and having been bred up (as we observed before), in cold and shady countries, were overcome with the excessive heat; they sweated extremely, and were much out of breath, being
forced to hold their shields before their faces; for the battle was fought
not long after the summer solstice, or, as the Romans reckon, upon the
third day before the new moon of the month now called August and
then Sextilis. The dust, too, gave the Romans no small addition to their
courage, inasmuch as it hid the enemy. For afar off they could not discover their number; but every one advancing to encounter those that
were nearest to them, they came to fight hand to hand, before the sight
of so vast a multitude had struck terror into them. They were so much
used to labor, and so well exercised, that in all the heat and toil of the encounter, not one of them was observed either to sweat or to be out of
breath; so much so, that Catulus himself, they say, recorded it in commendation of his soldiers.

Here the greatest part and most valiant of the enemies were cut in
pieces; for those that fought in the front, that they might not break their
ranks, were fast tied to one another, with long chains put through their
belts. But as they pursued those that fled to their camp they witnessed a
most fearful tragedy; the women, standing in black clothes on their wagons, slew all that fled, some their husbands, some their brethren, others
their fathers; and strangling their little children with their own hands,
threw them under the wheels, and the feet of the cattle, and then killed
themselves. They tell of one who hung herself from the end of the pole
of a wagon, with her children tied dangling at her heels. The men, for
want of trees, tied themselves, some to the horns of the oxen, others by
the neck to their legs, that so pricking them on, by the starting and
springing of the beasts, they might be torn and trodden to pieces. Yet for
all they thus massacred themselves, above sixty thousand were taken prisoners, and those that were slain were said to be twice as many.

The ordinary plunder was taken by Marius's soldiers, but the other
spoils, as ensigns, trumpets, and the like, they say, were brought to

Catulus's camp; which he used for the best argument that the victory was obtained by himself and his army. Some dissensions arising, as was natural, among the soldiers, the deputies from Parma, being then present, were made judges of the controversy; whom Catulus's men carried about among their slain enemies, and manifestly showed them that they were slain by their javelins, which were known by the inscriptions, having Catulus's name cut in the wood. Nevertheless, the whole glory of the action was ascribed to Marius, on account of his former victory, and under color of his present authority; the populace more especially styling him the third founder of their city, as having diverted a danger no less threatening than was that when the Gauls sacked Rome; and every one, in their feasts and rejoicings at home with their wives and children, made offerings and libations in honor of "*The Gods and Marius*"; and would have had him solely have the honor of both the triumphs. However, he did not do so, but triumphed together with Catulus, being desirous to show his moderation even in such great circumstances of good fortune; besides, he was not a little afraid of the soldiers in Catulus's army, lest, if he should wholly bereave their general of the honor, they should endeavor to hinder him of his triumph.

Marius was now in his fifth consulship, and he sued for his sixth in such a manner as never any man before him had done, even for his first; he courted the people's favor and ingratiated himself with the multitude by every sort of complaisance; not only derogating from the state and dignity of his office, but also belying his own character, by attempting to seem popular and obliging, for which nature had never designed him. His passion for distinction did, indeed, they say, make him exceedingly timorous in any political matters, or in confronting public assemblies; and that undaunted presence of mind he always showed in battle against the enemy forsook him when he was to address the people; he was easily upset by the most ordinary commendation or dispraise. It is told of him, that having at one time given the freedom of the city to one thousand men of Camerinum who had behaved valiantly in this war, and this seeming to be illegally done, upon some one or other calling him to an account for it, he answered, that the law spoke too softly to be heard in such a noise of war; yet he himself appeared to be more disconcerted and overcome by the clamor made in the assemblies. The need they had of him in time of war procured him power and dignity; but in civil affairs, when he despaired of getting the first place, he was forced to betake himself to the favor of the people, never caring to be a good man, so that he were but a great one.

He thus became very odious to all the nobility; and, above all, he feared Metellus, who had been so ungratefully used by him, and whose true virtue made him naturally an enemy to those that sought influence with the people, not by the honorable course, but by subservience and complaisance. Marius, therefore, endeavored to banish him from the city, and for this purpose he contracted a close alliance with Glaucia and Saturninus, a couple of daring fellows, who had the great mass of the indigent and seditious multitude at their control; and by their assistance he enacted various laws, and bringing the soldiers, also, to attend the assembly, he was enabled to overpower Metellus. And as Rutilius relates (in all other respects a fair and faithful authority, but, indeed, privately an enemy to Marius), he obtained his sixth consulship by distributing vast sums of money among the tribes, and by this bribery kept out Metellus, and had Valerius Flaccus given him as his instrument, rather than his colleague, in the consulship. The people had never before bestowed so many consulships on any one man, except on Valerius Corvinus only, and he, too, they say, was forty-five years between his first and last; but Marius, from his first, ran through five more, with one current of good fortune.

In the last, especially, he contracted a great deal of hatred, by committing several gross misdemeanors in compliance with the desires of Saturninus; among which was the murder of Nonius, whom Saturninus slew because he stood in competition with him for the tribuneship. And when, afterwards, Saturninus, on becoming tribune, brought forward his law for the division of lands, with a clause enacting that the senate publicly swear to confirm whatever the people should vote, and not to oppose them in anything, Marius, in the senate, cunningly feigned to be against this provision, and said that he would not take any such oath, nor would any man, he thought, who was wise; for if there were no ill design in the law, still it would be an affront to the senate to be compelled to give their approbation, and not to do it willingly and upon persuasion. This he said, not that it was agreeable to his own sentiments, but that he might entrap Metellus beyond any possibility of escape. For Marius, in whose ideas virtue and capacity consisted largely in deceit, made very little account of what he had openly professed to the senate; and knowing that Metellus was one of a fixed resolution, and, as Pindar has it, esteemed "truth the first principle of heroic virtue," he hoped to ensnare him into a declaration before the senate, and on his refusing, as he was sure to do, afterwards to take the oath, he expected to bring him into such odium with the people as should never be wiped off. The design succeeded to his wish. As soon as Metellus had declared that he would not swear to it, the senate adjourned. A few days after, on Saturninus citing the senators to make their appearance and take the oath before the people, Marius stepped forth, amidst a profound silence, every one being intent to hear him, and bidding farewell to those fine speeches he had before made in the senate, said, that his back was not so broad that he should think himself bound, once for all, by any opinion once given on so important a matter; he would willingly swear and submit to the law, if so be it were one, a proviso which he added as a mere cover for his effrontery. The people, in great joy at his taking the oath, loudly clapped and applauded him, while the nobility stood by ashamed and vexed at his inconstancy; but they submitted out of fear of the people, and all in order took the oath, till it came to Metellus's turn. But he, though his friends begged and entreated him to take it, and not to plunge himself irrecoverably into the penalties which Saturninus had provided for those that should refuse it, would not flinch from his resolution, nor swear; but, according to his fixed custom, being ready to suffer anything rather than do a base, unworthy action, he left the forum, telling those that were with him that to do a wrong thing is base, and to do well where there is no danger, common; the good man's characteristic is to do so where there is danger.

Hereupon Saturninus put it to the vote, that the consuls should place Metellus under their interdict, and forbid him fire, water, and lodging. There were enough, too, of the basest of people ready to kill him. Nevertheless, when many of the better sort were extremely concerned, and gathered about Metellus, he would not suffer them to raise a sedition upon his account, but with this calm reflection left the city, "Either when the posture of affairs is mended and the people repent, I shall be recalled, or if things remain in their present condition, it will be best to be absent." But what great favor and honor Metellus received in his banishment, and in what manner he spent his time at Rhodes, in philosophy, will be more fitly our subject when we write his life.

Marius, in return for this piece of service, was forced to connive at Saturninus, now proceeding to the very height of insolence and violence, and was, without knowing it, the instrument of mischief beyond endurance, the only course of which was through outrages and massacres to tyranny and the subversion of the government. Standing in some awe of the nobility, and, at the same time, eager to court the commonalty, he was guilty of a most mean and dishonest action. When some of the great men came to him at night to stir him up against Saturninus, at the other door, unknown to them, he let him in; then making the same pretence of some disorder of body to both, he ran from one party to the other, and staying at one time with them and another with him, he instigated and exasperated them one against another. At length when the senate and equestrian order concerted measures together, and openly manifested their resentment, he did bring his soldiers into the forum, and driving the insurgents into the capitol, and then cutting off the conduits, forced them to surrender by want of water. They, in this distress, addressing themselves to him, surrendered, as it is termed, on the *public faith*. He did his utmost to save their lives, but so wholly in vain, that when they came down into the forum they were all basely murdered. Thus he had made himself equally odious both to the nobility and commons, and when the time was come to create censors, though he was the most obvious man, yet he did not petition for it; but fearing the disgrace of being repulsed, permitted others, his inferiors, to be elected, though he pleased himself by giving out that he was not willing to disoblige too many by undertaking a severe inspection into their lives and conduct.

There was now an edict preferred to recall Metellus from banishment; this he vigorously, but in vain, opposed both by word and deed, and was at length obliged to desist. The people unanimously voted for it; and he, not able to endure the sight of Metellus's return, made a voyage to Cappadocia and Galatia; giving out that he had to perform the sacrifices which he had vowed to Cybele; but actuated really by other less apparent reasons. For, in fact, being a man altogether ignorant of civil life and ordinary politics, he received all his advancement from war; and supposing his power and glory would by little and little decrease by his lying quietly out of action, he was eager by every means to excite some new commotions, and hoped that by setting at variance some of the kings, and by exasperating Mithridates, especially, who was then apparently making preparations for war, he himself should be chosen general against him, and so furnish the city with new matter of triumph, and his own house with the plunder of Pontus and the riches of its king. Therefore, though Mithridates entertained him with all imaginable attention and respect, yet he was not at all wrought upon or softened by it; but said, "O king, either endeavor to be stronger than the Romans, or else quietly submit to their commands." With which he left Mithridates astonished, as he indeed had often heard the fame of the bold speaking of the Romans, but now for the first time experienced it.

When Marius returned again to Rome, he built a house close by the forum, either, as he himself gave out, that he was not willing his clients should be tired with going far, or that he imagined distance was the reason why more did not come. This, however, was not so; the real reason was that, being inferior to others in agreeableness of conversation and the arts of political life, like a mere tool and implement of war, he was thrown aside in time of peace. Amongst all those whose brightness eclipsed his glory, he was most incensed against Sylla, who had owed his rise to the hatred which the nobility bore Marius; and had made his disagreement with him the one principle of his political life. When Bocchus, king of Numidia, who was styled the associate of the Romans, dedicated some figures of Victory in the capitol, and with them a representation in gold of himself delivering Jugurtha to Sylla, Marius upon this was almost distracted with rage and ambition, as though Sylla had arrogated this honor to himself, and endeavored forcibly to pull down these presents; Sylla, on the other side, as vigorously resisted him; but the Social War, then on a sudden threatening the city, put a stop to this sedition when just ready to break out. For the most warlike and best-peopled countries of all Italy formed a confederacy together against Rome, and were within a little of subverting the empire; as they were indeed strong, not only in their weapons and the valor of their soldiers, but stood nearly upon equal terms with the Romans as to the skill and daring of their commanders.

As much glory and power as this war, so various in its events and so uncertain as to its success, conferred upon Sylla, so much it took away from Marius, who was thought tardy, unenterprising, and timid, whether it were that his age was now quenching his former heat and vigor (for he was above sixty-five years old), or that having, as he himself said, some distemper that affected his muscles, and his body being unfit for action, he did service above his strength. Yet, for all this, he came off victor in a considerable battle, wherein he slew six thousand of the enemies, and never once gave them any advantage over him; and when he was surrounded by the works of the enemy, he contained himself, and though insulted over, and challenged, did not yield to the provocation. The story is told that when Publius Silo, a man of the greatest repute and authority among the enemies, said to him, "If you are indeed a great general, Marius, leave your camp and fight a battle," he replied, "If you are one, make me do so." And another time, when the enemy gave them a good opportunity of a battle, and the Romans through fear durst not charge, so that both parties retreated, he called an assembly of his soldiers and said, "It is no small question whether I should call the enemies or you the greater cowards, for neither did they dare to face your backs, nor you to confront theirs." At length, professing to be worn out with the infirmity of his body, he laid down his command.

Afterwards, when the Italians were worsted, there were several candidates suing, with the aid of the popular leaders, for the chief command in the war with Mithridates. Sulpicius, tribune of the people, a bold and confident man, contrary to everybody's expectation, brought forward Marius, and proposed him as proconsul and general in that war. The people were divided; some were on Marius's side, others voted for Sylla, and jeeringly bade Marius go to his baths at Baiæ, to cure his body, worn out, as himself confessed, with age and catarrhs. Marius had, indeed, there, about Misenum, a villa more effeminately and luxuriously furnished than seemed to become one that had seen service in so many and great wars and expeditions. This same house Cornelia bought for seventy-five thousand drachmas, and not long after Lucius Lucullus, for two million five hundred thousand; so rapid and so great was the growth of Roman sumptuosity. Yet, in spite of all this, out of a mere boyish passion for distinction, affecting to shake off his age and weakness, he went down daily to the Campus Martius, and exercising himself with the youth, showed

himself still nimble in his armor, and expert in riding; though he was undoubtedly grown bulky in his old age, and inclining to excessive fatness
and corpulency.

Some people were pleased with this, and went continually to see him
competing and displaying himself in these exercises; but the better sort
that saw him pitied the cupidity and ambition that made one who had
risen from utter poverty to extreme wealth, and out of nothing into
greatness, unwilling to admit any limit to his high fortune, or to be content with being admired, and quietly enjoying what he had already got;
why, as if he still were indigent, should he at so great an age leave his
glory and his triumphs to go into Cappadocia and the Euxine Sea, to
fight Archelaus and Neoptolemus, Mithridates's generals? Marius's pretenses for this action of his seemed very ridiculous; for he said he wanted
to go and teach his son to be a general.

The condition of the city, which had long been unsound and diseased,
became hopeless now that Marius found so opportune an instrument for
the public destruction as Sulpicius's insolence. This man professed, in all
other respects, to admire and imitate Saturninus; only he found fault with
him for backwardness and want of spirit in his designs. He, therefore, to
avoid this fault, got six hundred of the equestrian order about him as his
guard, whom he named anti-senators; and with these confederates he set
upon the consuls, whilst they were at the assembly, and took the son of
one of them who fled from the forum and slew him. Sylla, being hotly
pursued, took refuge in Marius's house, which none could suspect, by
that means escaping those that sought him, who hastily passed by there,
and, it is said, was safely conveyed by Marius himself out at the other
door, and came to the camp. Yet Sylla, in his memoirs, positively denies
that he fled to Marius, saying he was carried thither to consult upon the
matters to which Sulpicius would have forced him, against his will, to
consent; that he, surrounding him with drawn swords, hurried him to
Marius, and constrained him thus, till he went thence to the forum and
removed, as they required him to do, the interdict on business.

Sulpicius, having thus obtained the mastery, decreed the command of
the army to Marius, who proceeded to make preparations for his march,
and sent two tribunes to receive the charge of the army from Sylla. Sylla
hereupon exasperating his soldiers, who were about thirty-five thousand
full-armed men, led them towards Rome. First falling upon the tribunes
Marius had sent, they slew them; Marius having done as much for several of Sylla's friends in Rome, and now offering their freedom to the
slaves on condition of their assistance in the war; of whom, however, they
say, there were but three who accepted his proposal. For some small time
he made head against Sylla's assault, but was soon overpowered and fled;
those that were with him, as soon as he had escaped out of the city, were

dispersed, and night coming on, he hastened to a country house of his, called Solonium. Hence he sent his son to some neighboring farms of his father-in-law, Mucius, to provide necessaries; he went himself to Ostia, where his friend Numerius had prepared him a ship, and hence, not staying for his son, he took with him his son-in-law Granius, and weighed anchor.

Young Marius, coming to Mucius's farms, made his preparations; and the day breaking, was almost discovered by the enemy. For there came thither a party of horse that suspected some such matter; but the farm steward, foreseeing their approach, hid Marius in a cart full of beans, then yoking in his team and driving toward the city, met those that were in search of him. Marius, thus conveyed home to his wife, took with him some necessaries, and came at night to the seaside; where, going on board a ship that was bound for Africa, he went away thither. Marius, the father, when he had put to sea, with a strong gale passing along the coast of Italy, was in no small apprehension of one Geminius, a great man at Terracina, and his enemy; and therefore bade the seamen hold off from that place. They were, indeed, willing to gratify him, but the wind now blowing in from the sea and making the waves swell to a great height, they were afraid the ship would not be able to weather out the storm, and Marius, too, being indisposed and seasick, they made for land, and not without some difficulty reached the shore near Circeium.

The storm now increasing and their victuals failing, they left their ship and wandered up and down without any certain purpose, simply as in great distresses people shun the present as the greatest evil, and rely upon the hopes of uncertainties. For the land and sea were both equally unsafe for them; it was dangerous to meet with people, and it was no less so to meet with none, on account of their want of necessaries. At length, though late, they lighted upon a few poor shepherds, that had not anything to relieve them; but knowing Marius, advised him to depart as soon as might be, for they had seen a little beyond that place a party of horse that were gone in search of him. Finding himself in a great straight, especially because those that attended him were not able to go further, being spent with their long fasting, for the present he turned aside out of the road, and hid himself in a thick wood, where he passed the night in great wretchedness. The next day, pinched with hunger, and willing to make use of the little strength he had, before it were all exhausted, he traveled by the seaside, encouraging his companions not to fall away from him before the fulfillment of his final hopes, for which, in reliance on some old predictions, he professed to be sustaining himself. For when he was yet but very young, and lived in the country, he caught in the skirt of his garment an eagle's nest, as it was falling, in which were seven young ones, which his parents seeing and much admiring, consulted the augurs about it, who told them that he should become the greatest man in the world, and that the fates had decreed he should seven times be possessed of the supreme power and authority. Some are of opinion that this really happened to Marius, as we have related it; others say, that those who then and through the rest of his exile heard him tell these stories, and believed him, have merely repeated a story that is altogether fabulous; for an eagle never hatches more than two; and even Musæus was deceived, who, speaking of the eagle, says that—

> "She lays three eggs, hatches two, and rears one."

However this be, it is certain Marius, in his exile and greatest extremities, would often say that he should attain a seventh consulship.

When Marius and his company were now about twenty furlongs distant from Minturnæ, a city in Italy, they espied a troop of horse making up toward them with all speed, and by chance, also, at the same time, two ships under sail. Accordingly, they ran every one with what speed and strength they could to the sea and, plunging into it, swam to the ships. Those that were with Granius, reaching one of them, passed over to an island opposite, called Ænaria; Marius himself, whose body was heavy and unwieldy, was with great pains and difficulty kept above the water by two servants, and put into the other ship. The soldiers were by this time come to the seaside, and from thence called out to the seamen to put to shore, or else to throw out Marius, and then they might go whither they would. Marius besought them with tears to the contrary, and the masters of the ship, after frequent changes, in a short space of time, of their purpose, inclining first to one, then to the other side, resolved at length to answer the soldiers that they would not give up Marius. As soon as they had ridden off in a rage, the seamen, again changing their resolution, came to land, and casting anchor at the mouth of the river Liris, where it overflows and makes a great marsh, they advised him to land, refresh himself on shore, and take some care of his discomposed body, till the wind came fairer; which, said they, will happen at such an hour, when the wind from the sea will calm, and that from the marshes rise. Marius, following their advice, did so, and when the seamen had set him on shore, he laid him down in an adjacent field, suspecting nothing less than what was to befall him. They, as soon as they had got into the ship, weighed anchor and departed, as thinking it neither honorable to deliver Marius into the hands of those that sought him, nor safe to protect him.

He thus, deserted by all, lay a good while silently on the shore; at length collecting himself, he advanced with pain and difficulty, without any path, till, wading through deep bogs and ditches full of water and mud, he came upon the hut of an old man that worked in the fens, and falling at his feet besought him to assist and preserve one who, if he es-

caped the present danger, would make him returns beyond his expectation. The poor man, whether he had formerly known him, or were then
moved with his superior aspect, told him that if he wanted only rest, his
cottage would be convenient; but if he were flying from anybody's
search, he would hide him in a more retired place. Marius desiring him
to do so, he carried him into the fens and bade him hide himself in an
hollow place by the riverside, where he laid upon him a great many
reeds, and other things that were light, and would cover, but not oppress
him. But within a very short time he was disturbed with a noise and tumult from the cottage, for Geminius had sent several from Terracina in
pursuit of him; some of whom, happening to come that way, frightened
and threatened the old man for having entertained and hid an enemy of
the Romans. Wherefore Marius, arising and stripping himself, plunged
into a puddle full of thick muddy water; and even there he could not escape their search, but was pulled out covered with mire, and carried away
naked to Minturnæ, and delivered to the magistrates. For there had been
orders sent through all the towns to make public search for Marius, and
if they found him to kill him; however, the magistrates thought convenient to consider a little better of it first, and sent him prisoner to the
house of one Fannia.

This woman was supposed not very well affected towards him upon
an old account. One Tinnius had formerly married this Fannia; from
whom she afterwards, being divorced, demanded her portion, which was
considerable, but her husband accused her of adultery; so the controversy
was brought before Marius in his sixth consulship. When the cause was
examined thoroughly, it appeared both that Fannia had been incontinent,
and that her husband knowing her to be so, had married and lived a considerable time with her. So that Marius was severe enough with both,
commanding him to restore her portion, and laying a fine of four copper coins upon her by way of disgrace. But Fannia did not then behave
like a woman that had been injured, but as soon as she saw Marius, remembered nothing less than old affronts; took care of him according to
her ability, and comforted him. He made her his returns and told her he
did not despair, for he had met with a lucky omen, which was thus.
When he was brought to Fannia's house, as soon as the gate was opened,
an ass came running out to drink at a spring hard by, and giving a bold
and encouraging look, first stood still before him, then brayed aloud and
pranced by him. From which Marius drew his conclusion, and said that
the fates designed his safety rather by sea than land, because the ass neglected his dry fodder and turned from it to the water. Having told
Fannia this story, he bade the chamber door to be shut and went to rest.

Meanwhile the magistrates and councilors of Minturnæ consulted together, and determined not to delay any longer, but immediately to kill

Marius; and when none of their citizens durst undertake the business, a certain soldier, a Gaulish or Cimbrian horseman (the story is told both ways), went in with his sword drawn to him. The room itself was not very light, that part of it especially where he then lay was dark, from whence Marius's eyes, they say, seemed to the fellow to dart out flames at him, and a loud voice to say, out of the dark, "Fellow, darest thou kill Caius Marius?" The barbarian hereupon immediately fled, and leaving his sword in the place rushed out of doors, crying only this, "I cannot kill Caius Marius." At which they were all at first astonished, and presently began to feel pity, and remorse, and anger at themselves for making so unjust and ungrateful a decree against one who had preserved Italy, and whom it was bad enough not to assist. "Let him go," said they, "where he please to banishment, and find his fate somewhere else; we only entreat pardon of the gods for thrusting Marius distressed and deserted out of our city."

Impelled by thoughts of this kind, they went in a body into the room, and taking him amongst them, conducted him towards the seaside; on his way to which, though everyone was very officious to him, and all made what haste they could, yet a considerable time was likely to be lost. For the grove of Marica (as she is called), which the people hold sacred and make it a point of religion not to let anything that is once carried into it be taken out, lay just in their road to the sea, and if they should go round about, they must needs come very late thither. At length one of the old men cried out and said, there was no place so sacred but they might pass through it for Marius's preservation; and thereupon, first of all, he himself, taking up some of the baggage that was carried for his accommodation to the ship, passed through the grove, all the rest immediately, with the same readiness, accompanying him. And one Belæus (who afterwards had a picture of these things drawn, and put it in a temple at the place of embarkation), having by this time provided him a ship, Marius went on board, and, hoisting sail, was by fortune thrown upon the island Ænaria, where meeting with Granius, and his other friends, he sailed with them for Africa. But their water failing them in the way, they were forced to put in near Eryx, in Sicily, where was a Roman quæstor on the watch, who all but captured Marius himself on his landing, and did kill sixteen of his retinue that went to fetch water. Marius, with all expedition loosing thence, crossed the sea to the isle of Meninx, where he first heard the news of his son's escape with Cethegus, and of his going to implore the assistance of Hiempsal, king of Numidia.

With this news, being somewhat comforted, he ventured to pass from that isle towards Carthage. Sextilius, a Roman, was then governor in Africa; one that had never received either any injury or any kindness from Marius; but who from compassion, it was hoped, might lend him some help. But he was scarce got ashore with a small retinue when an of-

ficer met him, and said, "Sextilius, the governor, forbids you, Marius, to
set foot in Africa; if you do, he says, he will put the decree of the senate
in execution, and treat you as an enemy to the Romans." When Marius
heard this, he wanted words to express his grief and resentment, and for
a good while held his peace, looking sternly upon the messenger, who
asked him what he should say, or what answer he should return to the
governor? Marius answered him with a deep sigh: "Go tell him that you
have seen Caius Marius sitting in exile among the ruins of Carthage";
appositely applying the example of the fortune of that city to the change
of his own condition.

In the interim, Hiempsal, king of Numidia, dubious of what he should
determine to do, treated young Marius and those that were with him very
honorably; but when they had a mind to depart, he still had some pretense
or other to detain them, and it was manifest he made these delays upon
no good design. However, there happened an accident that made well for
their preservation. The hard fortune which attended young Marius, who
was of a comely aspect, touched one of the king's concubines, and this pity
of hers was the beginning and occasion of love for him. At first he declined the woman's solicitations, but when he perceived that there was no
other way of escaping, and that her offers were more serious than for the
gratification of intemperate passion, he accepted her kindness, and she
finding means to convey them away, he escaped with his friends and fled
to his father. As soon as they had saluted each other, and were going by
the seaside, they saw some scorpions fighting, which Marius took for an
ill omen, whereupon they immediately went on board a little fisher-boat,
and made toward Cercinas, an island not far distant from the continent.
They had scarce put off from shore when they espied some horse, sent
after them by the king, with all speed making toward that very place from
which they were just retired. And Marius thus escaped a danger, it might
be said, as great as any he ever incurred.

At Rome news came that Sylla was engaged with Mithridates's generals in Bœotia; the consuls, from factious opposition, were fallen to downright fighting, wherein Octavius prevailing, drove Cinna out of the city
for attempting despotic government, and made Cornelius Merula consul
in his stead; while Cinna, raising forces in other parts of Italy, carried the
war against them. As soon as Marius heard of this he resolved, with all expedition, to put to sea again, and taking with him from Africa some
Mauritanian horse, and a few of the refugees out of Italy, all together not
above one thousand, he, with this handful, began his voyage. Arriving at
Telamon, in Etruria, and coming ashore, he proclaimed freedom for the
slaves; and many of the countrymen, also, and shepherds thereabouts, who
were already freemen, at the hearing his name flocked to him to the seaside. He persuaded the youngest and strongest to join him, and in a small

time got together a competent force with which he filled forty ships. Knowing Octavius to be a good man and willing to execute his office with the greatest justice imaginable, and Cinna to be suspected by Sylla, and in actual warfare against the established government, he determined to join himself and his forces with the latter. He therefore sent a message to him, to let him know that he was ready to obey him as consul.

When Cinna had joyfully received his offer, naming him proconsul, and sending him the fasces and other ensigns of authority, he said that grandeur did not become his present fortune; but wearing an ordinary habit, and still letting his hair grow as it had done, from that very day he first went into banishment, and being now above threescore and ten years old, he came slowly on foot, designing to move people's compassion; which did not prevent, however, his natural fierceness of expression from still predominating, and his humiliation still let it appear that he was not so much dejected as exasperated by the change of his condition. Having saluted Cinna and the soldiers, he immediately prepared for action, and soon made a considerable alteration in the posture of affairs. He first cut off the provision ships, and plundering all the merchants, made himself master of the supplies of corn; then bringing his navy to the seaport towns, he took them, and at last, becoming master of Ostia by treachery, he pillaged that town, and slew a multitude of the inhabitants, and, blocking up the river, took from the enemy all hopes of supply by the sea; then marched with his army toward the city, and posted himself upon the hill called Janiculum.

The public interest did not receive so great damage from Octavius's unskillfulness in his management of affairs as from his omitting needful measures through too strict observance of the law. As when several advised him to make the slaves free, he said that he would not give slaves the privilege of the country from which he then, in defense of the laws, was driving away Marius. When Metellus, son to that Metellus who was general in the war in Africa, and afterwards banished through Marius's means, came to Rome, being thought a much better commander than Octavius, the soldiers, deserting the consul, came to him and desired him to take the command of them and preserve the city; that they, when they had got an experienced valiant commander, should fight courageously, and come off conquerors. But when Metellus, offended at it, commanded them angrily to return to the consul, they revolted to the enemy. Metellus, too, seeing the city in a desperate condition, left it; but a company of Chaldæans, sacrificers, and interpreters of the Sibyl's books persuaded Octavius that things would turn out happily, and kept him at Rome. He was, indeed, of all the Romans the most upright and just, and maintained the honor of the consulate, without cringing or compliance, as strictly in accordance with ancient laws and usages as though they had been immutable mathematical truths; and yet fell, I know not how, into some weaknesses, giving more observance to fortune-tellers and diviners, than to men skilled in civil and military affairs. He therefore, before Marius entered the city, was pulled down from the rostra and murdered by those that were sent before by Marius; and it is reported there was a Chaldæan writing found in his gown when he was slain. And it seemed a thing very unaccountable, that of two famous generals, Marius should be often successful by the observing divinations, and Octavius ruined by the same means.

When affairs were in this posture, the senate assembled, and sent a deputation to Cinna and Marius, desiring them to come into the city peaceably and spare the citizens. Cinna, as consul, received the embassy, sitting in the curule chair, and returned a kind answer to the messengers; Marius stood by him and said nothing, but gave sufficient testimony, by the gloominess of his countenance and the sternness of his looks, that he would in a short time fill the city with blood. As soon as the council arose, they went toward the city, where Cinna entered with his guards, but Marius stayed at the gates, and, dissembling his rage, professed that he was then an exile and banished his country by course of law; that if his presence were necessary, they must, by a new decree, repeal the former act by which he was banished; as though he were, indeed, a religious observer of the laws, and as if he were returning to a city free from fear or oppression. Hereupon the people were assembled, but before three or four tribes had given their votes, throwing up his pretenses and his legal scruples about his banishment, he came into the city with a select guard of the slaves who had joined him, whom he called Bardyæi. These proceeded to murder a number of citizens, as he gave command, partly by word of mouth, partly by the signal of his nod. At length Ancharius, a senator, and one that had been prætor, coming to Marius, and not being resaluted by him, they with their drawn swords slew him before Marius's face; and henceforth this was their token, immediately to kill all those who met Marius and saluting him were taken no notice of, nor answered with the like courtesy; so that his very friends were not without dreadful apprehensions and horror, whensoever they came to speak with him.

When they had now butchered a great number, Cinna grew more remiss and cloyed with murders; but Marius's rage continued still fresh and unsatisfied, and he daily sought for all that were any way suspected by him. Now was every road and every town filled with those that pursued and hunted them that fled and hid themselves; and it was remarkable that there was no more confidence to be placed, as things stood, either in hospitality or friendship; for there were found but a very few that did not betray those that fled to them for shelter. And thus the servants of Cornutus deserve the greater praise and admiration, who, having concealed their master in the house, took the body of one of the slain, cut off the head, put a gold ring on the finger, and showed it to Marius's guards, and buried it with the same solemnity as if it had been their own master. This trick was perceived by nobody, and so Cornutus escaped, and was conveyed by his domestics into Gaul.

Marcus Antonius, the orator, though he, too, found a true friend, had ill fortune. The man was but poor and a plebeian, and as he was entertaining a man of the greatest rank in Rome, trying to provide for him with the best he could, he sent his servant to get some wine of a neighboring vintner. The servant carefully tasting it and bidding him draw better, the fellow asked him what was the matter, that he did not buy new and ordinary wine as he used to do, but richer and of a greater price; he, without any design, told him as his old friend and acquaintance, that his master entertained Marcus Antonius, who was concealed with him. The villainous vintner, as soon as the servant was gone, went himself to Marius, then at supper, and being brought into his presence, told him he would deliver Antonius into his hands. As soon as he heard it, it is said he gave a great shout, and clapped his hands for joy, and had very nearly risen up and gone to the place himself; but being detained by his friends, he sent Annius, and some soldiers with him, and commanded him to bring Antonius's head to him with all speed. When they came to the house, Annius stayed at the door, and the soldiers went upstairs into the chamber; where, seeing Antonius, they endeavored to shuffle off the murder from one to another; for so great it seems were the graces and charms of his oratory, that as soon as he began to speak and beg his life, none of them durst touch or so much as look upon him; but hanging down their heads, every one fell aweeping. When their stay seemed something tedious, Annius came up himself and found Antonius discoursing, and the soldiers astonished and quite softened by it, and calling them cowards, went himself and cut off his head.

Catulus Lutatius, who was colleague with Marius, and his partner in the triumph over the Cimbri, when Marius replied to those that interceded for him and begged his life, merely with the words, "He must die," shut himself up in a room, and making a great fire, smothered himself. When maimed and headless carcasses were now frequently thrown about and trampled upon in the streets, people were not so much moved with compassion at the sight, as struck into a kind of horror and consternation. The outrages of those that were called Bardyæi, was the greatest grievance. These murdered the masters of families in their own houses, abused their children, and ravished their wives, and were uncontrollable in their rapine and murders, till those of Cinna's and Sertorius's party, taking counsel together, fell upon them in the camp and killed them every man.

In the interim, as if a change of wind was coming on, there came news from all parts that Sylla, having put an end to the war with Mithridates, and taken possession of the provinces, was returning into Italy with a great army. This gave some small respite and intermission to these unspeakable calamities. Marius and his friends believing war to be close at hand, Marius was chosen consul the seventh time, and appearing on the very calends of January, the beginning of the year, threw one Sextus Lucinus from the Tarpeian precipice; an omen, as it seemed, portending the renewed misfortunes both of their party and of the city. Marius, himself now worn out with labor and sinking under the burden of anxieties, could not sustain his spirits, which shook within him with the apprehension of a new war and fresh encounters and dangers, the formidable character of which he knew by his own experience. He was not now to hazard the war with Octavius or Merula, commanding an inexperienced multitude or seditious rabble; but Sylla himself was approaching, the same who had formerly banished him, and since that, had driven Mithridates as far as the Euxine Sea.

Perplexed with such thoughts as these, and calling to mind his banishment, and the tedious wanderings and dangers he underwent, both by sea and land, he fell into despondency, nocturnal frights, and unquiet sleep, still fancying that he heard some one telling him, that—

> "—the lion's lair
> Is dangerous, though the lion be not there."

Above all things fearing to lie awake, he gave himself up to drinking deep and besotting himself at night in a way most unsuitable to his age, by all means provoking sleep, as a diversion to his thoughts. At length, on the arrival of a messenger from the sea, he was seized with new alarms, and so what with his fear for the future, and what with the burden and satiety of the present, on some slight predisposing cause, he fell into a pleurisy, as Posidonius the philosopher relates, who says he visited and conversed with him when he was sick, about some business relating to his embassy. Caius Piso, a historian, tells us that Marius, walking after supper with his friends, fell into a conversation with them about his past life, and after reckoning up the several changes of his condition that from the beginning had happened to him, said that it did not become a prudent man to trust himself any longer with fortune; and, thereupon taking leave of those that were with him, he kept his bed seven days, and then died.

Some say his ambition betrayed itself openly in his sickness. and that he ran into an extravagant frenzy, fancying himself to be general in the war against Mithridates, throwing himself into such postures and motions of his body as he had formerly used when he was in battle, with frequent shouts and loud cries. With so strong and invincible a desire of being employed in that business had he been possessed through his pride and emulation. Though he had now lived seventy years, and was the first man that ever was chosen seven times consul, and had an establishment and riches sufficient for many kings, he yet complained of his ill fortune, that he must now die before he had attained what he desired. Plato, when he saw his death approaching, thanked the guiding providence and fortune of his life, first, that he was born a man and a Grecian, not a barbarian or a brute, and next, that he happened to live in Socrates's age. And so, indeed, they say Antipater of Tarsus, in like manner, at his death, calling to mind the happiness that he had enjoyed, did not so much as omit his prosperous voyage to Athens; thus recognizing every favor of his indulgent fortune with the greatest acknowledgments, and carefully saving all to the last in that safest of human treasure chambers, the memory. Unmindful and thoughtless persons, on the contrary, let all that occurs to them slip away from them as time passes on. Retaining and preserving nothing, they lose the enjoyment of their present prosperity by fancying something better to come; whereas by fortune we may be prevented of this, but that cannot be taken from us. Yet they reject their present success, as though it did not concern them, and do nothing but dream of future uncertainties; not indeed unnaturally; as till men have by reason and education laid good foundation for external superstructures, in the seeking after and gathering them they can never satisfy the unlimited desires of their mind.

Thus died Marius on the seventeenth day of his seventh consulship, to the great joy and content of Rome, which thereby was in good hopes to be delivered from the calamity of a cruel tyranny; but in a small time they found that they had only changed their old and worn-out master for another young and vigorous; so much cruelty and savageness did his son Marius show in murdering the noblest and most approved citizens. At first, being esteemed resolute and daring against his enemies, he was named the son of Mars, but afterwards, his actions betraying his contrary disposition, he was called the son of Venus. At last, besieged by Sylla in Præneste, where he endeavored in many ways, but in vain, to save his life, when on the capture of the city there was no hope of escape, he killed himself with his own hand.

SULLA (SYLLA)[1]

Lucius Cornelius Sylla was descended of a patrician or noble family. Of his ancestors, Rufinus, it is said, had been consul, and incurred a disgrace more signal than his distinction. For being found possessed of more than ten pounds of silver plate, contrary to the law, he was for this reason put out of the senate. His posterity continued ever after in obscurity, nor had Sylla himself any opulent parentage. In his younger days he lived in hired lodgings, at a low rate, which in after times was adduced against him as proof that he had been fortunate above his quality. When he was boasting and magnifying himself for his exploits in Libya, a person of noble station made answer, "And how can you be an honest man, who, since the death of a father who left you nothing, have become so rich?" The time in which he lived was no longer an age of pure and upright manners, but had already declined, and yielded to the appetite for riches and luxury; yet still, in the general opinion, they who deserted the hereditary poverty of their family were as much blamed as those who had run out a fair patrimonial estate. And afterwards, when he had seized the power into his hands, and was putting many to death, a freedman suspected of having concealed one of the proscribed, and for that reason sentenced to be thrown down the Tarpeian rock, in a reproachful way recounted how they had lived long together under the same roof, himself for the upper rooms paying two thousand sesterces, and Sylla for the lower three thousand; so that the difference between their fortunes then was no more than one thousand sesterces, equivalent in Attic coin to two hundred and fifty drachmas. And thus much of his early fortune.

His general personal appearance may be known by his statues; only his blue eyes, of themselves extremely keen and glaring, were rendered all the more forbidding and terrible by the complexion of his face, in which white was mixed with rough blotches of fiery red. Hence, it is said, he was surnamed Sylla, and in allusion to it one of the scurrilous jesters at Athens made the verse upon him—

"Sylla is a mulberry sprinkled o'er with meal."

---

[1] [Plutarch calls him "Sylla," but he is more widely known as "Sulla."]

Nor is it out of place to make use of marks of character like these, in the case of one who was by nature so addicted to raillery, that in his youthful obscure years he would converse freely with players and professed jesters, and join them in all their low pleasures. And when supreme master of all, he was often wont to muster together the most impudent players and stage followers of the town, and to drink and bandy jests with them without regard to his age or the dignity of his place, and to the prejudice of important affairs that required his attention. When he was once at table, it was not in Sylla's nature to admit of anything that was serious, and whereas at other times he was a man of business, and austere of countenance, he underwent all of a sudden, at his first entrance upon wine and good-fellowship, a total revolution, and was gentle and tractable with common singers and dancers, and ready to oblige anyone that spoke with him. It seems to have been a sort of diseased result of this laxity that he was so prone to amorous pleasures, and yielded without resistance to any temptations of voluptuousness, from which even in his old age he could not refrain. He had a long attachment for Metrobius, a player. In his first amours, it happened that he made court to a common but rich lady, Nicopolis by name, and, what by the air of his youth, and what by long intimacy, won so far on her affections, that she rather than he was the lover, and at her death she bequeathed him her whole property. He likewise inherited the estate of a stepmother who loved him as her own son. By these means he had pretty well advanced his fortunes.

He was chosen quæstor to Marius in his first consulship, and set sail with him for Libya, to war upon Jugurtha. Here, in general, he gained approbation; and more especially, by closing in dexterously with an accidental occasion, made a friend of Bocchus, king of Numidia. He hospitably entertained the king's ambassadors on their escape from some Numidian robbers, and after showing them much kindness, sent them on their journey with presents, and an escort to protect them. Bocchus had long hated and dreaded his son-in-law, Jugurtha, who had now been worsted in the field and had fled to him for shelter; and it so happened he was at this time entertaining a design to betray him. He accordingly invited Sylla to come to him, wishing the seizure and surrender of Jugurtha to be effected rather through him than directly by himself. Sylla, when he had communicated the business to Marius and received from him a small detachment, voluntarily put himself into this imminent danger; and confiding in a barbarian who had been unfaithful to his own relations to apprehend another man's person, made surrender of his own. Bocchus, having both of them now in his power, was necessitated to betray one or other, and after long debate with himself, at last resolved on his first design, and gave up Jugurtha into the hands of Sylla.

For this Marius triumphed, but the glory of the enterprise, which through people's envy of Marius was ascribed to Sylla, secretly grieved him. And the truth is, Sylla himself was by nature vainglorious, and this being the first time that from a low and private condition he had risen to esteem amongst the citizens and tasted of honor, his appetite for distinction carried him to such a pitch of ostentation, that he had a representation of this action engraved on a signet ring; which he carried about with him, and made use of ever after. The impress was Bocchus delivering, and Sylla receiving, Jugurtha. This touched Marius to the quick; however, judging Sylla to be beneath his rivalry, he made use of him as lieutenant in his second consulship, and in his third as tribune; and many considerable services were effected by his means. When acting as lieutenant he took Copillus, chief of the Tectosages, prisoner, and compelled the Marsians, a great and populous nation, to become friends and confederates of the Romans.

Henceforward, however, Sylla, perceiving that Marius bore a jealous eye over him, and would no longer afford him opportunities of action, but rather opposed his advance, attached himself to Catulus, Marius's colleague, a worthy man, but not energetic enough as a general. And under this commander, who entrusted him with the highest and most important commissions, he rose at once to reputation and to power. He subdued by arms most part of the Alpine barbarians; and when there was a scarcity in the armies, he took that care upon himself, and brought in such a store of provisions as not only to furnish the soldiers of Catulus with abundance, but likewise to supply Marius. This, as he writes himself, wounded Marius to the very heart. So slight and childish were the first occasions and motives of that enmity between them, which, passing afterwards through a long course of civil bloodshed and incurable divisions to find its end in tyranny, and the confusion of the whole state, proved Euripides to have been truly wise and thoroughly acquainted with the causes of disorders in the body politic, when he forewarned all men to beware of Ambition, as of all the higher Powers, the most destructive and pernicious to her votaries.

Sylla, by this time thinking that the reputation of his arms abroad was sufficient to entitle him to a part in the civil administration, betook himself immediately from the camp to the assembly, and offered himself as a candidate for a prætorship, but failed. The fault of this disappointment he wholly ascribes to the populace, who, knowing his intimacy with King Bocchus, and for that reason expecting, that if he was made ædile before his prætorship, he would then show them magnificent hunting shows and combats between Libyan wild beasts, chose other prætors, on purpose to force him into the ædileship. The vanity of this pretext is sufficiently disproved by matter of fact. For the year following, partly by flatteries to the people, and partly by money, he got himself elected prætor. Accordingly, once while he was in office, on his angrily telling Cæsar that he should make use of his authority against him, Cæsar answered him with a smile, "You do well to call it your own, as you bought it." At the end of his prætorship he was sent over into Cappadocia, under the pretense of reestablishing Ariobarzanes in his kingdom, but in reality to keep in check the restless movements of Mithridates, who was gradually procuring himself as vast a new acquired power and dominion, as was that of his ancient inheritance. He carried over with him no great forces of his own, but making use of the cheerful aid of the confederates, succeeded, with considerable slaughter of the Cappadocians, and yet greater of the Armenian succors, in expelling Gordius and establishing Ariobarzanes as king.

During his stay on the banks of the Euphrates, there came to him Orobazus, a Parthian, ambassador from King Arsaces, as yet there having been no correspondence between the two nations. And this also we may lay to the account of Sylla's felicity, that he should be the first Roman to whom the Parthians made address for alliance and friendship. At the time of which reception, the story is that, having ordered three chairs of state to be set, one for Ariobarzanes, one for Orobazus, and a third for himself, he placed himself in the middle, and so gave audience. For this the king of Parthia afterwards put Orobazus to death. Some people commended Sylla for his lofty carriage towards the barbarians; others again accused him of arrogance and unseasonable display. It is reported that a certain Chaldæan, of Orobazus's retinue, looking Sylla wistfully in the face, and observing carefully the motions of his mind and body and forming a judgment of his nature, according to the rules of his art, said that it was impossible for him not to become the greatest of men; it was rather a wonder how he could even then abstain from being head of all.

At his return, Censorinus impeached him of extortion, for having exacted a vast sum of money from a well-affected and associate kingdom. However, Censorinus did not appear at the trial, but dropped his accusation. His quarrel, meantime, with Marius began to break out afresh, receiving new material from the ambition of Bocchus, who, to please the people of Rome, and gratify Sylla, set up in the temple of Jupiter Capitolinus images bearing trophies, and a representation in gold of the surrender of Jugurtha to Sylla. When Marius, in great anger, attempted to pull them down, and others aided Sylla, the whole city would have been in tumult and commotion with this dispute, had not the Social War, which had long lain smoldering, blazed forth at last, and for the present put an end to the quarrel.

In the course of this war, which had many great changes of fortune, and which, more than any, afflicted the Romans, and, indeed, endangered the very being of the Commonwealth, Marius was not able to signalize his valor in any action, but left behind him a clear proof, that warlike excellence requires a strong and still vigorous body. Sylla, on the other hand, by his many achievements, gained himself, with his fellow citizens, the name of a great commander, while his friends thought him the greatest of all commanders, and his enemies called him the most fortunate. Nor did this make the same sort of impression on him as it made on Timotheus the son of Conon, the Athenian; who, when his adversaries ascribed his successes to his good luck, and had a painting made, representing him asleep, and Fortune by his side, casting her nets over the cities, was rough and violent in his indignation at those who did it, as if, by attributing all to Fortune, they had robbed him of his just honors; and said to the people on one occasion at his return from war, "In this, ye men of Athens, Fortune had no part." A piece of boyish petulance, which the deity, we are told, played back upon Timotheus; who from that time was never able to achieve anything that was great, but proving altogether unfortunate in his attempts, and falling into discredit with the people, was at last banished the city. Sylla, on the contrary, not only accepted with pleasure the credit of such divine felicities and favors, but joining himself in extolling and glorifying what was done, gave the honor of all to Fortune, whether it were out of boastfulness, or a real feeling of divine agency. He remarks, in his Memoirs, that of all his well-advised actions, none proved so lucky in the execution as what he had boldly enterprised, not by calculation, but upon the moment. And in the character which he gives of himself, that he was born for fortune rather than war, he seems to give Fortune a higher place than merit, and, in short, makes himself entirely the creature of a superior power, accounting even his concord with Metellus, his equal in office, and his connection by marriage, a piece of preternatural felicity. For expecting to have met in him a most troublesome, he found him a most accommodating, colleague. Moreover, in the Memoirs which he dedicated to Lucullus, he admonished him to esteem nothing more trustworthy than what the divine powers advise him by night. And when he was leaving the city with an army, to fight in the Social War, he relates that the earth near the Laverna opened, and a quantity of fire came rushing out of it, shooting up with a bright flame into the heavens. The soothsayers upon this foretold that a person of great qualities, and of a rare and singular aspect, should take the government in hand, and quiet the present troubles of the city. Sylla affirms he was the man, for his golden head of hair made him an extraordinary-looking man, nor had he any shame, after the great actions he had done, in testifying to his own great qualities. And thus much of his opinion as to divine agency.

In general he would seem to have been of a very irregular character, full of inconsistencies with himself; much given to rapine, to prodigality yet more; in promoting or disgracing whom he pleased, alike unaccountable; cringing to those he stood in need of, and domineering over others who stood in need of him, so that it was hard to tell whether his nature had more in it of pride or of servility. As to his unequal distribution of punishments, as, for example, that upon slight grounds he would put to the torture, and again would bear patiently with the greatest wrongs; would readily forgive and be reconciled after the most heinous acts of enmity, and yet would visit small and inconsiderable offenses with death and confiscation of goods; one might judge that in himself he was really of a violent and revengeful nature, which however he could qualify, upon reflection, for his interest. In this very Social War, when the soldiers with stones and clubs had killed an officer of prætorian rank, his own lieutenant, Albinus by name, he passed by this flagrant crime without any inquiry, giving it out moreover in a boast, that the soldiers would behave all the better now, to make amends, by some special bravery, for their breach of discipline. He took no notice of the clamors of those that cried for justice, but designing already to supplant Marius, now that he saw the Social War near its end, he made much of his army, in hopes to get himself declared general of the forces against Mithridates.

At his return to Rome he was chosen consul with Quintus Pompeius, in the fiftieth year of his age, and made a most distinguished marriage with Cæcilia, daughter of Metellus, the chief priest.[2] The common people made a variety of verses in ridicule of the marriage, and many of the nobility also were disgusted at it, esteeming him, as Livy writes, unworthy of this connection, whom before they thought worthy of a consulship. This was not his only wife, for first, in his younger days, he was married to Ilia, by whom he had a daughter; after her to Ælia; and thirdly to Clœlia, whom he dismissed as barren, but honorably, and with professions of respect, adding, moreover, presents. But the match between him and Metella, falling out a few days after, occasioned suspicions that he had complained of Clœlia without due cause. To Metella he always showed great deference, so much so that the people, when anxious for the recall of the exiles of Marius's party, upon his refusal entreated the intercession of Metella. And the Athenians, it is thought, had harder measure, at the capture of their town because they used insulting language to Metella in their jests from the walls during the siege. But of this hereafter.

At present esteeming the consulship but a small matter in comparison of things to come, he was impatiently carried away in thought to the Mithridatic War. Here he was withstood by Marius; who out of mad affectation of glory and thirst for distinction, those never-dying passions, though he were now unwieldy in body, and had given up service, on ac-

---

[2][Her full name was Cæcilia Metella Dalmatica, so Plutarch also refers to her below as "Metella." When she married Sulla she was a widow with two children.]

count of his age, during the late campaigns, still coveted after command in a distant war beyond the seas. And whilst Sylla was departed for the camp, to order the rest of his affairs there, he sat brooding at home, and at last hatched that execrable sedition, which wrought Rome more mischief than all her enemies together had done, as was indeed foreshown by the gods. For a flame broke forth of its own accord, from under the staves of the ensigns, and was with difficulty extinguished. Three ravens brought their young into the open road, and ate them, carrying the relics into the nest again. Mice having gnawed the consecrated gold in one of the temples, the keepers caught one of them, a female, in a trap; and she bringing forth five young ones in the very trap, devoured three of them. But what was greatest of all, in a calm and clear sky there was heard the sound of a trumpet, with such a loud and dismal blast, as struck terror and amazement into the hearts of the people. The Etruscan sages affirmed that this prodigy betokened the mutation of the age, and a general revolution in the world. For according to them there are in all eight ages, differing one from another in the lives and the characters of men, and to each of these God has allotted a certain measure of time, determined by the circuit of the great year. And when one age is run out, at the approach of another, there appears some wonderful sign from earth or heaven, such as makes it manifest at once to those who have made it their business to study such things, that there has succeeded in the world a new race of men, differing in customs and institutes of life, and more or less regarded by the gods than the preceding. Among other great changes that happen, as they say, at the turn of ages, the art of divination, also, at one time rises in esteem and is more successful in its predictions, clearer and surer tokens being sent from God, and then again, in another generation, declines as low, becoming mere guesswork for the most part, and discerning future events by dim and uncertain intimations. This was the mythology of the wisest of the Tuscan sages, who were thought to possess a knowledge beyond other men. Whilst the senate sat in consultation with the soothsayers, concerning these prodigies, in the temple of Bellona, a sparrow came flying in, before them all, with a grasshopper in its mouth, and letting fall one part of it, flew away with the remainder. The diviners foreboded commotions and dissensions between the great landed proprietors and the common city populace; the latter, like the grasshopper, being loud and talkative; while the sparrow might represent the "dwellers in the field."

Marius had taken into alliance Sulpicius, the tribune, a man second to none in any villainies, so that it was less the question what others he surpassed, but rather in what respects he most surpassed himself in wickedness. He was cruel, bold, rapacious, and in all these points utterly shameless and unscrupulous; not hesitating to offer Roman citizenship by public sale to freed slaves and aliens, and to count out the price on public money-tables in the forum. He maintained three thousand swordsmen, and had always about him a company of young men of the equestrian class ready for all occasions, whom he styled his Anti-senate. Having had a law enacted, that no senator should contract a debt of above two thousand drachmas, he himself, after death, was found indebted three millions. This was the man whom Marius let in upon the Commonwealth, and who, confounding all things by force and the sword, made several ordinances of dangerous consequence, and amongst the rest one giving Marius the conduct of the Mithridatic war. Upon this the consuls proclaimed a public cessation of business, but as they were holding an assembly near the temple of Castor and Pollux, he let loose the rabble upon them, and amongst many others slew the consul Pompeius's young son in the forum, Pompeius himself hardly escaping in the crowd. Sylla, being closely pursued into the house of Marius, was forced to come forth and dissolve the cessation; and for his doing this, Sulpicius, having deposed Pompeius, allowed Sylla to continue his consulship, only transferring the Mithridatic expedition to Marius.

There were immediately dispatched to Nola tribunes, to receive the army and bring it to Marius; but Sylla having got first to the camp, and the soldiers, upon hearing of the news, having stoned the tribunes, Marius, in requital, proceeded to put the friends of Sylla in the city to the sword, and rifled their goods. Every kind of removal and flight went on, some hastening from the camp to the city, others from the city to the camp. The senate, no more in its own power, but wholly governed by the dictates of Marius and Sulpicius, alarmed at the report of Sylla's advancing with his troops towards the city, sent forth two of the prætors, Brutus and Servilius, to forbid his nearer approach. The soldiers would have slain these prætors in a fury, for their bold language to Sylla; contenting themselves, however, with breaking their rods, and tearing off their purple-edged robes, after much contumelious usage they sent them back, to the sad dejection of the citizens, who beheld their magistrates despoiled of their badges of office, and announcing to them that things were now manifestly come to a rupture past all cure. Marius put himself in readiness, and Sylla with his colleague moved from Nola, at the head of six complete legions, all of them willing to march up directly against the city, though he himself as yet was doubtful in thought, and apprehensive of the danger. As he was sacrificing, Postumius the soothsayer, having inspected the entrails, stretching forth both hands to Sylla, required to be bound and kept in custody till the battle was over, as willing, if they had not speedy and complete success, to suffer the utmost punishment. It is said, also, that there appeared to Sylla himself, in a dream, a certain goddess, whom the Romans learnt to worship from the Cappadocians, whether it be the Moon, or Pallas, or Bellona. This same goddess, to his thinking, stood by him, and put into his hand thunder and lightning, then naming his enemies one by one, bade him strike them, who, all of them, fell on the discharge and disappeared. Encouraged by this vision, and relating it to his colleague, next day he led on towards Rome. About Picinæ being met by a deputation, beseeching him not to attack at once, in the heat of a march, for that the senate had decreed to do him all the right imaginable, he consented to halt on the spot, and sent his officers to measure out the ground, as is usual, for a camp; so that the deputation, believing it, returned. They were no sooner gone, but he sent a party on under the command of Lucius Basillus and Caius Mummius, to secure the city gate, and the walls on the side of the Esquiline hill, and then close at their heels followed himself with all speed. Basillus made his way successfully into the city, but the unarmed multitude, pelting him with stones and tiles from off the houses, stopped his further progress, and beat him back to the wall. Sylla by this time was come up, and seeing what was going on, called aloud to his men to set fire to the houses, and taking a flaming torch, he himself led the way, and commanded the archers to make use of their fire-darts, letting fly at the tops of houses; all which he did, not upon any plan, but simply in his fury, yielding the conduct of that day's work to passion, and as if all he saw were enemies, without respect or pity either to friends, relations, or acquaintance, made his entry by fire, which knows no distinction betwixt friend or foe.

In this conflict, Marius, being driven into the temple of Mother Earth, thence invited the slaves by proclamation of freedom, but the enemy coming on he was overpowered and fled the city.

Sylla, having called a senate, had sentence of death passed on Marius and some few others, amongst whom was Sulpicius, tribune of the people. Sulpicius was killed, being betrayed by his servant, whom Sylla first made free, and then threw him headlong down the Tarpeian rock. As for Marius, he set a price on his life, by proclamation, neither gratefully nor politicly, if we consider into whose house, not long before, he put himself at mercy, and was safely dismissed. Had Marius at that time not let Sylla go, but suffered him to be slain by the hands of Sulpicius, he might have been lord of all; nevertheless he spared his life, and a few days after, when in a similar position himself, received a different measure.

By these proceedings, Sylla excited the secret distaste of the senate; but the displeasure and free indignation of the commonalty showed itself plainly by their actions. For they ignominiously rejected Nonius, his nephew, and Servius, who stood for offices of state by his interest, and elected others as magistrates, by honoring whom they thought they should most annoy him. He made semblance of extreme satisfaction at all this, as if the people by his means had again enjoyed the liberty of doing what seemed best to them. And to pacify the public hostility, he created Lucius Cinna consul, one of the adverse party, having first bound him under oaths and imprecations to be favorable to his interest. For Cinna, ascending the capitol with a stone in his hand, swore solemnly, and prayed with direful curses, that he himself, if he were not true to his friendship with Sylla, might be cast out of the city, as that stone out of his hand; and thereupon cast the stone to the ground, in the presence of many people. Nevertheless Cinna had no sooner entered on his charge but he took measures to disturb the present settlement, and, having prepared an impeachment against Sylla, got Virginius, one of the tribunes of the people, to be his accuser; but Sylla, leaving him and the court of judicature to themselves, set forth against Mithridates.

About the time that Sylla was making ready to put off with his forces from Italy, besides many other omens which befell Mithridates, then staying at Pergamus, there goes a story that a figure of Victory, with a crown in her hand, which the Pergamenians by machinery from above let down on him, when it had almost reached his head, fell to pieces, and the crown tumbling down into the midst of the theater, there broke against the ground, occasioning a general alarm among the populace, and considerably disquieting Mithridates himself, although his affairs at that time were succeeding beyond expectation. For having wrested Asia from the Romans, and Bithynia and Cappadocia from their kings, he made Pergamus his royal seat, distributing among his friends riches, principalities, and kingdoms. Of his sons, one residing in Pontus and Bosporus held his ancient realm as far as the deserts beyond the lake Mæotis, without molestation; while Ariarathes, another, was reducing Thrace and Macedon, with a great army, to obedience. His generals, with forces under them, were establishing his supremacy in other quarters. Archelaus, in particular, with his fleet, held absolute mastery of the sea, and was bringing into subjection the Cyclades, and all the other islands as far as Malea, and had taken Eubœa itself. Making Athens his headquarters, from thence as far as Thessaly he was withdrawing the states of Greece from the Roman allegiance, without the least ill success, except at Chæronea. For here Bruttius Sura, lieutenant to Sentius, governor of Macedon, a man of singular valor and prudence, met him, and, though he came like a torrent pouring over Bœotia, made stout resistance, and thrice giving him battle near Chæronea, repulsed and forced him back to the sea. But being commanded by Lucius Lucullus to give place to his successor, Sylla, and resign the war to whom it was decreed, he presently left Bœotia, and retired back to Sentius, although his success had outgone all hopes, and Greece was well disposed to a new revolution, upon account of his gallant behavior. These were the glorious actions of Bruttius.

Sylla, on his arrival, received by their deputations the compliments of all the cities of Greece, except Athens, against which, as it was compelled by the tyrant Aristion to hold for the king, he advanced with all his forces, and investing the Piræus, laid formal siege to it, employing every variety of engines, and trying every manner of assault; whereas, had he forborne but a little while, he might without hazard have taken the Upper City by famine, it being already reduced to the last extremity, through want of necessaries. But eager to return to Rome, and fearing innovation there, at great risk, with continual fighting and vast expense, he pushed on the war. Besides other equipage, the very work about the engines of battery was supplied with no less than ten thousand yoke of mules, employed daily in that service. And when timber grew scarce, for many of the works failed, some crushed to pieces by their own weight, others taking fire by the continual play of the enemy, he had recourse to the sacred groves, and cut down the trees of the Academy, the shadiest of all the suburbs, and the Lyceum. And a vast sum of money being wanted to carry on the war, he broke into the sanctuaries of Greece, that of Epidaurus and that of Olympia, sending for the most beautiful and precious offerings deposited there. He wrote, likewise, to the Amphictyons, at Delphi, that it were better to remit the wealth of the god to him, for that he would keep it more securely, or in case he made use of it, restore as much. He sent Caphis, the Phocian, one of his friends, with this message, commanding him to receive each item by weight. Caphis came to Delphi, but was loath to touch the holy things, and with many tears, in the presence of the Amphictyons, bewailed the necessity. And on some of them declaring they heard the sound of a harp from the inner shrine, he, whether he himself believed it, or was willing to try the effect of religious fear upon Sylla, sent back an express. To which Sylla replied in a scoffing way, that it was surprising to him that Caphis did not know that music was a sign of joy, not anger; he should, therefore, go on boldly, and accept what a gracious and bountiful god offered.

Other things were sent away without much notice on the part of the Greeks in general, but in the case of the silver tun, that only relic of the regal donations, which its weight and bulk made it impossible for any carriage to receive, the Amphictyons were forced to cut it into pieces, and called to mind in so doing, how Titus Flamininus, and Manius Acilius, and again Paulus Æmilius, one of whom drove Antiochus out of Greece, and the others subdued the Macedonian kings, had not only abstained from violating the Greek temples, but had even given them new gifts and honors, and increased the general veneration for them. They, indeed, the lawful commanders of temperate and obedient soldiers, and themselves great in soul, and simple in expenses, lived within the bounds of the ordinary established charges, accounting it a greater disgrace to seek popularity with their men, than to feel fear of their enemy. Whereas the commanders of these times, attaining to superiority by force, not worth, and having need of arms one against another, rather than against the public enemy, were constrained to temporize in authority, and in order to pay for the gratifications with which they purchased the labor of their soldiers, were driven, before they knew it, to sell the commonwealth itself, and, to gain the mastery over men better than themselves, were content to become slaves to the vilest of wretches. These practices drove Marius into exile, and again brought him in against Sylla. These made Cinna the assassin of Octavius, and Fimbria of Flaccus. To which courses Sylla contributed not the least; for to corrupt and win over those who were under the command of others, he would be munificent and profuse towards those who were under his own; and so, while tempting the soldiers of other generals to treachery, and his own to dissolute living, he was naturally in want of a large treasury, and especially during that siege.

Sylla had a vehement and an implacable desire to conquer Athens, whether out of emulation, fighting as it were against the shadow of the once famous city, or out of anger, at the foul words and scurrilous jests with which the tyrant Aristion, showing himself daily, with unseemly gesticulations, upon the walls, had provoked him and Metella.

The tyrant Aristion had his very being compounded of wantonness and cruelty, having gathered into himself all the worst of Mithridates's diseased and vicious qualities, like some fatal malady which the city, after its deliverance from innumerable wars, many tyrannies and seditions, was in its last days destined to endure. At the time when a medimnus of wheat was sold in the city for one thousand drachmas and men were forced to live on the feverfew growing round the citadel, and to boil down shoes and oil bags for their food, he, carousing and feasting in the open face of day, then dancing in armor, and making jokes at the enemy, suffered the holy lamp of the goddess to expire for want of oil, and to the chief priestess, who demanded of him the twelfth part of a medimnus of wheat, he sent the like quantity of pepper. The senators and priests who came as suppliants to beg of him to take compassion on the city, and treat for peace with Sylla, he drove away and dispersed with a flight of arrows. At last, with much ado, he sent forth two or three of his reveling companions to parley, to whom Sylla, perceiving that they made no serious overtures towards an accommodation, but went on haranguing in praise of Theseus, Eumolpus, and the Median trophies, replied, "My good friends, you may put up your speeches and be gone. I was sent by the Romans to Athens, not to take lessons, but to reduce rebels to obedience."

In the meantime news came to Sylla that some old men, talking in the Ceramicus, had been overheard to blame the tyrant for not securing the passages and approaches near the Heptachalcum, the one point where the enemy might easily get over. Sylla neglected not the report, but going in the night, and discovering the place to be assailable, set instantly to work. Sylla himself makes mention in his Memoirs that Marcus Teius, the first man who scaled the wall, meeting with an adversary, and striking him on the headpiece a home stroke, broke his own sword, but, notwithstanding, did not give ground, but stood and held him fast. The city was certainly taken from that quarter, according to the tradition of the oldest of the Athenians.

When they had thrown down the wall, and made all level betwixt the Piraic and Sacred Gate, about midnight Sylla entered the breach, with all the terrors of trumpets and cornets sounding, with the triumphant shout and cry of an army let loose to spoil and slaughter, and scouring through the streets with swords drawn. There was no numbering the slain; the amount is to this day conjectured only from the space of ground overflowed with blood. For without mentioning the execution done in other quarters of the city, the blood that was shed about the marketplace spread over the whole Ceramicus within the Double Gate, and, according to most writers, passed through the gate and overflowed the suburb. Nor did the multitudes which fell thus exceed the number of those who, out of pity and love for their country, which they believed was now finally to perish, slew themselves; the best of them, through despair of their country's surviving, dreading themselves to survive, expecting neither humanity nor moderation in Sylla. At length, partly at the instance of Midias and Calliphon, two exiled men, beseeching and casting themselves at his feet, partly by the intercession of those senators who followed the camp, having had his fill of revenge, and making some honorable mention of the ancient Athenians, "I forgive," said he, "the many for the sake of the few, the living for the dead." He took Athens, according to his own Memoirs, on the calends of March, coinciding pretty nearly with the new moon of Anthesterion, on which day it is the Athenian usage to perform various acts in commemoration of the ruins and devastations occasioned by the deluge, that being supposed to be the time of its occurrence.

At the taking of the town, the tyrant fled into the citadel, and was there besieged by Curio, who had that charge given him. He held out a considerable time, but at last yielded himself up for want of water, and divine power immediately intimated its agency in the matter. For on the same day and hour that Curio conducted him down, the clouds gathered in a clear sky, and there came down a great quantity of rain and filled the citadel with water.

Not long after, Sylla won the Piræus, and burnt most of it; amongst the rest, Philo's arsenal, a work very greatly admired.

In the meantime Taxiles, Mithridates's general, coming down from Thrace and Macedon, with an army of one hundred thousand foot, ten thousand horse, and ninety chariots, armed with scythes at the wheels, would have joined Archelaus, who lay with a navy on the coast near Munychia, reluctant to quit the sea, and yet unwilling to engage the Romans in battle, but desiring to protract the war and cut off the enemy's supplies. Which Sylla perceiving much better than himself, passed with his forces into Bœotia, quitting a barren district which was inadequate to maintain an army even in time of peace. He was thought by some to have taken false measures in thus leaving Attica, a rugged country, and ill suited for cavalry to move in, and entering the plain and open fields of Bœotia, knowing as he did the barbarian strength to consist most in horses and chariots. But as was said before, to avoid famine and scarcity, he was forced to run the risk of a battle. Moreover he was in anxiety for Hortensius, a bold and active officer, whom on his way to Sylla with forces from Thessaly, the barbarians awaited in the straits. For these reasons Sylla drew off into Bœotia. Hortensius, meantime, was conducted by Caphis, our countryman, another way unknown to the barbarians, by Parnassus, just under Tithora, which was then not so large a town as it is now, but a mere fort, surrounded by steep precipices, whither the Phocians also, in old times, when flying from the invasion of Xerxes, carried themselves and their goods and were saved. Hortensius, encamping here, kept off the enemy by day, and at night descending by difficult passages to Patronis, joined the forces of Sylla, who came to meet him. Thus united they posted themselves on a fertile hill in the middle of the plain of Elatea, shaded with trees and watered at the foot. It is called Philobœotus, and its situation and natural advantages are spoken of with great admiration by Sylla.

As they lay thus encamped, they seemed to the enemy a contemptible number, for they were not above fifteen hundred horse, and less than fifteen thousand foot. Therefore the rest of the commanders, overpersuading Archelaus, and drawing up the army, covered the plain with horses, chariots, bucklers, targets. The clamor and cries of so many nations forming for battle rent the air, nor was the pomp and ostentation of their costly array altogether idle and unserviceable for terror; for the brightness of their armor, embellished magnificently with gold and silver, and the rich colors of their Median and Scythian coats, intermixed with brass and shining steel, presented a flaming and terrible sight as they swayed about and moved in their ranks, so much so that the Romans shrunk within their trenches, and Sylla, unable by any arguments to remove their fear, and unwilling to force them to fight against their wills, was fain to sit down in quiet, ill brooking to become the subject of barbarian insolence and laughter. This, however, above all advantaged him, for the enemy, from contemning of him, fell into disorder amongst themselves, being already less thoroughly under command, on account of the number of their leaders. Some few of them remained within the encampment, but others, the major part, lured out with hopes of prey and rapine, strayed about the country many days' journey from the camp, and are related to have destroyed the city of Panope, to have plundered Lebadea, and robbed the oracle without any orders from their commanders.

Sylla, all this while, chafing and fretting to see the cities all around destroyed, suffered not the soldiery to remain idle, but leading them out, compelled them to divert the Cephisus from its ancient channel by casting up ditches, and giving respite to none, showed himself rigorous in punishing the remiss that, growing weary of labor, they might be induced by hardship to embrace danger. Which fell out accordingly, for on the third day, being hard at work as Sylla passed by, they begged and clamored to be led against the enemy. Sylla replied, that this demand of war proceeded rather from a backwardness to labor than any forwardness to fight, but if they were in good earnest martially inclined, he bade them take their arms and get up thither, pointing to the ancient citadel of the Parapotamians, of which at present, the city being laid waste, there remained only the rocky hill itself, steep and craggy on all sides, and severed from Mount Hedylium by the breadth of the river Assus, which, running between, and at the bottom of the same hill falling into the Cephisus with an impetuous confluence, makes this eminence a strong position for soldiers to occupy. Observing that the enemy's division, called the Brazen Shields, were making their way up thither, Sylla was willing to take first possession, and by the vigorous efforts of the soldiers, succeeded. Archelaus, driven from hence, bent his forces upon Chæronea. The Chæroneans who bore arms in the Roman camp beseeching Sylla not to abandon the city, he dispatched Gabinius, a tribune, with one legion, and sent out also the Chæroneans, who endeavored, but were not able to get in before Gabinius; so active was he, and more zealous to bring relief than those who had entreated it. Juba writes that Ericius was the man sent, not Gabinius. Thus narrowly did our native city escape.

From Lebadea and the cave of Trophonius there came favorable rumors and prophecies of victory to the Romans, of which the inhabitants of those places give a fuller account, but as Sylla himself affirms in the tenth book of his Memoirs, Quintus Titius, a man of some repute among the Romans who were engaged in mercantile business in Greece, came to him after the battle won at Chæronea, and declared that Trophonius had foretold another fight and victory on the same place, within a short time. After him a soldier, by name Salvenius, brought an account from the god of the future issue of affairs in Italy. As to the vision, they both agreed in this, that they had seen one who in stature and in majesty was similar to Jupiter Olympius.

Sylla, when he had passed over the Assus, marching under the Mount Hedylium, encamped close to Archelaus, who had entrenched himself strongly between the mountains Acontium and Hedylium, close to what are called the Assia. The place of his entrenchment is to this day named from him, Archelaus. Sylla, after one day's respite, having left Murena behind him with one legion and two cohorts to amuse the enemy with continual alarms, himself went and sacrificed on the banks of Cephisus, and the holy rites ended, held on towards Chæronea to receive the forces there and view Mount Thurium, where a party of the enemy had posted themselves. This is a craggy height running up in a conical form to a point called by us Orthopagus; at the foot of it is the river Morius and the temple of Apollo Thurius. The god had his surname from Thuro, mother of Chæron, whom ancient record makes founder of Chæronea. Others assert that the cow which Apollo gave to Cadmus for a guide appeared there, and that the place took its name from the beast, Thor being the Phœnician word for cow.

At Sylla's approach to Chæronea, the tribune who had been appointed to guard the city led out his men in arms, and met him with a garland of laurel in his hand; which Sylla accepting, and at the same time saluting the soldiers and animating them to the encounter, two men of Chæronea, Homoloichus and Anaxidamus, presented themselves before him, and offered, with a small party, to dislodge those who were posted on Thurium. For there lay a path out of sight of the barbarians, from what is called Petrochus along by the Museum, leading right down from above upon Thurium. By this way it was easy to fall upon them and either stone them from above or force them down into the plain. Sylla, assured of their faith and courage by Gabinius, bade them proceed with the enterprise, and meantime drew up the army, and disposing the cavalry on both wings, himself took command of the right; the left being committed to the direction of Murena. In the rear of all, Galba and Hortensius, his lieutenants, planted themselves on the upper grounds with the cohorts of reserve, to watch the motions of the enemy, who with numbers of horse and swift-footed, light-armed infantry, were noticed to have so formed their wing as to allow it readily to change about and alter its position, and thus gave reason for suspecting that they intended to carry it far out and so to enclose the Romans.

In the meanwhile, the Chæroneans, who had Ericius for commander by appointment of Sylla, covertly making their way around Thurium, and then discovering themselves, occasioned a great confusion and rout among the barbarians, and slaughter, for the most part, by their own hands. For they kept not their place, but making down the steep descent, ran themselves on their own spears, and violently sent each other over the cliffs, the enemy from above pressing on and wounding them where they exposed their bodies; insomuch that there fell three thousand about Thurium. Some of those who escaped, being met by Murena as he stood in array, were cut off and destroyed. Others breaking through to their friends and falling pell-mell into the ranks, filled most part of the army with fear and tumult, and caused a hesitation and delay among the generals, which was no small disadvantage. For immediately upon the discomposure, Sylla coming full speed to the charge, and quickly crossing the interval between the armies, lost them the service of their armed chariots, which require a considerable space of ground to gather strength and impetuosity in their career, a short course being weak and ineffectual, like that of missiles without a full swing. Thus it fared with the barbarians at present, whose first chariots came feebly on and made but a faint impression; the Romans, repulsing them with shouts and laughter, called out, as they do at the races in the circus, for more to come. By this time the mass of both armies met; the barbarians on one side fixed their long pikes, and with their shields locked close together, strove so far as in them lay to preserve their line of battle entire. The Romans, on the other side, having discharged their javelins, rushed on with their drawn swords, and struggled to put by the pikes to get at them the sooner, in the fury that possessed them at seeing in the front of the enemy fifteen thousand slaves, whom the royal commanders had set free by proclamation, and ranged amongst the men of arms. And a Roman centurion is reported to have said at this sight, that he never knew servants allowed to play the masters, unless at the Saturnalia. These men, by their deep and solid array, as well as by their daring courage, yielded but slowly to the legions, till at last by slinging engines, and darts, which the Romans poured in upon them behind, they were forced to give way and scatter.

As Archelaus was extending the right wing to encompass the enemy, Hortensius with his cohorts came down in force, with intention to charge him in the flank. But Archelaus wheeling about suddenly with two thousand horse, Hortensius, outnumbered and hard pressed, fell back towards the higher grounds, and found himself gradually getting separated from the main body and likely to be surrounded by the enemy. When Sylla heard this, he came rapidly up to his succor from the right wing, which as yet had not engaged. But Archelaus, guessing the matter by the dust of his troops, turned to the right wing, from whence Sylla came, in hopes to surprise it without a commander. At the same instant, likewise, Taxiles, with his Brazen Shields, assailed Murena, so that a cry coming from both places, and the hills repeating it around, Sylla stood in suspense which way to move. Deciding to resume his own station, he sent in aid to Murena four cohorts under Hortensius, and commanding the fifth to follow him, returned hastily to the right wing, which of itself held its ground on equal terms against Archelaus; and, at his appearance, with one bold effort forced them back, and, obtaining the mastery, followed them, flying in disorder to the river and Mount Acontium. Sylla, however, did not forget the danger Murena was in; but hasting thither and finding him victorious also, then joined in the pursuit. Many barbarians were slain in the field, many more were cut in pieces as they were making into the camp. Of all the vast multitude, ten thousand only got safe into Chalcis. Sylla writes that there were but fourteen of his soldiers missing, and that two of these returned towards evening; he, therefore, inscribed on the trophies the names of Mars, Victory, and Venus, as having won the day no less by good fortune than by management and force of arms. This trophy of the battle in the plain stands on the place where Archelaus first gave way, near the stream of the Molus; another is erected high on the top of Thurium, where the barbarians were environed, with an inscription in Greek, recording that the glory of the day belonged to Homoloichus and Anaxidamus. Sylla celebrated his victory at Thebes with spectacles, for which he erected a stage, near Œdipus's well. The judges of the performances were Greeks chosen out of other cities; his hostility to the Thebans being implacable, half of whose territory he took away and consecrated to Apollo and Jupiter, ordering that out of the revenue compensation should be made to the gods for the riches himself had taken from them.

After this, hearing that Flaccus, a man of the contrary faction, had been chosen consul, and was crossing the Ionian Sea with an army, professedly to act against Mithridates, but in reality against himself, he hastened towards Thessaly, designing to meet him, but in his march, when near Melitea, received advices from all parts that the countries behind him were overrun and ravaged by no less a royal army than the former. For Dorylaus, arriving at Chalcis with a large fleet, on board of which he brought over with him eighty thousand of the best appointed and best disciplined soldiers of Mithridates's army, at once invaded Bœotia, and occupied the country in hopes to bring Sylla to a battle, making no account of the dissuasions of Archelaus, but giving it out as to the last fight, that without treachery so many thousand men could never have perished. Sylla, however, facing about expeditiously, made it clear to him that Archelaus was a wise man, and had good skill in the Roman valor; insomuch that he himself, after some small skirmishes with Sylla near Tilphossium, was the first of those who thought it not advisable to put things to the decision of the sword, but rather to wear out the war by expense of time and treasure. The ground, however, near Orchomenus, where they then lay encamped, gave some encouragement to Archelaus, being a battlefield admirably suited for an army superior in cavalry. Of all the plains in Bœotia that are renowned for their beauty and extent, this alone, which commences from the city of Orchomenus, spreads out unbroken and clear of trees to the edge of the fens in which the Melas, rising close under Orchomenus, loses itself, the only Greek river which is a deep and navigable water from the very head, increasing also about the summer solstice like the Nile, and producing plants similar to those that grow there, only small and without fruit. It does not run far before the main stream disappears among the blind and woody marsh grounds; a small branch, however, joins the Cephisus, about the place where the lake is thought to produce the best flute reeds.

Now that both armies were posted near each other, Archelaus lay still, but Sylla employed himself in cutting ditches from either side; that if possible, by driving the enemies from the firm and open champaign, he might force them into the fens. They, on the other hand, not enduring this, as soon as their leaders allowed them the word of command, issued out furiously in large bodies; when not only the men at work were dispersed, but most part of those who stood in arms to protect the work fled in disorder. Upon this, Sylla leaped from his horse, and snatching hold of an ensign, rushed through the midst of the rout upon the enemy, crying out aloud, "To me, O Romans, it will be glorious to fall here. As for you, when they ask you where you betrayed your general, remember and say, at Orchomenus." His men rallying again at these words, and two cohorts coming to his succor from the right wing, he led them to the charge and turned the day. Then retiring some short distance and refreshing his men, he proceeded again with his works to block up the enemy's camp. They again sallied out in better order than before. Here Diogenes, stepson to Archelaus, fighting on the right wing with much gallantry, made an honorable end. And the archers, being hard pressed by the Romans, and wanting space for a retreat, took their arrows by handfuls, and striking with these as with swords, beat them back. In the end, however, they were all driven into the entrenchment and had a sorrowful night of it with their slain and wounded. The next day again, Sylla, leading forth his men up to their quarters, went on finishing the lines of entrenchment, and when they issued out again with larger numbers to give him battle, fell on them and put them to the rout, and in the consternation ensuing, none daring to abide, he took the camp by storm. The marshes were filled with blood, and the lake with dead bodies, insomuch that to this day many bows, helmets, fragments of iron, breastplates, and swords of barbarian make continue to be found buried deep in mud, two hundred years after the fight. Thus much of the actions of Chæronea and Orchomenus.

At Rome, Cinna and Carbo were now using injustice and violence towards persons of the greatest eminence, and many of them to avoid this tyranny repaired, as to a safe harbor, to Sylla's camp, where, in a short space, he had about him the aspect of a senate. Metella, likewise, having with difficulty conveyed herself and children away by stealth, brought him word that his houses, both in town and country, had been burnt by

his enemies, and entreated his help at home. Whilst he was in doubt what
to do, being impatient to hear of his country being thus outraged, and
yet not knowing how to leave so great a work as the Mithridatic war unfinished, there comes to him Archelaus, a merchant of Delos, with hopes
of an accommodation, and private instructions from Archelaus, the king's
general. Sylla liked the business so well as to desire a speedy conference
with Archelaus in person, and a meeting took place on the seacoast near
Delium, where the temple of Apollo stands. When Archelaus opened the
conversation, and began to urge Sylla to abandon his pretensions to Asia
and Pontus, and to set sail for the war in Rome, receiving money and
shipping, and such forces as he should think fitting from the king, Sylla,
interposing, bade Archelaus take no further care for Mithridates, but assume the crown to himself, and become a confederate of Rome, delivering up the navy. Archelaus professing his abhorrence of such treason,
Sylla proceeded: "So you, Archelaus, a Cappadocian, and slave, or if it so
please you friend, to a barbarian king, would not, upon such vast considerations, be guilty of what is dishonorable, and yet dare to talk to me,
Roman general and Sylla, of treason? as if you were not the selfsame
Archelaus who ran away at Chæronea, with few remaining out of one
hundred and twenty thousand men; who lay for two days in the fens of
Orchomenus, and left Bœotia impassable for heaps of dead carcasses."
Archelaus, changing his tone at this, humbly besought him to lay aside
the thoughts of war, and make peace with Mithridates. Sylla consenting
to this request, articles of agreement were concluded on. That
Mithridates should quit Asia and Paphlagonia, restore Bithynia to
Nicomedes, Cappadocia to Ariobarzanes, and pay the Romans two thousand talents, and give him seventy ships of war with all their furniture.
On the other hand, that Sylla should confirm to him his other dominions, and declare him a Roman confederate. On these terms he proceeded by the way of Thessaly and Macedon towards the Hellespont,
having Archelaus with him, and treating him with great attention. For
Archelaus being taken dangerously ill at Larissa, he stopped the march of
the army, and took care of him, as if he had been one of his own captains, or his colleague in command. This gave suspicion of foul play in the
battle of Chæronea; as it was also observed that Sylla had released all the
friends of Mithridates taken prisoners in war, except only Aristion
the tyrant, who was at enmity with Archelaus, and was put to death by
poison; and, above all, ten thousand acres of land in Eubœa had been
given to the Cappadocian, and he had received from Sylla the style of
friend and ally of the Romans. On all which points Sylla defends himself in his Memoirs.

The ambassadors of Mithridates arriving and declaring that they accepted of the conditions, only Paphlagonia they could not part with; and

as for the ships, professing not to know of any such capitulation, Sylla in a rage exclaimed, "What say you? Does Mithridates then withhold Paphlagonia? and as to the ships, deny that article? I thought to have seen him prostrate at my feet to thank me for leaving him so much as that right hand of his, which has cut off so many Romans. He will shortly, at my coming over into Asia, speak another language; in the meantime, let him at his ease in Pergamus sit managing a war which he never saw." The ambassadors in terror stood silent by, but Archelaus endeavored with humble supplications to assuage his wrath, laying hold on his right hand and weeping. In conclusion he obtained permission to go himself in person to Mithridates; for that he would either mediate a peace to the satisfaction of Sylla, or if not, slay himself. Sylla having thus dispatched him away, made an inroad into Mædica, and after wide depopulations returned back again into Macedon, where he received Archelaus about Philippi, bringing word that all was well, and that Mithridates earnestly requested an interview. The chief cause of this meeting was Fimbria; for he, having assassinated Flaccus, the consul of the contrary faction, and worsted the Mithridatic commanders, was advancing against Mithridates himself, who, fearing this, chose rather to seek the friendship of Sylla.

And so met at Dardanus in the Troad, on one side Mithridates, attended with two hundred ships, and land forces consisting of twenty thousand men at arms, six thousand horse, and a large train of scythed chariots; on the other, Sylla, with only four cohorts and two hundred horse. As Mithridates drew near and put out his hand, Sylla demanded whether he was willing or no to end the war on the terms Archelaus had agreed to, but seeing the king made no answer, "How is this?" he continued, "ought not the petitioner to speak first, and the conqueror to listen in silence?" And when Mithridates, entering upon his plea, began to shift off the war, partly on the gods, and partly to blame the Romans themselves, he took him up, saying that he had heard, indeed, long since from others, and now he knew it himself for truth, that Mithridates was a powerful speaker, who in defense of the most foul and unjust proceedings, had not wanted for specious pretences. Then charging him with and inveighing bitterly against the outrages he had committed, he asked again whether he was willing or no to ratify the treaty of Archelaus? Mithridates answering in the affirmative, Sylla came forward, embraced and kissed him. Not long after he introduced Ariobarzanes and Nicomedes, the two kings, and made them friends, Mithridates, when he had handed over to Sylla seventy ships and five hundred archers, set sail for Pontus.

Sylla, perceiving the soldiers to be dissatisfied with the peace (as it seemed indeed a monstrous thing that they should see the king who was then bitterest enemy, and who had caused one hundred and fifty thousand Romans to be massacred in one day in Asia, now sailing off with the

·riches and spoils of Asia, which he had pillaged, and put under contribution for the space of four years), in his defense to them alleged, that he
could not have made head against Fimbria and Mithridates, had they
both withstood him in conjunction. Thence he set out and went in
search of Fimbria, who lay with the army about Thyatira, and pitching
his camp not far off, proceeded to fortify it with a trench. The soldiers of
Fimbria came out in their single coats and, saluting his men, lent ready
assistance to the work; which change Fimbria beholding, and apprehending Sylla as irreconcilable, laid violent hands on himself in the camp.

Sylla imposed on Asia in general a tax of twenty thousand talents, and
despoiled individually each family by the licentious behavior and long
residence of the soldiery in private quarters. For he ordained that every
host should allow his guest four tetradrachms each day, and moreover entertain him, and as many friends as he should invite, with a supper; that
a centurion should receive fifty drachmas a day, together with one suit of
clothes to wear within doors, and another when he went abroad.

Having set out from Ephesus with the whole navy, he came the third
day to anchor in the Piræus. Here he was initiated in the mysteries, and
seized for his use the library of Apellicon the Teian, in which were most
of the works of Theophrastus and Aristotle, then not in general circula-
tion. When the whole was afterwards conveyed to Rome, there, it is said,
the greater part of the collection passed through the hands of Tyrannion
the grammarian, and that Andronicus the Rhodian, having through his
means the command of numerous copies, made the treatises public, and
drew up the catalogues that are now current. The elder Peripatetics appear themselves, indeed, to have been accomplished and learned men, but
of the writings of Aristotle and Theophrastus they had no large or exact
knowledge, because Theophrastus bequeathing his books to the heir of
Neleus of Scepsis, they came into careless and illiterate hands.

During Sylla's stay about Athens, his feet were attacked by a heavy be-
numbing pain, which Strabo calls the first inarticulate sounds of the gout.
Taking, therefore, a voyage to Ædepsus, he made use of the hot waters
there, allowing himself at the same time to forget all anxieties, and
passing away his time with actors. As he was walking along the seashore,
certain fishermen brought him some magnificent fish. Being much delighted with the gift, and understanding, on inquiry, that they were men
of Halææ, "What," said he, "are there any men of Halææ surviving?" For
after his victory at Orchomenus, in the heat of a pursuit, he had destroyed
three cities of Bœotia, Anthedon, Larymna, and Halææ. The men not
knowing what to say for fear, Sylla with a smile bade them cheer up and
return in peace, as they had brought with them no insignificant interces-
sors. The Halæans say that this first gave them courage to reunite and return to their city.

Sylla, having marched through Thessaly and Macedon to the seacoast, prepared, with twelve hundred vessels, to cross over from Dyrrhachium to Brundisium. Not far from hence is Apollonia, and near it the Nymphæum, a spot of ground where, from among green trees and meadows, there are found at various points springs of fire continually streaming out. Here, they say, a satyr, such as statuaries and painters represent, was caught asleep, and brought before Sylla, where he was asked by several interpreters who he was, and, after much trouble, at last uttered nothing intelligible, but a harsh noise, something between the neighing of a horse and crying of a goat. Sylla, in dismay, and deprecating such an omen, bade it be removed.

At the point of transportation, Sylla being in alarm, lest at their first setting foot upon Italy the soldiers should disband and disperse one by one among the cities, they of their own accord first took an oath to stand firm by him, and not of their goodwill to injure Italy; then seeing him in distress for money, they made, so to say, a freewill offering, and contributed each man according to his ability. However, Sylla would not accept of their offering, but praising their goodwill and arousing up their courage, put over (as he himself writes) against fifteen hostile generals in command of four hundred and fifty cohorts; but not without the most unmistakable divine intimations of his approaching happy successes. For when he was sacrificing at his first landing near Tarentum, the victim's liver showed the figure of a crown of laurel with two fillets hanging from it. And a little while before his arrival in Campania, near the mountain Hephæus, two stately goats were seen in the daytime, fighting together, and performing all the motions of men in battle. It proved to be an apparition, and rising up gradually from the ground, dispersed in the air, like fancied representations in the clouds, and so vanished out of sight. Not long after, in the selfsame place, when Marius the younger and Norbanus the consul, attacked him with two great armies, without prescribing the order of battle, or arranging his men according to their divisions, by the sway only of one common alacrity and transport of courage, he overthrew the enemy, and shut up Norbanus into the city of Capua, with the loss of seven thousand of his men. And this was the reason, he says, that the soldiers did not leave him and disperse into the different towns, but held fast to him, and despised the enemy, though infinitely more in number.

At Silvium (as he himself relates it), there met him a servant of Pontius, in a state of divine possession, saying that he brought him the power of the sword and victory from Bellona, the goddess of war, and if he did not make haste, that the capitol would be burnt, which fell out on the same day the man foretold it, namely, on the sixth day of the month Quintilis, which we now call July.

At Fidentia, also, Marcus Lucullus, one of Sylla's commanders, reposed such confidence in the forwardness of the soldiers, as to dare to face fifty cohorts of the enemy with only sixteen of his own; but because many of them were unarmed delayed the onset. As he stood thus waiting, and considering with himself, a gentle gale of wind, bearing along with it from the neighboring meadows a quantity of flowers, scattered them down upon the army, on whose shields and helmets they settled, and arranged themselves spontaneously so as to give the soldiers, in the eyes of the enemy, the appearance of being crowned with chaplets. Upon this, being yet further animated, they joined battle, and victoriously slaying eight thousand men, took the camp. This Lucullus was brother to that Lucullus who in aftertimes conquered Mithridates and Tigranes.

Sylla, seeing himself still surrounded by so many armies, and such mighty hostile powers, had recourse to art, inviting Scipio, the other consul, to a treaty of peace. The motion was willingly embraced, and several meetings and consultations ensued, in all which Sylla, still interposing matter of delay and new pretenses, in the meanwhile debauched Scipio's men by means of his own, who were as well practiced as the general himself in all the artifices of inveigling. For entering into the enemy's quarters and joining in conversation, they gained some by present money, some by promises, others by fair words and persuasions; so that in the end, when Sylla with twenty cohorts drew near, on his men saluting Scipio's soldiers, they returned the greeting and came over, leaving Scipio behind them in his tent, where he was found all alone and dismissed. And having used his twenty cohorts as decoys to ensnare the forty of the enemy, he led them all back into the camp. On this occasion, Carbo was heard to say that he had both a fox and a lion in the breast of Sylla to deal with, and was most troubled with the fox.

Some time after, at Signia, Marius the younger, with eighty-five cohorts, offered battle to Sylla, who was extremely desirous to have it decided on that very day; for the night before he had seen a vision in his sleep, of Marius the elder, who had been some time dead, advising his son to beware of the following day, as of fatal consequence to him. For this reason, Sylla, longing to come to a battle, sent off for Dolabella, who lay encamped at some distance. But because the enemy had beset and blocked up the passes, his soldiers got tired with skirmishing and marching at once. To these difficulties was added, moreover, tempestuous rainy weather, which distressed them most of all. The principal officers therefore came to Sylla, and besought him to defer the battle that day, showing him how the soldiers lay stretched on the ground, where they had thrown themselves down in their weariness, resting their heads upon their shields to gain some repose. When, with much reluctance, he had yielded, and given order for pitching the camp, they had no sooner

begun to cast up the rampart and draw the ditch, but Marius came riding up furiously at the head of his troops, in hopes to scatter them in that
disorder and confusion. Here the gods fulfilled Sylla's dream. For the soldiers, stirred up with anger, left off their work, and sticking their javelins
into the bank, with drawn swords and a courageous shout, came to blows
with the enemy, who made but small resistance, and lost great numbers
in the flight. Marius fled to Præneste, but finding the gates shut, tied himself round by a rope that was thrown down to him, and was taken up on
the walls. Some there are (as Fenestella for one) who affirm that Marius
knew nothing of the fight, but, overwatched and spent with hard duty,
had reposed himself, when the signal was given, beneath some shade, and
was hardly to be awakened at the flight of his men. Sylla, according to his
own account, lost only twenty-three men in this fight, having killed of
the enemy twenty thousand, and taken alive eight thousand.

The like success attended his lieutenants, Pompey, Crassus, Metellus,
Servilius, who with little or no loss cut off vast numbers of the enemy,
insomuch that Carbo, the prime supporter of the cause, fled by night
from his charge of the army, and sailed over into Libya.

In the last struggle, however, the Samnite Telesinus, like some cham-
pion, whose lot it is to enter last of all into the lists and take up the wea-
ried conqueror, came nigh to have foiled and overthrown Sylla before the
gates of Rome. For Telesinus with his second, Lamponius the Lucanian,
having collected a large force, had been hastening towards Præneste, to
relieve Marius from the siege; but perceiving Sylla ahead of him, and
Pompey behind, both hurrying up against him, straightened thus before
and behind, as a valiant and experienced soldier, he arose by night, and
marching directly with his whole army, was within a little of making his
way unexpectedly into Rome itself. He lay that night before the city, at
ten furlongs' distance from the Colline gate, elated and full of hope at
having thus out-generalled so many eminent commanders. At break of
day, being charged by the noble youth of the city, among many others he
overthrew Appius Claudius, renowned for high birth and character. The
city, as is easy to imagine, was all in an uproar, the women shrieking and
running about, as if it had already been entered forcibly by assault, till at
last Balbus, sent forward by Sylla, was seen riding up with seven hundred
horse at full speed. Halting only long enough to wipe the sweat from the
horses, and then hastily bridling again, he at once attacked the enemy.
Presently Sylla himself appeared, and commanding those who were foremost to take immediate refreshment, proceeded to form in order for battle. Dolabella and Torquatus were extremely earnest with him to desist
awhile, and not with spent forces to hazard the last hope, having before
them in the field, not Carbo or Marius, but two warlike nations bearing
immortal hatred to Rome, the Samnites and Lucanians, to grapple with.

But he put them by, and commanded the trumpets to sound a charge, when it was now about four o'clock in the afternoon. In the conflict which followed, as sharp a one as ever was, the right wing where Crassus was posted had clearly the advantage; the left suffered and was in distress, when Sylla came to its succor, mounted on a white courser, full of mettle and exceedingly swift, which two of the enemy knowing him by, had their lances ready to throw at him; he himself observed nothing, but his attendant behind him giving the horse a touch, he was, unknown to himself, just so far carried forward that the points, falling beside the horse's tail, stuck in the ground. There is a story that he had a small golden image of Apollo from Delphi, which he was always wont in battle to carry about him in his bosom, and that he then kissed it with these words, "O Apollo Pythius, who in so many battles hast raised to honor and greatness the Fortunate Cornelius Sylla, wilt thou now cast him down, bringing him before the gate of his country, to perish shamefully with his fellow citizens?" Thus, they say, addressing himself to the god, he entreated some of his men, threatened some, and seized others with his hand, till at length the left wing being wholly shattered, he was forced in the general rout, to betake himself to the camp, having lost many of his friends and acquaintance. Many, likewise, of the city spectators who had come out were killed or trodden underfoot. So that it was generally believed in the city that all was lost, and the siege of Præneste was all but raised; many fugitives from the battle making their way thither, and urging Lucretius Ofella, who was appointed to keep on the siege, to rise in all haste, for that Sylla had perished, and Rome fallen into the hands of the enemy.

About midnight there came into Sylla's camp messengers from Crassus, to fetch provision for him and his soldiers; for having vanquished the enemy, they had pursued him to the walls of Antemna, and had sat down there. Sylla, hearing this, and that most of the enemy were destroyed, came to Antemna by break of day, where three thousand of the besieged having sent forth a herald, he promised to receive them to mercy, on condition they did the enemy some mischief in their coming over. Trusting to his word, they fell foul on the rest of their companions, and made a great slaughter one of another. Nevertheless, Sylla gathered together in the circus, as well these as other survivors of the party, to the number of six thousand, and just as he commenced speaking to the senate, in the temple of Bellona, proceeded to cut them down, by men appointed for that service. The cry of so vast a multitude put to the sword, in so narrow a space, was naturally heard some distance, and startled the senators. He, however, continuing his speech with a calm and unconcerned countenance, bade them listen to what he had to say, and not busy themselves with what was doing out of doors; he had given directions for the chastisement of some offenders. This gave the most stupid of the Romans to understand that they had merely exchanged, not escaped, tyranny. And Marius, being of a naturally harsh temper, had not altered, but merely continued what he had been, in authority; whereas Sylla, using his fortune moderately and unambitiously at first, and giving good hopes of a true patriot, firm to the interests both of the nobility and commonalty, being, moreover, of a gay and cheerful temper from his youth, and so easily moved to pity as to shed tears readily, has, perhaps deservedly, cast a blemish upon offices of great authority, as if they deranged men's former habits and character, and gave rise to violence, pride, and inhumanity. Whether this be a real change and revolution in the mind, caused by fortune, or rather a lurking viciousness of nature, discovering itself in authority, it were matter of another sort of disquisition to decide.

Sylla being thus wholly bent upon slaughter, and filling the city with executions without number or limit, many wholly uninterested persons falling a sacrifice to private enmity, through his permission and indulgence to his friends, Caius Metellus, one of the younger men, made bold in the senate to ask him what end there was of these evils, and at what point he might be expected to stop? "We do not ask you," said he, "to pardon any whom you have resolved to destroy, but to free from doubt those whom you are pleased to save." Sylla answering, that he knew not as yet whom to spare, "Why then," said he, "tell us whom you will punish." This Sylla said he would do. These last words, some authors say, were spoken not by Metellus, but by Afidius, one of Sylla's fawning companions. Immediately upon this, without communicating with any of the magistrates, Sylla proscribed eighty persons and, notwithstanding the general indignation, after one day's respite, he posted two hundred and twenty more, and on the third, again as many. In an address to the people on this occasion, he told them he had put up as many names as he could think of; those which had escaped his memory, he would publish at a future time. He issued an edict likewise, making death the punishment of humanity, proscribing any who should dare to receive and cherish a proscribed person without exception to brother, son, or parents. And to him who should slay any one proscribed person, he ordained two talents reward, even were it a slave who had killed his master, or a son his father. And what was thought most unjust of all, he caused the attainder to pass upon their sons, and son's sons, and made open sale of all their property. Nor did the proscription prevail only at Rome, but throughout all the cities of Italy the effusion of blood was such, that neither sanctuary of the gods, nor hearth of hospitality, nor ancestral home escaped. Men were butchered in the embraces of their wives, children in the arms of their mothers. Those who perished through public animosity or pri-

vate enmity, were nothing in comparison of the numbers of those who
suffered for their riches. Even the murderers began to say, that "his fine
house killed this man, a garden that, a third, his hot baths." Quintus
Aurelius, a quiet, peaceable man, and one who thought all his part in the
common calamity consisted in condoling with the misfortunes of others,
coming into the forum to read the list, and finding himself among the
proscribed, cried out, "Woe is me, my Alban farm has informed against
me." He had not gone far before he was dispatched by a ruffian, sent on
that errand.

In the meantime, Marius, on the point of being taken, killed himself;
and Sylla, coming to Præneste, at first proceeded judicially against each
particular person, till at last, finding it a work of too much time, he
cooped them up together in one place, to the number of twelve thousand men, and gave order for the execution of them all, his own host
alone excepted. But he, brave man, telling him he could not accept the
obligation of life from the hands of one who had been the ruin of his
country, went in among the rest, and submitted willingly to the stroke.
What Lucius Catilina did was thought to exceed all other acts. For having, before matters came to an issue, made away with his brother, he besought Sylla to place him in the list of proscription, as though he had
been alive, which was done; and Catiline, to return the kind office, assassinated a certain Marcus Marius, one of the adverse party, and brought
the head to Sylla, as he was sitting in the forum, and then going to the
holy water of Apollo, which was nigh, washed his hands.

There were other things, besides this bloodshed, which gave offense.
For Sylla had declared himself dictator, an office which had then been
laid aside for the space of one hundred and twenty years. There was, likewise, an act of grace passed on his behalf, granting indemnity for what
was passed, and for the future entrusting him with the power of life and
death, confiscation, division of lands, erecting and demolishing of cities,
taking away of kingdoms, and bestowing them at pleasure. He conducted
the sale of confiscated property after such an arbitrary, imperious way,
from the tribunal, that his gifts excited greater odium even than his
usurpations; women, mimes, and musicians, and the lowest of the freed
slaves had presents made them of the territories of nations and the revenues of cities; and women of rank were married against their will to
some of them. Wishing to insure the fidelity of Pompey the Great by a
nearer tie of blood, he bade him divorce his present wife, and forcing
Æmilia, the daughter of Scaurus and Metella, his own wife, to leave her
husband, Manius Glabrio, he bestowed her, though then with child, on
Pompey, and she died in childbirth at his house.

When Lucretius Ofella, the same who reduced Marius by siege, offered himself for the consulship, he first forbade him; then, seeing he

could not restrain him, on his coming down into the forum with a numerous train of followers, he sent one of the centurions who were immediately about him, and slew him, himself sitting on the tribunal in the
temple of Castor, and beholding the murder from above. The citizens apprehending the centurion, and dragging him to the tribunal, he bade
them cease their clamoring and let the centurion go, for he had commanded it.

His triumph was, in itself, exceedingly splendid, and distinguished by
the rarity and magnificence of the royal spoils; but its yet greatest glory
was the noble spectacle of the exiles. For in the rear followed the most
eminent and most potent of the citizens, crowned with garlands, and calling Sylla savior and father, by whose means they were restored to their
own country, and again enjoyed their wives and children. When the
solemnity was over, and the time come to render an account of his actions, addressing the public assembly, he was as profuse in enumerating
the lucky chances of war as any of his own military merits. And, finally,
from this felicity, he requested to receive the surname of Felix. In writing and transacting business with the Greeks, he styled himself
Epaphroditus, and on his trophies which are still extant with us, the name
is given Lucius Cornelius Sylla Epaphroditus. Moreover, when his wife
had brought him forth twins, he named the male Faustus and the female
Fausta, the Roman words for what is auspicious and of happy omen. The
confidence which he reposed in his good genius, rather than in any abilities of his own, emboldened him, though deeply involved in bloodshed,
and though he had been the author of such great changes and revolutions of state, to lay down his authority, and place the right of consular
elections once more in the hands of the people. And when they were
held, he not only declined to seek that office, but in the forum exposed
his person publicly to the people, walking up and down as a private man.
And contrary to his will, a certain bold man and his enemy, Marcus
Lepidus, was expected to become consul, not so much by his own interest, as by the power and solicitation of Pompey, whom the people were
willing to oblige. When the business was over, seeing Pompey going
home overjoyed with the success, he called him to him and said, "What
a politic act, young man, to pass by Catulus, the best of men, and choose
Lepidus, the worst! It will be well for you to be vigilant, now that you
have strengthened your opponent against yourself." Sylla spoke this, it
may seem, by a prophetic instinct, for, not long after, Lepidus grew insolent, and broke into open hostility to Pompey and his friends.

Sylla, consecrating the tenth of his whole substance to Hercules, entertained the people with sumptuous feastings. The provision was so
much above what was necessary, that they were forced daily to throw
great quantities of meat into the river, and they drank wine forty years

old and upwards. In the midst of the banqueting, which lasted many days, Metella died of a disease. And because that the priest forbade him to visit the sick, or suffer his house to be polluted with mourning, he drew up an act of divorce, and caused her to be removed into another house whilst alive. Thus far, out of religious apprehension, he observed the strict rule to the very letter, but in the funeral expenses he transgressed the law he himself had made, limiting the amount, and spared no cost. He transgressed, likewise, his own sumptuary laws respecting expenditure in banquets, thinking to allay his grief by luxurious drinking parties and revelings with common buffoons.

Some few months after, at a show of gladiators, when men and women sat promiscuously in the theater, no distinct places being as yet appointed, there sat down by Sylla a beautiful woman of high birth, by name Valeria, daughter of Messala, and sister to Hortensius the orator. Now it happened that she had been lately divorced from her husband. Passing along behind Sylla, she leaned on him with her hand, and plucking a bit of wool from his garment, so proceeded to her seat. And on Sylla looking up and wondering what it meant, "What harm, mighty sir," said she, "if I also was desirous to partake a little in your felicity?" It appeared at once that Sylla was not displeased, but even tickled in his fancy, for he sent out to inquire her name, her birth, and past life. From this time there passed between them many side glances, each continually turning round to look at the other, and frequently interchanging smiles. In the end, overtures were made, and a marriage concluded on. All which was innocent, perhaps, on the lady's side, but, though she had been never so modest and virtuous, it was scarcely a temperate and worthy occasion of marriage on the part of Sylla, to take fire, as a boy might, at a face and a bold look, incentives not seldom to the most disorderly and shameless passions.

Notwithstanding this marriage, he kept company with actresses, musicians, and dancers, drinking with them on couches night and day. His chief favorites were Roscius the comedian, Sorex the arch mime, and Metrobius the player, for whom, though past his prime, he still professed a passionate fondness. By these courses he encouraged a disease which had begun from some unimportant cause; and for a long time he failed to observe that his bowels were ulcerated, till at length the corrupted flesh broke out into lice. Many were employed day and night in destroying them, but the work so multiplied under their hands, that not only his clothes, baths, basins, but his very meat was polluted with that flux and contagion, they came swarming out in such numbers. He went frequently by day into the bath to scour and cleanse his body, but all in vain; the evil generated too rapidly and too abundantly for any ablutions to overcome it. There died of this disease, amongst those of the most ancient times, Acastus, the son of Pelias; of later date, Alcman the poet,

Pherecydes the theologian, Callisthenes the Olynthian, in the time of his imprisonment, as also Mucius the lawyer; and if we may mention ignoble but notorious names, Eunus the fugitive, who stirred up the slaves of Sicily to rebel against their masters, after he was brought captive to Rome, died of this creeping sickness.

Sylla not only foresaw his end, but may be also said to have written of it. For in the two-and-twentieth book of his Memoirs, which he finished two days before his death, he writes that the Chaldeans foretold him, that after he had led a life of honor, he should conclude it in fullness of prosperity. He declares, moreover, that in a vision he had seen his son, who had died not long before Metella, stand by in mourning attire, and beseech his father to cast off further care, and come along with him to his mother Metella, there to live at ease and quietness with her. However, he could not refrain from intermeddling in public affairs. For, ten days before his decease, he composed the differences of the people of Dicæarchia, and prescribed laws for their better government. And the very day before his end, it being told him that the magistrate Granius deferred the payment of a public debt, in expectation of his death, he sent for him to his house, and placing his attendants about him, caused him to be strangled; but through the straining of his voice and body, the imposthume breaking, he lost a great quantity of blood. Upon this, his strength failing him, after spending a troublesome night, he died, leaving behind him two young children by Metella. Valeria was afterwards delivered of a daughter, named Posthuma; for so the Romans call those who are born after the father's death.

Many ran tumultuously together, and joined with Lepidus to deprive the corpse of the accustomed solemnities; but Pompey, though offended at Sylla (for he alone of all his friends was not mentioned in his will), having kept off some by his interest and entreaty, others by menaces, conveyed the body to Rome, and gave it a secure and honorable burial. It is said that the Roman ladies contributed such vast heaps of spices, that besides what was carried on two hundred and ten litters, there was sufficient to form a large figure of Sylla himself, and another representing a lictor, out of the costly frankincense and cinnamon. The day being cloudy in the morning, they deferred carrying forth the corpse till about three in the afternoon, expecting it would rain. But a strong wind blowing full upon the funeral pile, and setting it all in a bright flame, the body was consumed so exactly in good time, that the pyre had begun to smolder, and the fire was upon the point of expiring, when a violent rain came down, which continued till night. So that his good fortune was firm even to the last, and did as it were officiate at his funeral. His monument stands in the Campus Martius, with an epitaph of his own

writing; the substance of it being, that he had not been outdone by any
of his friends in doing good turns, nor by any of his foes in doing bad.

POMPEY

THE people of Rome seem to have entertained for Pompey from his childhood the same affection that Prometheus, in the tragedy of Æschylus, expresses for Hercules, speaking of him as the author of his deliverance, in these words:—

> "Ah cruel Sire! how dear thy son to me!
> The generous offspring of my enemy!"

For on the one hand, never did the Romans give such demonstrations of a vehement and fierce hatred against any of their generals as they did against Strabo, the father of Pompey; during whose lifetime, it is true, they stood in awe of his military power, as indeed he was a formidable warrior, but immediately upon his death, which happened by a stroke of thunder, they treated him with the utmost contumely, dragging his corpse from the bier as it was carried to his funeral. On the other side, never had any Roman the people's goodwill and devotion more zealous throughout all the changes of fortune, more early in its first springing up, or more steadily rising with his prosperity, or more constant in his adversity than Pompey had. In Strabo, there was one great cause of their hatred, his insatiable covetousness; in Pompey, there were many that helped to make him the object of their love; his temperance, his skill and exercise in war, his eloquence of speech, integrity of mind, and affability in conversation and address; insomuch that no man ever asked a favor with less offense, or conferred one with a better grace. When he gave, it was without assumption; when he received, it was with dignity and honor.

In his youth, his countenance pleaded for him, seeming to anticipate his eloquence, and win upon the affections of the people before he spoke. His beauty even in his bloom of youth had something in it at once of gentleness and dignity; and when his prime of manhood came, the majesty and kingliness of his character at once became visible in it. His hair sat somewhat hollow or rising a little; and this, with the languishing motion of his eyes, seemed to form a resemblance in his face, though perhaps more talked of than really apparent, to the statues of King Alexander. And because many applied that name to him in his youth,

Pompey himself did not decline it, insomuch that some called him so in
derision. And Lucius Philippus, a man of consular dignity, when he was
pleading in favor of him, thought it not unfit to say that people could not
be surprised if Philip was a lover of Alexander.

It is related of Flora, the courtesan, that when she was now pretty old,
she took great delight in speaking of her early familiarity with Pompey,
and was wont to say that she could never part after being with him without a bite. She would further tell, that Geminius, a companion of
Pompey's, fell in love with her, and made his court with great importunity; and on her refusing, and telling him, however her inclinations were,
yet she could not gratify his desires for Pompey's sake, he therefore made
his request to Pompey, and Pompey frankly gave his consent, but never
afterwards would have any converse with her, notwithstanding that he
seemed to have a great passion for her; and Flora, on this occasion,
showed none of the levity that might have been expected of her, but lan-
guished for some time after under a sickness brought on by grief and desire. This Flora, we are told, was such a celebrated beauty, that Cæcilius
Metellus, when he adorned the temple of Castor and Pollux with paint-
ings and statues, among the rest dedicated hers for her singular beauty. In
his conduct also to the wife of Demetrius, his freed servant (who had
great influence with him in his lifetime, and left an estate of four thousand talents), Pompey acted contrary to his usual habits, not quite fairly
or generously, fearing lest he should fall under the common censure of
being enamored and charmed with her beauty, which was irresistible, and
became famous everywhere. Nevertheless, though he seemed to be so
extremely circumspect and cautious, yet even in matters of this nature he
could not avoid the calumnies of his enemies, but upon the score of married women, they accused him, as if he had connived at many things, and
embezzled the public revenue to gratify their luxury.

Of his easiness of temper and plainness, in what related to eating and
drinking, the story is told that, once in a sickness, when his stomach nau-
seated common meats, his physician prescribed him a thrush to eat, but
upon search, there was none to be bought, for they were not then in season, and one telling him they were to be had at Lucullus's, who kept
them all the year round, "So then," said he, "if it were not for Lucullus's
luxury, Pompey should not live;" and thereupon, not minding the pre-
scription of the physician, he contented himself with such meat as could
easily be procured. But this was at a later time.

Being as yet a very young man, and upon an expedition in which his
father was commanding against Cinna, he had in his tent with him one
Lucius Terentius, as his companion and comrade, who, being corrupted
by Cinna, entered into an engagement to kill Pompey, as others had done
to set the general's tent on fire. This conspiracy being discovered to

Pompey at supper, he showed no discomposure at it, but on the contrary drank more liberally than usual, and expressed great kindness to Terentius; but about bedtime, pretending to go to his repose, he stole away secretly out of the tent, and setting a guard about his father, quietly expected the event. Terentius, when he thought the proper time come, rose with his naked sword, and coming to Pompey's bedside, stabbed several strokes through the bedclothes, as if he were lying there. Immediately after this there was a great uproar throughout all the camp, arising from the hatred they bore to the general, and a universal movement of the soldiers to revolt, all tearing down their tents and betaking themselves to their arms. The general himself all this while durst not venture out because of the tumult; but Pompey, going about in the midst of them, besought them with tears; and at last threw himself prostrate upon his face before the gate of the camp, and lay there in the passage at their feet, shedding tears, and bidding those that were marching off, if they would go, trample upon him. Upon which, none could help going back again, and all, except eight hundred, either through shame or compassion, repented, and were reconciled to the general.

Immediately upon the death of Strabo, there was an action commenced against Pompey, as his heir, for that his father had embezzled the public treasure. But Pompey, having traced the principal thefts, charged them upon one Alexander, a freed slave of his father's, and proved before the judges that he had been the appropriator. But he himself was accused of having in his possession some hunting tackle, and books, that were taken at Asculum. To this he confessed thus far, that he received them from his father when he took Asculum, but pleaded further, that he had lost them since, upon Cinna's return to Rome, when his home was broken open and plundered by Cinna's guards. In this cause he had a great many preparatory pleadings against his accuser, in which he showed an activity and steadfastness beyond his years, and gained great reputation and favor; insomuch that Antistius, the prætor and judge of the cause, took a great liking to him, and offered him his daughter in marriage, having had some communications with his friends about it. Pompey accepted the proposal, and they were privately contracted; however, the secret was not so closely kept as to escape the multitude, but it was discernible enough from the favor shown him by Antistius in his cause. And at last, when Antistius pronounced the absolutory sentence of the judges, the people, as if it had been upon a signal given, made the acclamation used according to ancient custom, at marriages, *Talasio.* The origin of which custom is related to be this. At the time when the daughters of the Sabines came to Rome, to see the shows and sports there, and were violently seized upon by the most distinguished and bravest of the Romans for wives, it happened that some goatswains and herdsmen of the meaner rank were carrying off a beautiful and tall maiden; and lest any of their betters should meet them, and take her away, as they ran, they cried out with one voice, *Talasio,* Talasius being a well-known and popular person among them, insomuch that all that heard the name clapped their hands for joy, and joined with them in the shout, as applauding and congratulating the chance. Now, say they, because this proved a fortunate match to Talasius, hence it is that this acclamation is sportively used as a nuptial cry at all weddings. This is the most credible of the accounts that are given of the Talasio. And some few days after this judgment, Pompey married Antistia.

After this he went to Cinna's camp, where finding some false suggestions and calumnies prevailing against him, he began to be afraid, and presently withdrew himself secretly; which sudden disappearance occasioned great suspicion. And there went a rumor and speech through all the camp that Cinna had murdered the young man; upon which all that had been anyways disobliged, and bore any malice to him, resolved to make an assault upon him. He, endeavoring to make his escape, was seized by a centurion, who pursued him with his naked sword. Cinna, in this distress, fell upon his knees, and offered him his seal ring, of great value, for his ransom; but the centurion repulsed him insolently, saying, "I did not come to seal a covenant, but to be revenged upon a lawless and wicked tyrant;" and so dispatched him immediately.

Thus Cinna being slain, Carbo, a tyrant yet more senseless than he, took the command and exercised it, while Sylla meantime was approaching, much to the joy and satisfaction of most people, who in their present evils were ready to find some comfort if it were but in the exchange of a master. For the city was brought to that pass by oppression and calamities that, being utterly in despair of liberty, men were only anxious for the mildest and most tolerable bondage. At that time Pompey was in Picenum in Italy, where he spent some time amusing himself, as he had estates in the country there, though the chief motive of his stay was the liking he felt for the towns of that district, which all regarded him with hereditary feelings of kindness and attachment. But when he now saw that the noblest and best of the city began to forsake their homes and property, and fly from all quarters to Sylla's camp, as to their haven, he likewise was desirous to go; not, however, as a fugitive, alone and with nothing to offer, but as a friend rather than a suppliant, in a way that would gain him honor, bringing help along with him, and at the head of a body of troops. Accordingly he solicited the Picentines for their assistance, who as cordially embraced his motion, and rejected the messengers sent from Carbo; insomuch that a certain Vindius taking upon him to say that Pompey was come from the schoolroom to put himself at the head of the people, they were so incensed that they fell forthwith upon this Vindius and killed him.

From henceforward Pompey, finding a spirit of government upon him, though not above twenty-three years of age, nor deriving an authority by commission from any man, took the privilege to grant himself full power, and, causing a tribunal to be erected in the marketplace of Auximum, a populous city, expelled two of their principal men, brothers, of the name of Ventidius, who were acting against him in Carbo's interest, commanding them by a public edict to depart the city; and then proceeded to levy soldiers, issuing out commissions to centurions and other officers, according to the form of military discipline. And in this manner he went round all the rest of the cities in the district. So that those of Carbo's faction flying, and all others cheerfully submitting to his command, in a little time he mustered three entire legions, having supplied himself besides with all manner of provisions, beasts of burden, carriages, and other necessaries of war. And with this equipage he set forward on his march towards Sylla, not as if he were in haste, or desirous of escaping observation, but by small journeys, making several halts upon the road, to distress and annoy the enemy, and exerting himself to detach from Carbo's interest every part of Italy that he passed through.

Three commanders of the enemy encountered him at once, Carinna, Clœlius, and Brutus, and drew up their forces, not all in the front, nor yet together on any one part, but encamping three several armies in a circle about him, they resolved to encompass and overpower him. Pompey was no way alarmed at this but, collecting all his troops into one body, and placing his horse in the front of the battle, where he himself was in person, he singled out and bent all his forces against Brutus, and when the Celtic horsemen from the enemy's side rode out to meet him, Pompey himself encountering hand to hand with the foremost and stoutest among them, killed him with his spear. The rest seeing this turned their backs and fled, and breaking the ranks of their own foot, presently caused a general rout; whereupon the commanders fell out among themselves, and marched off, some one way, some another, as their fortunes led them, and the towns round about came in and surrendered themselves to Pompey, concluding that the enemy was dispersed for fear. Next after these, Scipio, the consul, came to attack him, and with as little success; for before the armies could join, or be within the throw of their javelins, Scipio's soldiers saluted Pompey's, and came over to them, while Scipio made his escape by flight. Last of all, Carbo himself sent down several troops of horse against him by the river Arsis, which Pompey assailed with the same courage and success as before; and having routed and put them to flight, he forced them in the pursuit into difficult ground, unpassable for horse, where, seeing no hopes of escape, they yielded themselves with their horses and armor, all to his mercy.

Sylla was hitherto unacquainted with all these actions; and on the first intelligence he received of his movements was in great anxiety about him, fearing lest he should be cut off among so many and such experienced commanders of the enemy, and marched therefore with all speed to his aid. Now Pompey, having advice of his approach, sent out orders to his officers to marshal and draw up all his forces in full array, that they might make the finest and noblest appearance before the commander-in-chief; for he expected indeed great honors from him, but met with even greater. For as soon as Sylla saw him thus advancing, his army so well appointed, his men so young and strong, and their spirits so high and hopeful with their successes, he alighted from his horse, and being first, as was his due, saluted by them with the title of Imperator, he returned the salutation upon Pompey, in the same term and style of Imperator, which might well cause surprise, as none could have ever anticipated that he would have imparted, to one so young in years and not yet a senator, a title which was the object of contention between him and the Scipios and Marii. And indeed all the rest of his deportment was agreeable to this first compliment; whenever Pompey came into his presence, he paid some sort of respect to him, either in rising and being uncovered, or the like, which he was rarely seen to do to anyone else, notwithstanding that there were many about him of great rank and honor. Yet Pompey was not puffed up at all, or exalted with these favors. And when Sylla would have sent him with all expedition into Gaul, a province in which it was thought Metellus, who commanded in it, had done nothing worthy of the large forces at his disposal, Pompey urged that it could not be fair or honorable for him to take a province out of the hands of his senior in command and his superior in reputation; however, if Metellus were willing, and should request his service, he should be very ready to accompany and assist him in the war; which when Metellus came to understand, he approved of the proposal, and invited him over by letter. And on this Pompey fell immediately into Gaul, where he not only achieved wonderful exploits of himself, but also fired up and kindled again that bold and warlike spirit, which old age had in a manner extinguished in Metellus, into a new heat; just as molten copper, they say, when poured upon that which is cold and solid, will dissolve and melt it faster than fire itself. But as when a famous wrestler has gained the first place among men, and borne away the prizes at all the games, it is not usual to take account of his victories as a boy, or to enter them upon record among the rest; so with the exploits of Pompey in his youth, though they were extraordinary in themselves, yet because they were obscured and buried in the multitude and greatness of his later wars and conquests, I dare not be particular in them, lest, by trifling away time in the lesser moments of his youth, we should be driven to omit those greater actions and fortunes which best illustrate his character.

Now, when Sylla had brought all Italy under his dominion, and was proclaimed dictator, he began to reward the rest of his followers, by giving them wealth, appointing them to offices in the state, and granting them freely and without restriction any favors they asked for. But as for Pompey, admiring his valor and conduct, and thinking that he might prove a great stay and support to him hereafter in his affairs, he sought means to attach him to himself by some personal alliance, and his wife Metella joining in his wishes, they two persuaded Pompey to put away Antistia, and marry Æmilia, the stepdaughter of Sylla, born by Metella to Scaurus, her former husband, she being at that very time the wife of another man, living with him, and with child by him. These were the very tyrannies of marriage, and much more agreeable to the times under Sylla than to the nature and habits of Pompey; that Æmilia great with child should be, as it were, ravished from the embraces of another for him, and that Antistia should be divorced with dishonor and misery by him, for whose sake she had been but just before bereft of her father. For Antistius was murdered in the senate because he was suspected to be a favorer of Sylla, for Pompey's sake; and her mother, likewise, after she had seen all these indignities, made away with herself; a new calamity to be added to the tragic accompaniments of this marriage, and that there might be nothing wanting to complete them, Æmilia herself died, almost immediately after entering Pompey's house, in childbed.

About this time news came to Sylla that Perpenna was fortifying himself in Sicily, that the island was now become a refuge and receptacle for the relics of the adverse party, that Carbo was hovering about those seas with a navy, that Domitius had fallen in upon Africa, and that many of the exiled men of note who had escaped from the proscriptions were daily flocking into those parts. Against these, therefore, Pompey was sent with a large force; and no sooner was he arrived in Sicily but Perpenna immediately departed, leaving the whole island to him. Pompey received the distressed cities into favor, and treated all with great humanity, except the Mamertines in Messena; for when they protested against his court and jurisdiction, alleging their privilege and exemption founded upon an ancient charter or grant of the Romans, he replied sharply, "What! will you never cease prating of laws to us that have swords by our sides?" It was thought, likewise, that he showed some inhumanity to Carbo, seeming rather to insult over his misfortunes than to chastise his crimes. For if there had been a necessity, as perhaps there was, that he should be taken off, that might have been done at first, as soon as he was taken prisoner, for then it would have been the act of him that commanded it. But here

Pompey commanded a man that had been thrice consul of Rome to be brought in fetters to stand at the bar, he himself sitting upon the bench in judgment, examining the cause with the formalities of law, to the offense and indignation of all that were present, and afterwards ordered him to be taken away and put to death. It is related, by the way, of Carbo, that as soon as he was brought to the place, and saw the sword drawn for execution, he was suddenly seized with a looseness or pain in his bowels, and desired a little respite of the executioner, and a convenient place to relieve himself. And yet further, Caius Oppius, the friend of Cæsar, tells us, that Pompey dealt cruelly with Quintus Valerius, a man of singular learning and science. For when he was brought to him, he walked aside, and drew him into conversation, and after putting a variety of questions to him, and receiving answers from him, he ordered his officers to take him away and put him to death. But we must not be too credulous in the case of narratives told by Oppius, especially when he undertakes to relate anything touching the friends or foes of Cæsar. This is certain, that there lay a necessity upon Pompey to be severe upon many of Sylla's enemies, those at least that were eminent persons in themselves, and notoriously known to be taken; but for the rest, he acted with all the clemency possible for him, conniving at the concealment of some, and himself being the instrument in the escape of others. So in the case of the Himeræans; for when Pompey had determined on severely punishing their city, as they had been abettors of the enemy, Sthenis, the leader of the people there, craving liberty of speech, told him that what he was about to do was not at all consistent with justice, for that he would pass by the guilty and destroy the innocent; and on Pompey demanding who that guilty person was that would assume the offenses of them all, Sthenis replied it was himself, who had engaged his friends by persuasion to what they had done, and his enemies by force; whereupon Pompey, being much taken with the frank speech and noble spirit of the man, first forgave his crime, and then pardoned all the rest of the Himeræans. Hearing, likewise, that his soldiers were very disorderly in their march, doing violence upon the roads, he ordered their swords to be sealed up in their scabbards, and whosoever kept them not so were severely punished.

Whilst Pompey was thus busy in the affairs and government of Sicily, he received a decree of the senate, and a commission from Sylla, commanding him forthwith to sail into Africa, and make war upon Domitius with all his forces: for Domitius had rallied up a far greater army than Marius had had not long since, when he sailed out of Africa into Italy, and caused a revolution in Rome, and himself, of a fugitive outlaw, became a tyrant. Pompey, therefore, having prepared everything with the utmost speed, left Memmius, his sister's husband, governor of Sicily, and set sail with one hundred and twenty galleys, and eight hundred other vessels laden with provisions, money, ammunition, and engines of battery. He arrived with his fleet, part at the port of Utica, part at Carthage; and no sooner was he landed, but seven thousand of the enemy revolted and came over to him, while his own forces that he brought with him consisted of six entire legions. Here they tell us of a pleasant incident that happened to him at his first arrival.

Some of his soldiers having by accident stumbled upon a treasure, by which they got a good sum of money, the rest of the army hearing this, began to fancy that the field was full of gold and silver, which had been hid there of old by the Carthaginians in the time of their calamities, and thereupon fell to work, so that the army was useless to Pompey for many days, being totally engaged in digging for the fancied treasure, he himself all the while walking up and down only, and laughing to see so many thousands together, digging and turning up the earth. Until at last, growing weary and hopeless, they came to themselves, and returned to their general, begging him to lead them where he pleased, for that they had already received the punishment of their folly.

By this time Domitius had prepared himself and drawn out his army in array against Pompey; but there was a watercourse betwixt them, craggy and difficult to pass over; and this, together with a great storm of wind and rain pouring down even from break of day, seemed to leave but little possibility of their coming together; so that Domitius, not expecting any engagement that day, commanded his forces to draw off and retire to the camp. Now Pompey, who was watchful upon every occasion, making use of the opportunity, ordered a march forthwith, and having passed over the torrent, fell in immediately upon their quarters. The enemy was in great disorder and tumult, and in that confusion attempted a resistance; but they neither were all there, nor supported one another; besides, the wind, having veered about, beat the rain full in their faces. Neither indeed was the storm less troublesome to the Romans, for that they could not clearly discern one another, insomuch that even Pompey himself, being unknown, escaped narrowly; for when one of his soldiers demanded of him the word of battle, it happened that he was somewhat slow in his answer, which might have cost him his life.

The enemy being routed with a great slaughter (for it is said that of twenty thousand there escaped but three thousand), the army saluted Pompey by the name of Imperator; but he declined it, telling them that he could not by any means accept of that title as long as he saw the camp of the enemy standing; but if they designed to make him worthy of the honor, they must first demolish that. The soldiers on hearing this went at once and made an assault upon the works and trenches, and there Pompey fought without his helmet, in memory of his former danger, and to avoid the like. The camp was thus taken by storm, and among the rest Domitius was slain. After that overthrow, the cities of the country thereabouts were all either secured by surrender, or taken by storm. King Iarbas, likewise, a confederate and auxiliary of Domitius, was taken prisoner, and his kingdom was given to Hiempsal.

Pompey could not rest here, but being ambitious to follow the good fortune and use the valor of his army, entered Numidia; and marching forward many days' journey up into the country, he conquered all wherever he came. And having revived the terror of the Roman power, which was now almost obliterated among the barbarous nations, he said likewise, that the wild beasts of Africa ought not to be left without some experience of the courage and success of the Romans, and therefore he bestowed some few days in hunting lions and elephants. And it is said that it was not above the space of forty days at the utmost in which he gave a total overthrow to the enemy, reduced Africa, and established the affairs of the kings and kingdoms of all that country, being then in the twenty-fourth year of his age.

When Pompey returned back to the city of Utica, there were presented to him letters and orders from Sylla, commanding him to disband the rest of his army, and himself with one legion only to wait there the coming of another general, to succeed him in the government. This, inwardly, was extremely grievous to Pompey, though he made no show of it. But the army resented it openly, and when Pompey besought them to depart and go home before him, they began to revile Sylla, and declared broadly that they were resolved not to forsake him, neither did they think it safe for him to trust the tyrant. Pompey at first endeavored to appease and pacify them by fair speeches; but when he saw that his persuasions were vain, he left the bench, and retired to his tent with tears in his eyes. But the soldiers followed him, and seizing upon him, by force brought him again, and placed him in his tribunal; where great part of that day was spent in dispute, they on their part persuading him to stay and command them, he, on the other side, pressing upon them obedience and the danger of mutiny. At last, when they grew yet more importunate and clamorous, he swore that he would kill himself if they attempted to force him; and scarcely even thus appeased them. Nevertheless, the first tidings brought to Sylla were that Pompey was up in rebellion; on which he remarked to some of his friends, "I see, then, it is my destiny to contend with children in my old age"; alluding at the same time to Marius, who, being but a mere youth, had given him great trouble, and brought him into extreme danger. But being undeceived afterwards by better intelligence, and finding the whole city prepared to meet Pompey, and receive him with every display of kindness and honor, he resolved to exceed them all. And, therefore, going out foremost to meet him, and embracing him with great cordiality, he gave him his welcome aloud in the title of Magnus, or the Great, and bade all that were present call him by that name. Others say that he had this title first given him by a general acclamation of all the army in Africa, but that it was fixed upon him by this ratification of Sylla. It is certain that he himself was the last that owned the title; for it was a long time after, when he was sent proconsul into Spain against Sertorius, that he began to write himself in his letters and commissions by the name of Pompeius Magnus; common and familiar use having then worn off the invidiousness of the title. And one cannot but accord respect and admiration to the ancient Romans, who did not reward the successes of action and conduct in war alone with such honorable titles, but adorned likewise the virtues and services of eminent men in civil government with the same distinctions and marks of honor. Two persons received from the people the name of Maximus, or the Greatest, Valerius, for reconciling the senate and people, and Fabius Rullus, because he put out of the senate certain sons of freed slaves who had been admitted into it because of their wealth.

Pompey now desired the honor of a triumph, which Sylla opposed, alleging that the law allowed that honor to none but consuls and prætors, and therefore Scipio the elder, who subdued the Carthaginians in Spain in far greater and nobler conflicts, never petitioned for a triumph, because he had never been consul or prætor; and if Pompey, who had scarcely yet fully grown a beard, and was not of age to be a senator, should enter the city in triumph, what a weight of envy would it bring, he said, at once upon his government and Pompey's honor. This was his language to Pompey, intimating that he could not by any means yield to his request, but if he would persist in his ambition, that he was resolved to interpose his power to humble him. Pompey, however, was not daunted; but bade Sylla recollect that more worshiped the rising than the setting sun; as if to tell him that his power was increasing and Sylla's in the wane. Sylla did not perfectly hear the words, but observing a sort of amazement and wonder in the looks and gestures of those that did hear them, he asked what it was that he said. When it was told him, he seemed astounded at Pompey's boldness, and cried out twice together, "Let him triumph," and when others began to show their disapprobation and offense at it, Pompey, it is said, to gall and vex them the more, designed to have his triumphant chariot drawn with four elephants (having brought over several which belonged to the African kings), but the gates of the city being too narrow, he was forced to desist from that project, and be content with horses. And when his soldiers, who had not received as large rewards as they had expected, began to clamor, and interrupt the triumph, Pompey regarded these as little as the rest, and plainly told them that he had rather lose the honor of his triumph than flatter them. Upon

which Servilius, a man of great distinction, and at first one of the chief
opposers of Pompey's triumph, said, he now perceived that Pompey was
truly great and worthy of a triumph. It is clear that he might easily have
been a senator, also, if he had wished, but he did not sue for that, being
ambitious, it seems, only of unusual honors. For what wonder had it been
for Pompey to sit in the senate before his time? But to triumph before
he was in the senate was really an excess of glory.

And, moreover, it did not a little ingratiate him with the people, who
were much pleased to see him after his triumph take his place again
among the Roman knights. On the other side, it was no less distasteful
to Sylla to see how fast he came on, and to what a height of glory and
power he was advancing; yet being ashamed to hinder him, he kept quiet.
But when, against his direct wishes, Pompey got Lepidus made consul,
having openly joined in the canvass and, by the goodwill the people felt
for himself, conciliated their favor for Lepidus, Sylla could forbear no
longer; but when he saw him coming away from the election through
the forum with a great train after him, cried out to him, "Well, young
man, I see you rejoice in your victory. And, indeed, is it not a most generous and worthy act, that the consulship should be given to Lepidus, the
vilest of men, in preference to Catulus, the best and most deserving in
the city, and all by your influence with the people? It will be well, however, for you to be wakeful and look to your interests; as you have been
making your enemy stronger than yourself." But that which gave the
clearest demonstration of Sylla's ill will to Pompey was his last will and
testament; for whereas he had bequeathed several legacies to all the rest
of his friends, and appointed some of them guardians to his son, he passed
by Pompey without the least remembrance. However, Pompey bore this
with great moderation and temper; and when Lepidus and others were
disposed to obstruct his interment in the Campus Martius, and to prevent any public funeral taking place, came forward in support of it, and
saw his obsequies performed with all honor and security.

Shortly after the death of Sylla, his prophetic words were fulfilled; and
Lepidus proposing to be the successor to all his power and authority,
without any ambiguities or pretences, immediately appeared in arms,
rousing once more and gathering about him all the long dangerous remains of the old factions, which had escaped the hand of Sylla. Catulus,
his colleague, who was followed by the sounder part of the senate and
people, was a man of the greatest esteem among the Romans for wisdom
and justice; but his talent lay in the government of the city rather than
the camp, whereas the exigency required the skill of Pompey. Pompey,
therefore, was not long in suspense which way to dispose of himself, but
joining with the nobility, was presently appointed general of the army
against Lepidus, who had already raised up war in great part of Italy, and

held Cisalpine Gaul in subjection with an army under Brutus. As for the rest of his garrisons, Pompey subdued them with ease in his march, but Mutina in Gaul resisted in a formal siege, and he lay here a long time encamped against Brutus. In the meantime Lepidus marched in all haste against Rome, and sitting down before it with a crowd of followers, to the terror of those within, demanded a second consulship. But that fear quickly vanished upon letters sent from Pompey, announcing that he had ended the war without a battle; for Brutus, either betraying his army, or being betrayed by their revolt, surrendered himself to Pompey, and receiving a guard of horse, was conducted to a little town upon the river Po; where he was slain the next day by Geminius, in execution of Pompey's commands. And for this Pompey was much censured; for, having at the beginning of the revolt written to the senate that Brutus had voluntarily surrendered himself, immediately afterward he sent other letters, with matter of accusation against the man, after he was taken off. Brutus, who with Cassius slew Cæsar, was son to this Brutus; neither in war nor in his death like his father, as appears at large in his life. Lepidus, upon this being driven out of Italy, fled to Sardinia, where he fell sick and died of sorrow, not for his public misfortunes, as they say, but upon the discovery of a letter proving his wife to have been unfaithful to him.

There yet remained Sertorius, a very different general from Lepidus, in possession of Spain, and making himself formidable to Rome; the final disease, as it were, in which the scattered evils of the civil wars had now collected. He had already cut off various inferior commanders, and was at this time coping with Metellus Pius, a man of repute and a good soldier, though perhaps he might now seem too slow, by reason of his age, to second and improve the happier moments of war, and might be sometimes wanting to those advantages which Sertorius, by his quickness and dexterity, would wrest out of his hands. For Sertorius was always hovering about, and coming upon him unawares, like a captain of thieves rather than soldiers, disturbing him perpetually with ambuscades and light skirmishes; whereas Metellus was accustomed to regular conduct, and fighting in battle array with full-armed soldiers. Pompey, therefore, keeping his army in readiness, made it his object to be sent in aid to Metellus; neither would he be induced to disband his forces, notwithstanding that Catulus called upon him to do so, but by some colorable device or other he still kept them in arms about the city, until the senate at last thought fit, upon the report of Lucius Philippus, to decree him that government. At that time, they say, one of the senators there expressing his wonder and demanding of Philippus whether his meaning was that Pompey should be sent into Spain as proconsul, "No," replied Philippus, "but as pro*consuls*," as if both consuls for that year were in his opinion wholly useless.

When Pompey was arrived in Spain, as is usual upon the fame of a new leader, men began to be inspired with new hopes, and those nations that had not entered into a very strict alliance with Sertorius began to waver and revolt; whereupon Sertorius uttered various arrogant and scornful speeches against Pompey, saying, in derision, that he should want no other weapon but a ferula and rod to chastise this boy with, if he were not afraid of that old woman, meaning Metellus. Yet in deed and reality he stood in awe of Pompey, and kept on his guard against him, as appeared by his whole management of the war, which he was observed to conduct much more warily than before: for Metellus, which one would not have imagined, was grown excessively luxurious in his habits, having given himself over to self-indulgence and pleasure, and from a moderate and temperate became suddenly a sumptuous and ostentatious liver, so that this very thing gained Pompey great reputation and goodwill, as he made himself somewhat specially an example of frugality, although that virtue was habitual in him, and required no great industry to exercise it, as he was naturally inclined to temperance, and no ways inordinate in his desires. The fortune of the war was very various; nothing, however, annoyed Pompey so much as the taking of the town of Lauron by Sertorius. For when Pompey thought he had him safe enclosed, and had boasted somewhat largely of raising the siege, he found himself all of a sudden encompassed; insomuch that he durst not move out of his camp, but was forced to sit still whilst the city was taken and burnt before his face. However, afterwards, in a battle near Valentia, he gave great defeat to Herennius and Perpenna, two commanders among the refugees who had fled to Sertorius, and now lieutenants under him, in which he slew above ten thousand men.

Pompey, being elated and filled with confidence by this victory, made all haste to engage Sertorius himself, and the rather lest Metellus should come in for a share in the honor of the victory. Late in the day towards sunset they joined battle near the river Sucro, both being in fear lest Metellus should come: Pompey, that he might engage alone, Sertorius, that he might have one alone to engage with. The issue of the battle proved doubtful, for a wing of each side had the better; but of the generals Sertorius had the greater honor, for that he maintained his post, having put to flight the entire division that was opposed to him, whereas Pompey was himself almost made a prisoner; for being set upon by a strong man-at-arms that fought on foot (he being on horseback), as they were closely engaged hand to hand the strokes of their swords chanced to light upon their hands, but with a different success; for Pompey's was a slight wound only, whereas he cut off the other's hand. However, it happened so, that many now falling upon Pompey together, and his own forces there being put to the rout, he made his escape beyond expectation, by quitting his horse, and turning him out among the enemy. For the horse being richly adorned with golden trappings, and having a caparison of great value, the soldiers quarreled among themselves for the booty, so that while they were fighting with one another, and dividing the spoil, Pompey made his escape. By break of day the next morning, each drew out his forces into the field to claim the victory; but Metellus coming up, Sertorius vanished, having broken up and dispersed his army. For this was the way in which he used to raise and disband his armies, so that sometimes he would be wandering up and down all alone, and at other times again he would come pouring into the field at the head of no less than one hundred and fifty thousand fighting men, swelling of a sudden like a winter-torrent.

When Pompey was going, after the battle, to meet and welcome Metellus, and when they were near one another, he commanded his attendants to lower their rods in honor of Metellus, as his senior and superior. But Metellus on the other side forbade it, and behaved himself in general very obligingly to him, not claiming any prerogative either in respect of his consular rank or seniority; excepting only that when they encamped together, the watchword was given to the whole camp by Metellus. But generally they had their camps asunder, being divided and distracted by the enemy, who took all shapes, and being always in motion, would by some skillful artifice appear in a variety of places almost in the same instant, drawing them from one attack to another, and at last keeping them from foraging, wasting the country, and holding the dominion of the sea, Sertorius drove them both out of that part of Spain which was under his control, and forced them, for want of necessaries, to retreat into provinces that did not belong to them.

Pompey, having made use of and expended the greatest part of his own private revenues upon the war, sent and demanded moneys of the senate, adding that, in case they did not furnish him speedily, he should be forced to return into Italy with his army. Lucullus being consul at that time, though at variance with Pompey, yet in consideration that he himself was a candidate for the command against Mithridates, procured and hastened these supplies, fearing lest there should be any pretense or occasion given to Pompey of returning home, who of himself was no less desirous of leaving Sertorius and of undertaking the war against Mithridates, as an enterprise which by all appearance would prove much more honorable and not so dangerous. In the meantime Sertorius died, being treacherously murdered by some of his own party; and Perpenna, the chief among them, took the command and attempted to carry on the same enterprises with Sertorius, having indeed the same forces and the same means, only wanting the same skill and conduct in the use of them. Pompey therefore marched directly against Perpenna, and finding him acting merely at random in his affairs, had a decoy ready for him, and sent out a detachment of ten cohorts into the level country with orders to range up and down and disperse themselves abroad. The bait took accordingly, and no sooner had Perpenna turned upon the prey and had them in chase, but Pompey appeared suddenly with all his army and, joining battle, gave him a total overthrow. Most of his officers were slain in the field, and he himself being brought prisoner to Pompey, was by his order put to death. Neither was Pompey guilty in this of ingratitude or unmindfulness of what had occurred in Sicily, which some have laid to his charge, but was guided by a highminded policy and a deliberate counsel for the security of his country. For Perpenna, having in his custody all Sertorius's papers, offered to produce several letters from the greatest men in Rome, who, desirous of a change and subversion of the government, had invited Sertorius into Italy. And Pompey, fearing that these might be the occasion of worse wars than those which were now ended, thought it advisable to put Perpenna to death, and burnt the letters without reading them.

Pompey continued in Spain after this so long a time as was necessary for the suppression of all the greatest disorders in the province; and after moderating and allaying the more violent heats of affairs there, returned with his army into Italy, where he arrived, as chance would have it, in the height of the servile war. Accordingly, upon his arrival, Crassus, the commander in that war, at some hazard precipitated a battle, in which he had great success, and slew upon the place twelve thousand three hundred of the insurgents. Nor yet was he so quick, but that fortune reserved to Pompey some share of honor in the success of this war, for five thousand of those that had escaped out of the battle fell into his hands; and when he had totally cut them off, he wrote to the senate, that Crassus had overthrown the slaves in battle, but that he had plucked up the whole war by the roots. And it was agreeable to the people in Rome both thus to say, and thus to hear said, because of the general favor of Pompey. But of the Spanish war and the conquest of Sertorius, no one, even in jest, could have ascribed the honor to anyone else. Nevertheless, all this high respect for him, and this desire to see him come home, were not unmixed with apprehensions and suspicions that he might perhaps not disband his army, but take his way by force of arms and a supreme command to the seat of Sylla. And so in the number of all those that ran out to meet him and congratulate his return, as many went out of fear as affection. But after Pompey had removed this alarm, by declaring beforehand that he would discharge the army after his triumph, those that envied him could now only complain that he affected popularity, courting the common people more than the nobility, and that whereas Sylla had abolished the tribuneship of the people, he designed to gratify the people by restoring that office, which was indeed the fact. For there was not any one thing that the people of Rome were more wildly eager for, or more passionately desired, than the restoration of that office, insomuch that Pompey thought himself extremely fortunate in this opportunity, despairing (if he were anticipated by someone else in this) of ever meeting with any other sufficient means of expressing his gratitude for the favors which he had received from the people.

Though a second triumph was decreed him, and he was declared consul, yet all these honors did not seem so great an evidence of his power and glory as the ascendant which he had over Crassus; for he, the wealthiest among all the statesmen of his time, and the most eloquent and greatest too, who had looked down on Pompey himself and on all others as beneath him, durst not appear a candidate for the consulship before he had applied to Pompey. The request was made accordingly, and was eagerly embraced by Pompey, who had long sought an occasion to oblige him in some friendly office; so that he solicited for Crassus, and entreated the people heartily, declaring that their favor would be no less to him in choosing Crassus his colleague, than in making himself consul. Yet for all this, when they were created consuls, they were always at variance, and opposing one another. Crassus prevailed most in the senate, and Pompey's power was no less with the people, he having restored to them the office of tribune, and having allowed the courts of judicature to be transferred back to the knights by a new law. He himself in person, too, afforded them a most grateful spectacle, when he appeared and craved his discharge from the military service. For it is an ancient custom among the Romans that the knights, when they had served out their legal time in the wars, should lead their horses into the marketplace before the two officers, called censors, and having given an account of the commanders and generals under whom they served, as also of the places and actions of their service, should be discharged, every man with honor or disgrace, according to his deserts. There were then sitting in state upon the bench two censors, Gellius and Lentulus, inspecting the knights, who were passing by in muster before them, when Pompey was seen coming down into the forum, with all the ensigns of a consul, but leading his horse in his hand. When he came up, he bade his lictors make way for him, and so he led his horse to the bench; the people being all this while in a sort of amaze, and all in silence, and the censors themselves regarding the sight with a mixture of respect and gratification. Then the senior censor examined him: "Pompeius Magnus, I demand of you whether you have served the full time in the wars that is prescribed by the law?" "Yes," replied Pompey, with a loud voice, "I have served all, and all under myself as general." The people hearing this gave a great shout, and made such an outcry for delight, that there was no appeasing it; and the censors, rising from their judgment seat, accompanied him home to gratify the multitude, who followed after, clapping their hands and shouting.

Pompey's consulship was now expiring, and yet his difference with Crassus increasing, when one Caius Aurelius, a knight, a man who had declined public business all his lifetime, mounted the hustings, and addressed himself in an oration to the assembly, declaring that Jupiter had appeared to him in a dream, commanding him to tell the consuls that they should not give up office until they were friends. After this was said, Pompey stood silent, but Crassus took him by the hand, and spoke in this manner: "I do not think, fellow citizens, that I shall do anything mean or dishonorable in yielding first to Pompey, whom you were pleased to ennoble with the title of Great, when as yet he scarce had a hair on his face; and granted the honor of two triumphs before he had a place in the senate." Hereupon they were reconciled and laid down their office. Crassus resumed the manner of life which he had always pursued before; but Pompey in the great generality of causes for judgment declined appearing on either side, and by degrees withdrew himself totally from the forum, showing himself but seldom in public; and, whenever he did, it was with a great train after him. Neither was it easy to meet or visit him without a crowd of people about him; he was most pleased to make his appearance before large numbers at once, as though he wished to maintain in this way his state and majesty, and as if he held himself bound to preserve his dignity from contact with the addresses and conversation of common people. And life in the robe of peace is only too apt to lower the reputation of men that have grown great by arms, who naturally find difficulty in adapting themselves to the habits of civil equality. They expect to be treated as the first in the city, even as they were in the camp; and on the other hand, men who in war were nobody think it intolerable if in the city at any rate they are not to take the lead. And so, when a warrior renowned for victories and triumphs shall turn advocate and appear among them in the forum, they endeavor their utmost to obscure and depress him; whereas, if he gives up any pretensions here and retires, they will maintain his military honor and authority beyond the reach of envy. Events themselves not long after showed the truth of this.

The power of the pirates first commenced in Cilicia, having in truth but a precarious and obscure beginning, but gained life and boldness afterwards in the wars of Mithridates, where they hired themselves out and took employment in the king's service. Afterwards, whilst the Romans were embroiled in their civil wars, being engaged against one another even before the very gates of Rome, the seas lay waste and unguarded, and by degrees enticed and drew them on not only to seize upon and spoil the merchants and ships upon the seas, but also to lay waste the islands and seaport towns. So that now there embarked with these pirates men of wealth and noble birth and superior abilities, as if it had been a natural occupation to gain distinction in. They had divers arsenals, or piratic harbors, as likewise watchtowers and beacons, all along the seacoast; and fleets were here received that were well manned with the finest mariners, and well served with the expertest pilots, and composed of swift-sailing and light-built vessels adapted for their special purpose. Nor was it merely their being thus formidable that excited indignation; they were even more odious for their ostentation than they were feared for their force. Their ships had gilded masts at their stems; the sails woven of purple, and the oars plated with silver, as if their delight were to glory in their iniquity. There was nothing but music and dancing, banqueting and revels, all along the shore. Officers in command were taken prisoners, and cities put under contribution, to the reproach and dishonor of the Roman supremacy.

There were of these corsairs above one thousand sail, and they had taken no less than four hundred cities, committing sacrilege upon the temples of the gods, and enriching themselves with the spoils of many never violated before, such as were those of Claros, Didyma, and Samothrace; and the temple of the Earth in Hermione, and that of Æsculapius in Epidaurus; those of Neptune at the Isthmus, at Tænarus, and at Calauria; those of Apollo at Actium and Leucas, and those of Juno in Samos, at Argos, and at Lacinium. They themselves offered strange sacrifices upon Mount Olympus, and performed certain secret rites or religious mysteries, among which those of Mithras have been preserved to our own time, having received their previous institution from them. But besides these insolencies by sea, they were also injurious to the Romans by land; for they would often go inland up the roads, plundering and destroying their villages and country houses. And once they seized upon two Roman prætors, Sextilius and Bellinus, in their purple-edged robes, and carried them off together with their officers and lictors. The daughter also of Antonius, a man that had had the honor of a triumph, taking a journey into the country, was seized, and redeemed upon payment of a large ransom. But it was most abusive of all that, when any of the captives declared himself to be a Roman, and told his name, they affected to be surprised, and feigning fear, smote their thighs and fell down at his feet, humbly beseeching him to be gracious and forgive them.

The captives, seeing them so humble and suppliant, believed them to be in earnest; and some of them now would proceed to put Roman shoes on his feet, and to dress him in a Roman gown, to prevent, they said, his being mistaken another time. After all this pageantry, when they had thus deluded and mocked him long enough, at last putting out a ship's ladder, when they were in the midst of the sea, they told him he was free to go, and wished him a pleasant journey; and if he resisted, they themselves threw him overboard and drowned him.

This piratic power having got the dominion and control of all the Mediterranean, there was left no place for navigation or commerce. And this it was which most of all made the Romans, finding themselves to be extremely straitened in their markets, and considering that if it should continue, there would be a dearth and famine in the land, determined at last to send out Pompey to recover the seas from the pirates. Gabinius, one of Pompey's friends, preferred a law, whereby there was granted to him, not only the government of the seas as admiral, but in direct words, sole and irresponsible sovereignty over all men. For the decree gave him absolute power and authority in all the seas within the pillars of Hercules, and in the adjacent mainland for the space of four hundred furlongs from the sea. Now there were but few regions in the Roman empire out of that compass; and the greatest of the nations and most powerful of the kings were included in the limit. Moreover, by this decree he had a power of selecting fifteen lieutenants out of the senate, and of assigning to each his province in charge; then he might take likewise out of the treasury and out of the hands of the revenue farmers what moneys he pleased; as also two hundred sail of ships, with a power to press and levy what soldiers and seamen he thought fit.

When this law was read, the common people approved of it exceedingly, but the chief men and most important among the senators looked upon it as an exorbitant power, even beyond the reach of envy, but well deserving their fears. Therefore concluding with themselves that such unlimited authority was dangerous, they agreed unanimously to oppose the bill, and all went against it, except Cæsar, who gave his vote for the law, not to gratify Pompey, but the people, whose favor he had courted underhand from the beginning, and hoped to compass for himself. The rest inveighed bitterly against Pompey, insomuch that one of the consuls told him that, if he was ambitious of the place of Romulus, he would scarce avoid his end, but he was in danger of being torn in pieces by the multitude for his speech. Yet when Catulus stood up to speak against the law, the people in reverence to him were silent and attentive. And when, after saying much in the most honorable terms in favor of Pompey, he proceeded to advise the people in kindness to spare him, and not to expose a man of his value to such a succession of dangers and wars, "For," said he, "where could you find another Pompey, or whom would you have in case you should chance to lose him?" they all cried out with one voice, "Yourself." And so Catulus, finding all his rhetoric ineffectual, desisted. Then Roscius attempted to speak, but could obtain no hearing, and made signs with his fingers, intimating, "Not him alone," but that there might be a second Pompey or colleague in authority with him.

Upon this, it is said, the multitude being extremely incensed, made such a loud outcry, that a crow flying over the marketplace at that instant was struck, and dropped down among the crowd; whence it would appear that the cause of birds falling down to the ground is not any rupture or division of the air causing a vacuum, but purely the actual stroke of the voice, which when carried up in a great mass and with violence, raises a sort of tempest and billow, as it were, in the air.

The assembly broke up for that day; and when the day was come on which the bill was to pass by suffrage into a decree, Pompey went privately into the country; but hearing that it was passed and confirmed, he returned again into the city by night, to avoid the envy that might be occasioned by the concourse of people that would meet and congratulate him. The next morning he came abroad and sacrificed to the gods, and having audience at an open assembly, so handled the matter that they enlarged his power, giving him many things besides what was already granted, and almost doubling the preparation appointed in the former decree. Five hundred ships were manned for him, and an army raised of one hundred and twenty thousand foot and five thousand horse. Twenty-four senators that had been generals of armies were appointed to serve as lieutenants under him, and to these were added two quæstors. Now it happened within this time that the prices of provisions were much reduced, which gave an occasion to the joyful people of saying that the very name of Pompey had ended the war. However, Pompey, in pursuance of his charge, divided all the seas and the whole Mediterranean into thirteen parts, allotting a squadron to each, under the command of his officers; and having thus dispersed his power into all quarters, and encompassed the pirates everywhere, they began to fall into his hands by whole shoals, which he seized and brought into his harbors. As for those that withdrew themselves betimes, or otherwise escaped his general chase, they all made to Cilicia, where they hid themselves as in their hive; against whom Pompey now proceeded in person with sixty of his best ships, not, however, until he had first scoured and cleared all the seas near Rome, the Tyrrhenian, and the African, and all the waters of Sardinia, Corsica, and Sicily; all which he performed in the space of forty days, by his own indefatigable industry and the zeal of his lieutenants.

Pompey met with some interruption in Rome, through the malice and envy of Piso, the consul, who had given some check to his proceedings by withholding his stores and discharging his seamen; whereupon he sent his fleet round to Brundusium, himself going the nearest way by land through Tuscany to Rome; which was no sooner known by the people than they all flocked out to meet him upon the way as if they had not sent him out but a few days before. What chiefly excited their joy was the unexpectedly rapid change in the markets, which abounded now

with the greatest plenty, so that Piso was in great danger to have been deprived of his consulship, Gabinius having a law ready prepared for that
purpose; but Pompey forbade it, behaving himself as in that, so in all
things else, with great moderation, and when he had made sure of all that
he wanted or desired, he departed for Brundusium, whence he set sail in
pursuit of the pirates. And though he was straitened in time, and his hasty
voyage forced him to sail by several cities without touching, yet he would
not pass by the city of Athens unsaluted; but landing there, after he had
sacrificed to the gods, and made an address to the people, as he was returning out of the city, he read at the gates two epigrams, each in a single line, written in his own praise; one within the gate:—

"Thy humbler thoughts make thee a god the more";

the other without:—

"Adieu we bid, who welcome bade before."

Now because Pompey had shown himself merciful to some of these pirates that were yet roving in bodies about the seas, having upon their supplication ordered a seizure of their ships and persons only, without any
further process or severity, therefore the rest of their comrades, in hopes
of mercy too, made their escape from his other commanders, and surrendered themselves with their wives and children into his protection.
He continued to pardon all that came in, and the rather because by them
he might make discovery of those who fled from his justice, as conscious
that their crimes were beyond an act of indemnity. The most numerous
and important part of these conveyed their families and treasures, with all
their people that were unfit for war, into castles and strong forts about
Mount Taurus; but they themselves, having well manned their galleys,
embarked for Coracesium in Cilicia, where they received Pompey and
gave him battle. Here they had a final overthrow, and retired to the land,
where they were besieged. At last, having dispatched their heralds to him
with a submission, they delivered up to his mercy themselves, their
towns, islands, and strongholds, all which they had so fortified that they
were almost impregnable, and scarcely even accessible.

Thus was this war ended, and the whole power of the pirates at sea
dissolved everywhere in the space of three months, wherein, besides a
great number of other vessels, he took ninety men-of-war with brazen
beaks; and likewise prisoners of war to the number of no less than twenty
thousand.

As regarded the disposal of these prisoners, he never so much as entertained the thought of putting them to death; and yet it might be no
less dangerous on the other hand to disperse them, as they might reunite
and make head again, being numerous, poor, and warlike. Therefore

wisely weighing with himself that man by nature is not a wild or unso-
cial creature, neither was he born so, but makes himself what he naturally
is not by vicious habit; and that again, on the other side, he is civilized
and grows gentle by a change of place, occupation, and manner of life, as
beasts themselves that are wild by nature become tame and tractable by
housing and gentler usage, upon this consideration he determined to
translate these pirates from sea to land, and give them a taste of an honest and innocent course of life by living in towns, and tilling the ground.
Some therefore were admitted into the small and half-peopled towns of
the Cilicians, who, for an enlargement of their territories, were willing to
receive them. Others he planted in the city of the Solians, which had
been lately laid waste by Tigranes, king of Armenia, and which he now
restored. But the largest number were settled in Dyme, the town of
Achæa, at that time extremely depopulated, and possessing an abundance
of good land.

   However, these proceedings could not escape the envy and censure of
his enemies; and the course he took against Metellus in Crete was disapproved of even by the chiefest of his friends. For Metellus, a relation of
Pompey's former colleague in Spain, had been sent prætor into Crete, before this province of the seas was assigned to Pompey. Now Crete was the
second source of pirates next to Cilicia, and Metellus, having shut up a
number of them in their strongholds there, was engaged in reducing and
extirpating them. Those that were yet remaining and besieged sent their
supplications to Pompey, and invited him into the island as a part of his
province, alleging it to fall, every part of it, within the distance from the
sea specified in his commission, and so within the precincts of his charge.
Pompey receiving the submission, sent letters to Metellus, commanding
him to leave off the war; and others in like manner to the cities, in which
he charged them not to yield any obedience to the commands of
Metellus. And after these, he sent Lucius Octavius, one of his lieutenants,
to act as general, who entering the besieged fortifications, and fighting in
defense of the pirates, rendered Pompey not odious only, but even ridiculous too; that he should lend his name as a guard to a nest of thieves that
knew neither god nor law, and make his reputation serve as a sanctuary
to them, only out of pure envy and emulation to Metellus. For neither
was Achilles thought to act the part of a man, but rather of a mere boy,
mad after glory, when by signs he forbade the rest of the Greeks to strike
at Hector—

> "For fear
> Some other hand should give the blow, and he
> Lose the first honor of the victory."

Whereas Pompey even sought to preserve the common enemies of the world only that he might deprive a Roman prætor, after all his labors, of the honor of a triumph. Metellus, however, was not daunted, but prosecuted the war against the pirates, expelled them from their strongholds and punished them; and dismissed Octavius with the insults and reproaches of the whole camp.

When the news came to Rome that the war with the pirates was at an end, and that Pompey was unoccupied, diverting himself in visits to the cities for want of employment, one Manlius, a tribune of the people, preferred a law that Pompey should have all the forces of Lucullus, and the provinces under his government, together with Bithynia, which was under the command of Glabrio; and that he should forthwith conduct the war against the two kings, Mithridates and Tigranes, retaining still the same naval forces and the sovereignty of the seas as before. But this was nothing less than to constitute one absolute monarch of all the Roman empire. For the provinces which seemed to be exempt from his commission by the former decree, such as were Phrygia, Lycaonia, Galatia, Cappadocia, Cilicia, the upper Colchis, and Armenia, were all added in by this latter law, together with all the troops and forces with which Lucullus had defeated Mithridates and Tigranes. And though Lucullus was thus simply robbed of the glory of his achievements in having a successor assigned him, rather to the honor of his triumph than the danger of the war; yet this was of less moment in the eyes of the aristocratical party, though they could not but admit the injustice and ingratitude to Lucullus. But their great grievance was that the power of Pompey should be converted into a manifest tyranny; and they therefore exhorted and encouraged one another privately to bend all their forces in opposition to this law, and not tamely to cast away their liberty; yet when the day came on which it was to pass into a decree, their hearts failed them for fear of the people, and all were silent except Catulus, who boldly inveighed against the law and its proposer, and when he found that he could do nothing with the people, turned to the senate, crying out and bidding them seek out some mountain as their forefathers had done, and fly to the rocks where they might preserve their liberty. The law passed into a decree, as it is said, by the suffrages of all the tribes. And Pompey, in his absence, was made lord of almost all that power which Sylla only obtained by force of arms, after a conquest of the very city itself.

When Pompey had advice by letters of the decree, it is said that in the presence of his friends, who came to give him joy of his honor, he seemed displeased, frowning and smiting his thigh, and exclaimed as one overburdened and weary of government, "Alas, what a series of labors upon labors! If I am never to end my service as a soldier, nor to escape from this invidious greatness and live at home in the country with my wife, I had better have been an unknown man." But all this was looked upon as mere trifling, neither indeed could the best of his friends call it anything else, well knowing that his enmity with Lucullus, setting a flame just now to his natural passion for glory and empire, made him feel more than usually gratified.

As indeed appeared not long afterwards by his actions, which clearly unmasked him; for in the first place, he sent out his proclamations into all quarters, commanding the soldiers to join him, and summoned all the tributary kings and princes within his charge; and in short, as soon as he had entered upon his province, he left nothing unaltered that had been done and established by Lucullus. To some he remitted their penalties, and deprived others of their rewards, and acted in all respects as if with the express design that the admirers of Lucullus might know that all his authority was at an end.

Lucullus expostulated by friends, and it was thought fitting that there should be a meeting betwixt them; and accordingly they met in the country of Galatia. As they were both great and successful generals, their officers bore their rods before them all wreathed with branches of laurel; Lucullus came through a country full of green trees and shady woods, but Pompey's march was through a cold and barren district. Therefore the lictors of Lucullus, perceiving that Pompey's laurels were withered and dry, helped him to some of their own, and adorned and crowned his rods with fresh laurels. This was thought ominous, and looked as if Pompey came to take away the reward and honor of Lucullus's victories. Lucullus had the priority in the order of consulships, and also in age; but Pompey's two triumphs made him the greater man. Their first addresses in this interview were dignified and friendly, each magnifying the other's actions, and offering congratulations upon his success. But when they came to the matter of their conference or treaty, they could agree on no fair or equitable terms of any kind, but even came to harsh words against each other, Pompey upbraiding Lucullus with avarice, and Lucullus retorting ambition upon Pompey, so that their friends could hardly part them. Lucullus remaining in Galatia, made a distribution of the lands within his conquests, and gave presents to whom he pleased; and Pompey encamping not far distant from him, sent out his prohibitions, forbidding the execution of any of the orders of Lucullus, and commanded away all his soldiers, except sixteen hundred, whom he thought likely to be unserviceable to himself, being disorderly and mutinous, and whom he knew to be hostile to Lucullus; and to these acts he added satirical speeches, detracting openly from the glory of his actions, and giving out that the battles of Lucullus had been but with the mere stage shows and idle pictures of royal pomp, whereas the real war against a genuine army, disciplined by defeat, was reserved to him, Mithridates having now begun to be in earnest, and having betaken himself to his shields, swords, and horses.

Lucullus, on the other side, to be even with him, replied, that Pompey came to fight with the mere image and shadow of war, it being his usual practice, like a lazy bird of prey, to come upon the carcass, when others had slain the dead, and to tear in pieces the relics of a war.

Thus he had appropriated to himself the victories over Sertorius, over Lepidus, and over the insurgents under Spartacus; whereas this last had been achieved by Crassus, that obtained by Catulus, and the first won by Metellus. And therefore it was no great wonder that the glory of the Pontic and Armenian war should be usurped by a man who had condescended to any artifices to work himself into the honor of a triumph over a few runaway slaves.

After this Lucullus went away, and Pompey having placed his whole navy in guard upon the seas betwixt Phœnicia and Bosphorus, himself marched against Mithridates, who had a phalanx of thirty thousand foot, with two thousand horse, yet durst not bid him battle. He had encamped upon a strong mountain where it would have been hard to attack him, but abandoned it in no long time as destitute of water. No sooner was he gone but Pompey occupied it, and observing the plants that were thriving there, together with the hollows which he found in several places, conjectured that such a plot could not be without springs, and therefore ordered his men to sink wells in every corner. After which there was, in a little time, great plenty of water throughout all the camp, insomuch that he wondered how it was possible for Mithridates to be ignorant of this, during all that time of his encampment there. After this Pompey followed him to his next camp, and there drawing lines round about him, shut him in. But he, after having endured a siege of forty-five days, made his escape secretly, and fled away with all the best part of his army, having first put to death all the sick and unserviceable. Not long after Pompey overtook him again near the banks of the river Euphrates, and encamped close by him; but fearing lest he should pass over the river and give him the slip there too, he drew up his army to attack him at midnight. And at that very time Mithridates, it is said, saw a vision in his dream foreshowing what should come to pass. For he seemed to be under sail in the Euxine Sea with a prosperous gale, and just in view of Bosphorus, discoursing pleasantly with the ship's company, as one overjoyed for his past danger and present security, when on a sudden he found himself deserted of all, and floating upon a broken plank of the ship at the mercy of the sea. Whilst he was thus laboring under these passions and phantasms, his friends came and awaked him with the news of Pompey's approach; who was now indeed so near at hand that the fight must be for the camp itself, and the commanders accordingly drew up the forces in battle array.

Pompey perceiving how ready they were and well prepared for defense began to doubt with himself whether he should put it to the haz-ard of a fight in the dark, judging it more prudent to encompass them only at present, lest they should fly, and to give them battle with the ad-vantage of numbers the next day. But his oldest officers were of another opinion, and by entreaties and encouragements obtained permission that they might charge them immediately. Neither was the night so very dark, but that, though the moon was going down, it yet gave light enough to discern a body. And indeed this was one especial disadvantage to the king's army. For the Romans coming upon them with the moon on their backs, the moon, being very low, and just upon setting, cast the shadows a long way before their bodies, reaching almost to the enemy, whose eyes were thus so much deceived that not exactly discerning the distance, but imagining them to be near at hand, they threw their darts at the shadows without the least execution. The Romans therefore perceiving this, ran in upon them with a great shout; but the barbarians, all in a panic, un-able to endure the charge, turned and fled, and were put to great slaugh-ter, above ten thousand being slain; the camp also was taken. As for Mithridates himself, he at the beginning of the onset, with a body of eight hundred horse, charged through the Roman army, and made his es-cape. But before long all the rest dispersed, some one way, some another, and he was left only with three persons, among whom was his concu-bine, Hypsicratia, a girl always of a manly and daring spirit, and the king called her on that account Hypsicrates. She being attired and mounted like a Persian horseman, accompanied the king in all his flight, never weary even in the longest journey, nor ever failing to attend the king in person, and look after his horse too, until they came to Inora, a castle of the king's well stored with gold and treasure. From thence Mithridates took his richest apparel, and gave it among those that had resorted to him in their flight; and to every one of his friends he gave a deadly poison, that they might not fall into the power of the enemy against their wills. From thence he designed to have gone to Tigranes in Armenia, but being prohibited by Tigranes, who put out a proclamation with a reward of one hundred talents to any one that should apprehend him, he passed by the headwaters of the river Euphrates and fled through the country of Colchis.

Pompey in the meantime made an invasion into Armenia upon the in-vitation of young Tigranes, who was now in rebellion against his father, and gave Pompey a meeting about the river Araxes, which rises near the head of Euphrates, but turning its course and bending towards the east, falls into the Caspian Sea. They two, therefore, marched together through the country, taking in all the cities by the way, and receiving their sub-mission. But King Tigranes, having lately suffered much in the war with Lucullus, and understanding that Pompey was of a kind and gentle dis-

position, admitted Roman troops into his royal palaces, and taking along
with him his friends and relations, went in person to surrender himself
into the hands of Pompey. He came as far as the trenches on horseback,
but there he was met by two of Pompey's lictors, who commanded him
to alight and walk on foot, for no man ever was seen on horseback within
a Roman camp. Tigranes submitted to this immediately, and not only so,
but loosing his sword, delivered up that too; and last of all, as soon as he
appeared before Pompey, he pulled off his royal turban, and attempted to
have laid it at his feet. Nay, worst of all, even he himself had fallen prostrate as an humble suppliant at his knees had not Pompey prevented it,
taking him by the hand and placing him near him, Tigranes himself on
one side of him and his son upon the other. Pompey now told him that
the rest of his losses were chargeable upon Lucullus, by whom he had
been dispossessed of Syria, Phœnicia, Cilicia, Galatia, and Sophene; but
all that he had preserved to himself entire till that time he should peaceably enjoy, paying the sum of six thousand talents as a fine or penalty for
injuries done to the Romans, and that his son should have the kingdom
of Sophene. Tigranes himself was well pleased with these conditions of
peace, and when the Romans saluted him king, seemed to be overjoyed,
and promised to every common soldier half a mina of silver, to every
centurion ten minas, and to every tribune a talent; but the son was displeased, insomuch that when he was invited to supper, he replied that he
did not stand in need of Pompey for that sort of honor, for he would find
out some other Roman to sup with. Upon this he was put into close ar-
rest, and reserved for the triumph.

Not long after this Phraates, king of Parthia, sent to Pompey, and demanded to have young Tigranes, as his son-in-law, given up to him, and
that the river Euphrates should be the boundary of the empires. Pompey
replied, that for Tigranes, he belonged more to his own natural father
than his father-in-law, and for the boundaries, he would take care that
they should be according to right and justice.

So Pompey, leaving Armenia in the custody of Afranius, went himself
in chase of Mithridates; to do which he was forced of necessity to march
through several nations inhabiting about Mount Caucasus. Of these the
Albanians and Iberians were the two chiefest. The Iberians stretch out as
far as the Moschian mountains and the Pontus; the Albanians lie more
eastwardly, and towards the Caspian Sea. These Albanians at first permitted Pompey, upon his request, to pass through the country; but when
winter had stolen upon the Romans whilst they were still in the country, and they were busy celebrating the festival of Saturn, they mustered
a body of no less than forty thousand fighting men, and set upon them,
having passed over the river Cyrnus, which rising from the mountains of
Iberia, and receiving the river Araxes in its course from Armenia, dis-

charges itself by twelve mouths into the Caspian. Or, according to others, the Araxes does not fall into it, but they flow near one another, and so discharge themselves as neighbors into the same sea. It was in the power of Pompey to have obstructed the enemy's passage over the river, but he suffered them to pass over quietly; and then leading on his forces and giving battle, he routed them, and slew great numbers of them in the field. The king sent ambassadors with his submission, and Pompey upon his supplication pardoned the offense, and making a treaty with him, he marched directly against the Iberians, a nation no less in number than the other, but much more warlike, and extremely desirous of gratifying Mithridates and driving out Pompey.

These Iberians were never subject to the Medes or Persians, and they happened likewise to escape the dominion of the Macedonians, because Alexander was so quick in his march through Hyrcania. But these also Pompey subdued in a great battle, where there were slain nine thousand upon the spot, and more than ten thousand taken prisoners. From thence he entered into the country of Colchis, where Servilius met him by the river Phasis, bringing the fleet with which he was guarding the Pontus.

The pursuit of Mithridates, who had thrown himself among the tribes inhabiting Bosphorus and the shores of the Mæotian Sea, presented great difficulties. News was also brought to Pompey that the Albanians had again revolted. This made him turn back, out of anger and determination not to be beaten by them, and with difficulty and great danger he passed back over the Cyrnus, which the barbarous people had fortified a great way down the banks with palisadoes. And after this, having a tedious march to make through a waterless and difficult country, he ordered ten thousand skins to be filled with water, and so advanced towards the enemy, whom he found drawn up in order of battle near the river Abas, to the number of sixty thousand horse and twelve thousand foot, ill-armed generally, and most of them covered only with the skins of wild beasts. Their general was Cosis, the king's brother, who, as soon as the battle was begun, singled out Pompey, and rushing in upon him darted his javelin into the joints of his breastplate; while Pompey, in return, struck him through the body with his lance, and slew him. It is related that in this battle there were Amazons fighting as auxiliaries with the barbarians, and that they came down from the mountains by the river Thermodon. For that after the battle, when the Romans were taking the spoil and plunder of the field, they met with several targets and buskins of the Amazons; but no woman's body was found among the dead. They inhabit the parts of Mount Caucasus that reach down to the Hyrcanian Sea, not immediately bordering upon the Albanians, for the Gelæ and the Leges lie betwixt; and they keep company with these people yearly, for two

months only, near the river Thermodon; after which they retire to their
own habitations, and live alone all the rest of the year.

After this engagement, Pompey was eager to advance with his forces
upon the Hyrcanian and Caspian Sea, but was forced to retreat at a distance of three days' march from it, by the number of venomous serpents,
and so he retreated into Armenia the Less. Whilst he was there, the kings
of the Elymæans and Medes sent ambassadors to him, to whom he gave
friendly answer by letter; and sent against the king of Parthia, who had
made incursions upon Gordyene, and despoiled the subjects of Tigranes
an army under the command of Afranius, who put him to the rout, and
followed him in chase as far as the district of Arbela.

Of the concubines of King Mithridates that were brought before
Pompey, he took none to himself, but sent them all away to their parents
and relations; most of them being either the daughters or wives of
princes and great commanders. Stratonice, however, who had the greatest power and influence with him, and to whom he had committed the
custody of his best and richest fortress, had been, it seems, the daughter
of a musician, an old man, and of no great fortune, and happening to sing
one night before Mithridates at a banquet, she struck his fancy so that
immediately he took her with him, and sent away the old man much dissatisfied, the king having not so much as said one kind word to himself.
But when he rose in the morning, and saw tables in his house richly covered with gold and silver plate, a great retinue of servants, eunuchs, and
pages bringing him rich garments, and a horse standing before the door
richly caparisoned, in all respects as was usual with the king's favorites,
he looked upon it all as a piece of mockery, and thinking himself trifled
with, attempted to make off and run away. But the servants laying hold
upon him, and informing him really that the king had bestowed on him
the house and furniture of a rich man lately deceased, and that these were
but the first fruits or earnests of greater riches and possessions that were
to come, he was persuaded at last with much difficulty to believe them.
And so putting on his purple robes, and mounting his horse, he rode
through the city, crying out, "All this is mine"; and to those that laughed
at him, he said, there was no such wonder in this, but it was a wonder
rather that he did not throw stones at all he met, he was so transported
with joy. Such was the parentage and blood of Stratonice. She now delivered up this castle into the hands of Pompey, and offered him many
presents of great value, of which he accepted only such as he thought
might serve to adorn the temples of the gods, and add to the splendor of
his triumph; the rest he left to Stratonice's disposal, bidding her please
herself in the enjoyment of them.

And in the same manner he dealt with the presents offered him by the
king of Iberia, who sent him a bedstead, table, and a chair of state, all of

gold, desiring him to accept of them; but he delivered them all into the custody of the public treasurers, for the use of the commonwealth.

In another castle called Cænum, Pompey found and read with pleasure several secret writings of Mithridates, containing much that threw light on his character. For there were memoirs by which it appeared that, besides others, he had made away with his son Ariarathes by poison, as also with Alcæus the Sardian, for having robbed him of the first honors in a horse race. There were several judgments upon the interpretation of dreams, which either he himself or some of his mistresses had had; and besides these, there was a series of wanton letters to and from his concubine Monime. Theophanes tells us that there was found also an address by Rutilius, in which he attempted to exasperate him to the slaughter of all the Romans in Asia; though most men justly conjecture this to be a malicious invention of Theophanes, who probably hated Rutilius because he was a man in nothing like himself; or perhaps it might be to gratify Pompey, whose father is described by Rutilius in his history as the vilest man alive.

From thence Pompey came to the city of Amisus, where his passion for glory put him into a position which might be called a punishment on himself. For whereas he had often sharply reproached Lucullus, in that while the enemy was still living he had taken upon him to issue decrees, and distribute rewards and honors, as conquerors usually do only when the war is brought to an end, yet now was he himself, while Mithridates was paramount in the kingdom of Bosphorus, and at the head of a powerful army, as if all were ended, just doing the same thing, regulating the provinces, and distributing rewards, many great commanders and princes having flocked to him, together with no less than twelve barbarian kings; insomuch that to gratify these other kings, when he wrote to the king of Parthia, he would not condescend, as others used to do, in the superscription of his letter, to give him his title of king of kings.

Moreover, he had a great desire and emulation to occupy Syria, and to march through Arabia to the Red Sea, that he might thus extend his conquests every way to the great ocean that encompasses the habitable earth; as in Africa he was the first Roman that advanced his victories to the ocean; and again in Spain he made the Atlantic Sea the limit of the empire; and then thirdly, in his late pursuit of the Albanians, he had wanted but little of reaching the Hyrcanian Sea. Accordingly he raised his camp, designing to bring the Red Sea within the circuit of his expedition; especially as he saw how difficult it was to hunt after Mithridates with an army, and that he would prove a worse enemy flying than fighting. But yet he declared that he would leave a sharper enemy behind him than himself, namely, famine; and therefore he appointed a guard of ships to lie in wait for the merchants that sailed to

Bosphorus, death being the penalty for any who should attempt to carry provisions thither.

Then he set forward with the greatest part of his army, and in his march casually fell in with several dead bodies, still uninterred, of those soldiers who were slain with Triarius in his unfortunate engagement with Mithridates; these he buried splendidly and honorably. The neglect of whom, it is thought, caused, as much as anything, the hatred that was felt against Lucullus, and alienated the affections of the soldiers from him. Pompey having now by his forces under the command of Afranius subdued the Arabians about the mountain Amanus, himself entered Syria, and finding it destitute of any natural and lawful prince, reduced it into the form of a province, as a possession of the people of Rome. He conquered also Judæa, and took its king, Aristobulus, captive. Some cities he built anew, and to others he gave their liberty, chastising their tyrants. Most part of the time that he spent there was employed in the administration of justice, in deciding controversies of kings and states; and where he himself could not be present in person, he gave commissions to his friends, and sent them. Thus when there arose a difference betwixt the Armenians and Parthians about some territory, and the judgment was referred to him, he gave a power by commission to three judges and arbiters to hear and determine the controversy. For the reputation of his power was great; nor was the fame of his justice and clemency inferior to that of his power, and served indeed as a veil for a multitude of faults committed by his friends and familiars. For although it was not in his nature to check or chastise wrongdoers, yet he himself always treated those that had to do with him in such a manner that they submitted to endure with patience the acts of covetousness and oppression done by others.

Among these friends of his there was one Demetrius, who had the greatest influence with him of all; he was a freed slave, a youth of good understanding, but somewhat too insolent in his good fortune, of whom there goes this story. Cato, the philosopher, being as yet a very young man, but of great repute and a noble mind, took a journey of pleasure to Antioch, at a time when Pompey was not there, having a great desire to see the city. He, as his custom was, walked on foot, and his friends accompanied him on horseback; and seeing before the gates of the city a multitude dressed in white, the young men on one side of the road and the boys on the other, he was somewhat offended at it, imagining that it was officiously done in honor of him, which was more than he had any wish for. However, he desired his companions to alight and walk with him; but when they drew near, the master of the ceremonies in this procession came out with a garland and a rod in his hand and met them, inquiring where they had left Demetrius, and when he would come? Upon which Cato's companions burst out into laughter, but Cato said only, "Alas, poor city!" and passed by without any other answer. However, Pompey rendered Demetrius less odious to others by enduring his presumption and impertinence to himself. For it is reported how that Pompey, when he had invited his friends to an entertainment, would be very ceremonious in waiting till they all came and were placed, while Demetrius would be already stretched upon the couch as if he cared for no one, with his dress over his ears, hanging down from his head. Before his return into Italy, he had purchased the pleasantest country seat about Rome, with the finest walks and places for exercise, and there were sumptuous gardens, called by the name of Demetrius, while Pompey his master, up to his third triumph, was contented with an ordinary and simple habitation. Afterwards, it is true, when he had erected his famous and stately theater for the people of Rome, he built as a sort of appendix to it a house for himself, much more splendid than his former, and yet no object even this to excite men's envy, since he who came to be master of it after Pompey could not but express wonder and inquire where Pompey the Great used to sup. Such is the story told us.

The king of the Arabs near Petra, who had hitherto despised the power of the Romans, now began to be in great alarm at it, and sent letters to him promising to be at his commands, and to do whatever he should see fit to order. However, Pompey having a desire to confirm and keep him in the same mind, marched forwards for Petra, an expedition not altogether irreprehensible in the opinion of many; who thought it a mere running away from their proper duty, the pursuit of Mithridates, Rome's ancient and inveterate enemy, who was now rekindling the war once more, and making preparations, it was reported, to lead his army through Scythia and Pæonia into Italy. Pompey, on the other side, judging it easier to destroy his forces in battle than to seize his person in flight, resolved not to tire himself out in a vain pursuit, but rather to spend his leisure upon another enemy, as a sort of digression in the meanwhile. But fortune resolved the doubt, for when he was now not far from Petra, and had pitched his tents and encamped for that day, as he was taking exercise with his horse outside the camp, couriers came riding up from Pontus, bringing good news, as was known at once by the heads of their javelins, which it is the custom to carry crowned with branches of laurel. The soldiers, as soon as they saw them, flocked immediately to Pompey, who, notwithstanding, was minded to finish his exercise; but when they began to be clamorous and importunate, he alighted from his horse, and taking the letters went before them into the camp.

Now there being no tribunal erected there, not even that military substitute for one which they make by cutting up thick turfs of earth and piling them one upon another, they, through eagerness and impatience, heaped up a pile of packsaddles, and Pompey, standing upon that, told them the news of Mithridates's death, how that he had himself put an end to his life upon the revolt of his son Pharnaces, and that Pharnaces had taken all things there into his hands and possession, which he did, his letters said, in right of himself and the Romans. Upon this news the whole army, expressing their joy, as was to be expected, fell to sacrificing to the gods and feasting, as if in the person of Mithridates alone there had died many thousands of their enemies.

Pompey by this event having brought this war to its completion, with much more ease than was expected, departed forthwith out of Arabia, and passing rapidly through the intermediate provinces, he came at length to the city Amisus. There he received many presents brought from Pharnaces, with several dead bodies of the royal blood, and the corpse of Mithridates himself, which was not easy to be known by the face, for the physicians that embalmed him had not dried up his brain, but those who were curious to see him knew him by the scars there. Pompey himself would not endure to see him, but to deprecate the divine jealousy sent it away to the city of Sinope. He admired the richness of his robes no less than the size and splendor of his armor. His sword belt, however, which had cost four hundred talents, was stolen by Publius, and sold to Ariarathes; his tiara also, a piece of admirable workmanship, Gaius, the foster brother of Mithridates, gave secretly to Faustus, the son of Sylla, at his request. All which Pompey was ignorant of, but afterwards, when Pharnaces came to understand it, he severely punished those that embezzled them.

Pompey now having ordered all things, and established that province, took his journey homewards in greater pomp and with more festivity. For when he came to Mitylene, he gave the city their freedom upon the intercession of Theophanes, and was present at the contest, there periodically held, of the poets, who took at that time no other theme or subject than the actions of Pompey. He was extremely pleased with the theater itself, and had a model of it taken, intending to erect one in Rome on the same design, but larger and more magnificent. When he came to Rhodes, he attended the lectures of all the philosophers there, and gave to every one of them a talent. Posidonius has published the disputation which he held before him against Hermagoras the rhetorician, upon the subject of Invention in general. At Athens, also, he showed similar munificence to the philosophers, and gave fifty talents towards the repairing and beautifying the city. So that now by all these acts he well hoped to return into Italy in the greatest splendor and glory possible to man, and find his family as desirous to see him as he felt himself to come home to them. But that supernatural agency, whose province and charge it is always to mix some ingredient of evil with the greatest and most glorious goods of fortune, had for some time back been busy in his household, preparing him a sad welcome. For Mucia during his absence had dishonored his bed. Whilst he was abroad at a distance, he had refused all credence to the report; but when he drew nearer to Italy, where his thoughts were more at leisure to give consideration to the charge, he sent her a bill of divorce; but neither then in writing, nor afterwards by word of mouth, did he ever give a reason why he discharged her; the cause of it is mentioned in Cicero's epistles.

Rumors of every kind were scattered abroad about Pompey, and were carried to Rome before him, so that there was a great tumult and stir, as if he designed forthwith to march with his army into the city and establish himself securely as sole ruler. Crassus withdrew himself, together with his children and property, out of the city, either that he was really afraid, or that he counterfeited rather, as is most probable, to give credit to the calumny and exasperate the jealousy of the people. Pompey, therefore, as soon as he entered Italy, called a general muster of the army; and having made a suitable address and exchanged a kind farewell with his soldiers he commanded them to depart every man to his country and place of habitation, only taking care that they should not fail to meet again at his triumph. Thus the army being disbanded, and the news commonly reported, a wonderful result ensued. For when the cities saw Pompey the Great passing through the country unarmed, and with a small train of familiar friends only, as if he was returning from a journey of pleasure, not from his conquests, they came pouring out to display their affection for him, attending and conducting him to Rome with far greater forces than he disbanded; insomuch that if he had designed any movement or innovation in the state, he might have done it without his army.

Now, because the law permitted no commander to enter into the city before his triumph, he sent to the senate, entreating them as a favor to him to prorogue the election of consuls, that thus he might be able to attend and give countenance to Piso, one of the candidates. The request was resisted by Cato, and met with a refusal. However, Pompey could not but admire the liberty and boldness of speech which Cato alone had dared to use in the maintenance of law and justice. He therefore had a great desire to win him over, and purchase his friendship at any rate; and to that end, Cato having two nieces, Pompey asked for one in marriage for himself, the other for his son. But Cato looked unfavorably on the proposal, regarding it as a design for undermining his honesty, and in a manner bribing him by a family alliance; much to the displeasure of his wife and sister, who were indignant that he should reject a connection with Pompey the Great. About that time Pompey having a design of setting up Afranius for the consulship, gave a sum of money among the tribes for their votes, and people came and received it in his own gardens, a proceeding which, when it came to be generally known, excited great disapprobation, that he should thus, for the sake of men who could not obtain the honor by their own merits, make merchandise of an office which had been given to himself as the highest reward of his services. "Now," said Cato to his wife and sister, "had we contracted an alliance with Pompey, we had been allied to this dishonor too"; and this they could not but acknowledge, and allow his judgment of what was right and fitting to have been wiser and better than theirs.

The splendor and magnificence of Pompey's triumph was such that though it took up the space of two days, yet they were extremely straitened in time, so that of what was prepared for that pageantry, there was as much withdrawn as would have set out and adorned another triumph. In the first place, there were tables carried, inscribed with the names and titles of the nations over whom he triumphed, Pontus, Armenia, Cappadocia, Paphlagonia, Media, Colchis, the Iberians, the Albanians, Syria, Cilicia, and Mesopotamia, together with Phœnicia and Palestine, Judæa, Arabia, and all the power of the pirates subdued by sea and land. And in these different countries there appeared the capture of no less than one thousand fortified places, nor much less than nine hundred cities, together with eight hundred ships of the pirates, and the foundation of thirty-nine towns. Besides, there was set forth in these tables an account of all the tributes throughout the empire, and how that before these conquests the revenue amounted but to fifty millions, whereas from his acquisitions they had a revenue of eighty-five millions; and that in present payment he was bringing into the common treasury ready money, and gold and silver plate, and ornaments, to the value of twenty thousand talents, over and above what had been distributed among the soldiers, of whom he that had least had fifteen hundred drachmas for his share. The prisoners of war that were led in triumph, besides the chief pirates, were the son of Tigranes, king of Armenia, with his wife and daughter; as also Zosime, wife of King Tigranes himself, and Aristobulus, king of Judæa, the sister of King Mithridates, and her five sons, and some Scythian women. There were likewise the hostages of the Albanians and Iberians, and of the king of Commagene, besides a vast number of trophies, one for every battle in which he was conqueror, either himself in person or by his lieutenants. But that which seemed to be his greatest glory, being one which no other Roman ever attained to, was this, that he made his third triumph over the third division of the world. For others among the Romans had the honor of triumphing thrice, but his first triumph was over Africa, his second over Europe, and this last over Asia; so that he seemed in these three triumphs to have led the whole world captive.

As for his age, those who affect to make the parallel exact in all things betwixt him and Alexander the Great, do not allow him to have been quite thirty-four, whereas in truth at that time he was near forty. And well had it been for him had he terminated his life at this date, while he still enjoyed Alexander's fortune, since all his aftertime served only either to bring him prosperity that made him odious, or calamities too great to be retrieved. For that great authority which he had gained in the city by his merits he made use of only in patronizing the iniquities of others, so that by advancing their fortunes he detracted from his own glory, till at last he was overthrown even by the force and greatness of his own power. And as the strongest citadel or fort in a town, when it is taken by an enemy, does then afford the same strength to the foe as it had done to friends before, so Cæsar, after Pompey's aid had made him strong enough to defy his country, ruined and overthrew at last the power which had availed him against the rest. The course of things was as follows. Lucullus, when he returned out of Asia, where he had been treated with insult by Pompey, was received by the senate with great honor, which was yet increased when Pompey came home; to check whose ambition they encouraged him to assume the administration of the government, whereas he was now grown cold and disinclined to business, having given himself over to the pleasures of ease and the enjoyment of a splendid fortune. However, he began for the time to exert himself against Pompey, attacked him sharply, and succeeded in having his own acts and decrees, which were repealed by Pompey, reestablished, and, with the assistance of Cato, gained the superiority in the senate.

Pompey having fallen from his hopes in such an unworthy repulse, was forced to fly to the tribunes of the people for refuge, and to attach himself to the young men, among whom was Clodius, the vilest and most impudent wretch alive, who took him about, and exposed him as a tool to the people, carrying him up and down among the throngs in the marketplace, to countenance those laws and speeches which he made to cajole the people and ingratiate himself. And at last, for his reward, he demanded of Pompey, as if he had not disgraced, but done him great kindness, that he should forsake (as in the end he did forsake) Cicero, his friend, who on many public occasions had done him the greatest service. And so when Cicero was in danger, and implored his aid, he would not admit him into his presence, but shutting up his gates against those that came to mediate for him, slipped out at a back door, whereupon Cicero, fearing the result of his trial, departed privately from Rome.

About that time Cæsar, returning from military service, started a course of policy which brought him great present favor, and much increased his power for the future, and proved extremely destructive both to Pompey and the commonwealth. For now he stood candidate for his first consulship, and well observing the enmity betwixt Pompey and

Crassus, and finding that by joining with one he should make the other his enemy, he endeavored by all means to reconcile them, an object in itself honorable and tending to the public good, but, as he undertook it, a mischievous and subtle intrigue. For he well knew that opposite parties or factions in a commonwealth, like passengers in a boat, serve to trim and balance the unready motions of power there; whereas if they combine and come all over to one side, they cause a shock which will be sure to overset the vessel and carry down everything. And therefore Cato wisely told those who charged all the calamities of Rome upon the disagreement betwixt Pompey and Cæsar that they were in error in charging all the crime upon the last cause; for it was not their discord and enmity, but their unanimity and friendship, that gave the first and greatest blow to the commonwealth.

Cæsar, being thus elected consul, began at once to make an interest with the poor and meaner sort, by preferring and establishing laws for planting colonies and dividing lands, lowering the dignity of his office, and turning his consulship into a sort of tribuneship rather. And when Bibulus, his colleague, opposed him, and Cato was prepared to second Bibulus, and assist him vigorously, Cæsar brought Pompey upon the hustings, and addressing him in the sight of the people, demanded his opinion upon the laws that were proposed. Pompey gave his approbation. "Then," said Cæsar, "in case any man should offer violence to these laws, will you be ready to give assistance to the people?" "Yes," replied Pompey, "I shall be ready, and against those that threaten the sword, I will appear with sword and buckler." Nothing ever was said or done by Pompey up to that day that seemed more insolent or overbearing; so that his friends endeavored to apologize for it as a word spoken inadvertently; but by his actions afterwards it appeared plainly that he was totally devoted to Cæsar's service. For on a sudden, contrary to all expectation, he married Julia, the daughter of Cæsar, who had been affianced before and was to be married within a few days to Cæpio. And to appease Cæpio's wrath, he gave him his own daughter in marriage, who had been espoused before to Faustus, the son of Sylla. Cæsar himself married Calpurnia, the daughter of Piso.

Upon this Pompey, filling the city with soldiers, carried all things by force as he pleased. As Bibulus, the consul, was going to the forum, accompanied by Lucullus and Cato, they fell upon him on a sudden and broke his rods; and somebody threw a vessel of ordure upon the head of Bibulus himself; and two tribunes of the people, who escorted him, were desperately wounded in the fray. And thus having cleared the forum of all their adversaries, they got their bill for the division of lands established and passed into an act; and not only so, but the whole populace, being taken with this bait, became totally at their devotion, inquiring into nothing and without a word giving their suffrages to whatever they propounded. Thus they confirmed all those acts and decrees of Pompey which were questioned and contested by Lucullus; and to Cæsar they granted the provinces of Gaul, both within and without the Alps, together with Illyricum, for five years, and likewise an army of four entire legions; then they created consuls for the year ensuing, Piso, the father-in-law of Cæsar, and Gabinius, the most extravagant of Pompey's flatterers.

During all these transactions, Bibulus kept close within doors, nor did he appear publicly in person for the space of eight months together, notwithstanding he was consul, but sent out proclamations full of bitter invectives and accusations against them both. Cato turned prophet, and as if he had been possessed with a spirit of divination, did nothing else in the senate but foretell what evils should befall the commonwealth and Pompey. Lucullus pleaded old age, and retired to take his ease, as superannuated for affairs of state; which gave occasion to the saying of Pompey, that the fatigues of luxury were not more seasonable for an old man than those of government. Which in truth proved a reflection upon himself; for he not long after let his fondness for his young wife seduce him also into effeminate habits. He gave all his time to her, and passed his days in her company in country houses and gardens, paying no heed to what was going on in the forum. Insomuch that Clodius, who was then tribune of the people, began to despise him, and engage in the most audacious attempts. For when he had banished Cicero, and sent away Cato into Cyprus under pretence of military duty, and when Cæsar was gone upon his expedition to Gaul, finding the populace now looking to him as the leader who did everything according to their pleasure, he attempted forthwith to repeal some of Pompey's decrees; he took Tigranes, the captive, out of prison, and kept him about him as his companion; and commenced actions against several of Pompey's friends, thus designing to try the extent of his power. At last, upon a time when Pompey was present at the hearing of a certain cause, Clodius, accompanied with a crowd of profligate and impudent ruffians, standing up in a place above the rest, put questions to the populace as follows: "Who is the dissolute general? who is the man that seeks another man? who scratches his head with one finger?" and the rabble, upon the signal of his shaking his gown, with a great shout to every question, like singers making responses in a chorus, made answer, "Pompey."

This indeed was no small annoyance to Pompey, who was quite unaccustomed to hear anything ill of himself, and unexperienced altogether in such encounters; and he was yet more vexed when he saw that the senate rejoiced at this foul usage, and regarded it as a just punishment upon him for his treachery to Cicero. But when it came even to blows and wounds in the forum, and that one of Clodius's bondslaves was apprehended creeping through the crowd towards Pompey with a sword in his hand, Pompey laid hold of this pretense, though perhaps otherwise apprehensive of Clodius's insolence and bad language, and never appeared again in the forum during all the time he was tribune, but kept close at home, and passed his time in consulting with his friends by what means he might best allay the displeasure of the senate and nobles against him. Among other expedients, Culleo advised the divorce of Julia, and to abandon Cæsar's friendship to gain that of the senate; this he would not hearken to. Others again advised him to call home Cicero from banishment, a man who was always the great adversary of Clodius, and as great a favorite of the senate; to this he was easily persuaded. And therefore he brought Cicero's brother into the forum, attended with a strong party, to petition for his return; where, after a warm dispute, in which several were wounded and some slain, he got the victory over Clodius.

No sooner was Cicero returned home upon this decree, but immediately he used his efforts to reconcile the senate to Pompey; and by speaking in favor of the law upon the importation of corn, did again, in effect, make Pompey sovereign lord of all the Roman possessions by sea and land. For by that law there were placed under his control all ports, markets, and storehouses, and, in short, all the concerns both of the merchants and the husbandmen; which gave occasion to the charge brought against it by Clodius, that the law was not made because of the scarcity of corn, but the scarcity of corn was made that they might pass a law whereby that power of his, which was now grown feeble and consumptive, might be revived again, and Pompey reinstated in a new empire. Others look upon it as a politic device of Spinther, the consul, whose design it was to secure Pompey in a greater authority, that he himself might be sent in assistance to King Ptolemy. However, it is certain that Canidius, the tribune, preferred a law to dispatch Pompey in the character of an ambassador, without an army, attended only with two lictors, as a mediator betwixt the king and his subjects of Alexandria.

Neither did this proposal seem unacceptable to Pompey, though the senate cast it out upon the specious pretense that they were unwilling to hazard his person. However, there were found several writings scattered about the forum and near the senate house intimating how grateful it would be to Ptolemy to have Pompey appointed for his general instead of Spinther. And Timagenes even asserts that Ptolemy went away and left Egypt, not out of necessity, but purely upon the persuasion of Theophanes, who was anxious to give Pompey the opportunity for holding a new command and gaining further wealth. But Theophanes's want of honesty does not go so far to make this story credible as does Pompey's own nature, which was averse, with all its ambition, to such base and disingenuous acts, to render it improbable.

Thus Pompey, being appointed chief purveyor, and having within his administration and management all the corn trade, sent abroad his factors and agents into all quarters, and he himself sailing into Sicily, Sardinia and Africa, collected vast stores of corn. He was just ready to set sail upon his voyage home, when a great storm arose upon the sea, and the ships' commanders doubted whether it were safe. Upon which Pompey himself went first aboard, and bid the mariners weigh anchor, declaring with a loud voice that there was a necessity to sail, but no necessity to live. So that with this spirit and courage, and having met with favorable fortune, he made a prosperous return, and filled the markets with corn, and the sea with ships. So much so that this great plenty and abundance of provisions yielded a sufficient supply, not only to the city of Rome, but even to other places too, dispersing itself, like waters from a spring, into all quarters.

Meantime Cæsar grew great and famous with his wars in Gaul, and while in appearance he seemed far distant from Rome, entangled in the affairs of the Belgians, Suevians, and Britons, in truth he was working craftily by secret practices in the midst of the people, and countermining Pompey in all political matters of most importance. He himself, with his army close about him, as if it had been his own body, not with mere views of conquest over the barbarians, but as though his contests with them were but mere sports and exercises of the chase, did his utmost with this training and discipline to make it invincible and alarming. And in the meantime his gold and silver and other spoils and treasure which he took from the enemy in his conquests, he sent to Rome in presents, tempting people with his gifts, and aiding ædiles, prætors, and consuls, as also their wives, in their expenses, and thus purchasing himself numerous friends. Insomuch, that when he passed back again over the Alps, and took up his winter quarters in the city of Luca, there flocked to him an infinite number of men and women, striving who should get first to him, two hundred senators included, among whom were Pompey and Crassus; so that there were to be seen at once before Cæsar's door no less than six score rods of proconsuls and prætors. The rest of his addressers he sent all away full fraught with hopes and money; but with Crassus and Pompey he entered into special articles of agreement, that they should stand candidates for the consulship next year; that Cæsar on his part should send a number of his soldiers to give their votes at the election; that as soon as they were elected, they should use their interest to have the command of some provinces and legions assigned to themselves, and that Cæsar should have his present charge confirmed to him for five years more. When these arrangements came to be generally known, great indignation was excited among the chief men in Rome; and Marcellinus, in an open assembly of the people, demanded of them both, whether they designed to sue for the consulship or no. And being urged by the people for their answer, Pompey spoke first, and told them, perhaps he would sue for it, perhaps he would not. Crassus was more temperate, and said, that he would do what should be judged most agreeable with the interest of the commonwealth; and when Marcellinus persisted in his attack on Pompey, and spoke, as it was thought, with some vehemence, Pompey remarked that Marcellinus was certainly the unfairest of men, to show him no gratitude for having thus made him an orator out of a mute, and converted him from a hungry starveling into a man so full-fed that he could not contain himself.

Most of the candidates nevertheless abandoned their canvass for the consulship; Cato alone persuaded and encouraged Lucius Domitius not to desist, "since," said he, "the contest now is not for office, but for liberty against tyrants and usurpers." Therefore those of Pompey's party, fearing this inflexible constancy in Cato, by which he kept with him the whole senate, lest by this he should likewise pervert and draw after him all the well-affected part of the commonalty, resolved to withstand Domitius at once, and to prevent his entrance into the forum. To this end, therefore, they sent in a band of armed men, who slew the torch-bearer of Domitius, as he was leading the way before him, and put all the rest to flight; last of all, Cato himself retired, having received a wound in his right arm while defending Domitius. Thus by these means and practices they obtained the consulship; neither did they behave themselves with more decency in their further proceedings; but in the first place, when the people were choosing Cato prætor, and just ready with their votes for the poll, Pompey broke up the assembly, upon a pretext of some inauspicious appearance, and having gained the tribes by money, they publicly proclaimed Vatinius prætor. Then, in pursuance of their covenants with Cæsar, they introduced several laws by Trebonius, the tribune, continuing Cæsar's commission to another five years' charge of his province; to Crassus there were appointed Syria and the Parthian war; and to Pompey himself, all Africa, together with both Spains, and four legions of soldiers, two of which he lent to Cæsar upon his request for the wars in Gaul.

Crassus, upon the expiration of his consulship, departed forthwith into his province; but Pompey spent some time in Rome, upon the opening or dedication of his theater, where he treated the people with all sorts of games, shows, and exercises, in gymnastics alike and in music. There was likewise the hunting or baiting of wild beasts, and combats with them, in which five hundred lions were slain; but above all, the battle of elephants was a spectacle full of horror and amazement.

These entertainments brought him great honor and popularity; but on the other side he created no less envy to himself, in that he committed the government of his provinces and legions into the hands of friends as his lieutenants, whilst he himself was going about and spending his time with his wife in all the places of amusement in Italy; whether it were he was so fond of her himself, or she so fond of him, and he unable to distress her by going away, for this also is stated. And the love displayed by this young wife for her elderly husband was a matter of general note, to be attributed, it would seem, to his constancy in married life, and to his dignity of manner, which in familiar intercourse was tempered with grace and gentleness, and was particularly attractive to women, as even Flora, the courtesan, may be thought good enough evidence to prove.

It once happened in a public assembly, as they were at an election of the ædiles, that the people came to blows, and several about Pompey were slain, so that he, finding himself all bloody, ordered a change of apparel; but the servants who brought home his clothes, making a great bustle and hurry about the house, it chanced that the young lady, who was then with child, saw his gown all stained with blood; upon which she dropped immediately into a swoon, and was hardly brought to life again; however, what with her fright and suffering, she fell into labor and miscarried; even those who chiefly censured Pompey for his friendship to Cæsar could not reprove him for his affection to so attached a wife. Afterwards she was great again, and brought to bed of a daughter, but died in childbed; neither did the infant outlive her mother many days. Pompey had prepared all things for the interment of her corpse at his house near Alba, but the people seized upon it by force, and performed the solemnities in the field of Mars, rather in compassion for the young lady, than in favor either for Pompey or Cæsar; and yet of these two, the people seemed at that time to pay Cæsar a greater share of honor in his absence, than to Pompey, though he was present.

For the city now at once began to roll and swell, so to say, with the stir of the coming storm. Things everywhere were in a state of agitation, and everybody's discourse tended to division, now that death had put an end to that relation which hitherto had been a disguise rather than restraint to the ambition of these men. Besides, not long after came messengers from Parthia with intelligence of the death of Crassus there, by which another safeguard against civil war was removed, since both Cæsar and Pompey kept their eyes on Crassus, and awe of him held them together more or less within the bounds of fair dealing all his lifetime. But when fortune had taken away this second, whose province it might have been to revenge the quarrel of the conquered, you might then say with the comic poet—

"The combatants are waiting to begin,
  Smearing their hands with dust and oiling each his skin."

So inconsiderable a thing is fortune in respect of human nature, and so insufficient to give content to a covetous mind, that an empire of that mighty extent and sway could not satisfy the ambition of two men; and though they knew and had read, that—

"The gods, when they divided out 'twixt three,
  This massive universe, heaven, hell, and sea,
  Each one sat down contented on his throne,
  And undisturbed each god enjoys his own,"

yet they thought the whole Roman empire not sufficient to contain them, though they were but two.

Pompey once in an oration to the people told them that he had always come into office before he expected he should, and that he had always left it sooner than they expected he would; and, indeed, the disbanding of all his armies witnessed as much. Yet when he perceived that Cæsar would not so willingly discharge his forces, he endeavored to strengthen himself against him by offices and commands in the city; but beyond this he showed no desire for any change, and would not seem to distrust, but rather to disregard and contemn him. And when he saw how they bestowed the places of government quite contrary to his wishes, because the citizens were bribed in their elections, he let things take their course, and allowed the city to be left without any government at all. Hereupon there was mention straightaway made of appointing a dictator. Lucilius, a tribune of the people, was the man who first adventured to propose it, urging the people to make Pompey dictator. But the tribune was in danger of being turned out of his office by the opposition that Cato made against it. And for Pompey, many of his friends appeared and excused him, alleging that he never was desirous of that government, neither would he accept of it. And when Cato therefore made a speech in commendation of Pompey and exhorted him to support the cause of good order in the commonwealth, he could not for shame but yield to it, and so for the present Domitius and Messala were elected consuls. But shortly afterwards, when there was another anarchy, or vacancy in the government, and the talk of a dictator was much louder and more general than before, those of Cato's party, fearing lest they should be forced to appoint Pompey, thought it policy to keep him from that arbitrary and tyrannical power by giving him an office of more legal authority. Bibulus himself, who was Pompey's enemy, first gave his vote in the senate, that Pompey should be created consul alone; alleging, that by these means either the commonwealth would be freed from its present confusion, or that its bondage should be lessened by serving the worthiest. This was looked upon as a very strange opinion, considering the man that spoke it; and therefore on Cato's standing up, everybody expected that he would have opposed it; but after silence made, he said that he would never have been the author of that advice himself, but since it was propounded by another, his advice was to follow it, adding that any form of government was better than none at all; and that in a time so full of distraction, he thought no man fitter to govern than Pompey. This counsel was unanimously approved of, and a decree passed that Pompey should be made sole consul, with this clause, that if he thought it necessary to have a colleague, he might choose whom he pleased, provided it were not till after two months expired.

Thus was Pompey created and declared sole consul by Sulpicius, regent in this vacancy; upon which he made very cordial acknowledgments to Cato, professing himself much his debtor, and requesting his good advice in conducting the government; to this Cato replied that Pompey had no reason to thank him, for all that he had said was for the service of the commonwealth, not of Pompey; but that he would be always ready to give his advice privately, if he were asked for it; and if not, he should not fail to say what he thought in public. Such was Cato's conduct on all occasions.

On his return into the city Pompey married Cornelia, the daughter of Metellus Scipio, not a maiden, but lately left a widow by Publius, the son of Crassus, her first husband, who had been killed in Parthia. The young lady had other attractions besides those of youth and beauty; for she was highly educated, played well upon the lute, understood geometry, and had been accustomed to listen with profit to lectures on philosophy; all this, too, without in any degree becoming unamiable or pretentious, as sometimes young women do when they pursue such studies. Nor could any fault be found either with her father's family or reputation. The disparity of their ages was, however, not liked by everybody; Cornelia being in this respect a fitter match for Pompey's son. And wiser judges thought it rather a slight upon the commonwealth when he, to whom alone they had committed their broken fortunes, and from whom alone, as from their physician, they expected a cure to these distractions, went about crowned with garlands and celebrating his nuptial feasts; never considering that his very consulship was a public calamity, which would never have been given him, contrary to the rules of law, had his country been in a flourishing state. Afterwards, however, he took cognizance of the cases of those that had obtained offices by gifts and bribery, and enacted laws and ordinances, setting forth the rules of judgment by which they should be arraigned; and regulating all things with gravity and justice, he restored security, order, and silence to their courts of judicature, himself giving his presence there with a band of soldiers. But when his father-in-law, Scipio, was accused, he sent for the three hundred and sixty judges to his house, and entreated them to be favorable to him; whereupon his accuser, seeing Scipio come into the court accompanied by the judges themselves, withdrew the prosecution. Upon this Pompey was very ill spoken of, and much worse in the case of Plancus; for whereas he himself had made a law, putting a stop to the practice of making speeches in praise of persons under trial, yet, notwithstanding this prohibition, he came into court and spoke openly in commendation of Plancus, insomuch that Cato, who happened to be one of the judges at that time, stopping his ears with his hands, told him he could not in conscience listen to commendations contrary to law. Cato upon this was refused, and set aside from being a judge, before sentence was given, but Plancus was condemned by the rest of the judges, to Pompey's dishonor. Shortly after, Hypsæus, a man of consular dignity, who was under accusation, waited for Pompey's return from his bath to his supper and, falling down at his feet, implored his favor; but he disdainfully passed him by, saying, that he did nothing else but spoil his supper. Such partiality was looked upon as a great fault in Pompey and highly condemned; however, he managed all things else discreetly, and having put the government in very good order, he chose his father-in-law to be his colleague in the consulship for the last five months. His provinces were continued to him for the term of four years longer, with a commission to take one thousand talents yearly out of the treasury for the payment of his army.

This gave occasion to some of Cæsar's friends to think it reasonable that some consideration should be had of him too, who had done such signal services in war, and fought so many battles for the empire, alleging that he deserved at least a second consulship, or to have the government of his province continued, that so he might command and enjoy in peace what he had obtained in war, and no successor come in to reap the fruits of his labor and carry off the glory of his actions. There arising some debate about this matter, Pompey took upon him, as it were out of kindness to Cæsar, to plead his cause, and allay any jealousy that was conceived against him, telling them that he had letters from Cæsar, expressing his desire for a successor, and his own discharge from the command; but it would be only right that they should give him leave to stand for the consulship though in his absence. But those of Cato's party withstood this, saying, that if he expected any favor from the citizens, he ought to leave his army and come in a private capacity to canvass for it. And Pompey's making no rejoinder, but letting it pass as a matter in which he was overruled, increased the suspicion of his real feelings towards Cæsar. Presently, also, under pretense of a war with Parthia, he sent for his two legions which he had lent him. However, Cæsar, though he well knew why they were asked for, sent them home very liberally rewarded.

About that time Pompey recovered of a dangerous fit of sickness which seized him at Naples, where the whole city, upon the suggestion of Praxagoras, made sacrifices of thanksgiving to the gods for his recovery. The neighboring towns likewise happening to follow their example, the thing then went its course throughout all Italy, so that there was not a city, either great or small, that did not feast and rejoice for many days together. And the company of those that came from all parts to meet him was so numerous, that no place was able to contain them, but the villages, seaport towns, and the very highways, were all full of people, feasting and sacrificing to the gods. Nay, many went to meet him with garlands on their heads, and flambeaux in their hands, casting flowers and nosegays upon him as he went along; so that this progress of his, and reception, was one of the noblest and most glorious sights imaginable. And yet it is thought that this very thing was not one of the least causes and occasions of the civil war. For Pompey, yielding to a feeling of exultation, which in the greatness of the present display of joy lost sight of more solid grounds of consideration, and abandoning that prudent temper which had guided him hitherto to a safe use of all his good fortune and his successes, gave himself up to an extravagant confidence in his own, and contempt of Cæsar's power; insomuch that he thought neither force of arms nor care necessary against him, but that he could pull him down much easier than he had set him up. Besides this, Appius, under whose command those legions which Pompey lent to Cæsar were returned, coming lately out of Gaul, spoke slightingly of Cæsar's actions there, and spread scandalous reports about him, at the same time telling Pompey that he was unacquainted with his own strength and reputation, if he made use of any other forces against Cæsar than Cæsar's own; for such was the soldiers' hatred to Cæsar, and their love to Pompey so great, that they would all come over to him upon his first appearance. By these flatteries Pompey was so puffed up, and led on into such a careless security, that he could not choose but laugh at those who seemed to fear a war; and when some were saying, that if Cæsar should march against the city, they could not see what forces there were to resist him, he replied with a smile, bidding them be in no concern, "for," said he, "whenever I stamp with my foot in any part of Italy, there will rise up forces enough in an instant, both horse and foot."

Cæsar, on the other side, was more and more vigorous in his proceedings, himself always at hand about the frontiers of Italy, and sending his soldiers continually into the city to attend all elections with their votes. Besides, he corrupted several of the magistrates, and kept them in his pay; among others, Paulus, the consul, who was brought over by a bribe of one thousand and five hundred talents; and Curio, tribune of the people, by a discharge of the debts with which he was overwhelmed; together with Mark Antony, who, out of friendship to Curio, had become bound with him in the same obligations for them all. And it was stated as a fact that a centurion of Cæsar's, waiting at the senate house and hearing that the senate refused to give him a longer term of his government, clapped his hand upon his sword, and said, "But this shall give it." And indeed all his practices and preparations seemed to bear this appearance. Curio's demands, however, and requests in favor of Cæsar, were more popular in appearance; for he desired one of these two things, either that Pompey also should be called upon to resign his army, or that Cæsar's should not be taken away from him; for if both of them became private persons, both would be satisfied with simple justice; or if both retained their present power, each being a match for the other, they would be contented with what they already had; but he that weakens one, does at the same time strengthen the other, and so doubles that very strength and power which he stood in fear of before.

Marcellus, the consul, replied nothing to all this, but that Cæsar was a robber, and should be proclaimed an enemy to the state, if he did not disband his army. However, Curio, with the assistance of Antony and Piso, prevailed, that the matter in debate should be put to the question, and decided by vote in the senate. So that it being ordered upon the question for those to withdraw, who were of opinion that Cæsar only should lay down his army and Pompey command, the majority withdrew. But when it was ordered again for those to withdraw, whose vote was that both should lay down their arms and neither command, there were but twenty-two for Pompey, all the rest remained on Curio's side. Whereupon he, as one proud of his conquest, leaped out in triumph among the people, who received him with as great tokens of joy, clapping their hands and crowning him with garlands and flowers. Pompey was not then present in the senate, because it is not lawful for generals in command of an army to come into the city. But Marcellus, rising up, said that he would not sit there hearing speeches, when he saw ten legions already passing the Alps on their march toward the city, but on his own authority would send someone to oppose them in defense of the country.

Upon this the city went into mourning, as in a public calamity, and Marcellus, accompanied by the senate, went solemnly through the forum to meet Pompey, and made him this address: "I hereby give you orders, O Pompey, to defend your country, to employ the troops you now command, and to levy more." Lentulus, consul elect for the year following, spoke to the same purpose. Antony, however, contrary to the will of the senate, having in a public assembly read a letter of Cæsar's, containing various plausible overtures such as were likely to gain the common people, proposing, namely, that both Pompey and he, quitting their governments and dismissing their armies, should submit to the judgment of the people, and give an account of their actions before them, the consequence was that when Pompey began to make his levies, he found himself disappointed in his expectations. Some few, indeed, came in, but those very unwillingly; others would not answer to their names, and the generality cried out for peace. Lentulus, notwithstanding he was now entered upon his consulship, would not assemble the senate; but Cicero, who was lately returned from Cilicia, labored for a reconciliation, proposing that Cæsar should leave his province of Gaul and army, reserving two legions only, together with the government of Illyricum, and should thus be put in nomination for a second consulship. Pompey disliking this motion, Cæsar's friends were contented that he should surrender one of the two; but Lentulus still opposing, and Cato crying out that Pompey did ill to be deceived again, the reconciliation did not take effect.

In the meantime, news was brought that Cæsar had occupied Ariminum, a great city in Italy, and was marching directly towards Rome with all his forces. But this latter was altogether false, for he had no more with him at that time than three hundred horse and five thousand foot; and he did not mean to tarry for the body of his army, which lay beyond the Alps, choosing rather to fall in on a sudden upon his enemies, while they were in confusion, and did not expect him, than to give them time, and fight them after they had made preparations. For when he came to the banks of the Rubicon, a river that made the bounds of his province, there he made a halt, pausing a little, and considering, we may suppose, with himself the greatness of the enterprise which he had undertaken; then, at last, like men that are throwing themselves headlong from some precipice into a vast abyss, having shut, as it were, his mind's eyes and put away from his sight the idea of danger, he merely uttered to those near him in Greek the words, "Anerriphtho kubos" (let the die be cast), and led his army through it. No sooner was the news arrived, but there was an uproar throughout all the city, and a consternation in the people even to astonishment, such as never was known in Rome before; all the senate ran immediately to Pompey, and the magistrates followed. And when Tullus made inquiry about his legions and forces, Pompey seemed to pause a little, and answered with some hesitation that he had those two legions ready that Cæsar sent back, and that out of the men who had been previously enrolled he believed he could shortly make up a body of thirty thousand men. On which Tullus, crying out aloud, "O Pompey, you have deceived us," gave his advice to send off a deputation to Cæsar. Favonius, a man of fair character, except that he used to suppose his own petulance and abusive talking a copy of Cato's straightforwardness, bade Pompey stamp upon the ground, and call forth the forces he had promised. But Pompey bore patiently with this unseasonable raillery; and on Cato putting him in mind of what he had foretold from the very beginning about Cæsar, made this answer only, that Cato indeed had spoken more like a prophet, but he had acted more like a friend. Cato then advised them to choose Pompey general with absolute power and authority, saying that the same men who do great evils know best how to cure them. He himself went his way forthwith into Sicily, the province that was allotted him, and all the rest of the senators likewise departed every one to his respective government.

Thus all Italy in a manner being up in arms, no one could say what was best to be done. For those that were without came from all parts flocking into the city; and they who were within, seeing the confusion and disorder so great there, all good things impotent, and disobedience and insubordination grown too strong to be controlled by the magistrates, were quitting it as fast as the others came in. Nay, it was so far from being possible to allay their fears, that they would not suffer Pompey to follow out his own judgment, but every man pressed and urged him according to his particular fancy, whether it proceeded from doubt, fear, grief, or any meaner passion; so that even in the same day quite contrary counsels were acted upon. Then, again, it was as impossible to have any good intelligence of the enemy; for what each man heard by chance upon a flying rumor he would report for truth, and exclaim against Pompey if he did not believe it. Pompey, at length, seeing such a confusion in Rome, determined with himself to put an end to their clamors by his departure, and therefore commanding all the senate to follow him, and declaring that whosoever tarried behind should be judged a confederate of Cæsar's, about the dusk of the evening he went out and left the city. The consuls also followed after in a hurry, without offering the sacrifices to the gods usual before a war. But in all this, Pompey himself had the glory that, in the midst of such calamities, he had so much of men's love and goodwill. For though many found fault with the conduct of the war, yet no man hated the general; and there were more to be found of those that went out of Rome because that they could not forsake Pompey, than of those that fled for love of liberty.

Some few days after Pompey was gone out, Cæsar came into the city, and made himself master of it, treating everyone with a great deal of courtesy, and appeasing their fears, except only Metellus, one of the tribunes; on whose refusing to let him take any money out of the treasury, Cæsar threatened him with death, adding words yet harsher than the threat, that it was far easier for him to do it than say it. By this means removing Metellus, and taking what moneys were of use for his occasions, he set forwards in pursuit of Pompey, endeavoring with all speed to drive him out of Italy before his army, that was in Spain, could join him.

But Pompey arriving at Brundusium, and having plenty of ships there, bade the two consuls embark immediately, and with them shipped thirty cohorts of foot, bound before him for Dyrrhachium. He sent likewise his father-in-law Scipio, and Cnæus his son, into Syria, to provide and fit out a fleet there; himself in the meantime having blocked up the gates, placed his lightest soldiers as guards upon the walls; and giving express orders that the citizens should keep within doors, he dug up all the ground inside the city, cutting trenches, and fixing stakes and palisades throughout all the streets of the city, except only two that led down to the seaside. Thus in three days' space having with ease put all the rest of his army on shipboard, he suddenly gave the signal to those that guarded the walls, who nimbly repairing to the ships were received on board and carried off. Cæsar meantime perceiving their departure by seeing the walls unguarded, hastened after, and in the heat of pursuit was all but entangled himself among the stakes and trenches. But the Brundusians discovering the danger to him, and showing him the way, he wheeled about, and taking a circuit round the city, made towards the haven, where he found all the ships on their way, excepting only two vessels that had but a few soldiers aboard.

Most are of opinion that this departure of Pompey's is to be counted among the best of his military performances, but Cæsar himself could not but wonder that he, who was thus ingarrisoned in a city well fortified, who was in expectation of his forces from Spain, and was master of the sea besides, should leave and abandon Italy. Cicero accuses him of imitating the conduct of Themistocles, rather than of Pericles, when the circumstances were more like those of Pericles than they were like those of Themistocles. However, it appeared plainly, and Cæsar showed it by his actions, that he was in great fear of delay, for when he had taken Numerius, a friend of Pompey's, prisoner, he sent him as an ambassador to Brundusium, with offers of peace and reconciliation upon equal terms; but Numerius sailed away with Pompey. And now Cæsar, having become master of all Italy in sixty days, without a drop of blood shed, had a great desire forthwith to follow Pompey; but being destitute of shipping, he was forced to divert his course and march into Spain, designing to bring over Pompey's forces there to his own.

In the meantime Pompey raised a mighty army both by sea and land. As for his navy, it was irresistible. For there were five hundred men-of-war, besides an infinite company of light vessels, Liburnians, and others; and for his land forces, the cavalry made up a body of seven thousand horse, the very flower of Rome and Italy, men of family, wealth, and high spirit; but the infantry was a mixture of unexperienced soldiers drawn from different quarters, and these he exercised and trained near Berœa, where he quartered his army; himself noways slothful, but performing all his exercises as if he had been in the flower of his youth, conduct which raised the spirits of his soldiers extremely. For it was no small encouragement for them to see Pompey the Great, sixty years of age wanting two, at one time handling his arms among the foot, then again mounted among the horse, drawing out his sword with ease in full career, and sheathing it up as easily; and in darting the javelin, showing not only skill and dexterity in hitting the mark, but also strength and activity in throwing it so far that few of the young men went beyond him.

Several kings and princes of nations came thither to him, and there was a concourse of Roman citizens who had held the magistracies, so numerous that they made up a complete senate. Labienus forsook his old friend Cæsar, whom he had served throughout all his wars in Gaul, and came over to Pompey; and Brutus, son to that Brutus that was put to death in Gaul, a man of a high spirit, and one that to that day had never so much as saluted or spoke to Pompey, looking upon him as the murderer of his father, came then and submitted himself to him as the defender of their liberty. Cicero likewise, though he had written and advised otherwise, yet was ashamed not to be accounted in the number of those that would hazard their lives and fortunes for the safeguard of their country. There came to him also into Macedonia, Tidius Sextius, a man extremely old, and lame of one leg; so that others indeed mocked and laughed at the spectacle, but Pompey, as soon as he saw him, rose and ran to meet him, esteeming it no small testimony in his favor, when men of such age and infirmities should rather choose to be with him in danger than in safety at home. Afterwards in a meeting of their senate they passed a decree, on the motion of Cato, that no Roman citizen should be put to death but in battle, and that they should not sack or plunder any city that was subject to the Roman empire, a resolution which gained Pompey's party still greater reputation, insomuch that those who were noways at all concerned in the war, either because they dwelt afar off, or were thought incapable of giving help, were yet, in their good wishes, upon his side, and in all their words, so far as that went, supported the good or just cause, as they called it; esteeming those as enemies to the gods and men that wished not victory to Pompey.

Neither was Pompey's clemency such but that Cæsar likewise showed himself as merciful a conqueror; for when he had taken and overthrown all Pompey's forces in Spain, he gave them easy terms, leaving the commanders at their liberty, and taking the common soldiers into his own pay. Then repassing the Alps, and making a running march through Italy, he came to Brundusium about the winter solstice, and crossing the sea there, landed at the port of Oricum. And having Jubius, an intimate friend of Pompey's, with him as his prisoner, he dispatched him to Pompey with an invitation that they, meeting together in a conference, should disband both their armies within three days, and renewing their former friendship with solemn oaths, should return together into Italy. Pompey looked upon this again as some new stratagem, and therefore marching down in all haste to the seacoast, possessed himself of all forts and places of strength suitable to encamp in, and to secure his land forces, as likewise of all ports and harbors commodious to receive any that came by sea, so that what wind soever blew, it must needs in some way or other be favorable to him, bringing in either provision, men, or money; while Cæsar, on the contrary, was so hemmed in both by sea and land that he was forced to desire battle, daily provoking the enemy, and assailing them in their very forts; and in these light skirmishes for the most part had the better. Once only he was dangerously overthrown, and was within a little of losing his whole army, Pompey having fought nobly, routing the whole force and killing two thousand on the spot. But either he was not able, or was afraid, to go on and force his way into their camp with them; so that Cæsar made the remark, that "Today the victory had been the enemy's, had there been anyone among them to gain it." Pompey's soldiers were so encouraged by this victory that they were eager now to have all put to the decision of a battle; but Pompey himself, though he wrote to distant kings, generals, and states in confederacy with him as a conqueror, yet was afraid to hazard the success of a battle, choosing rather by delays and distress of provisions to tire out a body of men who had never yet been conquered by force of arms, and had long been used to fight and conquer together; while their time of life, now an advanced one, which made them quickly weary of those other hardships of war, such as were long marches and frequent decampings, making trenches, and building fortifications, made them eager to come to close combat and venture a battle with all speed.

Pompey had all along hitherto by his persuasions pretty well quieted his soldiers; but after this last engagement, when Cæsar, for want of provisions, was forced to raise his camp, and passed through Athamania into Thessaly, it was impossible to curb or allay the heat of their spirits any longer. For all crying out with a general voice that Cæsar was fled, some were for pursuing and pressing upon him, others for returning into Italy; some there were that sent their friends and servants beforehand to Rome, to hire houses near the forum, that they might be in readiness to sue for offices; several of their own motion sailed off at once to Lesbos to carry to Cornelia (whom Pompey had conveyed thither to be in safety), the joyful news that the war was ended. And a senate being called and the matter being under debate, Afranius was of opinion that Italy should first be regained, for that it was the grand prize and crown of all the war; and they who were masters of that would quickly have at their devotion all the provinces of Sicily, Sardinia, Corsica, Spain, and Gaul; but what was of greatest weight and moment to Pompey, it was his own native country that lay near, reaching out her hand for his help; and certainly it could not be consistent with his honor to leave her thus exposed to all indignities, and in bondage under slaves and the flatterers of a tyrant. But Pompey himself, on the contrary, thought it neither honorable to fly a second time before Cæsar, and be pursued, when fortune had given him the advantage of a pursuit; nor indeed lawful before the gods to forsake Scipio and divers other men of consular dignity dispersed throughout Greece and Thessaly, who must necessarily fall into Cæsar's hands, together with large sums of money and numerous forces; and as to his care for the city of Rome, that would most eminently appear by removing the scene of war to a greater distance, and leaving her, without feeling the distress or even hearing the sound of these evils, to await in peace the return of whichever should be the victor.

With this determination, Pompey marched forwards in pursuit of Cæsar, firmly resolved with himself not to give him battle, but rather to besiege and distress him, by keeping close at his heels, and cutting him short. There were other reasons that made him continue this resolution, but especially because a saying that was current among the Romans serving in the cavalry came to his ear, to the effect that they ought to beat Cæsar as soon as possible, and then humble Pompey too. And some report it was for this reason that Pompey never employed Cato in any matter of consequence during the whole war, but now, when he pursued Cæsar, left him to guard his baggage by sea, fearing lest, if Cæsar should be taken off, he himself also by Cato's means not long after should be forced to give up his power.

Whilst he was thus slowly attending the motions of the enemy, he was exposed on all sides to outcries and imputations of using his generalship to defeat, not Cæsar, but his country and the senate, that he might always continue in authority, and never cease to keep those for his guards and servants who themselves claimed to govern the world. Domitius Ænobarbus, continually calling him Agamemnon, and king of kings, excited jealousy against him; and Favonius, by his unseasonable raillery, did him no less injury than those who openly attacked him, as when he cried out, "Good friends, you must not expect to gather any figs in Tusculum this year." But Lucius Afranius, who had lain under an imputation of treachery for the loss of the army in Spain, when he saw Pompey purposely declining an engagement, declared openly that he could not but admire why those who were so ready to accuse him did not go themselves and fight this buyer and seller of their provinces.

With these and many such speeches they wrought upon Pompey, who never could bear reproach, or resist the expectations of his friends; and thus they forced him to break his measures, so that he forsook his own prudent resolution to follow their vain hopes and desires: weakness that would have been blamable in the pilot of a ship, how much more in the sovereign commander of such an army, and so many nations. But he, though he had often commended those physicians who did not comply with the capricious appetites of their patients, yet himself could not but yield to the malady and disease of his companions and advisers in the war, rather than use some severity in their cure. Truly who could have said that health was not disordered and a cure not required in the case of men who went up and down the camp, suing already for the consulship and office of prætor, while Spinther, Domitius, and Scipio made friends, raised factions, and quarrelled among themselves who should succeed Cæsar in the dignity of his high priesthood, esteeming all as lightly as if they were to engage only with Tigranes, king of Armenia, or some petty Nabathæan king, not with that Cæsar and his army that had stormed a thousand towns, and subdued more than three hundred several nations; that had fought innumerable battles with the Germans and Gauls, and always carried the victory; that had taken a million of men prisoners, and slain as many upon the spot in pitched battles?

But they went on soliciting and clamoring, and on reaching the plain of Pharsalia, they forced Pompey by their pressure and importunities to call a council of war, where Labienus, general of the horse, stood up first and swore that he would not return out of the battle if he did not rout the enemies; and all the rest took the same oath. That night Pompey dreamed that, as he went into the theater, the people received him with great applause, and that he himself adorned the temple of Venus the Victorious with many spoils. This vision partly encouraged, but partly also disheartened him, fearing lest that splendor and ornament to Venus should be made with spoils furnished by himself to Cæsar, who derived his family from that goddess. Besides there were some panic fears and alarms that ran through the camp, with such a noise that it awakened him out of his sleep. And about the time of renewing the watch towards morning, there appeared a great light over Cæsar's camp whilst they were all at rest, and from thence a ball of flaming fire was carried into Pompey's camp, which Cæsar himself says he saw as he was walking his rounds.

Now Cæsar having designed to raise his camp with the morning and move to Scotussa, whilst the soldiers were busy in pulling down their tents, and sending on their cattle and servants before them with their baggage, there came in scouts who brought word that they saw arms carried to and fro in the enemy's camp, and heard a noise and running up and down, as of men preparing for battle; not long after there came in other scouts with further intelligence, that the first ranks were already set in battle array. Thereupon Cæsar, when he had told them that the wished-for day was come at last, when they should fight with men, not with hunger and famine, instantly gave orders for the red colors to be set up before his tent, that being the ordinary signal of battle among the Romans. As soon as the soldiers saw that, they left their tents, and with great shouts of joy ran to their arms; the officers likewise, on their part, drawing up their companies in order of battle, every man fell into his proper rank without any trouble or noise, as quietly and orderly as if they had been in a dance.

Pompey himself led the right wing of his army against Antony, and placed his father-in-law, Scipio, in the middle against Lucius Calvinus. The left wing was commanded by Lucius Domitius, and supported by the great mass of the horse. For almost the whole cavalry was posted there in the hope of crushing Cæsar, and cutting off the tenth legion, which was spoken of as the stoutest in all the army, and in which Cæsar himself usually fought in person. Cæsar observing the left wing of the enemy to be lined and fortified with such a mighty guard of horse, and alarmed at the gallantry of their appearance, sent for a detachment of six cohorts out of the reserves, and placed them in the rear of the tenth legion, commanding them not to stir, lest they should be discovered by the enemy; but when the enemy's horse should begin to charge, and press upon them, that they should make up with all speed to the front through the foremost ranks, and not throw their javelins at a distance, as is usual with brave soldiers, that they may come to a close fight with their swords the sooner, but that they should strike them upwards into the eyes and faces of the enemy; telling them that those fine young dancers would never endure the steel shining in their eyes, but would fly to save their handsome faces. This was Cæsar's employment at that time. But while he was thus instructing his soldiers, Pompey on horseback was viewing the order of both armies, and when he saw how well the enemy kept their ranks, expecting quietly the signal of battle; and, on the contrary, how impatient and unsteady his own men were, waving up and down in disorder for want of experience, he was very much afraid that their ranks would be broken upon the first onset; and therefore he gave out orders that the van should make a stand and, keeping close in their ranks, should receive the enemy's charge. Cæsar much condemns this command; which, he says, not only took off from the strength of the blows, which would otherwise have been made with a spring; but also lost the men the impetus, which, more than anything, in the moment of their coming upon the enemy, fills soldiers with impulse and inspiration, the very shouts and rapid pace adding to their fury; of which Pompey deprived his men, arresting them in their course and cooling down their heat.

Cæsar's army consisted of twenty-two thousand, and Pompey's of somewhat above twice as many. When the signal of battle was given on both sides, and the trumpets began to sound a charge, most men of course were fully occupied with their own matters; only some few of the noblest Romans, together with certain Greeks there present, standing as spectators without the battle, seeing the armies now ready to join, could not but consider in themselves to what a pass private ambition and emulation had brought the empire. Common arms, and kindred ranks drawn up under the selfsame standards, the whole flower and strength of the same single city here meeting in collision with itself, offered plain proof how blind and how mad a thing human nature is when once possessed with any passion; for if they had been desirous only to rule, and enjoy in peace what they had conquered in war, the greatest and best part of the world was subject to them both by sea and land. But if there was yet a thirst in their ambition, that must still be fed with new trophies and triumphs, the Parthian and German wars would yield matter enough to satisfy the most covetous of honor. Scythia, moreover, was yet unconquered, and the Indians too, where their ambition might be colored over with the specious pretext of civilizing barbarous nations. And what Scythian horse, Parthian arrows, or Indian riches could be able to resist seventy thousand Roman soldiers, well appointed in arms, under the command of two such generals as Pompey and Cæsar, whose names they had heard of before that of the Romans, and whose prowess, by their conquests of such wild, remote, savage, and brutish nations, was spread further than the fame of the Romans themselves? Today they met in conflict, and could no longer be induced to spare their country, even out of regard for their own glory or the fear of losing the name which till this day both had held, of having never yet been defeated. As for their former private ties, and the charms of Julia, and the marriage that had made them near connections, these could now only be looked upon as tricks of state, the mere securities of a treaty made to serve the needs of an occasion, not the pledges of any real friendship.

Now, therefore, as soon as the plains of Pharsalia were covered with men, horse, and armor, and that the signal of battle was raised on either side, Caius Crassianus, a centurion, who commanded a company of one hundred and twenty men, was the first that advanced out of Cæsar's army, to give the charge, and acquit himself of a solemn engagement that he had made to Cæsar. He had been the first man that Cæsar had seen going out of the camp in the morning, and Cæsar, after saluting him, had asked him what he thought of the coming battle. To which he, stretching out his right hand, replied aloud, "Thine is the victory, O Cæsar, thou shalt conquer gloriously, and I myself this day will be the subject of thy praise either alive or dead." In pursuance of this promise he hastened forward, and being followed by many more, charged into the midst of the enemy.

There they came at once to a close fight with their swords, and made a great slaughter; but as he was still pressing forward, and breaking the ranks of the vanguard, one of Pompey's soldiers ran him in at the mouth, so that the point of the sword came out behind at his neck; and Crassianus being thus slain, the fight became doubtful, and continued equal on that part of the battle.

Pompey had not yet brought on the right wing, but stayed and looked about, waiting to see what execution his cavalry would do on the left. They had already drawn out their squadrons in form, designing to turn Cæsar's flank, and force those few horse, which he had placed in the front, to give back upon the battalion of foot. But Cæsar, on the other side, having given the signal, his horse retreated back a little, and gave way to those six subsidiary cohorts, which had been posted in the rear, as a reserve to cover the flank; and which now came out, three thousand men in number, and met the enemy; and when they came up, standing by the horses, struck their javelins upwards, according to their instructions, and hit the horsemen full in their faces. They, unskillful in any manner of fight, and least of all expecting or understanding such a kind as this, had not courage enough to endure the blows upon their faces, but turning their backs, and covering their eyes with their hands, shamefully took to flight. Cæsar's men, however, did not follow them, but marched upon the foot, and attacked the wing, which the flight of the cavalry had left unprotected, and liable to be turned and taken in the rear, so that this wing now being attacked in the flank by these, and charged in the front by the tenth legion, was not able to abide the charge, or make any longer resistance, especially when they saw themselves surrounded and circumvented in the very way in which they had designed to invest the enemy. Thus these being likewise routed and put to flight, when Pompey, by the dust flying in the air, conjectured the fate of his horse, it were very hard to say what his thoughts or intentions were, but looking like one distracted and beside himself, and without any recollection or reflection that he was Pompey the Great, he retired slowly towards his camp, without speaking a word to any man, exactly according to the description in the verses—

"But Jove from heaven struck Ajax with a fear;
Ajax the bold then stood astonished there,
Flung o'er his back the mighty sevenfold shield,
And trembling gazed and spied about the field."

In this state and condition he went into his own tent and sat down, speechless still, until some of the enemy fell in together with his men that were flying into the camp, and then he let fall only this one word, "What!

into the very camp?" and said no more; but rose up, and putting on a dress suitable to his present fortune, made his way secretly out.

By this time the rest of the army was put to flight, and there was a great slaughter in the camp among the servants and those that guarded the tents, but of the soldiers themselves there were not above six thousand slain, as is stated by Asinius Pollio, who himself fought in this battle on Cæsar's side. When Cæsar's soldiers had taken the camp, they saw clearly the folly and vanity of the enemy; for all their tents and pavilions were richly set out with garlands of myrtle, embroidered carpets and hangings, and tables laid and covered with goblets. There were large bowls of wine ready, and everything prepared and put in array, in the manner rather of people who had offered sacrifice and were going to celebrate a holiday, than of soldiers who had armed themselves to go out to battle, so possessed with the expectation of success and so full of empty confidence had they gone out that morning.

When Pompey had got a little way from the camp, he dismounted and forsook his horse, having but a small retinue with him; and finding that no man pursued him, walked on softly afoot, taken up altogether with thoughts, such as probably might possess a man that for the space of thirty-four years together had been accustomed to conquest and victory, and was then at last, in his old age, learning for the first time what defeat and flight were. And it was no small affliction to consider, that he had lost in one hour all that glory and power which he had been getting in so many wars, and bloody battles; and that he who but a little before was guarded with such an army of foot, so many squadrons of horse, and such a mighty fleet, was now flying in so mean a condition, and with such a slender retinue, that his very enemies who fought him could not know him. Thus, when he had passed by the city of Larissa, and came into the pass of Tempe, being very thirsty, he kneeled down and drank out of the river; then rising up again, he passed through Tempe, until he came to the seaside, and there he betook himself to a poor fisherman's cottage, where he rested the remainder of the night. The next morning about break of day he went into one of the river boats, and taking none of those that followed him except such as were free, dismissed his servants, advising them to go boldly to Cæsar and not be afraid. As he was rowing up and down near the shore, he chanced to spy a large merchant ship, lying off, just ready to set sail; the master of which was a Roman citizen, named Peticius, who, though he was not familiarly acquainted with Pompey, yet knew him well by sight. Now it happened that this Peticius dreamed, the night before, that he saw Pompey, not like the man he had often seen him, but in a humble and dejected condition, and in that posture discoursing with him. He was then telling his dream to the people on board, as men do when at leisure, and especially dreams of that conse-

quence, when of a sudden one of the mariners told him he saw a river
boat with oars putting off from shore, and that some of the men there
shook their garments, and held out their hands, with signs to take them
in; thereupon Peticius, looking attentively, at once recognized Pompey,
just as he appeared in his dream, and smiting his hand on his head, ordered the mariners to let down the ship's boat, he himself waving his
hand, and calling to him by his name, already assured of his change and
the change of his fortune by that of his garb. So that without waiting for
any further entreaty or discourse, he took him into his ship, together with
as many of his company as he thought fit, and hoisted sail. There were
with him the two Lentuli, and Favonius; and a little after they spied King
Deiotarus, making up towards them from the shore; so they stayed and
took him in along with them. At supper time, the master of the ship having made ready such provisions as he had aboard, Pompey, for want of his
servants, began to undo his shoes himself; which Favonius, noticing, ran
to him and undid them, and helped him to anoint himself, and always
after continued to wait upon and attend him in all things, as servants do
their masters, even to the washing of his feet and preparing his supper.
Insomuch that anyone there present, observing the free and unaffected
courtesy of these services, might have well exclaimed—

> "O heavens, in those that noble are,
> Whate'er they do is fit and fair."

Pompey, sailing by the city of Amphipolis, crossed over from thence to
Mitylene, with a design to take in Cornelia and his son; and as soon as
he arrived at the port in that island, he dispatched a messenger into the
city with news very different from Cornelia's expectation. For she, by all
the former messages and letters sent to please her, had been put in hopes
that the war was ended at Dyrrhachium, and that there was nothing more
remaining for Pompey but the pursuit of Cæsar. The messenger, finding
her in the same hopes still, was not able to salute or speak to her, but declaring the greatness of her misfortune by his tears rather than by his
words, desired her to make haste if she would see Pompey, with one ship
only, and that not of his own. The young lady hearing this, fell down in
a swoon, and continued a long time senseless and speechless. And when
with some trouble she was brought to her senses again, being conscious
to herself that this was no time for lamentation and tears, she started up
and ran through the city towards the seaside, where Pompey meeting and
embracing her, as she sank down, supported by his arms, "This, sir," she
exclaimed, "is the effect of my fortune, not of yours, that I see you thus
reduced to one poor vessel, who before your marriage with Cornelia
were wont to sail in these seas with a fleet of five hundred ships. Why
therefore should you come to see me, or why not rather have left to her

evil genius one who has brought upon you her own ill fortune? How happy a woman had I been, if I had breathed out my last before the news came from Parthia of the death of Publius, the husband of my youth, and how prudent if I had followed his destiny, as I designed! But I was reserved for a greater mischief, even the ruin of Pompey the Great."

Thus, they say, Cornelia spoke to him, and this was Pompey's reply: "You have had, Cornelia, but one season of a better fortune, which, it may be, gave you unfounded hopes, by attending me a longer time than is usual. It behooves us, who are mortals born, to endure these events, and to try fortune yet again; neither is it any less possible to recover our former state than it was to fall from that into this." Thereupon Cornelia sent for her servants and baggage out of the city. The citizens also of Mitylene came out to salute and invite Pompey into the city, but he refused, advising them to be obedient to the conqueror and fear not, for that Cæsar was a man of great goodness and clemency. Then turning to Cratippus, the philosopher, who came among the rest out of the city to visit him, he began to find some fault, and briefly argued with him upon Providence, but Cratippus modestly declined the dispute, putting him in better hopes only, lest by opposing he might seem too austere or unseasonable. For he might have put Pompey a question in his turn, in defense of Providence; and might have demonstrated the necessity there was that the commonwealth should be turned into a monarchy, because of their ill government in the state; and could have asked, "How, O Pompey, and by what token or assurance can we ascertain, that if the victory had been yours, you would have used your fortune better than Cæsar? We must leave the divine power to act as we find it do."

Pompey having taken his wife and friends aboard, set sail, making no port, nor touching anywhere, but when he was necessitated to take in provisions, or fresh water. The first city he entered was Attalia, in Pamphylia, and whilst he was there, there came some galleys thither to him out of Cilicia, together with a small body of soldiers, and he had almost sixty senators with him again; then hearing that his navy was safe too, and that Cato had rallied a considerable body of soldiers after their overthrow, and was crossing with them over into Africa, he began to complain and blame himself to his friends that he had allowed himself to be driven into engaging by land, without making use of his other forces, in which he was irresistibly the stronger, and had not kept near enough to his fleet, that failing by land, he might have reinforced himself from the sea, and would have been again at the head of a power quite sufficient to encounter the enemy on equal terms. And in truth, neither did Pompey during all the war commit a greater oversight, nor Cæsar use a more subtle stratagem, than in drawing the fight so far off from the naval forces.

As it now was, however, since he must come to some decision, and try some plan within his present ability, he dispatched his agents to the neighboring cities, and himself sailed about in person to others, requiring their aid in money and men for his ships. But, fearing lest the rapid approach of the enemy might cut off all his preparations, he began to consider what place would yield him the safest refuge and retreat at present. A consultation was held, and it was generally agreed that no province of the Romans was secure enough. As for foreign kingdoms, he himself was of opinion that Parthia would be the fittest to receive and defend them in their present weakness, and best able to furnish them with new means and send them out again with large forces. Others of the council were for going into Africa, and to King Juba. But Theophanes the Lesbian thought it madness to leave Egypt, that was but at a distance of three days' sailing, and make no use of Ptolemy, who was still a boy, and was highly indebted to Pompey for the friendship and favor he had shown to his father, only to put himself under the Parthian, and trust the most treacherous nation in the world; and rather than make any trial of the clemency of a Roman, and his own near connection, to whom if he would but yield to be second, he might be the first and chief over all the rest, to go and place himself at the mercy of Arsaces, which even Crassus had not submitted to while alive; and, moreover, to expose his young wife, of the family of the Scipios, among a barbarous people, who govern by their lusts, and measure their greatness by their power to commit affronts and insolences; from whom, though she suffered no dishonor, yet it might be thought she did, being in the hands of those who had the power to do it. This argument alone, they say, was persuasive enough to divert his course, that was designed towards Euphrates, if it were so indeed that any counsel of Pompey's, and not some superior power, made him take this other way.

As soon, therefore, as it was resolved upon that he should fly into Egypt, setting sail from Cyprus in a galley of Seleucia, together with Cornelia, while the rest of his company sailed along near him, some in ships of war, and others in merchant vessels, he passed over sea without danger. But on hearing that King Ptolemy was posted with his army at the city of Pelusium, making war against his sister, he steered his course that way, and sent a messenger before to acquaint the king with his arrival, and to crave his protection. Ptolemy himself was quite young, and therefore Pothinus, who had the principal administration of all affairs, called a council of the chief men, those being the greatest whom he pleased to make so, and commanded them every man to deliver his opinion touching the reception of Pompey. It was, indeed, a miserable thing that the fate of the great Pompey should be left to the determinations of Pothinus the eunuch, Theodotus of Chios, the paid rhetoric master, and

Achillas the Egyptian. For these, among the chamberlains and menial domestics that made up the rest of the council, were the chief and leading
men. Pompey, who thought it dishonorable for him to owe his safety to
Cæsar, riding at anchor at a distance from shore, was forced to wait the
sentence of this tribunal. It seems they were so far different in their opinions that some were for sending the man away, and others, again, for
inviting and receiving him; but Theodotus, to show his cleverness and the
cogency of his rhetoric, undertook to demonstrate that neither the one
nor the other was safe in that juncture of affairs. For if they entertained
him, they would be sure to make Cæsar their enemy, and Pompey their
master; or if they dismissed him, they might render themselves hereafter
obnoxious to Pompey, for that inhospitable expulsion, and to Cæsar, for
the escape; so that the most expedient course would be to send for him
and take away his life, for by that means they would ingratiate themselves
with the one, and have no reason to fear the other; adding, it is related,
with a smile, that "a dead man cannot bite."

This advice being approved of, they committed the execution of it to
Achillas. He, therefore, taking with him as his accomplices one Septimius,
a man that had formerly held a command under Pompey, and Salvius, another centurion, with three or four attendants, made up towards
Pompey's galley. In the meantime, all the chiefest of those who accompanied Pompey in this voyage were come into his ship to learn the event
of their embassy. But when they saw the manner of their reception, that
in appearance it was neither princely nor honorable, nor indeed in any
way answerable to the hopes of Theophanes, or their expectation (for
there came but a few men in a fisherman's boat to meet them), they
began to suspect the meanness of their entertainment, and gave warning
to Pompey that he should row back his galley, whilst he was out of their
reach, and make for the sea. By this time the Egyptian boat drew near,
and Septimius standing up first, saluted Pompey, in the Latin tongue, by
the title of imperator. Then Achillas, saluting him in the Greek language,
desired him to come aboard his vessel, telling him that the sea was very
shallow towards the shore, and that a galley of that burden could not
avoid striking upon the sands. At the same time they saw several of the
king's galleys getting their men on board, and all the shore covered with
soldiers; so that even if they changed their minds, it seemed impossible
for them to escape, and besides, their distrust would have given the assassins a pretense for their cruelty. Pompey, therefore, taking his leave of
Cornelia, who was already lamenting his death before it came, bade two
centurions, with Philip, one of his freedmen, and a slave called Scythes,
go on board the boat before him. And as some of the crew with Achillas
were reaching out their hands to help him, he turned about towards his
wife and son, and repeated those iambics of Sophocles—

"He that once enters at a tyrant's door,
Becomes a slave, though he were free before."

These were the last words he spoke to his friends, and so he went aboard. Observing presently that notwithstanding there was a considerable distance betwixt his galley and the shore, yet none of the company addressed any words of friendliness or welcome to him all the way, he looked earnestly upon Septimius, and said, "I am not mistaken, surely, in believing you to have been formerly my fellow soldier." But he only nodded with his head, making no reply at all, nor showing any other courtesy. Since, therefore, they continued silent, Pompey took a little book in his hand, in which was written out an address in Greek, which he intended to make to King Ptolemy, and began to read it. When they drew near to the shore, Cornelia, together with the rest of his friends in the galley, was very impatient to see the event, and began to take courage at last when she saw several of the royal escort coming to meet him, apparently to give him a more honorable reception; but in the meantime, as Pompey took Philip by the hand to rise up more easily, Septimius first stabbed him from behind with his sword; and after him likewise Salvius and Achillas drew out their swords. He, therefore, taking up his gown with both hands, drew it over his face, and neither saying nor doing anything unworthy of himself, only groaning a little, endured the wounds they gave him, and so ended his life, in the fifty-ninth year of his age, the very next day after the day of his birth.

Cornelia, with her company from the galley, seeing him murdered, gave such a cry that it was heard to the shore, and weighing anchor with all speed, they hoisted sail, and fled. A strong breeze from the shore assisted their flight into the open sea, so that the Egyptians, though desirous to overtake them, desisted from the pursuit. But they cut off Pompey's head, and threw the rest of his body overboard, leaving it naked upon the shore, to be viewed by any that had the curiosity to see so sad a spectacle. Philip stayed by and watched till they had glutted their eyes in viewing it; and then washing it with seawater, having nothing else, he wrapped it up in a shirt of his own for a winding sheet. Then seeking up and down about the sands, at last he found some rotten planks of a little fisher boat, not much, but yet enough to make up a funeral pile for a naked body, and that not quite entire. As Philip was busy in gathering and putting these old planks together, an old Roman citizen, who in his youth had served in the wars under Pompey, came up to him and demanded who he was that was preparing the funeral of Pompey the Great. And Philip making answer that he was his freedman, "Nay, then," said he, "you shall not have this honor alone; let even me, too, I pray you, have my share in such a pious office, that I may not altogether repent me of this pilgrimage in a strange land, but in compensation of many misfortunes may obtain this happiness at last, even with mine own hands to touch the body of Pompey, and do the last duties to the greatest general among the. Romans." And in this manner were the obsequies of Pompey performed. The next day Lucius Lentulus, not knowing what had passed, came sailing from Cyprus along the shore of that coast, and seeing a funeral pile, and Philip standing by, exclaimed, before he was yet seen by any one, "Who is this that has found his end here?" adding, after a short pause, with a sigh, "Possibly even thou, Pompeius Magnus!" and so going ashore, he was presently apprehended and slain. This was the end of Pompey.

Not long after, Cæsar arrived in the country that was polluted with this foul act, and when one of the Egyptians was sent to present him with Pompey's head, he turned away from him with abhorrence as from a murderer; and on receiving his seal, on which was engraved a lion holding a sword in his paw, he burst into tears. Achillas and Pothinus he put to death; and King Ptolemy himself, being overthrown in battle upon the banks of the Nile, fled away and was never heard of afterwards. Theodotus, the rhetorician, flying out of Egypt, escaped the hands of Cæsar's justice, but lived a vagabond in banishment; wandering up and down, despised and hated of all men, till at last Marcus Brutus, after he had killed Cæsar, finding him in his province of Asia, put him to death, with every kind of ignominy. The ashes of Pompey were carried to his wife Cornelia, who deposited them at his country house near Alba.

CÆSAR

AFTER SYLLA became master of Rome, he wished to make Cæsar put away his wife Cornelia, daughter of Cinna, the late sole ruler of the commonwealth, but was unable to effect it either by promises or intimidation, and so contented himself with confiscating her dowry. The ground of Sylla's hostility to Cæsar was the relationship between him and Marius; for Marius, the elder, married Julia, the sister of Cæsar's father, and had by her the younger Marius, who consequently was Cæsar's first cousin. And though at the beginning, while so many were to be put to death, and there was so much to do, Cæsar was overlooked by Sylla, yet he would not keep quiet, but presented himself to the people as a candidate for the priesthood, though he was yet a mere boy. Sylla, without any open opposition, took measures to have him rejected, and in consultation whether he should be put to death, when it was urged by some that it was not worth his while to contrive the death of a boy, he answered, that they knew little who did not see more than one Marius in that boy. Cæsar, on being informed of this saying, concealed himself, and for a considerable time kept out of the way in the country of the Sabines, often changing his quarters, till one night, as he was removing from one house to another on account of his health, he fell into the hands of Sylla's soldiers, who were searching those parts in order to apprehend any who had absconded. Cæsar, by a bribe of two talents, prevailed with Cornelius, their captain, to let him go, and was no sooner dismissed but he put to sea and made for Bithynia. After a short stay there with Nicomedes, the king, in his passage back he was taken near the island of Pharmacusa by some of the pirates, who, at that time, with large fleets of ships and innumerable smaller vessels, infested the seas everywhere.

When these men at first demanded of him twenty talents for his ransom, he laughed at them for not understanding the value of their prisoner, and voluntarily engaged to give them fifty. He presently dispatched those about him to several places to raise the money, till at last he was left among a set of the most bloodthirsty people in the world, the Cilicians, only with one friend and two attendants. Yet he made so little of them, that when he had a mind to sleep, he would send to them, and order them to make no noise. For thirty-eight days, with all the freedom in the world, he amused himself with joining in their exercises and games, as if they had not been his keepers, but his guards. He wrote verses and speeches, and made them his auditors, and those who did not admire them, he called to their faces illiterate and barbarous, and would often, in raillery, threaten to hang them. They were greatly taken with this, and attributed his free talking to a kind of simplicity and boyish playfulness. As soon as his ransom was come from Miletus, he paid it, and was discharged, and proceeded at once to man some ships at the port of Miletus, and went in pursuit of the pirates, whom he surprised with their ships still stationed at the island, and took most of them. Their money he made his prize, and the men he secured in prison at Pergamus, and made application to Junius, who was then governor of Asia, to whose office it belonged, as prætor, to determine their punishment. Junius, having his eye upon the money, for the sum was considerable, said he would think at his leisure what to do with the prisoners, upon which Cæsar took his leave of him, and went off to Pergamus, where he ordered the pirates to be brought forth and crucified; the punishment he had often threatened them with whilst he was in their hands, and they little dreamt he was in earnest.

In the meantime Sylla's power being now on the decline, Cæsar's friends advised him to return to Rome, but he went to Rhodes, and entered himself in the school of Apollonius, Molon's son, a famous rhetorician, one who had the reputation of a worthy man, and had Cicero for one of his scholars. Cæsar is said to have been admirably fitted by nature to make a great statesman and orator, and to have taken such pains to improve his genius this way that without dispute he might challenge the second place. More he did not aim at, as choosing to be first rather amongst men of arms and power, and, therefore, never rose to that height of eloquence to which nature would have carried him, his attention being diverted to those expeditions and designs, which at length gained him the empire. And he himself, in his answer to Cicero's panegyric on Cato, desires his reader not to compare the plain discourse of a soldier with the harangues of an orator who had not only fine parts, but had employed his life in this study.

When he was returned to Rome, he accused Dolabella of maladministration, and many cities of Greece came in to attest it. Dolabella was acquitted, and Cæsar, in return for the support he had received from the Greeks, assisted them in their prosecution of Publius Antonius for corrupt practices, before Marcus Lucullus, prætor of Macedonia. In this cause he so far succeeded, that Antonius was forced to appeal to the tribunes at Rome, alleging that in Greece he could not have fair play against Grecians. In his pleadings at Rome, his eloquence soon obtained him great credit and favor, and he won no less upon the affections of the people by the affability of his manners and address, in which he showed a tact and consideration beyond what could have been expected at his age; and the open house he kept, the entertainments he gave, and the general splendor of his manner of life contributed little by little to create and increase his political influence. His enemies slighted the growth of it at first, presuming it would soon fail when his money was gone; whilst in the meantime it was growing up and flourishing among the common people. When his power at last was established and not to be overthrown, and now openly tended to the altering of the whole constitution, they were aware too late that there is no beginning so mean, which continued application will not make considerable, and that despising a danger at first will make it at last irresistible. Cicero was the first who had any suspicions of his designs upon the government, and, as a good pilot is apprehensive of a storm when the sea is most smiling, saw the designing temper of the man through this disguise of good humor and affability, and said that, in general, in all he did and undertook, he detected the ambition for absolute power, "but when I see his hair so carefully arranged, and observe him adjusting it with one finger, I cannot imagine it should enter into such a man's thoughts to subvert the Roman state." But of this more hereafter.

The first proof he had of the people's goodwill to him was when he received by their suffrages a tribuneship in the army, and came out on the list with a higher place than Caius Popilius. A second and clearer instance of their favor appeared upon his making a magnificent oration in praise of his aunt Julia, wife to Marius, publicly in the forum, at whose funeral he was so bold as to bring forth the images of Marius, which nobody had dared to produce since the government came into Sylla's hands, Marius's party having from that time been declared enemies of the state. When some who were present had begun to raise a cry against Cæsar, the people answered with loud shouts and clapping in his favor, expressing their joyful surprise and satisfaction at his having, as it were, brought up again from the grave those honors of Marius, which for so long a time had been lost to the city. It had always been the custom at Rome to make funeral orations in praise of elderly matrons, but there was no precedent of any upon young women till Cæsar first made one upon the death of his own wife. This also procured him favor, and by this show of affection he won upon the feelings of the people, who looked upon him as a man of great tenderness and kindness of heart. After he had buried his wife, he went as quæstor into Spain under one of the prætors, named Vetus, whom he honored ever after, and made his son his own quæstor, when he himself came to be prætor. After this employment was ended, he married Pompeia, his third wife, having then a daughter by Cornelia, his first

wife, whom he afterwards married to Pompey the Great. He was so profuse in his expenses that, before he had any public employment, he was
in debt thirteen hundred talents, and many thought that by incurring
such expense to be popular, he changed a solid good for what would
prove but short and uncertain return; but in truth he was purchasing
what was of the greatest value at an inconsiderable rate. When he was
made surveyor of the Appian Way, he disbursed, besides the public money,
a great sum out of his private purse; and when he was ædile, he provided
such a number of gladiators that he entertained the people with three
hundred and twenty single combats, and by his great liberality and magnificence in theatrical shows, in processions, and public feastings, he
threw into the shade all the attempts that had been made before him, and
gained so much upon the people that everyone was eager to find out
new offices and new honors for him in return for his munificence.

There being two factions in the city, one that of Sylla, which was
very powerful, the other that of Marius, which was then broken and in
a very low condition, he undertook to revive this and to make it his
own. And to this end, whilst he was in the height of his repute with the
people for the magnificent shows he gave as ædile, he ordered images
of Marius and figures of Victory, with trophies in their hands, to be carried privately in the night and placed in the capitol. Next morning,
when some saw them bright with gold and beautifully made, with inscriptions upon them, referring them to Marius's exploits over the
Cimbrians, they were surprised at the boldness of him who had set
them up, nor was it difficult to guess who it was. The fame of this soon
spread and brought together a great concourse of people. Some cried
out that it was an open attempt against the established government thus
to revive those honors which had been buried by the laws and decrees
of the senate; that Cæsar had done it to sound the temper of the people whom he had prepared before, and to try whether they were tame
enough to bear his humor, and would quietly give way to his innovations. On the other hand, Marius's party took courage, and it was incredible how numerous they were suddenly seen to be, and what a
multitude of them appeared and came shouting into the capitol. Many,
when they saw Marius's likeness, cried for joy, and Cæsar was highly
extolled as the one man, in the place of all others, who was a relation
worthy of Marius. Upon this the senate met, and Catulus Lutatius, one
of the most eminent Romans of that time, stood up and inveighed
against Cæsar, closing his speech with the remarkable saying that Cæsar
was now not working mines, but planting batteries to overthrow the
state. But when Cæsar had made an apology for himself, and satisfied
the senate, his admirers were very much animated, and advised him not
to depart from his own thoughts for anyone, since with the people's

good favor he would erelong get the better of them all, and be the first man in the commonwealth.

At this time, Metellus, the high priest, died, and Catulus and Isauricus, persons of the highest reputation, and who had great influence in the senate, were competitors for the office; yet Cæsar would not give way to them, but presented himself to the people as a candidate against them. The several parties seeming very equal, Catulus, who, because he had the most honor to lose, was the most apprehensive of the event, sent to Cæsar to buy him off, with offers of a great sum of money. But his answer was that he was ready to borrow a larger sum than that, to carry on the contest. Upon the day of election, as his mother conducted him out of doors with tears, after embracing her, "My mother," he said, "today you will see me either high priest or an exile." When the votes were taken, after a great struggle, he carried it, and excited among the senate and nobility great alarm lest he might now urge on the people to every kind of insolence. And Piso and Catulus found fault with Cicero for having let Cæsar escape, when in the conspiracy of Catiline he had given the government such advantage against him. For Catiline, who had designed not only to change the present state of affairs, but to subvert the whole empire and confound all, had himself taken to flight, while the evidence was yet incomplete against him, before his ultimate purposes had been properly discovered. But he had left Lentulus and Cethegus in the city to supply his place in the conspiracy, and whether they received any secret encouragement and assistance from Cæsar is uncertain; all that is certain, is, that they were fully convicted in the senate, and when Cicero, the consul, asked the several opinions of the senators, how they would have them punished, all who spoke before Cæsar sentenced them to death; but Cæsar stood up and made a set speech, in which he told them that he thought it without precedent and not just to take away the lives of persons of their birth and distinction before they were fairly tried, unless there was an absolute necessity for it; but that if they were kept confined in any towns of Italy Cicero himself should choose till Catiline was defeated, then the senate might in peace and at their leisure determine what was best to be done.

This sentence of his carried so much appearance of humanity, and he gave it such advantage by the eloquence with which he urged it, that not only those who spoke after him closed with it, but even they who had before given a contrary opinion now came over to his, till it came about to Catulus's and Cato's turn to speak. They warmly opposed it, and Cato intimated in his speech the suspicion of Cæsar himself, and pressed the matter so strongly that the criminals were given up to suffer execution. As Cæsar was going out of the senate, many of the young men who at that time acted as guards to Cicero ran in with their naked swords to assault him. But Curio, it is said, threw his gown over him, and conveyed him away, and Cicero himself, when the young men looked up to see his wishes, gave a sign not to kill him, either for fear of the people or because he thought the murder unjust and illegal. If this be true, I wonder how Cicero came to omit all mention of it in his book about his consulship. He was blamed, however, afterwards, for not having made use of so fortunate an opportunity against Cæsar, as if he had let it escape him out of fear of the populace, who, indeed, showed remarkable solicitude about Cæsar, and some time after, when he went into the senate to clear himself of the suspicions he lay under, and found great clamors raised against him, upon the senate in consequence sitting longer than ordinary, they went up to the house in a tumult, and beset it, demanding Cæsar, and requiring them to dismiss him. Upon this, Cato, much fearing some movement among the poor citizens, who were always the first to kindle the flame among the people, and placed all their hopes in Cæsar, persuaded the senate to give them a monthly allowance of corn, an expedient which put the commonwealth to the extraordinary charge of seven million five hundred thousand drachmas in the year, but quite succeeded in removing the great cause of terror for the present, and very much weakened Cæsar's power, who at that time was just going to be made prætor, and consequently would have been more formidable by his office.

But there was no disturbance during his prætorship, only what misfortune he met with in his own domestic affairs. Publius Clodius was a patrician by descent, eminent both for his riches and eloquence, but in licentiousness of life and audacity exceeded the most noted profligates of the day. He was in love with Pompeia, Cæsar's wife, and she had no aversion to him. But there was strict watch kept on her apartment, and Cæsar's mother, Aurelia, who was a discreet woman, being continually about her, made any interview very dangerous and difficult. The Romans have a goddess whom they call Bona, the same whom the Greeks call Gynæcea. The Phrygians, who claim a peculiar title to her, say she was mother to Midas. The Romans profess she was one of the Dryads, and married to Faunus. The Grecians affirm that she is that mother of Bacchus whose name is not to be uttered, and, for this reason, the women who celebrate her festival cover the tents with vine branches, and, in accordance with the fable, a consecrated serpent is placed by the goddess. It is not lawful for a man to be by, nor so much as in the house, whilst the rites are celebrated, but the women by themselves perform the sacred offices, which are said to be much the same with those used in the solemnities of Orpheus. When the festival comes, the husband, who is either consul or prætor, and with him every male creature, quits the house. The wife then taking it under her care, sets it in order, and the principal ceremonies are performed during the night, the women playing together amongst themselves as they keep watch, and music of various kinds going on.

As Pompeia was at that time celebrating this feast, Clodius, who as yet had no beard, and so thought to pass undiscovered, took upon him the dress and ornaments of a singing woman, and so came thither, having the air of a young girl. Finding the doors open, he was without any stop introduced by the maid, who was in the intrigue. She presently ran to tell Pompeia, but as she was away a long time, he grew uneasy in waiting for her, and left his post and traversed the house from one room to another, still taking care to avoid the lights, till at last Aurelia's woman met him, and invited him to play with her, as the women did among themselves. He refused to comply, and she presently pulled him forward, and asked him who he was and whence he came. Clodius told her he was waiting for Pompeia's own maid, Abra, being in fact her own name also, and as he said so, betrayed himself by his voice. Upon which the woman, shrieking, ran into the company where there were lights, and cried out she had discovered a man. The women were all in a fright. Aurelia covered up the sacred things and stopped the proceedings, and having ordered the doors to be shut, went about with lights to find Clodius, who was got into the maid's room that he had come in with, and was seized there. The women knew him, and drove him out of doors, and at once, that same night, went home and told their husbands the story. In the morning, it was all about the town, what an impious attempt Clodius had made, and how he ought to be punished as an offender, not only against those whom he had offended, but also against the public and the gods. Upon which one of the tribunes impeached him for profaning the holy rites, and some of the principal senators combined together and gave evidence against him, that besides many other horrible crimes, he had been guilty of incest with his own sister, who was married to Lucullus. But the people set themselves against this combination of the nobility, and defended Clodius, which was of great service to him with the judges, who took alarm and were afraid to provoke the multitude. Cæsar at once dismissed Pompeia, but being summoned as a witness against Clodius, said he had nothing to charge him with. This looking like a paradox, the accuser asked him why he parted with his wife. Cæsar replied, "I wished my wife to be not so much as suspected." Some say that Cæsar spoke this as his real thought; others, that he did it to gratify the people, who were very earnest to save Clodius. Clodius, at any rate, escaped; most of the judges giving their opinions so written as to be illegible, that they might not be in danger from the people by condemning him, nor in disgrace with the nobility by acquitting him.

Cæsar, in the meantime, being out of his prætorship, had got the province of Spain, but was in great embarrassment with his creditors, who, as he was going off, came upon him, and were very pressing and importunate. This led him to apply himself to Crassus, who was the richest man in Rome, but wanted Cæsar's youthful vigor and heat to sustain the opposition against Pompey. Crassus took upon him to satisfy those creditors who were most uneasy to him, and would not be put off any longer, and engaged himself to the amount of eight hundred and thirty talents, upon which Cæsar was now at liberty to go to his province. In his journey, as he was crossing the Alps, and passing by a small village of the barbarians with but few inhabitants, and those wretchedly poor, his companions asked the question among themselves by way of mockery, if there were any canvassing for offices there; any contention which should be uppermost, or feuds of great men one against another. To which Cæsar made answer seriously, "For my part, I had rather be the first man among these fellows, than the second man in Rome." It is said that another time, when free from business in Spain, after reading some part of the history of Alexander, he sat a great while very thoughtful, and at last burst out into tears. His friends were surprised, and asked him the reason of it. "Do you think," said he, "I have not just cause to weep, when I consider that Alexander at my age had conquered so many nations, and I have all this time done nothing that is memorable?" As soon as he came into Spain he was very active, and in a few days had got together ten new cohorts of foot in addition to the twenty which were there before. With these he marched against the Calaici and Lusitani and conquered them, and advancing as far as the ocean, subdued the tribes which never before had been subject to the Romans. Having managed his military affairs with good success, he was equally happy in the course of his civil government. He took pains to establish a good understanding amongst the several states, and no less care to heal the differences between debtors and creditors. He ordered that the creditor should receive two parts of the debtor's yearly income, and that the other part should be managed by the debtor himself, till by this method the whole debt was at last discharged. This conduct made him leave his province with a fair reputation; being rich himself, and having enriched his soldiers, and having received from them the honorable name of Imperator.

There is a law among the Romans, that whoever desires the honor of a triumph must stay without the city and expect his answer. And another, that those who stand for the consulship shall appear personally upon the place. Cæsar was come home at the very time of choosing consuls, and being in a difficulty between these two opposite laws, sent to the senate to desire that, since he was obliged to be absent, he might sue for the consulship by his friends. Cato, being backed by the law, at first opposed his request; afterwards perceiving that Cæsar had prevailed with a great part of the senate to comply with it, he made it his business to gain time, and went on wasting the whole day in speaking. Upon which Cæsar thought fit to let the triumph fall, and pursued the consulship. Entering the town and coming forward immediately, he had recourse to a piece of state policy by which everybody was deceived but Cato. This was the reconciling of Crassus and Pompey, the two men who then were most powerful in Rome. There had been a quarrel between them, which he now succeeded in making up, and by this means strengthened himself by the united power of both, and so, under the cover of an action which carried all the appearance of a piece of kindness and good nature, caused what was in effect a revolution in the government. For it was not the quarrel between Pompey and Cæsar, as most men imagine, which was the origin of the civil wars, but their union, their conspiring together at first to subvert the aristocracy, and so quarreling afterwards between themselves. Cato, who often foretold what the consequence of this alliance would be, had then the character of a sullen, interfering man, but in the end the reputation of a wise but unsuccessful counselor.

Thus Cæsar, being doubly supported by the interests of Crassus and Pompey, was promoted to the consulship, and triumphantly proclaimed with Calpurnius Bibulus. When he entered on his office he brought in bills which would have been preferred with better grace by the most audacious of the tribunes than by a consul, in which he proposed the plantation of colonies and division of lands, simply to please the commonalty. The best and most honorable of the senators opposed it, upon which, as he had long wished for nothing more than for such a colorable pretext, he loudly protested how much against his will it was to be driven to seek support from the people, and how the senate's insulting and harsh conduct left no other course possible for him than to devote himself henceforth to the popular cause and interest. And so he hurried out of the senate, and presenting himself to the people, and there placing Crassus and Pompey, one on each side of him, he asked them whether they consented to the bills he had proposed. They owned their assent, upon which he desired them to assist him against those who had threatened to oppose him with their swords. They engaged they would, and Pompey added further, that he would meet their swords with a sword and buckler too. These words the nobles much resented, as neither suitable to his own dignity, nor becoming the reverence due to the senate, but resembling rather the vehemence of a boy or the fury of a madman. But the people were pleased with it. In order to get a yet firmer hold upon Pompey, Cæsar having a daughter, Julia, who had been before contracted to Servilius Cæpio, now betrothed her to Pompey, and told Servilius he should have Pompey's daughter, who was not unengaged either, but promised to Sylla's son, Faustus. A little time after, Cæsar married

Calpurnia, the daughter of Piso, and got Piso made consul for the year following. Cato exclaimed loudly against this, and protested, with a great deal of warmth, that it was intolerable the government should be prostituted by marriages, and that they should advance one another to the commands of armies, provinces, and other great posts, by means of women. Bibulus, Cæsar's colleague, finding it was to no purpose to oppose his bills, but that he was in danger of being murdered in the forum, as also was Cato, confined himself to his house, and there let the remaining part of his consulship expire. Pompey, when he was married, at once filled the forum with soldiers, and gave the people his help in passing the new laws, and secured Cæsar the government of all Gaul, both on this and the other side of the Alps, together with Illyricum, and the command of four legions for five years. Cato made some attempts against these proceedings, but was seized and led off on the way to prison by Cæsar, who expected that he would appeal to the tribunes. But when he saw that Cato went along without speaking a word, and not only the nobility were indignant, but that the people, also, out of respect for Cato's virtue, were following in silence, and with dejected looks, he himself privately desired one of the tribunes to rescue Cato. As for the other senators, some few of them attended the house, the rest, being disgusted, absented themselves. Hence Considius, a very old man, took occasion one day to tell Cæsar that the senators did not meet because they were afraid of his soldiers. Cæsar asked, "Why don't you, then, out of the same fear, keep at home?" To which Considius replied, that age was his guard against fear, and that the small remains of his life were not worth much caution. But the most disgraceful thing that was done in Cæsar's consulship was his assisting to gain the tribuneship for the same Clodius who had made the attempt upon his wife's chastity and intruded upon the secret vigils. He was elected on purpose to effect Cicero's downfall; nor did Cæsar leave the city to join his army till they two had overpowered Cicero and driven him out of Italy.

Thus far have we followed Cæsar's actions before the wars of Gaul. After this, he seems to begin his course afresh, and to enter upon a new life and scene of action. And the period of those wars which he now fought, and those many expeditions in which he subdued Gaul, showed him to be a soldier and general not in the least inferior to any of the greatest and most admired commanders who had ever appeared at the head of armies. For if we compare him with the Fabii, the Metelli, the Scipios, and with those who were his contemporaries, or not long before him, Sylla, Marius, the two Luculli, or even Pompey himself, whose glory, it may be said, went up at that time to heaven for every excellence in war, we shall find Cæsar's actions to have surpassed them all. One he may be held to have outdone in consideration of the difficulty of the country in which he fought, another in the extent of territory which he conquered; some, in the number and strength of the enemies whom he defeated; one man, because of the wildness and perfidiousness of the tribes whose goodwill he conciliated, another in his humanity and clemency to those he overpowered; others, again, in his gifts and kindnesses to his soldiers; all alike in the number of the battles which he fought and the enemies whom he killed. For he had not pursued the wars in Gaul full ten years when he had taken by storm above eight hundred towns, subdued three hundred states, and of the three millions of men, who made up the gross sum of those with whom at several times he engaged, he had killed one million and taken captive a second.

He was so much master of the goodwill and hearty service of his soldiers that those who in other expeditions were but ordinary men displayed a courage past defeating or withstanding when they went upon any danger where Cæsar's glory was concerned. Such a one was Acilius, who, in the sea fight before Marseilles, had his right hand struck off with a sword, yet did not quit his buckler out of his left, but struck the enemies in the face with it, till he drove them off and made himself master of the vessel. Such another was Cassius Scæva, who, in a battle near Dyrrhachium, had one of his eyes shot out with an arrow, his shoulder pierced with one javelin, and his thigh with another; and having received one hundred and thirty darts upon his target, called to the enemy, as though he would surrender himself. But when two of them came up to him, he cut off the shoulder of one with a sword, and by a blow over the face forced the other to retire, and so with the assistance of his friends, who now came up, made his escape. Again, in Britain, when some of the foremost officers had accidentally got into a morass full of water, and there were assaulted by the enemy, a common soldier, whilst Cæsar stood and looked on, threw himself into the midst of them, and after many signal demonstrations of his valor, rescued the officers and beat off the barbarians. He himself, in the end, took to the water, and with much difficulty, partly by swimming, partly by wading, passed it, but in the passage lost his shield. Cæsar and his officers saw it and admired, and went to meet him with joy and acclamation. But the soldier, much dejected and in tears, threw himself down at Cæsar's feet and begged his pardon for having let go his buckler. Another time in Africa, Scipio having taken a ship of Cæsar's in which Granius Petro, lately appointed quæstor, was sailing, gave the other passengers as free prize to his soldiers, but thought fit to offer the quæstor his life. But he said it was not usual for Cæsar's soldiers to take but give mercy, and having said so, fell upon his sword and killed himself.

This love of honor and passion for distinction were inspired into them and cherished in them by Cæsar himself, who, by his unsparing distribution of money and honors, showed them that he did not heap up wealth from the wars for his own luxury, or the gratifying his private pleasures, but that all he received was but a public fund laid by for the reward and encouragement of valor, and that he looked upon all he gave to deserving soldiers as so much increase to his own riches. Added to this, also, there was no danger to which he did not willingly expose himself, no labor from which he pleaded an exemption. His contempt of danger was not so much wondered at by his soldiers, because they knew how much he coveted honor. But his enduring so much hardship, which he did to all appearance beyond his natural strength, very much astonished them. For he was a spare man, had a soft and white skin, was distempered in the head, and subject to an epilepsy, which, it is said, first seized him at Corduba. But he did not make the weakness of his constitution a pretext for his ease, but rather used war as the best physic against his indispositions; whilst by indefatigable journeys, coarse diet, frequent lodging in the field, and continual laborious exercise, he struggled with his diseases and fortified his body against all attacks. He slept generally in his chariots or litters, employing even his rest in pursuit of action. In the day he was thus carried to the forts, garrisons, and camps, one servant sitting with him, who used to write down what he dictated as he went, and a soldier attending behind with his sword drawn. He drove so rapidly that when he first left Rome he arrived at the river Rhone within eight days. He had been an expert rider from his childhood; for it was usual with him to sit with his hands joined together behind his back, and so to put his horse to its full speed. And in this war he disciplined himself so far as to be able to dictate letters from on horseback, and to give directions to two who took notes at the same time, or, as Oppius says, to more. And it is thought that he was the first who contrived means for communicating with friends by cipher, when either press of business, or the large extent of the city, left him no time for a personal conference about matters that required dispatch. How little nice he was in his diet may be seen in the following instance. When at the table of Valerius Leo, who entertained him at supper at Milan, a dish of asparagus was put before him, on which his host instead of oil had poured sweet ointment, Cæsar partook of it without any disgust, and reprimanded his friends for finding fault with it. "For it was enough," said he, "not to eat what you did not like; but he who reflects on another man's want of breeding, shows he wants it as much himself." Another time upon the road he was driven by a storm into a poor man's cottage, where he found but one room, and that such as would afford but a mean reception to a single person, and therefore told his companions places of honor should be given up to the greater men, and necessary accommodations to the weaker, and accordingly ordered that

Oppius, who was in bad health, should lodge within, whilst he and the rest slept under a shed at the door.

His first war in Gaul was against the Helvetians and Tigurini, who having burnt their own towns, twelve in number, and four hundred villages, would have marched forward through that part of Gaul which was included in the Roman province, as the Cimbrians and Teutons formerly had done. Nor were they inferior to these in courage; and in numbers they were equal, being in all three hundred thousand, of which one hundred and ninety thousand were fighting men. Cæsar did not engage the Tigurini in person, but Labienus, under his directions, routed them near the river Arar. The Helvetians surprised Cæsar, and unexpectedly set upon him as he was conducting his army to a confederate town. He succeeded, however, in making his retreat into a strong position, where, when he had mustered and marshalled his men, his horse was brought to him; upon which he said, "When I have won the battle, I will use my horse for the chase, but at present let us go against the enemy," and accordingly charged them on foot. After a long and severe combat, he drove the main army out of the field, but found the hardest work at their carriages and ramparts, where not only the men stood and fought, but the women also and children defended themselves till they were cut to pieces; insomuch that the fight was scarcely ended till midnight. This action, glorious in itself, Cæsar crowned with another yet more noble, by gathering in a body all the barbarians that had escaped out of the battle, above one hundred thousand in number, and obliging them to reoccupy the country which they had deserted, and the cities which they had burnt. This he did for fear the Germans should pass in and possess themselves of the land whilst it lay uninhabited.

His second war was in defense of the Gauls against the Germans, though some time before he had made Ariovistus, their king, recognized at Rome as an ally. But they were very insufferable neighbors to those under his government; and it was probable, when occasion offered, they would renounce the present arrangements, and march on to occupy Gaul. But finding his officers timorous, and especially those of the young nobility who came along with him in hopes of turning their campaigns with him into a means for their own pleasure or profit, he called them together, and advised them to march off, and not run the hazard of a battle against their inclinations, since they had such weak and unmanly feelings; telling them that he would take only the tenth legion and march against the barbarians, whom he did not expect to find an enemy more formidable than the Cimbri, nor, he added, should they find him a general inferior to Marius. Upon this, the tenth legion deputed some of their body to pay him their acknowledgments and thanks, and the other legions blamed their officers, and all, with great vigor and zeal, followed him many days' journey, till they encamped within two hundred furlongs of the enemy. Ariovistus's courage to some extent was cooled upon their very approach; for never expecting the Romans would attack the Germans, whom he had thought it more likely they would not venture to withstand even in defense of their own subjects, he was the more surprised at Cæsar's conduct, and saw his army to be in consternation. They were still more discouraged by the prophecies of their holy women, who foretell the future by observing the eddies of rivers, and taking signs from the windings and noise of streams, and who now warned them not to engage before the next new moon appeared. Cæsar having had intimation of this, and seeing the Germans lie still, thought it expedient to attack them whilst they were under these apprehensions, rather than sit still and wait their time. Accordingly he made his approaches to the strongholds and hills on which they lay encamped, and so galled and fretted them that at last they came down with great fury to engage. But he gained a signal victory, and pursued them for four hundred furlongs, as far as the Rhine; all which space was covered with spoils and bodies of the slain. Ariovistus made shift to pass the Rhine with the small remains of an army, for it is said the number of the slain amounted to eighty thousand.

After this action, Cæsar left his army at their winter quarters in the country of the Sequani, and in order to attend to affairs at Rome, went into that part of Gaul which lies on the Po, and was part of his province; for the river Rubicon divides Gaul, which is on this side the Alps, from the rest of Italy. There he sat down and employed himself in courting people's favor; great numbers coming to him continually, and always finding their requests answered; for he never failed to dismiss all with present pledges of his kindness in hand, and further hopes for the future. And during all this time of the war in Gaul, Pompey never observed how Cæsar was on the one hand using the arms of Rome to effect his conquests, and on the other was gaining over and securing to himself the favor of the Romans, with the wealth which those conquests obtained him. But when he heard that the Belgæ, who were the most powerful of all the Gauls, and inhabited a third part of the country, were revolted, and had got together a great many thousand men in arms, he immediately set out and took his way thither with great expedition, and falling upon the enemy as they were ravaging the Gauls, his allies, he soon defeated and put to flight the largest and least scattered division of them. For though their numbers were great, yet they made but a slender defense, and the marshes and deep rivers were made passable to the Roman foot by the vast quantity of dead bodies. Of those who revolted, all the tribes that lived near the ocean came over without fighting, and he, therefore, led his army against the Nervii, the fiercest and most warlike people of all in those parts. These live in a country covered with continuous woods, and having lodged their children and property out of the way in the depth of the forest, fell upon Cæsar with a body of sixty thousand men, before he was prepared for them, while he was making his encampment. They soon routed his cavalry, and having surrounded the twelfth and seventh legions, killed all the officers, and had not Cæsar himself snatched up a buckler and forced his way through his own men to come up to the barbarians, or had not the tenth legion, when they saw him in danger, run in from the tops of the hills, where they lay, and broken through the enemy's ranks to rescue him, in all probability not a Roman would have been saved. But now, under the influence of Cæsar's bold example, they fought a battle, as the phrase is, of more than human courage, and yet with their utmost efforts they were not able to drive the enemy out of the field, but cut them down fighting in their defense. For out of sixty thousand men, it is stated that not above five hundred survived the battle, and of four hundred of their senators not above three.

When the Roman senate had received news of this, they voted sacrifices and festivals to the gods, to be strictly observed for the space of fifteen days, a longer space than ever was observed for any victory before. The danger to which they had been exposed by the joint outbreak of such a number of nations was felt to have been great; and the people's fondness for Cæsar gave additional luster to successes achieved by him. He now, after settling everything in Gaul, came back again, and spent the winter by the Po, in order to carry on the designs he had in hand at Rome. All who were candidates for offices used his assistance, and were supplied with money from him to corrupt the people and buy their votes, in return of which, when they were chosen, they did all things to advance his power. But what was more considerable, the most eminent and powerful men in Rome in great numbers came to visit him at Lucca, Pompey, and Crassus, and Appius, the governor of Sardinia, and Nepos, the proconsul of Spain, so that there were in the place at one time one hundred and twenty lictors, and more than two hundred senators. In deliberation here held, it was determined that Pompey and Crassus should be consuls again for the following year; that Cæsar should have a fresh supply of money, and that his command should be renewed to him for five years more. It seemed very extravagant to all thinking men that those very persons who had received so much money from Cæsar should persuade the senate to grant him more, as if he were in want. Though in truth it was not so much upon persuasion as compulsion that, with sorrow and groans for their own acts, they passed the measure. Cato was not present, for they had sent him seasonably out of the way into Cyprus; but Favonius, who was a zealous imitator of Cato, when he found he could do no good by opposing it, broke out of the house and loudly declaimed against these proceedings to the people, but none gave him any hearing; some slighting him out of respect to Crassus and Pompey, and the greater part to gratify Cæsar, on whom depended their hopes.

After this, Cæsar returned again to his forces in Gaul, where he found that country involved in a dangerous war, two strong nations of the Germans having lately passed the Rhine to conquer it; one of them called the Usipes, the other the Tenteritæ. Of the war with this people, Cæsar himself has given this account in his commentaries, that the barbarians, having sent ambassadors to treat with him, did, during the treaty, set upon him in his march, by which means with eight hundred men they routed five thousand of his horse, who did not suspect their coming; that afterwards they sent other ambassadors to renew the same fraudulent practices, whom he kept in custody, and led on his army against the barbarians, as judging it mere simplicity to keep faith with those who had so faithlessly broken the terms they had agreed to. But Tanusius states that when the senate decreed festivals and sacrifices for this victory, Cato declared it to be his opinion that Cæsar ought to be given into the hands of the barbarians, that so the guilt which this breach of faith might otherwise bring upon the state might be expiated by transferring the curse on him, who was the occasion of it. Of those who passed the Rhine, there were four hundred thousand cut off; those few who escaped were sheltered by the Sugambri, a people of Germany. Cæsar took hold of this pretense to invade the Germans, being at the same time ambitious of the honor of being the first man that should pass the Rhine with an army. He carried a bridge across it, though it was very wide, and the current at that particular point very full, strong, and violent, bringing down with its waters trunks of trees, and other lumber, which much shook and weakened the foundations of his bridge. But he drove great piles of wood into the bottom of the river above the passage, to catch and stop these as they floated down, and thus fixing his bridle upon the stream, successfully finished this bridge, which no one who saw could believe to be the work but of ten days.

In the passage of his army over it, he met with no opposition; the Suevi themselves, who are the most warlike people of all Germany, flying with their effects into the deepest and most densely wooded valleys. When he had burnt all the enemy's country, and encouraged those who embraced the Roman interest, he went back into Gaul, after eighteen days' stay in Germany. But his expedition into Britain was the most famous testimony of his courage. For he was the first who brought a navy into the western ocean, or who sailed into the Atlantic with an army to make war; and by invading an island, the reported extent of which had made its existence a matter of controversy among historians, many of whom questioned whether it were not a mere name and fiction, not a real place, he might be said to have carried the Roman empire beyond the limits of the known world. He passed thither twice from that part of Gaul which lies over against it, and in several battles which he fought did more hurt to the enemy than service to himself, for the islanders were so miserably poor that they had nothing worth being plundered of. When he found himself unable to put such an end to the war as he wished, he was content to take hostages from the king, and to impose a tribute, and then quitted the island. At his arrival in Gaul, he found letters which lay ready to be conveyed over the water to him from his friends at Rome, announcing his daughter's death, who died in labor of a child by Pompey. Cæsar and Pompey both were much afflicted with her death, nor were their friends less disturbed, believing that the alliance was now broken which had hitherto kept the sickly commonwealth in peace, for the child also died within a few days after the mother. The people took the body of Julia, in spite of the opposition of the tribunes, and carried it into the field of Mars, and there her funeral rites were performed, and her remains are laid.

Cæsar's army was now grown very numerous, so that he was forced to disperse them into various camps for their winter quarters, and he having gone himself to Italy as he used to do, in his absence a general outbreak throughout the whole of Gaul commenced, and large armies marched about the country, and attacked the Roman quarters, and attempted to make themselves masters of the forts where they lay. The greatest and strongest party of the rebels, under the command of Abriorix, cut off Cotta and Titurius with all their men, while a force sixty thousand strong besieged the legion under the command of Cicero, and had almost taken it by storm, the Roman soldiers being all wounded, and having quite spent themselves by a defense beyond their natural strength. But Cæsar, who was at a great distance, having received the news, quickly got together seven thousand men and hastened to relieve Cicero. The besiegers were aware of it, and went to meet him with great confidence that they should easily overpower such a handful of men. Cæsar, to increase their presumption, seemed to avoid fighting, and still marched off till he found a place conveniently situated for a few to engage against many, where he encamped. He kept his soldiers from making any attack upon the enemy, and commanded them to raise the ramparts higher and barricade the gates that, by show of fear they might heighten the enemy's contempt of them. Till at last they came without any order in great security to make an assault, when he issued forth and put them to flight with the loss of many men.

This quieted the greater part of the commotions in these parts of Gaul, and Cæsar, in the course of the winter, visited every part of the country, and with great vigilance took precautions against all innovations. For there were three legions now come to him to supply the place of the men he had lost, of which Pompey furnished him with two out of those under his command; the other was newly raised in the part of Gaul by the Po. But in a while the seeds of war, which had long since been secretly sown and scattered by the most powerful men in those warlike nations, broke forth into the greatest and most dangerous war that ever was in those parts, both as regards the number of men in the vigor of their youth who were gathered and armed from all quarters, the vast funds of money collected to maintain it, the strength of the towns, and the difficulty of the country where it was carried on. It being winter, the rivers were frozen, the woods covered with snow, and the level country flooded, so that in some places the ways were lost through the depth of the snow; in others, the overflowing of marshes and streams made every kind of passage uncertain. All which difficulties made it seem impracticable for Cæsar to make any attempt upon the insurgents. Many tribes had revolted together, the chief of them being the Arverni and Carnutini; the general who had the supreme command in war was Vergentorix, whose father the Gauls had put to death on suspicion of his aiming at absolute government.

He having disposed his army in several bodies, and set officers over them, drew over to him all the country round about as far as those that lie upon the Arar, and having intelligence of the opposition which Cæsar now experienced at Rome, thought to engage all Gaul in the war. Which if he had done a little later, when Cæsar was taken up with the civil wars, Italy had been put into as great a terror as before it was by the Cimbri. But Cæsar, who above all men was gifted with the faculty of making the right use of everything in war, and most especially of seizing the right moment, as soon as he heard of the revolt, returned immediately the same way he went, and showed the barbarians, by the quickness of his march in such a severe season, that an army was advancing against them which was invincible. For in the time that one would have thought it scarce credible that a courier or express should have come with a message from him, he himself appeared with all his army, ravaging the country, reducing their posts, subduing their towns, receiving into his protection those who declared for him. Till at last the Edui, who hitherto had styled themselves brethren to the Romans, and had been much honored by them, declared against him, and joined the rebels, to the great discouragement of his army. Accordingly he removed thence, and passed the country of the Lingones, desiring to reach the territories of the Sequani, who were his friends, and who lay like a bulwark in front of Italy against the other tribes of Gaul. There the enemy came upon him, and surrounded him with many myriads, whom he also was eager to engage; and at last, after some time and with much slaughter, gained on the whole a complete victory; though at first he appears to have met with some reverse, and the Aruveni show you a small sword hanging up in a temple, which they say was taken from Cæsar. Cæsar saw this afterwards himself, and smiled, and when his friends advised it should be taken down, would not permit it, because he looked upon it as consecrated.

After the defeat, a great part of those who had escaped fled with their king into a town called Alesia, which Cæsar besieged, though the height of the walls, and number of those who defended them, made it appear impregnable; and meantime, from without the walls, he was assailed by a greater danger than can be expressed. For the choice men of Gaul, picked out of each nation, and well armed, came to relieve Alesia, to the number of three hundred thousand; nor were there in the town less than one hundred and seventy thousand. So that Cæsar being shut up betwixt two such forces, was compelled to protect himself by two walls, one towards the town, the other against the relieving army, as knowing if these forces should join, his affairs would be entirely ruined. The danger that he underwent before Alesia justly gained him great honor on many accounts, and gave him an opportunity of showing greater instances of his valor and conduct than any other contest had done. One wonders much how he should be able to engage and defeat so many thousands of men without the town, and not be perceived by those within, but yet more, that the Romans themselves, who guarded their wall which was next to the town, should be strangers to it. For even they knew nothing of the victory, till they heard the cries of the men and lamentations of the women who were in the town, and had from thence seen the Romans at a distance carrying into their camp a great quantity of bucklers, adorned with gold and silver, many breastplates stained with blood, besides cups and tents made in the Gallic fashion. So soon did so vast an army dissolve and vanish like a ghost or dream, the greatest part of them being killed upon the spot. Those who were in Alesia, having given themselves and Cæsar much trouble, surrendered at last; and Vergentorix, who was the chief spring of all the war, putting his best armor on, and adorning his horse, rode out of the gates, and made a turn about Cæsar as he was sitting, then quitted his horse, threw off his armor, and remained seated quietly at Cæsar's feet until he was led away to be reserved for the triumph.

Cæsar had long ago resolved upon the overthrow of Pompey, as had Pompey, for that matter, upon his. For Crassus, the fear of whom had hitherto kept them in peace, having now been killed in Parthia, if the one of them wished to make himself the greatest man in Rome, he had only to overthrow the other; and if he again wished to prevent his own fall, he had nothing for it but to be beforehand with him whom he feared. Pompey had not been long under any such apprehensions, having till lately despised Cæsar, as thinking it no difficult matter to put down him whom he himself had advanced. But Cæsar had entertained this design from the beginning against his rivals, and had retired, like an expert wrestler, to prepare himself apart for the combat. Making the Gallic wars his exercise ground, he had at once improved the strength of his soldiery, and had heightened his own glory by his great actions, so that he was looked on as one who might challenge comparison with Pompey. Nor did he let go any of those advantages which were now given him both by Pompey himself and the times, and the ill government of Rome, where all who were candidates for offices publicly gave money, and without any shame bribed the people, who having received their pay, did not contend for their benefactors with their bare suffrages, but with bows, swords, and slings. So that after having many times stained the place of election with the blood of men killed upon the spot, they left the city at last without a government at all, to be carried about like a ship without a pilot to steer her; while all who had any wisdom could only be thankful if a course of such wild and stormy disorder and madness might end no worse than in a monarchy. Some were so bold as to declare openly that the government was incurable but by a monarchy, and that they ought to take that remedy from the hands of the gentlest physician, meaning Pompey, who, though in words he pretended to decline it, yet in reality made his utmost efforts to be declared dictator. Cato, perceiving his design, prevailed with the senate to make him sole consul, that with the offer of a more legal sort of monarchy he might be withheld from demanding the dictatorship. They over and above voted him the continuance of his provinces, for he had two, Spain and all Africa, which he governed by his lieutenants, and maintained armies under him, at the yearly charge of a thousand talents out of the public treasury.

Upon this Cæsar also sent and petitioned for the consulship and the continuance of his provinces. Pompey at first did not stir in it, but Marcellus and Lentulus opposed it, who had always hated Cæsar, and now did everything, whether fit or unfit, which might disgrace and affront him. For they took away the privilege of Roman citizens from the people of New Comum, who were a colony that Cæsar had lately planted in Gaul, and Marcellus, who was then consul, ordered one of the senators of that town, then at Rome, to be whipped, and told him he laid that mark upon him to signify he was no citizen of Rome, bidding him, when he went back again, to show it to Cæsar. After Marcellus's consulship, Cæsar began to lavish gifts upon all the public men out of the riches he had taken from the Gauls; discharged Curio, the tribune, from his great debts; gave Paulus, then consul, fifteen hundred talents, with which he built the noble court of justice adjoining the forum, to supply the place of that called the Fulvian. Pompey, alarmed at these preparations, now openly took steps, both by himself and his friends, to have a successor appointed in Cæsar's room, and sent to demand back the soldiers whom he had lent him to carry on the wars in Gaul. Cæsar returned them, and made each soldier a present of two hundred and fifty drachmas. The officer who brought them home to Pompey spread amongst the people no very fair or favorable report of Cæsar, and flattered Pompey himself with false suggestions that he was wished for by Cæsar's army; and though his affairs here were in some embarrassment through the envy of some, and the ill state of the government, yet there the army was at his command, and, if they once crossed into Italy, would presently declare for him; so weary were they of Cæsar's endless expeditions, and so suspicious of his designs for a monarchy. Upon this Pompey grew presumptuous, and neglected all warlike preparations, as fearing no danger, and used no other means against him than mere speeches and votes, for which Cæsar cared nothing. And one of his captains, it is said, who was sent by him to Rome, standing before the senate house one day, and being told that the senate would not give Cæsar a longer time in his government, clapped his hand on the hilt of his sword and said, "But this shall."

Yet the demands which Cæsar made had the fairest colors of equity imaginable. For he proposed to lay down his arms, and that Pompey should do the same, and both together should become private men, and each expect a reward of his services from the public. For that those who proposed to disarm him, and at the same time to confirm Pompey in all the power he held, were simply establishing the one in the tyranny which they accused the other of aiming at. When Curio made these proposals to the people in Cæsar's name, he was loudly applauded, and some threw garlands towards him, and dismissed him as they do successful wrestlers, crowned with flowers. Antony, being tribune, produced a letter sent from Cæsar on this occasion, and read it though the consuls did what they could to oppose it. But Scipio, Pompey's father-in-law, proposed in the senate, that if Cæsar did not lay down his arms within such a time, he should be voted an enemy; and the consuls putting it to the question, whether Pompey should dismiss his soldiers, and again, whether Cæsar should disband his, very few assented to the first, but almost all to the latter. But Antony proposing again, that both should lay down their commissions, all but a very few agreed to it. Scipio was upon this very violent, and Lentulus, the consul, cried aloud that they had need of arms, and not of suffrages, against a robber; so that the senators for the present adjourned, and appeared in mourning as a mark of their grief for the dissension.

Afterwards there came other letters from Cæsar, which seemed yet more moderate, for he proposed to quit everything else, and only to retain Gaul within the Alps, Illyricum, and two legions, till he should stand a second time for consul. Cicero, the orator, who was lately returned from Cilicia, endeavored to reconcile differences, and softened Pompey, who was willing to comply in other things, but not to allow him the soldiers. At last Cicero used his persuasions with Cæsar's friends to accept of the provinces and six thousand soldiers only, and so to make up the quarrel. And Pompey was inclined to give way to this, but Lentulus, the consul, would not hearken to it, but drove Antony and Curio out of the senate house with insults, by which he afforded Cæsar the most plausible pretense that could be, and one which he could readily use to inflame the soldiers, by showing them two persons of such repute and authority who were forced to escape in a hired carriage in the dress of slaves. For so they were glad to disguise themselves when they fled out of Rome.

There were not about him at that time above three hundred horse and five thousand foot; for the rest of his army, which was left behind the Alps, was to be brought after him by officers who had received orders for that purpose. But he thought the first motion towards the design which he had on foot did not require large forces at present, and that what was wanted was to make this first step suddenly, and so as to astound his enemies with the boldness of it; as it would be easier, he thought, to throw them into consternation by doing what they never anticipated, than fairly to conquer them, if he had alarmed them by his preparations. And therefore he commanded his captains and other officers to go only with their swords in their hands, without any other arms, and make themselves masters of Ariminum, a large city of Gaul, with as little disturbance and bloodshed as possible. He committed the care of these forces to Hortensius, and himself spent the day in public as a stander-by and spectator of the gladiators, who exercised before him. A little before night he attended to his person, and then went into the hall, and conversed for some time with those he had invited to supper, till it began to grow dusk, when he rose from table and made his excuses to the company, begging them to stay till he came back, having already given private directions to a few immediate friends that they should follow him, not all the same way, but some one way, some another. He himself got into one of the hired carriages, and drove at first another way, but presently turned towards Ariminum. When he came to the river Rubicon, which parts Gaul within the Alps from the rest of Italy, his thoughts began to work, now he was just entering upon the danger, and he wavered much in his mind when he considered the greatness of the enterprise into which he was throwing himself. He checked his course and ordered a halt, while he revolved with himself, and often changed his opinion one way and the other, without speaking a word. This was when his purposes fluctuated most; presently he also discussed the matter with his friends who were about him (of which number Asinius Pollio was one), computing how many calamities his passing that river would bring upon mankind, and what a relation of it would be transmitted to posterity. At last, in a sort of passion, casting aside calculation, and abandoning himself to what might come, and using the proverb frequently in their mouths who enter upon dangerous and bold attempts, "The die is cast," with these words he took the river. Once over, he used all expedition possible, and before it was day reached Ariminum and took it. It is said that the night before he passed the river he had an impious dream, that he was unnaturally familiar with his own mother.

As soon as Ariminum was taken, wide gates, so to say, were thrown open, to let in war upon every land alike and sea, and with the limits of the province, the boundaries of the laws were transgressed. Nor would one have thought that, as at other times, the mere men and women fled from one town of Italy to another in their consternation, but that the very towns themselves left their sites, and fled for succor to each other. The city of Rome was overrun, as it were, with a deluge, by the conflux of people flying in from all the neighboring places. Magistrates could no longer govern, nor the eloquence of any orator quiet it; it was all but suffering shipwreck by the violence of its own tempestuous agitation. The most vehement contrary passions and impulses were at work everywhere. Nor did those who rejoiced at the prospect of the change altogether conceal their feelings, but when they met, as in so great a city they frequently must, with the alarmed and dejected of the other party, they provoked quarrels by their bold expressions of confidence in the event. Pompey, sufficiently disturbed of himself, was yet more perplexed by the clamors of others; some telling him that he justly suffered for having armed Cæsar against himself and the government; others blaming him for permitting Cæsar to be insolently used by Lentulus, when he made such ample concessions, and offered such reasonable proposals towards an accommodation. Favonius bade him now stamp upon the ground; for once talking big in the senate, he desired them not to trouble themselves about making any preparations for the war, for that he himself, with one stamp of his foot, would fill all Italy with soldiers. Yet still Pompey at that time had more forces than Cæsar; but he was not permitted to pursue his own thoughts, but being continually disturbed with false reports and alarms, as if the enemy was close upon him and carrying all before him, he gave way, and let himself be borne down by the general cry. He put forth an edict declaring the city to be in a state of anarchy, and left it with orders that the senate should follow him, and that no one should stay behind who did not prefer tyranny to their country and liberty.

The consuls at once fled, without making even the usual sacrifices; so did most of the senators, carrying off their own goods in as much haste as if they had been robbing their neighbors. Some, who had formerly much favored Cæsar's cause, in the prevailing alarm quitted their own sentiments, and without any prospect of good to themselves, were carried along by the common stream. It was a melancholy thing to see the city tossed in these tumults, like a ship given up by her pilots, and left to run, as chance guides her, upon any rock in her way. Yet, in spite of their sad condition, people still esteemed the place of their exile to be their country for Pompey's sake, and fled from Rome, as if it had been Cæsar's camp. Labienus even, who had been one of Cæsar's nearest friends, and his lieutenant, and who had fought by him zealously in the Gallic wars, now deserted him, and went over to Pompey. Cæsar sent all his money and equipage after him and then sat down before Corfinium, which was garrisoned with thirty cohorts under the command of Domitius. He, in despair of maintaining the defense, requested a physician, whom he had among his attendants, to give him poison; and taking the dose, drank it, in hopes of being dispatched by it. But soon after, when he was told that Cæsar showed the utmost clemency towards those he took prisoners, he lamented his misfortune, and blamed the hastiness of his resolution. His physician consoled him by informing him that he had taken a sleeping draught, not a poison; upon which, much rejoiced, and rising from his bed, he went presently to Cæsar and gave him the pledge of his hand, yet afterwards again went over to Pompey. The report of these actions at Rome quieted those who were there, and some who had fled thence returned.

Cæsar took into his army Domitius's soldiers, as he did all those whom he found in any town enlisted for Pompey's service. Being now strong and formidable enough, he advanced against Pompey himself, who did not stay to receive him, but fled to Brundusium, having sent the consuls before with a body of troops to Dyrrhachium. Soon after, upon Cæsar's approach, he set to sea, as shall be more particularly related in his Life. Cæsar would have immediately pursued him, but wanted shipping, and therefore went back to Rome, having made himself master of all Italy without bloodshed in the space of sixty days. When he came thither, he found the city more quiet than he expected, and many senators present, to whom he addressed himself with courtesy and deference, desiring them to send to Pompey about any reasonable accommodation towards a peace. But nobody complied with this proposal; whether out of fear of Pompey, whom they had deserted, or that they thought Cæsar did not mean what he said, but thought it his interest to talk plausibly. Afterwards, when Metellus, the tribune, would have hindered him from taking money out of the public treasure, and adduced some laws against it, Cæsar replied that arms and laws had each their own time; "If what I do displeases you, leave the place; war allows no free talking. When I have laid down my arms, and made peace, come back and make what speeches you please. And this," he added, "I tell you in diminution of my own just right, as indeed you and all others who have appeared against me and are now in my power may be treated as I please." Having said this to Metellus, he went to the doors of the treasury, and the keys being not to be found, sent for smiths to force them open. Metellus again making resistance, and some encouraging him in it, Cæsar, in a louder tone, told him he would put him to death if he gave him any further disturbance. "And this," said he, "you know, young man, is more disagreeable for me to say than to do." These words made Metellus withdraw for fear, and obtained speedy execution henceforth for all orders that Cæsar gave for procuring necessaries for the war.

He was now proceeding to Spain, with the determination of first crushing Afranius and Varro, Pompey's lieutenants, and making himself master of the armies and provinces under them, that he might then more securely advance against Pompey, when he had no enemy left behind him. In this expedition his person was often in danger from ambuscades, and his army by want of provisions, yet he did not desist from pursuing the enemy, provoking them to fight, and hemming them with his fortifications, till by main force he made himself master of their camps and their forces. Only the generals got off, and fled to Pompey.

When Cæsar came back to Rome, Piso, his father-in-law, advised him to send men to Pompey to treat of a peace; but Isauricus, to ingratiate himself with Cæsar, spoke against it. After this, being created dictator by the senate, he called home the exiles, and gave back their rights as citizens to the children of those who had suffered under Sylla; he relieved the debtors by an act remitting some part of the interest on their debts, and passed some other measures of the same sort, but not many. For within eleven days he resigned his dictatorship, and having declared himself consul, with Servilius Isauricus, hastened again to the war. He marched so fast that he left all his army behind him, except six hundred chosen horse and five legions, with which he put to sea in the very middle of winter, about the beginning of the month January (which corresponds pretty nearly with the Athenian month Posideon), and having past the Ionian Sea, took Oricum and Apollonia, and then sent back the ships to Brundusium, to bring over the soldiers who were left behind in the march. They, while yet on the march, their bodies now no longer in the full vigor of youth, and they themselves weary with such a multitude of wars, could not but exclaim against Cæsar, "When at last, and where, will this Cæsar let us be quiet? He carries us from place to place, and uses us as if we were not to be worn out, and had no sense of labor. Even our iron itself is spent by blows, and we ought to have some pity on our bucklers and breastplates, which have been used so long. Our wounds, if nothing else, should make him see that we are mortal men whom he commands, subject to the same pains and sufferings as other human beings. The very gods themselves cannot force the winter season, or hinder the storms in their time; yet he pushes forward, as if he were not pursuing, but flying from an enemy." So they talked as they marched leisurely towards Brundusium. But when they came thither, and found Cæsar gone off before them, their feelings changed, and they blamed themselves as traitors to their general. They now railed at their officers for marching so slowly, and placing themselves on the heights overlooking the sea towards Epirus, they kept watch to see if they could espy the vessels which were to transport them to Cæsar.

He in the meantime was posted in Apollonia, but had not an army with him able to fight the enemy, the forces from Brundusium being so long in coming, which put him to great suspense and embarrassment what to do. At last he resolved upon a most hazardous experiment, and embarked, without anyone's knowledge, in a boat of twelve oars, to cross over to Brundusium, though the sea was at that time covered with a vast fleet of the enemies. He got on board in the nighttime, in the dress of a slave and, throwing himself down like a person of no consequence, lay along at the bottom of the vessel. The river Anius was to carry them down to sea, and there used to blow a gentle gale every morning from the land, which made it calm at the mouth of the river, by driving the waves forward; but this night there had blown a strong wind from the sea, which overpowered that from the land, so that where the river met the influx of the seawater and the opposition of the waves it was extremely rough and angry; and the current was beaten back with such a violent swell that the master of the boat could not make good his passage, but ordered his sailors to tack about and return. Cæsar, upon this, discovers himself, and taking the man by the hand, who was surprised to see him there, said, "Go on, my friend, and fear nothing; you carry Cæsar and his fortune in your boat." The mariners, when they heard that, forgot the storm, and laying all their strength to their oars, did what they could to force their way down the river. But when it was to no purpose, and the vessel now took in much water, Cæsar finding himself in such danger in the very mouth of the river, much against his will permitted the master to turn back. When he was come to land, his soldiers ran to him in a multitude, reproaching him for what he had done, and indignant that he should think himself not strong enough to get a victory by their sole assistance, but must disturb himself, and expose his life for those who were absent, as if he could not trust those who were with him.

After this, Antony came over with the forces from Brundusium, which encouraged Cæsar to give Pompey battle, though he was encamped very advantageously, and furnished with plenty of provisions both by sea and land, whilst he himself was at the beginning but ill supplied, and before the end was extremely pinched for want of necessaries, so that his soldiers were forced to dig up a kind of root which grew there, and tempering it with milk, to feed on it. Sometimes they made a kind of bread of it, and advancing up to the enemy's outposts, would throw in these loaves, telling them, that as long as the earth produced such roots they would not give up blockading Pompey. But Pompey took what care he could that neither the loaves nor the words should reach his men, who were out of heart and despondent through terror at the fierceness and hardiness of their enemies, whom they looked upon as a sort of wild beasts. There were continual skirmishes about Pompey's outworks, in all which Cæsar had the better, except one, when his men were forced to fly in such a manner that he had like to have lost his camp. For Pompey made such a vigorous sally on them that not a man stood his ground; the trenches were filled with the slaughter, many fell upon their own ramparts and bulwarks, whither they were driven in flight by the enemy. Cæsar met them, and would have turned them back, but could not. When he went to lay hold of the ensigns, those who carried them threw them down, so that the enemies took thirty-two of them. He himself narrowly escaped; for taking hold of one of his soldiers, a big and strong man, that was flying by him, he bade him stand and face about; but the fellow, full of apprehensions from the danger he was in, laid hold of his sword, as if he would strike Cæsar, but Cæsar's armor bearer cut off his arm. Cæsar's affairs were so desperate at that time that when Pompey, either through overcautiousness or his ill fortune, did not give the finishing stroke to that great success, but retreated after he had driven the routed enemy within their camp, Cæsar, upon seeing his withdrawal, said to his friends, "The victory today had been on the enemies' side, if they had had a general who knew how to gain it." When he was retired into his tent, he laid himself down to sleep, but spent that night as miserably as ever he did any, in perplexity and consideration with himself, coming to the conclusion that he had conducted the war amiss. For when he had a fertile country before him, and all the wealthy cities of Macedonia and Thessaly, he had neglected to carry the war thither, and had sat down by the seaside, where his enemies had such a powerful fleet, so that he was in fact rather besieged by the want of necessaries, than besieging others with his arms. Being thus distracted in his thoughts with the view of the difficulty and distress he was in, he raised his camp with the intention of advancing towards Scipio, who lay in Macedonia; hoping either to entice Pompey into a country where he should fight without the advantage he now had of supplies from the sea, or to overpower Scipio, if not assisted.

This set all Pompey's army and officers on fire to hasten and pursue Cæsar, whom they concluded to be beaten and flying. But Pompey was afraid to hazard a battle on which so much depended, and being himself provided with all necessaries for any length of time, thought to tire out and waste the vigor of Cæsar's army, which could not last long. For the best part of his men, though they had great experience and showed an irresistible courage in all engagements, yet by their frequent marches, changing their camps, attacking fortifications, and keeping long night-watches, were getting worn out and broken; they being now old, their bodies less fit for labor, and their courage, also, beginning to give way with the failure of their strength. Besides, it was said that an infectious disease, occasioned by their irregular diet, was prevailing in Cæsar's army, and what was of greatest moment, he was neither furnished with money nor provisions, so that in a little time he must needs fall of himself.

For these reasons Pompey had no mind to fight him, but was thanked for it by none but Cato, who rejoiced at the prospect of sparing his fellow citizens. For he, when he saw the dead bodies of those who had fallen in the last battle on Cæsar's side, to the number of a thousand, turned away, covered his face, and shed tears. But everyone else upbraided Pompey for being reluctant to fight, and tried to goad him on by such nicknames as Agamemnon, and king of kings, as if he were in no hurry to lay down his sovereign authority, but was pleased to see so many commanders attending on him, and paying their attendance at his tent. Favonius, who affected Cato's free way of speaking his mind, complained bitterly that they should eat no figs even this year at Tusculum, because of Pompey's love of command. Afranius, who was lately returned out of Spain, and on account of his ill success there, labored under the suspicion of having been bribed to betray the army, asked why they did not fight this purchaser of provinces. Pompey was driven, against his own will, by this kind of language, into offering battle, and proceeded to follow Cæsar. Cæsar had found great difficulties in his march, for no country would supply him with provisions, his reputation being very much fallen since his late defeat. But after he took Gomphi, a town of Thessaly, he not only found provisions for his army, but physic too. For there they met with plenty of wine, which they took very freely, and heated with this, sporting and reveling on their march in bacchanalian fashion, they shook off the disease, and their whole constitution was relieved and changed into another habit.

When the two armies were come into Pharsalia, and both encamped there, Pompey's thoughts ran the same way as they had done before, against fighting, and the more because of some unlucky presages, and a vision he had in a dream. But those who were about him were so confident of success, that Domitius, and Spinther, and Scipio, as if they had already conquered, quarreled which should succeed Cæsar in the pontificate. And many sent to Rome to take houses fit to accommodate consuls and prætors, as being sure of entering upon those offices as soon as the battle was over. The cavalry especially were obstinate for fighting, being splendidly armed and bravely mounted, and valuing themselves upon the fine horses they kept, and upon their own handsome persons; as also upon the advantage of their numbers, for they were five thousand against one thousand of Cæsar's. Nor were the numbers of the infantry less disproportionate, there being forty-five thousand of Pompey's against twenty-two thousand of the enemy.

Cæsar, collecting his soldiers together, told them that Corfinius was coming up to them with two legions, and that fifteen cohorts more under Calenus were posted at Megara and Athens; he then asked them whether they would stay till these joined them, or would hazard the battle by themselves. They all cried out to him not to wait, but on the contrary to do whatever he could to bring about an engagement as soon as possible. When he sacrificed to the gods for the lustration of his army, upon the death of the first victim, the augur told him, within three days he should come to a decisive action. Cæsar asked him whether he saw anything in the entrails which promised a happy event. "That," said the priest, "you can best answer yourself; for the gods signify a great alteration from the present posture of affairs. If, therefore, you think yourself well off now, expect worse fortune; if unhappy, hope for better." The night before the battle, as he walked the rounds about midnight, there was a light seen in the heaven, very bright and flaming, which seemed to pass over Cæsar's camp and fall into Pompey's. And when Cæsar's soldiers came to relieve the watch in the morning, they perceived a panic disorder among the enemies. However, he did not expect to fight that day, but set about raising his camp with the intention of marching towards Scotussa.

But when the tents were now taken down, his scouts rode up to him, and told him the enemy would give him battle. With this news he was extremely pleased, and having performed his devotions to the gods, set his army in battle array, dividing them into three bodies. Over the middlemost he placed Domitius Calvinus; Antony commanded the left wing, and he himself the right, being resolved to fight at the head of the tenth legion. But when he saw the enemy's cavalry taking position against him, being struck with their fine appearance and their number, he gave private orders that six cohorts from the rear of the army should come round and join him, whom he posted behind the right wing, and instructed them what they should do when the enemy's horse came to charge. On the other side, Pompey commanded the right wing, Domitius the left, and Scipio, Pompey's father-in-law, the center. The whole weight of the cavalry was collected on the left wing, with the intent that they should outflank the right wing of the enemy, and rout that part where the general himself commanded. For they thought no phalanx of infantry could be solid enough to sustain such a shock, but that they must necessarily be broken and shattered all to pieces upon the onset of so immense a force of cavalry. When they were ready on both sides to give the signal for battle, Pompey commanded his foot, who were in the front, to stand their ground, and without breaking their order, receive quietly the enemy's first attack, till they came within javelin's cast. Cæsar, in this respect, also, blames Pompey's generalship, as if he had not been aware how the first encounter, when made with an impetus and upon the run, gives weight and force to the strokes, and fires the men's spirits into a flame, which the general concurrence fans to full heat. He himself was just putting the troops into motion and advancing to the action, when he found one of his captains, a trusty and experienced soldier, encouraging his men to exert their utmost. Cæsar called him by his name, and said, "What hopes, Caius Crassinius, and what grounds for encouragement?" Crassinius stretched out his hand, and cried in a loud voice, "We shall conquer nobly, Cæsar; and I this day will deserve your praises, either alive or dead." So he said, and was the first man to run in upon the enemy, followed by the hundred and twenty soldiers about him, and breaking through the first rank, still pressed on forwards with much slaughter of the enemy, till at last he was struck back by the wound of a sword, which went in at his mouth with such force that it came out at his neck behind.

Whilst the foot was thus sharply engaged in the main battle, on the flank Pompey's horse rode up confidently, and opened their ranks very wide, that they might surround the right wing of Cæsar. But before they engaged, Cæsar's cohorts rushed out and attacked them, and did not dart their javelins at a distance, nor strike at the thighs and legs, as they usually did in close battle, but aimed at their faces. For thus Cæsar had instructed them, in hopes that young gentlemen, who had not known much of battles and wounds, but came wearing their hair long, in the flower of their age and height of their beauty, would be more apprehensive of such blows, and not care for hazarding both a danger at present and a blemish for the future. And so it proved, for they were so far from bearing the stroke of the javelins, that they could not stand the sight of them, but turned about, and covered their faces to secure them. Once in disorder, presently they turned about to fly; and so most shamefully ruined all. For those who had beat them back at once outflanked the infantry, and falling on their rear, cut them to pieces. Pompey, who commanded the other wing of the army, when he saw his cavalry thus broken and flying, was no longer himself, nor did he now remember that he was Pompey the Great, but like one whom some god had deprived of his senses, retired to his tent without speaking a word, and there sat to expect the event, till the whole army was routed and the enemy appeared upon the works which were thrown up before the camp, where they closely engaged with his men who were posted there to defend it. Then first he seemed to have recovered his senses, and uttering, it is said, only these words, "What, into the camp too?" he laid aside his general's habit, and putting on such clothes as might best favor his flight, stole off. What fortune he met with afterwards, how he took shelter in Egypt, and was murdered there, we tell you in his Life.

Cæsar, when he came to view Pompey's camp, and saw some of his opponents dead upon the ground, others dying, said, with a groan, "This they would have; they brought me to this necessity. I, Caius Cæsar, after succeeding in so many wars, had been condemned had I dismissed my army." These words, Pollio says, Cæsar spoke in Latin at that time, and that he himself wrote them in Greek; adding, that those who were killed at the taking of the camp, were most of them servants; and that not above six thousand soldiers fell. Cæsar incorporated most of the foot whom he took prisoners with his own legions, and gave a free pardon to many of the distinguished persons, and amongst the rest to Brutus, who afterwards killed him. He did not immediately appear after the battle was over, which put Cæsar, it is said, into great anxiety for him; nor was his pleasure less when he saw him present himself alive.

There were many prodigies that foreshadowed this victory, but the most remarkable that we are told of was that at Tralles. In the temple of Victory stood Cæsar's statue. The ground on which it stood was naturally hard and solid, and the stone with which it was paved still harder; yet it is said that a palm tree shot itself up near the pedestal of this statue. In the city of Padua, one Caius Cornelius, who had the character of a good augur, the fellow citizen and acquaintance of Livy, the historian, happened to be making some augural observations that very day when the battle was fought. And first, as Livy tells us, he pointed out the time of the fight, and said to those who were by him that just then the battle was begun and the men engaged. When he looked a second time, and observed the omens, he leaped up as if he had been inspired, and cried out, "Cæsar, you are victorious." This much surprised the standers-by, but he took the garland which he had on from his head, and swore he would never wear it again till the event should give authority to his art. This Livy positively states for a truth.

Cæsar, as a memorial of his victory, gave the Thessalians their freedom, and then went in pursuit of Pompey. When he was come into Asia, to gratify Theopompus, the author of the collection of fables, he enfranchised the Cnidians, and remitted one-third of their tribute to all the people of the province of Asia. When he came to Alexandria, where Pompey was already murdered, he would not look upon Theodotus, who presented him with his head, but taking only his signet, shed tears. Those of Pompey's friends who had been arrested by the king of Egypt, as they were wandering in those parts, he relieved, and offered them his own friendship. In his letter to his friends at Rome, he told them that the greatest and most signal pleasure his victory had given him was to be able continually to save the lives of fellow citizens who had fought against him. As to the war in Egypt, some say it was at once dangerous and dishonorable, and noways necessary, but occasioned only by his passion for Cleopatra. Others blame the ministers of the king, and especially the eunuch Pothinus, who was the chief favorite, and had lately killed Pompey, who had banished Cleopatra, and was now secretly plotting Cæsar's destruction (to prevent which, Cæsar from that time began to sit up whole nights, under pretense of drinking, for the security of his person), while openly he was intolerable in his affronts to Cæsar, both by his words and actions. For when Cæsar's soldiers had musty and unwholesome corn measured out to them, Pothinus told them they must be content with it, since they were fed at another's cost. He ordered that his table should be served with wooden and earthen dishes, and said Cæsar had carried off all the gold and silver plate, under pretense of arrears of debt. For the present king's father owed Cæsar one thousand seven hundred and fifty myriads of money. Cæsar had formerly remitted to his children the rest, but thought fit to demand the thousand myriads at that time to maintain his army. Pothinus told him that he had better go now and attend to his other affairs of greater consequence, and that he should receive his money at another time with thanks. Cæsar replied that he did not want Egyptians to be his counselors, and soon after privately sent for Cleopatra from her retirement.

She took a small boat, and one only of her confidants, Apollodorus, the Sicilian, along with her, and in the dusk of the evening landed near the palace. She was at a loss how to get in undiscovered, till she thought of putting herself into the coverlet of a bed and lying at length, whilst Apollodorus tied up the bedding and carried it on his back through the gates to Cæsar's apartment. Cæsar was first captivated by this proof of Cleopatra's bold wit, and was afterwards so overcome by the charm of her society that he made a reconciliation between her and her brother, on condition that she should rule as his colleague in the kingdom. A festival was kept to celebrate this reconciliation, where Cæsar's barber, a busy, listening fellow, whose excessive timidity made him inquisitive into everything, discovered that there was a plot carrying on against Cæsar by Achillas, general of the king's forces, and Pothinus, the eunuch. Cæsar, upon the first intelligence of it, set a guard upon the hall where the feast was kept and killed Pothinus. Achillas escaped to the army, and raised a troublesome and embarrassing war against Cæsar, which it was not easy for him to manage with his few soldiers against so powerful a city and so large an army. The first difficulty he met with was want of water, for the enemies had turned the canals. Another was, when the enemy endeavored to cut off his communication by sea, he was forced to divert that danger by setting fire to his own ships, which, after burning the docks, thence spread on and destroyed the great library. A third was, when in an engagement near Pharos, he leaped from the mole into a small boat to assist his soldiers who were in danger, and when the Egyptians pressed him on every side, he threw himself into the sea, and with much difficulty swam off. This was the time when, according to the story, he had a number of manuscripts in his hand, which, though he was continually darted at, and forced to keep his head often under water, yet he did not let go, but held them up safe from wetting in one hand, whilst he swam with the other. His boat, in the meantime, was quickly sunk. At last, the king having gone off to Achillas and his party, Cæsar engaged and conquered them. Many fell in that battle, and the king himself was never seen after. Upon this, he left Cleopatra queen of Egypt, who soon after had a son by him, whom the Alexandrians called Cæsarion, and then departed for Syria.

Thence he passed to Asia, where he heard that Domitius was beaten by Pharnaces, son of Mithridates, and had fled out of Pontus with a handful of men; and that Pharnaces pursued the victory so eagerly, that though he was already master of Bithynia and Cappadocia, he had a further design of attempting the Lesser Armenia, and was inviting all the kings and tetrarchs there to rise. Cæsar immediately marched against him with three legions, fought him near Zela, drove him out of Pontus, and totally defeated his army. When he gave Amantius, a friend of his at Rome, an account of this action, to express the promptness and rapidity of it he used three words, I came, saw, and conquered, which in Latin, having all the same cadence, carry with them a very suitable air of brevity.[1]

Hence he crossed into Italy, and came to Rome at the end of that year, for which he had been a second time chosen dictator, though that office had never before lasted a whole year, and was elected consul for the next. He was ill spoken of, because upon a mutiny of some soldiers, who killed Cosconius and Galba, who had been prætors, he gave them only the slight reprimand of calling them *Citizens,* instead of *Fellow Soldiers,* and afterwards assigned to each man a thousand drachmas, besides a share of lands in Italy. He was also reflected on for Dolabella's extravagance, Amantius's covetousness, Antony's debauchery, and Corfinius's profuseness, who pulled down Pompey's house, and rebuilt it, as not magnificent enough; for the Romans were much displeased with all these. But Cæsar, for the prosecution of his own scheme of government, though he knew their characters and disapproved them, was forced to make use of those who would serve him.

After the battle of Pharsalia, Cato and Scipio fled into Africa, and

---

[1] ["Veni, vidi, vici."]

there, with the assistance of King Juba, got together a considerable force, which Cæsar resolved to engage. He, accordingly, passed into Sicily about the winter solstice, and to remove from his officers' minds all hopes of delay there, encamped by the seashore, and as soon as ever he had a fair wind, put to sea with three thousand foot and a few horse. When he had landed them, he went back secretly, under some apprehensions for the larger part of his army, but met them upon the sea, and brought them all to the same camp. There he was informed that the enemies relied much upon an ancient oracle, that the family of the Scipios should be always victorious in Africa. There was in his army a man, otherwise mean and contemptible, but of the house of the Africani, and his name Scipio Sallutio. This man Cæsar (whether in raillery, to ridicule Scipio, who commended the enemy, or seriously to bring over the omen to his side, it were hard to say) put at the head of his troops, as if he were general, in all the frequent battles which he was compelled to fight. For he was in such want both of victualing for his men, and forage for his horses, that he was forced to feed the horses with seaweed, which he washed thoroughly to take off its saltiness, and mixed with a little grass to give it a more agreeable taste. The Numidians, in great numbers, and well horsed, whenever he went, came up and commanded the country. Cæsar's cavalry, being one day unemployed, diverted themselves with seeing an African, who entertained them with dancing and at the same time playing upon the pipe to admiration. They were so taken with this, that they alighted, and gave their horses to some boys, when on a sudden the enemy surrounded them, killed some, pursued the rest, and fell in with them into their camp; and had not Cæsar himself and Asinius Pollio come to their assistance, and put a stop to their flight, the war had been then at an end. In another engagement, also, the enemy had again the better, when Cæsar, it is said, seized a standard bearer, who was running away, by the neck, and forcing him to face about, said, "Look, that is the way to the enemy."

Scipio, flushed with this success at first, had a mind to come to one decisive action. He therefore left Afranius and Juba in two distinct bodies not far distant and marched himself towards Thapsus, where he proceeded to build a fortified camp above a lake, to serve as a center point for their operations, and also as a place of refuge. Whilst Scipio was thus employed, Cæsar with incredible dispatch made his way through thick woods, and a country supposed to be impassable, cut off one party of the enemy, and attacked another in the front. Having routed these, he followed up his opportunity and the current of his good fortune, and on the first onset carried Afranius's camp, and ravaged that of the Numidians, Juba, their king, being glad to save himself by flight; so that in a small part of a single day he made himself master of three camps, and killed fifty thousand of the enemy, with the loss only of fifty of his own men. This is the account some give of that fight. Others say he was not in the action, but that he was taken with his usual distemper just as he was setting his army in order. He perceived the approaches of it, and before it had too far disordered his senses, when he was already beginning to shake under its influence, withdrew into a neighboring fort, where he reposed himself. Of the men of consular and prætorian dignity that were taken after the fight, several Cæsar put to death, others anticipated him by killing themselves.

Cato had undertaken to defend Utica, and for that reason was not in the battle. The desire which Cæsar had to take him alive made him hasten thither; and upon the intelligence that he had dispatched himself, he was much discomposed, for what reason is not so well agreed. He certainly said, "Cato, I must grudge you your death, as you grudged me the honor of saving your life." Yet the discourse he wrote against Cato after his death is no great sign of his kindness, or that he was inclined to be reconciled to him. For how is it probable that he would have been tender of his life when he was so bitter against his memory? But from his clemency to Cicero, Brutus, and many others who fought against him, it may be divined that Cæsar's book was not written so much out of animosity to Cato, as in his own vindication. Cicero had written an encomium upon Cato, and called it by his name. A composition by so great a master upon so excellent a subject was sure to be in everyone's hands. This touched Cæsar, who looked upon a panegyric on his enemy as no better than an invective against himself; and therefore he made in his Anti-Cato a collection of whatever could be said in his derogation. The two compositions, like Cato and Cæsar themselves, have each of them their several admirers.

Cæsar, upon his return to Rome, did not omit to pronounce before the people a magnificent account of his victory, telling them that he had subdued a country which would supply the public every year with two hundred thousand attic bushels of corn and three million pounds' weight of oil. He then led three triumphs for Egypt, Pontus, and Africa, the last for the victory over not Scipio, but King Juba, as it was professed, whose little son was then carried in the triumph, the happiest captive that ever was, who, of a barbarian Numidian, came by this means to obtain a place among the most learned historians of Greece. After the triumphs, he distributed rewards to his soldiers and treated the people with feasting and shows. He entertained the whole people together at one feast, where twenty-two thousand dining couches were laid out; and he made a display of gladiators, and of battles by sea, in honor, as he said, of his daughter Julia, though she had been long since dead. When these shows were over, an account was taken of the people who, from three hundred and twenty thousand, were now reduced to one hundred and fifty thousand. So great a waste had the civil war made in Rome alone, not to mention what the other parts of Italy and the provinces suffered.

He was now chosen a fourth time consul, and went into Spain against Pompey's sons. They were but young, yet had gathered together a very numerous army, and showed they had courage and conduct to command it, so that Cæsar was in extreme danger. The great battle was near the town of Munda, in which Cæsar, seeing his men hard pressed, and making but a weak resistance, ran through the ranks among the soldiers, and crying out, asked them whether they were not ashamed to deliver him into the hands of boys? At last, with great difficulty, and the best efforts he could make, he forced back the enemy, killing thirty thousand of them, though with the loss of one thousand of his best men. When he came back from the fight, he told his friends that he had often fought for victory, but this was the first time that he had ever fought for life. This battle was won on the feast of Bacchus, the very day in which Pompey, four years before, had set out for the war. The younger of Pompey's sons escaped; but Didius, some days after the fight, brought the head of the elder to Cæsar. This was the last war he was engaged in. The triumph which he celebrated for this victory displeased the Romans beyond anything. For he had not defeated foreign generals, or barbarian kings, but had destroyed the children and family of one of the greatest men of Rome, though unfortunate; and it did not look well to lead a procession in celebration of the calamities of his country, and to rejoice in those things for which no other apology could be made either to gods or men than their being absolutely necessary. Besides that, hitherto he had never sent letters or messengers to announce any victory over his fellow citizens, but had seemed rather to be ashamed of the action than to expect honor from it.

Nevertheless his countrymen, conceding all to his fortune, and accepting the bit, in the hope that the government of a single person would give them time to breathe after so many civil wars and calamities, made him dictator for life. This was indeed a tyranny avowed, since his power now was not only absolute, but perpetual too. Cicero made the first proposals to the senate for conferring honors upon him, which might in some sort be said not to exceed the limits of ordinary human moderation. But others, striving which should deserve most, carried them so excessively high, that they made Cæsar odious to the most indifferent and moderate sort of men, by the pretensions and the extravagance of the titles which they decreed him. His enemies, too, are thought to have had some share in this, as well as his flatterers. It gave them advantage against him, and would be their justification for any attempt they should make upon him; for since the civil wars were ended, he had nothing else that he could be charged with. And they had good reason to decree a temple to Clemency, in token of their thanks for the mild use he made of his victory. For he not only pardoned many of those who fought against him, but, further, to some gave honors and offices; as particularly to Brutus and Cassius, who both of them were prætors. Pompey's images that were thrown down he set up again, upon which Cicero also said that by raising Pompey's statues he had fixed his own. When his friends advised him to have a guard, and several offered their service, he would not hear of it; but said it was better to suffer death once than always to live in fear of it. He looked upon the affections of the people to be the best and surest guard, and entertained them again with public feasting and general distributions of corn; and to gratify his army, he sent out colonies to several places, of which the most remarkable were Carthage and Corinth; which as before they had been ruined at the same time, so now were restored and repeopled together.

As for the men of high rank, he promised to some of them future consulships and prætorships, some he consoled with other offices and honors, and to all held out hopes of favor by the solicitude he showed to rule with the general goodwill, insomuch that upon the death of Maximus one day before his consulship was ended, he made Caninius Revilius consul for that day. And when many went to pay the usual compliments and attentions to the new consul, "Let us make haste," said Cicero, "lest the man be gone out of his office before we come."

Cæsar was born to do great things, and had a passion after honor, and the many noble exploits he had done did not now serve as an inducement to him to sit still and reap the fruit of his past labors, but were incentives and encouragements to go on, and raised in him ideas of still greater actions, and a desire of new glory, as if the present were all spent. It was in fact a sort of emulous struggle with himself, as it had been with another, how he might outdo his past actions by his future. In pursuit of these thoughts, he resolved to make war upon the Parthians, and when he had subdued them, to pass through Hyrcania; thence to march along by the Caspian Sea to Mount Caucasus, and so on about Pontus till he came into Scythia; then to overrun all the countries bordering upon Germany, and Germany itself; and so to return through Gaul into Italy, after completing the whole circle of his intended empire, and bounding it on every side by the ocean. While preparations were making for this expedition, he proposed to dig through the isthmus on which Corinth stands; and appointed Anienus to superintend the work. He had also a design of diverting the Tiber, and carrying it by a deep channel directly from Rome to Circeii, and so into the sea near Tarracina, that there might be a safe and easy passage for all merchants who traded to Rome. Besides this, he intended to drain all the marshes by Pomentium and

Setia, and gain ground enough from the water to employ many thousands of men in tillage. He proposed further to make great mounds on the shore nearest Rome to hinder the sea from breaking in upon the land, to clear the coast at Ostia of all the hidden rocks and shoals that made it unsafe for shipping, and to form ports and harbors fit to receive the large number of vessels that would frequent them.

These things were designed without being carried into effect; but his reformation of the calendar in order to rectify the irregularity of time was not only projected with great scientific ingenuity, but was brought to its completion, and proved of very great use. For it was not only in ancient time that the Romans had wanted a certain rule to make the revolutions of their months fall in with the course of the year, so that their festivals and solemn days for sacrifice were removed by little and little, till at last they came to be kept at seasons quite the contrary to what was at first intended, but even at this time the people had no way of computing the solar year; only the priests could say the time, and they, at their pleasure, without giving any notice, slipped in the intercalary month, which they called Mercedonius. Numa was the first who put in this month, but his expedient was but a poor one and quite inadequate to correct all the errors that arose in the returns of the annual cycles, as we have shown in his life.[2] Cæsar called in the best philosophers and mathematicians of his time to settle the point, and out of the systems he had before him formed a new and more exact method of correcting the calendar, which the Romans use to this day, and seem to succeed better than any nation in avoiding the errors occasioned by the inequality of the cycles. Yet even this gave offense to those who looked with an evil eye on his position and felt oppressed by his power. Cicero, the orator, when someone in his company chanced to say the next morning Lyra would rise, replied, "Yes, in accordance with the edict," as if even this were a matter of compulsion.

But that which brought upon him the most apparent and mortal hatred, was his desire of being king; which gave the common people the first occasion to quarrel with him, and proved the most specious pretense to those who had been his secret enemies all along. Those who would have procured him that title gave it out that it was foretold in the Sybils' books that the Romans should conquer the Parthians when they fought against them under the conduct of a king, but not before. And one day, as Cæsar was coming down from Alba to Rome, some were so bold as to salute him by the name of king; but he finding the people disrelish it, seemed to resent it himself, and said his name was Cæsar, not king. Upon this, there was a general silence, and he passed on looking not very well pleased or

---

[2][Not included in this volume.]

contented. Another time, when the senate had conferred on him some extravagant honors, he chanced to receive the message as he was sitting on
the rostra, where, though the consuls and prætors themselves waited on
him, attended by the whole body of the senate, he did not rise, but behaved himself to them as if they had been private men, and told them his
honors wanted rather to be retrenched than increased. This treatment offended not only the senate, but the commonalty too, as if they thought
the affront upon the senate equally reflected upon the whole republic; so
that all who could decently leave him went off, looking much discomposed. Cæsar, perceiving the false step he had made, immediately retired
home; and laying his throat bare, told his friends that he was ready to offer
this to anyone who would give the stroke. But afterwards he made the
malady from which he suffered the excuse for his sitting, saying that those
who are attacked by it lose their presence of mind if they talk much standing; that they presently grow giddy, fall into convulsions, and quite lose
their reason. But this was not the reality, for he would willingly have stood
up to the senate, had not Cornelius Balbus, one of his friends, or rather
flatterers, hindered him. "Will you not remember," said he, "you are Cæsar,
and claim the honor which is due to your merit?"

He gave a fresh occasion of resentment by his affront to the tribunes.
The Lupercalia were then celebrated, a feast at the first institution belonging, as some writers say, to the shepherds, and having some connection with the Arcadian Lycæ. Many young noblemen and magistrates run
up and down the city with their upper garments off, striking all they
meet with thongs of hide, by way of sport; and many women, even of the
highest rank, place themselves in the way, and hold out their hands to the
lash, as boys in a school do to the master, out of a belief that it procures
an easy labor to those who are with child, and makes those conceive who
are barren. Cæsar, dressed in a triumphal robe, seated himself in a golden
chair at the rostra to view this ceremony. Antony, as consul, was one of
those who ran this course, and when he came into the forum, and the
people made way for him, he went up and reached to Cæsar a diadem
wreathed with laurel. Upon this there was a shout, but only a slight one,
made by the few who were planted there for that purpose; but when
Cæsar refused it, there was universal applause. Upon the second offer,
very few, and upon the second refusal, all again applauded. Cæsar finding
it would not take, rose up, and ordered the crown to be carried into the
capitol. Cæsar's statues were afterwards found with royal diadems on their
heads. Flavius and Marullus, two tribunes of the people, went presently
and pulled them off, and having apprehended those who first saluted
Cæsar as king committed them to prison. The people followed them
with acclamations, and called them by the name of Brutus, because
Brutus was the first who ended the succession of kings, and transferred

the power which before was lodged in one man into the hands of the senate and people. Cæsar so far resented this, that he displaced Marullus and Flavius; and in urging his charges against them, at the same time ridiculed the people, by himself giving the men more than once the names of Bruti and Cumæi.

This made the multitude turn their thoughts to Marcus Brutus, who, by his father's side, was thought to be descended from that first Brutus, and by his mother's side from the Servilii, another noble family, being besides nephew and son-in-law to Cato. But the honors and favors he had received from Cæsar, took off the edge from the desires he might himself have felt for overthrowing the new monarchy. For he had not only been pardoned himself after Pompey's defeat at Pharsalia, and had procured the same grace for many of his friends, but was one in whom Cæsar had a particular confidence. He had at that time the most honorable prætorship of the year, and was named for the consulship four years after, being preferred before Cassius, his competitor. Upon the question as to the choice, Cæsar, it is related, said that Cassius had the fairer pretensions, but that he could not pass by Brutus. Nor would he afterwards listen to some who spoke against Brutus, when the conspiracy against him was already afoot, but laying his hand on his body, said to the informers, "Brutus will wait for this skin of mine," intimating that he was worthy to bear rule on account of his virtue, but would not be base and ungrateful to gain it. Those who desired a change, and looked on him as the only, or at least the most proper, person to effect it, did not venture to speak with him; but in the nighttime laid papers about his chair of state, where he used to sit and determine causes, with such sentences in them as, "You are asleep, Brutus," "You are no longer Brutus." Cassius, when he perceived his ambition a little raised upon this, was more instant than before to work him yet further, having himself a private grudge against Cæsar for some reasons that we have mentioned in the Life of Brutus.[3] Nor was Cæsar without suspicions of him, and said once to his friends, "What do you think Cassius is aiming at? I don't like him, he looks so pale." And when it was told him that Antony and Dolabella were in a plot against him, he said he did not fear such fat, luxurious men, but rather the pale, lean fellows, meaning Cassius and Brutus.

Fate, however, is to all appearance more unavoidable than unexpected. For many strange prodigies and apparitions are said to have been observed shortly before the event. As to the lights in the heavens, the noises heard in the night, and the wild birds which perched in the forum, these are not perhaps worth taking notice of in so great a case as this. Strabo, the philosopher, tells us that a number of men were seen, looking as if

---

[3][Not included in this volume.]

they were heated through with fire, contending with each other; that a quantity of flame issued from the hand of a soldier's servant, so that they who saw it thought he must be burnt, but that after all he had no hurt. As Cæsar was sacrificing, the victim's heart was missing, a very bad omen, because no living creature can subsist without a heart. One finds it also related by many, that a soothsayer bade him prepare for some great danger on the Ides of March. When this day was come, Cæsar, as he went to the senate, met this soothsayer, and said to him by way of raillery, "The Ides of March are come"; who answered him calmly, "Yes, they are come, but they are not past." The day before his assassination, he supped with Marcus Lepidus; and as he was signing some letters according to his custom, as he reclined at table, there arose a question what sort of death was the best. At which he immediately, before anyone could speak, said, "A sudden one."

After this, as he was in bed with his wife, all the doors and windows of the house flew open together; he was startled at the noise, and the light which broke into the room, and sat up in his bed, where by the moonshine he perceived Calpurnia fast asleep, but heard her utter in her dream some indistinct words and inarticulate groans. She fancied at that time she was weeping over Cæsar, and holding him butchered in her arms. Others say this was not her dream, but that she dreamed that a pinnacle, which the senate, as Livy relates, had ordered to be raised on Cæsar's house by way of ornament and grandeur, was tumbling down, which was the occasion of her tears and ejaculations. When it was day, she begged of Cæsar, if it were possible, not to stir out, but to adjourn the senate to another time; and if he slighted her dreams, that he would be pleased to consult his fate by sacrifices, and other kinds of divination. Nor was he himself without some suspicion and fears; for he never before discovered any womanish superstition in Calpurnia, whom he now saw in such great alarm. Upon the report which the priests made to him, that they had killed several sacrifices, and still found them inauspicious, he resolved to send Antony to dismiss the senate.

In this juncture, Decimus Brutus, surnamed Albinus, one whom Cæsar had such confidence in that he made him his second heir, who nevertheless was engaged in the conspiracy with the other Brutus and Cassius, fearing lest if Cæsar should put off the senate to another day, the business might get wind, spoke scoffingly and in mockery of the diviners, and blamed Cæsar for giving the senate so fair an occasion of saying he had put a slight upon them, for that they were met upon his summons, and were ready to vote unanimously that he should be declared king of all the provinces out of Italy, and might wear a diadem in any other place but Italy, by sea or land. If anyone should be sent to tell them they might break up for the present, and meet again when Calpurnia should chance to have better dreams, what would his enemies say? Or who would with any patience hear his friends, if they should presume to defend his government as not arbitrary and tyrannical? But if he was possessed so far as to think this day unfortunate, yet it were more decent to go himself to the senate, and to adjourn it in his own person. Brutus, as he spoke these words, took Cæsar by the hand, and conducted him forth. He was not gone far from the door, when a servant of some other person's made towards him, but not being able to come up to him, on account of the crowd of those who pressed about him, he made his way into the house, and committed himself to Calpurnia, begging of her to secure him till Cæsar returned, because he had matters of great importance to communicate to him.

Artemidorus, a Cnidian, a teacher of Greek logic, and by that means so far acquainted with Brutus and his friends as to have got into the secret, brought Cæsar in a small written memorial the heads of what he had to depose. He had observed that Cæsar, as he received any papers, presently gave them to the servants who attended on him; and therefore came as near to him as he could, and said, "Read this, Cæsar, alone, and quickly, for it contains matter of great importance which nearly concerns you." Cæsar received it, and tried several times to read it, but was still hindered by the crowd of those who came to speak to him. However, he kept it in his hand by itself till he came into the senate. Some say it was another who gave Cæsar this note, and that Artemidorus could not get to him, being all along kept off by the crowd.

All these things might happen by chance. But the place which was destined for the scene of this murder, in which the senate met that day, was the same in which Pompey's statue stood, and was one of the edifices which Pompey had raised and dedicated with his theater to the use of the public, plainly showing that there was something of a supernatural influence which guided the action and ordered it to that particular place. Cassius, just before the act, is said to have looked towards Pompey's statue, and silently implored his assistance, though he had been inclined to the doctrines of Epicurus. But this occasion, and the instant danger, carried him away out of all his reasonings, and filled him for the time with a sort of inspiration. As for Antony, who was firm to Cæsar, and a strong man, Brutus Albinus kept him outside the house, and delayed him with a long conversation contrived on purpose. When Cæsar entered, the senate stood up to show their respect to him, and of Brutus's confederates, some came about his chair and stood behind it, others met him, pretending to add their petitions to those of Tillius Cimber, in behalf of his brother, who was in exile; and they followed him with their joint supplications till he came to his seat. When he was sat down, he refused to comply with their requests, and upon their urging him further began to reproach them severally for their importunities, when Tillius, laying hold of his robe with both his hands, pulled it down from his neck, which was the signal for the assault. Casca gave him the first cut, in the neck, which was not mortal nor dangerous, as coming from one who at the beginning of such a bold action was probably very much disturbed; Cæsar immediately turned about, and laid his hand upon the dagger and kept hold of it. And both of them at the same time cried out, he that received the blow, in Latin, "Vile Casca, what does this mean?" and he that gave it, in Greek, to his brother, "Brother, help!" Upon this first onset, those who were not privy to the design were astonished, and their horror and amazement at what they saw were so great that they durst not fly nor assist Cæsar, nor so much as speak a word. But those who came prepared for the business enclosed him on every side, with their naked daggers in their hands. Which way soever he turned, he met with blows, and saw their swords leveled at his face and eyes, and was encompassed, like a wild beast in the toils, on every side. For it had been agreed they should each of them make a thrust at him, and flesh themselves with his blood; for which reason Brutus also gave him one stab in the groin. Some say that he fought and resisted all the rest, shifting his body to avoid the blows, and calling out for help, but that when he saw Brutus's sword drawn, he covered his face with his robe and submitted, letting himself fall, whether it were by chance, or that he was pushed in that direction by his murderers, at the foot of the pedestal on which Pompey's statue stood, and which was thus wetted with his blood. So that Pompey himself seemed to have presided, as it were, over the revenge done upon his adversary, who lay here at his feet, and breathed out his soul through his multitude of wounds, for they say he received three and twenty. And the conspirators themselves were many of them wounded by each other, whilst they all leveled their blows at the same person.

When Cæsar was dispatched, Brutus stood forth to give a reason for what they had done, but the senate would not hear him, but flew out of doors in all haste, and filled the people with so much alarm and distraction, that some shut up their houses, others left their counters and shops. All ran one way or the other, some to the place to see the sad spectacle, others back again after they had seen it. Antony and Lepidus, Cæsar's most faithful friends, got off privately, and hid themselves in some friends' houses. Brutus and his followers, being yet hot from the deed, marched in a body from the senate house to the capitol with their drawn swords, not like persons who thought of escaping, but with an air of confidence and assurance, and as they went along, called to the people to resume their liberty, and invited the company of any more distinguished people whom they met. And some of these joined the procession and went up along with them, as if they also had been of the conspiracy, and

could claim a share in the honor of what had been done. As, for example, Caius Octavius and Lentulus Spinther, who suffered afterwards for
their vanity, being taken off by Antony and the young Cæsar, and lost the
honor they desired, as well as their lives, which it cost them, since no one
believed they had any share in the action. For neither did those who
punished them profess to revenge the fact, but the ill will. The day after,
Brutus with the rest came down from the capitol and made a speech to
the people, who listened without expressing either any pleasure or resentment, but showed by their silence that they pitied Cæsar and respected Brutus. The senate passed acts of oblivion for what was past, and
took measures to reconcile all parties. They ordered that Cæsar should be
worshipped as a divinity, and nothing, even of the slightest consequence,
should be revoked which he had enacted during his government. At the
same time they gave Brutus and his followers the command of provinces,
and other considerable posts. So that all people now thought things were
well settled, and brought to the happiest adjustment.

But when Cæsar's will was opened, and it was found that he had left
a considerable legacy to each one of the Roman citizens, and when his
body was seen carried through the marketplace all mangled with
wounds, the multitude could no longer contain themselves within the
bounds of tranquillity and order, but heaped together a pile of benches,
bars, and tables, which they placed the corpse on, and setting fire to it,
burnt it on them. Then they took brands from the pile, and ran some to
fire the houses of the conspirators, others up and down the city, to find
out the men and tear them to pieces, but met, however, with none of
them, they having taken effectual care to secure themselves.

One Cinna, a friend of Cæsar's, chanced the night before to have an
odd dream. He fancied that Cæsar invited him to supper, and that upon
his refusal to go with him, Cæsar took him by the hand and forced him,
though he hung back. Upon hearing the report that Cæsar's body was
burning in the marketplace, he got up and went thither, out of respect to
his memory, though his dream gave him some ill apprehensions, and
though he was suffering from a fever. One of the crowd who saw him
there asked another who that was, and having learned his name, told it
to his next neighbor. It presently passed for a certainty that he was one
of Cæsar's murderers, as, indeed, there was another Cinna, a conspirator,
and they, taking this to be the man, immediately seized him and tore him
limb from limb upon the spot.

Brutus and Cassius, frightened at this, within a few days retired out of
the city. What they afterwards did and suffered, and how they died, is
written in the Life of Brutus. Cæsar died in his fifty-sixth year, not having survived Pompey above four years. That empire and power which he
had pursued through the whole course of his life with so much hazard,

he did at last with much difficulty compass, but reaped no other fruits from it than the empty name and invidious glory. But the great genius which attended him through his lifetime even after his death remained as the avenger of his murder, pursuing through every sea and land all those who were concerned in it, and suffering none to escape, but reaching all who in any sort or kind were either actually engaged in the fact, or by their counsels any way promoted it.

The most remarkable of mere human coincidences was that which befell Cassius, who, when he was defeated at Philippi, killed himself with the same dagger which he had made use of against Cæsar. The most signal preternatural appearances were the great comet, which shone very bright for seven nights after Cæsar's death, and then disappeared, and the dimness of the sun, whose orb continued pale and dull for the whole of that year, never showing its ordinary radiance at its rising, and giving but a weak and feeble heat. The air consequently was damp and gross for want of stronger rays to open and rarify it. The fruits, for that reason, never properly ripened, and began to wither and fall off for want of heat before they were fully formed. But above all, the phantom which appeared to Brutus showed the murder was not pleasing to the gods. The story of it is this.

Brutus, being to pass his army from Abydos to the continent on the other side, laid himself down one night, as he used to do, in his tent, and was not asleep, but thinking of his affairs, and what events he might expect. For he is related to have been the least inclined to sleep of all men who have commanded armies, and to have had the greatest natural capacity for continuing awake, and employing himself without need of rest. He thought he heard a noise at the door of his tent, and looking that way, by the light of his lamp, which was almost out, saw a terrible figure, like that of a man, but of unusual stature and severe countenance. He was somewhat frightened at first, but seeing it neither did nor spoke anything to him, only stood silently by his bedside, he asked who it was. The specter answered him, "Thy evil genius, Brutus, thou shalt see me at Philippi." Brutus answered courageously, "Well, I shall see you," and immediately the appearance vanished. When the time was come, he drew up his army near Philippi against Antony and Cæsar, and in the first battle won the day, routed the enemy, and plundered Cæsar's camp. The night before the second battle, the same phantom appeared to him again, but spoke not a word. He presently understood his destiny was at hand, and exposed himself to all the danger of the battle. Yet he did not die in the fight, but seeing his men defeated, got up to the top of a rock, and there presenting his sword to his naked breast, and assisted, as they say, by a friend, who helped him to give the thrust, met his death.

CICERO

IT IS generally said, that Helvia, the mother of Cicero, was both well born and lived a fair life; but of his father nothing is reported but in extremes. For whilst some would have him the son of a fuller, and educated in that trade, others carry back the origin of his family to Tullus Attius, an illustrious king of the Volscians, who waged war not without honor against the Romans. However, he who first of that house was surnamed Cicero seems to have been a person worthy to be remembered; since those who succeeded him not only did not reject, but were fond of that name, though vulgarly made a matter of reproach. For the Latins call a vetch *Cicer,* and a nick or dent at the tip of his nose, which resembled the opening in a vetch, gave him the surname of *Cicero.*

Cicero, whose story I am writing, is said to have replied with spirit to some of his friends, who recommended him to lay aside or change the name when he first stood for office and engaged in politics, that he would make it his endeavor to render the name of Cicero more glorious than that of the Scauri and Catuli. And when he was quæstor in Sicily, and was making an offering of silver plate to the gods, and had inscribed his two names, Marcus and Tullius, instead of the third he jestingly told the artificer to engrave the figure of a vetch by them. Thus much is told us about his name.

Of his birth it is reported that his mother was delivered, without pain or labor, on the third of the new Calends, the same day on which now the magistrates of Rome pray and sacrifice for the emperor. It is said, also, that a vision appeared to his nurse, and foretold the child she then suckled should afterwards become a great benefit to the Roman states. To such presages, which might in general be thought mere fancies and idle talk, he himself ere long gave the credit of true prophecies. For as soon as he was of an age to begin to have lessons, he became so distinguished for his talent, and got such a name and reputation among the boys, that their fathers would often visit the school that they might see young Cicero, and might be able to say that they themselves had witnessed the quickness and readiness in learning for which he was renowned. And the more rude among them used to be angry with their children, to see them, as they walked together, receiving Cicero with respect into the middle place. And being, as Plato would have the scholar-like and philosophical temper, eager for every kind of learning and indisposed to no description of knowledge or instruction, he showed, however, a more peculiar propensity to poetry; and there is a poem now extant made by him when a boy, in tetrameter verse, called Pontius Glaucus. And afterwards, when he applied himself more curiously to these accomplishments, he had the name of being not only the best orator, but also the best poet of Rome. And the glory of his rhetoric still remains, notwithstanding the many new modes in speaking since his time; but his verses are forgotten and out of all repute, so many ingenious poets having followed him.

Leaving his juvenile studies, he became an auditor of Philo the Academic, whom the Romans, above all the other scholars of Clitomachus, admired for his eloquence and loved for his character. He also sought the company of the Mucii, who were eminent statesmen and leaders in the senate, and acquired from them a knowledge of the laws. For some short time he served in arms under Sylla, in the Marsian war. But perceiving the commonwealth running into factions, and from faction all things tending to an absolute monarchy, he betook himself to a retired and contemplative life, and conversing with the learned Greeks, devoted himself to study, till Sylla had obtained the government, and the commonwealth was in some kind of settlement.

At this time, Chrysogonus, Sylla's emancipated slave, having laid an information about an estate belonging to one who was said to have been put to death by proscription, had bought it himself for two thousand drachmas. And when Roscius, the son and heir of the dead, complained, and demonstrated the estate to be worth two hundred and fifty talents, Sylla took it angrily to have his actions questioned, and preferred a process against Roscius for the murder of his father, Chrysogonus managing the evidence. None of the advocates durst assist him, but, fearing the cruelty of Sylla, avoided the cause. The young man, being thus deserted, came for refuge to Cicero. Cicero's friends encouraged him, saying he was not likely ever to have a fairer and more honorable introduction to public life; he therefore undertook the defense, carried the cause, and got much renown for it.

But fearing Sylla, he traveled into Greece, and gave it out that he did so for the benefit of his health. And indeed he was lean and meager, and had such a weakness in his stomach that he could take nothing but a spare and thin diet, and that not till late in the evening. His voice was loud and good, but so harsh and unmanaged that in vehemence and heat of speaking he always raised it to so high a tone, that there seemed to be reason to fear about his health.

When he came to Athens, he was a hearer of Antiochus of Ascalon, with whose fluency and elegance of diction he was much taken, although he did not approve of his innovations in doctrine. For Antiochus had now fallen off from the New Academy, as they call it, and forsaken the sect of Carneades, whether that he was moved by the argument of manifestness and the senses, or, as some say, had been led by feelings of rivalry and opposition to the followers of Clitomachus and Philo to change his opinions, and in most things to embrace the doctrine of the Stoics. But Cicero rather affected and adhered to the doctrines of the New Academy; and purposed with himself, if he should be disappointed of any employment in the commonwealth, to retire hither from pleading and political affairs, and to pass his life with quiet in the study of philosophy.

But after he had received the news of Sylla's death, and his body, strengthened again by exercise, was come to a vigorous habit, his voice managed and rendered sweet and full to the ear and pretty well brought into keeping with his general constitution, his friends at Rome earnestly soliciting him by letters, and Antiochus also urging him to return to public affairs, he again prepared for use his orator's instrument of rhetoric, and summoned into action his political faculties, diligently exercising himself in declamations and attending the most celebrated rhetoricians of the time. He sailed from Athens for Asia and Rhodes. Amongst the Asian masters, he conversed with Xenocles of Adramyttium, Dionysius of Magnesia, and Menippus of Caria; at Rhodes, he studied oratory with Apollonius, the son of Molon, and philosophy with Posidonius. Apollonius, we are told, not understanding Latin, requested Cicero to declaim in Greek. He complied willingly, thinking that his faults would thus be better pointed out to him. And after he finished, all his other hearers were astonished, and contended who should praise him most, but Apollonius, who had shown no signs of excitement whilst he was hearing him, so also now, when it was over, sat musing for some considerable time, without any remark. And when Cicero was discomposed at this, he said, "You have my praise and admiration, Cicero, and Greece my pity and commiseration, since those arts and that eloquence which are the only glories that remain to her, will now be transferred by you to Rome."

And now when Cicero, full of expectation, was again bent upon political affairs, a certain oracle blunted the edge of his inclination; for consulting the god of Delphi how he should attain most glory, the Pythoness answered, by making his own genius and not the opinion of the people the guide of his life; and therefore at first he passed his time in Rome cautiously, and was very backward in pretending to public offices, so that he was at that time in little esteem, and had got the names, so readily given by low and ignorant people in Rome, of Greek and Scholar. But when his own desire of fame and the eagerness of his father and relations had made him take in earnest to pleading, he made no slow or gentle advance to the first place, but shone out in full luster at once, and far surpassed all the advocates of the bar. At first, it is said, he, as well as Demosthenes, was defective in his delivery, and on that account paid much attention to the instructions, sometimes of Roscius the comedian, and sometimes of Æsop the tragedian. They tell of this Æsop, that whilst he was representing on the theater Atreus deliberating the revenge of Thyestes, he was so transported beyond himself in the heat of action, that he struck with his scepter one of the servants, who was running across the stage, so violently that he laid him dead upon the place. And such afterwards was Cicero's delivery that it did not a little contribute to render his eloquence persuasive. He used to ridicule loud speakers, saying that they shouted because they could not speak, like lame men who get on horseback because they cannot walk. And his readiness and address in sarcasm, and generally in witty sayings, was thought to suit a pleader very well, and to be highly attractive, but his using it to excess offended many, and gave him the repute of ill nature.

He was appointed quæstor in a great scarcity of corn, and had Sicily for his province, where, though at first he displeased many by compelling them to send in their provisions to Rome, yet after they had had experience of his care, justice, and clemency, they honored him more than ever they did any of their governors before. It happened, also, that some young Romans of good and noble families, charged with neglect of discipline and misconduct in military service, were brought before the prætor in Sicily. Cicero undertook their defense, which he conducted admirably, and got them acquitted. So returning to Rome with a great opinion of himself for these things, a ludicrous incident befell him, as he tells us himself. Meeting an eminent citizen in Campania, whom he accounted his friend, he asked him what the Romans said and thought of his actions, as if the whole city had been filled with the glory of what he had done. His friend asked him in reply, "Where is it you have been, Cicero?" This for the time utterly mortified and cast him down, to perceive that the report of his actions had sunk into the city of Rome as into an immense ocean, without any visible effect or result in reputation. And afterwards considering with himself that the glory he contended for was an infinite thing, and that there was no fixed end nor measure in its pursuit, he abated much of his ambitious thoughts. Nevertheless, he was always excessively pleased with his own praise, and continued to the very last to be passionately fond of glory; which often interfered with the prosecution of his wisest resolutions.

On beginning to apply himself more resolutely to public business, he remarked it as an unreasonable and absurd thing that artificers, using vessels and instruments inanimate, should know the name, place, and use of every one of them, and yet the statesman, whose instruments for carrying out public measures are men, should be negligent and careless in the knowledge of persons. And so he not only acquainted himself with the names, but also knew the particular place where every one of the more eminent citizens dwelt, what lands he possessed, the friends he made use of, and those that were of his neighborhood, and when he traveled on any road in Italy, he could readily name and show the estates and seats of his friends and acquaintance. Having so small an estate, though a sufficient competency for his own expenses, it was much wondered at that he took neither fees nor gifts from his clients, and more especially that he did not do so when he undertook the prosecution of Verres. This Verres, who had been prætor of Sicily, and stood charged by the Sicilians of many evil practices during his government there, Cicero succeeded in getting condemned, not by speaking, but in a manner by holding his tongue. For the prætors, favoring Verres, had deferred the trial by several adjournments to the last day, in which it was evident there could not be sufficient time for the advocates to be heard, and the cause brought to an issue. Cicero, therefore, came forward, and said there was no need of speeches; and after producing and examining witnesses, he required the judges to proceed to sentence. However, many witty sayings are on record, as having been used by Cicero on the occasion. When a man named Cæcilius, one of the freed slaves, who was said to be given to Jewish practices, would have put by the Sicilians, and undertaken the prosecution of Verres himself, Cicero asked, "What has a Jew to do with swine?" *verres* being the Roman word for a boar. And when Verres began to reproach Cicero with effeminate living, "You ought," replied he, "to use this language at home, to your sons"; Verres having a son who had fallen into disgraceful courses. Hortensius the orator, not daring directly to undertake the defense of Verres, was yet persuaded to appear for him at the laying on of the fine, and received an ivory sphinx for his reward; and when Cicero, in some passage of his speech, obliquely reflected on him, and Hortensius told him he was not skillful in solving riddles, "No," said Cicero, "and yet you have the sphinx in your house!"

Verres was thus convicted; though Cicero, who set the fine at seventy-five myriads, lay under the suspicion of being corrupted by bribery to lessen the sum. But the Sicilians, in testimony of their gratitude, came and brought him all sorts of presents from the island, when he was ædile; of which he made no private profit himself, but used their generosity only to reduce the public price of provisions.

He had a very pleasant seat at Arpi, he had also a farm near Naples, and another about Pompeii, but neither of any great value. The portion of his wife, Terentia, amounted to ten myriads, and he had a bequest valued at nine myriads of denarii; upon these he lived in a liberal but temperate style with the learned Greeks and Romans that were his familiars. He rarely, if at any time, sat down to meat till sunset, and that not so much on account of business, as for his health and the weakness of his stomach. He was otherwise in the care of his body nice and delicate, appointing himself, for example, a set number of walks and rubbings. And after this manner managing the habit of his body, he brought it in time to be healthful, and capable of supporting many great fatigues and trials. His father's house he made over to his brother, living himself near the Palatine hill, that he might not give the trouble of long journeys to those that made suit to him. And, indeed, there were not fewer daily appearing at his door, to do their court to him, than there were that came to Crassus for his riches, or to Pompey for his power amongst the soldiers, these being at that time the two men of the greatest repute and influence in Rome. Nay, even Pompey himself used to pay court to Cicero, and Cicero's public actions did much to establish Pompey's authority and reputation in the state.

Numerous distinguished competitors stood with him for the prætor's office; but he was chosen before them all, and managed the decision of causes with justice and integrity. It is related that Licinius Macer, a man himself of great power in the city, and supported also by the assistance of Crassus, was accused before him of extortion, and that, in confidence on his own interest and the diligence of his friends, whilst the judges were debating about the sentence, he went to his house, where hastily trimming his hair and putting on a clean gown as already acquitted, he was setting off again to go to the Forum; but at his hall door meeting Crassus, who told him that he was condemned by all the votes, he went in again, threw himself upon his bed, and died immediately. This verdict was considered very creditable to Cicero, as showing his careful management of the courts of justice. On another occasion, Vatinius, a man of rude manners and often insolent in court to the magistrates, who had large swellings on his neck, came before his tribunal and made some request, and on Cicero's desiring further time to consider it, told him that he himself would have made no question about it had he been prætor. Cicero, turning quickly upon him, answered, "But I, you see, have not the neck that you have."

When there were but two or three days remaining in his office, Manilius was brought before him, and charged with peculation. Manilius had the good opinion and favor of the common people, and was thought to be prosecuted only for Pompey's sake, whose particular friend he was. And therefore, when he asked a space of time before his trial, and Cicero allowed him but one day, and that the next only, the common people grew highly offended, because it had been the custom of the prætors to allow ten days at least to the accused; and the tribunes of the people, having called him before the people and accused him, he, desiring to be heard, said that as he had always treated the accused with equity and humanity, as far as the law allowed, so he thought it hard to deny the same to Manilius, and that he had studiously appointed that day of which alone, as prætor, he was master, and that it was not the part of those that were desirous to help him to cast the judgment of his cause upon another prætor. These things being said made a wonderful change in the people, and, commending him much for it, they desired that he himself would undertake the defense of Manilius; which he willingly consented to, and that principally for the sake of Pompey, who was absent. And, accordingly, taking his place before the people again, he delivered a bold invective upon the oligarchical party and on those who were jealous of Pompey.

Yet he was preferred to the consulship no less by the nobles than the common people, for the good of the city; and both parties jointly assisted his promotion, upon the following reasons. The change of government made by Sylla, which at first seemed a senseless one, by time and usage had now come to be considered by the people no unsatisfactory settlement. But there were some that endeavored to alter and subvert the whole present state of affairs, not from any good motives, but for their own private gain; and Pompey being at this time employed in the wars with the kings of Pontus and Armenia, there was no sufficient force at Rome to suppress any attempts at a revolution. These people had for their head a man of bold, daring, and restless character, Lucius Catiline, who was accused, besides other great offenses, of deflowering his virgin daughter, and killing his own brother; for which latter crime, fearing to be prosecuted at law, he persuaded Sylla to set him down, as though he were yet alive, amongst those that were to be put to death by proscription. This man the profligate citizens choosing for their captain, gave faith to one another, amongst other pledges, by sacrificing a man and eating of his flesh; and a great part of the young men of the city were corrupted by him, he providing for everyone pleasures, drink, and women, and profusely supplying the expense of these debauches. Etruria, moreover, had all been excited to revolt, as well as a great part of Gaul within the Alps. But Rome itself was in the most dangerous inclination to change, on account of the unequal distribution of wealth and property, those of highest rank and greatest spirit having impoverished themselves by shows, entertainments, ambition of offices, and sumptuous buildings, and the riches of the city having thus fallen into the hands of mean and low-born persons. So that there wanted but a slight impetus to set all in motion, it being in the power of every daring man to overturn a sickly commonwealth.

Catiline, however, being desirous of procuring a strong position to carry out his designs, stood for the consulship, and had great hopes of success, thinking he should be appointed, with Caius Antonius as his colleague, who was a man fit to lead neither in a good cause nor in a bad one, but might be a valuable accession to another's power. These things the greatest part of the good and honest citizens apprehending, put Cicero upon standing for the consulship; whom the people readily receiving, Catiline was put by, so that he and Caius Antonius were chosen, although amongst the competitors he was the only man descended from a father of the equestrian and not of the senatorial order.

Though the designs of Catiline were not yet publicly known, yet considerable preliminary troubles immediately followed upon Cicero's entrance upon the consulship. For, on the one side, those who were disqualified by the laws of Sylla from holding any public offices, being neither inconsiderable in power nor in number, came forward as candidates and caressed the people for them; speaking many things truly and justly against the tyranny of Sylla, only that they disturbed the government at an improper and unseasonable time; on the other hand, the tribunes of the people proposed laws to the same purpose, constituting a commission of ten persons, with unlimited powers, in whom as supreme governors should be vested the right of selling the public lands of all Italy and Syria and Pompey's new conquests, of judging and banishing whom they pleased, of planting colonies, of taking moneys out of the treasury, and of levying and paying what soldiers should be thought needful. And several of the nobility favored this law, but especially Caius Antonius, Cicero's colleague, in hopes of being one of the ten. But what gave the greatest fear to the nobles was that he was thought privy to the conspiracy of Catiline, and not to dislike it, because of his great debts.

Cicero, endeavoring in the first place to provide a remedy against this danger, procured a decree assigning to him the province of Macedonia, he himself declining that of Gaul, which was offered to him. And this piece of favor so completely won over Antonius, that he was ready to second and respond to, like a hired player, whatever Cicero said for the good of the country. And now, having made his colleague thus tame and tractable, he could with greater courage attack the conspirators. And, therefore, in the senate, making an oration against the law of the ten commissioners, he so confounded those who proposed it, that they had nothing to reply. And when they again endeavored, and, having prepared things beforehand, had called the consuls before the assembly of the people, Cicero, fearing nothing, went first out, and commanded the senate to follow him, and not only succeeded in throwing out the law, but so entirely overpowered the tribunes by his oratory, that they abandoned all thought of their other projects.

For Cicero, it may be said, was the one man, above all others, who made the Romans feel how great a charm eloquence lends to what is good, and how invincible justice is, if it be well spoken; and that it is necessary for him who would dexterously govern a commonwealth, in action, always to prefer that which is honest before that which is popular, and in speaking, to free the right and useful measure from everything that may occasion offense. An incident occurred in the theater, during his consulship, which showed what his speaking could do. For whereas formerly the knights of Rome were mingled in the theater with the common people and took their places among them as it happened, Marcus Otho, when he was prætor, was the first who distinguished them from the other citizens and appointed them a proper seat, which they still enjoy as their special place in the theater. This the common people took as an indignity done to them, and, therefore, when Otho appeared in the theater they hissed him; the knights, on the contrary, received him with loud clapping. The people repeated and increased their hissing; the knights continued their clapping. Upon this, turning upon one another, they broke out into insulting words, so that the theater was in great disorder. Cicero, being informed of it, came himself to the theater, and summoning the people into the temple of Bellona, he so effectually chid and chastised them for it, that, again returning into the theater, they received Otho with loud applause, contending with the knights who should give him the greatest demonstrations of honor and respect.

The conspirators with Catiline, at first cowed and disheartened, began presently to take courage again. And assembling themselves together, they exhorted one another boldly to undertake the design before Pompey's return, who, as it was said, was now on his march with his forces for Rome. But the old soldiers of Sylla were Catiline's chief stimulus to action. They had been disbanded all about Italy, but the greatest number and the fiercest of them lay scattered among the cities of Etruria, entertaining themselves with dreams of new plunder and rapine amongst the hoarded riches of Italy. These, having for their leader Manlius, who had served with distinction in the wars under Sylla, joined themselves to Catiline and came to Rome to assist him with their suffrages at the election. For he again pretended to the consulship, having resolved to kill Cicero in a tumult at the elections. Also, the divine powers seemed to give intimation of the coming troubles, by earthquakes, thunderbolts, and strange appearances. Nor was human evidence wanting, certain enough in itself, though not sufficient for the conviction of the noble and powerful Catiline. Therefore Cicero, deferring the day of election, summoned Catiline into the senate, and questioned him as to the charges made against him. Catiline, believing there were many in the senate desirous of change, and to give a specimen of himself to the conspirators present, returned an audacious answer, "What harm," said he, "when I see two bodies, the one lean and consumptive with a head, the other great and strong without one, if I put a head to that body which wants one?" This covert representation of the senate and the people excited yet greater apprehensions in Cicero. He put on armor, and was attended from his house by the noble citizens in a body; and a number of the young men went with him into the Plain. Here, designedly letting his tunic slip partly off from his shoulders, he showed his armor underneath, and discovered his danger to the spectators; who, being much moved at it, gathered round about him for his defense. At length, Catiline was by a general suffrage again put by, and Silanus and Murena chosen consuls.

Not long after this, Catiline's soldiers got together in a body in Etruria and began to form themselves into companies, the day appointed for the design being near at hand. About midnight, some of the principal and most powerful citizens of Rome, Marcus Crassus, Marcus Marcellus, and Scipio Metellus, went to Cicero's house, where, knocking at the gate, and calling up the porter, they commanded him to awake Cicero and tell him they were there. The business was this: Crassus's porter after supper had delivered to him letters brought by an unknown person. Some of them were directed to others, but one to Crassus, without a name; this only Crassus read, which informed him that there was a great slaughter intended by Catiline, and advised him to leave the city. The others he did not open, but went with them immediately to Cicero, being affrighted at the danger, and to free himself of the suspicion he lay under for his familiarity with Catiline. Cicero, considering the matter, summoned the senate at break of day. The letters he brought with him, and delivered them to those to whom they were directed, commanding them to read them publicly; they all alike contained an account of the conspiracy. And when Quintus Arrius, a man of prætorian dignity, recounted to them how soldiers were collecting in companies in Etruria, and Manlius stated to be in motion with a large force, hovering about those cities, in expectation of intelligence from Rome, the senate made a decree to place all in the hands of the consuls, who should undertake the conduct of everything, and do their best to save the state. This was not a common thing, but only done by the senate in case of imminent danger.

After Cicero had received this power, he committed all affairs outside to Quintus Metellus, but the management of the city he kept in his own hands. Such a numerous attendance guarded him every day when he went abroad, that the greatest part of the marketplace was filled with his train when he entered it. Catiline, impatient of further delay, resolved himself to break forth and go to Manlius, but he commanded Marcius and Cethegus to take their swords, and go early in the morning to Cicero's gates, as if only intending to salute him, and then to fall upon him and slay him. This a noble lady, Fulvia, coming by night, discovered to Cicero, bidding him beware of Cethegus and Marcius. They came by break of day and, being denied entrance, made an outcry and disturbance at the gates, which excited all the more suspicion. But Cicero, going forth, summoned the senate into the temple of Jupiter Stator, which stands at the end of the Sacred Street, going up to the Palatine. And when Catiline with others of his party also came, as intending to make his defense, none of the senators would sit by him, but all of them left the bench where he had placed himself. And when he began to speak, they interrupted him with outcries. At length Cicero, standing up, commanded him to leave the city, for since one governed the commonwealth with words, the other with arms, it was necessary there should be a wall betwixt them. Catiline, therefore, immediately left the town, with three hundred armed men; and assuming, as if he had been a magistrate, the rods, axes, and military ensigns, he went to Manlius, and having got together a body of near twenty thousand men, with these he marched to the several cities, endeavoring to persuade or force them to revolt. So it being now come to open war, Antonius was sent forth to fight him.

The remainder of those in the city whom he had corrupted, Cornelius Lentulus kept together and encouraged. He had the surname Sura, and was a man of a noble family, but a dissolute liver, who for his debauchery was formerly turned out of the senate, and was now holding the office of prætor for the second time, as the custom is with those who desire to regain the dignity of senator. It is said that he got the surname Sura upon this occasion; being quæstor in the time of Sylla, he had lavished away and consumed a great quantity of the public moneys, at which Sylla being provoked, called him to give an account in the senate; he appeared with great coolness and contempt, and said he had no account to give, but they might take this, holding up the calf of his leg, as boys do at ball, when they have missed. Upon which he was surnamed *Sura, sura* being the Roman word for the calf of the leg. Being at another time prosecuted at law, and having bribed some of the judges, he escaped only by two votes, and complained of the needless expense he had gone to in paying for a second, as one would have sufficed to acquit him. This man, such in his own nature, and now inflamed by Catiline, false prophets and fortune tellers had also corrupted with vain hopes, quoting to him fictitious verses and oracles, and proving from the Sibylline prophecies that there were three of the name Cornelius designed by fate to be monarchs of Rome; two of whom, Cinna and Sylla, had already fulfilled the decree, and that divine fortune was now advancing with the gift of monarchy for the remaining third Cornelius; and that therefore he ought by all means to accept it, and not lose opportunity by delay, as Catiline had done.

Lentulus, therefore, designed no mean or trivial matter, for he had resolved to kill the whole senate, and as many other citizens as he could, to fire the city, and spare nobody, except only Pompey's children, intending to seize and keep them as pledges of his reconciliation with Pompey. For there was then a common and strong report that Pompey was on his way homeward from his great expedition. The night appointed for the design was one of the Saturnalia; swords, flax, and sulfur they carried and hid in the house of Cethegus; and providing one hundred men, and dividing the city into as many parts, they had allotted to every one singly his proper place, so that in a moment, many kindling the fire, the city might be in a flame all together. Others were appointed to stop up the aqueducts, and to kill those who should endeavor to carry water to put it out. Whilst these plans were preparing, it happened there were two ambassadors from the Allobroges staying in Rome; a nation at that time in a distressed condition, and very uneasy under the Roman government. These Lentulus and his party judging useful instruments to move and seduce Gaul to revolt, admitted into the conspiracy, and they gave them letters to their own magistrates and letters to Catiline; in those they promised liberty, in these they exhorted Catiline to set all slaves free and to bring them along with him to Rome. They sent also, to accompany them to Catiline, one Titus, a native of Croton, who was to carry those letters to him.

These counsels of inconsidering men, who conversed together over wine and with women, Cicero watched with sober industry and forethought, and with most admirable sagacity, having several emissaries abroad, who observed and traced with him all that was done, and keeping also a secret correspondence with many who pretended to join in the conspiracy. He thus knew all the discourse which passed betwixt them and the strangers; and lying in wait for them by night, he took the Crotonian with his letters, the ambassadors of the Allobroges acting secretly in concert with him.

By break of day, he summoned the senate into the temple of Concord, where he read the letters and examined the informers. Junius Silanus further stated that several persons had heard Cethegus say that three consuls and four prætors were to be slain. Piso, also, a person of consular dignity, testified other matters of the like nature; and Caius Sulpicius, one of the prætors, being sent to Cethegus's house, found there a quantity of darts and of armor, and a still greater number of swords and daggers, all recently whetted. At length, the senate decreeing indemnity to the Crotonian upon his confession of the whole matter, Lentulus was convicted, abjured his office (for he was then prætor), and put off his robe edged with purple in the senate, changing it for another garment more agreeable to his present circumstances. He thereupon, with the rest of his confederates present, was committed to the charge of the prætors in free custody.

It being evening, and the common people in crowds expecting without, Cicero went forth to them, and told them what was done, and then, attended by them, went to the house of a friend and near neighbor; for his own was taken up by the women who were celebrating with secret rites the feast of the goddess whom the Romans call the Good, and the Greeks the Women's goddess. For a sacrifice is annually performed to her in the consul's house, either by his wife or mother, in the presence of the vestal virgins. And having got into his friend's house privately, a few only being present, he began to deliberate how he should treat these men. The severest, and the only punishment fit for such heinous crimes, he was somewhat shy and fearful of inflicting, as well from the clemency of his nature, as also lest he should be thought to exercise his authority too insolently, and to treat too harshly men of the noblest birth and most powerful friendships in the city; and yet, if he should use them more mildly, he had a dreadful prospect of danger from them. For there was no likelihood, if they suffered less than death, they would be reconciled, but rather, adding new rage to their former wickedness, they would rush into every kind of audacity, while he himself, whose character for courage already did not stand very high with the multitude, would be thought guilty of the greatest cowardice and want of manliness.

Whilst Cicero was doubting what course to take, a portent happened to the women in their sacrificing. For on the altar, where the fire seemed wholly extinguished, a great and bright flame issued forth from the ashes of the burnt wood; at which others were affrighted, but the holy virgins called to Terentia, Cicero's wife, and bade her haste to her husband, and command him to execute what he had resolved for the good of his country, for the goddess had sent a great light to the increase of his safety and glory. Terentia, therefore, as she was otherwise in her own nature neither tenderhearted nor timorous, but a woman eager for distinction (who, as Cicero himself says, would rather thrust herself into his public affairs, than communicate her domestic matters to him), told him these things, and excited him against the conspirators. So also did Quintus his brother, and Publius Nigidius, one of his philosophical friends, whom he often made use of in his greatest and most weighty affairs of state.

The next day, a debate arising in the senate about the punishment of the men, Silanus, being the first who was asked his opinion, said it was fit they should be all sent to the prison, and there suffer the utmost penalty. To him all consented in order till it came to Caius Cæsar, who was afterwards dictator. He was then but a young man, and only at the outset of his career, but had already directed his hopes and policy to that course by which he afterwards changed the Roman state into a monarchy. Of this others foresaw nothing; but Cicero had seen reason for strong suspicion, though without obtaining any sufficient means of proof. And there were some indeed that said that he was very near being discovered, and only just escaped him; others are of opinion that Cicero voluntarily overlooked and neglected the evidence against him, for fear of his friends and power; for it was very evident to everybody that if Cæsar was to be accused with the conspirators, they were more likely to be saved with him, than he to be punished with them.

When, therefore, it came to Cæsar's turn to give his opinion, he stood up and proposed that the conspirators should not be put to death, but their estates confiscated, and their persons confined in such cities in Italy as Cicero should approve, there to be kept in custody till Catiline was conquered. To this sentence, as it was the most moderate, and he that delivered it a most powerful speaker, Cicero himself gave no small weight, for he stood up and, turning the scale on either side, spoke in favor partly of the former, partly of Cæsar's sentence. And all Cicero's friends, judging Cæsar's sentence most expedient for Cicero, because he would incur the less blame if the conspirators were not put to death, chose rather the latter; so that Silanus, also, changing his mind, retracted his opinion, and said he had not declared for capital, but only the utmost punishment, which to a Roman senator is imprisonment. The first man who spoke against Cæsar's motion was Catulus Lutatius. Cato followed, and so vehemently urged in his speech the strong suspicion about Cæsar himself, and so filled the senate with anger and resolution, that a decree was passed for the execution of the conspirators. But Cæsar opposed the confiscation of their goods, not thinking it fair that those who had rejected the mildest part of his sentence should avail themselves of the severest. And when many insisted upon it, he appealed to the tribunes, but they would do nothing; till Cicero himself, yielding, remitted that part of the sentence.

After this, Cicero went out with the senate to the conspirators; they were not all together in one place, but the several prætors had them, some one, some another, in custody. And first he took Lentulus from the Palatine, and brought him by the Sacred Street, through the middle of the marketplace, a circle of the most eminent citizens encompassing and protecting him. The people, affrighted at what was doing, passed along in silence, especially the young men; as if, with fear and trembling, they were undergoing a rite of initiation into some ancient, sacred mysteries of aristocratic power. Thus passing from the marketplace, and coming to the gaol, he delivered Lentulus to the officer, and commanded him to execute him; and after him Cethegus, and so all the rest in order, he brought and delivered up to execution. And when he saw many of the conspirators in the marketplace, still standing together in companies, ignorant of what was done, and waiting for the night, supposing the men were still alive and in a possibility of being rescued, he called out in a loud voice, and said, "*They did live*"; for so the Romans, to avoid inauspicious language, name those that are dead.

It was now evening, when he returned from the marketplace to his own house, the citizens no longer attending him with silence, nor in order, but receiving him, as he passed, with acclamations and applauses, and saluting him as the savior and founder of his country. A bright light shone through the streets from the lamps and torches set up at the doors, and the women showed lights from the tops of the houses, to honor Cicero, and to behold him returning home with a splendid train of the most principal citizens; amongst whom were many who had conducted great wars, celebrated triumphs, and added to the possessions of the Roman empire, both by sea and land. These, as they passed along with him, acknowledged to one another, that though the Roman people were indebted to several officers and commanders of that age for riches, spoils, and power, yet to Cicero alone they owed the safety and security of all these, for delivering them from so great and imminent a danger. For though it might seem no wonderful thing to prevent the design, and punish the conspirators, yet to defeat the greatest of all conspiracies with so little disturbance, trouble, and commotion, was very extraordinary. For the greater part of those who had flocked in to Catiline, as soon as they heard the fate of Lentulus and Cethegus, left and forsook him, and he himself, with his remaining forces, joining battle with Antonius, was destroyed with his army.

And yet there were some who were very ready both to speak ill of Cicero, and to do him hurt for these actions; and they had for their leaders some of the magistrates of the ensuing year, as Cæsar, who was one of the prætors, and Metellus and Bestia, the tribunes. These, entering upon their office some few days before Cicero's consulate expired, would not permit him to make any address to the people, but, throwing the benches before the rostra, hindered his speaking, telling him he might, if he pleased, make the oath of withdrawal from office, and then come down again. Cicero, accordingly, accepting the conditions, came forward to make his withdrawal; and silence being made, he recited his oath, not in the usual, but in a new and peculiar form, namely, that he had saved his country, and preserved the empire; the truth of which oath all the people confirmed with theirs. Cæsar and the tribunes, all the more exasperated by this, endeavored to create him further trouble, and for this purpose proposed a law for calling Pompey home with his army, to put an end to Cicero's usurpation. But it was a very great advantage for Cicero and the whole commonwealth that Cato was at that time one of the tribunes. For he, being of equal power with the rest and of greater reputation, could oppose their designs. He easily defeated their other projects, and, in an oration to the people, so highly extolled Cicero's con-

sulate, that the greatest honors were decreed him, and he was publicly declared the Father of his Country, which title he seems to have obtained,
the first man who did so, when Cato gave it to him in this address to the
people.

At this time, therefore, his authority was very great in the city; but he
created himself much envy, and offended very many, not by any evil action, but because he was always lauding and magnifying himself. For neither senate, nor assembly of the people, nor court of judicature could
meet, in which he was not heard to talk of Catiline and Lentulus. Indeed,
he also filled his books and writings with his own praises, to such an excess as to render a style, in itself most pleasant and delightful, nauseous
and irksome to his hearers; this ungrateful humor, like a disease, always
cleaving to him. Nevertheless, though he was intemperately fond of his
own glory, he was very free from envying others, and was, on the contrary, most liberally profuse in commending both the ancients and his
contemporaries, as anyone may see in his writings. And many such sayings of his are also remembered; as that he called Aristotle a river of flowing gold, and said of Plato's Dialogues, that if Jupiter were to speak, it
would be in language like theirs. He used to call Theophrastus his special
luxury. And being asked which of Demosthenes's orations he liked best,
he answered, the longest. And yet some affected imitators of
Demosthenes have complained of some words that occur in one of his
letters, to the effect that Demosthenes sometimes falls asleep in his
speeches; forgetting the many high encomiums he continually passes
upon him, and the compliment he paid him when he named the most
elaborate of all his orations, those he wrote against Antony, Philippics.
And as for the eminent men of his own time, either in eloquence or philosophy, there was not one of them whom he did not, by writing or
speaking favorably of him, render more illustrious. He obtained of Cæsar,
when in power, the Roman citizenship for Cratippus, the Peripatetic, and
got the court of Areopagus, by public decree, to request his stay at Athens,
for the instruction of their youth and the honor of their city. There are
letters extant from Cicero to Herodes, and others to his son, in which he
recommends the study of philosophy under Cratippus. There is one in
which he blames Gorgias, the rhetorician, for enticing his son into luxury and drinking, and, therefore, forbids him his company. And this, and
one other to Pelops, the Byzantine, are the only two of his Greek epistles which seem to be written in anger. In the first, he justly reflects on
Gorgias, if he were what he was thought to be, a dissolute and profligate
character; but in the other, he rather meanly expostulates and complains
with Pelops for neglecting to procure him a decree of certain honors
from the Byzantines.

Another illustration of his love of praise is the way in which sometimes, to make his orations more striking, he neglected decorum and dignity. When Munatius, who had escaped conviction by his advocacy, immediately prosecuted his friend Sabinus, he said in the warmth of his resentment, "Do you suppose you were acquitted for your own merits, Munatius, and was it not that I so darkened the case, that the court could not see your guilt?" When from the rostra he had made a eulogy on Marcus Crassus, with much applause, and within a few days after again as publicly reproached him, Crassus called to him, and said, "Did not you yourself two days ago, in this same place, commend me?" "Yes," said Cicero, "I exercised my eloquence in declaiming upon a bad subject." At another time, Crassus had said that no one of his family had ever lived beyond sixty years of age, and afterwards denied it, and asked, "What should put it into my head to say so?" "It was to gain the people's favor," answered Cicero; "you knew how glad they would be to hear it." When Crassus expressed admiration of the Stoic doctrine, that *the good man is always rich*, "Do you not mean," said Cicero, "their doctrine that *all things belong to the wise?*" Crassus being generally accused of covetousness. One of Crassus's sons, who was thought so exceedingly like a man of the name of Axius as to throw some suspicion on his mother's honor, made a successful speech in the senate. Cicero on being asked how he liked it, replied with the Greek words, *Axios Crassou.*[1]

When Crassus was about to go into Syria, he desired to leave Cicero rather his friend than his enemy, and, therefore, one day saluting him, told him he would come and sup with him, which the other as courteously received. Within a few days after, on some of Cicero's acquaintances interceding for Vatinius, as desirous of reconciliation and friendship, for he was then his enemy, "What," he replied, "does Vatinius also wish to come and sup with me?" Such was his way with Crassus. When Vatinius, who had swellings in his neck, was pleading a cause, he called him the *tumid* orator; and having been told by someone that Vatinius was dead, on hearing presently after, that he was alive, "May the rascal perish," said he, "for his news not being true."

Upon Cæsar's bringing forward a law for the division of the lands in Campania amongst the soldiers, many in the senate opposed it; amongst the rest, Lucius Gellius, one of the oldest men in the house, said it should never pass whilst he lived. "Let us postpone it," said Cicero, "Gellius does not ask us to wait long." There was a man of the name of Octavius, suspected to be of African descent. He once said, when Cicero was pleading, that he could not hear him; "Yet there are holes," said Cicero, "in your ears."[2] When Metellus Nepos told him that he had ruined more as

---

[1] ["Worthy of Crassus."]
[2] [The mark of a slave.]

a witness than he had saved as an advocate, "I admit," said Cicero, "that I have more truth than eloquence." To a young man who was suspected of having given a poisoned cake to his father, and who talked largely of the invectives he meant to deliver against Cicero, "Better these," replied he, "than your cakes." Publius Sextius, having amongst others retained Cicero as his advocate in a certain cause, was yet desirous to say all for himself, and would not allow anybody to speak for him; when he was about to receive his acquittal from the judges, and the ballots were passing, Cicero called to him, "Make haste, Sextius, and use your time; tomorrow you will be nobody." He cited Publius Cotta to bear testimony in a certain cause, one who affected to be thought a lawyer, though ignorant and unlearned; to whom, when he had said, "I know nothing of the matter," he answered, "You think, perhaps, we ask you about a point of law." To Metellus Nepos, who, in a dispute between them, repeated several times, "Who was your father, Cicero?" he replied, "Your mother has made the answer to such a question in your case more difficult"; Nepos's mother having been of ill repute. The son, also, was of a giddy, uncertain temper. At one time, he suddenly threw up his office of tribune, and sailed off into Syria to Pompey; and immediately after, with as little reason, came back again. He gave his tutor, Philagrus, a funeral with more than necessary attention, and then set up the stone figure of a crow over his tomb. "This," said Cicero, "is really appropriate; as he did not teach you to speak, but to fly about." When Marcus Appius, in the opening of some speech in a court of justice, said that his friend had desired him to employ industry, eloquence, and fidelity in that cause, Cicero answered, "And how have you had the heart not to accede to any one of his requests?"

To use this sharp raillery against opponents and antagonists in judicial pleading seems allowable rhetoric. But he excited much ill feeling by his readiness to attack anyone for the sake of a jest. A few anecdotes of this kind may be added. Marcus Aquinius, who had two sons-in-law in exile, received from him the name of King Adrastus.[3] Lucius Cotta, an intemperate lover of wine, was censor when Cicero stood for the consulship. Cicero being thirsty at the election, his friends stood round about him while he was drinking. "You have reason to be afraid," he said, "lest the censor should be angry with me for drinking water." Meeting one day Voconius with his three very ugly daughters, he quoted the verse—

"He reared a race without Apollo's leave."

When Marcus Gellius, who was reputed the son of a slave, had read several letters in the senate with a very shrill and loud voice, "Wonder not,"

[3][A mythical king of Argos whose two sons-in-law were exiles.]

said Cicero, "he comes of the criers." When Faustus Sylla, the son of Sylla the dictator, who had, during his dictatorship, by public bills proscribed and condemned so many citizens, had so far wasted his estate, and got into debt, that he was forced to publish his bills of sale, Cicero told him that he liked these bills much better than those of his father. By this habit he made himself odious with many people.

But Clodius's faction conspired against him upon the following occasion. Clodius was a member of a noble family, in the flower of his youth, and of a bold and resolute temper. He, being in love with Pompeia, Cæsar's wife, got privately into his house in the dress and attire of a music girl; the women being at that time offering there the sacrifice which must not be seen by men, and there was no man present. Clodius, being a youth and beardless, hoped to get to Pompeia among the women without being taken notice of. But coming into a great house by night, he missed his way in the passages, and a servant belonging to Aurelia, Cæsar's mother, spying him wandering up and down, inquired his name. Thus being necessitated to speak, he told her he was seeking for one of Pompeia's maids, Abra by name; and she, perceiving it not to be a woman's voice, shrieked out, and called in the women; who, shutting the gates, and searching every place, at length found Clodius hidden in the chamber of the maid with whom he had come in. This matter being much talked about, Cæsar put away his wife, Pompeia, and Clodius was prosecuted for profaning the holy rites.

Cicero was at this time his friend, for he had been useful to him in the conspiracy of Catiline, as one of his forwardest assistants and protectors. But when Clodius rested his defense upon this point, that he was not then at Rome, but at a distance in the country, Cicero testified that he had come to his house that day, and conversed with him on several matters; which thing was indeed true, although Cicero was thought to testify it not so much for the truth's sake as to preserve his quiet with Terentia his wife. For she bore a grudge against Clodius on account of his sister Clodia's wishing, as it was alleged, to marry Cicero, and having employed for this purpose the intervention of Tullus, a very intimate friend of Cicero's; and his frequent visits to Clodia, who lived in their neighborhood, and the attentions he paid to her had excited Terentia's suspicions, and, being a woman of a violent temper, and having the ascendant over Cicero, she urged him on to taking a part against Clodius, and delivering his testimony. Many other good and honest citizens also gave evidence against him, for perjuries, disorders, bribing the people, and debauching women. Lucullus proved, by his women-servants, that he had debauched his youngest sister when she was Lucullus's wife; and there was a general belief that he had done the same with his two other sisters, Tertia, whom Marcius Rex, and Clodia, whom Metellus Celer had married; the latter of whom was called Quadrantia, because one of her lovers had deceived her with a purse of small copper money instead of silver, the smallest copper coin being called a *quadrant*. Upon this sister's account, in particular, Clodius's character was attacked. Notwithstanding all this, when the common people united against the accusers and witnesses and the whole party, the judges were affrighted, and a guard was placed about them for their defense; and most of them wrote their sentences on the tablets in such a way that they could not well be read. It was decided, however, that there was a majority for his acquittal, and bribery was reported to have been employed; in reference to which Catulus remarked, when he next met the judges, "You were very right to ask for a guard, to prevent your money being taken from you." And when Clodius upbraided Cicero that the judges had not believed his testimony, "Yes," said he, "five-and-twenty of them trusted me, and condemned you, and the other thirty did not trust you, for they did not acquit you till they had got your money."

Cæsar, though cited, did not give his testimony against Clodius, and declared himself not convinced of his wife's adultery, but that he had put her away because it was fit that Cæsar's house should not be only free of the evil fact, but of the fame too.

Clodius, having escaped this danger, and having got himself chosen one of the tribunes, immediately attacked Cicero, heaping up all matters and inciting all persons against him. The common people he gained over with popular laws; to each of the consuls he decreed large provinces, to Piso, Macedonia, and to Gabinius, Syria; he made a strong party among the indigent citizens, to support him in his proceedings, and had always a body of armed slaves about him. Of the three men then in greatest power, Crassus was Cicero's open enemy, Pompey indifferently made advances to both, and Cæsar was going with an army into Gaul. To him, though not his friend (what had occurred in the time of the conspiracy having created suspicions between them), Cicero applied, requesting an appointment as one of his lieutenants in the province. Cæsar accepted him, and Clodius, perceiving that Cicero would thus escape his tribunician authority, professed to be inclinable to a reconciliation, laid the greatest fault upon Terentia, made always a favorable mention of him, and addressed him with kind expressions, as one who felt no hatred or ill will, but who merely wished to urge his complaints in a moderate and friendly way. By these artifices, he so freed Cicero of all his fears, that he resigned his appointment to Cæsar, and betook himself again to political affairs. At which Cæsar, being exasperated, joined the party of Clodius against him, and wholly alienated Pompey from him; he also himself declared in a public assembly of the people, that he did not think Lentulus and Cethegus, with their accomplices, were fairly and legally put to death

without being brought to trial. And this, indeed, was the crime charged
upon Cicero, and this impeachment he was summoned to answer. And
so, as an accused man, and in danger for the result, he changes his dress,
and went round with his hair untrimmed, in the attire of a suppliant, to
beg the people's grace. But Clodius met him in every corner, having a
band of abusive and daring fellows about him, who derided Cicero for
his change of dress and his humiliation, and often, by throwing dirt and
stones at him, interrupted his supplication to the people.

However, first of all, almost the whole equestrian order changed their
dress with him, and no less than twenty thousand young gentlemen followed him with their hair untrimmed, and supplicating with him to the
people. And then the senate met, to pass a decree that the people should
change their dress as in time of public sorrow. But the consuls opposing
it, and Clodius with armed men besetting the senate house, many of the
senators ran out, crying out and tearing their clothes. But this sight
moved neither shame nor pity; Cicero must either fly or determine it by
the sword with Clodius. He entreated Pompey to aid him, who was on
purpose gone out of the way, and was staying at his country house in the
Alban hills; and first he sent his son-in-law Piso to intercede with him,
and afterwards set out to go himself. Of which Pompey being informed,
would not stay to see him, being ashamed at the remembrance of the
many conflicts in the commonwealth which Cicero had undergone in
his behalf, and how much of his policy he had directed for his advantage.
But being now Cæsar's son-in-law, at his instance he had set aside all former kindness, and, slipping out at another door, avoided the interview.
Thus being forsaken by Pompey, and left alone to himself, he fled to the
consuls. Gabinius was rough with him, as usual, but Piso spoke more
courteously, desiring him to yield and give place for a while to the fury
of Clodius, and to await a change of times, and to be now, as before, his
country's savior from the peril of these troubles and commotions which
Clodius was exciting.

Cicero, receiving this answer, consulted with his friends. Lucullus advised him to stay, as being sure to prevail at last; others to fly, because the
people would soon desire him again, when they should have enough of
the rage and madness of Clodius. This last Cicero approved. But first he
took a statue of Minerva, which had been long set up and greatly honored in his house, and carrying it to the capitol, there dedicated it, with
the inscription, "To Minerva, Patroness of Rome." And receiving an escort from his friends, about the middle of the night he left the city and
went by land through Lucania, intending to reach Sicily.

But as soon as it was publicly known that he was fled, Clodius proposed to the people a decree of exile, and by his own order interdicted
him fire and water, prohibiting any within five hundred miles in Italy to

receive him into their houses. Most people, out of respect for Cicero, paid no regard to this edict, offering him every attention and escorting him on his way. But at Hipponium, a city of Lucania, now called Vibo, one Vibius, a Sicilian by birth, who, amongst many other instances of Cicero's friendship, had been made head of the state engineers when he was consul, would not receive him into his house, sending him word he would appoint a place in the country for his reception. Caius Vergilius, the prætor of Sicily, who had been on the most intimate terms with him, wrote to him to forbear coming into Sicily. At these things Cicero, being disheartened, went to Brundusium, whence putting forth with a prosperous wind, a contrary gale blowing from the sea carried him back to Italy the next day. He put again to sea, and having reached Dyrrachium, on his coming to shore there, it is reported that an earthquake and a convulsion in the sea happened at the same time, signs which the diviners said intimated that his exile would not be long, for these were prognostics of change. Although many visited him with respect, and the cities of Greece contended which should honor him most, he yet continued disheartened and disconsolate, like an unfortunate lover, often casting his looks back upon Italy; and, indeed, he was become so poor-spirited, so humiliated and dejected by his misfortunes, as none could have expected in a man who had devoted so much of his life to study and learning. And yet he often desired his friends not to call him orator, but philosopher, because he had made philosophy his business, and had only used rhetoric as an instrument for attaining his objects in public life. But the desire of glory has great power in washing the tinctures of philosophy out of the souls of men, and in imprinting the passions of the common people, by custom and conversation, in the minds of those that take a part in governing them, unless the politician be very careful so to engage in public affairs as to interest himself only in the affairs themselves, but not participate in the passions that are consequent to them.

Clodius, having thus driven away Cicero, fell to burning his farms and villas, and afterwards his city house, and built on the site of it a temple to Liberty. The rest of his property he exposed to sale by daily proclamation, but nobody came to buy. By these courses he became formidable to the noble citizens, and, being followed by the commonalty, whom he had filled with insolence and licentiousness, he began at last to try his strength against Pompey, some of whose arrangements in the countries he conquered, he attacked. The disgrace of this made Pompey begin to reproach himself for his cowardice in deserting Cicero, and, changing his mind, he now wholly set himself with his friends to contrive his return. And when Clodius opposed it, the senate made a vote that no public measure should be ratified or passed by them till Cicero was recalled. But when Lentulus was consul, the commotions grew so high upon this matter, that the tribunes were wounded in the Forum, and Quintus, Cicero's brother, was left as dead, lying unobserved amongst the slain. The people began to change in their feelings; and Annius Milo, one of their tribunes, was the first who took confidence to summon Clodius to trial for acts of violence. Many of the common people and out of the neighboring cities formed a party with Pompey, and he went with them, and drove Clodius out of the Forum, and summoned the people to pass their vote. And, it is said, the people never passed any suffrage more unanimously than this. The senate, also, striving to outdo the people, sent letters of thanks to those cities which had received Cicero with respect in his exile, and decreed that his house and his country places, which Clodius had destroyed, should be rebuilt at the public charge.

Thus Cicero returned sixteen months after his exile, and the cities were so glad, and people so zealous to meet him, that what he boasted of afterwards, that Italy had brought him on her shoulders home to Rome, was rather less than the truth. And Crassus himself, who had been his enemy before his exile, went then voluntarily to meet him, and was reconciled, to please his son Publius, as he said, who was Cicero's affectionate admirer.

Cicero had not been long at Rome when, taking the opportunity of Clodius's absence, he went, with a great company, to the capitol, and there tore and defaced the tribunician tables, in which were recorded the acts done in the time of Clodius. And on Clodius calling him in question for this, he answered, that he, being of the patrician order, had obtained the office of tribune against law, and therefore nothing done by him was valid. Cato was displeased at this, and opposed Cicero, not that he commended Clodius, but rather disapproved of his whole administration; yet, he contended, it was an irregular and violent course for the senate to vote the illegality of so many decrees and acts, including those of Cato's own government in Cyprus and at Byzantium. This occasioned a breach between Cato and Cicero, which, though it came not to open enmity, yet made a more reserved friendship between them.

After this, Milo killed Clodius, and, being arraigned for the murder, he procured Cicero as his advocate. The senate, fearing lest the questioning of so eminent and high-spirited a citizen as Milo might disturb the peace of the city, committed the superintendence of this and of the other trials to Pompey, who should undertake to maintain the security alike of the city and of the courts of justice. Pompey, therefore, went in the night, and occupying the high grounds about it, surrounded the Forum with soldiers. Milo, fearing lest Cicero, being disturbed by such an unusual sight, should conduct his cause the less successfully, persuaded him to come in a litter into the Forum, and there repose himself till the judges were set and the court filled. For Cicero, it seems, not only wanted courage in arms, but in his speaking also began with timidity, and in many cases scarcely left off trembling and shaking when he had got thoroughly into the current and the substance of his speech. Being to defend Licinius Murena against the prosecution of Cato, and being eager to outdo Hortensius, who had made his plea with great applause, he took so little rest that night, and was so disordered with thought and overwatching, that he spoke much worse than usual. And so now, on quitting his litter to commence the cause of Milo, at the sight of Pompey posted, as it were, and encamped with his troops above, and seeing arms shining round about the Forum, he was so confounded that he could hardly begin his speech for the trembling of his body and hesitance of his tongue; whereas Milo, meantime, was bold and intrepid in his demeanor, disdaining either to let his hair grow or to put on the mourning habit. And this, indeed, seems to have been one principal cause of his condemnation. Cicero, however, was thought not so much to have shown timidity for himself as anxiety about his friend.

He was made one of the priests, whom the Romans call Augurs, in the room of Crassus the younger, dead in Parthia. Then he was appointed by lot to the province of Cilicia, and set sail thither with twelve thousand foot and two thousand six hundred horse. He had orders to bring back Cappadocia to its allegiance to Ariobarzanes, its king; which settlement he effected very completely without recourse to arms. And perceiving the Cilicians, by the great loss the Romans had suffered in Parthia, and the commotions in Syria, to have become disposed to attempt a revolt, by a gentle course of government he soothed them back into fidelity. He would accept none of the presents that were offered him by the kings; he remitted the charge of public entertainments, but daily at his own house received the ingenious and accomplished persons of the province, not sumptuously, but liberally. His house had no porter, nor was he ever found in bed by any man, but early in the morning, standing or walking before his door, he received those who came to offer their salutations. He is said never once to have ordered any of those under his command to be beaten with rods, or to have their garments rent. He never gave contumelious language in his anger, nor inflicted punishment with reproach. He detected an embezzlement, to a large amount, in the public money, and thus relieved the cities from their burdens, at the same time that he allowed those who made restitution to retain without further punishment their rights as citizens. He engaged too, in war, so far as to give a defeat to the banditti who infested Mount Amanus, for which he was saluted by his army Imperator. To Cæcilius, the orator, who asked him to send him some panthers from Cilicia, to be exhibited on the theater at Rome, he wrote, in commendation of his own actions, that there were no panthers in Cilicia, for they were all fled to Caria, in anger that in so general a peace they had become the sole objects of attack. On leaving his province, he touched at Rhodes, and tarried for some length of time at Athens, longing much to renew his old studies. He visited the eminent men of learning, and saw his former friends and companions; and after receiving in Greece the honors that were due to him, returned to the city, where everything was now just as it were in a flame, breaking out into a civil war.

When the senate would have decreed him a triumph, he told them he had rather, so differences were accommodated, follow the triumphal chariot of Cæsar. In private, he gave advice to both, writing many letters to Cæsar, and personally entreating Pompey; doing his best to soothe and bring to reason both the one and the other. But when matters became incurable and Cæsar was approaching Rome, and Pompey durst not abide it, but, with many honest citizens, left the city, Cicero as yet did not join in the flight, and was reputed to adhere to Cæsar. And it is very evident he was in his thoughts much divided, and wavered painfully between both, for he writes in his epistles, "To which side should I turn? Pompey has the fair and honorable plea for war; and Cæsar, on the other hand, has managed his affairs better, and is more able to secure himself and his friends. So that I know whom I should fly, not whom I should fly to." But when Trebatius, one of Cæsar's friends, by letter signified to him that Cæsar thought it was his most desirable course to join his party, and partake his hopes, but if he considered himself too old a man for this, then he should retire into Greece, and stay quietly there, out of the way of either party, Cicero, wondering that Cæsar had not written himself, gave an angry reply, that he should not do anything unbecoming his past life. Such is the account to be collected from his letters.

But as soon as Cæsar was marched into Spain, he immediately sailed away to join Pompey. And he was welcomed by all but Cato; who, taking him privately, chid him for coming to Pompey. As for himself, he said, it had been indecent to forsake that part in the commonwealth which he had chosen from the beginning; but Cicero might have been more useful to his country and friends, if, remaining neuter, he had attended and used his influence to moderate the result, instead of coming hither to make himself, without reason or necessity, an enemy to Cæsar, and a partner in such great dangers.

By this language, partly, Cicero's feelings were altered, and partly, also, because Pompey made no great use of him. Although, indeed, he was himself the cause of it, by his not denying that he was sorry he had come, by his depreciating Pompey's resources, finding fault underhand with his counsels, and continually indulging in jests and sarcastic remarks on his fellow soldiers. Though he went about in the camp with a gloomy and melancholy face himself, he was always trying to raise a laugh in others, whether they wished it or not. It may not be amiss to mention a few instances. To Domitius, on his preferring to a command one who was no soldier, and saying, in his defense, that he was a modest and prudent person, he replied, "Why did not you keep him for a tutor for your children?" On hearing Theophanes, the Lesbian, who was master of the engineers in the army, praised for the admirable way in which he had consoled the Rhodians for the loss of their fleet, "What a thing it is," he said, "to have a Greek in command!" When Cæsar had been acting successfully, and in a manner blockading Pompey, Lentulus was saying it was reported that Cæsar's friends were out of heart; "Because," said Cicero, "they do not wish Cæsar well." To one Marcius, who had just come from Italy and told them that there was a strong report at Rome that Pompey was blocked up, he said, "And you sailed hither to see it with your own eyes." To Nonius, encouraging them after a defeat to be of good hope because there were seven eagles still left in Pompey's camp, "Good reason for encouragement," said Cicero, "if we were going to fight with jackdaws." Labienus insisted on some prophecies to the effect that Pompey would gain the victory; "Yes," said Cicero, "and the first step in the campaign has been losing our camp."

After the battle of Pharsalia was over, at which he was not present for want of health, and Pompey was fled, Cato, having considerable forces and a great fleet at Dyrrachium, would have had Cicero commander-in-chief, according to law and the precedence of his consular dignity. And on his refusing the command, and wholly declining to take part in their plans for continuing the war, he was in the greatest danger of being killed, young Pompey and his friends calling him traitor, and drawing their swords upon him; only that Cato interposed, and hardly rescued and brought him out of the camp.

Afterwards, arriving at Brundusium, he tarried there sometime in expectation of Cæsar, who was delayed by his affairs in Asia and Egypt. And when it was told him that he was arrived at Tarentum, and was coming thence by land to Brundusium, he hastened towards him, not altogether without hope, and yet in some fear of making experiment of the temper of an enemy and conqueror in the presence of many witnesses. But there was no necessity for him either to speak or do anything unworthy of himself; for Cæsar, as soon as he saw him coming a good way before the rest of the company, came down to meet him, saluted him, and, leading the way, conversed with him alone for some furlongs. And from that time forward he continued to treat him with honor and respect; so that, when Cicero wrote an oration in praise of Cato, Cæsar, in writing an answer to it, took occasion to commend Cicero's own life and eloquence, comparing him to Pericles and Theramenes. Cicero's oration was called Cato; Cæsar's, anti-Cato.

So also it is related that when Quintus Ligarius was prosecuted for having been in arms against Cæsar, and Cicero had undertaken his defense, Cæsar said to his friends, "Why might we not as well once more hear a speech from Cicero? Ligarius, there is no question, is a wicked man and an enemy." But when Cicero began to speak, he wonderfully moved him, and proceeded in his speech with such varied pathos, and such a charm of language, that the color of Cæsar's countenance often changed, and it was evident that all the passions of his soul were in commotion. At length, the orator touching upon the Pharsalian battle, he was so affected that his body trembled, and some of the papers he held dropped out of his hands. And thus he was overpowered, and acquitted Ligarius.

Henceforth, the commonwealth being changed into a monarchy, Cicero withdrew himself from public affairs, and employed his leisure in instructing those young men that would, in philosophy; and by the near intercourse he thus had with some of the noblest and highest in rank, he again began to possess great influence in the city. The work and object which he set himself was to compose and translate philosophical dialogues and to render logical and physical terms into the Roman idiom. For he it was, as it is said, who first or principally gave Latin names to *phantasia, syncatathesis, epokhe, catalepsis, atomon, ameres, kenon,* and other such technical terms, which, either by metaphors or other means of accommodation, he succeeded in making intelligible and expressible to the Romans. For his recreation, he exercised his dexterity in poetry, and when he was set to it, would make five hundred verses in a night. He spent the greatest part of his time at his country house near Tusculum. He wrote to his friends that he led the life of Laertes, either jestingly, as his custom was, or rather from a feeling of ambition for public employment, which made him impatient under the present state of affairs. He rarely went to the city, unless to pay his court to Cæsar. He was commonly the first amongst those who voted him honors, and sought out new terms of praise for himself and for his actions. As, for example, what he said of the statues of Pompey, which had been thrown down, and were afterwards by Cæsar's orders set up again: that Cæsar, by this act of humanity, had indeed set up Pompey's statues, but he had fixed and established his own.

He had a design, it is said, of writing the history of his country, combining with it much of that of Greece, and incorporating in it all the stories and legends of the past that he had collected. But his purposes were interfered with by various public and various private unhappy occurrences and misfortunes; for most of which he was himself in fault. For first of all, he put away his wife Terentia, by whom he had been neglected in the time of the war, and sent away destitute of necessaries for his jour-

ney; neither did he find her kind when he returned into Italy, for she did
not join him at Brundusium, where he stayed a long time, nor would
allow her young daughter, who undertook so long a journey, decent attendance, or the requisite expenses; besides, she left him a naked and
empty house, and yet had involved him in many and great debts. These
were alleged as the fairest reasons for the divorce. But Terentia, who denied them all, had the most unmistakable defense furnished her by her
husband himself, who not long after married a young maiden for the
love of her beauty, as Terentia upbraided him; or as Tiro, his emancipated
slave, has written, for her riches, to discharge his debts. For the young
woman was very rich, and Cicero had the custody of her estate, being left
guardian in trust; and being indebted many myriads of money, he was
persuaded by his friends and relations to marry her, notwithstanding his
disparity of age, and to use her money to satisfy his creditors. Antony,
who mentions this marriage in his answer to the Philippics, reproaches
him for putting away a wife with whom he had lived to old age; adding
some happy strokes of sarcasm on Cicero's domestic, inactive, unsoldier-
like habits. Not long after this marriage, his daughter died in childbed at
Lentulus's house, to whom she had been married after the death of Piso,
her former husband. The philosophers from all parts came to comfort
Cicero; for his grief was so excessive, that he put away his new-married
wife, because she seemed to be pleased at the death of Tullia. And thus
stood Cicero's domestic affairs at this time.

He had no concern in the design that was now forming against Cæsar,
although, in general, he was Brutus's most principal confidant, and one
who was as aggrieved at the present and as desirous of the former state
of public affairs, as any other whatsoever. But they feared his temper, as
wanting courage, and his old age, in which the most daring dispositions
are apt to be timorous.

As soon, therefore, as the act was committed by Brutus and Cassius, and
the friends of Cæsar were got together, so that there was fear the city
would again be involved in a civil war, Antony, being consul, convened the
senate, and made a short address recommending concord. And Cicero, following with various remarks such as the occasion called for, persuaded the
senate to imitate the Athenians, and decree an amnesty for what had been
done in Cæsar's case, and to bestow provinces on Brutus and Cassius. But
neither of these things took effect. For as soon as the common people, of
themselves inclined to pity, saw the dead body of Cæsar borne through the
marketplace, and Antony showing his clothes filled with blood, and pierced
through in every part with swords, enraged to a degree of frenzy, they made
a search for the murderers, and with firebrands in their hands ran to their
houses to burn them. They, however, being forewarned, avoided this danger; and expecting many more and greater to come, they left the city.

Antony on this was at once in exultation, and everyone was in alarm with the prospect that he would make himself sole ruler, and Cicero in more alarm than anyone. For Antony, seeing his influence reviving in the commonwealth, and knowing how closely he was connected with Brutus, was ill-pleased to have him in the city. Besides, there had been some former jealousy between them, occasioned by the difference of their manners. Cicero, fearing the event, was inclined to go as lieutenant with Dolabella into Syria. But Hirtius and Pansa, consuls elect as successors of Antony, good men and lovers of Cicero, entreated him not to leave them, undertaking to put down Antony if he would stay in Rome. And he, neither distrusting wholly, nor trusting them, let Dolabella go without him, promising Hirtius that he would go and spend his summer at Athens, and return again when he entered upon his office. So he set out on his journey; but some delay occurring in his passage, new intelligence, as often happens, came suddenly from Rome, that Antony had made an astonishing change, and was doing all things and managing all public affairs at the will of the senate, and that there wanted nothing but his presence to bring things to a happy settlement. And therefore, blaming himself for his cowardice, he returned again to Rome, and was not deceived in his hopes at the beginning. For such multitudes flocked out to meet him, that the compliments and civilities which were paid him at the gates, and at his entrance into the city, took up almost one whole day's time.

On the morrow, Antony convened the senate, and summoned Cicero thither. He came not, but kept his bed, pretending to be ill with his journey; but the true reason seemed the fear of some design against him, upon a suspicion and intimation given him on his way to Rome. Antony, however, showed great offense at the affront, and sent soldiers, commanding them to bring him or burn his house; but many interceding and supplicating for him, he was contented to accept sureties. Ever after, when they met, they passed one another with silence, and continued on their guard, till Cæsar, the younger, coming from Apollonia, entered on the first Cæsar's inheritance, and was engaged in a dispute with Antony about two thousand five hundred myriads of money, which Antony detained from the estate.

Upon this, Philippus, who married the mother, and Marcellus, who married the sister of young Cæsar, came with the young man to Cicero, and agreed with him that Cicero should give them the aid of his eloquence and political influence with the senate and people, and Cæsar give Cicero the defense of his riches and arms. For the young man had already a great party of the soldiers of Cæsar about him. And Cicero's readiness to join him was founded, it is said, on some yet stronger motives; for it seems, while Pompey and Cæsar were yet alive, Cicero, in his sleep, had fancied himself engaged in calling some of the sons of the senators into the capitol, Jupiter being about, according to the dream, to declare one of them the chief ruler of Rome. The citizens, running up with curiosity, stood about the temple, and the youths, sitting in their purple-bordered robes, kept silence. On a sudden the doors opened, and the youths, arising one by one in order, passed round the god, who reviewed them all, and, to their sorrow, dismissed them; but when this one was passing by, the god stretched forth his right hand and said, "O ye Romans, this young man, when he shall be lord of Rome, shall put an end to all your civil wars." It is said that Cicero formed from his dream a distinct image of the youth, and retained it afterwards perfectly, but did not know who it was. The next day, going down into the Campus Martius, he met the boys resuming from their gymnastic exercises, and the first was he, just as he had appeared to him in his dream. Being astonished at it, he asked him who were his parents. And it proved to be this young Cæsar, whose father was a man of no great eminence, Octavius, and his mother, Attia, Cæsar's sister's daughter; for which reason, Cæsar, who had no children, made him by will the heir of his house and property. From that time, it is said that Cicero studiously noticed the youth whenever he met him, and he as kindly received the civility; and by fortune he happened to be born when Cicero was consul.

These were the reasons spoken of; but it was principally Cicero's hatred of Antony, and a temper unable to resist honor, which fastened him to Cæsar, with the purpose of getting the support of Cæsar's power for his own public designs. For the young man went so far in his court to him, that he called him Father; at which Brutus was so highly displeased, that, in his epistles to Atticus, he reflected on Cicero saying, it was manifest, by his courting Cæsar for fear of Antony, he did not intend liberty to his country, but an indulgent master to himself. Notwithstanding, Brutus took Cicero's son, then studying philosophy at Athens, gave him a command, and employed him in various ways, with a good result. Cicero's own power at this time was at the greatest height in the city, and he did whatsoever he pleased; he completely overpowered and drove out Antony, and sent the two consuls, Hirtius and Pansa, with an army, to reduce him; and, on the other hand, persuaded the senate to allow Cæsar the lictors and ensigns of a prætor, as though he were his country's defender. But after Antony was defeated in battle, and the two consuls slain, the armies united, and ranged themselves with Cæsar. And the senate, fearing the young man, and his extraordinary fortune, endeavored, by honors and gifts, to call off the soldiers from him, and to lessen his power; professing there was no further need of arms, now Antony was put to flight.

This giving Cæsar an affright, he privately sends some friends to en-

treat and persuade Cicero to procure the consular dignity for them both
together; saying he should manage the affairs as he pleased, should have
the supreme power, and govern the young man who was only desirous
of name and glory. And Cæsar himself confessed that, in fear of ruin and
in danger of being deserted, he had seasonably made use of Cicero's ambition, persuading him to stand with him, and to accept the offer of his
aid and interest for the consulship.

And now, more than at any other time, Cicero let himself be carried
away and deceived, though an old man, by the persuasion of a boy. He
joined him in soliciting votes, and procured the goodwill of the senate,
not without blame at the time on the part of his friends; and he, too, soon
enough after, saw that he had ruined himself, and betrayed the liberty of
his country. For the young man, once established, and possessed of the office of consul, bade Cicero farewell; and, reconciling himself to Antony
and Lepidus, joined his power with theirs, and divided the government,
like a piece of property, with them. Thus united, they made a schedule of
above two hundred persons who were to be put to death. But the greatest contention in all their debates was on the question of Cicero's case.
Antony would come to no conditions, unless he should be the first man
to be killed. Lepidus held with Antony, and Cæsar opposed them both.
They met secretly and by themselves, for three days together, near the
town of Bononia. The spot was not far from the camp, with a river surrounding it. Cæsar, it is said, contended earnestly for Cicero the first two
days; but on the third day he yielded, and gave him up. The terms of their
mutual concessions were these; that Cæsar should desert Cicero, Lepidus
his brother Paulus, and Antony, Lucius Cæsar, his uncle by his mother's
side. Thus they let their anger and fury take from them the sense of humanity, and demonstrated that no beast is more savage than man, when
possessed with power answerable to his rage.

Whilst these things were contriving, Cicero was with his brother at his
country house near Tusculum; whence, hearing of the proscriptions, they
determined to pass to Astura, a villa of Cicero's near the sea, and to take
shipping from thence for Macedonia to Brutus, of whose strength in that
province news had already been heard. They traveled together in their
separate litters, overwhelmed with sorrow; and often stopping on the way
till their litters came together, condoled with one another. But Quintus
was the more disheartened when he reflected on his want of means for
his journey; for, as he said, he had brought nothing with him from home.
And even Cicero himself had but a slender provision. It was judged,
therefore, most expedient that Cicero should make what haste he could
to fly, and Quintus return home to provide necessaries, and thus resolved,
they mutually embraced, and parted with many tears.

Quintus, within a few days after, betrayed by his servants to those who came to search for him, was slain, together with his young son. But Cicero was carried to Astura, where, finding a vessel, he immediately went on board her, and sailed as far as Circæum with a prosperous gale; but when the pilots resolved immediately to set sail from thence, whether fearing the sea, or not wholly distrusting the faith of Cæsar, he went on shore, and passed by land a hundred furlongs, as if he was going for Rome. But losing resolution and changing his mind, he again returned to the sea, and there spent the night in fearful and perplexed thoughts. Sometimes he resolved to go into Cæsar's house privately, and there kill himself upon the altar of his household gods, to bring divine vengeance upon him; but the fear of torture put him off this course. And after passing through a variety of confused and uncertain counsels, at last he let his servants carry him by sea to Capitæ, where he had a house, an agreeable place to retire to in the heat of summer, when the Etesian winds are so pleasant.

There was at that place a chapel of Apollo, not far from the seaside, from which a flight of crows rose with a great noise, and made towards Cicero's vessel as it rowed to land, and lighting on both sides of the yard, some croaked, others pecked the ends of the ropes. This was looked upon by all as an ill omen; and, therefore, Cicero went again ashore, and entering his house, lay down upon his bed to compose himself to rest. Many of the crows settled about the window, making a dismal cawing; but one of them alighted upon the bed where Cicero lay covered up, and with its bill by little and little pecked off the clothes from his face. His servants, seeing this, blamed themselves that they should stay to be spectators of their master's murder, and do nothing in his defense, whilst the brute creatures came to assist and take care of him in his undeserved affliction; and therefore, partly by entreaty, partly by force, they took him up, and carried him in his litter towards the seaside.

But in the meantime the assassins were come with a band of soldiers, Herennius, a centurion, and Popillius, a tribune, whom Cicero had formerly defended when prosecuted for the murder of his father. Finding the doors shut, they broke them open, and Cicero not appearing, and those within saying they knew not where he was, it is stated that a youth, who had been educated by Cicero in the liberal arts and sciences, an emancipated slave of his brother Quintus, Philologus by name, informed the tribune that the litter was on its way to the sea through the close and shady walks. The tribune, taking a few with him, ran to the place where he was to come out. And Cicero, perceiving Herennius running in the walks, commanded his servants to set down the litter; and stroking his chin, as he used to do, with his left hand, he looked steadfastly upon his murderers, his person covered with dust, his beard and hair untrimmed, and his face worn with his troubles. So that the greatest part of those that stood by covered their faces whilst Herennius slew him. And thus was he murdered, stretching forth his neck out of the litter, being now in his sixty-fourth year. Herennius cut off his head, and, by Antony's command, his hands also, by which his Philippics were written; for so Cicero styled those orations he wrote against Antony, and so they are called to this day.

When these members of Cicero were brought to Rome, Antony was holding an assembly for the choice of public officers; and when he heard it, and saw them, he cried out, "Now let there be an end of our proscriptions." He commanded his head and hands to be fastened up over the rostra, where the orators spoke; a sight which the Roman people shuddered to behold, and they believed they saw there not the face of Cicero, but the image of Antony's own soul. And yet amidst these actions he did justice in one thing, by delivering up Philologus to Pomponia, the wife of Quintus; who, having got his body into her power, besides other grievous punishments, made him cut off his own flesh by pieces, and roast and eat it; for so some writers have related. But Tiro, Cicero's emancipated slave, has not so much as mentioned the treachery of Philologus.

Some long time after, Cæsar, I have been told, visiting one of his daughter's sons, found him with a book of Cicero's in his hand. The boy for fear endeavored to hide it under his gown; which Cæsar perceiving, took it from him, and, turning over a great part of the book standing, gave it him again, and said, "My child, this was a learned man, and a lover of his country." And immediately after he had vanquished Antony, being then consul, he made Cicero's son his colleague in the office; and under that consulship the senate took down all the statues of Antony, and abolished all the other honors that had been given him, and decreed that none of that family should thereafter bear the name of Marcus; and thus the final acts of the punishment of Antony were, by the divine powers, devolved upon the family of Cicero.

POETRY

La Vita Nuova, Dante Alighieri. 56pp. 0-486-41915-0

101 Great American Poems, The American Poetry & Literacy Project (ed.). (Available in U.S. only.) 96pp. 0-486-40158-8

English Romantic Poetry: An Anthology, Stanley Appelbaum (ed.). 256pp. 0-486-29282-7

Bhagavadgita, Bhagavadgita. 112pp. 0-486-27782-8

The Book of Psalms, King James Bible. 128pp. 0-486-27541-8

Imagist Poetry: An Anthology, Bob Blaisdell (ed.). 176pp. (Available in U.S. only.) 0-486-40875-2

Blake's Selected Poems, William Blake. 96pp. 0-486-28517-0

Songs of Innocence and Songs of Experience, William Blake. 64pp. 0-486-27051-3

The Classic Tradition of Haiku: An Anthology, Faubion Bowers (ed.). 96pp. 0-486-29274-6

To My Husband and Other Poems, Anne Bradstreet (Robert Hutchinson, ed.). 80pp. 0-486-41408-6

Best Poems of the Brontë Sisters (ed. by Candace Ward), Emily, Anne, and Charlotte Brontë. 64pp. 0-486-29529-X

Sonnets from the Portuguese and Other Poems, Elizabeth Barrett Browning. 64pp. 0-486-27052-1

My Last Duchess and Other Poems, Robert Browning. 128pp. 0-486-27783-6

Poems and Songs, Robert Burns. 96pp. 0-486-26863-2

Selected Poems, George Gordon, Lord Byron. 112pp. 0-486-27784-4

Jabberwocky and Other Poems, Lewis Carroll. 64pp. 0-486-41582-1

Selected Canterbury Tales, Geoffrey Chaucer. 144pp. 0-486-28241-4

The Rime of the Ancient Mariner and Other Poems, Samuel Taylor Coleridge. 80pp. 0-486-27266-4

The Cavalier Poets: An Anthology, Thomas Crofts (ed.). 80pp. 0-486-28766-1

Selected Poems, Emily Dickinson. 64pp. 0-486-26466-1

Selected Poems, John Donne. 96pp. 0-486-27788-7

Selected Poems, Paul Laurence Dunbar. 80pp. 0-486-29980-5

"The Waste Land" and Other Poems, T. S. Eliot. 64pp. (Available in U.S. only.) 0-486-40061-1

The Rubáiyát of Omar Khayyám: First and Fifth Editions, Edward FitzGerald. 64pp. 0-486-26467-X

A Boy's Will and North of Boston, Robert Frost. 112pp. (Available in U.S. only.) 0-486-26866-7

The Road Not Taken and Other Poems, Robert Frost. 64pp. (Available in U.S. only.) 0-486-27550-7

The Garden of Heaven: Poems of Hafiz, Hafiz. 112pp. 0-486-43161-4

Hardy's Selected Poems, Thomas Hardy. 80pp. 0-486-28753-X

A Shropshire Lad, A. E. Housman. 64pp. 0-486-26468-8

Lyric Poems, John Keats. 80pp. 0-486-26871-3

Gunga Din and Other Favorite Poems, Rudyard Kipling. 80pp. 0-486-26471-8

Snake and Other Poems, D. H. Lawrence. 64pp. 0-486-40647-4

PLAYS

FICTION

FICTION

THE QUEEN OF SPADES AND OTHER STORIES, Alexander Pushkin. 128pp. 0-486-28054-3
THE STORY OF AN AFRICAN FARM, Olive Schreiner. 256pp. 0-486-40165-0
FRANKENSTEIN, Mary Shelley. 176pp. 0-486-28211-2
THE JUNGLE, Upton Sinclair. 320pp. (Available in U.S. only.) 0-486-41923-1
THREE LIVES, Gertrude Stein. 176pp. (Available in U.S. only.) 0-486-28059-4
THE BODY SNATCHER AND OTHER TALES, Robert Louis Stevenson. 80pp. 0-486-41924-X
THE STRANGE CASE OF DR. JEKYLL AND MR. HYDE, Robert Louis Stevenson. 64pp.
   0-486-26688-5
TREASURE ISLAND, Robert Louis Stevenson. 160pp. 0-486-27559-0
GULLIVER'S TRAVELS, Jonathan Swift. 240pp. 0-486-29273-8
THE KREUTZER SONATA AND OTHER SHORT STORIES, Leo Tolstoy. 144pp. 0-486-27805-0
THE WARDEN, Anthony Trollope. 176pp. 0-486-40076-X
FATHERS AND SONS, Ivan Turgenev. 176pp. 0-486-0073-5
ADVENTURES OF HUCKLEBERRY FINN, Mark Twain. 224pp. 0-486-28061-6
THE ADVENTURES OF TOM SAWYER, Mark Twain. 192pp. 0-486-40077-8
THE MYSTERIOUS STRANGER AND OTHER STORIES, Mark Twain. 128pp. 0-486-27069-6
HUMOROUS STORIES AND SKETCHES, Mark Twain. 80pp. 0-486-29279-7
AROUND THE WORLD IN EIGHTY DAYS, Jules Verne. 160pp. 0-486-41111-7
CANDIDE, Voltaire (François-Marie Arouet). 112pp. 0-486-26689-3
GREAT SHORT STORIES BY AMERICAN WOMEN, Candace Ward (ed.). 192pp. 0-486-28776-9
"THE COUNTRY OF THE BLIND" AND OTHER SCIENCE-FICTION STORIES, H. G. Wells. 160pp.
   (Not available in Europe or United Kingdom.) 0-486-29569-9
THE ISLAND OF DR. MOREAU, H. G. Wells. 112pp. (Not available in Europe or United
   Kingdom.) 0-486-29027-1
THE INVISIBLE MAN, H. G. Wells. 112pp. (Not available in Europe or United Kingdom.)
   0-486-27071-8
THE TIME MACHINE, H. G. Wells. 80pp. (Not available in Europe or United Kingdom.)
   0-486-28472-7
THE WAR OF THE WORLDS, H. G. Wells. 160pp. (Not available in Europe or United
   Kingdom.) 0-486-29506-0
ETHAN FROME, Edith Wharton. 96pp. 0-486-26690-7
SHORT STORIES, Edith Wharton. 128pp. 0-486-28235-X
THE AGE OF INNOCENCE, Edith Wharton. 288pp. 0-486-29803-5
THE PICTURE OF DORIAN GRAY, Oscar Wilde. 192pp. 0-486-27807-7
JACOB'S ROOM, Virginia Woolf. 144pp. (Not available in Europe or United Kingdom.)
   0-486-40109-X
MONDAY OR TUESDAY: Eight Stories, Virginia Woolf. 64pp. (Not available in Europe or
   United Kingdom.) 0-486-29453-6

NONFICTION

POETICS, Aristotle. 64pp. 0-486-29577-X
POLITICS, Aristotle. 368pp. 0-486-41424-8
NICOMACHEAN ETHICS, Aristotle. 256pp. 0-486-40096-4
MEDITATIONS, Marcus Aurelius. 128pp. 0-486-29823-X
THE LAND OF LITTLE RAIN, Mary Austin. 96pp. 0-486-29037-9
THE DEVIL'S DICTIONARY, Ambrose Bierce. 144pp. 0-486-27542-6
THE ANALECTS, Confucius. 128pp. 0-486-28484-0
CONFESSIONS OF AN ENGLISH OPIUM EATER, Thomas De Quincey. 80pp. 0-486-28742-4
THE SOULS OF BLACK FOLK, W. E. B. Du Bois. 176pp. 0-486-28041-1

NONFICTION

NARRATIVE OF THE LIFE OF FREDERICK DOUGLASS, Frederick Douglass. 96pp. 0-486-28499-9

SELF-RELIANCE AND OTHER ESSAYS, Ralph Waldo Emerson. 128pp. 0-486-27790-9

THE LIFE OF OLAUDAH EQUIANO, OR GUSTAVUS VASSA, THE AFRICAN, Olaudah Equiano. 192pp. 0-486-40661-X

THE AUTOBIOGRAPHY OF BENJAMIN FRANKLIN, Benjamin Franklin. 144pp. 0-486-29073-5

TOTEM AND TABOO, Sigmund Freud. 176pp. (Not available in Europe or United Kingdom.) 0-486-40434-X

LOVE: A Book of Quotations, Herb Galewitz (ed.). 64pp. 0-486-40004-2

PRAGMATISM, William James. 128pp. 0-486-28270-8

THE STORY OF MY LIFE, Helen Keller. 80pp. 0-486-29249-5

TAO TE CHING, Lao Tze. 112pp. 0-486-29792-6

GREAT SPEECHES, Abraham Lincoln. 112pp. 0-486-26872-1

THE PRINCE, Niccolò Machiavelli. 80pp. 0-486-27274-5

THE SUBJECTION OF WOMEN, John Stuart Mill. 112pp. 0-486-29601-6

SELECTED ESSAYS, Michel de Montaigne. 96pp. 0-486-29109-X

UTOPIA, Sir Thomas More. 96pp. 0-486-29583-4

BEYOND GOOD AND EVIL: Prelude to a Philosophy of the Future, Friedrich Nietzsche. 176pp. 0-486-29868-X

THE BIRTH OF TRAGEDY, Friedrich Nietzsche. 96pp. 0-486-28515-4

COMMON SENSE, Thomas Paine. 64pp. 0-486-29602-4

SYMPOSIUM AND PHAEDRUS, Plato. 96pp. 0-486-27798-4

THE TRIAL AND DEATH OF SOCRATES: Four Dialogues, Plato. 128pp. 0-486-27066-1

A MODEST PROPOSAL AND OTHER SATIRICAL WORKS, Jonathan Swift. 64pp. 0-486-28759-9

CIVIL DISOBEDIENCE AND OTHER ESSAYS, Henry David Thoreau. 96pp. 0-486-27563-9

WALDEN; OR, LIFE IN THE WOODS, Henry David Thoreau. 224pp. 0-486-28495-6

NARRATIVE OF SOJOURNER TRUTH, Sojourner Truth. 80pp. 0-486-29899-X

THE THEORY OF THE LEISURE CLASS, Thorstein Veblen. 256pp. 0-486-28062-4

DE PROFUNDIS, Oscar Wilde. 64pp. 0-486-29308-4

OSCAR WILDE'S WIT AND WISDOM: A Book of Quotations, Oscar Wilde. 64pp. 0-486-40146-4

UP FROM SLAVERY, Booker T. Washington. 160pp. 0-486-28738-6

A VINDICATION OF THE RIGHTS OF WOMAN, Mary Wollstonecraft. 224pp. 0-486-29036-0

All books complete and unabridged. All 5³⁄₁₆" x 8¼", paperbound. Available at your book dealer, online at **www.doverpublications.com**, or by writing to Dept. GI, Dover Publications, Inc., 31 East 2nd Street, Mineola, NY 11501. For current price information or for free catalogs (please indicate field of interest), write to Dover Publications or log on to **www.doverpublications.com** and see every Dover book in print. Dover publishes more than 500 books each year on science, elementary and advanced mathematics, biology, music, art, literary history, social sciences, and other areas.